Mathematics FOR Business

Mathematics FOR Business

Fifth Edition

Stanley A. Salzman
American River College

Charles D. Miller

Louis F. Hoelzle
Bucks County Community College

HarperCollinsCollegePublishers

Chuck, you are greatly missed by colleagues and friends.

Sponsoring Editor: Anne Kelly
Developmental Editor: Elizabeth Lee
Project Editor: Ann-Marie Buesing
Design Supervisor: Jess Schaal
Text Design: Jeanne Calabrese
Cover Design: Jeanne Calabrese
Cover Photo: Judith Turner
Photo Researcher: Leslie Coopersmith
Production Administrator: Randee Wire
Compositor: Publication Services, Inc.
Printer and Binder: R. R. Donnelley & Sons Company
Cover Printer: Lehigh Press Lithographers

Mathematics for Business, 5th edition

Library of Congress Cataloging-in-Publication Data
Salzman, Stanley A.
    Mathematics for business/ Stanley A. Salzman, Charles D. Miller,
Louis F. Hoelzle.—5th edition.
    p.   cm.
    Includes index.
    ISBN 0-673-46740-6.—ISBN 0-673-99009-5 (instructor's ed.)
    1. Business mathematics. I. Miller, Charles David
II. Hoelzle, Louis F. III. Title.
    HF5691.S26 1993
    650′.01′513—dc20   93-14230
                                                                           CIP

94 95 96 9 8 7 6 5 4 3 2

To the Instructor

Mathematics for Business, Fifth Edition, provides solid, practical, and up-to-date coverage of those topics students need to master to attain success in business today. The fifth edition incorporates the most current business procedures, tax laws, and government forms, as well as new pedagogical features. Many examples and exercises, plus portions of instructional text, have been revised in response to current educational thinking and the comments of reviewers and users of the fourth edition.

Following a brief review of operations with fractions and calculators, and a discussion of formulas and algebra, the book introduces elementary business topics such as bank services, payroll, taxes, risk management, discount, and markup. More advanced topics, such as interest, annuities, depreciation, financial statements, and business statistics, complete the coverage. Strong examples, the most accurate and current forms and business documents available, and numerous exercises provide solid preparation for students going on to further study in accounting, management, marketing, retailing, real estate, or office administration. More than enough topics are included for a one-year course. For shorter courses, the wide range of topics permits you to select those chapters that best fit your needs.

The supplemental package continues to be extensive. For students we offer a computer tutorial program. For instructors, we provide an Instructor's Edition with all answers in place on the page; an Instructor's Testing Manual containing alternative forms of tests, additional test items, and teaching tips; color transparencies; and a computerized test generator. In addition, a videotape series and telecourse designed around the textbook plus *The Electronic Calculator Workbook with Business Applications* are available.

IMPORTANT FEATURES

Several features designed to assist students in the learning process have been integrated into this edition. The following pages illustrate many of these.

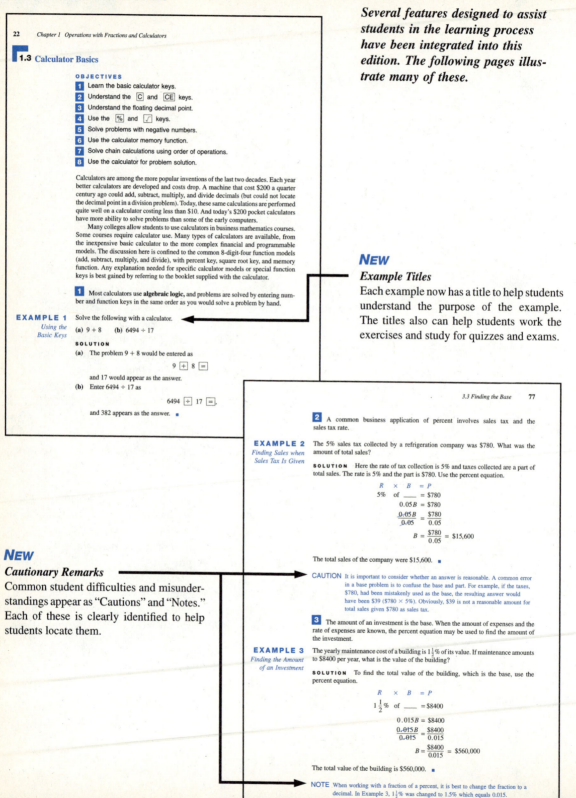

1.3 Calculator Basics

OBJECTIVES

1 Learn the basic calculator keys.
2 Understand the C and CE keys.
3 Understand the floating decimal point.
4 Use the % and √ keys.
5 Solve problems with negative numbers.
6 Use the calculator memory function.
7 Solve chain calculations using order of operations.
8 Use the calculator for problem solution.

Calculators are among the more popular inventions of the last two decades. Each year better calculators are developed and costs drop. A machine that cost $200 a quarter century ago could add, subtract, multiply, and divide decimals (but could not locate the decimal point in a division problem). Today, these same calculations are performed quite well on a calculator costing less than $10. And today's $200 pocket calculators have more ability to solve problems than some of the early computers.

Many colleges allow students to use calculators in business mathematics courses. Some courses require calculator use. Many types of calculators are available, from the inexpensive basic calculator to the more complex financial and programmable models. The discussion here is confined to the common 8-digit-four function models (add, subtract, multiply, and divide), with percent key, square root key, and memory function. Any explanation needed for specific calculator models or special function keys is best gained by referring to the booklet supplied with the calculator.

1 Most calculators use **algebraic logic,** and problems are solved by entering number and function keys in the same order as you would solve a problem by hand.

EXAMPLE 1
Using the Basic Keys

Solve the following with a calculator.

(a) 9 + 8   (b) 6494 ÷ 17

SOLUTION

(a) The problem 9 + 8 would be entered as

$$9 \boxed{+} 8 \boxed{=}$$

and 17 would appear as the answer.

(b) Enter 6494 ÷ 17 as

$$6494 \boxed{÷} 17 \boxed{=},$$

and 382 appears as the answer. ■

NEW

Example Titles

Each example now has a title to help students understand the purpose of the example. The titles also can help students work the exercises and study for quizzes and exams.

2 A common business application of percent involves sales tax and the sales tax rate.

EXAMPLE 2
Finding Sales when Sales Tax Is Given

The 5% sales tax collected by a refrigeration company was $780. What was the amount of total sales?

SOLUTION   Here the rate of tax collection is 5% and taxes collected are a part of total sales. The rate is 5% and the part is $780. Use the percent equation.

$$R \quad × \quad B \quad = P$$
$$5\% \quad \text{of} \quad \underline{\quad} = \$780$$
$$0.05B = \$780$$
$$\frac{0.05B}{0.05} = \frac{\$780}{0.05}$$
$$B = \frac{\$780}{0.05} = \$15,600$$

The total sales of the company were $15,600. ■

CAUTION   It is important to consider whether an answer is reasonable. A common error in a base problem is to confuse the base and part. For example, if the taxes, $780, had been mistakenly used as the base, the resulting answer would have been $39 ($780 × 5%). Obviously, $39 is not a reasonable amount for total sales given $780 as sales tax.

3 The amount of an investment is the base. When the amount of expenses and the rate of expenses are known, the percent equation may be used to find the amount of the investment.

EXAMPLE 3
Finding the Amount of an Investment

The yearly maintenance cost of a building is $1\frac{1}{2}\%$ of its value. If maintenance amounts to $8400 per year, what is the value of the building?

SOLUTION   To find the total value of the building, which is the base, use the percent equation.

$$R \quad × \quad B \quad = P$$
$$1\frac{1}{2}\% \quad \text{of} \quad \underline{\quad} = \$8400$$
$$0.015B = \$8400$$
$$\frac{0.015B}{0.015} = \frac{\$8400}{0.015}$$
$$B = \frac{\$8400}{0.015} = \$560,000$$

The total value of the building is $560,000. ■

NEW

Cautionary Remarks

Common student difficulties and misunderstandings appear as "Cautions" and "Notes." Each of these is clearly identified to help students locate them.

NOTE   When working with a fraction of a percent, it is best to change the fraction to a decimal. In Example 3, $1\frac{1}{2}\%$ was changed to 1.5% which equals 0.015.

NEW

Summary Exercise

Every chapter ends with a Summary Exercise, designed to help students apply what they have learned in the chapter. These problems require students to synthesize most or all of the topics they have covered in the chapter to be able to solve one cumulative exercise.

SUMMARY EXERCISE

Many people collect baseball cards as a hobby, some collect them as an investment, and a few people support themselves through college by buying and selling cards. A 1952 Jackie Robinson card recently sold for $4675. (The one pictured here is from 1953.)

In the past year some cards have gone up in value while others have gone down.

THE UPS AND DOWNS OF LAST YEAR		
ROOKIE CARD	CARD PRICE*	% CHANGE FROM LAST YEAR
Frank Thomas	$ 4.50	+13
Cal Ripken Jr.	65.00	+117
Dave Justice	4.00	+167
Nolan Ryan	1200.00	Unch.
Ken Griffey Jr.	9.00	Unch.
José Canseco	10.00	−44
Will Clark	15.00	−40
Mark McGwire	12.00	−20

*Average prices for rookie cards

National Baseball Library and Archive, Cooperstown, New York

FIGURE 3.5

Find the price of each of the cards last year for each of the players listed. (Round to the nearest half dollar.)

Frank Thomas

Cal Ripken Jr.

Dave Justice

Nolan Ryan

Ken Griffey Jr.

Jose Canseco

Will Clark

Mark McGwire

---

65. A classmate of yours is confused on how to convert a decimal to a fraction. Write an explanation of this to your classmate including changing the fraction to lowest terms. (See Objective 3.)

66. Explain how to convert a fraction to a decimal. Be sure to mention rounding in your explanation. (See Objective 5.)

67. Explain in your own words the difference between thousands and thousandths. (See Objective 3.)

68. Write the directions for rounding a money answer to the nearest cent.

Work each of the following word problems.

69. Kevin Howell allows $1\frac{1}{3}$ bottles of beverage for each guest at his party. If he expects 35 guests, how many bottles of beverage will he need?

70. Sandy Yost bought 12 shares of stock at $18\frac{3}{4}$ per share, 24 shares at $36\frac{3}{8}$ per share, and 16 shares at $74\frac{1}{8}$ per share. Her broker charged her a commission of $12. Find the total amount that she paid.

71. It takes $\frac{4}{5}$ pound of salt to fill a large salt shaker. How many salt shakers can be filled with 28 pounds of salt?

72. How many $\frac{1}{8}$-ounce vials of medicine can be filled with 7 ounces of medicine?

73. A will states that $\frac{7}{8}$ of the estate is to be divided among relatives. Of the remaining $\frac{1}{8}$, $\frac{1}{4}$ goes to the American Cancer Society. What fraction of the estate goes to the American Cancer Society?

74. A couple invested $\frac{1}{5}$ of their total investment in stocks. Of the $\frac{1}{5}$ invested in stocks, $\frac{1}{8}$ is invested in General Motors. What fraction of the total investment is invested in General Motors?

75. A photographer uses $4\frac{1}{4}$ rolls of film at a wedding and $2\frac{3}{8}$ rolls of film at a retirement party. Find the total number of rolls needed for 28 weddings and 16 retirement parties.

76. One necklace can be completed in $6\frac{1}{2}$ minutes, while a bracelet takes $3\frac{1}{8}$ minutes. Find the total time that it takes to complete 36 necklaces and 22 bracelets.

77. The Bridge Lighting Committee has raised $\frac{7}{8}$ of the funds necessary for their lighting project. If this amounts to $840,000, how much additional money must be raised?

78. A mountain guide has used pack animals for $\frac{14}{17}$ of a trip and must finish the trip on foot. The distance covered with pack animals is 98 miles. Find the number of miles to be completed on foot.

NEW

Writing Exercises

Designed to help students better understand and relate the concepts within a section, these exercises require a written answer of a few sentences. These exercises often are referenced to a specific learning objective to help students formulate an answer.

Numerous Exercises

Mastering business mathematics requires working many exercises, so we have included nearly 3500 in the fifth edition. They range from simple drill problems to word problems that require several steps to solve. All problems have been independently checked to ensure accuracy.

Quick Reviews. At the end of each chapter a concise review helps reinforce student understanding of chapter topics and formulas. It identifies the key topics, describes the method of approach to solution, and presents a detailed, worked-out example for each topic.

Review Exercises. Each chapter contains a set of review problems that provide the student with the opportunity to practice the ideas of the entire chapter. They are referenced to the sections.

Supplementary Exercises. Two sets of supplementary exercises in Chapter 3 require students to distinguish among the different elements of a percent problem and decide on the correct method of solution.

Flexibility. After basic prerequisites have been met, the chapters in this book have been made as independent as possible to give instructors freedom in choosing course sequences. Chapter prerequisites are as follows.

Chapter	Prerequisite	Chapter	Prerequisite
1	None	12	Chapter 11, simple interest
2	Chapter 1, fractions	13	Chapter 2, equations and
3	Chapter 2, equations and formulas		formulas, and Chapter 11, simple interest
4	Chapter 1, fractions	14	Chapter 11, simple interest
5	Chapter 3, percent	15	Chapter 13, compound interest
6	Chapter 3, percent	16	Chapter 3, percent
7	Chapter 1, fractions	17	Chapter 3, percent
8	Chapter 3, percent	18	Chapter 1, fractions
9	Chapter 3, percent	19	Chapter 3, percent
10	Chapter 3, percent		
11	Chapter 2, equations and formulas		

Pretests. *Mathematics for Business* offers two different pretests. One shows the students the type of questions they may see in preemployment tests, and the other tests students' skills in basic mathematics and their knowledge of business mathematics.

Appendixes. Appendix A provides an arithmetic review for those students needing to review whole numbers and decimals. Appendix B presents the powers of e. Appendix C includes all interest tables.

Summary of Formulas. The endpapers of *Mathematics for Business* provide a handy summary of commonly used business formulas from the book.

Glossary. A glossary of key words, located at the back of the book, provides a quick reference for the main ideas of the course.

The material in Chapter 4 has been updated to reflect current banking trends and practices. Banking charges and credit card deposit slips are the latest available. The bank reconciliation form has been simplified to reflect current industry changes.

In Chapter 5 all wages and salaries have been updated along with FICA and tax withholding rates. FICA and medicare rates have been separated to reflect the latest government practices. The percentage method of determining federal tax withholding is now explained along with the wage bracket method. A simplified calculation of state withholding tax is now shown.

The interest rates and loan terms have been changed throughout the book to reflect the most recent market conditions in banking and finance.

In Chapter 18 the sections on stocks and bonds have been updated and show currently traded securities using current market practices.

Throughout the book, examples and exercises have been updated and replaced with new ones to provide realistic applications for the student in today's world.

Supplements

Our complete supplementary package includes an instructor's edition, testing materials, teaching tips, instructor's solution manual, software, videotapes, and a student's solution manual.

Instructor's Edition. In this volume instructors have immediate access to all answers to exercises directly on the page. In addition, the writing exercises are marked by a symbol, ✎, so instructors may use discretion in assigning these problems.

Instructor's Testing Manual. An extensive instructor's testing manual contains suggested course outlines, teaching tips, answers to even-numbered exercises, alternative pretests in both basic mathematics and business mathematics, six different test forms for each chapter (two are multiple choice), two final examinations, answers to all test materials, and transparency masters.

Instructor's Solution Manual. This volume contains solutions to all even-numbered exercises in the textbook, with the exception of writing exercises, for which many answers are possible.

Transparencies. Color overhead transparencies of forms, tables, and schedules help instructors present and review important points during lecture.

Electronic Calculator Workbook. *The Electronic Calculator Workbook with Business Applications* by Rita Evans Bowtell, Bakersfield College, may be used with this textbook in a standard course, or may become the central text for an electronic calculator-based course.

HarperCollins Test Generator/Editor for Mathematics QuizMaster. This software is available in IBM and Macintosh versions and is fully networkable. The test generator enables instructors to select questions by objective, section, or chapter, or to use a ready-made test for each chapter. The editor enables instructors to edit any preexisting data or to easily create their own questions. The software is algorithm driven, allowing the instructor to regenerate constants while maintaining problem type, providing a nearly unlimited number of available tests or quiz items in multiple-choice or open-response format. The system features printed graphics and accurate mathematics symbols. QuizMaster enables instructors to create tests and quizzes using the Test Generator/Editor and save them to disk so students can take the test or quiz on a stand-alone computer or network. QuizMaster then grades the test or quiz and allows the instructor to create reports on individual students or classes.

Videotape Series and Telecourse. The Southern California Consortium has produced a videotape series called *By the Numbers,* based on *Mathematics for Business.* The series has been aired over the Public Broadcasting System (PBS). Your school can offer a telecourse using *Mathematics for Business* and the teleguide for *By the Numbers,* or the videotapes can be used for a traditional lecture course.

Computer Tutorial. This innovative package is available in IBM and Macintosh versions and is fully networkable. As with the Test Generator/Editor, this software is algorithm driven, which automatically regenerates constants so a student will not see the numbers repeat in a problem type if he or she revisits any particular section. The tutorial is self-paced and provides unlimited opportunities to review lessons and to practice problem solving. When students give a wrong answer, they can request to see the problem worked out. The program is menu-driven for ease of use, and on-screen help can be obtained at any time with a single keystroke. Students' scores are automatically recorded and can be printed for a permanent record. The optional management system lets instructors record student scores on disk and print diagnostic reports for individual students or classes.

Student's Solution Manual. The *Student's Solution Manual,* by Paul J. Eldersveld, College of DuPage, provides students with detailed solutions to the odd-numbered exercises and solutions to all of the chapter review exercises. The only exception is writing exercises, for which many answers exist.

Acknowledgments

We would like to thank the many users of the fourth edition for their insightful observations and suggestions for improving the book. We also wish to express our appreciation and thanks to the following reviewers for their contributions.

Carl Ballard, Central Piedmont Community College

Maryann Birdsall, Ocean County College

Ruth Ann Edwards, Craven Community College

Norman Eric Ellis, Essex Community College

Patricia H. Eyer, Northern Virginia Community College-Annandale Campus

Andrea Goehner, Catawba Valley Community College

Dennis A. Gutting, Orange County Community College

Dianne Hendrickson, Becker College-Leicester

Linda L. Hermann, Parkland College

Janice L. Hoeweler, Cincinnati Technical College

Larry C. Hollar, Catawba Valley Community College

Marjorie Lapham, Quinsigamond Valley Community College

Yvonne P. Mangan, Niagara County Community College

Michel C. Marette, Northern Virginia Community College-Loudoun Campus

David C. Mayne, Anne Arundel Community College

A. Ally Mishal, Stark Technical College

David T. Nakamaejo, Kapiolani Community College

Ned W. Schillow, Lehigh County Community College

Steven Sodergren, Antelope Valley College

Chris Widmer, Tidewater Community College, Virginia Beach

Our appreciation goes to John Garlow, Tarrant County Junior College, Northwest Campus, for his careful work checking all the exercises and examples in the book.

We also would like to express our gratitude to our colleagues at American River College and Bucks County Community College who have helped us immeasurably with their support and encouragement: Gilbert Eckern, Richard McIntosh, Paul Plescia, Barbara Weeks, Richard Wright, Robert Garrett, James Bralley, Richard Gonsalves, Bill Monroe, Bernie Bieg, and Lee Neumann.

Also, special thanks and appreciation go to Sheri Minkner and Judy Martinez for their neat and accurate manuscript typing.

At HarperCollins, we would like to thank Anne Kelly, Linda Youngman, Liz Lee, Ann-Marie Buesing, and Laura Taber. These very talented and focused people made sure that all the elements of this project came together in superb fashion.

Stanley A. Salzman
Louis F. Hoelzle

Contents

19 Business Statistics 651

Appendixes

Answers to Selected Exercises A-47

Glossary A-77

Index A-93

Introduction to Students:
Why Business Mathematics?

With a growing need for recordkeeping, establishing budgets, and understanding finance, taxation, and investment opportunities, mathematics has become a greater part of our daily lives. This text applies mathematics to daily business experiences. Your success in future business courses and pursuits will be enhanced by the knowledge and skills you will learn in this business mathematics course.

Your need for skills in business mathematics will be apparent when you apply for your first permanent job. Many companies follow a well-organized three-part employment process: application, testing, and interview. Poor results on the mathematics test often eliminate a large number of applicants from further consideration for employment. To give you an idea of what to expect, the mathematics section of a preemployment test is included here. This preemployment test contains questions from federal and state civil service examinations and from a major public utility examination.

A second test is designed to test your skills in business mathematics before beginning this course. This pretest is composed of problems used later as examples throughout the text so that you may study the solutions to those you find difficult.

**Test 1
Preemployment
Test**

These problems are selected from federal and state personnel board preemployment examinations and from a major public utility examination. Work each problem; then select the best answer from the five choices given.

1. $\frac{3}{4} \times \frac{9}{14} =$

    (a) $8\frac{3}{14}$ (b) $\frac{1}{2}$ (c) $\frac{27}{56}$ (d) $\frac{12}{16}$ (e) $\frac{27}{65}$

2. Add: 9 years 8 months
              5 years 4 months
        + 6 years 9 months

    (a) 21 years 9 months   (b) 20 years 9 months   (c) 22 years 2 months
    (d) 20 years 8 months   (e) None of these

3. $\frac{7}{8} \div 3\frac{1}{2} =$

    (a) $3\frac{1}{16}$ (b) $\frac{1}{4}$ (c) $\frac{16}{49}$ (d) 4   (e) $\frac{1}{3}$

4. What is the least common denominator of the fractions $\frac{1}{8}$ and $\frac{1}{36}$?

    (a) 96   (b) 36   (c) 108   (d) 288   (e) None of these

5. $\frac{1}{2} + \frac{5}{8} + \frac{9}{10} =$

    (a) $2\frac{1}{40}$ (b) $\frac{19}{30}$ (c) $\frac{37}{60}$ (d) $1\frac{1}{40}$ (e) $2\frac{3}{40}$

6. 18% of 78% is:

    (a) 15.6%   (b) 18%   (c) 14.4%   (d) $14\frac{1}{4}$%   (e) None of these

7. $0.052 \times 0.03 =$

    (a) 1.56   (b) 0.0156   (c) 15.6   (d) 0.00156   (e) 156

8. What is $\frac{1}{4}$% in decimal form?

    (a) 2.5   (b) 0.25   (c) 0.025   (d) 0.0025   (e) None of these

9. What is $\frac{1}{2}$% of $1300?

    (a) $.65   (b) $6.50   (c) $65.00   (d) $650   (e) $6500

10. Three yards most nearly equals

    (a) 80 in.   (b) 90 in.   (c) 100 in.   (d) 110 in.   (3) None of these

11. $113\frac{17}{52} - 33\frac{5}{13} =$

    (a) $79\frac{49}{52}$ (b) $80\frac{3}{52}$ (c) $80\frac{12}{52}$ (d) $80\frac{49}{52}$ (e) None of these

12. $221\frac{1}{119} \times 10\frac{11}{35} =$

    (a) 80.3   (b) 2510.0   (c) 2510.1   (d) 2280.0   (e) None of these

13. $\dfrac{(418 + 56 - 8)313}{77 + (50 + 9)7 - 24} =$

(a) $-12,378$ (b) 310   (c) 313   (d) 1246.649   (e) None of these

14. The sum of two numbers is 63, and one is 27 larger than the other. What is the smaller number?

(a) 18   (b) 26   (c) 31   (d) 45   (e) None of these

15. If upholstery material sells for $12.76 per yard, how much would it cost to buy 144 inches of material?

(a) $3.19   (b) $51.04   (c) $12.76   (d) $25.52   (e) None of these

16. An importer has a shipment of 2000 pens of equal value with a total value of $800. The duty rate on pens valued at 10¢ or more but not over 50¢ per pen is 8% of their value; the duty on pens valued over 50¢ but not more than $1 per pen is 6% of their value. How much duty is paid on the shipment of pens?

(a) $48   (b) $64   (c) $160   (d) $180   (e) None of these

17. If a strip of cloth 36 inches long will shrink 3 inches when washed, how many inches long will a 48-inch strip be after shrinking?

(a) 44   (b) 45   (c) 46   (d) 47   (e) None of these

18. If an automobile travels 8 miles in 12 minutes, what is its average speed in mph?

(a) 40   (b) 50   (c) 60   (d) 70   (e) None of these

19. An office supply store buys 100 reams of special quality paper for $400. If 1 ream = 500 sheets of paper, how much must the store receive per 100 sheets to obtain a 20% gain on its cost?

(a) 83¢   (b) 85¢   (c) 96¢   (d) 98¢   (e) None of these

20. A vase is packed in a carton with a 10″ diameter and is surrounded by packing 2″ thick at the mouth. If the diameter of the base is $\frac{1}{2}$ the diameter of the mouth, what is the diameter of the base?

(a) 3″   (b) 4″   (c) 6″   (d) 8″   (e) None of these

21. A company bidding for a contract to produce aircraft engine parts is planning production time. A machinist has 74 equal units of work to complete in 8 hours. During the first 2 hours, the machinist averages $8\frac{1}{2}$ units per hour. How many units per hour must be completed in the remaining time to complete the job?

(a) $7\frac{1}{8}$ (b) $9\frac{1}{4}$ (c) $9\frac{1}{2}$ (d) $12\frac{1}{3}$ (e) None of these

22. An invoice contained the following items:

6 desks @ $89.20	$525.20
8 chairs @ $32.50	260.00
Total	$885.20

The terms given on the invoice were 3% 10 days, net 30 days. Verify the computations, which may be incorrect, and calculate the correct amount to be paid if payment is made within the discount period.

(a) $761.64   (b) $771.85   (c) $795.20   (d) $858.64
(e) None of these

23. Full-time employees earn sick leave at the rate of 4 hours per 2-week pay period. Four work hours are equal to $\frac{1}{2}$ workday; a workweek consists of five 8-hour days, and the leave year consists of 26 biweekly pay periods. The following table gives the sick-leave record of the full-time employee for the current leave year. Determine the balance of accumulated sick leave to the credit of the employee at the end of the current leave year.

Employee	Accumulated Sick Leave from the Previous Year	Sick Leave Used During Current Year
2208	8 days 4 hours	2 days 1 hour

(a) 6 days 3 hours   (b) 19 days 3 hours   (c) 23 days 5 days
(d) 32 days 3 hours   (e) None of these

24. A supply depot had an inventory of $24,625 on January 1. During the year, purchases made by the depot amounted to $60,000, and the cost of goods issued amounted to $28,000. The inventory on December 31 was

(a) $25,065   (b) $28,500   (c) $49,560   (d) $57,005
(e) None of these

25. Dividends are earnings distributed among stockholders of a corporation in proportion of their holdings. In today's market, a person who received $54.40 on 32 shares of common stock from a large defense contractor during any given quarter would consider that the stock is reasonably valuable, although he or she is receiving very little return for capital invested in conditions of risk. If, additionally, this investor owns 51 shares of the same stock, how much did the investor receive in dividends during the same quarter for these 51 shares?

(a) $85.40   (b) $86.70   (c) $87.40   (d) $87.62   (e) None of these

---

Answers: 1. (c)   **2.** (a)   **3.** (b)   **4.** (e)   **5.** (a)   **6.** (e)   **7.** (d)   **8.** (d)
9. (b)   **10.** (d)   **11.** (a)   **12.** (d)   **13.** (c)   **14.** (a)   **15.** (b)   **16.** (b)
17. (a)   **18.** (a)   **19.** (c)   **20.** (a)   **21.** (c)   **22.** (e)   **23.** (b)   **24.** (e)
25. (b)

Test 2 Pretest in Business Mathematics

This pretest measures your business mathematics skills at the beginning of the course. The solutions to each of these problems are to be found in this book on the given page.

(page 3)   1. Convert to an improper fraction: $7\frac{2}{3}$

(page 3)   2. Convert to a mixed number: $\frac{17}{5}$

(page 6)   3. Find the least common denominator of the fractions $\frac{5}{12}$, $\frac{7}{18}$, and $\frac{11}{20}$.

(page 8)   4. Mixed numbers—add: $17\frac{5}{6} + 11\frac{1}{4} + 43\frac{9}{16}$

(page 9)   5. Common fractions—subtract: $\frac{17}{18} - \frac{20}{27}$

(page 9)   6. Mixed numbers—subtract: $36\frac{2}{9}$
$$-27\frac{5}{6}$$

(page 14)   7. Mixed numbers—multiply: $5\frac{5}{8} \times 4\frac{1}{6}$

(page 14)   8. Common fractions—divide: $\frac{25}{36} \div \frac{15}{18}$

(page 16)   9. Convert the decimal 0.028 to a fraction.

(page 37)   10. Solve $k + 7 = 18$ for k.

(page 40)   11. Solve $5r - 2 = 2(r + 5)$ for r.

(page 50)   12. Solve for W in the formula $P = 2L + 2W$.

(page 56)   13. Find x in the proportion: $\dfrac{3}{5} = \dfrac{x}{40}$

(page 65)   14. Express as a percent: 0.7

(page 66)   15. Express as a decimal: 142%

(page 70)   16. Solve for part: 1.2% of 180 is ———.

(page 76)   17. Solve for base: 135 is 15% of ———.

(page 77)   18. The 5% sales tax collected by a refrigeration company amounted to $780. What was the amount of total sales?

(page 88)   19. At one firm, this year's sales were $121,000, which was 10% more than last year's sales. Find last year's sales.

(page 91)   20. After a dealer deducted 10% from the price of a pair of skis, a customer paid $135. What was the original price of the skis?

(page 171)   21. Suppose that during a certain quarter a firm has collected $1382.71 from its employees for FICA tax, $319.09 for medicare tax, and $1786.43 in federal withholding tax. Compute the total amount due to the government form the firm.

(page 193)   22. Find the taxes on each of the following pieces of property. Assessed valuations and tax rates are given.
(a) $58,975; 8.4%   (b) $74,500; $7.82 per $100
(c) $129,600; $64.21 per $1000   (d) $221,750; 94 mills

(page 203) **23.** Adam Strong is single, has no dependents and had an adjusted gross income of $15,353 last year, with deductions of $1352 for other taxes, $2616 for mortgage interest, and $317 for charity. Find his taxable income and his income tax.

(page 220) **24.** Talaya Turner owns a factory valued at $560,000. Her fire insurance policy (with an 80% coinsurance clause) has a face value of $420,000. The building suffers a fire loss of $112,000. Find the amount of loss that the insurance company will pay.

(page 260) **25.** Suppose a series discount of 20/10 is offered on a circular saw with a list price of $150. Find the net cost after the series discount.

(page 275) **26.** An invoice of $450 is dated July 1 and offers terms of 2/10, n/30. If the invoice is paid on July 8 and the shipping and insurance charges are $23.40, find the total amount due.

(page 295) **27.** Find the percent of markup based on cost if a washing machine costing $350 is sold for $420.

(page 309) **28.** An athletic shoe manufacturer makes a walking shoe at a cost of $16.80 per pair. Based on past experience 10% of the shoes will be defective and must be sold as irregulars for $24 per pair. If the manufacturer produces 1000 pairs of the shoes and desires a markup of 100% on cost, find the selling price per pair.

(page 332) **29.** Suppose Shasta Office Products made the following purchases of the same model of file cabinets during the year.

January	50 file cabinets at $80 each
March	60 file cabinets at $85 each
July	40 file cabinets at $75 each
October	100 file cabinets at $90 each

At the end of the year there are 125 file cabinets in inventory. Use the weighted average method to find the inventory value.

(page 358) **30.** Suppose $3400 is invested for 135 days and earns $89.25 interest. Find the rate of interest.

(page 406) **31.** On February 27, Andrews Lincoln-Mercury receives a 150-day note with a face value of $3500 at 8% interest per year. On March 27, the firm discounts the note at the bank. Find the proceeds if the discount rate is 12%.

(page 419) **32.** Find the interest earned on $800 at 8% per year, compounded semiannually for $2\frac{1}{2}$ years.

(page 453) **33.** A 120-day note is made on May 9, has a face value of $4000, and carries interest on 10%. On June 17, payment of $1500 is made. Find the balance owed on the principal. If no additional payments are made, find the amount that will be due on the maturity date of the loan.

(page 512) **34.** Prepare a repayment schedule for the first month on a loan of $60,000 at 8% interest for 30 years. The monthly payment on this loan is $440.40.

(page 545) **35.** Using the sum-of-the-years'-digits method of depreciation, find the first and second year's depreciation for an asset which has a cost of $2000, an estimated life of 4 years, and no salvage value.

(page 554) **36.** An asset with a life of 10 years is purchased on April 1 at a cost of $12,000. If the double-declining-balance method is used, find the depreciation for the first partial year and the next full year.

(page 579) **37.** Write each of the following items as a percent of net sales.

Gross sales	$209,000	Salaries and wages	$11,000
Returns	$9000	Rent	$6000
Cost of goods sold	$145,000	Advertising	$11,000

(page 613) **38.** Because of a steep drop in the price of beef last year, Rocky Mountain Land paid no dividend. This year, the board of directors has set aside $175,000 for the payment of dividends. The company has outstanding 12,500 shares of cumulative preferred stock having par value of $50, with an 8% dividend. The company also has 40,000 shares of common stock. What dividend will be paid to the owners of each type of stock?

(page 631) **39.** Lin Chao and Joan Frisk start a new dry-cleaning business. Frisk contributed $50,000, while Chao contributed $25,000. The business will be run by Chao. The partners have agreed to pay Chao a salary of $14,000 per year, and then divide the remaining profits according to the original investment. Find the amount each partner would get from a profit of $26,000.

(page 678) **40.** Suppose an instructor gives a test to 300 students. Suppose further that the grades are closely approximated by a normal curve with mean 75 and standard deviation 8. Find the number of scores: (a) within 1 standard deviation of the mean; (b) within 2 standard deviations.

Answers: 1. $\frac{23}{3}$ **2.** $3\frac{2}{5}$ **3.** 180 **4.** $72\frac{31}{48}$ **5.** $\frac{11}{54}$ **6.** $8\frac{7}{18}$ **7.** $23\frac{7}{16}$
8. $\frac{5}{6}$ **9.** $\frac{7}{250}$ **10.** 11 **11.** 4 **12.** $\frac{P-2L}{2} = W$ **13.** 24 **14.** 70%
15. 1.42 **16.** 2.160 **17.** 900 **18.** $15,600 **19.** $110,000 **20.** $150
21. $5190.03 **22. (a)** $4953.90 **(b)** $5825.90 **(c)** $8321.62 **(d)** $20,844.50
23. $8918; $1337.70 **24.** $105,000 **25.** $108 **26.** $464.40 **27.** 20%
28. $34.67 **29.** $10,550 **30.** 7% **31.** $3469.59 **32.** $173.33 **33.** $2543.33;
$2600.55 **34.** Interest Payment $400; Principal Payment $40.40; Balance of Principal $59,959.60 **35.** $800; $600 **36.** $1800; $2040 **37.** 104.5%; 4.5%; 72.5%; 5.5%; 3%; 5.5% **38.** $8; $1.88 **39.** $18,000; $8000 **40. (a)** 204 **(b)** 285

Operations with Fractions and Calculators

Businesses use mathematics every day: to calculate employee payrolls, find the interest on loans, determine the markups on items to be sold, or maintain the firm's financial records, for example.

It is important to understand the fundamentals of mathematics, so that the more advanced problems in business mathematics can be solved. The first chapter reviews fractions and introduces calculators, Chapter 2 looks briefly at basic equations and formulas, and Chapter 3 discusses percent. The rest of the chapters apply these mathematical skills to actual business situations.

1.1 Addition and Subtraction of Fractions

OBJECTIVES

1. Learn the basic terminology of fractions.
2. Convert mixed numbers.
3. Write fractions in lowest terms.
4. Use rules for divisibility.
5. Add like fractions.
6. Find the least common denominator.
7. Add unlike fractions.
8. Add mixed numbers.
9. Subtract fractions.
10. Subtract mixed numbers.

1 A **fraction** is an indicated quotient that represents part of a whole. Fractions are written as one number over another, with a line between the two numbers, as in the following.

$$\frac{5}{8} \qquad \frac{1}{4} \qquad \frac{9}{7} \qquad \frac{12}{10}$$

The number above the line is called the **numerator,** and the number below the line is called the **denominator.** In the fraction $\frac{2}{3}$, for example, the numerator is 2 and the denominator is 3. The denominator tells the number of parts into which the whole is divided and the numerator tells how many parts are needed. For example, $\frac{2}{3}$ is "2 parts out of 3 equal parts." (See Figure 1.1.)

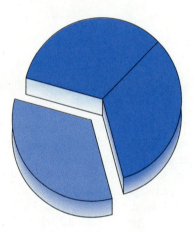

$\frac{2}{3}$ means 2 parts out of 3 equal parts

FIGURE 1.1

If the numerator of the fraction is smaller than the denominator, the fraction is a **proper fraction.** Examples of proper fractions include $\frac{2}{3}$, $\frac{3}{4}$, $\frac{15}{16}$, and $\frac{1}{8}$. A fraction with a numerator greater than or equal to the denominator is an **improper fraction.** Examples of improper fractions include $\frac{17}{8}$, $\frac{19}{12}$, $\frac{11}{2}$, and $\frac{5}{3}$. A proper fraction has a value less than 1, while an improper fraction has a value greater than or equal to 1.

To write a whole number as a fraction, place the whole number over 1; for example,

$$7 = \frac{7}{1} \quad \text{and} \quad 12 = \frac{12}{1}.$$

2 The sum of a fraction and a whole number is called a **mixed number.** Examples of mixed numbers include $2\frac{2}{3}$, $3\frac{5}{8}$, and $9\frac{5}{6}$. The mixed number $2\frac{2}{3}$ is a short way of writing $2 + \frac{2}{3}$. A mixed number can be converted to an improper fraction. For example, to convert the mixed number $4\frac{5}{8}$ to an improper fraction, first multiply the denominator of the fraction part, 8, by the whole number part, 4. This gives $4 \times 8 = 32$. Then add the product (32) to the numerator (in this case, 5). This gives $32 + 5 = 37$. This sum is the numerator of the new improper fraction. The denominator stays the same.

$$4\frac{5}{8} = \frac{37}{8} \quad \leftarrow (4 \times 8) + 5$$

EXAMPLE 1

Converting Mixed Numbers to Improper Fractions

Convert $7\frac{2}{3}$ to an improper fraction.

SOLUTION First multiply 3 by 7, then add 2. This gives $(3 \times 7) + 2 = 21 + 2 = 23$. The parentheses are used to show that 3 and 7 are multiplied first.

$$7\frac{2}{3} = \frac{23}{3} \quad \leftarrow (3 \times 7) + 2 \quad \blacksquare$$

Convert an improper fraction to a mixed number by dividing the numerator of the improper fraction by the denominator. The quotient is the whole number part of the mixed number, and the remainder is used as the numerator of the fraction part. The denominator stays the same.

EXAMPLE 2

Converting Improper Fractions to Mixed Numbers

Convert $\frac{17}{5}$ to a mixed number.

SOLUTION Divide 17 by 5.

$$
\begin{array}{r}
3 \\
5\overline{)17} \\
15 \\
\hline
2
\end{array}
$$

The whole number part is the quotient 3. The remainder 2 is used as the numerator of the fraction part. Keep 5 as the denominator.

$$\frac{17}{5} = 3\frac{2}{5} \quad \blacksquare$$

3 If no number except 1 divides without remainder into both numerator and denominator of a fraction, the fraction is in **lowest terms.** For example, only 1 divides without remainder into both 2 and 3, so that $\frac{2}{3}$ is in lowest terms. In the same way, $\frac{1}{9}, \frac{4}{11}, \frac{12}{17}, \frac{8}{9}$, and $\frac{11}{15}$ are all in lowest terms. The fraction $\frac{15}{25}$ is *not* in lowest terms, however, because both 15 and 25 may be divided by 5. Write $\frac{15}{25}$ in lowest terms by dividing numerator and denominator by 5.

$$\frac{15}{25} = \frac{15 \div 5}{25 \div 5} = \frac{3}{5}$$

EXAMPLE 3

Writing Fractions in Lowest Terms

Write the following in lowest terms.

(a) $\dfrac{30}{42}$ (b) $\dfrac{32}{40}$

SOLUTION   Look for the largest number that can be divided into both numerator and denominator.

(a) 6 is the largest divisor of both 30 and 42.

$$\frac{30}{42} = \frac{30 \div 6}{42 \div 6} = \frac{5}{7}$$

(b) Divide by 8.

$$\frac{32}{40} = \frac{32 \div 8}{40 \div 8} = \frac{4}{5} \quad \blacksquare$$

4 Deciding which numbers will divide into another number is sometimes difficult. The following **rules for divisibility** can help.

A number can be divided by:

2, if the last digit is 0, 2, 4, 6, or 8;

3, if the sum of the digits is divisible by 3;

4, if the last two digits are divisible by 4;

5, if the last digit is 0 or 5;

6, if the number is even and the sum of the digits is divisible by 3;

8, if the last three digits are divisible by 8;

9, if the sum of the digits is divisible by 9;

10, if the last digit is 0.

EXAMPLE 4

Using Rules for Divisibility

Determine whether the following statements are true.

(a) 3,746,892 is divisible by 4

(b) 15,974,802 is divisible by 9

SOLUTION

(a)   The number 3,746,892 is divisible by 4, since the last two digits form a number divisible by 4.

$$3,746,892$$

→ 92 is divisible by 4.

(b)   See if 15,974,802 is divisible by 9 by adding the digits of the number.

$$1 + 5 + 9 + 7 + 4 + 8 + 0 + 2 = 36$$

→ 36 is divisible by 9.

Since 36 is divisible by 9, the given number is divisible by 9. (Be careful: testing for divisibility by adding the digits works only for 3 and 9.) ■

5 Fractions with the same denominator are called **like fractions.** Such fractions have a **common denominator.** For example, $\frac{3}{4}$ and $\frac{1}{4}$ are like fractions, but $\frac{4}{7}$ and $\frac{4}{9}$ are not. To add like fractions, add the numerators and place this sum over the common denominator. The answer can then be written in lowest terms, if necessary.

EXAMPLE 5

Adding Like Fractions

Add the following fractions.

(a) $\frac{3}{4} + \frac{1}{4} + \frac{5}{4}$ (b) $\frac{4}{5} + \frac{3}{5} + \frac{2}{5} + \frac{1}{5}$

SOLUTION   The fractions in both parts of this example have common denominators, so add the numerators and place this sum over the common denominators. Write as a mixed number in lowest terms, as necessary.

(a) $\dfrac{3}{4} + \dfrac{1}{4} + \dfrac{5}{4} = \dfrac{3 + 1 + 5}{4} = \dfrac{9}{4} = 2\dfrac{1}{4}$

(b) $\dfrac{4}{5} + \dfrac{3}{5} + \dfrac{2}{5} + \dfrac{1}{5} = \dfrac{4 + 3 + 2 + 1}{5} = \dfrac{10}{5} = 2$ ■

6 Fractions having different denominators are called **unlike fractions.** To add unlike fractions, first rewrite the fractions with a common denominator.

The **least common denominator (LCD)** for two or more fractions is the smallest whole number that can be divided, without remainder, by all the denominators of the fractions. For example, the least common denominator of the fractions $\frac{3}{4}$, $\frac{5}{6}$, and $\frac{1}{2}$ is 12, since 12 is the smallest number that can be divided by 4, 6, and 2.

There are two ways to find the least common denominator.

Inspection.   Check to see if the least common denominator can be found by inspection. For example, the least common denominator of $\frac{1}{3}$ and $\frac{1}{4}$ is 12, since 12 is the smallest number into which 3 and 4 both divide with remainder zero. This method works best when the denominators involved are small.

Method of Prime Numbers.   If you cannot find the least common denominator by inspection, use the method of prime numbers, as shown in the next example.

> A **prime number** is a number that can be divided without remainder only by itself and by 1. Prime numbers are 2, 3, 5, 7, 11, 13, 17, and so on.

NOTE All prime numbers other than 2 are odd numbers. All odd numbers however, are not prime numbers. The number 1 is not a prime number.

EXAMPLE 6
Finding the
Least Common
Denominator

Use the method of prime numbers to find the least common denominator of the fractions $\frac{5}{12}$, $\frac{7}{18}$, and $\frac{11}{20}$.

SOLUTION   First write down the three denominators.

$$12 \quad 18 \quad 20$$

Begin by trying to divide the three denominators by the first prime number, 2. Write each quotient directly above the given denominator. (This way of writing the division process is just a handy way of writing the separate problems $2\overline{)12}$, $2\overline{)18}$, and $2\overline{)20}$.)

$$
\begin{array}{r}
6 \quad 9 \; 10 \\
\hline
2\,\lfloor\, 12 \;\; 18 \;\; 20
\end{array}
$$

Two of the new quotients, 6 and 10, can still be divided by 2, so perform the division again. Since 9 cannot be divided by 2, just bring up the 9.

$$
\begin{array}{r}
3 \quad 9 \quad 5 \\
\hline
2\,\lfloor\, 6 \quad 9 \; 10 \\
\hline
2\,\lfloor\, 12 \;\; 18 \;\; 20
\end{array}
$$

None of the new quotients in the top row can be divided by 2, so try the next prime number, 3. The number 9 can be divided twice by 3 as shown on the left.

	1	1	5			1	1	1
3	1	3	5		5	1	1	5
3	3	9	5		3	1	3	5
2	6	9	10		3	3	9	5
2	12	18	20		2	6	9	10
					2	12	18	20

Since none of the new quotients in the top row can be divided by 3, try the next prime number, 5. The number 5 can be used only once, as shown on the right. Now that the top row contains only 1s, find the least common denominator by multiplying the prime numbers in the left column.

$$2 \times 2 \times 3 \times 3 \times 5 \;=\; 180$$

The least common denominator is 180. ■

NOTE It is not necessary to start with the smallest prime number as shown in Example 6. In fact, no matter which prime number we start with, we will still get the same least common denominator.

7 Add unlike fractions by rewriting the fractions with a common denominator. Since Example 6 shows that 180 is the least common denominator for $\frac{5}{12}$, $\frac{7}{18}$, and $\frac{11}{20}$, these three fractions can be added if each fraction is first written with a denominator of 180.

$$\frac{5}{12} = \frac{\quad}{180} \qquad \frac{7}{18} = \frac{\quad}{180} \qquad \frac{11}{20} = \frac{\quad}{180}$$

Rewrite these fractions with a common denominator by first dividing the common denominator by the denominator of the original fractions.

$$180 \div 12 = 15 \qquad 180 \div 18 = 10 \qquad 180 \div 20 = 9$$

Next, multiply each quotient by the original numerator.

$$15 \times 5 = 75 \qquad 10 \times 7 = 70 \qquad 9 \times 11 = 99$$

Finally, rewrite the fractions.

$$\frac{5}{12} = \frac{75}{180} \qquad \frac{7}{18} = \frac{70}{180} \qquad \frac{11}{20} = \frac{99}{180}$$

Now add the fractions.

$$\frac{5}{12} + \frac{7}{18} + \frac{11}{20} = \frac{75}{180} + \frac{70}{180} + \frac{99}{180} = \frac{75 + 70 + 99}{180} = \frac{244}{180} = 1\frac{64}{180} = 1\frac{16}{45}$$

EXAMPLE 7   Add the following fractions.

Adding Unlike
Fractions   **(a)** $\dfrac{3}{4} + \dfrac{1}{2} + \dfrac{5}{8}$ **(b)** $\dfrac{9}{10} + \dfrac{4}{5} + \dfrac{3}{8}$

SOLUTION

(a)   Inspection shows that the least common denominator is 8. Rewrite the fractions so they each have a denominator of 8. Then add.

$$\frac{3}{4} + \frac{1}{2} + \frac{5}{8} = \frac{6}{8} + \frac{4}{8} + \frac{5}{8} = \frac{6 + 4 + 5}{8} = \frac{15}{8} = 1\frac{7}{8}$$

(b)   The method of prime numbers shows that the least common denominator is 40. Rewrite the fractions so they each have a denominator of 40. Then add.

$$\frac{9}{10} + \frac{4}{5} + \frac{3}{8} = \frac{36}{40} + \frac{32}{40} + \frac{15}{40} = \frac{36 + 32 + 15}{40} = \frac{83}{40} = 2\frac{3}{40} \quad \blacksquare$$

8   Add two mixed numbers by first adding the whole number parts. Then add the fraction parts and combine the two sums. For example, add $16\frac{1}{8}$ and $5\frac{5}{8}$ as shown.

$$
\begin{aligned}
16\tfrac{1}{8} \\
+\ 5\tfrac{5}{8} \\
\hline
21\tfrac{6}{8}
\end{aligned}
$$

— sum of fractions
— sum of whole numbers

Write $\frac{6}{8}$ in lowest terms as $\frac{3}{4}$, with $16\frac{1}{8} + 5\frac{5}{8} = 21\frac{3}{4}$.

The sum of the fraction parts of mixed numbers is sometimes greater than one. In that case, carry the excess from the fraction part to the whole number part.

EXAMPLE 8

Adding Mixed Numbers

Add the following mixed numbers.

(a) Add $9\frac{2}{3}$ and $6\frac{3}{4}$

(b) $17\frac{5}{6} + 11\frac{1}{4} + 43\frac{9}{16}$

SOLUTION

(a) Inspection shows that 12 is the least common denominator. Write $9\frac{2}{3}$ as $9\frac{8}{12}$, and $6\frac{3}{4}$ as $6\frac{9}{12}$. Then add. The work can be organized as shown.

$$9\frac{2}{3} = 9\frac{8}{12}$$
$$+\ 6\frac{3}{4} = 6\frac{9}{12}$$
$$\overline{\phantom{+\ 6\frac{3}{4} = }\ 15\frac{17}{12}} \quad \longleftarrow \text{ Add } \frac{8}{12} \text{ and } \frac{9}{12} \text{ to get } \frac{17}{12}.$$

$\text{Add 9 and 6 to get 15.}$

$$15\frac{17}{12} = 15 + \frac{17}{12} = 15 + 1\frac{5}{12} = 16\frac{5}{12} \quad \blacksquare$$

(b) Before adding these mixed numbers, first write the fractions with their least common denominator, 48.

$$17\frac{5}{6} = 17\frac{40}{48}$$
$$11\frac{1}{4} = 11\frac{12}{48}$$
$$+\ 43\frac{9}{16} = 43\frac{27}{48}$$
$$\overline{71\frac{79}{48}} = 71 + \frac{79}{48} = 71 + 1\frac{31}{48} = 72\frac{31}{48} \quad \blacksquare$$

9 To subtract fractions, first find the least common denominator, if necessary. Then subtract the numerators and place this difference over the common denominator. For example, the fractions $\frac{3}{4}$ and $\frac{1}{4}$ have the same denominator. Subtract these fractions by subtracting the numerators and placing the difference over 4.

$$\frac{3}{4} - \frac{1}{4} = \frac{3-1}{4} = \frac{2}{4} = \frac{1}{2}$$

If the fractions to be subtracted have different denominators, first find the least common denominator. For example, to subtract $\frac{1}{3}$ from $\frac{5}{8}$, first find the least common denominator, 24. Now write each fraction with a denominator of 24 and subtract.

$$\frac{5}{8} - \frac{1}{3} = \frac{15}{24} - \frac{8}{24} = \frac{15-8}{24} = \frac{7}{24}$$

EXAMPLE 9

Subtracting Fractions

Subtract the following fractions.

(a) $\dfrac{3}{4} - \dfrac{5}{9}$ (b) $\dfrac{17}{18} - \dfrac{20}{27}$

SOLUTION   Find the common denominator and then subtract.

(a) $\dfrac{3}{4} - \dfrac{5}{9} = \dfrac{27}{36} - \dfrac{20}{36} = \dfrac{7}{36}$ (b) $\dfrac{17}{18} - \dfrac{20}{27} = \dfrac{51}{54} - \dfrac{40}{54} = \dfrac{11}{54}$ ■

10 Subtract two mixed numbers by changing the mixed numbers, if necessary, so that the fraction parts have a common denominator. Then subtract the fraction parts and the whole number parts separately. For example, subtract $3\frac{1}{12}$ from $8\frac{5}{8}$ by first finding the least common denominator, 24. Then rewrite the problem.

$$
\begin{aligned}
8\,\tfrac{5}{8} &= 8\,\tfrac{15}{24} \\
-\ 3\,\tfrac{1}{12} &= 3\,\tfrac{2}{24}
\end{aligned}
$$

Now subtract the fraction parts and subtract the whole number parts.

$$
\begin{aligned}
8\,\tfrac{15}{24} \\
-\ 3\,\tfrac{2}{24} \\
\hline
5\,\tfrac{13}{24}
\end{aligned}
$$

— Subtract fractions.
— Subtract whole numbers.

The following example shows how to subtract when borrowing is needed.

EXAMPLE 10

Subtracting with Borrowing

Subtract $27\frac{5}{6}$ from $36\frac{2}{9}$.

SOLUTION   Start by rewriting the problem with a common denominator.

$$
\begin{aligned}
36\,\tfrac{2}{9} &= 36\,\tfrac{4}{18} \\
-\ 27\,\tfrac{5}{6} &= 27\,\tfrac{15}{18}
\end{aligned}
$$

Subtracting $\frac{15}{18}$ from $\frac{4}{18}$ requires borrowing 1 from 36.

$$
\begin{aligned}
36\,\tfrac{4}{18} &= 35 + 1 + \tfrac{4}{18} \\
&= 35 + \tfrac{18}{18} + \tfrac{4}{18} \qquad 1 = \tfrac{18}{18} \\
&= 35\,\tfrac{22}{18}
\end{aligned}
$$

$$
\begin{aligned}
35\,\tfrac{22}{18} \\
-\ 27\,\tfrac{15}{18} \\
\hline
8\,\tfrac{7}{18}
\end{aligned}
$$

■

Rewrite the problem as shown at the right. Check by adding $8\frac{7}{18}$ and $27\frac{5}{6}$. The answer should be $36\frac{2}{9}$.

1.1 Exercises

Convert each of the following mixed numbers to an improper fraction.

1. $1\frac{5}{9}$ **2.** $3\frac{8}{9}$ **3.** $2\frac{9}{10}$ **4.** $6\frac{2}{3}$

5. $11\frac{12}{13}$ **6.** $2\frac{8}{11}$ **7.** $12\frac{5}{8}$ **8.** $17\frac{5}{8}$

Write each of the following fractions in lowest terms. Use the divisibility rules as needed.

9. $\frac{20}{30}$ **10.** $\frac{40}{80}$ **11.** $\frac{40}{75}$ **12.** $\frac{36}{42}$

13. $\frac{63}{70}$ **14.** $\frac{27}{45}$ **15.** $\frac{120}{150}$ **16.** $\frac{30}{66}$

17. $\frac{132}{144}$ **18.** $\frac{40}{96}$ **19.** $\frac{96}{180}$ **20.** $\frac{65}{85}$

Convert each of the following improper fractions to a mixed number and write it in lowest terms.

21. $\frac{18}{7}$ **22.** $\frac{21}{15}$ **23.** $\frac{19}{5}$ **24.** $\frac{26}{15}$

25. $\frac{14}{11}$ **26.** $\frac{55}{8}$ **27.** $\frac{40}{11}$ **28.** $\frac{85}{52}$

29. $\frac{125}{63}$ **30.** $\frac{187}{35}$ **31.** $\frac{82}{37}$ **32.** $\frac{720}{149}$

33. Define in your own words what a mixed number is. Give three examples of mixed numbers. (See Objective 2.)

34. What does it mean when a fraction is expressed in lowest terms? (See Objective 3.)

Add each of the following and reduce to lowest terms.

35. $\frac{3}{5} + \frac{3}{5}$ **36.** $\frac{2}{7} + \frac{4}{7}$ **37.** $\frac{7}{10} + \frac{3}{20}$ **38.** $\frac{5}{8} + \frac{1}{4}$

39. $\frac{7}{12} + \frac{8}{15}$ **40.** $\frac{5}{8} + \frac{7}{12}$ **41.** $\frac{9}{11} + \frac{1}{22}$ **42.** $\frac{5}{6} + \frac{7}{9}$

43. $\frac{3}{4} + \frac{5}{9} + \frac{1}{3}$ **44.** $\frac{9}{10} + \frac{2}{5} + \frac{3}{20}$ **45.** $\frac{5}{6} + \frac{3}{4} + \frac{5}{8}$ **46.** $\frac{7}{10} + \frac{8}{15} + \frac{5}{6}$

47. $21\frac{1}{7}$

$+ 49\frac{3}{7}$

_____

48. $28\frac{1}{6}$

$+ 43\frac{2}{3}$

_____

49. $51\frac{1}{4}$

$+ 29\frac{1}{2}$

_____

50. $38\frac{5}{6}$

$29\frac{1}{3}$

$+ 47\frac{1}{2}$

_____

51. $46\frac{3}{4}$

$12\frac{5}{8}$

$+ 37\frac{4}{5}$

_____

52. $26\frac{5}{8}$

$17\frac{3}{14}$

$+ 32\frac{2}{7}$

_____

53. $89\frac{5}{9}$

$10\frac{1}{3}$

$+ 87\frac{1}{9}$

_____

54. $74\frac{1}{5}$

$58\frac{3}{7}$

$+ 21\frac{3}{10}$

_____

Subtract each of the following and reduce to lowest terms.

55. $\frac{5}{6} - \frac{1}{6}$

56. $\frac{11}{12} - \frac{5}{12}$

57. $\frac{2}{3} - \frac{1}{6}$

58. $\frac{7}{8} - \frac{1}{2}$

59. $\frac{5}{12} - \frac{1}{4}$

60. $\frac{5}{6} - \frac{7}{9}$

61. $\frac{3}{4} - \frac{5}{12}$

62. $\frac{9}{16} - \frac{1}{3}$

63. $21\frac{5}{8}$

$- 9\frac{1}{2}$

_____

64. $76\frac{11}{24}$

$- 3\frac{5}{36}$

_____

65. $9\frac{7}{8}$

$- 6\frac{5}{12}$

_____

66. $24\frac{5}{6}$

$- 18\frac{5}{9}$

_____

67. $71\frac{3}{8}$

$- 62\frac{1}{3}$

_____

68. $19\frac{5}{6}$

$- 12\frac{3}{4}$

_____

69. $6\frac{1}{3}$

$- 2\frac{5}{12}$

_____

70. $72\frac{3}{10}$

$- 25\frac{8}{15}$

_____

71. Prime numbers are used to find the least common denominator. Give the definition of a prime number in your own words. (See Objective 6.)

72. Can you add or subtract fractions without using the least common denominator? Describe how you would do this.

73. Where are fractions used in everday life? Think in terms of business applications, hobbies, and vacations. Give three examples.

74. With the exception of the number 2, all prime numbers are odd numbers. But, all odd numbers are not prime numbers. Explain why these statements are true. (See Objective 6.)

Work each of the following word problems.

75. Donald Cole bought a $\frac{3}{8}$ interest in The Sub-Shop last year, and made two additional $\frac{1}{4}$ interest investments this year. Find his total ownership in The Sub-Shop.

76. A wetlands reserve has four sides which measure $1\frac{7}{8}$ mile, $\frac{1}{2}$ mile, $1\frac{2}{3}$ mile, and $\frac{1}{3}$ mile. What is the total distance around the wetlands reserve?

77. Three sides of a parking lot are $108\frac{1}{4}$ feet, $162\frac{3}{8}$ feet, and $143\frac{11}{12}$ feet. If the distance around the lot is $518\frac{23}{24}$ feet, find the fourth side.

78. Hermitage Office Supply sold $\frac{1}{4}$ gross of pencils on December 8, $\frac{3}{8}$ gross on December 10, and $\frac{5}{12}$ gross on December 12. How many gross were sold all together on these three days?

79. Frank Capek paid $\frac{1}{8}$ of a debt in January, $\frac{1}{3}$ in February, $\frac{1}{4}$ in March, and $\frac{1}{12}$ in April. What portion of his debt was paid in these four months?

80. Earl Karn drove for $6\frac{5}{6}$ hours on the first day of his vacation, $5\frac{1}{3}$ hours on the second day, $3\frac{3}{4}$ hours on the third day, and $9\frac{1}{6}$ hours on the fourth day. Find the total hours he drove on the first four days of his vacation.

81. Jane Gunton worked overtime at the Telescope Place. Her overtime hours are shown in the following table. Find the total number of overtime hours she worked.

Date	Aug. 1	2	3	4	5	6	7
Overtime	$1\frac{1}{4}$	$\frac{3}{8}$	$4\frac{1}{2}$	0	$1\frac{7}{12}$	$4\frac{3}{4}$	$2\frac{1}{2}$

82. Karen La Bonte owns $83\frac{5}{8}$ acres of land in Mexico, $76\frac{3}{4}$ acres in the United States, and $182\frac{1}{3}$ acres in Canada. Find the total number of acres that she owns in these three countries.

83. Last month Lim's Wholesale Vegetable Market sold $3\frac{1}{4}$ tons of broccoli, $2\frac{3}{8}$ tons of spinach, $7\frac{1}{2}$ tons of corn, and $1\frac{5}{16}$ tons of turnips. Find the total number of tons of these vegetables sold by the firm last month.

84. Last week Action Auto Parts sold $5\frac{1}{8}$ cases of cheap spark plugs, $8\frac{3}{4}$ cases of medium-priced plugs, and $12\frac{5}{8}$ cases of their best plugs. Find the total number of cases of spark plugs they sold last week.

85. Goldi's Resort decided to expand by buying a piece of property next to the resort. The property is irregularly shaped, with five sides. The lengths of the five sides are $146\frac{1}{2}$ feet, $98\frac{3}{4}$ feet, $196\frac{2}{3}$ feet, $76\frac{5}{8}$ feet, and $100\frac{7}{8}$ feet. Find the total distance around the piece of property.

86. In order to sample a shipment of grain, an inspector took $1\frac{5}{8}$ bushels from one part of a load, $3\frac{1}{4}$ bushels from a second part, $2\frac{3}{8}$ bushels from a third part, and $3\frac{1}{3}$ bushels from a fourth. Find the total number of bushels inspected.

87. Pam Harder worked 40 hours during one week. She worked $8\frac{1}{4}$ hours on Monday, $6\frac{1}{6}$ hours on Tuesday, $7\frac{2}{3}$ hours on Wednesday, and $8\frac{3}{4}$ hours on Thursday. How many hours did she work on Friday?

88. Dana Genzel-Diaz bought four shares of stock. The prices for three of the shares were $\$71\frac{3}{8}$, $\$18\frac{1}{2}$, and $\$143\frac{5}{8}$. Find the price of the fourth share if she paid a total of $\$352\frac{1}{8}$.

89. A contractor has a truck loaded with $9\frac{5}{8}$ cubic yards of peatmoss. The driver gives out $1\frac{1}{2}$ cubic yards at the first stop and $2\frac{3}{4}$ cubic yards at the second stop. At a third stop, the landscaper delivers $3\frac{5}{12}$ cubic yards. How much peatmoss is then left in the truck?

90. Steve Saling is restoring an antique airplane and bought 15 yards of fabric. He repaired the wing with $3\frac{3}{4}$ yards of the material, the fuselage with $4\frac{1}{8}$ yards, and the stabilizer with $3\frac{7}{8}$ yards. How many yards of material did he have left?

1.2 Multiplication and Division of Fractions

OBJECTIVES

1 Multiply fractions.

2 Divide fractions.

3 Convert decimals to fractions.

4 Round decimals.

5 Convert fractions to decimals.

Multiply two fractions by first multiplying the numerator and then multiplying the denominators (forming a new denominator). Write the answer in lowest terms. For example, multiply $\frac{2}{3}$ and $\frac{5}{8}$.

Multiply numerators.

$$\frac{2}{3} \times \frac{5}{8} = \frac{2 \times 5}{3 \times 8} = \frac{10}{24} = \frac{5}{12} \quad (\text{in lowest terms})$$

Multiply denominators.

1 This problem can be simplified by using **cancellation,** a modification of the method of writing fractions in lowest terms. For example, find the product of $\frac{2}{3}$ and $\frac{5}{8}$ by cancelling as follows.

$$\frac{\overset{1}{\cancel{2}}}{3} \times \frac{5}{\underset{4}{\cancel{8}}} = \frac{1 \times 5}{3 \times 4} = \frac{5}{12} \qquad \text{Divide 2 into both 2 and 8.}$$

EXAMPLE 1
Multiplying Common Fractions

Multiply the following fractions.

(a) $\dfrac{6}{11} \times \dfrac{7}{8}$ **(b)** $\dfrac{35}{12} \times \dfrac{32}{25}$

SOLUTION Use cancellation in both of these problems.

(a) $\dfrac{\overset{3}{\cancel{6}}}{11} \times \dfrac{7}{\underset{4}{\cancel{8}}} = \dfrac{3 \times 7}{11 \times 4} = \dfrac{21}{44}$ 2 was divided into both 6 and 8.

(b) $\dfrac{\overset{7}{\cancel{35}}}{\underset{3}{\cancel{12}}} \times \dfrac{\overset{8}{\cancel{32}}}{\underset{5}{\cancel{25}}} = \dfrac{7 \times 8}{3 \times 5} = \dfrac{56}{15} = 3\dfrac{11}{15}$ 4 was divided into both
12 and 32, while 5 was
divided into both 35 and 25. ∎

NOTE When cancelling, be certain that a numerator and a denominator are both divided by the same number.

To multiply mixed numbers, change the mixed numbers to improper fractions, then multiply. For example, multiply $6\frac{1}{4}$ and $2\frac{2}{3}$.

$$6\frac{1}{4} \times 2\frac{2}{3} = \frac{25}{4} \times \frac{8}{3} = \frac{25}{\cancel{4}} \times \frac{\overset{2}{\cancel{8}}}{3} = \frac{25 \times 2}{1 \times 3} = \frac{50}{3} = 16\frac{2}{3}$$

EXAMPLE 2   Multiply the following.

*Multiplying
Mixed Numbers* **(a)** $5\frac{5}{8} \times 4\frac{1}{6}$ **(b)** $1\frac{3}{5} \times 3\frac{1}{3}$ **(c)** $5 \times 2\frac{3}{5}$

SOLUTION

(a) $\dfrac{\overset{15}{\cancel{45}}}{8} \times \dfrac{25}{\underset{2}{\cancel{6}}} = \dfrac{15 \times 25}{8 \times 2} = \dfrac{375}{16} = 23\dfrac{7}{16}$

(b) $\dfrac{8}{\underset{1}{\cancel{5}}} \times \dfrac{\overset{2}{\cancel{10}}}{3} = \dfrac{8 \times 2}{1 \times 3} = \dfrac{16}{3} = 5\dfrac{1}{3}$

(c) Write the whole number 5 as $\frac{5}{1}$. Then multiply.

$$\dfrac{\overset{1}{\cancel{5}}}{1} \times \dfrac{13}{\underset{1}{\cancel{5}}} = \dfrac{1 \times 13}{1 \times 1} = \dfrac{13}{1} = 13 \quad ∎$$

2 Divide two fractions by inverting and multiplying by the second fraction. (Invert the second fraction by exchanging numerator and denominator.)

EXAMPLE 3   Divide.

*Dividing
Common Fractions* **(a)** $\dfrac{25}{36} \div \dfrac{15}{18}$ **(b)** $\dfrac{21}{8} \div \dfrac{14}{16}$

SOLUTION   Invert the second fraction and multiply.

(a) $\dfrac{25}{36} \div \dfrac{15}{18} = \dfrac{\overset{5}{\cancel{25}}}{\underset{2}{\cancel{36}}} \times \dfrac{\overset{1}{\cancel{18}}}{\underset{3}{\cancel{15}}} = \dfrac{5 \times 1}{2 \times 3} = \dfrac{5}{6}$

(b) $\dfrac{21}{8} \div \dfrac{14}{16} = \dfrac{\overset{3}{\cancel{21}}}{\underset{1}{\cancel{8}}} \times \dfrac{\overset{2}{\cancel{16}}}{\underset{2}{\cancel{14}}} = \dfrac{3 \times \overset{1}{\cancel{2}}}{1 \times \cancel{2}} = 3$ ■

NOTE The second fraction (divisor) is inverted when dividing by a fraction. Cancellation is done *only after inverting.*

Divide mixed numbers by changing all mixed numbers to improper fractions, as follows.

$$3\frac{5}{9} \div 2\frac{2}{5} = \frac{32}{9} \div \frac{12}{5} = \frac{\overset{8}{\cancel{32}}}{9} \times \frac{5}{\underset{3}{\cancel{12}}} = \frac{8 \times 5}{9 \times 3} = \frac{40}{27} = 1\frac{13}{27}$$

Multiply or divide by a whole number by writing the whole number as a fraction over 1.

$$3\frac{3}{4} \times 16 = 3\frac{3}{4} \times \frac{16}{1} \qquad \textcolor{blue}{\text{whole number over 1}}$$

$$= \frac{15}{4} \times \frac{16}{1}$$

$$= \frac{15}{\underset{1}{\cancel{4}}} \times \frac{\overset{4}{\cancel{16}}}{1} = 15 \times 4 = 60$$

Also:

$$2\frac{2}{5} \div 3 = \frac{12}{5} \div \frac{3}{1} = \frac{\overset{4}{\cancel{12}}}{5} \times \frac{1}{\underset{1}{\cancel{3}}} = \frac{4 \times 1}{5 \times 1} = \frac{4}{5}$$

EXAMPLE 4
Multiplying a Whole Number by a Mixed Number

Edward Roberts earns \$12 per hour. On Saturday he is paid time and a half. How much does he earn per hour on Saturday?

SOLUTION   Multiply the regular rate by $1\frac{1}{2}$, or $\frac{3}{2}$.

$$12 \times \frac{3}{2} = \frac{\overset{6}{\cancel{12}}}{1} \times \frac{3}{\underset{1}{\cancel{2}}} = \frac{6 \times 3}{1 \times 1} = \frac{18}{1} = 18$$

Roberts earns \$18 per hour when he is paid time and a half.   ■

3   A **decimal number** is really a fraction with a denominator that is a power of ten. The digits written to the right of the decimal point have place values as shown in Figure 1.2.

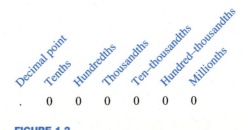

FIGURE 1.2

Convert a decimal to a fraction by thinking of the decimal as being written in words. For example, think of 0.47 as "forty-seven hundredths." Then write this in fraction form.

$$0.47 = \frac{47}{100}$$

In the same way, 0.3, read as "three tenths," is written in fraction form as follows.

$$0.3 = \frac{3}{10}$$

Also, 0.963, read "nine hundred sixty-three thousandths," is written $\frac{963}{1000}$.

EXAMPLE 5

Converting Decimals to Fractions

Convert the following decimals to fractions.

(a) 0.75   **(b)** 0.028

SOLUTION

(a)   0.75 is read as "seventy-five hundredths."

$$0.75 = \frac{75}{100} = \frac{3}{4}$$

Here $\frac{75}{100}$ is written in lowest terms as $\frac{3}{4}$.

(b)   0.028 is read as "twenty-eight thousandths," and the resulting fraction is written in lowest terms.

$$0.028 = \frac{28}{1000} = \frac{7}{250} \quad ∎$$

4   Decimals are often rounded to make the numbers easier to work with and understand. To round 17.639 to the nearest tenth, first look at the tenths digit, 6. Then look at the first digit to the right of the tenths digit, 3. If this digit is 0, 1, 2, 3, or 4, leave the tenths digit unchanged and drop the digits to its right. If this digit is 5, 6, 7, 8, or 9, increase the tenths digit by 1 and drop the digits to its right. With this rule, 17.639 rounds to the nearest tenth as 17.6.

EXAMPLE 6

Rounding to the Nearest Tenth

Round 98.5892 to the nearest tenth.

SOLUTION

Step 1 Locate the tenths digit.

$$98.5892$$
tenths digit

The tenths digit is 5.

Step 2 Locate the digit just to the right of the tenths digit.

$$98.5892$$
just to the right of the tenths digit

The digit just to the right of the tenths digit is 8.

Step 3 If the digit found in Step 2 is 0, 1, 2, 3, or 4, leave the digit of Step 1 alone. If the digit found in Step 2 is 5, 6, 7, 8, or 9, increase the digit of Step 1 by 1. The digit found in Step 2 is 8, so 98.5892 rounded to the nearest tenth is 98.6. ■

EXAMPLE 7

Rounding to the Nearest Thousandth

Round 0.008572 to the nearest thousandth.

SOLUTION   Locate the thousandths digit.

$$0.008572$$

thousandths digit

Since the digit to the right of the thousandths digit is 5, increase the thousandths digit by 1, with 0.008572 rounding to the nearest thousandth as 0.009. ■

EXAMPLE 8

Rounding Decimals

Round 24.6483 to the nearest:

(a)   thousandth
(b)   hundredth
(c)   tenth

SOLUTION   Use the method described.

(a)   24.6483 to the nearest thousandth is 24.648
(b)   24.6483 to the nearest hundredth is 24.65
(c)   24.6483 to the nearest tenth is 24.6 ■

The answer to part (c) in Example 8 may be surprising because of the answer in (b). However, keep the following rule in mind.

NOTE When rounding the same number to different places as in Example 8, always go back to the *original number,* and not to some number that was rounded from the original number.

5   To convert a fraction to a decimal, divide the numerator of the fraction by the denominator. Place a decimal point after the numerator and attach additional zeros, one at a time, to the right of the decimal point as the division is performed. Keep going until the division ends or until the desired degree of precision is reached. As a general rule, divide until the quotient has one more digit than the desired degree of precision, then round from the last digit. **The result is the decimal equivalent to the fraction.**

For example, to convert $\frac{1}{8}$ to a decimal, divide 1 by 8.

$$8\overline{)1.}$$

Since 8 will not divide into 1, place a 0 to the right of the decimal point. Now 8 divides into 10 once, with a remainder of 2.

$$\begin{array}{r} .1 \\ 8\overline{)1.0} \\ \underline{8} \\ 2 \end{array}$$ Be sure to move the decimal point up.

Continue placing 0's to the right of the decimal point.

$$
\begin{array}{r}
.12 \\
8\overline{)1.00} \\
8 \\
\overline{20} \\
16 \\
\overline{4}
\end{array}
$$

Place another 0 to the right of the decimal point. The division now gives a remainder of 0.

$$
\begin{array}{r}
.125 \\
8\overline{)1.000} \\
8 \\
\overline{20} \\
16 \\
\overline{40} \\
40 \\
\overline{0}
\end{array}
$$ Keep attaching zeros.

remainder of 0

Therefore, $\frac{1}{8} = 0.125$.

NOTE The decimal answer, .125, was not rounded; instead, the division was continued until there was no remainder. In most problems the answer will be rounded to the required accuracy.

EXAMPLE 9   Convert $\frac{2}{3}$ to a decimal. Round to the nearest ten-thousandth.

Rounding a
Repeating Decimal   **SOLUTION**   Divide 2 by 3.

$$
\begin{array}{r}
.66666 \\
3\overline{)2.00000} \\
1\,8 \\
\overline{20} \\
18 \\
\overline{20} \\
18 \\
\overline{20} \\
18 \\
\overline{2}
\end{array}
$$

This division results in a **repeating decimal,** which is often indicated by placing a bar over the digit or digits that repeat. The answer could be written as follows.

$$0.\overline{6} \quad \text{or} \quad 0.6\overline{6} \quad \text{or} \quad 0.666\overline{66}$$

However, round to the nearest ten-thousandth:

$$\frac{2}{3} = 0.6667 \quad \blacksquare$$

Since decimal equivalents of fractions are often needed, some of the more common ones are listed here. (Results that do not come out even were rounded to the nearest ten-thousandth.) These decimals appear from least to greatest value.

$\frac{1}{16} = 0.0625$	$\frac{1}{4} = 0.25$	$\frac{5}{8} = 0.625$
$\frac{1}{9} = 0.1111$	$\frac{5}{16} = 0.3125$	$\frac{2}{3} = 0.6667$
$\frac{1}{8} = 0.125$	$\frac{1}{3} = 0.3333$	$\frac{11}{16} = 0.6875$
$\frac{1}{7} = 0.1429$	$\frac{3}{8} = 0.375$	$\frac{3}{4} = 0.75$
$\frac{1}{6} = 0.1667$	$\frac{7}{16} = 0.4375$	$\frac{13}{16} = 0.8125$
$\frac{3}{16} = 0.1875$	$\frac{1}{2} = 0.5$	$\frac{5}{6} = 0.8333$
$\frac{1}{5} = 0.2$	$\frac{9}{16} = 0.5625$	$\frac{7}{8} = 0.875$

1.2 Exercises

Multiply each of the following and write in lowest terms.

1. $\frac{3}{4} \times \frac{5}{6}$

2. $\frac{3}{8} \times \frac{2}{3}$

3. $\frac{21}{30} \times \frac{5}{7}$

4. $6\frac{1}{4} \times 3\frac{1}{5}$

5. $3\frac{1}{9} \times 1\frac{2}{7}$

6. $6 \times 4\frac{2}{3}$

7. $4\frac{3}{5} \times 15$

8. $\frac{3}{4} \times \frac{8}{9} \times 2\frac{1}{2}$

9. $\frac{1}{4} \times 6\frac{2}{3} \times \frac{1}{5}$

10. $\frac{2}{3} \times \frac{9}{8} \times 3\frac{1}{4}$

11. $12 \times 2\frac{1}{2} \times 3$

12. $18 \times 1\frac{2}{3} \times 2$

Divide each of the following and write in lowest terms.

13. $\frac{7}{12} \div \frac{5}{18}$

14. $\frac{13}{20} \div \frac{26}{30}$

15. $\frac{7}{9} \div \frac{12}{5}$

16. $\frac{7}{8} \div \frac{3}{4}$

17. $\frac{15}{16} \div \frac{5}{8}$

18. $\frac{12}{11} \div \frac{3}{22}$

19. $2\frac{1}{2} \div 3\frac{3}{4}$ **20.** $5\frac{1}{2} \div \frac{1}{4}$ **21.** $3\frac{1}{8} \div \frac{15}{16}$

22. $3\frac{4}{5} \div 2$ **23.** $4 \div 5\frac{1}{2}$ **24.** $3 \div 1\frac{1}{4}$

25. Cancellation is used when multiplying and dividing fractions. How can you benefit by using cancellation?

26. Describe in your own words how proper cancellation is done. (See Objective 1.)

Find the total price for each of the following purchases of stock.

27. 8 shares of IBM at $282\frac{1}{2}$ per share

28. 20 shares of General Motors at $70\frac{1}{4}$ per share

29. 24 shares of Merck at $55\frac{7}{8}$ per share

30. 48 shares of International Paper at $69\frac{5}{8}$ per share

31. 32 shares of Ford Motor at $57\frac{1}{8}$ per share

32. 56 shares of McDonald's at $47\frac{3}{8}$ per share

Convert each of the following decimals to fractions and reduce to lowest terms.

33. 0.36 **34.** 0.72 **35.** 0.336 **36.** 0.215

37. 0.096 **38.** 0.012 **39.** 0.875 **40.** 0.375

41. 0.255 **42.** 0.8125 **43.** 0.1875 **44.** 0.3125

Round each of the following decimals to the nearest tenth and to the nearest hundredth.

45. 78.414   **46.** 3689.537   **47.** 0.0837   **48.** 2.548

49. 7.446   **50.** 86.472   **51.** 58.956   **52.** 7.014

Convert each of the following fractions to decimals. Round the answer to the nearest thousandth if necessary.

53. $\frac{5}{8}$ **54.** $\frac{7}{16}$ **55.** $\frac{15}{16}$ **56.** $\frac{5}{6}$

57. $\frac{1}{6}$ **58.** $\frac{2}{3}$ **59.** $\frac{13}{16}$ **60.** $\frac{1}{8}$

61. $\frac{1}{9}$ **62.** $\frac{1}{3}$ **63.** $\frac{83}{97}$ **64.** $\frac{73}{93}$

65. A classmate of yours is confused on how to convert a decimal to a fraction. Write an explanation of this to your classmate including changing the fraction to lowest terms. (See Objective 3.)

66. Explain how to convert a fraction to a decimal. Be sure to mention rounding in your explanation. (See Objective 5.)

67. Explain in your own words the difference between thousands and thousandths. (See Objective 3.)

68. Write the directions for rounding a money answer to the nearest cent.

Work each of the following word problems.

69. Kevin Howell allows $1\frac{3}{5}$ bottles of beverage for each guest at his party. If he expects 35 guests, how many bottles of beverage will he need?

70. Sandy Yost bought 12 shares of stock at $18\frac{3}{4}$ per share, 24 shares at $36\frac{3}{8}$ per share, and 16 shares at $74\frac{1}{8}$ per share. Her broker charged her a commission of $12. Find the total amount that she paid.

71. It takes $\frac{4}{5}$ pound of salt to fill a large salt shaker. How many salt shakers can be filled with 28 pounds of salt?

72. How many $\frac{1}{8}$-ounce vials of medicine can be filled with 7 ounces of medicine?

73. A will states that $\frac{7}{8}$ of the estate is to be divided among relatives. Of the remaining $\frac{1}{8}$, $\frac{1}{4}$ goes to the American Cancer Society. What fraction of the estate goes to the American Cancer Society?

74. A couple invested $\frac{1}{5}$ of their total investment in stocks. Of the $\frac{1}{5}$ invested in stocks, $\frac{1}{8}$ is invested in General Motors. What fraction of the total investment is invested in General Motors?

75. A photographer uses $4\frac{1}{4}$ rolls of film at a wedding and $2\frac{3}{8}$ rolls of film at a retirement party. Find the total number of rolls needed for 28 weddings and 16 retirement parties.

76. One necklace can be completed in $6\frac{1}{2}$ minutes, while a bracelet takes $3\frac{1}{8}$ minutes. Find the total time that it takes to complete 36 necklaces and 22 bracelets.

77. The Bridge Lighting Committee has raised $\frac{7}{8}$ of the funds necessary for their lighting project. If this amounts to $840,000, how much additional money must be raised?

78. A mountain guide has used pack animals for $\frac{14}{15}$ of a trip and must finish the trip on foot. The distance covered with pack animals is 98 miles. Find the number of miles to be completed on foot.

1.3 Calculator Basics

OBJECTIVES

1. Learn the basic calculator keys.
2. Understand the $\boxed{C}$ and $\boxed{CE}$ keys.
3. Understand the floating decimal point.
4. Use the $\boxed{\%}$ and $\boxed{\sqrt{\ }}$ keys.
5. Solve problems with negative numbers.
6. Use the calculator memory function.
7. Solve chain calculations using order of operations.
8. Use the calculator for problem solution.

Calculators are among the more popular inventions of the last two decades. Each year better calculators are developed and costs drop. A machine that cost $200 a quarter century ago could add, subtract, multiply, and divide decimals (but could not locate the decimal point in a division problem). Today, these same calculations are performed quite well on a calculator costing less than $10. And today's $200 pocket calculators have more ability to solve problems than some of the early computers.

Many colleges allow students to use calculators in business mathematics courses. Some courses require calculator use. Many types of calculators are available, from the inexpensive basic calculator to the more complex financial and programmable models. The discussion here is confined to the common 8-digit-four function models (add, subtract, multiply, and divide), with percent key, square root key, and memory function. Any explanation needed for specific calculator models or special function keys is best gained by referring to the booklet supplied with the calculator.

1 Most calculators use **algebraic logic,** and problems are solved by entering number and function keys in the same order as you would solve a problem by hand.

EXAMPLE 1
Using the Basic Keys

Solve the following with a calculator.

(a) $9 + 8$ **(b)** $6494 \div 17$

SOLUTION

(a)   The problem $9 + 8$ would be entered as

$$9 \;\boxed{+}\; 8 \;\boxed{=}$$

and 17 would appear as the answer.

(b)   Enter $6494 \div 17$ as

$$6494 \;\boxed{\div}\; 17 \;\boxed{=},$$

and 382 appears as the answer.   ■

2 All calculators have a ⊡C⊡ key. Pressing this key erases everything in the calculator and prepares it for a new problem. Some calculators have a ⊡CE⊡ key. Pressing this key erases only the number displayed, thus allowing for correction of a mistake without having to start the problem over. Many calculators combine the ⊡C⊡ key and ⊡CE⊡ key and use an ⊡ON/C⊡ key. This key turns the calculator on and is also used to erase the calculator display. If the ⊡ON/C⊡ is pressed after the ⊡=⊡ , or after one of the operation keys (⊡+⊡, ⊡−⊡, ⊡×⊡, ⊡÷⊡), everything in the calculator is erased. If the wrong operation key is pressed, simply press the correct key and the error is corrected. For example, in 7 ⊡+⊡ ⊡−⊡ 3 ⊡=⊡ 4, pressing the ⊡−⊡ key cancels out the previous ⊡+⊡ key entry.

3 Most calculators have a **floating decimal** which locates the decimal point in the final result.

EXAMPLE 2
Calculating with Decimal Numbers

A contractor purchased 55.75 square yards of vinyl floor covering, at $18.99 per square yard. Find her total cost.

SOLUTION   Proceed as follows.

$$55.75 \; \boxed{\times} \; 18.99 \; \boxed{=} \; 1058.6925$$

The decimal point is automatically placed in the answer. Since money answers are usually rounded to the nearest cent, the answer is $1058.69. ■

In using a machine with a floating decimal, enter the decimal point as needed. For example, enter $47 as

$$47$$

with no decimal point, but enter 95¢ as follows.

$$\boxed{\cdot} \; 95$$

One problem utilizing a floating decimal is shown by the following example.

EXAMPLE 3
Placing the Decimal Point in Money Answers

Add $21.38 and $1.22.

SOLUTION

$$21.38 \; \boxed{+} \; 1.22 \; \boxed{=} \; 22.6$$

The final 0 is left off. Remember that the problem deals with dollars and cents, and write the answer as $22.60. ■

4 The ⊡%⊡ key moves the decimal point two places to the left when used following multiplication or division.

EXAMPLE 4
Using the ⊡%⊡ Key

Find 8% of $4205.

SOLUTION

$$4205 \; \boxed{\times} \; 8 \; \boxed{\%} \; \boxed{=} \; 336.4 = \$336.40 \quad ■$$

Although square root is not used often in business, it is important to understand the $\boxed{\sqrt{}}$ key and its function. The product 3×3 can be written as 3^2. The small number 2, called an **exponent,** says to multiply 3 by itself. The number 3 is called the **base.** The number 3^2 is simplified by writing it as 9. Since $3^2 = 9$, the number 3 is called the **square root** of 9. Square roots of numbers are written with the symbol $\sqrt{}$.

$$\sqrt{9} = 3$$

EXAMPLE 5

Using the $\boxed{\sqrt{}}$ *Key*

Find each square root.

(a) $\sqrt{144}$ **(b)** $\sqrt{20}$

SOLUTION

(a)   Using the calculator, enter

$$144 \ \boxed{\sqrt{}}$$

and 12 appears in the display. The square root of 144 is 12.

(b)   The square root of 20 is

$$20 \ \boxed{\sqrt{}} \ 4.4721359$$

which may be rounded to the desired position.   ■

5   There are several calculations in business that result in a **negative number** or **deficit amount.**

EXAMPLE 6

Working with Negative Numbers

The amount in the advertising account last month was \$4800 while \$5200 was actually spent. Find the balance remaining in the advertising account.

SOLUTION   Enter the numbers in the calculator.

$$4800 \ \boxed{-} \ 5200 \ \boxed{=} \ 400-$$

Notice that there is a minus after the 400, which indicates that there is a deficit, or negative number. On many calculators the minus sign appears as -400. The answer to Example 6 is written as $-\$400$, with the minus sign on the left, or by placing the amount in parentheses, as (\$400).   ■

Negative numbers may be entered into the calculator by using the $\boxed{-}$ before entering the number. For example, if \$3000 is now added to the advertising account in Example 6, the new balance is calculated as follows.

$$\boxed{-} \ 400 \ \boxed{+} \ 3000 \ \boxed{=} \ 2600$$

The new account balance is \$2600.

6   Many calculators feature memory keys, which are a sort of electronic scratch paper. These **memory keys** are used to store intermediate steps in a calculation. On some calculators, a key labeled $\boxed{M}$ is used to store the numbers in the display, with $\boxed{MR}$ used to recall the numbers from memory.

Other calculators have M+ and M− keys. The M+ key adds the number displayed to the number already in memory. For example, if the memory contains the number 0 at the beginning of a problem, and the calculator display contains the number 29.4, then pushing M+ will cause 29.4 to be stored in the memory (the result of adding 0 and 29.4). If 57.8 is then entered into the display, pushing M+ will cause

$$29.4 + 57.8 = 87.2$$

to be stored. If 11.9 is then entered into the display, with M− pushed, the memory will contain

$$87.2 - 11.9 = 75.3.$$

The MR key is used to recall the number in memory as needed, with MC used to clear the memory. (Always clear the memory before starting a problem—not doing so is a very common error.)

CAUTION *Using the memory function of a calculator varies from one model to another. Some calculators have a* STO *or a* Min *button which is used with the memory function. BE SURE TO READ THE OPERATING MANUAL FOR YOUR CALCULATOR.*

7 Memory keys are useful when working long calculations where several numbers are being added, subtracted, multiplied, or divided in a specific sequence. These calculations are called **chain calculations.** When working with chain calculations some rules must be followed. These rules are called **order of operations.**

1. Do all operations inside parentheses first.
2. Simplify any expressions with exponents (squares) and find any square roots.
3. Multiply and divide from left to right.
4. Add and subtract from left to right.

EXAMPLE 7
Using the Order of Operations

Solve the following problem.

$$\frac{8 \times 19.4}{15.7 + (11.8 \times 4.6)}$$

SOLUTION Find the denominator first. Start by calculating 11.8×4.6.

$$11.8 \;\boxed{\times}\; 4.6 \;\boxed{=}\; 54.28$$

Then add 15.7.

$$\boxed{+}\; 15.7 \;\boxed{=}\; 69.98$$

Store this result in memory, using $\boxed{\text{M}}$ or $\boxed{\text{M+}}$ depending on your machine. Then find the numerator.

$$8 \ \boxed{\times} \ 19.4 \ \boxed{=} \ 155.2$$

To divide, push $\boxed{\div}$ and then $\boxed{\text{MR}}$ $\boxed{=}$, which will give the final quotient.

$$\frac{8 \times 19.4}{15.7 + (11.8 \times 4.6)} = 2.218 \qquad \text{(rounded)} \quad \blacksquare$$

NOTE The denominator was found first in Example 7 so that it could be stored in memory. After calculating the numerator, the numerator is then divided by the amount stored in memory. Working the problem this way saves at least one step.

The following examples show how the calculator can be used to solve business problems.

EXAMPLE 8

Solving a Business Problem with a Calculator

A furniture store has a sofa with an original price of $470 on sale at 15% off. Find the sale price of the sofa.

SOLUTION

$$470 \ \boxed{\times} \ 15 \ \boxed{\%} \ \boxed{=} \ 70.5 \qquad \text{\$70.50 discount}$$

Store this result in memory, using $\boxed{\text{M}}$ or $\boxed{\text{M+}}$. Then find the actual price.

$$470 \ \boxed{-} \ \boxed{\text{MR}} \ = 399.5 = \$399.50 \quad \blacksquare$$

8 Business mathematics involves many problems with several varied steps, as shown in Example 9.

EXAMPLE 9

Applying Calculator Use to Problem Solving

A home purchaser borrows $86,400 at 10% for 30 years. The monthly payment on the loan is $8.78 per $1000 borrowed. Annual taxes are $780, and fire insurance is $453 a year. Find the total monthly payment including taxes and insurance.

SOLUTION   To find the monthly loan payment, multiply the number of thousands, 86.4, by 8.78.

$$86.4 \ \boxed{\times} \ 8.78 \ \boxed{=} \ 758.59 \qquad \text{(rounded)}$$

Store this in memory, using $\boxed{\text{M}}$ or $\boxed{\text{M+}}$. Next, find the monthly taxes.

$$780 \ \boxed{\div} \ 12 \ \boxed{=} \ 65$$

Add this result to memory using $\boxed{\text{M}}$ or $\boxed{\text{M+}}$. Now find the monthly insurance.

$$453 \ \boxed{\div} \ 12 \ \boxed{=} \ 37.75$$

Add this to memory, using $\boxed{\text{M}}$ or $\boxed{\text{M+}}$. Finally, push $\boxed{\text{MR}}$, giving the total payment of $861.34. $\blacksquare$

1.3 Exercises

Work each of the following problems on a calculator. Round each answer to the nearest hundredth.

1.
$$\begin{array}{r} 28.96 \\ 34.25 \\ 19.78 \\ + 21.59 \end{array}$$

2.
$$\begin{array}{r} 758.42 \\ 76.98 \\ + 217.91 \end{array}$$

3.
$$\begin{array}{r} 28{,}974.2 \\ 15{,}892 \\ + \quad 38.55 \end{array}$$

4.
$$\begin{array}{r} 21.5 \\ - 13.82 \end{array}$$

5.
$$\begin{array}{r} 769.2 \\ - \quad 35.75 \end{array}$$

6. $12 - 10.798$

7.
$$\begin{array}{r} 89.7 \\ \times \quad .63 \end{array}$$

8.
$$\begin{array}{r} 47.82 \\ \times \quad .13 \end{array}$$

9.
$$\begin{array}{r} 3409 \\ \times \quad .006 \end{array}$$

10. $\dfrac{9225}{25}$

11. $\dfrac{4594.2}{78}$

12. $\dfrac{3676.5}{142.9}$

13. $1.705\overline{)\,.8359}$

14. $.0028\overline{)\,.00719}$

15. $\dfrac{222.34}{1.67}$

16. $\dfrac{79{,}693.8}{365}$

Work each of the following chain calculations. Round each answer to the nearest hundredth. Remember to find the denominator first and store it in the memory.

17. $\dfrac{9 \times 9}{2 \times 5}$

18. $\dfrac{15 \times 8 \times 3}{11 \times 7 \times 4}$

19. $\dfrac{87 \times 24 \times 47.2}{13.6 \times 12.8}$

20. $\dfrac{2 \times (3+4)}{6+10}$

21. $\dfrac{2 \times 3 + 4}{6 + 10}$

22. $\dfrac{4200 \times .12 \times 90}{365}$

23. $\dfrac{74{,}500 \times .14 \times 200}{360}$

24. $\dfrac{47 \times 1256}{14.93 + (85.77 \times .663)}$

25. $\dfrac{633 \times .0299}{8.911 + (525 \times .399)}$

26. $200\left(1 + 0.07 \times \dfrac{60}{360}\right)$

27. Describe in your own words the order of operations to be used when solving chain calculations. (See Objective 7.)

28. Explain how the memory function of a calculator can be used when solving chain calculations.

Work each of the following word problems on a calculator. Round each answer to the nearest cent.

29. Bucks County Community College Bookstore bought 397 copies of a computer science book at a net cost of $23.86 each; 125 copies of an accounting book at $28.74 each; and 740 copies of a real estate text at $21.76 each. Find the total paid by the bookstore.

30. To find the monthly interest due on a certain home mortgage, multiply the mortgage balance by .007292. Find the monthly interest on a mortgage having a balance of $95,830.

31. Find the monthly interest on a mortgage having a balance of $113,720. (See Exercise 30.)

32. Judy Martinez needs to file her expense account claims. She spent 5 nights at the Macon Holiday Inn at $47.46 per night, 4 nights at the Charlotte Sheraton at $51.62 per night, and rented a car for 7.6 days at $29.95 per day. She drove the car 916 miles with a charge of 24¢ per mile. Find her total expenses.

33. In Virginia City, the sales tax is 6.5%. Find the tax on each of the following items: (a) a new car costing $17,908.43 and (b) an office word processor costing $1463.58.

34. Marja Strutz bought a new commericial fishing boat equipped for sardine fishing at a cost of $78,250. Additional safety equipment was needed at a cost of $4820 and sales tax of $7\frac{1}{4}\%$ was due on the boat and safety equipment. In addition she was charged a licensing fee of $1135 and a Coast Guard registration fee of $428. Strutz will pay $\frac{1}{3}$ of the total cost as a down payment and will borrow the balance. How much will she borrow?

CHAPTER 1 QUICK REVIEW

TOPIC	APPROACH	EXAMPLE
1.1 Identifying types of fractions	Proper: Numerator smaller than denominator.	$\dfrac{2}{3}, \dfrac{3}{4}, \dfrac{15}{16}, \dfrac{1}{8}$
	Improper: Numerator equal to or greater than denominator.	$\dfrac{17}{8}, \dfrac{19}{12}, \dfrac{11}{2}, \dfrac{5}{3}, \dfrac{4}{4}$
	Mixed: Whole number plus proper fraction.	$2\dfrac{2}{3}, 3\dfrac{5}{8}, 9\dfrac{5}{6}$

TOPIC	APPROACH	EXAMPLE
1.1 Converting fractions	Mixed to improper: Multiply denominator by whole number and add numerator.	$7\frac{2}{3} = \frac{23}{3}$
	Improper to mixed: Divide numerator by denominator and place remainder over denominator.	$\frac{17}{5} = 3\frac{2}{5}$
1.1 Writing fractions in lowest terms	Divide numerator and denominator by the same number.	$\frac{30}{42} = \frac{30 \div 6}{42 \div 6} = \frac{5}{7}$
1.1 Adding like fractions	Add numerators and reduce to lowest terms.	$\frac{3}{4} + \frac{1}{4} + \frac{5}{4} = \frac{3 + 1 + 5}{4}$ $= \frac{9}{4} = 2\frac{1}{4}$
1.1 Finding a least common denominator (LCD)	Inspection method: Look to see if the LCD can be found.	$\frac{1}{3} + \frac{1}{4} + \frac{1}{10}$
	Method of prime numbers: Divide by prime numbers to find LCD.	$\begin{array}{r|ccc} 5 & 1 & 1 & 5 \\ 3 & 3 & 1 & 5 \\ 2 & 3 & 2 & 5 \\ 2 & 3 & 4 & 10 \end{array}$
	Multiply the prime numbers.	$2 \times 2 \times 3 \times 5 = 60 \text{ LCD}$
1.1 Adding unlike fractions	1. Find the LCD.	$\frac{1}{3} + \frac{1}{4} + \frac{1}{10}; \text{LCD} = 60$
	2. Rewrite fractions with LCD.	$\frac{1}{3} = \frac{20}{60}, \frac{1}{4} = \frac{15}{60}, \frac{1}{10} = \frac{6}{60}$
	3. Add numerators, placing answer over LCD.	$\frac{20 + 15 + 6}{60} = \frac{41}{60}$
1.1 Adding mixed numbers	1. Add fractions. 2. Add whole numbers. 3. Combine sums of whole numbers and fractions and simplify answer.	$9\frac{2}{3} = 9\frac{8}{12}$ $+6\frac{3}{4} = 6\frac{9}{12}$ $\overline{\phantom{+6\frac{3}{4} = }}$ $15\frac{17}{12} = 16\frac{5}{12}$

TOPIC	APPROACH	EXAMPLE
1.1 Subtracting fractions	1. Find the LCD. 2. Subtract numerator of number being subtracted. 3. Write difference over LCD.	$\dfrac{5}{8} - \dfrac{1}{3} = \dfrac{15}{24} - \dfrac{8}{24} = \dfrac{7}{24}$
1.1 Subtracting mixed numbers	1. Subtract fractions, borrowing if necessary. 2. Subtract whole numbers. 3. Combine the differences of whole numbers and fractions.	$\begin{aligned}8\tfrac{5}{8} &= 8\tfrac{15}{24}\\ -3\tfrac{1}{12} &= 3\tfrac{2}{24}\\ \hline &\;\;5\tfrac{13}{24}\end{aligned}$
1.2 Multiplying proper fractions	Multiply numerators and denominators, cancelling if possible.	$\dfrac{6}{11} \times \dfrac{7}{8} = \dfrac{\overset{3}{\cancel{6}}}{11} \times \dfrac{7}{\underset{4}{\cancel{8}}} = \dfrac{21}{44}$
1.2 Multiplying mixed numbers	1. Change mixed numbers to improper fractions, cancelling if possible. 2. Multiply as proper fractions.	$1\tfrac{3}{5} \times 3\tfrac{1}{3} = \dfrac{8}{\underset{1}{\cancel{5}}} \times \dfrac{\overset{2}{\cancel{10}}}{3} = \dfrac{8}{1} \times \dfrac{2}{3}$ $= \dfrac{16}{3} = 5\tfrac{1}{3}$
1.2 Dividing proper fractions	Invert the divisor and multiply.	$\dfrac{25}{36} \div \dfrac{15}{18} = \dfrac{\overset{5}{\cancel{25}}}{\underset{2}{\cancel{36}}} \times \dfrac{\overset{1}{\cancel{18}}}{\underset{3}{\cancel{15}}} = \dfrac{5}{2} \times \dfrac{1}{3} = \dfrac{5}{6}$
1.2 Dividing mixed numbers	1. Change mixed numbers to improper fractions. 2. Invert the divisor, cancelling if possible. 3. Multiply.	$3\tfrac{5}{9} \div 2\tfrac{2}{5} = \dfrac{32}{9} \div \dfrac{12}{5} = \dfrac{\overset{8}{\cancel{32}}}{9} \times \dfrac{5}{\underset{3}{\cancel{12}}}$ $= \dfrac{40}{27} = 1\tfrac{13}{27}$
1.2 Converting decimals to fractions	Think of the decimal as being written in words, then write it in fraction form. Reduce to lowest terms.	To convert 0.47 to a fraction, think of 0.47 as "forty-seven-hundredths," then write it as $\dfrac{47}{100}$.

TOPIC	APPROACH	EXAMPLE

1.2 Rounding decimals

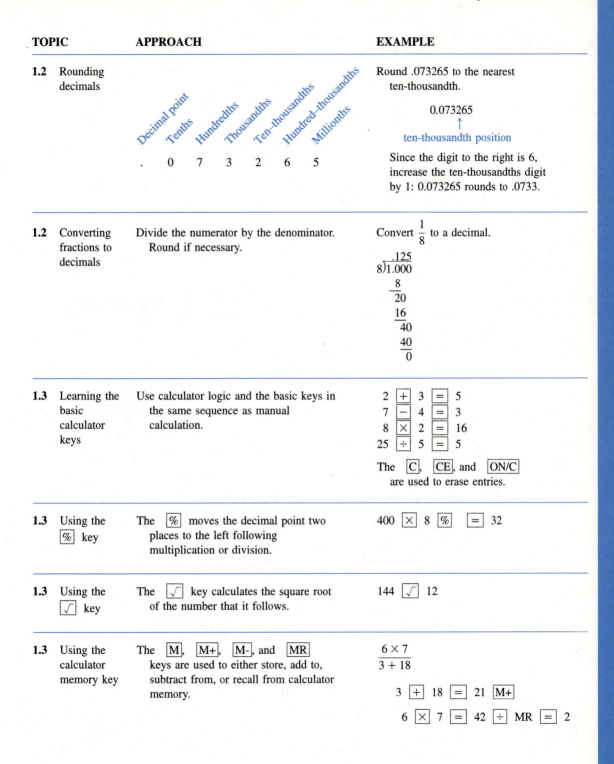

Round .073265 to the nearest ten-thousandth.

0.073265

↑

ten-thousandth position

Since the digit to the right is 6, increase the ten-thousandths digit by 1: 0.073265 rounds to .0733.

1.2 Converting fractions to decimals

Divide the numerator by the denominator. Round if necessary.

Convert $\frac{1}{8}$ to a decimal.

$$\begin{array}{r} .125 \\ 8\overline{)1.000} \\ \underline{8} \\ 20 \\ \underline{16} \\ 40 \\ \underline{40} \\ 0 \end{array}$$

1.3 Learning the basic calculator keys

Use calculator logic and the basic keys in the same sequence as manual calculation.

2 $+$ 3 $=$ 5
7 $-$ 4 $=$ 3
8 $\times$ 2 $=$ 16
25 $\div$ 5 $=$ 5

The C, CE, and ON/C are used to erase entries.

1.3 Using the $\%$ key

The $\%$ moves the decimal point two places to the left following multiplication or division.

400 $\times$ 8 $\%$ $=$ 32

1.3 Using the $\sqrt{}$ key

The $\sqrt{}$ key calculates the square root of the number that it follows.

144 $\sqrt{}$ 12

1.3 Using the calculator memory key

The M, $M+$, $M-$, and MR keys are used to either store, add to, subtract from, or recall from calculator memory.

$$\frac{6 \times 7}{3 + 18}$$

3 $+$ 18 $=$ 21 $M+$

6 $\times$ 7 $=$ 42 $\div$ MR $=$ 2

SUMMARY EXERCISE

Walt Hardin, a full-time accounting professor and experienced investor, had been following the stock price of Roadmaster Industries, Incorporated. The price of the stock had been just slightly over $1 per share. On January 29, Hardin purchased 1000 shares of Roadmaster Industries at 1\frac{1}{32}$ per share and agreed to pay a purchase commission of $90. The price of Roadmaster Industries showed increases in value over the next two weeks and Hardin phoned his stock broker with an order to sell the stock on February 13 at 1\frac{5}{8}$ per share agreeing to a sales commission of $90.

(a) Find the purchase price of the stock excluding the commission.
(b) Find the purchase price of the stock including the commission.
(c) Find the selling price of the stock excluding the commission.
(d) Find the amount Hardin received after deducting the commission.
(e) How much profit did Hardin make on the investment?

CHAPTER 1 REVIEW EXERCISES

Write each of the following fractions in lowest terms. [1.1]

1. $\dfrac{20}{25}$

2. $\dfrac{42}{84}$

3. $\dfrac{27}{81}$

4. $\dfrac{147}{294}$

5. $\dfrac{63}{70}$

6. $\dfrac{264}{288}$

7. $\dfrac{24}{1200}$

8. $\dfrac{192}{264}$

Convert each of the following improper fractions to mixed numbers and write in lowest terms. [1.1]

9. $\dfrac{19}{6}$

10. $\dfrac{25}{16}$

11. $\dfrac{38}{24}$

12. $\dfrac{55}{7}$

13. $\dfrac{135}{65}$

14. $\dfrac{196}{24}$

15. $\dfrac{246}{111}$

16. $\dfrac{531}{256}$

Work each of the following problems and write in lowest terms. [1.1]

17. $\dfrac{9}{11} + \dfrac{1}{22}$

18. $\dfrac{1}{4} + \dfrac{1}{8} + \dfrac{5}{12}$

19. $\dfrac{2}{3} - \dfrac{1}{6}$

20. $\dfrac{5}{8} - \dfrac{1}{3}$

21. $\begin{aligned} 25\tfrac{1}{6} \\ + \ 46\tfrac{2}{3} \\ \hline \end{aligned}$

22. $\begin{aligned} 18\tfrac{3}{5} \\ 47\tfrac{7}{10} \\ + \ 25\tfrac{8}{15} \\ \hline \end{aligned}$

23. $\begin{aligned} 6\tfrac{7}{12} \\ - \ 2\tfrac{1}{3} \\ \hline \end{aligned}$

24. $\begin{aligned} 15\tfrac{13}{24} \\ - \ 8\tfrac{15}{16} \\ \hline \end{aligned}$

Work each of the following word problems. [1.1]

25. A baker used $2\frac{1}{4}$ cans of baking powder one day and $1\frac{7}{8}$ cans the next day. How many cans did she use altogether?

26. A water heater contains $58\frac{2}{3}$ gallons of water. If $43\frac{1}{2}$ gallons are drained out, how many gallons still remain in the water heater?

27. Three sides of Sheri Minkner's kiwi ranch are $202\frac{1}{8}$ feet, $370\frac{3}{4}$ feet, and $274\frac{1}{2}$ feet. If the distance around the ranch is $1166\frac{7}{8}$ feet, find the length of the fourth side.

28. The Cheese Company sold $2\frac{2}{3}$ pounds of American cheese, $6\frac{1}{8}$ pounds of jack cheese, $15\frac{1}{2}$ pounds of sharp cheddar cheese, and $10\frac{1}{6}$ pounds of meunster cheese to a caterer. Find the total weight of the products sold.

Work each problem. [1.2]

29. $\dfrac{3}{5} \times \dfrac{3}{8}$

30. $\dfrac{7}{8} \times \dfrac{1}{3} \times \dfrac{3}{5}$

31. $\dfrac{5}{6} \div \dfrac{1}{2}$

32. $10 \div \dfrac{5}{8}$

33. $3\dfrac{1}{4} \times 1\dfrac{1}{8}$

34. $3\dfrac{1}{8} \div 5\dfrac{5}{7}$

35. $12\dfrac{1}{2} \times 1\dfrac{2}{3}$

36. $12\dfrac{1}{3} \div 2$

Work each of the following word problems. [1.2]

37. Tracy Copley worked $18\frac{3}{10}$ hours at \$8 per hour. How much did she earn?

38. How many athletic bags can be made from $78\frac{3}{4}$ yards of material if each bag requires $4\frac{3}{8}$ yards?

39. A company will share $\frac{5}{8}$ of its profits with 4 employees. What fraction of the total profits will each employee receive?

40. The directions on a can of fabric glue say to apply $3\frac{1}{2}$ ounces of glue per square yard. How many ounces are needed for $43\frac{5}{9}$ square yards?

Convert each of the following decimals to a fraction and reduce to lowest terms. [1.2]

41. 0.28

42. 0.875

43. 0.1875

44. 0.005

Round each of the following decimals to the nearest tenth and to the nearest hundredth. [1.2]

45. 56.214

46. 7215.636

47. 0.7189

48. 8.025

Convert each of the following fractions to a decimal. Round to the nearest thousandth. [1.2]

49. $\dfrac{5}{8}$

50. $\dfrac{1}{9}$

51. $\dfrac{5}{6}$

52. $\dfrac{73}{96}$

Work each of the following problems on a calculator. Round each answer to the nearest hundredth. [1.3]

53.   16.75
    2.09
  371.765
+ 86.008

54.   768.728
− 54.617

55. 87.008×0.69

56.   7218.5
   36.09

57. $\dfrac{215.68 \times 16.7}{0.79 \times 23.72}$

58. $\dfrac{79.28 \times 5.71 \times 623.92}{0.07 \times 395.63}$

59. $\dfrac{376.72 \times 138.62}{13.29 + (713.9 \times 22.07)}$

60. $\dfrac{731.08 \times (10.02 + 1.98)}{(22.79 \times 2.65) + 71.9}$

Equations and Formulas

Formulas occur again and again throughout business mathematics. For example, formulas are used for finding markup, interest, depreciation, and in other important areas of business. This chapter discusses various ways of working with formulas, starting with a brief look at methods of solving equations.

2.1 Solving Equations

OBJECTIVES

1 Learn the basic terminology of equations.

2 Use basic rules to solve equations.

3 Combine similar terms in equations.

4 Use the distributive property to simplify equations.

An **equation** is a statement that says two expressions are equal. For example, the equation

$$x + 5 = 9$$

says that the expressions $x + 5$ and 9 are equal. In dealing with an equation certain terminology is used.

1 The letter x is called a **variable**—a letter that represents a number. The variable x, as well as the numbers 5 and 9, are called terms. A **term** is a single letter, a single number, or the product of a number and one or more letters. The expression $x + 5$ is called the **left side** of the equation while 9 is the **right side**. A **solution** to the equation is any number which can replace the variable and result in a true statement.

The solution for this equation is the number 4, since the replacement of the variable x with the number 4 results in a true statement.

$$x + 5 = 9$$

$$4 + 5 = 9 \qquad \text{Let } x = 4.$$

$$9 = 9 \qquad \text{True.}$$

The preceding check is an example of **substitution**: the variable x was replaced with 4.

2 In solving equations, the object is to find numbers that can be used to replace the variable so that the equation is a true statement. This is accomplished by changing the equation so that all the terms containing a variable are on one side of the equation and all the numbers are on the other side. Since an equation states that two expressions are equal, as long as both sides of the equation are changed in the same way the resulting expressions remain equal. The rules for solving equations follow.

Addition Rule. The same number may be added or subtracted on both sides of an equation.

Multiplication Rule. The same nonzero number may be multiplied or divided on both sides of an equation.

EXAMPLE 1

Solving Equations Using Addition

Solve $x - 6 = 13$

SOLUTION   To solve this equation, x must be alone on one side of the equal sign, and all numbers collected on the other side. To change the $x - 6$ to x, perform the opposite operation to "undo" what was done. The opposite of subtraction is addition, so add 6 to both sides.

$$x - 6 = 13$$

$$x - 6 + 6 = 13 + 6 \qquad \text{Add 6 on both sides.}$$

$$x + 0 = 19$$

$$x = 19$$

To check this answer, substitute 19 for x in the original equation.

$$x - 6 = 13 \qquad \text{Original equation.}$$

$$19 - 6 = 13 \qquad \text{Let } x = 19.$$

$$13 = 13 \qquad \text{True.}$$

The answer, 19, checks. ■

EXAMPLE 2

Solving Equations Using Subtraction

Solve $k + 7 = 18$.

SOLUTION   To isolate k on the left side, do the opposite of adding 7, which is *subtracting* 7.

$$k + 7 = 18$$

$$k + 7 - 7 = 18 - 7 \qquad \text{Subtract 7.}$$

$$k + 0 = 11$$

$$k = 11 \qquad \blacksquare$$

In formulas, the product of a number and a variable is often written without any special symbol for multiplication. As an example, the product of 5 and p could be written as $5p$, instead of $5 \times p$. The number 5 in the term $5p$ is the **coefficient** of p. Also, $\frac{1}{2}$ is the coefficient of z in the term $\frac{1}{2}z$.

EXAMPLE 3

Solving Equations Using Division

Solve $5p = 60$.

SOLUTION   The term $5p$ indicates the product of 5 and p. Since the opposite of multiplication is division, solve the equation by *dividing* both sides by 5.

$$5p = 60$$

$$\frac{5p}{5} = \frac{60}{5} \qquad \text{Divide by 5.}$$

$$p = 12$$

Check by substituting 12 for p in the original equation. $\blacksquare$

EXAMPLE 4

Solving Equations Using Multiplication

Solve $\dfrac{y}{3} = 9$.

SOLUTION   The bar in $\frac{y}{3}$ means to divide ($y \div 3 = 9$), so solve the equation by multiplying both sides by 3. (The opposite of division is multiplication.) As in the following solution, it is common to use a dot to indicate multiplication.

$$\frac{y}{3} = 9$$

$$3 \cdot \frac{y}{3} = 3 \cdot 9 \qquad \text{Multiply by 3.}$$

$$\cancel{3} \cdot \frac{y}{\cancel{3}} = 3 \cdot 9$$

$$y = 27 \qquad \blacksquare$$

Example 5 shows how to solve an equation using a reciprocal. To get the **reciprocal** of a nonzero fraction, exchange the numerator and the denominator. For example, the reciprocal of $\frac{7}{9}$ is $\frac{9}{7}$.

EXAMPLE 5

Solving Equations Using Reciprocals

Solve $\frac{3}{4}z = 9$.

SOLUTION   Solve this equation by multiplying both sides by $\frac{4}{3}$, the reciprocal of $\frac{3}{4}$. This process will give just $1z$, or z, on the left.

$$\frac{3}{4}z = 9$$

$$\frac{4}{3} \cdot \frac{3}{4}z = \frac{4}{3} \cdot 9 \qquad \text{Multiply by } \frac{4}{3}.$$

$$z = 12 \quad \blacksquare$$

The equation in Example 6 requires two steps to solve.

EXAMPLE 6

Solving Equations Involving Several Steps

Solve $2m + 5 = 17$.

SOLUTION   To solve equations that require more than one step, first isolate the terms involving the unknown on one side of the equation and constants on the other side by using addition and subtraction.

$$2m + 5 = 17$$

$$2m + 5 - 5 = 17 - 5 \qquad \text{Subtract 5.}$$

$$2m = 12$$

Now divide both sides by 2.

$$\frac{2m}{2} = \frac{12}{2} \qquad \text{Divide by 2.}$$

$$m = 6$$

As before, check by substituting 6 for m in the original equation. $\blacksquare$

NOTE   The unknown can be on either side of the equal sign. $6 = m$ is the same as $m = 6$. The number is the solution when the equation has the variable on the left *or* the right.

3   Some equations have more than one term with the same variable. Terms with the same variables can be *combined* by adding or subtracting the coefficients, as shown.

$$5y + 2y = 7y$$

$$11k - 8k = 3k$$

$$12p - 5p + 2p = 9p$$

$$2z + z = 2z + 1z = 3z$$

NOTE   Since multiplying by 1 does not change the value of a quantity, $1 \cdot z$ is the same as z.

EXAMPLE 7

Combining Similar Terms

Solve $8y - 6y + 4y = 24$

SOLUTION Start by combining terms on the left: $8y - 6y + 4y = 2y + 4y = 6y$. This gives the simplified equation:

$$6y = 24$$

$$\frac{6y}{6} = \frac{24}{6} \qquad \text{Divide by 6.}$$

$$y = 4 \quad \blacksquare$$

4 Some of the more advanced formulas used later in this book involve a coefficient in front of parentheses. These formulas often require the use of the **distributive property**, by which a number on the outside of parentheses can be multiplied times each term inside the parentheses, as shown here.

$$a(b + c) = ab + ac$$

The following diagram may help in remembering the distributive property.

$$a\,(b + c) = ab + ac$$

The *a* is *distributed* over the *b* and the *c*, as in the following examples.

$$2\,(m + 7) = 2\,m + 2 \cdot 7 = 2m + 14$$
$$8\,(k - 5) = 8\,k - 8 \cdot 5 = 8\,k - 40$$

EXAMPLE 8

Solving Equations Using the Distributive Property

Solve $6(p - 2) = 30$.

SOLUTION First use the distributive property on the left to remove the parentheses.

$$6(p - 2) = 30$$

$$6p - 12 = 30$$

Add 12 to both sides, then divide.

$$6p - 12 + 12 = 30 + 12$$

$$6p = 42$$

$$\frac{6p}{6} = \frac{42}{6} \qquad \text{Divide by 6.}$$

$$p = 7 \quad \blacksquare$$

To solve an equation, go through the following steps.

1. Remove all parentheses on both sides of the equation using the distributive property.

2. Combine all similar terms on both sides of the equation.

3. Add to or subtract from both sides whatever is needed to produce a term with the variable on one side and a number on the other side.

4. Multiply or divide the variable term by whatever is needed to produce a term with a coefficient of 1. Multiply or divide the number by the same quantity.

EXAMPLE 9

Solving Equations Involving Several Steps

Solve $5r - 2 = 2(r + 5)$.

SOLUTION

$$5r - 2 = 2r + 10$$ Use distributive property on the right.

$$5r - 2 + 2 = 2r + 10 + 2$$ Add 2 to both sides to get all numbers on the right side.

$$5r = 2r + 12$$

$$5r - 2r = 2r + 12 - 2r$$ Subtract 2r from both sides to get all variables on the left side.

$$5r - 2r = 12$$ Combine similar terms on the left.

$$3r = 12$$

$$\frac{3r}{3} = \frac{12}{3}$$ Divide both sides by 3 to get 1 as a coefficient.

$$r = 4 \quad \blacksquare$$

CAUTION Be sure to check the answer in the *original* equation and not in any other step.

2.1 Exercises

Solve each equation. Check each answer.

1. $y + 4 = 9$

2. $k + 8 = 15$

3. $s - 2 = 8$

4. $a - 7 = 3$

5. $14 = c + 8$

6. $7 = m - 3$

7. $9k = 72$

8. $2y = 16$

9. $4q = 140$

10. $8z = 136$

11. $60 = 30m$

12. $94 = 2z$

13. $1.7p = 5.1$

14. $3.5k = 24.5$

15. $4.2m = 25.2$

16. $3.9a = 15.6$

17. $3.92w = 3.136$

18. $2.773m = 3.3276$

19. $0.03751k = 0.135036$

20. $0.98145p = 1.668465$

21. $\frac{b}{4} = 5$

22. $\frac{m}{5} = 6$

23. $\frac{r}{7} = 1$

24. $\frac{c}{7} = 2$

25. $\dfrac{3}{5}a = 4$

26. $\dfrac{3}{4}m = 18$

27. $\dfrac{9}{4}z = 27$

28. $\dfrac{7}{3}s = 21$

29. $2x = \dfrac{5}{3}$

30. $4y = \dfrac{1}{3}$

31. $3m = \dfrac{6}{11}$

32. $7q = \dfrac{3}{4}$

33. $5p + 2 = 27$

34. $3m + 5 = 17$

35. $4y - 2 = 30$

36. $9p - 7 = 11$

37. $3r + 2 = 7$

38. $7z + 5 = 9$

39. $4p + \dfrac{1}{4} = 5$

40. $5z + \dfrac{2}{3} = 2$

41. $7q - \dfrac{2}{3} = 4$

42. $7a - \dfrac{5}{4} = \dfrac{9}{4}$

43. $\dfrac{2}{3}m - 5 = 1$

44. $\dfrac{3}{2}k + 1 = 13$

45. $6 + \dfrac{5}{4}m = 10$

46. $5 + \dfrac{8}{5}y = 13$

47. $7m + 4m - 5m = 78$

48. $13r - 7r + 3r = 81$

49. $k + k + 2k = 80$

50. $4z + z + 2z = 28$

51. $4x + 10 = 2(3x + 2)$

52. $4z + 2 = 2(z + 2)$

53. $3(m - 4) = m + 2$

54. $s + 8 = 3(s - 6)$

55. $3(2x + 12) = 8(4 + x)$

56. $5(2r - 1) = 3(r + 10)$

57. $\dfrac{1}{2}m + \dfrac{2}{3} = \dfrac{1}{4}m + \dfrac{17}{12}$

58. $\dfrac{3}{4}q - \dfrac{1}{9} = \dfrac{1}{3} + \dfrac{1}{4}q$

59. $\dfrac{3}{8}y + \dfrac{1}{4} = \dfrac{9}{8}y - \dfrac{1}{4}$

60. $3(2m - 2) = 4(5 - m)$

61. $2(4 - p) = 3(2 + p) - 6$

62. $9.1765y + 0.3284y = 6.65343$

63. $0.7452(3k - 1) = 3.94956$

64. $0.1325(4 + 3m) = 1.20575$

65. $0.234(3 + 4p) = .5286(p + 3)$

66. A student obtains the equation $6x = 5x$ after applying several steps correctly. The student then divides both sides by x and obtains the result $6 = 5$ and gives "no solution" as the answer. Is this correct? If not, state why not and give the correct solution. (See Objective 3.)

67. Solving the equation $3(5x - 2) = 15x - 6$ a student obtains the result $0 = 0$ and gives the value of "0" as the solution. Is this correct? If not, state why not and give the correct solution. (See Objective 4.)

2.2 Applications of Equations

OBJECTIVES

1 Translate phrases into mathematical expressions.

2 Write equations from given information.

3 Solve applied problems.

Most problems in business are expressed in words. Before these problems can be solved, they must be converted into mathematical language.

1   Applied problems tend to have certain phrases that occur again and again. The key to solving such problems is to correctly translate these phrases into mathematical expressions. The next few examples illustrate this process.

EXAMPLE 1
Translating Phrases into Expressions

Write the following verbal expressions as mathematical expressions. Use x to represent the unknown. (Other letters could be used to represent this unknown quantity.)

Verbal Expression	Mathematical Expression	Comments
(a) 7 plus a number	$7 + x$	x represents the number and "plus" means addition
(b) Add 20 to a number	$x + 20$	x represents the number to which 20 is added
(c) The sum of a number and 12	$x + 12$	"sum" indicates addition
(d) 6 more than a number	$x + 6$	"more than" indicates addition ∎

EXAMPLE 2
Translating Phrases Involving Subtraction

Write each of the following verbal expressions as a mathematical expression. Use x as a variable.

Verbal Expression	Mathematical Expression	Comments
(a) 3 less than a number	$x - 3$	"less than" indicates subtraction
(b) A number decreased by 8	$x - 8$	"decreased" indicates subtraction
(c) Ten fewer than a number	$x - 10$	"fewer than" indicates subtraction ∎

EXAMPLE 3
Translating Phrases Involving Multiplication and Division

Write the following verbal expressions as mathematical expressions. Use x as the variable.

Verbal Expression	Mathematical Expression	Comments
(a) The product of a number and 5	$5x$	"product" indicates multiplication
(b) Four times a number	$4x$	"times" indicates multiplication
(c) Two thirds of a number	$\frac{2}{3}x$	"of" indicates multiplication
(d) The quotient of a number and 3	$\frac{x}{3}$	"quotient" indicates division
(e) The sum of 3 and a number, multiplied by 5	$5(3 + x)$ or $5(x + 3)$	multiplying a sum requires parentheses ∎

Now that statements have been translated into mathematical expressions, you can use this knowledge to solve problems. The following steps represent a systematic approach to solving applied problems.

---

1. To solve an applied problem: Read the problem very carefully. Reread the problem to make sure that its meaning is clear.

2. Decide on the unknown. Choose a variable to represent the unknown number.

3. Identify the knowns. Use the given information to write an equation describing the relationship given in the problem.

4. Solve the equation.

5. Answer the question asked in the problem.

6. Check the solution by using the original words of the problem.

NOTE   The third step is often the hardest. To write an equation from the information given in the problem, convert the facts stated in words into mathematical expressions. This converted mathematical expression, or equation, is called the *mathematical model* of the situation described in the original words.

2 Since equal mathematical expressions represent the same number, any words that mean *equals* or *same* translate as $=$. The $=$ sign produces an equation which can be solved.

EXAMPLE 4
Solving Number Problems

Translate "the product of 4, and a number decreased by 7, is 100" into an equation. Use x as the variable. Solve the equation.

SOLUTION   Translate as follows.

the product of 4		and a number	decreased by	7	is	100
↓	↓	↓	↓	↓		↓
4	·	(x	−	7)	=	100

Simplify and complete the solution of the equation.

$$4 \cdot (x - 7) = 100$$

$$4x - 28 = 100 \qquad \text{Apply the distributive property.}$$

$$4x = 128 \qquad \text{Add 28 to both sides.}$$

$$x = 32 \qquad \text{Divide by 4.} \quad ■$$

EXAMPLE 5

Solving Applied Number Problems

At a business meeting there were 25 more women than men. The total number of people at the meeting was 139. Find the number of men.

3 **SOLUTION**

$$x = \text{number of men}$$

$$x + 25 = \text{number of women (There were 25 more women than men.)}$$

$$139 = \text{total number of people at the meeting}$$

Now, use this information to write an equation.

the total	is	the number of men	plus	the number of women
↓	↓	↓	↓	↓
139	=	x	+	$x + 25$

Solve the equation.

$$139 = 2x + 25$$

$$139 - 25 = 2x + 25 - 25 \qquad \text{Subtract 25.}$$

$$114 = 2x$$

$$57 = x \qquad \text{Divide by 2.}$$

There were 57 men at the meeting. Also, there were $57 + 25 = 82$ women at the meeting. Check this answer in the words of the original problem: 82 women is 25 more than 57 men, and $82 + 57 = 139$. ■

EXAMPLE 6

Solving Number and Cost Problems

The Eastside Nursery ordered 27 trees. Some of the trees were elms, costing $17 each, while the rest of the trees were maples at $11 each. The total cost of the trees was $375. Find the number of elms and the number of maples.

SOLUTION   A table can be very helpful in identifying the knowns and unknowns.

	Number of Trees	Cost per Tree	Total Cost
Elms	x	$17	$17x$
Maples	$27 - x$	$11	$11(27 - x)$
Totals	27		375

NOTE The shipment contained 27 trees so the number of maples is found by subtracting the number of elms, x, from 27.

The information in the table is used to get the following equation.

Cost of elms + Cost of maples = Total cost

$$17x + 11(27 - x) \quad\quad = 375$$

Now solve this equation. First use the distributive property.

$$17x + 297 - 11x = 375$$

$$6x + 297 = 375 \quad\quad \text{Combine terms.}$$

$$6x = 78 \quad\quad \text{Subtract 297 from each side.}$$

$$x = 13 \quad\quad \text{Divide each side by 6.}$$

There were 13 elm trees and $27 - 13$, or 14, maple trees. Check this answer.

Cost of elms + Cost of maples = Total cost

$$17(13) + 11(14) \quad\quad = 375$$

$$221 + 154 \quad\quad = 375$$

$$375 \quad\quad = 375$$

The answer checks. ■

EXAMPLE 7

Solving Interest Problems

Mike Lutz has $25,000. He puts some of the money into a passbook account and invests $5000 more than 3 times this amount in savings bonds. How much is put into the passbook account? How much is invested in bonds?

SOLUTION   Let x represent the amount invested in the passbook account. To find the amount invested in savings bonds, translate as follows.

5000	more than	3 times the amount
↓	↓	↓
5000	+	3 x

Since the sum of the two investments must be $25,000, an equation can be formed as follows.

Amount invested in passbook	+	Amount invested in savings bonds	=	Total amount invested
x	+	$(5000 + 3x)$	=	$25,000

Now solve the equation.

$$x + 5000 + 3x = 25000$$

$$4x + 5000 = 25000$$

$$4x + 5000 - 5000 = 25000 - 5000$$

$$4x = 20000$$

$$x = 5000$$

In answer to the question in the problem, the amount invested in the passbook account is x, or $5000, and the amount invested in savings bonds is $5000 + 3x$, or $5000 + 3(5000)$, or $20,000. ■

2.2 Exercises

Write the following as mathematical expressions. Use x as the variable.

1. 5 plus a number
2. a number added to 9
3. 1 added to a number
4. the sum of a number and 12
5. a quantity is increased by 16
6. the total of x and 17
7. 3 less than a number
8. a number decreased by 6
9. subtract 15 from a number
10. 16 fewer than a number
11. the product of a number and 9
12. triple a number
13. double a number
14. three fifths of a number
15. the quotient of a number and 11
16. the quotient of 9 and a number
17. a number divided by 4
18. 16 divided by a number
19. the product of 8 and the sum of a number and 3
20. a number is added to twice the number
21. 7 times the difference of a number and 3
22. the difference of a number and 2, multiplied by 7

Write mathematical expressions for each of the following.

23. Find the cost of x apples at 53 cents each.
24. Find the cost of x small trucks at $5625 each.
25. A company has 73 employees of whom x are union. How many employees are nonunion?
26. The inventory of a small card shop is valued at $73,000. The value of the greeting cards is x. Find the value of the rest of the inventory.
27. A market paid $172 for x crates of berries. Find the cost of one crate of berries.
28. A lodge paid $1853 for tickets for its x members to visit the state capitol. Find the cost of one ticket.
29. Robin has 21 books on computers. She donates x of them to the school library. How many does she have left?
30. A video rental store is x years old. How old will it be in 8 years?
31. A plane ticket costs b dollars for an adult and d dollars for a child. Find the total cost for 2 adults and 5 children.
32. A bank teller has f five dollar bills and t ten dollar bills. Find the total value of the money.

Solve the following word problems. Follow steps 1–6.

1. Read the problem carefully.
2. Choose a variable to represent the unknown quantity.
3. Translate the problem into an equation.
4. Solve the equation.
5. Answer the question asked in the problem.
6. Check your solution by using the original words of the problem.

33. If 5 times a number is decreased by 3, the result is 27. Find the number.

34. When 6 is added to 4 times a number, the result is 42. Find the number.

35. The sum of a number and 5 is multiplied by 6, giving 42 as a result. Find the number.

36. The sum of a number and 8 is multiplied by 5, giving 60 as the answer. Find the number.

37. When 6 is added to a number, the result is 7 times the number. Find the number.

38. If 6 is subtracted from three times a number, the result is 4 more than the number. Find the number.

39. When 5 times a number is added to twice the number, the result is 10. Find the number.

40. If 7 times a number is subtracted from 11 times the number, the result is 9. Find the number.

41. In an executive fitness test, Oscar did 15 more pushups than Lou did. The total number of pushups for both men was 193. Find the number of pushups that Lou did.

42. A pharmacist found that at the end of the day she had 12 more prescriptions for antibiotics than she had for tranquilizers. She had 84 prescriptions altogether for these two types of drugs. How many did she have for tranquilizers?

43. At one company, 15 more people work in the production department than work in the packaging department. The total number of people in the two departments is 277. Find the number of people in the production department.

44. A company with 111 employees offers a choice of two different health plans. Suppose 15 more people signed up for Blue Cross than took a plan from a doctor's organization. How many people took the doctor's plan?

45. A mattress is on sale for $250, which is $\frac{5}{6}$ of its original price. Find the original price.

46. Because of handling and freight charges, Western Oil Equipment charges $\frac{5}{4}$ of the list price for an item shipped to Indonesia. Find the list price of an item that was charged at $725.

47. A contractor built 105 homes last year, some economy models and some deluxe models. The number of economy models was $\frac{3}{2}$ the number of deluxe models. Find the number of each type of home that was built.

48. Jose's Auto Parts spent $14,000 last year on advertising. Jose advertises only on the radio and in newspapers. The amount spent in the newspapers was $\frac{7}{3}$ the amount spent on the radio. Find the amount spent on each type of advertising.

49. Johnson Computer Products has declared a dividend of $44,000 to be divided between its founder and its president. The founder gets $1\frac{1}{2}$ times as much as the president. Find the amount received by each.

50. A building can be used either for retail stores or for offices. The owner wants to receive a total annual rent of $67,500, with $3\frac{1}{2}$ times as much rent coming from retail stores as from offices. How much rent will come from offices? How much from retail stores?

51. Karen has a piece of material that is 106 inches long. She wishes to cut it into two pieces so that one piece is 12 inches longer than the other. What should be the length of each piece?

52. Rose earns $8000 less than twice as much as Lou. If their two incomes total $76,000, how much does each earn?

53. There are 63 people employed at Dewey's Department Store. New workers receive $6 per hour while experienced workers receive $9 per hour. If the company spends a total of $483 per hour in wages, find the number of each type of worker the company employs.

54. Jumbo Market makes 5¢ on a head of lettuce and 4¢ on a bunch of carrots. Last week, a total of 12,900 heads of lettuce and bunches of carrots were sold, with a total profit of $587. How many heads of lettuce and how many bunches of carrots were sold?

55. Is "solving the equation" the final step in solving an applied problem? If not, what remains to be done? (See Objective 3.)

56. Write out the steps necessary to solve an applied problem. (See Objective 3.)

2.3 Formulas

OBJECTIVES

1 Evaluate formulas for given values of the variables.

2 Solve formulas for a specific variable.

3 Use standard business formulas to solve word problems.

Many of the most useful rules and procedures in business are given as a **formula**, an equation showing how one number is found from other numbers. One of the single most useful formulas in business is the one for simple interest.

$$\text{Interest} = \text{Principal} \times \text{Rate} \times \text{Time}$$

1   When written out in words, as shown, a formula can take up too much space and be hard to remember. For this reason, it is common to use letters as variables for the words in a formula. Many times the first letter in each word of a formula is used, to make it easier to remember the formula. By this method, the formula for simple interest is written as follows.

$$I = PRT$$

EXAMPLE 1
Finding Interest

Use the formula $I = PRT$ and find I if $P = 7000$, $R = 0.07$, and $T = 2$.

SOLUTION   Substitute 7000 for P, 0.07 for R, and 2 for T in the formula $I = PRT$. (Remember that writing P, R, and T together as PRT indicates the product of the three letters.)

$$I = PRT$$

$$I = 7000(0.07)(2)$$

Multiply on the right to get the solution.

$$I = 980 \quad \blacksquare$$

EXAMPLE 2
Finding Principal

Use the formula $I = PRT$ and find P if $I = 5760$, $R = 0.12$, and $T = 3$.

SOLUTION   Substitute the given numbers for the letters of the formula.

$$I = PRT$$

$$5760 = P(0.12)(3)$$

On the right, $(0.12)(3) = 0.36$.

$$5760 = 0.36P$$

To find P, divide both sides of this equation by 0.36.

$$\frac{5760}{0.36} = \frac{0.36P}{0.36}$$

$$16{,}000 = P \quad \blacksquare$$

2   In Example 2 we found the value of P when given the values of I, R and T. If several problems of this type must be solved, it may be better to rewrite the formula $I = PRT$ so that P is alone on one side of the equation. Do this with the rules of equations given earlier. Since P is multiplied by RT, get P alone by dividing both sides of the equation by RT.

$$I = PRT$$

$$\frac{I}{RT} = \frac{PRT}{RT} \qquad \text{Divide by } RT.$$

$$\frac{I}{RT} = P$$

This process of rearranging a formula is sometimes called *solving a formula for a specific variable.*

EXAMPLE 3   Solve for T in the formula $M = P(1 + RT)$.

Solving for a Specific Variable

SOLUTION   This formula expresses the maturity value (M) of an initial amount of money (P) invested at a specified rate (R) for a certain period of time (T).

Start by using the distributive property on the right side.

$$M = P(1 + RT)$$

$$M = P + PRT$$

Now subtract P from both sides.

$$M - P = P + PRT - P$$

$$M - P = PRT$$

Divide each side by PR.

$$\frac{M - P}{PR} = \frac{PRT}{PR}$$

$$\frac{M - P}{PR} = T$$

The original formula is now solved for T.   ■

EXAMPLE 4   Solve for W in the formula $P = 2L + 2W$.

Solving for a Specific Variable

SOLUTION   This formula gives the perimeter, or distance around, a rectangle if the length and width of the rectangle are known. (For example, this formula could be used to find the distance around the edge of this page.) To solve for W, get W alone on one side of the equal sign. Start by subtracting $2L$ from each side.

$$P = 2L + 2W$$

$$P - 2L = 2L - 2L + 2W$$

$$P - 2L = 2W$$

Now divide each side by 2.

$$\frac{P - 2L}{2} = \frac{2W}{2}$$

$$\frac{P - 2L}{2} = W$$

The original formula is now solved for W.   ■

3   In the following two examples applied problems that use some common business formulas are solved. (These formulas are discussed in more detail later in the book.)

EXAMPLE 5

Finding Gross Sales

Find the gross sales from selling 186 gallons of diesel fuel at $1.28 gallon.

SOLUTION   The formula for gross sales is

$$G = NP.$$

For this formula, N is the number of items sold and P is the price per item. To find the gross sales from selling 186 gallons of diesel fuel at $1.28 per gallon, use the formula as shown.

$$G = NP$$

$$G = 186(\$1.28)$$

$$G = \$238.08$$

The gross sales will be $238.08. ∎

EXAMPLE 6

Finding Selling Price

Find the selling price if the cost of an item is $5.15 and its markup is $2.11.

SOLUTION   The selling price of an item is found by adding the cost of the item and the markup.

$$S = C + M$$

The variable C is the cost of the item, and M is the markup (an amount added to cover expenses and profit). If an item costs $5.15, and has a markup of $2.11, the selling price would be found as shown.

$$S = \$5.15 + \$2.11$$

$$S = \$7.26$$

The selling price is $7.26. ∎

2.3 Exercises

In the following exercises a formula is given, along with the values of all but one of the variables in the formula. Find the value of the variable that is not given.

1. $P = M - B; P = 150, B = 35$

2. $I = PRT; P = 1000, R = 0.04, T = 2$

3. $M = P(1 + RT);$
    $P = 500, R = 0.02, M = 530$

4. $P = RB; P = 85, B = 1700$

5. $R = \dfrac{D}{1 - DT}; D = 0.05, T = 4$

6. $\dfrac{I}{PR} = T; P = 100, R = 0.02, T = 500$

7. $P = 2L + 2W; P = 40, W = 6$

8. $P = 2L + 2W; P = 340, L = 70$

9. $V = \dfrac{1}{3}Bh; V = 160, B = 48$

10. $V = \dfrac{1}{3}Bh; V = 52, h = 13$

11. $A = \dfrac{1}{2}(b + B)h; b = 6, B = 8, h = 3$

12. $A = \dfrac{1}{2}(b + B)h; b = 15, B = 13, h = 4$

13. $I = PRT; I = 100, P = 500, R = 0.10$

14. $I = PRT; I = 60, P = 250, R = 0.04$

15. $V = LWH; V = 150, L = 10, W = 5$

16. $V = LWH; V = 800, L = 40, W = 10$

17. $A = \frac{1}{2}(b + B)h; A = 105, b = 19, B = 11$

18. $A = \frac{1}{2}(b + B)h; A = 70, b = 15, B = 20$

19. $P = \frac{S}{1 + RT}; S = 24,600, R = 0.06, T = \frac{5}{12}$

20. $P = \frac{S}{1 + RT}; S = 23,815, R = 0.09, T = \frac{11}{12}$

Solve each formula for the indicated variable.

21. $A = LW$; for W

22. $d = rt$; for r

23. $V = LWH$; for H

24. $I = PRT$; for R

25. $I = PRT$; for T

26. $A = \frac{1}{2}bh$; for b

27. $P = 2L + 2W$; for L

28. $a + b + c = P$; for c

29. $A = \frac{1}{2}(b + B)h$; for h

30. $M = P + PRT$; for R

31. $M = P(1 + RT)$; for R

32. $P = M(1 - DT)$; for D

33. $P = \frac{A}{1 + i}$; for i

34. $d = r(c - s)$; for s

In problems 35–56 the following formulas may be needed for solution.

$$I = PRT \qquad G = NP$$
$$P = 2L + 2W \qquad S = C + M$$
$$M = P(1 + RT)$$

35. A lawn mower shop buys 52 lawn mowers for $6123. Find the cost of one lawn mower.

36. Wood's Television and Stereo bought 17 table model television sets for $1942.25. Find the cost of one set.

37. Thompson Cleaning Service bought 8 vacuum cleaners and 19 drums of cleaning solvent for $3403. Each vacuum cleaner cost $176. Find the cost of a drum of solvent.

38. Lake Boating bought 5 small boats and 3 large boats for $14,878. A small boat cost $1742. Find the cost of a large boat.

39. An employee of Wilson's Department Store is paid a weekly salary given by the formula $S = 160 + 0.03x$, where x is the total sales of the employee for the week. Find the salary of employees having the following weekly sales. (a) $1152 (b) $1796 (c) $2314

40. The Green Lawn Company charges a $60 flat fee for its lawn service in addition to a charge of $.006 per square foot of lawn maintained. Find the total charges for the following size lawns. (a) 3200 square feet (b) 6600 square feet (c) 12,785 square feet

41. In June, Hany's Hardware had net sales (net sales = gross sales − returns) in the amount of $56,000. The returns were $\frac{1}{15}$ of gross sales. Find the gross sales.

42. The Bridal Shop has net sales of $33,000 and a return of $\frac{1}{12}$ of gross sales. If net sales equal gross sales minus returns, find the gross sales.

43. One store sets markup at $\frac{3}{4}$ of its cost for the item. Find the cost of an item if the selling price is $84.

44. The bookstore at Ironwood Community College has a markup that is $\frac{1}{4}$ its cost on a book. Find the cost to the bookstore of a book selling for $20.

45. Last year, the expenses at the Taco Mary Restaurant were $\frac{5}{6}$ of the revenue. The profit (the difference between revenue and expenses) was $15,000. Find the revenue.

46. Computerworld has expenses that run $\frac{15}{16}$ of revenue. Profit (the difference between revenue and expenses) was $9000. Find the revenue.

47. A bank teller has some five-dollar bills and some twenty-dollar bills. The teller has 5 more of the twenties. The total value of the money is $725. Find the number of five-dollar bills that the teller has.

48. A convention manager finds that she has $1290, made up of twenties and fifties. She has a total of 42 bills. How many fifty-dollar bills does the manager have?

49. Find the principal if interest of $2325 is earned in 3 years at 5% (or 0.05).

50. How much money must be invested for 3 years at 11% (or 0.11) to earn interest of $4620?

51. Miriam Cross loaned $12,000 to Don Reynolds. The loan was for 4 years, with interest of $3840. Find the rate of interest.

52. Terry Twitty made a $22,000 loan so that Melissa Graves could start an auto parts business. The loan was for 2 years, and interest was $5720. Find the rate of interest.

53. Fred Tausz loaned $39,000 to Anne Topsy. The loan was at 7% (or 0.07), with interest of $13,650. Find the time for the loan.

54. Jackie Williams loaned $18,200 to Colleen Sullivan. The two agreed on an interest rate of 11% (or 0.11), with interest of $8008. Find the time for the loan.

55. Mary Scott invests $1000 at 8% (or 0.08) for 5 years. How much did Mary have in her account at the end of 5 years?

56. John Wood had $4560 in his account after 2 years. If the account paid 7% (or 0.07) interest, how much did John initially deposit in his account?

57. Write a step-by-step explanation of the procedure you would use to solve the equation $A = P + PRT$ for R. (See Objective 2.)

58. Explain why the equation $T = \dfrac{A - P}{PR}$ is equivalent to the equation $T = \dfrac{A}{PR} - \dfrac{1}{R}$. (See Objective 2.)

2.4 Ratios and Proportions

OBJECTIVES

1 Define a ratio.

2 Set up a proportion.

3 Solve a proportion for unknown values.

4 Use proportions to solve problems.

1 A **ratio** is a quotient of two quantities. It can be used to compare the quantities. The ratio of the number a to the number b is written in any of the following ways.

$$a \text{ to } b \qquad a : b \qquad \text{or} \qquad \frac{a}{b}$$

This last way of writing a ratio is most common in algebra, while $a : b$ is perhaps most common in business.

EXAMPLE 1

Writing Ratios from Words

Write a ratio in the form $\frac{a}{b}$ for each word phrase. (Notice in each phrase that the number mentioned first always gives the numerator.)

SOLUTION

(a) The ratio of 5 hours to 3 hours is $\frac{5}{3}$.

(b) To find the ratio of 5 hours to 3 days, first convert 3 days to hours. This is needed, since both quantities in the ratio must be in the same units. There are 24 hours in 1 day so 3 days $= 3 \cdot 24 = 72$ hours. Then the ratio of 5 hours to 3 days is the quotient of 5 hours and 72 hours.

$$\frac{5}{72}$$

(c) The ratio of $700,000 in sales to $950,000 in sales is written this way.

$$\frac{\$700,000}{\$950,000}$$

Write this ratio in lowest terms.

$$\frac{\$700,000}{\$950,000} = \frac{14}{19} \quad \blacksquare$$

NOTE In the ratios of Example 1, the quantities had to have the same units (hours to hours, dollars to dollars).

2 A ratio is used to compare two numbers or amounts. A **proportion** says that two ratios are equal, as in the following example.

$$\frac{3}{4} = \frac{15}{20}$$

This proportion says that the ratios $\frac{3}{4}$ and $\frac{15}{20}$ are equal.

To see if a proportion is true, use the method of **cross-products** as shown.

The proportion

$$\frac{a}{b} = \frac{c}{d}$$

is true if the cross-products $b \cdot c$ and $a \cdot d$ are equal, that is, if $ad = bc$.

EXAMPLE 2
Determining True Proportions

Decide if the following proportions are true.

(a) $\dfrac{3}{5} = \dfrac{12}{20}$

(b) $\dfrac{2\frac{1}{4}}{3\frac{1}{2}} = \dfrac{9}{16}$

SOLUTION

(a) Find each cross-product.

$$\frac{3}{5} = \frac{12}{20}$$

$$3 \cdot 20 = 5 \cdot 12$$

$$60 = 60$$

Since the cross-products are equal, the proportion is true.

(b) Find each cross-product.

$$\frac{2\frac{1}{4}}{3\frac{1}{2}} = \frac{9}{16}$$

$$\left(2\frac{1}{4}\right)(16) = (9)\left(3\frac{1}{2}\right)$$

$$\left(\frac{9}{4}\right)(16) = (9)\left(\frac{7}{2}\right)$$

$$36 = \frac{63}{2}$$

This proportion is false because 36 does not equal $\frac{63}{2}$. ∎

NOTE The numbers in a proportion need not be whole numbers.

We might mention that the method of cross-products is just a shortcut version of solving an equation. To see how, start with the proportion

$$\frac{a}{b} = \frac{c}{d}$$

and multiply both sides by bd.

$$bd \cdot \frac{a}{b} = bd \cdot \frac{c}{d}$$

$$ad = bc$$

The expressions ad and bc are the cross-products, and this solution shows that they are equal.

3   Four numbers are used in a proportion. If any three of these numbers are known, the fourth can be found.

EXAMPLE 3

Finding Unknown Values in a Proportion

Find x in this proportion.

$$\frac{3}{5} = \frac{x}{40}$$

SOLUTION   In a proportion, the cross-products are equal. The cross-products in this proportion are $3 \cdot 40 = 5 \cdot x$. Placing these equal gives the following equation.

$$3 \cdot 40 = 5 \cdot x$$

$$120 = 5x$$

Divide both sides by 5 to find the solution.

$$24 = x \qquad ■$$

EXAMPLE 4

Finding Unknown Values in a Proportion

Solve this proportion to find k.

$$\frac{3}{10} = \frac{5}{k}$$

SOLUTION   Find the two cross-products and place them equal.

$$3k = 10 \cdot 5$$

$$3k = 50$$

$$k = \frac{50}{3}$$

Write the answer as the mixed number $16\frac{2}{3}$, if desired.   ■

4 Proportions are used in many practical applications, as Example 5 shows.

EXAMPLE 5
Solving Applications

A hospital charges a patient $7.80 for 12 capsules. How much should it charge for 18 capsules?

SOLUTION Let x be the cost of 18 capsules. Set up a proportion: one ratio in the proportion can involve the number of capsules, while the other ratio can use the costs. Make sure that corresponding numbers appear in the numerator and the denominator. Use this pattern.

$$\frac{\text{capsules}}{\text{capsules}} = \frac{\text{cost}}{\text{cost}}$$

Now substitute the given information.

$$\frac{12}{18} = \frac{7.80}{x}$$

Use cross-products to solve the proportion.

$$12x = 18(7.80)$$
$$12x = 140.40$$
$$x = 11.70$$

The 18 capsules should cost $11.70. ∎

EXAMPLE 6
Solving Applications

Lou and Stan are partners in a business. They agree to divide the profits of the business in the ratio 3 : 5, respectively. Find Lou's share of the profits if Stan receives $5700. Find Lou's share with the following proportion.

$$\frac{\text{Lou's share}}{\text{Stan's share}} = \frac{3}{5}$$

SOLUTION Let x represent Lou's share. Since Stan's share is $5700, substitute to get the following proportion.

$$\frac{x}{5700} = \frac{3}{5}$$

Find the cross-products and solve the resulting equation.

$$5x = 3(\$5700)$$
$$5x = \$17,100$$
$$x = \$3420$$

Lou's share of the profits is $3420. ∎

2.4 Exercises

Write the following ratios. Write each ratio in lowest terms.

1. 50 miles to 30 miles

2. 70 feet to 110 feet

3. 86 dollars to 102 dollars

4. 180 people to 160 people

5. 6 feet to 5 yards

6. 10 yards to 8 feet

7. 40 inches to 5 feet

8. 100 inches to 5 yards

9. 24 minutes to 3 hours

10. 148 minutes to 4 hours

11. 4 dollars to 10 quarters

12. 35 dimes to 6 dollars

13. 20 hours to 5 days

14. 6 days to 9 hours

15. 80¢ to $3

16. $1.20 to 75¢

17. $3.24 to 72¢

18. $3.57 to 42¢

Decide whether the following proportions are true.

19. $\dfrac{2}{5} = \dfrac{8}{20}$

20. $\dfrac{9}{10} = \dfrac{18}{20}$

21. $\dfrac{84}{48} = \dfrac{14}{8}$

22. $\dfrac{12}{18} = \dfrac{8}{12}$

23. $\dfrac{7}{10} = \dfrac{82}{120}$

24. $\dfrac{17}{19} = \dfrac{72}{84}$

25. $\dfrac{19}{32} = \dfrac{33}{77}$

26. $\dfrac{19}{30} = \dfrac{57}{90}$

27. $\dfrac{110}{18} = \dfrac{160}{27}$

28. $\dfrac{420}{600} = \dfrac{14}{20}$

29. $\dfrac{216}{95} = \dfrac{864}{380}$

30. $\dfrac{174}{97} = \dfrac{4350}{2425}$

31. $\dfrac{2\frac{1}{4}}{5} = \dfrac{9}{20}$

32. $\dfrac{5\frac{3}{4}}{9} = \dfrac{23}{36}$

33. $\dfrac{11}{34} = \dfrac{3\frac{5}{8}}{7}$

34. $\dfrac{16}{13} = \dfrac{2}{1\frac{5}{8}}$

35. $\dfrac{3\frac{3}{8}}{5\frac{1}{4}} = \dfrac{27}{42}$

36. $\dfrac{28}{17} = \dfrac{9\frac{2}{3}}{5\frac{2}{3}}$

37. $\dfrac{8.15}{2.03} = \dfrac{61.125}{15.225}$

38. $\dfrac{423.88}{17.119} = \dfrac{330.6264}{13.35282}$

Solve each of the following proportions.

39. $\dfrac{x}{24} = \dfrac{2}{3}$

40. $\dfrac{5}{y} = \dfrac{20}{8}$

41. $\dfrac{a}{35} = \dfrac{5}{7}$

42. $\dfrac{6}{x} = \dfrac{4}{18}$

43. $\dfrac{z}{20} = \dfrac{80}{100}$

44. $\dfrac{25}{100} = \dfrac{8}{m}$

45. $\dfrac{1}{2} = \dfrac{r}{7}$

46. $\dfrac{2}{3} = \dfrac{5}{s}$

47. $\dfrac{\frac{3}{4}}{6} = \dfrac{3}{x}$

48. $\dfrac{3}{x} = \dfrac{11}{9}$

49. $\dfrac{12}{p} = \dfrac{23.571}{15.714}$

50. $\dfrac{86.112}{57.408} = \dfrac{k}{15}$

51. Explain the difference between ratio and proportion. (See Objective 2.)

52. Describe the process used to determine if a proportion is true or false. (See Objective 3.)

Solve each of the following word problems.

53. A basketball player scores 152 points in her first 8 games. At the same rate, how many points will she score in the 25-game season?

54. A lawn mower used 24 tanks of gas to cut 60 acres of lawn. How many tanks of gas were needed for each 5-acre parcel?

55. A new compact car travels 324 miles on 9 gallons of gas. If the tank holds 16 usable gallons, how many miles will the car travel before it runs out of gas?

56. If you pay $7.60 tax on a $114 item, find the tax on a $456 item.

57. The ratio of yes to no votes in an election was 8 to 7. How many no votes were cast if 4400 people voted yes?

58. If 22 children's dresses cost $176, find the cost of 12 dresses.

59. Jose paid $199,500 for a 7-unit apartment house. Find the cost for a 16-unit apartment house.

60. Eight yards of material are needed for 5 dresses. How much material is needed for 12 dresses?

61. Suppose that 7 sacks of fertilizer cover 3325 square feet of lawn. Find the number of sacks needed for 7125 square feet.

62. The distance between two cities on a road map is 2 inches. Actually, the cities are 120 miles apart. The distance between two other cities is 17 inches. How far apart are these cities?

63. The charge to move a load of freight 750 miles is $90. Find the charge to move the freight 1200 miles.

64. To ride a bus 80 miles costs $5. Find the charge to ride 180 miles.

65. Hite and Clark are partners who agree to divide any profits in the ratio 4 : 7. Find Clark's profit if Hite gets $8000.

66. Suppose two partners agree to divide their profits in the ratio 5 : 8. If the first partner receives $15,000 in profits, how much does the second get?

67. The owner of a factory has always kept the ratio of salespeople to production employees at 2:7. If she currently has 24 salespeople, how many production employees are there?

68. At one company, sales of the Texas plant are in the ratio 5 : 4 with sales of the Michigan plant. Find the sales of the Michigan plant if Texas sales are $30,000.

69. A 16-ounce box of cereal sells for $2.40. What is the cost per ounce?

70. What is the best buy for a box of pretzels: the 15-ounce size for $2.69 or the 20-ounce size for $3.29?

CHAPTER 2 QUICK REVIEW

TOPIC	APPROACH	EXAMPLE
2.1 Solving equations	1. Use addition and multiplication rules to move all variables to one side of the equation and constants to the other. 2. Combine all similar terms. 3. Divide both sides of equation by the coefficient.	$13x + 5 - 8x = 20$ $13x - 8x = 20 - 5$ $5x = 15$ $x = 3$
2.2 Translating phrases	Use mathematical symbols to represent verbal expressions.	2 plus a number: $2 + x$ 5 less than a number: $x - 5$
2.3 Solving applied problems	1. Read problem carefully. 2. Choose a variable to represent the unknown. 3. Write an equation describing the relationship among the quantities. 4. Solve the equation. 5. Answer the problem. 6. Check solution.	A committee had 7 fewer men than women. The total number of people on the committee was 19. Find the number of women. Let x represent the number of women. $x + (x - 7) = 19$ $2x - 7 = 19$ $2x = 26$ $x = 13$ women
2.3 Evaluating formulas for given values of the variable	Substitute numerical values for variables and evaluate.	Use the formula $M = P(1 + RT)$ to find M if $P = \$5000$, $R = .05$, and $T = 6$. $M = 5000(1 + (.05)(6))$ $M = 5000(1 + .3)$ $M = 5000(1.3) = \$6500$
2.3 Solving formulas for specific variables	Use the rules for solving equations.	Solve $M = P + PRT$ for T. $M - P = PRT$ $\dfrac{M - P}{PR} = T$

TOPIC	APPROACH	EXAMPLE
2.4 Solving a proportion for a missing part	Use the principle of cross-products: $\dfrac{a}{b} = \dfrac{c}{d}$ if $a \cdot d = b \cdot c$.	Find x in the proportion. $\dfrac{6}{5} = \dfrac{x}{20}$ $6 \cdot 20 = 5 \cdot x$ $120 = 5x$ $24 = x$
2.4 Using proportions to solve problems	Set up the proportion and use the principle of cross-products.	A video store charges \$12 to rent 5 tapes. How much does it charge for 8 tapes? $\dfrac{\$12}{5} = \dfrac{x}{8}$ $\$12 \cdot 8 = 5 \cdot x$ $\$96 = 5x$ $\$19.20 = x$

SUMMARY EXERCISE

A local bookstore had a going-out-of-business sale. The store had two prices for its books, one for hardcover books and a different price for softbound books. Hardcover books cost 3 times as much as the softbound books. Jim notices that Sam bought 5 hardcover and 8 softbound books and spent a total of \$159.85.

(a) What was the store's price for hardcover books?

(b) What was the store's price for softbound books?

(c) If Jim wanted to buy twice as many softbound books and three times as many hardcover books as Sam bought, how much money would he need?

CHAPTER 2 REVIEW EXERCISES

Solve each equation. [2.1]

1. $x - 7 = 20$

2. $x + 5 = 15$

3. $3x - 8 = 13$

4. $6x + 7 = 11$

5. $\dfrac{k}{3} = 10$

6. $\dfrac{2k}{5} = 12$

7. $\dfrac{m}{4} - 5 = 9$

8. $2(x - 3) = 3(x + 4)$

9. $\dfrac{2p}{3} - 5 = 6p - 1$

10. $3m - 7 = -2(4 - 3m) + 8$

11. $.147(2x - 3) = 5.239$

12. $.621(x - 2) = .324x$

Write a mathematical expression. Use x as the variable.[2.2]

13. 5 times a number
14. $\frac{1}{2}$ times a number
15. 6 times a number is added to the number
16. 5 times a number is decreased by 11
17. The sum of 3 times a number and 7

Solve each word problem.[2.2]

18. One-third of a shoe store's sales were charges. What were their total sales if charges totaled $750?

19. A video store rents movies at $3.50 per day. If the total income for one day was $630, how many movies did the store rent?

20. Phone and water bills together cost a company $540 for March. If the phone cost 4 times as much as the water, how much was each utility?

21. Five more than $\frac{1}{4}$ of the employees of a company have 25 years or more of service. If 24 employees have 25 or more years of service, how many employees does the company have?

22. The local movie theater sold 100 tickets for $390. If children's tickets cost $3 and adult tickets $6, how many of each were sold?

For each problem, use the formula to find the value of the variable that is not given.[2.3]

23. $I = PRT; I = \$960, R = 0.12, T = 2$
24. $M = P(1 + RT); M = \$3770, R = 0.04, T = 4$
25. $P = 2L + 2W; P = 360, L = 20$

Solve each equation for the variable indicated.[2.3]

26. $P = tv + kx^2$; for t

27. $A = 2L + 2W$; for W

28. $C = \dfrac{5}{9}(F - 32)$; for F

Write the following ratios.[2.4]

29. 40 feet to 10 yards

30. 9 days to 12 hours

31. $5000 to $250

32. 3 years to 15 months

33. 2 dollars to 75 cents

Solve the following proportions.[2.4]

34. $\dfrac{5}{x} = \dfrac{15}{4}$

35. $\dfrac{x}{5} = \dfrac{2}{3}$

36. $\dfrac{5}{9} = \dfrac{x}{4}$

37. $\dfrac{5}{12} = \dfrac{4}{x}$

38. $\dfrac{27}{36} = \dfrac{x}{5}$

Work the following word problems.[2.4]

39. The ratio of management to marketing majors is $\frac{2}{3}$. If 48 students are enrolled in management, how many students are marketing majors?

40. Mary can read 3 books in 7 weeks. How many weeks will it take her to read 6 books?

41. Gas costs $1.02 per gallon. If Joe fills his tank with 12.5 gallons, how much does the gas cost?

42. John proofreads 7 pages in 12 minutes. How many pages does he proofread in 3 hours?

43. A company spends three times as much on training as it does on company cars. If $19,000 is spent on cars, how much is spent on training?

44. If 8 shirts cost $223.20, how much would 5 shirts cost?

45. If 4 video cassettes cost $75, how many did Kim buy if she received $31.25 in change from her $500 check?

3

Percent

Percents are widely used in business and everyday life. For example, interest rates on automobile loans, home loans, and other installment loans are almost always given as percents. Advertisers often claim that their products perform a certain "percent better" than other products or cost some "percent less." Stores often advertise sale items as being a certain "percent off" the regular price. In business, marketing costs, damage, and theft may be expressed as a percent of sales; profit as a percent of investment; and labor as a percent of production costs. Current numbers about inflation, recession, and unemployment are also reported as percents. This chapter discusses the various types of percent problems that will be used throughout this text.

3.1 Writing Decimals and Fractions as Percents

OBJECTIVES

1 Write a decimal as a percent.

2 Write a fraction as a percent.

3 Write a percent as a decimal.

4 Write a fractional percent as a decimal.

Percents represent parts of a whole, just as fractions or decimals do. **Percents** are *hundredths* or parts of a hundred. "One percent" means one of one hundred parts. Percents are written with a percent sign, %. For example, 25% refers to 25 parts out of 100 equal parts $\left(\frac{25}{100}\right)$, just as 50% refers to 50 out of 100 equal parts $\left(\frac{50}{100}\right)$, and 100% refers to all 100 of the 100 equal parts $\left(\frac{100}{100}\right)$. If a percent is larger than 100% (for example 150%), more than one item has been divided into 100 equal parts, and 150 of the parts are being considered $\left(\frac{150}{100}\right)$.

1   Write a decimal as a percent by moving the decimal point two places to the right and attaching a % sign.

For example, write 0.75 as a percent by moving the decimal point two places to the right and attaching a % sign, giving 75% as the result.

Decimal   *Percent*

0.75 (.75.)   75% ← attach percent sign

             2 places to the right

EXAMPLE 1
Changing Decimals to Percents

Write the following decimals as percents.

(a) 0.25   **(b)** 0.38   **(c)** 0.65

SOLUTION Move the decimal point two places to the right and attach a percent sign.

(a) 25%   **(b)** 38%   **(c)** 65% ■

If there is nothing in the hundredths position, place zeros to the right of the number to hold the hundredths position. For example, the decimal 0.5 is expressed as 50%, and the number 1.2 is 120%.

$$0.5 = 0.50.\% = 50\% \qquad 1.2 = 1.20.\% = 120\%$$
            attach zero   attach zero

EXAMPLE 2
Writing Decimals as Percents

Write the following decimals as percents.

(a) 0.7   **(b)** 1.3   **(c)** 0.1   **(d)** 3

SOLUTION It is necessary to attach zeros to these decimals.

(a) 70%   **(b)** 130%   **(c)** 10%   **(d)** 300% ■

If the decimal extends farther than the hundredths position, the resulting percent includes decimal parts of whole percents.

EXAMPLE 3
Writing Decimals as Percents

Write the following decimals as percents.

(a) 0.857   **(b)** 0.0057   **(c)** 0.0025

SOLUTION

(a) 85.7%   **(b)** 0.57%   **(c)** 0.25% ■

NOTE In Example 3 both (b) and (c) are less than 1%; they are decimal parts of 1%.

2 There are two ways to write a fraction as a percent. One way is to first convert the fraction to a decimal, as explained in Section 1.2. For example, to express the fraction $\frac{2}{5}$ as a percent, write $\frac{2}{5}$ as a decimal by dividing 2 by 5. Then write the decimal as a percent.

Fraction	*Decimal*	*Percent*
$\dfrac{2}{5}$	0.4	40%

EXAMPLE 4

Writing Fractions as Percents

Write the following fractions as percents.

(a) $\frac{1}{4}$ **(b)** $\frac{3}{5}$ **(c)** $\frac{7}{8}$

SOLUTION First write each fraction as a decimal. Then write the decimal as a percent.

(a) $\frac{1}{4} = 0.25 = 25\%$ **(b)** $\frac{3}{5} = 0.6 = 60\%$ **(c)** $\frac{7}{8} = 0.875 = 87.5\%$ ■

A second way to write a fraction as a percent is to multiply the fraction by 100%. For example, write the fraction $\frac{2}{5}$ as a percent by multiplying $\frac{2}{5}$ by 100%.

$$\frac{2}{5} = \frac{2}{5} \times 100\% = \frac{200}{5}\% = 40\%$$

EXAMPLE 5

Writing Fractions as Percents

Write the following fractions as percents.

(a) $\frac{3}{4}$ **(b)** $\frac{1}{3}$ **(c)** $\frac{7}{8}$

SOLUTION Write these fractions as percents by multiplying each by 100%.

(a) $\frac{3}{4} \times 100\% = 75\%$ **(b)** $\frac{1}{3} \times 100\% = 33.3\%$ (rounded)

(c) $\frac{7}{8} \times 100\% = 87.5\%$ ■

NOTE When writing the fraction $\frac{1}{3}$ as a percent it is often expressed as $33\frac{1}{3}\%$. It is expressed this way because $\frac{1}{3} \times 100\% = 33\frac{1}{3}\%$. Also, $\frac{2}{3}$ is expressed as $66\frac{2}{3}\%$ ($\frac{2}{3} \times 100\% = 66\frac{2}{3}\%$).

3 Write a percent as a decimal by moving the decimal point two places to the left and dropping the percent sign. For example, 50% becomes 0.50 or 0.5, 100% becomes 1, and 352% becomes 3.52.

EXAMPLE 6

Writing Percents as Decimals

Write the following percents as decimals.

(a) 25%   **(b)** 142%   **(c)** $37\frac{1}{2}\%$

(Hint: $37\frac{1}{2}\% = 37.5\%$)

SOLUTION Move the decimal point two places to the left and drop the percent sign.

(a) 0.25   **(b)** 1.42   **(c)** 0.375 ■

NOTE In Example 6(c) change $37\frac{1}{2}\%$ to 37.5%. It is usually best to change fractional percents to the decimal form and then change the percent to a decimal.

4 A fractional percent such as $\frac{1}{4}\%$ has a value less than 1%. In fact, $\frac{1}{4}\%$ is equal to $\frac{1}{4}$ of 1%. Write a fractional percent as a decimal by first changing the fraction to a decimal, leaving the percent sign. For example, first write $\frac{1}{2}\%$ as 0.5%. Then write 0.5% as a decimal by moving the decimal point two places to the left and dropping the percent sign.

$$\frac{1}{2}\% = 0.5\% = 0.005$$

                └── written as decimal with percent sign remaining

TABLE 3.1 Common Fractions and Their Equivalent Percents

$\dfrac{1}{100} = 1\%$	$\dfrac{1}{9} = 11\dfrac{1}{9}\%$	$\dfrac{1}{4} = 25\%$	$\dfrac{5}{8} = 62\dfrac{1}{2}\%$
$\dfrac{1}{50} = 2\%$	$\dfrac{1}{8} = 12\dfrac{1}{2}\%$	$\dfrac{1}{3} = 33\dfrac{1}{3}\%$	$\dfrac{3}{4} = 75\%$
$\dfrac{1}{25} = 4\%$	$\dfrac{1}{7} = 14\dfrac{2}{7}\%$	$\dfrac{3}{8} = 37\dfrac{1}{2}\%$	$\dfrac{4}{5} = 80\%$
$\dfrac{1}{20} = 5\%$	$\dfrac{1}{6} = 16\dfrac{2}{3}\%$	$\dfrac{2}{4} = 40\%$	$\dfrac{5}{6} = 83\dfrac{1}{3}\%$
$\dfrac{1}{16} = 6\dfrac{1}{4}\%$	$\dfrac{3}{16} = 18\dfrac{3}{4}\%$	$\dfrac{1}{2} = 50\%$	$\dfrac{7}{8} = 85\dfrac{1}{2}\%$
$\dfrac{1}{12} = 8\dfrac{1}{3}\%$	$\dfrac{1}{5} = 20\%$	$\dfrac{3}{5} = 60\%$	$1 = 100\%$
$\dfrac{1}{10} = 10\%$			

EXAMPLE 7

Writing Fractional Percents as Decimals

Write each of the following fractional percents as decimals.

(a) $\frac{1}{5}\%$ **(b)** $\frac{3}{4}\%$ **(c)** $1\frac{1}{8}\%$

SOLUTION   Begin by writing the fraction as a decimal.

(a) $\frac{1}{5}\% = 0.2\% = 0.002$ **(b)** $\frac{3}{4}\% = 0.75\% = 0.0075$

(c) $1\frac{1}{8}\% = 1.125\% = 0.01125$ ■

Table 3.1 shows many fractions and their percent equivalents. It is often helpful to memorize those which are most commonly used.

3.1 Exercises

Write the following decimals as percents.

1. 0.8

2. 0.75

3. 0.007

4. 0.045

5. 1.4

6. 3.017

7. 0.375

8. 0.875

9. 4.125

10. 5.3

11. 0.0025

12. 0.0008

Write the following fractions as percents.

13. $\dfrac{3}{4}$

14. $\dfrac{3}{8}$

15. $\dfrac{1}{10}$

16. $\dfrac{1}{20}$

17. $\dfrac{2}{5}$

18. $\dfrac{1}{2}$

19. $\dfrac{5}{8}$

20. $\dfrac{7}{8}$

21. $\dfrac{1}{8}$

22. $\dfrac{13}{20}$

23. $\dfrac{1}{200}$

24. $\dfrac{1}{400}$

Write the following percents as decimals.

25.	18%	**26.**	24%	**27.**	65%	**28.**	72%
29.	0.6%	**30.**	0.5%	**31.**	0.25%	**32.**	0.125%
33.	125%	**34.**	175%	**35.**	200.6%	**36.**	475.6%

37. Explain in your own words how to write a decimal as a percent. (See Objective 1.)

38. Explain in your own words how to write a percent as a decimal. (See Objective 3.)

39. To change a fraction to a percent you must first change the fraction to a decimal. Why is this true? (See Objective 2.)

40. The fractional percent $\frac{1}{2}\%$ is equal to 0.005. Explain each step as you change $\frac{1}{2}\%$ to its decimal equivalent. (See Objective 4.)

Determine the fraction, decimal, or percent equivalents for each of the following, as necessary. Write fractions in lowest terms.

	Fraction	**Decimal**	**Percent**
41.	$\frac{1}{4}$	————	————
42.	$\frac{1}{8}$	————	————
43.	————	————	5%
44.	————	————	87.5%
45.	————	0.75	————
46.	————	0.35	————
47.	$6\frac{1}{8}$	————	————
48.	$3\frac{1}{2}$	————	————
49.	————	7.25	————
50.	$1\frac{3}{4}$	————	————
51.	————	0.0025	————

Fraction	Decimal	Percent
52. _____	0.00125	_____
53. $\frac{1}{3}$	_____	_____
54. _____	_____	$4\frac{1}{4}\%$
55. _____	_____	$\frac{3}{4}\%$
56. _____	_____	12.5%
57. _____	0.025	_____
58. _____	2.5	_____
59. _____	_____	35%
60. _____	_____	1038.35%
61. _____	23.82	_____
62. $4\frac{3}{8}$	_____	_____
63. _____	_____	$37\frac{1}{2}\%$
64. _____	_____	$6\frac{3}{4}\%$

3.2 Finding Part

OBJECTIVES

1. Identify the three elements of a percent problem.
2. Use the percent formula.
3. Apply the percent formula to a business problem.
4. Recognize the terms associated with base, rate, and part.
5. Use the basic percent equation.

1 Problems in percent have three main quantities. Usually two of these quantities are given and the third must be found. You must be able to recognize each of these three quantities to work successfully with percents. The three key quantities in a percent problem are as follows.

Base. The "starting point," the "whole of something," or "that to which something is compared." The base is often preceded by "of."

Rate. A number followed by "%" or "percent."

Part. The result of multiplying the base and the rate. Part is often preceded by "is" and is always part of the base.

NOTE Percent and part are different quantities. The stated percent in a given problem is always the rate. The part is the product of the base and the rate. It is a portion of the base, as sales tax is a portion of the total sales and as the number of sports cars is a portion of the total number of cars. This makes part a number and it never appears with "percent" or "%" following it.

2 The above three quantities are related by the basic **percent formula**.

Percent Formula

$$\text{Part} = \text{Base} \times \text{Rate} \quad \text{or} \quad P = B \times R \quad \text{or} \quad P = BR$$

For example, find 15% of 780 by using $P = BR$, with $B = 780$ and $R = 15\%$ (the rate). The rate must be changed to a decimal before multiplying.

$$P = BR$$
$$P = 780 \times 15\%$$
$$P = 780 \times 0.15 \quad \text{or} \quad$$
$$P = 117$$

$$\begin{array}{r} 780 \\ \times\ 0.15 \\ \hline 117.00 \end{array}$$

Finally, 15% of 780 is 117.

EXAMPLE 1
Solving for Part

Solve for part using $P = B \times R$.
(a) 4% of 50   **(b)** 1.2% of 180   **(c)** 140% of 225   **(d)** $\frac{1}{4}$% of 560
(Hint: $\frac{1}{4}\% = 0.25\%$)

SOLUTION

(a)
$$\begin{array}{r} 50 \\ \times\ 0.04 \\ \hline 2.00 \end{array}$$

(b)
$$\begin{array}{r} 180 \\ \times\ 0.012 \\ \hline 2.160 \end{array}$$

(c)
$$\begin{array}{r} 225 \\ \times\ 1.4 \\ \hline 315.0 \end{array}$$

(d)
$$\begin{array}{r} 560 \\ \times\ 0.0025 \\ \hline 1.4000 \end{array}$$ ■

3 Calculating *sales tax* is an excellent example of finding part. States, counties, and cities often collect taxes on sales to the consumer. The sales tax is a percent of the sale. This percent varies from as low as 3% in some states to 8% or more in other states. The percent formula is used for finding sales tax.

$$P \quad = \quad B \quad \times \quad R$$
$$\text{Sales tax} = \text{Sales} \times \text{Sales tax rate}$$

EXAMPLE 2
Calculating Sales Tax

Racy Feed and Pet Supply sold $284.50 worth of merchandise. If the sales tax was 4%, how much tax was paid?

SOLUTION The amount of sales, $284.50, is the starting point or base, and 4% is the rate. Since the tax is a *part* of total sales, use the formula $P = BR$ to find part.

$$P = BR$$

$$P = \$284.50 \times 4\%$$

$$P = \$284.50 \times 0.04 \quad \text{or}$$

$$P = \$11.38$$

$$
\begin{array}{r}
\$284.50 \\
\times \quad 0.04 \\
\hline
\$ \ 11.38
\end{array}
$$

The tax, or part, was $11.38 ■

NOTE If the total amount of sales and tax was needed in Example 2, the amount of sales, $284.50, would be added to the sales tax ($11.38). The total sales and tax would be $295.88 ($248.50 + $11.38). An alternative approach would be to multiply $284.50 by 104% (100% sales + 4% sales tax) to get $284.50 × 104% = $295.88.

EXAMPLE 3
Finding Part

Pay 'N' Save Stores employ 600 people, with $35\frac{1}{2}\%$ being students. How many students does Pay 'N' Save employ?

SOLUTION The total number of employees, 600, is the starting point, or base. The rate, $35\frac{1}{2}\%$, is the portion of the total number of employees who are students. Since the number of students employed is a part of the total, find the number of students employed by using the formula to find part.

$$P = BR$$

$$P = 600 \times 35\frac{1}{2}\%$$

$$P = 600 \times 0.355$$

$$P = 213$$

Pay 'N' Save Stores has 213 student employees. ■

4 Percent problems have certain similarities. For example, some phrases are associated with the base in the problem. Other phrases lead to the part, while "%" or "percent" following a number identifies the rate. Table 3.2 helps distinguish between the base and the part.

TABLE 3.2   **Distinguishing the Base from the Part**

Usually the Base	Usually the Part
Sales	Sales tax
Investment	Return
Savings	Interest
Value of bonds	Interest
Retail price	Discount
Last year's anything	Increase or decrease
Value of real estate	Rents
Old salary	Raise
Total sales	Commission
Value of stocks	Dividends
Earnings	Expenditures
Original	Change

Most percent problems can be written in the following form.

_____% of _____ is _____

5 This is known as the **basic percent equation**, several examples of which follow.

5% of the automobiles are red.
4.2% of the workers are unemployed.
20% of the income is income tax.
75% of the students are full-time.

When expressed in this standard form, the elements in the percent problem appear in the following order.

$$
\begin{array}{ccccc}
R & \times & B & & P \\
\text{Rate} & \times & \text{Base} & = & \text{Part} \\
\downarrow & \downarrow & \downarrow & \downarrow & \downarrow \\
\underline{\quad}\% & \text{of} & \underline{\quad} & \text{is} & \underline{\quad}
\end{array}
$$

NOTE Rate is identified by "%" (the percent sign); the word "of" means "×" (multiplication); the *multiplicand*, or number being multiplied, is the base; the word "is" means "=" (equals); and the product, or answer, is part of the base.

EXAMPLE 4
Identifying the Elements in Percent Problems

Identify the elements given in the following percent problems and determine which element must be found.

(a) During a recent sale, Stockdale Marine offered a 15% discount on all new recreation equipment. Find the discount on a jet ski originally priced at $2895.

SOLUTION   First arrange this problem using the basic percent equation.

$$R \times B = P$$

_____% of _____ is _____

% of price is discount

15% of $2895 = discount

$$R \quad \times \quad B \quad = P$$

$$0.15 \times \$2895 = P$$

$$0.15 \times \$2895 = \$434.25 \text{ discount}$$

At this point, check that rate is given, base is given, and part must be found. To find the discount, multiply 0.15 by $2895.

The discount is $434.25.

(b) Round Table Pizza spends an amount equal to 5.8% of its sales on advertising. If sales for the month were $12,500, find the amount spent on advertising.

SOLUTION   Use the basic percent equation.

$$R \times B = P$$

_____% of _____ is _____

% of sales is advertising

5.8% of $12,500 = advertising

$$R \quad \times \quad B \quad = P$$

Rate is given as 5.8%, base (sales) is $12,500, and part (advertising) must be found. Find the amount spent on advertising by multiplying 0.058 and $12,500.

$$0.058 \times \$12,500 = P$$

$$0.058 \times \$12,500 = \$725$$

The amount spent on advertising is $725. ■

3.2 Exercises

Solve for part in each of the following. Round to the nearest hundredth.

1. 14% of 78	**2.** 12% of 350	**3.** 22.5% of 1086
4. 20.5% of 1500	**5.** 5% of 80	**6.** 125% of 2000
7. 175% of 5820	**8.** ·15% of 75	**9.** 25% of 484
10. 400% of 3008	**11.** 118% of 125.8	**12.** 3% of 128
13. $90\frac{1}{2}$% of 5930	**14.** $7\frac{1}{2}$% of 150	**15.** 12.5% of 56

16. 18.5% of 780

17. List the three elements in a percent problem and tell how you can identify each of the elements. (See Objective 1.)

18. Name three terms that are usually associated with base in a percent problem, in business. (See Objective 4.)

Solve for part in each of the following. Round to the nearest cent unless otherwise indicated.

19. Marc Garza Appliance had sales of $297,500 last month and spent 7% of this amount on advertising. Find the amount that they spent on advertising.

20. Dime Savings Bank of New York announced that 97% of its $4.5 billion home loans are adjustable rate mortgages (ARMs). Find the dollar amount of these ARMs.

21. A collection agency specializing in collecting past-due child support charges $25 as an application fee plus 20% of the amount collected. What is the total charge for collecting $3100 of past-due child support?

22. A retailer has $123,000 invested in her business and finds that she is earning 12% per year on her investment. How much money is she earning per year?

23. A family of four with a monthly income of $2900 spends 90% of its earnings and saves the balance. Find (a) the monthly savings and (b) the annual savings of this family.

24. John Cross recently purchased a duplex for $124,000. If he expects a return on his investment of 8% a year, what will this amount to in dollars per year?

25. The Yale University marching band has 250 members. If 18.4% of the band members are senior class students, find the number of students who are seniors.

26. A shipment of posters valued at $175 was damaged in transit. The estimated damage was 35%. What was the value of the undamaged posters?

27. A U.S. Food and Drug Administration (FDA) biologist found that canned tuna is "relatively clean." Extraneous matter was found in 5% of the 1600 cans of tuna tested. How many cans of tuna contained extraneous matter?

28. An investment valued at $95,000 today is gaining value at the rate of 6% per year. Find the value of the investment at the end of one year.

29. Doug Gilbert must pay $5\frac{1}{2}$% sales tax on his total sales of $11,500. Find the amount of tax he must pay.

30. Mercury Savings Bank pays $5\frac{1}{4}$% interest per year. What is the annual interest on an account of $830?

31. Marketing Intelligence Service says that there were 15,401 new products introduced last year. If 86% of the products introduced last year failed to reach their business objectives, find the number of products that did reach their objectives. (Round to the nearest whole number.)

32. An ad for steel-belted radial tires promises 15% better mileage. If mileage has been 25.6 mpg in the past, what mileage could be expected after new tires are installed? (Round to the nearest tenth of a mile.)

33. Pam Fullerton owns 350 shares of Tri-Mart Construction common stock valued at $38\frac{1}{2}$ dollars per share. After an increase in value of 23%, find the total value of the 350 shares.

34. Rancher Supply loses 4.8% of its livestock feed to spoilage. In an inventory of 4.75 tons, find the number of pounds that are not spoiled. (1 ton = 2000 pounds)

35. A retailer must collect $6\frac{1}{2}$% of the amount of each sale for sales tax. If sales for the month are $48,680, find the combined amount of sales and tax.

36. Sales at Coast Lumber were $268,500 last month. If sales this month are down 18.8% from last month, find the amount of sales this month.

37. J & K Mustang has increased the sale of auto parts by $32\frac{1}{2}$% over last year. If the sale of parts last year amounted to $385,200, find the volume of parts sales this year.

38. The value of Brookefield stock rose 6.25% from yesterday's $100 per share. Find the value of the stock after the increase. (Do not round.)

39. Jack Armstrong owns 65% of a trucking company. If the company has a value of $280,000, and Armstrong receives an income of 25% of his ownership, find the amount of his income.

40. Rick Wilson has an 82% ownership in a company called Puppets and Clowns. If the company has a value of $49,200 and Wilson receives an income of 30% of his ownership, find the amount of his income.

3.3 Finding the Base

OBJECTIVES

1 Use the basic percent equation to solve for base.

2 Find the amount of sales when taxes and rate of tax are known.

3 Find the amount of investment when expense and rate of expense are known.

4 Find base when rate and part are for different quantities.

1   In some problems, the rate and part are given and the base must be found. For example, suppose that 8% of a company's employees are supplied with a company car and that 24 cars have been supplied. To find the total number of employees, use the rate (8%) and part (24) to find the base by using the basic percent equation, Rate × Base = Part. The key word here indicating that the number of company employees is the base is "of."

$$R \times B = P$$

$$8\% \text{ of } \text{_____} = 24$$

$$0.08 \times B = 24$$

Now divide both sides by 0.08, as explained in Chapter 2.

$$\frac{0.08\,B}{0.08} = \frac{24}{0.08}$$

$$B = \frac{24}{0.08}$$

$$B = 300$$

The company has 300 employees.

EXAMPLE 1   Solve for base using the basic percent equation.

Solving for Base   **(a)** 8 is 4% of _____   **(b)** 135 is 15% of _____

(c) 1.25 is 25% of _____

SOLUTION

(a) $8 = 4\% \text{ of } \text{\_\_\_\_}$ **(b)** $135 = 15\% \text{ of } \text{\_\_\_\_}$

$8 = 4\% \times B$ $135 = 15\% \times B$

$8 = 0.04\,B$ $135 = 0.15\,B$

$\dfrac{8}{0.04} = \dfrac{0.04\,B}{0.04}$ $\dfrac{135}{0.15} = \dfrac{0.15\,B}{0.15}$

$B = \dfrac{8}{0.04} = 200$ $B = \dfrac{135}{0.15} = 900$

(c) $1.25 = 25\% \text{ of } \text{\_\_\_\_}$

$1.25 = 25\% \times B$

$1.25 = 0.25\,B$

$\dfrac{1.25}{0.25} = \dfrac{0.25\,B}{0.25}$

$B = \dfrac{1.25}{0.25} = 5$ ▪

2 A common business application of percent involves sales tax and the sales tax rate.

EXAMPLE 2
Finding Sales when Sales Tax Is Given

The 5% sales tax collected by a refrigeration company was $780. What was the amount of total sales?

SOLUTION Here the rate of tax collection is 5% and taxes collected are a part of total sales. The rate is 5% and the part is $780. Use the percent equation.

$$R \quad \times \quad B \quad = \quad P$$
$$5\% \quad \text{of} \quad \underline{\quad} \quad = \$780$$
$$0.05B = \$780$$
$$\frac{0.05B}{0.05} = \frac{\$780}{0.05}$$
$$B = \frac{\$780}{0.05} = \$15,600$$

The total sales of the company were $15,600. ■

CAUTION It is important to consider whether an answer is reasonable. A common error in a base problem is to confuse the base and part. For example, if the taxes, $780, had been mistakenly used as the base, the resulting answer would have been $39 ($780 × 5%). Obviously, $39 is not a reasonable amount for total sales given $780 as sales tax.

3 The amount of an investment is the base. When the amount of expenses and the rate of expenses are known, the percent equation may be used to find the amount of the investment.

EXAMPLE 3
Finding the Amount of an Investment

The yearly maintenance cost of a building is $1\frac{1}{2}\%$ of its value. If maintenance amounts to $8400 per year, what is the value of the building?

SOLUTION To find the total value of the building, which is the base, use the percent equation.

$$R \quad \times \quad B \quad = \quad P$$
$$1\frac{1}{2}\% \quad \text{of} \quad \underline{\quad} \quad = \$8400$$
$$0.015B = \$8400$$
$$\frac{0.015B}{0.015} = \frac{\$8400}{0.015}$$
$$B = \frac{\$8400}{0.015} = \$560,000$$

The total value of the building is $560,000. ■

NOTE When working with a fraction of a percent, it is best to change the fraction to a decimal. In Example 3, $1\frac{1}{2}\%$ was changed to 1.5% which equals 0.015.

4   The rate used and the part given in a problem do not always refer to the same quantity. Always pay careful attention to reading and understanding a problem.

EXAMPLE 4
Finding Base when Rate and Part Are for Different Quantities

A company finds that 25% of its employees are women and 180 are men. Find the total number of employees.

SOLUTION   The rate given, 25%, refers to women employees, while 180, the part, is the number of men. A rate of 75% (100% of all employees − 25% women employees) must be used to solve for the total number of employees, which is the base. Use the percent equation.

$$R \quad \times \quad B \quad = P$$
$$75\% \quad \text{of} \ \underline{\quad} = 180$$
$$0.75B = 180$$
$$\frac{0.75B}{0.75} = \frac{180}{0.75}$$
$$B = \frac{180}{0.75} = 240$$

The total number of employees is 240. ∎

3.3 Exercises

Solve for base in each of the following. Round to the nearest hundredth.

1. 625 is 25% of _____.

2. 300 is 75% of _____.

3. 75 is 40% of _____.

4. 128 is 32% of _____.

5. 850 is $4\frac{1}{4}$% of _____.

6. 15 is 0.75% of _____.

7. 32 is $33\frac{1}{3}$% of _____.

8. 53,700 is $66\frac{2}{3}$% of _____.

9. 50 is 0.25% of _____.

10. 39 is 0.78% of _____.

11. 40% of _____ is 350.

12. 32% of _____ is 180.

13. 75% of _____ is 5024.

14. 22.2% of _____ is 1320.

15. 0.5% of _____ is 654.

16. 6.5 is 0.05% of _____.

17. 18 is $66\frac{2}{3}$% of _____.

18. 93 is $16\frac{2}{3}$% of _____.

19. The basic percent formula is $P = B \times R$. Show how to solve for B (base). (See Objective 1.)

20. A problem includes amount of sales, sales tax, and a sales tax rate. Explain how you could identify the base, rate, and part in this problem. (See Objective 2.)

Solve for base in each of the following problems. Round to the nearest hundredth, unless otherwise noted.

21. Woolworth Corporation will close, sell, or change the format of 900 stores, or about 9.7% of its total. How many stores does the Woolworth Corporation have? (Round to the nearest whole number.)

22. One survey reported that 6.8% of the people in a certain city were in business for themselves. The same survey reported that 10,800 people in the city were in business for themselves. How many people live in the city? (Round to the nearest whole number.)

23. This semester there are 1785 married students on campus. If this figure represents 23% of the total enrollment, what is the total enrollment? (Round to the nearest whole number.)

24. Americans who are 65 years of age or older make up 12.7% of the total population. If there are 31.5 million Americans in this group, find the total American population. (Round to the nearest tenth of a million.)

25. Raw steel production by the nation's steel mills decreased by 2.5% from last week. If the decrease amounted to 50,475 tons, find the steel production last week.

26. Kent Merrill spends 22% of his income on housing, 24% on food, 8% on clothing, 15% on transportation, 11% on education, and 7% on recreation, and saves the balance. If his savings amount to $154 per month, what are his monthly earnings?

27. Lillie Chalmers owns common stock valued at $8078, which amounts to 17% of her total investments. What is the value of her total investments?

28. In analyzing the success of license applicants, the state finds that 58.3% of those examined received a passing mark. If the records show that 8370 new licenses were issued, what was the number of applicants? (Round to the nearest whole number.)

29. Mama Bacchi's recipe for pizza sauce says that herbs and spices should amount to 11.3% of the sauce, with the balance made up of tomato products. The use of $5\frac{1}{2}$ gallons of herbs and spices should yield how many gallons of pizza sauce? (Round to the nearest tenth of a gallon.)

30. Erin Kelly saves 23% of her salary toward the down payment on a larger home. If this amounts to $828 per month, find her annual salary.

31. An Atlantic City casino advertises that it gives a 97.4% payback on slot machines, and the balance is retained by the casino. If the amount retained by the casino is $4823, find the total amount played on the slot machines.

32. A resort hotel states that 35% of its rooms are for nonsmokers. If the resort allows smoking in 468 rooms, find the total number of rooms.

Supplementary Exercises on Base and Part

Solve for base or part as indicated in the following.

1. The Chevy Camaro was introduced in 1967. Sales that year were 220,917 which was 46.2% of the number of Ford Mustangs sold in the same year. Find the number of Mustangs sold in the same year. (Round to the nearest whole number.)

2. The Bureau of Labor Statistics states that the number of unemployed people is 8.9 million, or 7.1% of all workers. What is the size of the total workforce? (Round to the nearest tenth of a billion.)

3. A building is valued at $423,750 and is insured for 68% of its value. Find the amount of insurance coverage.

4. Cherie Norvell has 11.5% of her earnings deposited into a stock purchase plan. If this amounts to $138 per month, find her annual earnings.

5. The manager of Oakland Computer Supplies contributes 8.75% of her salary to a retirement plan. If her annual salary is $43,600, find the annual amount of her retirement contribution.

6. The Northridge PTA received $79.75 in annual interest on its bank account. If the bank paid $5\frac{1}{2}\%$ interest per year, how much money was in the account?

7. Curt Reynolds received a $7\frac{1}{4}\%$ return on a real estate investment. If the amount of his investment was $17,400, find the amount of the return.

8. At one store, losses to shrinkage (employee and customer theft) amounted to $4129.50, which was $1\frac{1}{2}\%$ of total sales. Find the total sales.

9. A shipping company finds that $3\frac{3}{4}\%$ of its shipments are damaged. If shipments for the month are $783,200, find the amount of damage.

10. The State License Board says that there are 186,000 building contractors in the state. If 48% of the contractors are self-employed, find the number who are self-employed.

11. A teacher's union chief says that 145,050 of the teachers are on strike and that this number represents 75% of the total number of teachers. Find the total number of teachers.

12. An airline ticket from Portland to Los Angeles cost $292 last year. If the same flight costs 35% less this year, find the cost of the flight this year.

13. International Chemical Laboratories, Inc., stock soared $7.25—a 46% increase in value. Find the value of the stock after the increase. (Round to the nearest dollar.)

14. Roper Corporation stock rose $11—a 29% increase in value. Find the value of the stock after the increase. (Round to the nearest dollar.)

3.4 Finding the Rate

OBJECTIVES

1 Use the percent equation to solve for rate.

2 Find the rate of return when the amount of the return and the investment are known.

3 Solve for the percent remaining when the total amount and amount used are given.

4 Find the percent of change.

In the third type of percent problem, the part and base are given and the rate must be found. The rate is identified by the "%" sign, "percent," or "rate percent." For example, what part of 32 is 8? Use the percent equation as shown.

1

$$R \times B = P$$

$$\underline{\hspace{1cm}}\% \text{ of } 32 = 8$$

$$R \times 32 = 8$$

$$32R = 8$$

Now divide both sides by 32.

$$\frac{\cancel{32}R}{\cancel{32}} = \frac{8}{32}$$

$$R = \frac{8}{32} = 0.25 = 25\%$$

Finally, 8 is 25% of 32, or 25% of 32 is 8.

EXAMPLE 1
Solving for Rate

Solve for rate.

(a) 13 is what percent of 52?

(b) What percent of 500 is 100?

(c) 48 is what percent of 12?

SOLUTION

(a) 13 is $\underline{\hspace{0.8cm}}$% of 52

$$\underline{\hspace{0.8cm}}\% \text{ of } 52 = 13$$

$$52R = 13$$

$$\frac{\cancel{52}R}{\cancel{52}} = \frac{13}{52}$$

$$R = \frac{13}{52} = 0.25 = 25\%$$

(b) 100 is ____% of 500

$$\underline{\hspace{1cm}}\% \text{ of } 500 = 100$$

$$500\,R = 100$$

$$\frac{\cancel{500}\,R}{\cancel{500}} = \frac{100}{500}$$

$$R = \frac{100}{500} = 0.2 = 20\%$$

(c) 48 is ____% of 12

$$\underline{\hspace{1cm}}\% \text{ of } 12 = 48$$

$$12\,R = 48$$

$$\frac{\cancel{12}\,R}{\cancel{12}} = \frac{48}{12}$$

$$R = \frac{48}{12} = 4. = 400\% \quad \blacksquare$$

2 It is often necessary to find the rate of return when the amount of the return and investment are known.

EXAMPLE 2

Finding the Rate of Return

What rate of return is needed to earn $960 on an investment of $6840?

SOLUTION The amount of investment, $6840, is the base, and the return, $960, is the part. The return is a part of the total investment. Start with $R \times B = P$.

$$\underline{\hspace{1cm}}\% \text{ of } \$6840 = \$960$$

$$R \times \$6840 = \$960$$

$$\$6840\,R = \$960$$

$$\frac{6840\,R}{6840} = \frac{960}{6840}$$

$$R = \frac{960}{6840} = 0.1404 = 14.0\% \qquad \text{rounded to the nearest tenth of a percent} \quad \blacksquare$$

NOTE The rate in Example 2 had to be rounded. The rules for rounding percents are identical to the rules for rounding discussed in Chapter 1. Change the decimal answer to percent and round as indicated. Here, 14.04% rounds to the nearest tenth as 14.0%.

3 When the total amount of something and the amount used are known, it is common to solve for the percent remaining.

EXAMPLE 3

Solving for the Percent Remaining

A roof is expected to last 12 years before it needs replacement. If the roof is 10 years old, what percent of the roof's life remains? Round to the nearest tenth of a percent.

SOLUTION The total life of the roof, 12 years, is the base. Subtract the amount of life already used, 10 years, from the total life, 12 years, to find the number of years remaining.

$$12 \text{ yrs. (total life)} - 10 \text{ yrs. (life used)} = 2 \text{ yrs. (life remaining)}$$

Use the equation $R \times B = P$ to find the solution.

_____% of 12 is 2

$$R \times 12 = 2$$

$$12\,R = 2$$

$$\frac{\cancel{12}\,R}{\cancel{12}} = \frac{2}{12}$$

$$R = \frac{2}{12} = \frac{1}{6} = 0.166 \ldots = 16.7\% \qquad \text{rounded to the nearest tenth of a percent}$$

If the age of the roof (10 years) had been used as part, the resulting answer, 83.3% (rounded), would be the percent of life used. Find the percent of remaining life by subtracting 83.3% from 100%. The result, 16.7% (the same answer), would be the percent of life remaining. ∎

NOTE Remember that the base is always 100%.

4 A common business problem is to find the percent of change in amounts involved in operating a business, such as sales and returns and to determine the percent of gain or loss on an investment.

EXAMPLE 4
Finding the Percent of Increase

Lisa King purchased stock in a small company for $9300 and sold it for $10,416. What percent of her original investment was her gain?

SOLUTION The original purchase price or investment, $9300, is the base. Profit (sale price − cost) is the part.

$$\$10,416 \text{ (sale price)} - \$9300 \text{ (cost)} = \$1116 \text{ (profit)}$$

Use the basic percent equation as follows.

$$\text{_____\% of } \$9300 = \$1116$$

$$R \times \$9300 = \$1116$$

$$\$9300R = \$1116$$

$$\frac{9300R}{9300} = \frac{1116}{9300}$$

$$R = \frac{1116}{9300} = 0.12 = 12\% \quad \blacksquare$$

CAUTION Remember, to find the percent of increase, the first step is to determine the amount of increase. The base is *always* the original amount, or last year's or last month's amount, and the amount of increase is the part.

EXAMPLE 5
Finding the Percent of Decrease

Judy Lewis Decorators had sales of $52,000 in June and $48,000 in August of the same year. Calculate the percent of change in sales. Round to the nearest tenth of a percent.

SOLUTION   The amount of sales in June, $52,000, is the base because June sales are the "starting point" or "reference point." The decrease in sales (June sales − August sales) is the part.

$$\$52{,}000 \text{ (June sales)} - \$48{,}000 \text{ (August sales)} = \$4000 \text{ (decrease in sales)}$$

Use the basic percent equation.

$$\underline{\hspace{2cm}}\% \text{ of } \$52{,}000 = \$4000$$

$$R \times \$52{,}000 = \$4000$$

$$\$52{,}000R = \$4000$$

$$\frac{52{,}000R}{52{,}000} = \frac{4000}{52{,}000}$$

$$R = \frac{4000}{52{,}000} = 0.076923 = 7.7\% \qquad \text{rounded to the nearest tenth of a percent} \blacksquare$$

CAUTION   To find the percent of decrease, the first step is to determine the amount of decrease. The amount of decrease is the part in the problem and the base is *always* the original amount or last year's, last month's, or last week's amount.

3.4 Exercises

Solve for rate in each of the following. Round to the nearest tenth of a percent.

1. _____% of 2636 is 1318.
2. _____% of 34.5 is 13.8.
3. 217 is _____% of 124.
4. _____% of 78.57 is 22.2.
5. _____% of 27 is 1.36.
6. 5.2 is _____% of 28.4.
7. 310.75 is _____% of 124.3.
8. _____% of 2 is 2.05.
9. _____% of 5 is 0.04.
10. 13,830 is _____% of 78,400.
11. $8.63 is _____% of $613.
12. $39.42 is _____% of $76.11.
13. _____% of 115 is 16.
14. _____% of 105 is 39.4.
15. $26.50 is_____% of $385.
16. _____% of 73 is 350.4.
17. _____% of $16,800 is $4316.
18. 2520 is _____% of 9086.

19. The basic percent formula is $P = B \times R$. Show how to solve for R (rate). (See Objective 1.)

20. A problem includes last year's sales, this year's sales, and asks for the percent of increase. Explain how you could identify the base, rate, and part in this problem. (See Objective 4.)

Solve for rate in each of the following. Round to the nearest tenth of a percent.

21. A coronary bypass operation costs $41,000. If Medicare will pay the hospital $27,000 toward this cost, find the percent of the cost paid by Medicare.

22. There are 55,000-plus words in Webster's Dictionary, but most educated people can identify only 20,000 of these words. What percent of the words in the dictionary can these people identify?

23. Meadow Vista Water estimates that $117,000 will be spent this year on delivery costs alone. If total sales are estimated at $755,000, what percent of total sales will be spent on delivery?

24. Sid's Pharmacy has a total monthly payroll of $6875, of which $1450 goes toward employee fringe benefits. What percent of the total payroll goes to fringe benefits?

25. Advertising expenditures for Bailey's Roofers are as follows:

Newspaper	$2250	Television	$1425
Radio	$954	Yellow Pages	$1605
Outdoor	$1950	Miscellaneous	$2775

What percent of the total advertising expenditures is spent on radio advertising?

26. Barbara's Antiquery says that of its 3800 items in inventory, 3344 are just plain junk, while the rest are antiques. What percent of the total inventory is antiques?

27. A revenue passenger mile in the airline industry is one paying passenger flown one mile. Last month America West Airlines flew 1.09 billion revenue passenger miles, up from 947 million miles the same month a year earlier. Find the percent of increase.

28. For the entire year America West Airlines flew 13.03 billion revenue passenger miles, up from 11.11 billion miles the previous year. Find the percent of increase.

29. The price per share of Pacific Enterprise common stock fell from $38\frac{7}{8}$ per share to $26\frac{1}{4}$ per share in one year. Find the percent of decrease.

30. In the past five years, the cost of generating electricity from the sun has been brought down from 24 cents per kilowatt hour to 8 cents (less than the newest nuclear power plants). Find the percent of decrease.

Supplementary Exercises on Rate, Base, and Part

Solve for rate, base, or part as indicated in the following. Round rates to the nearest tenth of a percent.

1. In a test by Consumer Reports, six of the 123 cans of tuna that it analyzed contained more than the 30 microgram intake limit of mercury. What percent of the cans contained this level of mercury?

2. According to industry figures there are 44,500 hotels and motels in America. Economy hotels and motels account for 38% of this total. Find the number of economy hotels and motels.

3. A PC-Compatible Deskjet 500 printer priced at $599 is sold for $498. Find the percent of price reduction.

4. The Nestlé Company made an offer of 1500 francs a share ($281.57) to buy the Perrier Company whose value is 1295 francs a share. What percent greater than the value of each share was the offer to purchase price?

5. A cellular phone priced at $398 is marked down 7% to promote the new model. If the sales tax is also 7%, find the cost of the cellular phone including sales tax.

6. College students are offered a 6% discount on a dictionary which sells for $18.50. If the sales tax is 6%, find the cost of the dictionary including the sales tax.

7. Children's videotape sales last year amounted to 37% of all videos sold. If the number of children's videotapes sold last year was 92 million, find the total number of videos sold. (Round to the nearest tenth of a million.)

8. In a national Teamsters Union election, the three candidates for president of the union received the following votes: Ronald Carey, 205,830 votes; R. V. Durham, 129,538 votes; Walter Shea, 71,227 votes. The balance of the votes were received by several other candidates. If the total number of ballots was 424,392, find the percent of the total votes received by each candidate.

9. There are 1,560,000 members in the Teamsters Union. In the first direct, secret ballot election of Teamsters officers, election monitors counted 424,392 ballots. What percent of the members voted in this election?

10. The Boston Water and Sewer Commission says that by the year 2000, the average household water and sewer bills in Boston will rise to about $1600 from the current average of $500. Find the percent of increase.

11. Americans are eating more fish. This year the average American will eat $15\frac{1}{2}$ pounds compared to only $12\frac{1}{2}$ pounds per year a decade ago. Find the percent of increase.

12. In the past year 51,156 airline workers have lost their jobs through layoffs. If this was a 9.8% reduction in the number of workers, find the number of workers after the layoffs.

13. According to the National Association of Realtors the median national sales price of a house was down 1.4%, or $1390 from last month. Find the median national sales price this month. (Round to the nearest dollar.)

14. According to a recent report, a person owes more than $30,000 to 15 different credit card companies. If his payments on this debt amount to $1220 each month and $298 of this is interest, what percent of his payment is interest?

15. The average number of hours worked in manufacturing jobs last week fell from 41.1 to 40.9. Find the percent of decrease.

16. Weekly hours of employment last week rose to 34.9 from 34.7. Find the percent of increase.

17. If the sales tax rate is 6% and the sales tax collected is $478.20, find the total sales.

18. A young couple established a budget allowing 25 percent for rent, 30 percent for food, 8 percent for clothing, 20 percent for travel and recreation, and the remainder for savings. The man takes home $1950 per month, and the woman takes home $28,500 per year. How much will the couple save in a year?

19. Julie Rislov sold a mountain cabin for $64,980. If she originally paid $28,500 for the cabin, find her percent of gain.

20. Alan's Shoes sells shoes for 25% off the regular price of $30. The employee discount is 20% of the sale price. Find the total amount an employee must pay for a pair of shoes, including a sales tax of 6%.

21. Campbell Soup sells 80% of the canned soup sold in this country. The total market for canned soup is worth $843 million. What is the value of the Campbell soup sold in a year?

22. The local real estate agents' association collects a fee of 2% of all money received by its members. The members charge 6% of the selling price of a property as their fee. How much does the association get if its members sell property worth a total of $8,680,000?

23. American River Auto Dismantlers purchased 386 vehicles in one month. Of the total number, 180 units were parted out, 85 units were sold as scrap, and the remaining vehicles were sold to rebuilders. What percent of the total vehicles were (a) parted out, (b) sold as scrap, and (c) sold to rebuilders?

24. The Dravo Corporation slashed its work force of 15,400 by laying off 48% of its employees. Find the size of the work force after the layoffs.

25. Annual business defaults climbed from $60 million one year to $840 million the next year. Find the percent of increase.

26. The Dow Jones Industrial Average roared up 62.39 points to a record of 3163.91 in one day. Find (a) the average the day before this increase and (b) the percent of increase.

27. The average price of a new home rose 4.2%. If the average price of a new home was $131,500, find the average price after the increase.

28. An AT&T Videophone (model 2500) designed for the mass consumer market sells for $1500, while the model designed for big corporations costs $25,000. What percent of the corporate model price is the price of the consumer model?

3.5 Increase and Decrease Problems

OBJECTIVES

1. Learn to identify an increase or a decrease problem.
2. Apply the basic diagram for increase problems.
3. Use an equation to solve increase problems.
4. Apply the basic diagram for decrease problems.
5. Use an equation to solve decrease problems.

As mentioned earlier, it is common to look at how amounts change, either up or down. For example, a manager might need to know the percent by which sales have increased, or the percent by which costs have decreased, while a consumer might need to know the percent by which the price of an item has changed. Identify these **increase** and **decrease** problems as follows.

1

Increase or Amount Problem. The part equals the base (100%) plus some portion of the base, resulting in a new value. Phrases such as "after an increase of," "more than," or "greater than" often indicate an increase problem. The basic formula for an increase problem is

Original + Increase = New value.

Decrease or Difference Problem. The part equals the base (100%) minus some portion of the base, resulting in a new value. Phrases such as "after a decrease of," "less than," or "after a reduction of" often indicate a decrease problem. The basic formula for a decrease problem is

Original − Decrease = New value.

NOTE Base is always the original amount and both increase and decrease problems are base problems. Base is always 100%.

EXAMPLE 1
Using a Diagram to Understand an Increase Problem

At one firm, this year's sales were $121,000, which was 10% more than last year's sales. Find last year's sales.

SOLUTION   Use a diagram to help solve this problem. Since base is the starting point, or that to which something is compared, the base here is last year's sales. Call base 100% and remember that

2   Original + Increase = New Value.

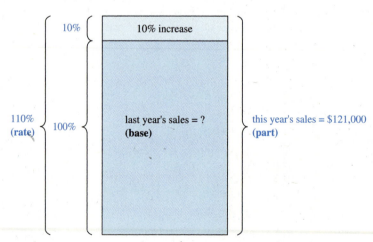

10%   10% increase

110%   100%   last year's sales = ?   this year's sales = $121,000
(rate)   (base)   (part)

FIGURE 3.1

3   As shown in Figure 3.1, the 10% increase is based on last year's sales (which are unknown) and not on this year's sales of $121,000. This year's sales are the result of adding 10% of last year's sales to the amount of last year's sales. Therefore, this year's sales are all of last year's sales (100%) plus 10% (100% + 10% = 110%). Solve with the increase formula, using B to represent base.

$$\text{Original} + \text{Increase} = \text{New value}$$

$$\text{Last year's sales} + 10\% \text{ of last year's sales} = \text{This year's sales}$$

$$100\% \times B + 10\% \times B = \$121,000$$

$$110\% \times B = \$121,000$$

$$1.1B = \$121,000$$

$$\frac{\cancel{1.1}B}{\cancel{1.1}} = \frac{\$121,000}{1.1}$$

$$B = \frac{\$121,000}{1.1}$$

$$B = \$110,000 \qquad \text{last year's sales}$$

Check the answer by taking 10% of last year's sales and adding it to last year's sales.

$$
\begin{array}{ll}
\$110,000 & \text{last year's sales} \\
+\ \ 11,000 & \text{(10\% of \$110,000)} \\
\hline
\$121,000 & \text{this year's sales} \ \blacksquare
\end{array}
$$

CAUTION The common error in solving an increase problem is thinking that the base is given and that the solution can be found by solving for part. Remember that the number given in Example 1, $121,000, is the result of having added 10% of the base to the base (100% + 10% = 110%). In fact, the $121,000 is the part, and base must be found.

Example 2 shows how to solve a problem with two increases.

EXAMPLE 2
Finding Base After Two Increases

At one factory, production last year was 20% more than the year before. This year's production is 93,600 units, which is 20% more than last year's. Find the number of units produced two years ago.

SOLUTION The two 20% increases cannot be added together because these increases are from two different years, with two separate bases. The problem must be solved in two steps. First, use a diagram to find last year's production.

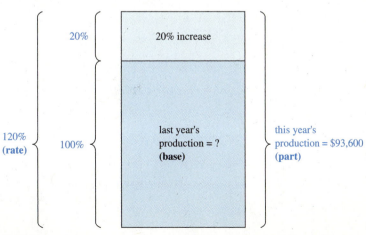

20%

20% increase

120%
(rate)

100%

last year's
production = ?
(base)

this year's
production = $93,600
(part)

FIGURE 3.2

From Figure 3.2, last year's production plus 20% of last year's production equals this year's production. Use the formula as follows.

$$100\% \times B + 20\% \times B = 93,600$$
$$120\% \times B = 93,600$$
$$1.2\,B = 93,600$$
$$\frac{\cancel{1.2}\,B}{\cancel{1.2}} = \frac{93,600}{1.2}$$
$$B = \frac{93,600}{1.2}$$
$$B = 78,000 \qquad \text{last year's production}$$

Production last year was 78,000 units. Production for the preceding year (two years ago) must now be found. Use another diagram.

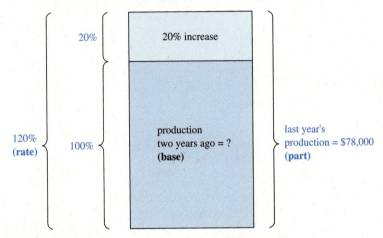

20%

20% increase

120% (rate)

100%

production two years ago = ? (base)

last year's production = $78,000 (part)

FIGURE 3.3

Thus, production two years ago + 20% of production two years ago = last year's production. In the following solution b is used since B was used before.

$$100\% \times b + 20\% \times b = 78,000$$
$$120\% \times b = 78,000$$
$$1.2b = 78,000$$
$$\frac{\cancel{1.2}b}{\cancel{1.2}} = \frac{78,000}{1.2}$$
$$b = \frac{78,000}{1.2}$$
$$b = 65,000 \qquad \text{production two years ago}$$

Check the answer.

65,000	production two years ago
+13,000	20% increase
78,000	production last year
+15,600	20% increase
93,600	production this year ∎

CAUTION It is important to realize that the two 20% increases cannot be added together to equal one increase of 40%. Each 20% increase is calculated on a different base.

The final example shows a decrease problem.

EXAMPLE 3
Using a Diagram to Understand a Decrease Problem

After a dealer deducted 10% from the price of a pair of skis, a customer paid $135. What was the original price of the skis?

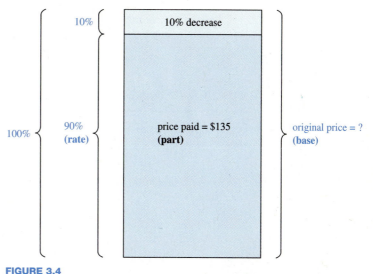

10%

10% decrease

100%

90%
(rate)

price paid = $135
(part)

original price = ?
(base)

FIGURE 3.4

4 **SOLUTION**   Use a diagram again and remember that the base is the starting point—in this case, the original price. As always, the base is 100%. Use the decrease formula.

5   As Figure 3.4 shows, 10% was deducted from the original price. The result equals the price paid, which is 90% of the original price.

Be careful in finding the rate: 10% cannot be used because the original price to which 10% was applied is not given. The rate 90% (the difference, 100% − 10% = 90%) must be used since 90% of the original price is the resulting $135 price paid. Now find the original price.

$$\text{Original} - \text{Decrease} = \text{New value}$$

$$\text{Original price} - 10\% \text{ of the original price} = \text{Price paid}$$

$$100\% \times B - 10\% \times B = \$135$$

$$90\% \times B = \$135$$

$$0.9B = \$135$$

$$\frac{0.9B}{0.9} = \frac{\$135}{0.9}$$

$$B = \frac{\$135}{0.9}$$

$$B = \$150 \qquad \text{original price}$$

Check the answer.

$150	original price
− 15	10% discount
$135	price paid ∎

CAUTION The common mistake made in Example 3 is thinking that the reduced price, $135 is the base. The original price is the base while the reduced price, $135, is a result of subtracting 10% from the base. The reduced price is the part or 90% of the base (100% − 10% = 90%).

3.5 Exercises

Solve for base in each of the following. Round to the nearest cent.

Part (Amount After Increase)	Rate of Increase
1. $770	10%
2. $9.80	25%
3. $20.18	8%
4. $8790	18%

Solve for base in each of the following. Round to the nearest cent.

Part (Amount After Decrease)	Rate of Decrease
5. $19	5%
6. $68	10%
7. $720	12%
8. $9680	50%

9. Certain words or word phrases help to identify an increase problem. Discuss how you will identify an increase problem. (See Objective 1.)

10. Certain words or word phrases help to identify a decrease problem. Discuss how you will identify a decrease problem. (See Objective 1.)

Solve each of the following problems. Read each carefully to determine which are increase or decrease problems and work accordingly. Round to the nearest cent, when necessary.

11. This year Ed Moura paid an income tax of $4026, an increase of 10% over last year's tax. How much did Mr. Moura pay in taxes last year?

12. A tire manufacturer advertises that his tire will give 25% longer wear than Brand X. If the advertised brand gives 49,600 miles of service, how many miles would be expected from Brand X?

13. An auto accessories dealer sold some merchandise for $225.28, a loss of 12% on her original cost. What was her original cost?

14. Estelle Zagorin agrees to allow a real estate broker to sell her townhouse and charge a 6% brokerage fee. Zagorin, however, states that she must receive $79,900 after the real estate broker has deducted the 6% fee. At what amount should the townhouse be priced?

15. In a local election, 205,850 people cast their votes. If this number represents a gain of 15% over the last election, what was the number of voters in the last election?

16. Gail Kelly bought a steering wheel lock for her pickup truck for $34.64 including $6\frac{1}{4}\%$ sales tax. (a) How much of the $34.64 was for the lock and (b) how much was the sales tax?

17. In a recent test of an automobile antilock braking system (ABS) on wet pavement the stopping distance was 114 feet. If this was 28.75% less than the distance needed to stop the same automobile without the ABS, find the distance needed to stop without the antilock braking system.

18. Alice Cramden installed an electronic alarm and several simple auto-theft devices in her car. As a result her auto insurance policy premium was reduced by 5.2% to $1147 per year. Find the amount of her insurance premium before installing these devices. (Round to the nearest cent.)

19. Sara's Plant World collects 4% state sales tax on all sales. If total sales including tax are $1648.40, find the portion that is tax.

20. In 1993 the population of Stamford was 10% more than it was in 1992. If the population was 26,620 in 1994, which was 10% more than in 1993, find the population in 1992.

21. Jim Tecu, a metal sculptor, says that his sales have increased exactly 20% per year for the last 2 years. His sales this year are $14,169.60. Find his sales two years ago.

22. Physicians services, the second largest component of health care expenditures (hospital care is the largest), is expected to rise 11% next year to $155 billion. Find the amount spent on physicians services this year. (Round to the nearest tenth of a billion.)

23. The cost of nursing home care in the United States will jump nearly 12% to $66 billion next year. Find the cost of nursing home care this year. (Round to the nearest tenth of a billion.)

24. The number of new jobless claims this week is 305,000, which is a decrease of 1.6% from last week. Find the number of new jobless claims last week. (Round to the nearest whole number.)

25. In a three-day public sale of Jackson County surplus equipment, the first day brought $5750 in sales and the second day brought $4186 in sales, with 28% of the value of the equipment left to be sold on the third day. Find the value of the equipment left to sell.

26. After spending $1650 for tuition and $2250 for dormitory fees, George Duda finds that 35% of his original savings remain. Find the remaining amount of his savings.

27. At an auto parts store, this year's inventory of 73,008 items is 6.4% fewer items than last year's. Find last year's inventory.

28. If the owner of a condominium quickly sold his unit for $86,330, at a loss of 11% of the original purchase price, how much did the owner pay originally?

29. Even though wheat prices are rising during the planting season, farmers have planted only 50.2 million acres of winter wheat varieties. If this is 2% fewer acres than last year, find the number of acres planted last year. (Round to the nearest tenth of a million.)

30. Boise Cascade Corporation reported annual revenue of $963.2 million which was a drop of 3.5% from the previous year. Find the revenue in the previous year. (Round to the nearest tenth of a million.)

31. In 1993 the student enrollment at American River College was 8% more than it was in 1992. If the enrollment was 23,328 students in 1994, which was 8% more than it was in 1993, find the student enrollment in 1992.

32. Students at the state universities are outraged. The annual university fees were 30% more last year than they were the year before. If the fees are $2704 per year this year, which is 30% more than they were last year, find the annual student fees two years ago.

33. The price per share of Wal-Mart stock rose to $58\frac{7}{8}$ after an increase of 94.6%. Find the price per share before the increase.

34. The stock of International Game Technology, a primary manufacturer of slot machines, rose to $46 per share after an increase of 449.3%. Find the price per share before this increase. (Round to the nearest cent.)

CHAPTER 3 QUICK REVIEW

TOPIC	APPROACH	EXAMPLE
3.1 Writing a decimal as a percent	Move the decimal point two places to the right and attach a % sign.	$0.75(.75.) = 75\%$
3.1 Writing a fraction as a percent	First change the fraction to a decimal, then write the decimal as a percent.	$\frac{2}{5} = 0.4$ $0.4(.40.) = 40\%$
3.1 Writing a percent as a decimal	Move the decimal point two places to the left and drop the % sign.	$50\% \quad (.50.\%) = 0.5$
3.1 Writing a fractional percent as a decimal	First change the fraction to a decimal leaving the % sign, then move the decimal point two places to the left and drop the % sign.	$\frac{1}{2}\% = 0.5\%$ $0.5\% = 0.00.5$

TOPIC	APPROACH	EXAMPLE
3.2 Solving for part using the percent formula	**Part** = Base × Rate $P = B \times R$ $P = BR$ ___% of ___ is ___	A company offered a 15% discount on all sales. Find the discount on sales of $1850. ___% of <u>sales</u> is <u>discount</u> 15% of $1850 = discount $R \times B = P$ $0.15 \times \$1850 = P$ $0.15 \times \$1850 = \$277.50$ discount
3.3 Using the basic percent equation to solve for base	Remember that base is the starting point, reference point, all of something, or 100%. Rate × **Base** = Part ___% × ___ is ___	If the sales tax rate is 4%, find the sales if the sales tax is $18. $R \times B = P$ $4\% \times$ ___ $= \$18$ $0.04\,B = \$18$ $\dfrac{0.04\,B}{0.04} = \dfrac{\$18}{0.04}$ $B = \dfrac{18}{0.04} = \$450$ sales
3.4 Using the basic percent equation to solve for rate	Remember that rate is a percent and is followed by a % sign. **Rate** × Base = Part ___% × ___ is ___	The return is $307.80 on an investment of $3420. Find the rate of return. $R \times B = P$ ___% of $3420 is $307.80 $R \times \$3420 = \$307.80$ $\$3420R = \$307.80$ $\dfrac{3420R}{3420} = \dfrac{307.8}{3420} = 0.09$ $R = 9\%$
3.4 Finding the percent of change	Calculate the change (increase or decrease), which is the part. Base is the amount before the change. Use $R = \dfrac{P}{B}$	Production rose from 3820 units to 5157 units. Find the percent of increase. $5157 - 3820 = 1337$ increase $R = \dfrac{1337}{3820} = 0.35 = 35\%$

TOPIC	APPROACH	EXAMPLE

3.5 Drawing a diagram and using an equation to solve an increase problem

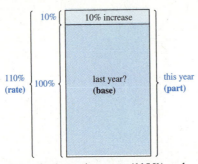

Solve for base given rate (110%) and part (after increase).

This year's sales are \$121,000, which is 10% more than last year's sales. Find last year's sales.

Original + Increase = New value

$$100\% \times B + 10\% \times B = \$121,000$$

$$1B + 0.1B = \$121,000$$

$$1.1B = \$121,000$$

$$B = \frac{\$121,000}{1.1} = \$110,000 \text{ last year's sales}$$

3.5 Drawing a diagram and using an equation to solve a decrease problem

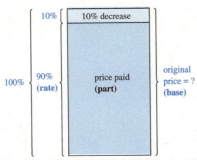

Solve for base given rate (90%) and part (after decrease).

After a deduction of 10% from the price, a customer paid \$135. Find the original price.

Original − Decrease = New value

$$100\% \times B - 10\% \times B = \$135$$

$$1B - 0.1B = \$135$$

$$0.9B = \$135$$

$$B = \frac{\$135}{0.9}$$

$$B = \$150 \text{ original price}$$

SUMMARY EXERCISE

Many people collect baseball cards as a hobby, some collect them as an investment, and a few people support themselves through college by buying and selling cards. A 1952 Jackie Robinson card recently sold for $4675. (The one pictured here is from 1953.)

In the past year some cards have gone up in value while others have gone down.

National Baseball Library and Archive, Cooperstown, New York

THE UPS AND DOWNS OF LAST YEAR		
ROOKIE CARD	CARD PRICE*	% CHANGE FROM LAST YEAR
Frank Thomas	$ 4.50	+13
Cal Ripkin Jr.	65.00	+117
Dave Justice	4.00	+167
Nolan Ryan	1200.00	Unch.
Ken Griffey Jr.	9.00	Unch.
José Canseco	10.00	−44
Will Clark	15.00	−40
Mark McGwire	12.00	−20

*Average prices for rookie cards

FIGURE 3.5

Find the price of each of the cards last year for each of the players listed. (Round to the nearest half dollar.)

Frank Thomas

Cal Ripken Jr.

Dave Justice

Nolan Ryan

Ken Griffey Jr.

Jose Canseco

Will Clark

Mark McGwire

CHAPTER 3 REVIEW EXERCISES

Solve each of the following. [3.1 through 3.4]

1. Find the decimal equivalent of 12%.

2. What is 10% of 376?

3. Change $3\frac{1}{2}$% to its decimal equivalent.

4. 66 is 6% of what number?

5. 6898.5 is what percent of 54,750?

6. 36 is what percent of 720?

7. Change $\frac{3}{4}$% to its decimal equivalent.

8. 44 is $5\frac{1}{2}$% of what number?

9. 60 is $12\frac{1}{2}$% of what number?

10. What is $\frac{1}{2}$% of $1300?

Solve each of the following problems, reading each carefully to determine whether base, part, or rate is being asked for. Also, check to see which are increase or decrease problems, and work accordingly. (Round to the nearest cent or tenth of a percent, as necessary.)

11. A savings account paying 6% interest earns $51 in a year. Find the amount of the savings account. [3.3]

12. A bond selling for $650 pays a return of $26. Find the rate of return. [3.4]

13. In past years at Freeport Line and Fasteners, 7.6% of all employees have been absent during November. This November, 173 employees were absent. The total number of employees is 1620. (a) Is the percent absent this year higher or lower than in other years? (b) Subtract the two percents to find by how much. [3.4]

14. Gross earnings minus employee deductions equal net earnings. If employee deductions are 21.2% of gross earnings, find the gross earnings if employee deductions are $232.50. [3.3]

15. After properly tuning his car, Murray Grannard found that he used 8.3% less gasoline on a 425-mile trip. If the trip took 19.3 gallons after the tuneup, find the number of gallons that would have been needed before. (Round to the nearest tenth of a gallon.) [3.4]

16. A new union contract allows for an increase of 14.8% in fringe benefits. If total fringe benefits are $875 per year after the increase, find the amount of fringe benefits before the increase. [3.5]

17. Highlands Upholstery had sales of $187,450 last year and sales of $200,946.40 this year. Find the percent of increase in sales. [3.4]

18. The inventory at Wilmington Appliance was $186,250 last month. If inventory this month is $156,450, find the percent of decrease. [3.4]

19. After losing 22 golf balls, Al Zagorin finds that he has 35 balls remaining. What percent of the original number of balls remains? [3.4]

20. In the processing of raisins, grapes lose 76% of their weight. How many pounds of grapes are needed to yield 1200 pounds of raisins? [3.3]

21. Linda Youngman bought 10 pounds of gold at $380 per ounce. (Gold is measured in troy weight, 12 ounces per pound.) She paid a brokerage fee of $540, and shipping and insurance charges of $620. (a) What total amount did she spend for the gold, including the brokerage fee and shipping and insurance charges? (b) What percent (rounded to the nearest tenth) of her total investment were her charges for brokerage, shipping, and insurance? [3.4]

22. A customer at Bobbie's Boutique says, "I hate short pants. I'd rather they be a little long than a little short." The customer needs a 30-inch length. The pants come in whole-inch lengths only, and there will be 3.6% shrinkage after washing. What length of pants should the customer buy? [3.5]

23. The local bank says that on home purchases, it will loan 97% of the first $50,000 of the home cost, 90% of the next $20,000, and 80% of the balance of the purchase price. Kerry Williams buys a home for $105,800. Find her down payment. (Hint: The portion that the lender will not loan is the down payment.) [3.2]

24. Ann Felsted, an artist, says that her sales have increased exactly 20% per year for the last 3 years. Her sales this year are $14,169.60. Find her sales 3 years ago. [3.5]

25. This year, Julie Stevens earned $18,900, an increase of 12.5% over last year. Find her salary last year. [3.5]

26. Steel production this year rose 16% from the 1,702,000 tons produced last year. Find this year's steel production.

27. The value of Businessland's stock rose 6.25% from yesterday's $10 per share. Find the value of the stock after the increase. (Do not round.)

28. Pilferage at Jungleland Pet Centre is $2732 per year, which is 3.2% of sales. Find the total sales. [3.3]

29. Gerald Brian buys five $5000 bonds and receives interest of $2125 per year. Find his rate of return. [3.4]

30. Your school bookstore keeps 20% of the price of a new book. The remainder goes to the publisher. The authors get 15% of all money received by the publisher. Anne and Jen split evenly all authors' money paid. If students at your school buy a total of 250 copies, at $42 per copy, how much does Anne get? [3.2]

31. The head accountant at Village Floral finds that her firm has spent 30% of its advertising budget on television and $20,855 on radio spots. The firm has $13,095 left. What percent of the total advertising budget does the firm still have? [3.3]

32. John Young sells some stock at $48 per share. This is a loss of 62.5% of the original price per share. What was the original price? [3.5]

4

Banking Services

Modern banks and savings institutions today offer so many services that they have become more than places to deposit savings and take out loans. These financial institutions now offer a wide range of services to individuals and business customers. Today, many types of savings and checking accounts are offered, as well as services such as computerized home and business banking, automated teller machines (ATMs), credit cards, investment securities services, and even payroll services to the business owner.

This chapter examines checking accounts and check registers, and how to use them. It also discusses business checking account services, the depositing of credit card transactions, and bank reconciliation (balancing the checking account).

4.1 Checking Accounts and Check Registers

OBJECTIVES

1. Identify the parts of a check.
2. Know the types of checking accounts.
3. Find the monthly service charges.
4. Identify the parts of a deposit slip.
5. Identify the parts of a check stub.
6. Complete the parts of a check register.

Over 90 percent of all business transactions today involve checks. Goods are purchased by check, and bills are paid by check. A small business may write several hundred checks each month and take in several thousand, while large businesses can take in several million checks in a month. This heavy reliance on checks makes it important for all people in business to have a good understanding of checks and checking accounts. The various parts of a check are explained in Figure 4.1.

1

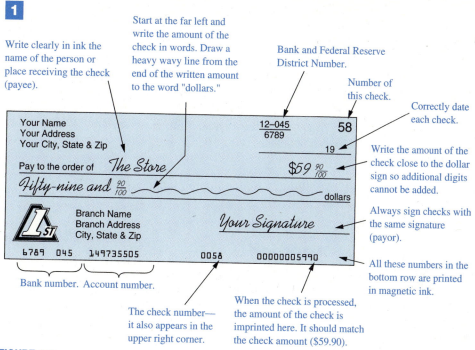

Write clearly in ink the name of the person or place receiving the check (payee).

Start at the far left and write the amount of the check in words. Draw a heavy wavy line from the end of the written amount to the word "dollars."

Bank and Federal Reserve District Number.

Number of this check.

Correctly date each check.

Write the amount of the check close to the dollar sign so additional digits cannot be added.

Always sign checks with the same signature (payor).

All these numbers in the bottom row are printed in magnetic ink.

Bank number.   Account number.

The check number—it also appears in the upper right corner.

When the check is processed, the amount of the check is imprinted here. It should match the check amount ($59.90).

FIGURE 4.1

2   Two main types of checking accounts are available, and are explained here.

Personal checking accounts are used by individuals. The bank supplies printed checks (normally charging a check-printing fee) for the customer to use. Some banks offer the checking account at no charge to the customer but most require that a minimum monthly balance remain in the checking account. If the minimum balance is not maintained during any month, a service charge is applied to the account. Today, the **flat fee checking account** is common. For a fixed charge per month, the bank supplies the checking account, check printing, a bank charge card, and a host of other services. Interest paid on checking account balances is common with personal checking accounts. These accounts are offered by savings and loan associations, credit unions, and banks, and are available to individuals as well as a few business customers. These accounts often require much higher minimum balances than regular accounts.

Business checking accounts often receive more services than do personal accounts. For example, banks often arrange to receive payments on debts due to business firms. The bank automatically credits the amount to the business account.

A popular service available to personal and business customers is the **automated teller machine (ATM)**. Offered by many banks, savings and loans, and credit unions, an ATM allows customers to perform a great number of transactions on a 24-hour basis. The customer can make cash withdrawals and deposits, transfer funds from one account to another (including the paying of credit card accounts or other loans), and make account-balance inquiries. In addition, through several networking arrangements, the customer may make purchases and receive cash advances from hundreds, and in some cases thousands, of participating businesses nationally, and often worldwide.

For example, through one computer networking system, the use of the customer ATM card and a personal code will give the customer access to their account at over 100,000 STARSYSTEM®, CIRRUS, or Plus ATM locations.*

The customer may pay a transaction charge ranging from less than $1.00 to about $2.00 for each transaction.

NOTE   When using the ATM card remember to keep receipts so that the transaction can be subtracted from your bank balance. Be certain to subtract any charge made for using the ATM card.

3   Service charges for business checking accounts are based on the average balance for the period covered by the statement. This average balance determines the **maintenance charge per month**, to which a **per debit charge** (per check charge) is added. The charges generally apply regardless of the amount of account activity. Some typical bank charges for a business checking account appear in Table 4.1.

EXAMPLE 1
*Finding the
Checking Account
Service Charge*

Find the monthly service charge for the following business accounts.
(a) Pittsburgh Glass, 38 checks written, average balance $833

SOLUTION   From Table 4.1, an account having an average balance between $500 and $1999 will have a maintenance charge of $5.00 for the month. In addition, there is a per debit (check) charge of $.20. Since 38 checks were written during the month, the monthly service charge is calculated as follows.

$$\$5.00 + 38(\$.20) = \$5.00 + \$7.60 = \$12.60$$

(b) Fargo Western Auto, 87 checks written average balance $2367

SOLUTION   Since the average balance is between $2000 and $4999, the maintenance charge for the month is $2.50, to which a $.10 per debit (check) charge is added. The monthly service charge is $2.50 + 87($.10) = $11.20.   ■

TABLE 4.1   Typical Bank Charges for a Business Checking Account

Average Balance	Maintenance Charge Per Month	Per Check Charge
Less than $500	$7.50	$.20
$500–$1999	$5.00	$.20
$2000–$4999	$2.50	$.10
$5000 or more	$0	$0

*Reprinted by permission of Star System, Inc., CIRRUS System, Inc., and Plus System, Inc.

4 Money, either cash or checks, is placed into a checking account with a **deposit slip** or **deposit ticket** such as the one in Figure 4.2. The account number is written at the bottom of the slip in magnetic ink. The slip contains blanks in which are entered any cash (either currency or coins), as well as checks that are to be deposited.

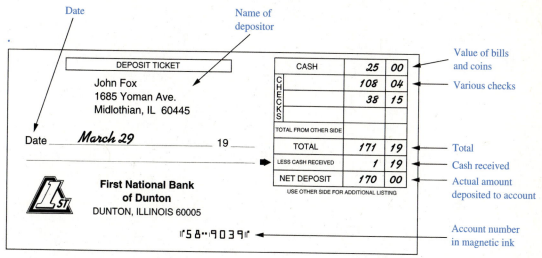

FIGURE 4.2

FIGURE 4.3

A two-sided commercial deposit slip is shown in Figure 4.3. Notice that much more space is allowed for an itemized list of the customers' checks being deposited into the business account. Many financial institutions require that the bank and federal reserve district numbers be shown in the description column of the deposit slip. These numbers appear in the upper right hand corner of the check and are identified in the sample check on page 101.

When a check is deposited, it should have "for deposit only" and either the depositor's signature or the company stamp placed on the back within 1.5 inches of the vertical top edge. In this way, if a check is lost or stolen on the way to the bank, it will be worthless to anyone finding it. Such an endorsement, which limits the ability to cash a check, is called a **restricted endorsement**. An example of a restricted endorsement is shown in Figure 4.4, along with two other types of endorsements. The most common endorsement by individuals is the **blank endorsement**, where only the name of the person being paid is signed. This endorsement should be used only at the moment of cashing a check. The **special endorsement**, used to pass on the check to someone else, might be used to pay a bill on another account.

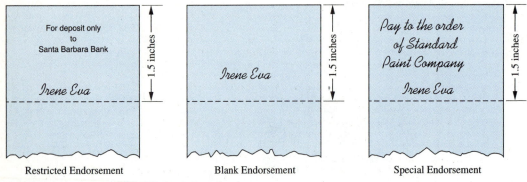

Restricted Endorsement   Blank Endorsement   Special Endorsement

FIGURE 4.4

5   A record must be kept of every deposit made and every check written. Business firms normally do this with one **check stub** for each check. These stubs provide room to list the date, the person or firm to whom the check will be paid, and the purpose of the check. Also, the stub provides space to record the balance in the account after the last check was written (called the **balance brought forward**, abbreviated Bal. Bro't. For'd., on the stub), and any money deposited since the last check was written. The balance brought forward and amount deposited are added to provide the current balance in the checking account. The amount of the current check is then subtracted, and a new balance is found. This balance forward from the bottom of the stub should be written on the next stub. Figure 4.5 shows a typical check stub.

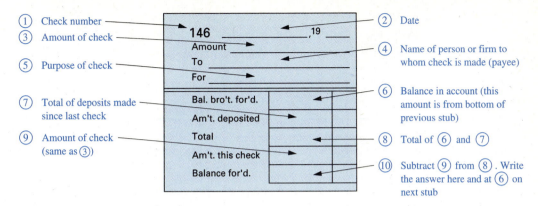

FIGURE 4.5

EXAMPLE 2

Completing a Check Stub

Check number 724 is made out on April 15 to the Internal Revenue Service for federal income tax. Assume that the check is for $248.93, that the balance forward is $3748.12, and that deposits of $182.74 and $98.12 have been made since the last check was written. The stub would then be completed as shown in Figure 4.6.

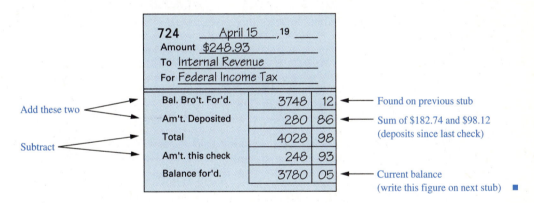

FIGURE 4.6

Banks offer many styles of checkbooks. Notice that the style shown in Figure 4.7 offers two stubs and is designed to be used for payroll. The stub next to the check can be used as the employee's record of earnings and deductions. Business checks are generally larger in size than personal checks.

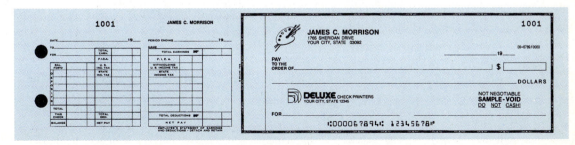

Reprinted by permission of Deluxe Corporation.

FIGURE 4.7

6   Some depositors prefer a check register to the check stubs, while others use both. The **check register** shows at a glance the checks written and deposits made, as seen in Figure 4.8. The column headed ✔ is used to check off each check after it is received back from the bank.

CHECK NO.	DATE	CHECK ISSUED TO	AMOUNT OF CHECK	✔	DATE OF DEP.	AMOUNT OF DEPOSIT	BALANCE	
		BALANCE BROUGHT FORWARD →					3518	72
1435	5/8	SWAN BROTHERS	378 93				3139	79
1436	5/8	CLASS ACTS	25 14				3114	65
1437	5/9	MIRROR LIGHTING	519 65				2595	00
		DEPOSIT			5/10	3821 17	6416	17
1438	5/10	WOODLAKE AUDITORIUM	750 00				5666	17
		DEPOSIT			5/12	500 00	6166	17
1439	5/12	RICK'S CLOWNS	170 80				5995	37
1440	5/14	Y.M.C.A.	219 17				5776	20
ATM	5/14	ATM (cash)	120 00				5656	20
		DEPOSIT			5/15	326 15	5982	35
1441	5/16	STAGE DOOR PLAYHOUSE	825 00				5157	35
1442	5/17	GILBERT ECKERN	1785 00				3372	35
		DEPOSIT			5/19	1580 25	4952	60

FIGURE 4.8

CAUTION   ATM transactions for cash withdrawals and purchases must be entered on check stubs or in the check register. The transaction amount and the charge for each transaction must then be subtracted to maintain an accurate balance.

4.1 Exercises

Use Table 4.1 to find the monthly checking account service charge for the following business accounts.

1. Carl's Garage, 39 checks, average balance $677
2. Hall's Television Repair, 43 checks, average balance $1905
3. Pest-X, 40 checks, average balance $491
4. Video Warehouse, 27 checks, average balance $103
5. Coco's Sandwiches, 50 checks, average balance $5847
6. Columbus Manufacturing, 87 checks, average balance $6560
7. CompuTech, 117 checks, average balance $1993
8. Mart & Bottle, 74 checks, average balance $875

Use the information supplied to complete the stubs that follow.

	Date	To	For	Amount	Balance Bro't. For'd.	Deposits
9.	Jan 8	Mark Badgett	Handyman work	$276.32	$4780.92	$12.74
10.	Mar. 13	Diane Grey	Consulting service	$850.00	$2973.09	$1853.24
11.	Nov. 29	Payless Laundry	Uniforms	$29.38	$1768.92	—

9.

85

_Jan 8_____ , 19 _____

Amount *$276.32*

To *Mark Badgett*

For *handyman work*

Bal. bro't. for'd.	4780	92
Am't. deposited	12	74
Total	4793	66
Am't. this check	276	32
Balance for'd.		

10.

12

_Mar 13_____ , 19 _____

Amount *$850.00*

To *Diane Grey*

For *consulting service*

Bal. bro't. for'd.	2973	09
Am't. deposited	1853	24
Total	4826	33
Am't. this check	850	00
Balance for'd.		

11.

73

_Nov 29_____ , 19 _____

Amount *$29.38*

To *Payless Laundry*

For *uniforms*

Bal. bro't. for'd.	1768	92
Am't. deposited		
Total	1768	92
Am't. this check	29	38
Balance for'd.		

12. List and explain at least six parts of a check. Draw a sketch showing where these parts appear on a check. (See Objective 1.)

13. Suppose you have a personal and a business checking account. List and explain some differences between the two accounts. Consider volume of use, account balances, and banking charges. (See Objective 2.)

14. Explain to a friend at least two advantages and two possible disadvantages of using an ATM card. Do this in writing.

15. Explain in your own words the factors that determine the service charges on a business checking account. (See Objective 3.)

Complete the check stubs on the next page for Twin Rivers Mobile Homes. The balance forward for stub 4286 is $9748.12.

Checks written:

Number	Date	To	For	Amount
4286	April 1	Lida Lee Finance	Interest	$389.12
4287	April 5	Computer Center	Software	$39.12
4288	April 15	IRS	Income tax	$212.40

Deposits:

Date	Amount
April 3	$176.09
April 4	$23.32
April 7	$980.24
April 17	$273.09
April 17	$87.26
April 23	$187.62

16.

4286	
_____ , 19 ____	
Amount _____	
To _____	
For _____	

Bal. bro't. for'd.	
Am't. deposited	
Total	
Am't. this check	
Balance for'd.	

17.

4287	
_____ , 19 ____	
Amount _____	
To _____	
For _____	

Bal. bro't. for'd.	
Am't. deposited	
Total	
Am't. this check	
Balance for'd.	

18.

4288	
_____ , 19 ____	
Amount _____	
To _____	
For _____	

Bal. bro't. for'd.	
Am't. deposited	
Total	
Am't. this check	
Balance for'd.	

Complete the balance column in the following check registers after each check or deposit transaction.

19.

CHECK NO.	DATE	CHECK ISSUED TO	AMOUNT OF CHECK		✓	DATE OF DEP.	AMOUNT OF DEPOSIT		BALANCE	
		BALANCE BROUGHT FORWARD →							1629	86
861	7/3	AHWAHNEE HOTEL	250	45						
862	7/5	WILLOW CREEK	149	00						
863	7/5	VOID								
		DEPOSIT				7/7	117	73		
864	7/9	DEL CAMPO HIGH SCH.	69	80						
		DEPOSIT				7/10	329	86		
		DEPOSIT				7/12	418	30		
865	7/14	BIG 5 SPORTING GOODS	109	76						
866	7/14	DR. YATES	614	12						
867	7/16	GREYHOUND	32	18						
		DEPOSIT				7/16	520	95		

20.

CHECK NO.	DATE	CHECK ISSUED TO	AMOUNT OF CHECK		✓	DATE OF DEP.	AMOUNT OF DEPOSIT		BALANCE	
		BALANCE BROUGHT FORWARD →							832	15
1121	3/17	WORLDBOOK INC.	257	29						
1122	3/18	CURRY VILLAGE	190	50						
		DEPOSIT				3/19	78	29		
		DEPOSIT				3/21	157	42		
1123	3/22	SAN JUAN DISTRICT	38	76						
1124	3/23	MACY'S GOURMET	175	88						
		DEPOSIT				3/23	379	28		
1125	3/24	CLASS VIDEO	197	20						
1126	3/24	WATER WORLD	20	10						
1127	3/25	ATM (cash)	80	00						
		DEPOSIT				3/28	722	35		

21.

CHECK NO.	DATE	CHECK ISSUED TO	AMOUNT OF CHECK		✓	DATE OF DEP.	AMOUNT OF DEPOSIT		BALANCE	
			BALANCE BROUGHT FORWARD →						3852	48
2308	12/6	Village Printing	143	16						
2309	12/7	Water and Power	118	40						
		Deposit				12/8	286	32		
	12/10	ATM (cash)	80	00						
2310	12/11	Clare Lynch Suppliers	986	22						
2311	12/11	Account Temps	375	50						
		Deposit				12/14	1201	82		
2312	12/14	Central Chevrolet	735	68						
2313	12/15	Miller Mining	223	94						
		Deposit				12/17	498	01		
2314	12/18	Federal Parcel	78	24						

22.

CHECK NO.	DATE	CHECK ISSUED TO	AMOUNT OF CHECK		✓	DATE OF DEP.	AMOUNT OF DEPOSIT		BALANCE	
			BALANCE BROUGHT FORWARD →						8284	18
1917	6/4	Valley Electric	188	18						
1918	6/5	Harrold Ford	433	56						
1919	6/5	Sheila Jones (photography)	138	17						
		Deposit				6/6	453	28		
		Deposit				6/8	1475	69		
1920	6/9	U.S. Rentals	335	82						
1921	6/11	Quick Turn Merchandise	573	27						
	6/11	ATM (gas)	16	35						
1922	6/14	Broadly Plumbing	195	15						
		Deposit				6/16	635	85		
1923	6/16	National Dues (F.F.A.)	317	20						

4.2 Checking Services and Depositing Credit Card Transactions

OBJECTIVES

1 Identify bank services available to customers.

2 Understand interest-paying checking plans.

3 Deposit credit card transactions.

4 Calculate discount fee on credit card deposits.

Most business checking account charges are based on either the average balance or minimum balance in the account, together with specific charges for each service performed by the bank. Following are explanations of some of the more common services provided by banks, along with the typical charges. (These charges may vary from bank to bank.)

1 An **overdraft** occurs when checks are written for which there are insufficient funds in the checking account and when the customer has no overdraft protection. (This may also be referred to as *bouncing a check*.) A typical charge is $10 to $20 per check. The same charges occur when a check is returned because it was improperly completed.

Overdraft protection is given when an account balance is insufficient to cover the amount of a check and an overdraft occurs. Minimum transfer amounts and transfer charges vary among banks.

A **returned deposit item** is a check which was deposited and then returned to the bank, usually because of lack of funds in the account of the person or firm writing the check ($5.00 per item).

A **stop payment order** is a request to the bank that it not honor a check which the depositor has written ($10.00 per request).

A **cashier's check** is a check written by the financial institution itself. It therefore has the full faith and backing of the institution ($5.00).

A **money order** is an instrument which is purchased and is often used in place of cash. It is sometimes required by the payee instead of a personal or business check ($4.00).

Noncustomer check cashing is sometimes offered to an individual who does not have an account with the institution ($5.00).

A **notary service** is often given free to customers. This is a service which is required on certain business documents. To a noncustomer there is usually a charge ($5.00).

Telephone transfer of funds allows the customer to make fund transfers by telephone ($2.00 per transfer after the third transfer each month).

2 Federal banking regulations now allow both personal and business interest-paying checking plans. Some of the plans combine two accounts—a savings account and a checking account—while others are simply checking accounts which pay interest on the average daily balance.

A **NOW account** is technically a savings account with special withdrawal privileges. For all practical purposes, it functions as a checking account that pays interest. Instead of writing a check, however, the customer writes a "negotiable order of withdrawal" (NOW), which looks and works like a check.

NOW accounts were introduced by a savings bank in Massachusetts in the early 1970s. In the mid '70s, Congress used the New England states as a testing ground to determine whether federal banking laws should be revised to allow NOW accounts or other types of interest-bearing checking accounts nationwide. The test was a success and helped change the 1933 law against paying interest on checking accounts.

Credit union share draft accounts are offered to members by many credit unions. Share drafts look like checks and are used in the same ways checks are used. Members of credit unions can write share drafts against their credit union shares (savings). The major difference between share drafts and personal checks is that share drafts usually are not returned to members after they have been processed and paid, while regular checks are usually returned to the customer by the bank.

3 Credit cards are used in a very large number of today's retail purchases. These credit card sales are deposited into a business checking account with a **merchant batch header ticket** such as the one in Figure 4.9 in Example 1. This form is used with VISA or MasterCard credit card deposits. Notice that the form lists both sales slips and credit slips (refunds). Entries in each of these categories are totaled, and the total credits are subtracted from the total sales to give the net amount of deposit.

The merchant batch header ticket is a triplicate form and the bank copy along with the charge slips, credit slips, and a printed calculator tape showing the itemized deposits and credits is deposited in the business checking account.

EXAMPLE 1

Determining Deposits with Credit Card Transactions

The Athletic Shoe Shop had the following credit card sales and refunds on athletic shoes and accessories. Complete a merchant batch header ticket.

Sales		Refunds (Credit)
$12.31	$44.31	$13.83
$38.18	$78.80	$25.19
$65.29	$63.14	$78.56
$178.22	$11.92	

SOLUTION   All credit slips and sales slips must be totaled. The number of each of these and the totals are written at the right. The total sales slips are $492.17, and the credit slips total $117.58. The difference is the net deposit; here $374.59 is the net deposit. The completed merchant batch header ticket is show in Figure 4.9. ■

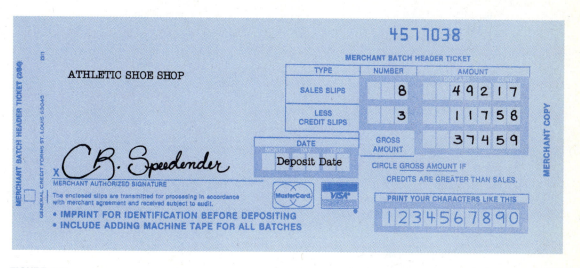

FIGURE 4.9

4 The bank collects a fee (a percent of sales) from the merchant and also an interest charge from the card user on all accounts not paid in full at the first billing. Although credit card transactions are deposited frequently by a business, the bank calculates the discount fee on the net amount of the credit card deposits since the last bank statement date. The fee paid by the merchant varies from 2% to 5% of the sales slip amount and is determined by the type of processing used (electronic or manual), the dollar volume of credit card usage by the merchant, and the average amount of the sale at the merchant's store. All credit card deposits for the month are added, and the fee is subtracted from the total at the statement date.

EXAMPLE 2
Finding the Discount on a Credit Card Deposit

If the deposit in Example 1 represented total credit card deposits for the month, find the discount charged at the statement date if the Athletic Shoe Shop pays a 3% fee.

SOLUTION   Since the total credit card deposit for the Athletic Shoe Shop is $374.59 and the fee is 3%, the discount charged is

$$\$374.59 \times .03(3\%) = \$11.24 \text{ discount charge}$$

Out of a deposit of $374.59, the merchant would actually receive only

$$\$374.59 - \$11.24 = \$363.35. \quad \blacksquare$$

4.2 Exercises

For each of the following businesses, find (a) the total charges, (b) the total credits, (c) the amount of the net deposit, and (d) the amount of the discount charged at the statement date.

1. In addition to videotape rentals, Captain Video sells audio and videotapes, compact discs, and various electronic video equipment and accessories. In a recent period, the company had the following credit card charges and credits. The bank charges a 3% discount.

Charges		Credits
$37.27	$228.17	$72.89
$418.75	$152.68	$61.54
$77.16	$47.19	$19.15
$14.95	$637.15	
$64.13	$22.97	

2. Amber Tune Up and Brake accepts travel and leisure cards from customers for auto repairs and the sale of parts. The following credit card transactions occurred during a recent period. The bank charges a 4% discount.

Charges		Credits
$66.68	$18.95	$62.16
$119.63	$496.28	$106.62
$53.86	$21.85	$38.91
$178.62	$242.78	
$219.78	$176.93	

3. North Avea Dodge does most of its business on a cash basis or through its own credit department, although it does honor major bank charge cards. In a recent period, the business had the following credit card charges and credits. The bank charges a 4% discount.

Charges			Credits
$25.18	$77.51	$14.73	$38.15
$15.73	$357.18	$106.78	$106.86
$138.97	$72.73	$88.34	$44.38
$58.73	$29.68	$72.21	
$255.18	$15.76	$262.73	

4. Stork's Maternity Shop had the following credit card transactions during a recent period. The bank charges a $4\frac{1}{2}$% discount.

Charges		Credits
$42.60	$29.50	$22.10
$38.25	$72.85	$14.67
$16.60	$19.30	$30.30
$52.40	$6.75	
$14.38	$88.98	

5. Mollie Schlue Gifts had the following credit card transactions during a recent period. The bank charges a 3% discount.

Charges		Credits
$7.84	$98.56	$13.86
$33.18	$318.72	$58.97
$50.76	$116.35	$17.29
$12.72	$23.78	
$9.36	$38.95	

6. David Fleming owns Campus Bicycle Shop near a college campus. The shop sells new and used bicycle parts, and does a major portion of its business in adjustments and repairs. The following credit card charges and credits took place during a recent period. The bank charges a 5% discount.

Charges		Credits
$16.40	$184.16	$23.17
$18.98	$137.61	$7.26
$6.76	$24.69	$14.53
$11.75	$86.17	
$29.63		

7. List and describe in your own words four services offered to business checking account customers. (See Objective 1.)
8. The merchant accepting a credit card from a customer must pay a fee of 2% to 5% of the transaction amount. Why is the merchant willing to do this? Who really pays this fee?

4.3 Reconciliation

OBJECTIVES

1 Reconcile a bank statement with checkbook.

2 List outstanding checks.

3 Find the adjusted bank balance or current balance.

4 Use the T-account form of reconciliation.

Each month, banks send depositors, both individual and business, a bank statement. This **bank statement** shows all deposits made during the period covered by the statement, as well as all checks paid by the bank and any automated teller machine (ATM) transactions. Bank charges for the month covered by the statement are also listed. This is especially important with a business checking account because the bank charge normally varies from month to month. On occasion, a customer's check that was deposited must be returned due to **nonsufficient funds (NSF)** in the account. This amount must be subtracted from the checkbook balance along with any other charges. The business must then resolve this matter with the writer of the bad check.

CAUTION Reconciling the bank statement is an important step in maintaining accurate checking account records and in helping to avoid writing checks for which there are nonsufficient funds. In addition to nonsufficient funds charges, which can be costly, a certain amount of irresponsibility is associated with the person or business who writes "bad checks."

1 Many businesses have automatic deposits from customers and other sources made to their accounts. These amounts must be added to the checkbook balance. When the bank statement is received, it is very important to verify its accuracy. In addition, it is a good time to check the accuracy of the check register, making certain that all checks written have been listed and subtracted and that all deposits have been added to the checking account balance. This process of checking the bank statement and the check register is called **reconciliation.**

Reconciliation is best done using the forms usually printed on the back of the bank statement. A sample bank statement is shown in Figure 4.10, and an example of the reconciliation process follows. The codes on the bank statement indicate the following: RC means Returned Check, SC means Service Charge, IC means Interest Credit, ATM means Automated Teller Machine.

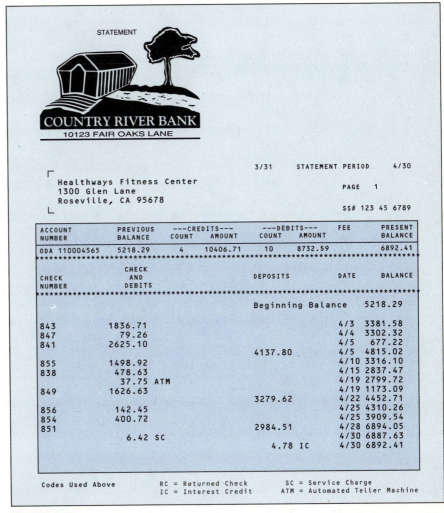

FIGURE 4.10

EXAMPLE 1
Reconciling a
Checking Account

Healthways Fitness Center received its bank statement. The statement shows a balance of $6892.41, after a bank service charge of $6.42 and an interest credit of $4.78. Healthways' checkbook now shows a balance of $7576.38. Reconcile the account using the following steps (illustrated in Figure 4.11).

SOLUTION

2 Compare the list of checks on the bank statement with the list of checks written by the firm. Checks that have been written by the firm but do not yet appear on the bank statement were not paid by the bank as of the date of the statement. These unpaid checks are called **checks outstanding**. The firm finds that the following checks are outstanding.

Number	Amount	Number	Amount
846	$42.73	857	$79.80
852	$598.71	858	$160.30
853	$68.12		

After listing the outstanding checks in the space provided on the form, total them. The total is $949.66.

The following steps are used to reconcile the checking account of Healthways Fitness Center.

Step 1.   Enter the new balance from the front of the bank statement. As given, the new balance is $6892.41. Write this number in the space provided on the reconcilement form.

Step 2.   List any deposits made that have not yet been recorded by the bank (deposits in transit). Suppose that the fitness center has deposits of $892.41 and $739.58 that are not yet recorded. These numbers are written at step 2 on the form.

Step 3.   All the numbers from steps 1 and 2 are added. Here the total is $8524.40.

Step 4.   Write down the total of outstanding checks. The total is $949.66.

Step 5.   Subtract the total in step 4 from the number in step 3. The result here is $7574.74, called the **adjusted bank balance** or the **current balance**. This number should represent the current checking account balance.

3 Now look at the firm's own records.

Step 6.   List the firm's checkbook balance. As mentioned before, the checkbook balance for Healthways Fitness Center is $7576.38. This number is entered on line 6.

Step 7.   Enter any charges not yet deducted. The check charge here is $6.42. Enter $6.42 on line 7.

Step 8.   Enter the interest credit on line 8. The interest credit here is $4.78. (This amount is interest paid on the money in the account.)

Step 9.   Subtract the charges in step 7 from line 6 and add the interest on line 8 to get $7574.74, the same result as in step 5.

Since the result from step 9 is the same as the result from step 5, the account is **balanced** (reconciled). The correct current balance in the account is $7574.74. ∎

Checks Outstanding		
Number	**Amount**	
846	$ 42	73
852	598	71
853	68	12
857	79	80
858	160	30
Total	$ 949	66

Compare the list of checks paid by the bank with your records. List and total the checks not yet paid.

(1)   Enter new balance from bank statement: $ 6892.41

(2)   List any deposits made by you and not   +   892.41
yet recorded by the bank: +   739.58
+ _____
+ _____

(3)   Add all numbers from lines above.
Total: 8524.40

(4)   Write total of checks outstanding   −   949.66

(5)   Subtract (4) from (3).
This is adjusted bank balance: $ 7574.74

To reconcile your records:

(6)   List your checkbook balance: $ 7576.38

(7)   Write the total of any fees or charges deducted
by the bank and not yet subtracted by you from
your checkbook: −   6.42

(8)   Enter interest credit: (Add to your checkbook)   +   4.78

(9)   Adjusted checkbook balance: (Subtract line (7)
from line (6) and add line (8).) $ 7574.74

New balance of your
account; these numbers
should be the same.

FIGURE 4.11

4   Many business people and accountants prefer a *T-account form* for bank reconciliation. With this method, the bank statement is written on the left and the checkbook balance is written on the right. Adjustments are made to either the bank balance or the checkbook balance, depending on which side was unaware of the transaction or charge. T-account reconciliation uses the format in Figure 4.12. The adjusted balances must agree, with the result showing the actual amount remaining in the account.

Bank Reconciliation

Bank statement balance	$		Checkbook balance	$	
Add:			Add:		
1) Add all deposits not yet recorded.			1) Add all miscellaneous credits, collections, and interest.		
Less:			Less:		
2) Subtract all outstanding checks.			2) Subtract previously deposited overdrafts and bank charges.		
Adjusted balance	$ _____		Adjusted balance	$ _____	

FIGURE 4.12

EXAMPLE 2

Using the
T-Account Form

The bank statement of Hazel Nut Gifts shows a balance of $4385.88. Checks outstanding are $292.70, $75.16, and $636.55; deposits not yet recorded are $483.11 and $89.95. Also appearing are a service charge of $7.90, a check printing charge of $9.20, a returned check for $94.25, and an interest credit of $10.06. The checkbook now shows a balance of $4055.82. Use the T-method to reconcile the checking account.

SOLUTION The reconciliation is shown in Figure 4.13. ∎

Bank Reconciliation

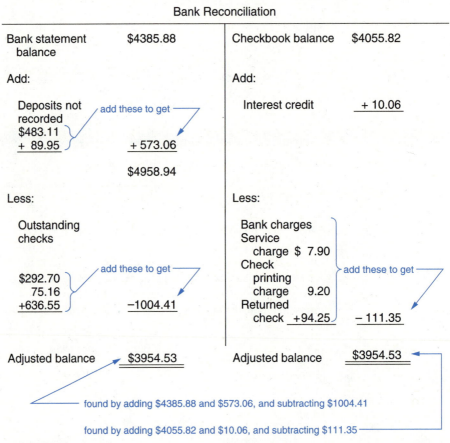

| Bank statement balance | $4385.88 | Checkbook balance | $4055.82 |

Add:

Deposits not recorded
$483.11
+ 89.95   *add these to get* → + 573.06

$4958.94

Less:

Outstanding checks

$292.70
75.16
+636.55   *add these to get* → −1004.41

Adjusted balance $3954.53

Add:

Interest credit   + 10.06

Less:

Bank charges
Service
charge $ 7.90
Check
printing
charge   9.20   *add these to get* →
Returned
check +94.25   − 111.35

Adjusted balance $3954.53

found by adding $4385.88 and $573.06, and subtracting $1004.41

found by adding $4055.82 and $10.06, and subtracting $111.35

FIGURE 4.13

If the account does not balance, either the bank or the customer has made an error. Typically, errors are made when customers forget to enter a deposit or check in the check register, transpose figures (writing 961 as 916, for example), or make an addition or subtraction error. Often customers forget to subtract one of the bank service fees from the account balance. Occasionally the bank may charge the customer an amount different from the check amount. This can be checked by comparing the number entered by the bank in magnetic ink in the lower right-hand corner of the check to the amount for which the check was written. (See Figure 4.1.) If the checking account cannot be balanced, the bank will work with the customer to help balance the account. There is often a charge for this service.

EXAMPLE 3

Reconciling a Checking Account

A checking account register is shown in Figure 4.14. A ✔ on the register indicates that the check appeared on the previous month's bank statement. Reconcile the account with a bank statement shown in Figure 4.15. (Codes on the statement have the following meaning: RC, Returned Check; SC, Service Charge; IC, Interest Credit; ATM, Automated Teller Machine.)

SOLUTION Follow the instructions on the form in Figure 4.12. The completed reconciliation is shown in T-form in Figure 4.16. ■

CHECK NO.	DATE	CHECK ISSUED TO	AMOUNT OF CHECK	✓	DATE OF DEP	AMOUNT OF DEPOSIT	BALANCE
						BALANCE BROUGHT FORWARD →	2782 95
721	7/11	MILLER'S OUTPOST	138 50	✓			2644 45
722	7/12	BARBER ADVERTISING	73 08				2571 37
723	7/18	WAYSIDE LUMBER	318 62	✓			2252 75
		DEPOSIT			7/20	1060 37	3313 12
724	7/25	I.R.S.	836 15				2476 97
725	7/26	JOHN LESSOR	450 00				2026 97
726	7/28	CHRIS BATCHELOR	67 80				1959 17
727	8/2	T.V.A.	59 25				1899 92
728	8/3	CARMICHAEL OFFICE	97 37				1802 55
		DEPOSIT			8/4	795 45	2598 00
	8/5	ATM (CASH)	80 00				2518 00

FIGURE 4.14

Bank Statement

Checks and Debits		Deposits	Date	Balance
			7/20	2325.83
73.08			7/22	2252.75
		1060.37	7/24	3313.12
836.15			7/28	2476.97
450.00	49.07RC		7/30	1977.90
59.25		3.22IC	8/4	1921.87
	80.00ATM		8/5	1841.87
	7.60SC		8/5	1834.27

FIGURE 4.15

Bank Reconciliation

Bank statement balance	$1834.27	Checkbook balance		$2518.00
Add:		Add:		
Deposits not recorded	+ 795.45	Interest credit (IC)		+3.22
	2629.72			2521.22
Less:		Less:		
Outstanding checks		Bank charges Returned check (RC)	$49.07	
$67.80 +97.37	−165.17	Service charge (SC)	+7.60	−56.67
Adjusted balance	$2464.55	Adjusted balance		$2464.55

FIGURE 4.16

4.3 Exercises

Find the current balance for each of the following accounts.

	Balance from Bank Statement	Checks Outstanding		Deposits Not Yet Recorded
1.	$4974.12	$85.13 $296.45	$172.11	$892.04 $320.50
2.	$9876.53	$921.11 $42.53	$872.10 $46.58	$92.50 $83.72
3.	$7911.42	$52.38 $95.42	$528.02 $76.50	$492.80 $38.72
4.	$8742.83	$970.42 $63.21	$782.40 $93.00	$758.92 $1921.40
5.	$27,642.40	$2781.02 $486.50	$290.00 $38.20	$5874.20 $60.80
6.	$32,489.50	$3589.70 $263.15	$18,702.15 $7269.78	$7110.65 $2218.63

Use the steps given in Example 1 and Figure 4.11 to reconcile the following accounts.

		7.		8.
Balance from bank statement		$7408.36		$4721.30
Checks outstanding (check number	851	$429.63	21	$82.74
is given first)	854	$584.09	29	$69.08
	857	$721.73	30	$124.73
	859	$29.87	32	$51.20
Deposits not yet recorded		$508.64		$758.06
		$293.82		$32.51
		$574.02		$298.06
Bank charge		$4.58		$2.00
Interest credit		$11.57		$9.58
Checkbook balance		$7012.53		$5474.60

Use the T-account form, Figure 4.12, to reconcile the following accounts.

9. A checkbook shows a balance of $3889.50. When the bank statement is received, it shows a balance of $3118.72, a returned check amounting to $123.35, a service charge of $7.80, and a check printing charge of $9.25. There are unrecorded deposits of $721.22 and $239.75, and checks outstanding of $73.18, $45.76, $21.89, and $189.76.

10. Stuart Miller received a bank statement showing a balance of $1248.63, a returned check amounting to $35.17, a service charge of $7.70, and an interest credit of $2.51. Checks outstanding are $380, $36.66, $15.29, and $143.18; deposits not yet recorded are $478.18 and $359.12. The checkbook shows a balance of $1551.16. Reconcile the checking account.

11. The bank statement of Vicky Valerin Interiors showed a bank balance of $4074.65, a returned check amounting to $168.40, a service charge of $7.08, and an interest credit of $10.18. There were unrecorded deposits of $907.82 and $1784.15, and checks outstanding of $642.55, $1082.98, $73.25 and $471.83. The checkbook shows a balance of $4661.31.

12. A bank statement has a balance of $1270.08. The checkbook balance showed $1626.63. There were unrecorded deposits of $370.64 and $219.38 and outstanding checks of $38.18, $185.10, $14.75, and $90.14. Check printing charges were $8.50; the service charge was $3.80; there was a returned check of $83.85, and an interest credit of $1.45.

13. Explain in your own words the significance of writing a bad check. What might the cost be in dollars? What are the other consequences? (See Objective 1.)

14. As a business person, what happens when you receive a bad check? What are the financial costs to the business? What are you likely to do regarding this customer? (See Objective 1.)

15. Briefly describe the importance of reconciling a checking account. What are the benefits derived from keeping good checking records? (See Objective 2.)

16. Suppose your checking account will not balance. Name four types of errors that you will look for in trying to correct this problem.

Reconcile the following checking accounts. Compare the items appearing on the bank statement to the check register. A ✔ indicates that the check appeared on the previous month's statement. (Codes indicate the following: RC means Returned Check, SC means Service Charge, CP means Check Printing Charge, IC means Interest Credit, ATM means Automated Teller Machine.)

17.

CHECK NO.	DATE	CHECK ISSUED TO	AMOUNT OF CHECK		✔	DATE OF DEP	AMOUNT OF DEPOSIT		BALANCE	
			BALANCE BROUGHT FORWARD →						6669	34
760	2/8	FLOORS TO GO	248	96					6420	38
762	2/9	HEALTHWAYS DIST.	137	22					6283	16
		DEPOSIT				2/11	618	34	6901	50
763	2/12	FRANCHISE TAX	770	41	✔				6131	09
764	2/14	FOOTHILL REPAIR	22	86	✔				6108	23
765	2/15	YELLOW PAGES	91	24					6016	99
		DEPOSIT				2/17	826	03	6843	02
766	2/17	ATM (CASH)	60	00					6783	02
767	2/18	SAN JUAN ELECTRIC	63	24					6719	78
768	2/22	HOME FINDERS	15	26					6704	52
769	2/23	WEST CONSTRUCTION	405	07					6299	45
770	2/24	RENT	525	00					5774	45
		DEPOSIT				2/26	220	16	5994	61
771	2/28	CAPITAL ALARM	135	76					5858	85

Bank Statement

Checks and Debits		Deposits	Date	Balance
			2/14	5876.07
91.24		618.34	2/16	6403.17
248.96		826.03	2/17	6980.24
	60.00 ATM		2/19	6920.24
137.22			2/21	6783.02
	198.17RC		2/22	6584.85
15.26		8.12IC	2/24	6577.71
405.07	4.85CP		2/26	6167.79
	6.28SC		2/27	6161.51
525.00			2/28	5636.51

18.

CHECK NO.	DATE	CHECK ISSUED TO	AMOUNT OF CHECK		✓	DATE OF DEP	AMOUNT OF DEPOSIT		BALANCE	
		BALANCE BROUGHT FORWARD →							1876	93
318	9/6	MUIR TRAVEL	76	18	✓				1800	75
319	9/6	NORTH COAST TOURS	322	40					1478	35
320	9/8	AMES PHOTO	41	12	✓				1437	23
		DEPOSIT				9/10	851	62	2288	85
321	9/14	AMERICAN FLYERS	970	40					1318	45
322	9/15	REVERE INTER.	386	92					931	53
		DEPOSIT				9/18	995	20	1926	73
324	9/20	IDAHO EDISON	68	17					1858	56
325	9/20	WESSON SUPPLY	195	76					1662	80
326	9/22	PARKER PACKERS	348	33					1314	47
327	9/23	FREEZE DRY SUPPLY	215	84					1098	63
328	9/24	COUNTY WATER	169	56					929	07
		DEPOSIT				9/28	418	35	1347	42

Bank Statement

Checks and Debits		Deposits	Date	Balance
			9/9	1759.63
		851.62	9/10	2611.25
970.40			9/15	1640.85
322.40			9/18	1318.45
386.92	78.93RC	995.20	9/20	1847.80
195.76		6.52IC	9/23	1658.56
348.33	7.80SC		9/25	1302.43

CHAPTER 4 QUICK REVIEW

TOPIC	APPROACH	EXAMPLE
4.1 Checking account service charges	There is usually a checking account maintenance charge and often a per check charge.	Find the monthly checking account service charge for a business with 36 checks and transactions, given a monthly maintenance charge of $7.50 and a $.20 per check charge. $7.50 + 36($.20) = $7.50 + $7.20 = $14.70

TOPIC	APPROACH	EXAMPLE
4.2 Banking services offered	The checking account customer must be aware of various banking services.	Overdraft protection Stop payment order Cashier's check Money order Noncustomer check cashing Notary service Telephone transfer

4.2 Depositing credit card transactions	Subtract credit card refunds from total credit card sales to find the net deposit. Then subtract the discount charge from this total.	**Charges** **Credits**
		$28.15 $78.59 $21.86
		$36.92 $63.82 $79.62
		(a) Find total charges.
		  $28.15 + $36.92 + $78.59 + $63.82 = $207.48
		(b) Find total credits.
		  $21.86 + $79.62 = $101.48
		(c) Find net deposit.
		  $207.48 − $101.48 = $106
		(d) Given a 3% discount charge, find the discount amount.
		  $106 × .03 = $3.18

4.3 Reconciliation of a checking account	Periodically, verify checking account records with those of the bank or financial institution, using the bank statement.	Verify all checks, deposits, service charges, and interest. The checkbook balance and bank balance must be the same for the account to reconcile, or balance.

S U M M A R Y   E X E R C I S E

Philip Howrigan owns a used book store and accepts credit cards to better serve his customers. During a recent month Howrigan had credit card sales slips amounting to $389.20 and credits of $25.18. The discount fee that he pays on credit card deposits is $3\frac{1}{2}\%$.

When receiving his bank statement the balance was $2984.61. The checks outstanding were found to be $2.58, $39.12, $71.62, $85.30, $117.20, $89.10, and $38.20. Howrigan had deposits that were not recorded in the amounts of $72.10, $158.96, $60.51, and $38.20, and his bank credit card deposits and credit slips.

Find the current balance in Philip Howrigan's checking account.

CHAPTER 4 REVIEW EXERCISES

Complete the check stubs for Saving Center. The balance brought forward for stub 6381 is $43,150.23. [4.1]

Checks Written:

Number	Date	To	For	Amount
6381	July 5	Town Properties	Rent	$8400.00
6382	July 7	Swanson, Inc.	Bookkeeping	$380.50
6383	July 11	County Billing	Utilities	$375.18
6384	July 12	Western Supply	Merchandise	$14,320.15
6385	July 14	Fair Oaks Post	Advertising	$5621.82

Deposits:

Date	Amount
July 6	$180.18
July 8	$917.13
July 9	$72.18
July 10	$228.73
July 13	$1296.15

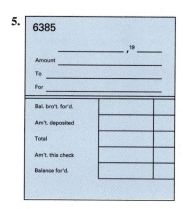

1. **6381**

_____, 19 _____

Amount _____
To _____
For _____

Bal. bro't. for'd.		
Am't. deposited		
Total		
Am't. this check		
Balance for'd.		

2. **6382**

_____, 19 _____

Amount _____
To _____
For _____

Bal. bro't. for'd.		
Am't. deposited		
Total		
Am't. this check		
Balance for'd.		

3. **6383**

_____, 19 _____

Amount _____
To _____
For _____

Bal. bro't. for'd.		
Am't. deposited		
Total		
Am't. this check		
Balance for'd.		

4. **6384**

_____, 19 _____

Amount _____
To _____
For _____

Bal. bro't. for'd.		
Am't. deposited		
Total		
Am't. this check		
Balance for'd.		

5. **6385**

_____, 19 _____

Amount _____
To _____
For _____

Bal. bro't. for'd.		
Am't. deposited		
Total		
Am't. this check		
Balance for'd.		

The following credit card transactions were made at Roanoke Lumber Company. Use this information to solve exercises 6 through 9. [4.2]

Charges		Credits
$21.63	$89.98	$17.73
$75.98	$37.15	$75.26
$29.67	$216.82	$21.28
$113.72	$77.65	
$79.16	$186.39	

6. Find the total charges for the store.

7. What is the total amount of the credit?

8. Find the amount of the net deposit when these credit card transactions are deposited.

9. If the bank charges the retailer $2\frac{1}{2}\%$ discount charge, find the amount of the discount charge at the statement date.

Solve the following word problems.

10. Melissa Dietz Marketing received a bank statement showing a balance of $2497.26, a returned check amounting to $70.34, a service charge of $15.42, and an interest credit of $5.02. Checks outstanding are $760, $73.32, $30.58, and $286.38; deposits not yet recorded are $956.36 and $718.24. The checkbook shows a balance of $3102.32. Use Figure 4.11 to reconcile the checking account. [4.3]

11. The bank statement of Superior Bushings showed a bank balance of $8149.30, a returned check amounting to $336.80, a service charge of $14.16, and an interest credit of $20.36. There were unrecorded deposits of $1815.64 and $3568.30, and checks outstanding of $1285.10, $2165.96, $146.50, and $943.66. The checkbook shows a balance of $9322.62. Use Figure 4.12 to reconcile the checking account. [4.3]

12. Use Figure 4.12 and the following check register and bank statement to reconcile the checking account. Compare the items appearing on the bank statement to the check register. A ✔ indicates that the check appeared on the previous month's statement. (Codes indicate the following: RC means Returned Check, SC means Service Charge, CP means Check Printing Charge, IC means Interest Credit, ATM means Automated Teller Machine.) [4.3]

CHECK NO.	DATE	CHECK ISSUED TO	AMOUNT OF CHECK		✓	DATE OF DEP.	AMOUNT OF DEPOSIT		BALANCE	
			BALANCE BROUGHT FORWARD →						7682	07
662	3/3	Action Packing Supplies	451	16					7230	91
663	3/3	Crown Paper	772	34	✓				6458	57
664	3/5	Moore Forms	261	95	✓				6196	62
		Deposit				3/7	913	28	7109	90
665	3/10	Fairless Water District	72	37					7037	53
666	3/12	Audia Temporary	340	88					6696	65
667	3/13	Lionel Toys	618	65					6078	
668	3/14	Fairless Hills Power	100	50					5977	50
		Deposit				3/16	450	18	6427	68
		Deposit				3/18	163	55	6591	23
669	3/20	Hunt Roofing	238	50					6352	73
670	3/22	Standard Brands	315	62					6037	11
671	3/23	Pennye Saver Products	67	29					5969	82
		Deposit				3/24	830	75	6800	57

Bank Statement

Checks and Debits		Deposits	Date	Balance
			3/5	6647.78
		913.28	3/7	7561.06
451.16			3/11	7109.90
340.88	82.15RC	450.18	3/16	7137.05
72.37		22.48IC	3/20	7087.16
618.65		163.55	3/22	6632.06
238.50	12.70SC		3/26	6380.86

5

Payroll

Preparing the payroll is one of the most important jobs in any office. Payroll records must be accurate, and the payroll must be prepared on time so that the necessary checks can be written. The first step in preparing the payroll is to determine the **gross earnings** (the total amount earned) for each employee. There are many methods used to find gross earnings and several of these are discussed in this chapter. A number of **deductions** may be subtracted from gross earnings to find **net pay,** the amount actually received by the employee. These various deductions also will be discussed in this chapter. Finally, the employer must keep records to maintain an efficient business and to satisfy legal requirements.

5.1 Gross Earnings (Wages and Salaries)

OBJECTIVES

1 Use hourly rate to calculate gross earnings.

2 Use time-and-a-half rate for over 40 hours to find overtime earnings.

3 Use overtime premium method of calculating gross earnings.

4 Find overtime earnings using time-and-a-half rate for over 8 hours of work per day.

5 Understand double-time, shift differential, and split-shift premiums.

6 Find equivalent earnings for different pay periods.

7 Find gross earnings when overtime is paid to salaried employees.

Several methods are used for finding an employee's pay. Two of these methods, salaries and wages, are discussed in this section; two additional methods, piecework and commission, will be discussed in the next two sections.

In many businesses, the first step in preparing the payroll is to look at the **time card** maintained for each employee. An example of a time card is shown in Figure 5.1. The card includes the dates of the pay period; the employee's name and other personal information; the days, times, and hours worked; the total number of hours worked; and a signature verification by the employee as to the accuracy of the card. While the card in Figure 5.1 is filled in by hand, many companies use a time clock that automatically stamps the days, dates, and times on the card. The information on these cards is then transferred to a **payroll ledger** (a chart showing all payroll information), as shown in Example 1.

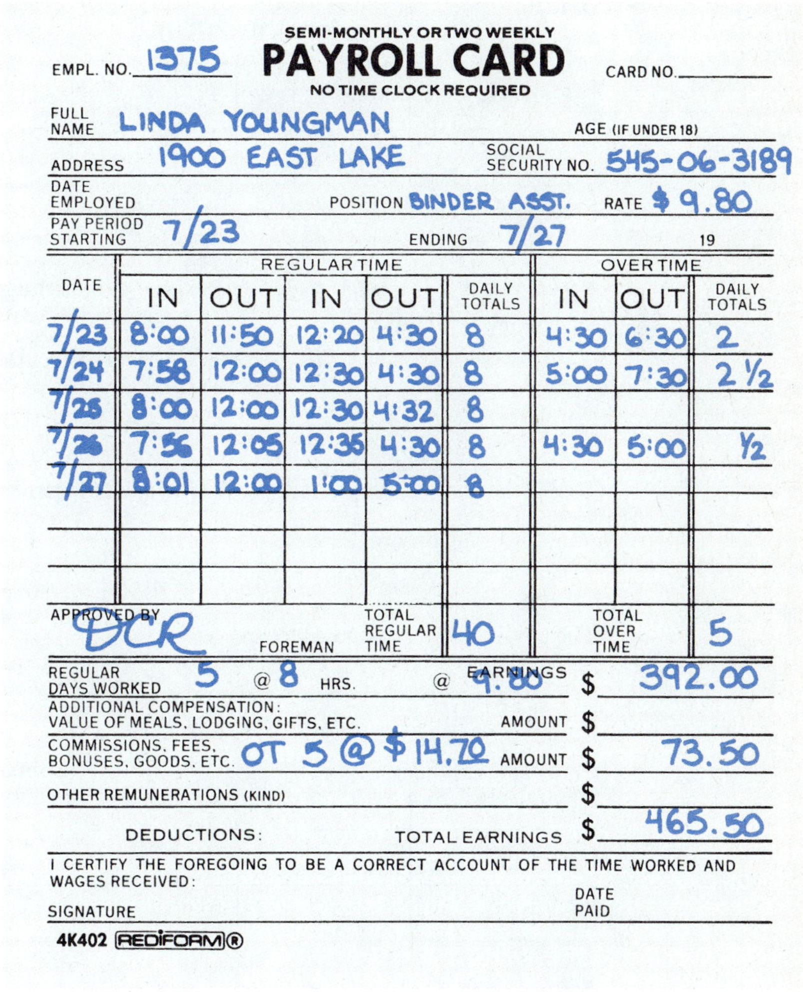

SEMI-MONTHLY OR TWO WEEKLY

PAYROLL CARD

NO TIME CLOCK REQUIRED

EMPL. NO. 1375   CARD NO. _____

FULL NAME LINDA YOUNGMAN   AGE (IF UNDER 18)

ADDRESS 1900 EAST LAKE   SOCIAL SECURITY NO. 545-06-3189

DATE EMPLOYED   POSITION BINDER ASST.   RATE $ 9.80

PAY PERIOD STARTING 7/23   ENDING 7/27   19

DATE	REGULAR TIME					OVER TIME		
	IN	OUT	IN	OUT	DAILY TOTALS	IN	OUT	DAILY TOTALS
7/23	8:00	11:50	12:20	4:30	8	4:30	6:30	2
7/24	7:58	12:00	12:30	4:30	8	5:00	7:30	2 1/2
7/25	8:00	12:00	12:30	4:32	8			
7/26	7:56	12:05	12:35	4:30	8	4:30	5:00	1/2
7/27	8:01	12:00	1:00	5:00	8			

APPROVED BY *DCR*

FOREMAN   TOTAL REGULAR TIME 40   TOTAL OVER TIME 5

REGULAR DAYS WORKED 5 @ 8 HRS.   @ 9.80 EARNINGS $ 392.00

ADDITIONAL COMPENSATION: VALUE OF MEALS, LODGING, GIFTS, ETC.   AMOUNT $

COMMISSIONS, FEES, BONUSES, GOODS, ETC. OT 5 @ $14.70 AMOUNT $ 73.50

OTHER REMUNERATIONS (KIND) $

DEDUCTIONS: TOTAL EARNINGS $ 465.50

I CERTIFY THE FOREGOING TO BE A CORRECT ACCOUNT OF THE TIME WORKED AND WAGES RECEIVED:

SIGNATURE   DATE PAID

4K402 REDIFORM®

FIGURE 5.1

1 Linda Youngman, whose time card is shown in Figure 5.1, is paid an **hourly wage** of $9.80 (see the time card). Her **gross earnings** would be calculated with the formula

Gross earnings = Number of hours worked × Rate per hour.

For example, if Youngman works 7 hours at $9.80 per hour, her gross earnings would be

$$\text{Gross earnings} = 7 \times \$9.80 = \$68.60.$$

EXAMPLE 1   Complete the following payroll ledger.

Completing a
Payroll Ledger

Employee	Hours Worked							Total Hours	Rate	Gross Earnings
	S	M	T	W	Th	F	S			
Goshorn, S.	–	2	4	8	6	3	–		$8.43	
Adams, P.	–	$3\frac{1}{2}$	$2\frac{1}{4}$	$7\frac{3}{4}$	$6\frac{1}{4}$	$7\frac{1}{2}$	–		$6.08	

SOLUTION   The first step is to find the total number of hours worked by each person.

$$\text{Goshorn: } 2 + 4 + 8 + 6 + 3 = 23 \text{ hours}$$

$$\text{Adams: } 3\frac{1}{2} + 2\frac{1}{4} + 7\frac{3}{4} + 6\frac{1}{4} + 7\frac{1}{2} = 27\frac{1}{4} \text{ hours}$$

To find the gross earnings, multiply the number of hours worked and the rate per hour.

$$\text{Goshorn: } 23 \times \$8.43 = \$193.89$$

$$\text{Adams: } 27.25 \times \$6.08 = \$165.68 \qquad 27\frac{1}{4} = 27.25 \text{ hours}$$

The payroll ledger can now be completed.

Employee	Hours Worked							Total Hours	Rate	Gross Earnings
	S	M	T	W	Th	F	S			
Goshorn, S.	–	2	4	8	6	3	–	23	$8.43	$193.89
Adams, P.	–	$3\frac{1}{2}$	$2\frac{1}{4}$	$7\frac{3}{4}$	$6\frac{1}{4}$	$7\frac{1}{2}$	–	$27\frac{1}{4}$	$6.08	$165.68

2   The **Fair Labor Standards Act,** which covers the majority of full-time employees in this country, was passed by Congress in 1938. It establishes minimum hourly wages, overtime pay, and other labor standards for workers. This law does not cover all employees. Those specifically excluded from coverage are business executives and administrators; commission salespeople; professionals such as doctors, lawyers, and teachers; employees of small retail businesses; and many seasonal agricultural workers. The law states that **overtime** (a higher than usual hourly rate) must be paid for all hours worked in excess of 40 per week. A great number of companies not covered by the Fair Labor Standards Act have voluntarily followed the practice of paying a **time-and-a-half rate** ($1\frac{1}{2}$ times the normal rate) for any work over 40 hours per week. With the time-and-a-half rate, gross earnings are found by the formula

Gross earnings =
Earnings at regular rate + Earnings at time-and-a-half rate.

EXAMPLE 2

Completing a Payroll Ledger with Overtime

Complete the following payroll ledger.

Employee	\multicolumn{7}{c}{Hours Worked}			\multicolumn{2}{c}{Total Hours}	Reg. Rate	\multicolumn{3}{c}{Gross Earnings}		
	S	M	T	W	Th	F	S	Reg.	O.T.	Reg. Rate	Reg.	O.T.	Total
Neal, S.	6	$9\frac{1}{2}$	$8\frac{1}{4}$	$7\frac{1}{2}$	$8\frac{3}{4}$	$4\frac{3}{4}$	–			$7.08			
Keen, C.	–	$9\frac{1}{2}$	7	9	$6\frac{1}{4}$	$9\frac{3}{4}$	$4\frac{3}{4}$			$9.48			

SOLUTION First find the total number of hours worked.

$$\text{Neal: } 6 + 9\frac{1}{2} + 8\frac{1}{4} + 7\frac{1}{2} + 8\frac{3}{4} + 4\frac{3}{4} = 44\frac{3}{4} \text{ hours}$$

$$\text{Keen: } 9\frac{1}{2} + 7 + 9 + 6\frac{1}{4} + 9\frac{3}{4} + 4\frac{3}{4} = 46\frac{1}{4} \text{ hours}$$

Both employees worked more than 40 hours. Gross earnings at the regular rate can now be found as discussed previously. Neal earned $40 \times \$7.08 = \$283.20$ at the regular rate, and Keen earned $40 \times \$9.48 = \$379.20$ at the regular rate. To find overtime earnings, first find the number of overtime hours worked by each employee.

$$\text{Neal: } 44\frac{3}{4} - 40 = 4\frac{3}{4} \text{ overtime hours}$$

$$\text{Keen: } 46\frac{1}{4} - 40 = 6\frac{1}{4} \text{ overtime hours}$$

The regular rate given for each employee can be used to find the time-and-a-half rate.

$$\text{Neal: } 1\frac{1}{2} \times \$7.08 = \$10.62$$

$$\text{Keen: } 1\frac{1}{2} \times \$9.48 = \$14.22$$

Now find the overtime earnings.

$$\text{Neal: } 4\frac{3}{4} \text{ hours} \times \$10.62 \text{ per hour } = \$50.45 \qquad \text{(rounded to the nearest cent)}$$

$$\text{Keen: } 6\frac{1}{4} \text{ hours} \times \$14.22 \text{ per hour } = \$88.88 \qquad \text{(rounded)}$$

The ledger can now be completed.

Employee	\multicolumn{7}{c}{Hours Worked}							Total Hours		Reg. Rate	\multicolumn{3}{c}{Gross Earnings}		
	S	M	T	W	Th	F	S	Reg.	O.T.	Reg. Rate	Reg.	O.T.	Total
Neal, S.	6	$9\frac{1}{2}$	$8\frac{1}{4}$	$7\frac{1}{2}$	$8\frac{3}{4}$	$4\frac{3}{4}$	–	40	$4\frac{3}{4}$	$7.08	$283.20	$50.45	$333.65
Keen, C.	–	$9\frac{1}{2}$	7	9	$6\frac{1}{4}$	$9\frac{3}{4}$	$4\frac{3}{4}$	40	$6\frac{1}{4}$	$9.48	$379.20	$88.88	$468.08

3 Gross earnings with overtime is sometimes calculated with the **overtime premium method** (sometimes called the **overtime excess method**). With this method, which produces the same result as the method just described, the total hours at the regular rate are added to the overtime hours at one half of the regular rate to arrive at gross earnings.

$$\text{Total hours} \times \text{Regular rate } = \text{Straight-time earnings}$$

$$+ \text{ Overtime hours} \times \frac{1}{2} \text{ regular rate } = \text{Overtime premium (Overtime excess)}$$

$$= \text{Gross earnings}$$

EXAMPLE 3
Using the Overtime Premium Method

Lucinda Turley worked 40 regular hours and 12 overtime hours during the week. If her regular rate of pay is $12.38 per hour, find her total gross pay using the overtime premium method.

SOLUTION   The total number of hours worked by Turley is 52 (40 + 12) and her overtime premium is $6.19 $\left(\frac{1}{2} \times \$12.38\right)$.

$$52 \text{ hours} \times \$12.38 = \$643.76 \qquad \text{regular-rate earnings}$$
$$12 \text{ overtime hours} \times \$6.19 = \underline{\ \ \$74.28} \qquad \text{overtime}$$
$$\$718.04 \qquad \text{gross earnings} \ \blacksquare$$

NOTE Some companies prefer the overtime premium method since it readily identifies the extra cost of overtime labor and can be seen easily. Quite often, excessive use of overtime indicates inefficiencies in management.

4   Some companies pay the time-and-a-half rate for all time worked over 8 hours in any one day, no matter how many hours are worked in a week. This *daily overtime* is shown in the next example.

EXAMPLE 4

Finding Overtime Each Day

Mark Spangler worked 10 hours on Monday, 5 on Tuesday, 7 on Wednesday, and 12 on Thursday. His regular rate of pay is $10.10. Find his gross earnings for the week.

	S	M	T	W	T	F	S	Total Hours
Reg.	–	8	5	7	8	–	–	28
O.T.	–	2	–	–	4	–	–	6

SOLUTION   Spangler worked more than 8 hours on both Monday and Thursday. On Monday, he had $10 - 8 = 2$ hours of overtime, with $12 - 8 = 4$ hours of overtime on Thursday. For the week, he earned $2 + 4 = 6$ hours of overtime. His regular hours are 8 on Monday, 5 on Tuesday, 7 on Wednesday, and 8 on Thursday, or

$$8 + 5 + 7 + 8 = 28$$

hours at the regular rate. His hourly earnings are $10.10, giving

$$28 \times \$10.10 = \$282.80$$

at the regular rate. If the regular rate is $10.10, the time-and-a-half rate is

$$\$10.10 \times 1\frac{1}{2} = \$15.15.$$

He earned time and a half for 6 hours.

$$6 \times \$15.15 = \$90.90$$

Gross earnings are found by adding regular earnings and overtime earnings.

$$\$282.80 + \$90.90 = \$373.70 \quad \blacksquare$$

NOTE   There are many careers that require unusual schedules and do not pay overtime for over 40 hours worked in one week or over 8 hours worked in one day. An obvious example is the work schedule of a firefighter where the employee may work 24 hours and then get 48 hours off.

5   Other **premium payment** plans include **double time** for holidays and, in some industries, Saturdays and Sundays. A **shift-differential** is often given to compensate employees for working less desirable hours. For example, an additional amount per hour or per shift might be paid to swing shift (4 P.M. to midnight) and graveyard (midnight to 8:00 A.M.) employees.

Restaurant employees and telephone operators often receive a **split-shift premium.** The employees' hours are staggered so that the employees are on the job only during the busiest times. For example, an employee may work 4 hours, be off 4 hours, then work 4 hours. The employee is paid a premium because of this less desirable schedule.

Some employers offer **compensatory time,** or **comp time,** for overtime hours worked. Instead of receiving additional money, an employee is given time off from the regular work schedule as compensation for overtime hours already worked. Quite often, the compensatory time is given at $1\frac{1}{2}$ times the overtime hours worked. For example, 12 hours might be given as compensation for 8 hours of previously worked overtime. Occasionally an employee is given a choice of overtime pay or comp time. Many companies reserve the use of compensatory time for their supervisors or managerial employees. Also, compensatory time is very common in government agencies.

6 The second common method of finding gross earnings uses a **salary,** an amount given as so much per **pay period** (time between pay checks). Common pay periods are weekly, biweekly, semimonthly, and monthly.

TABLE 5.1   Common Pay Periods

Monthly	12 paychecks each year
Semimonthly	Twice each month; 24 paychecks each year
Biweekly	Every two weeks; 26 paychecks each year
Weekly	52 paychecks each year

NOTE One person's salary might be a certain amount per month, while someone else might earn a certain amount every two weeks. Many people receive an annual salary, divided among shorter pay periods.

EXAMPLE 5
Determining Equivalent Salaries

Michael Anderson receives a weekly salary of $273, Beth Darden a biweekly salary of $1686, Debbie Roper a semimonthly salary of $736, and Brett Sullivan a monthly salary of $1818. For each worker, find the following: (a) earnings per year, (b) earnings per month, and (c) earnings per week.

SOLUTION
Michael Anderson's earnings are calculated as follows.

(a) $273 \times 52 = \$14,196$ per year
(b) $14,196 \div 12 = \$1183$ per month
(c) $273 per week

Beth Darden's earnings are found as shown.

(a) $1686 \times 26 = \$43,836$ per year (biweekly = 26 per year)
(b) $43,836 \div 12 = \$3653$ per month
(c) $1686 \div 2 = \$843$ per week

Debbie Roper's earnings follow.

(a) $736 \times 24 = \$17,664$ per year
(b) $736 \times 2 = \$1472$ per month
(c) $17,664 \div 52 = \$339.69$

Brett Sullivan has the following earnings.

(a) $1818 \times 12 = \$21,816$ per year
(b) $1818 per month
(c) $21,816 \div 52 = \$419.54$ ■

7 A salary is paid for the performance of a certain job, without keeping track of the number or hours worked. However, the Fair Labor Standards Act requires that certain salaried positions receive additional compensation for overtime. Just as with wage-earners, the salaried employee is often paid time and a half for all hours worked over the normal number of hours per week.

EXAMPLE 6
Finding Overtime for Salaried Employees

Alice Lavin is paid $448 a week as an executive assistant. If her normal work week is 40 hours, find her gross earnings for a week in which she works 46 hours.

SOLUTION The executive assistant's salary has an hourly equivalent of

$$\frac{\$448}{40 \text{ hours}} = \$11.20 \text{ per hour.}$$

Since she must be paid overtime at the rate of $1\frac{1}{2}$ times her regular pay, she will get $16.80 per hour ($1\frac{1}{2} \times \$11.20$) for overtime. Her gross earnings for the week are calculated as follows.

Salary for 40 hours	$= \$448.00$	regular-rate earnings
Overtime for 6 hours ($6 \times \$16.80$)	$= \underline{\ \ 100.80}$	overtime
	$\$548.80$	gross earnings ∎

EXAMPLE 7
Finding Gross Earnings with Overtime

A conference coordinator is paid a salary of $324 per week. If his regular work week is 36 hours, find his gross earnings for a week in which he works 46 hours.

SOLUTION The coordinator's salary has an hourly equivalent of

$$\frac{\$324}{36 \text{ hours}} = \$9 \text{ per hour.}$$

Since he is paid $1\frac{1}{2}$ times the regular rate per hour, he will receive $13.50 per hour ($1\frac{1}{2} \times \$9$) for overtime. His gross earnings for the week are found as follows.

Salary for 36 hours	$= \$324$	regular-rate earnings
Overtime for 10 hours ($10 \times \$13.50$)	$= \underline{\ \ 135}$	overtime
	$\$459$	gross earnings ∎

Calculator Approach to Example 7

Store the weekly salary in memory for later use at the same time the hourly rate is found.

$$324 \boxed{M+} \quad \boxed{\div} \ 36 \ \boxed{=} \ 9$$

Without clearing the calculator, find the time-and-a-half rate by multiplying by $1\frac{1}{2}$ (the decimal 1.5) and also by 10, the number of overtime hours ($46 - 36 = 10$).

$$\boxed{\times} \ 1.5 \ \boxed{\times} \ 10 \ \boxed{=} \ 135$$

Finally, recall $324 from memory and add to get the gross earnings for the week.

$$\boxed{+} \quad \boxed{MR} \quad \boxed{=} \ 459$$

Some calculators can do the steps above without all the equal signs. The calculation would look like this.

$$324 \boxed{M+} \quad \boxed{\div} \ 36 \ \boxed{\times} \ 1.5 \ \boxed{\times} \ 10 \ \boxed{M+} \quad \boxed{MR} \ 459$$

This abbreviated form is used throughout the text.

5.1 Exercises

Find the number of regular hours and overtime hours (any hours over 40) for each of the following employees. Then calculate the overtime rate (time and a half) for each employee.

	Employee	S	M	T	W	Th	F	S	Reg. Hrs.	O.T. Hrs.	Reg. Rate	O.T. Rate
1.	Glen, D.	—	8	6	7	11	5	2			$6.12	
2.	Paluch, M.	—	$7\frac{1}{2}$	8	$8\frac{1}{2}$	9	$8\frac{1}{2}$	8			$9.04	
3.	Gowing, J.	4	$3\frac{3}{4}$	$9\frac{1}{2}$	$8\frac{3}{4}$	$7\frac{3}{4}$	5	—			$6.20	
4.	Ertl, J.	$8\frac{1}{2}$	9	$7\frac{1}{2}$	8	$9\frac{3}{4}$	$8\frac{1}{2}$	—			$8.10	
5.	Noble, S.	—	$7\frac{1}{2}$	8	$9\frac{3}{4}$	$8\frac{1}{2}$	$9\frac{1}{2}$	—			$10.28	
6.	Camp, J.	—	8	$7\frac{1}{2}$	9	$7\frac{1}{4}$	$6\frac{1}{2}$	7			$9.80	

Find the earnings at the regular rate, the earnings at the overtime rate, and the gross earnings for each of the employees in problems 1–6.

7. Glen, D.

8. Paluch, M.

9. Gowing, J.

10. Ertl, J.

11. Noble, S.

12. Camp, J.

Complete the following partial payroll ledger by finding the overtime rate, the amount of earnings at regular pay, the amount at overtime pay, and the total gross wages for each employee.

	Employee	Total Hours Reg.	Total Hours O.T.	Reg. Rate	O.T. Rate	Gross Earnings Reg.	Gross Earnings O.T.	Gross Earnings Total
13.	Burnett, B.	$37\frac{1}{2}$	—	$5.10				
14.	Hadd, D.	$39\frac{1}{4}$	—	$7.90				
15.	Cooper, D.	40	$5\frac{1}{2}$	$6.20				
16.	Quinlan, P.	40	$6\frac{3}{4}$	$8.06				
17.	Stowe, L.	40	$3\frac{1}{2}$	$8.18				
18.	Wolfe, C.	40	$4\frac{3}{4}$	$7.10				

Some companies use the overtime premium method to determine gross earnings. Use this method to complete the following partial payroll ledger. Overtime is paid at time-and-a-half rate for all hours over 40.

	Employee	S	M	T	W	Th	F	S	Total Hours	Reg. Rate	O.T. Hours	O.T. Pre-mium	Gross Earnings Reg.	Gross Earnings O.T.	Gross Earnings Total
19.	Granger, L.	8	5	12	7	9	10	—		$5.80					
20.	Harr, M.	$7\frac{1}{2}$	$10\frac{1}{4}$	5	$9\frac{1}{2}$	$8\frac{1}{4}$	10	—		$6.10					
21.	Miller, E.	—	9	12	$11\frac{1}{2}$	$9\frac{3}{4}$	10	—		$10.60					
22.	Martin, M.	—	$5\frac{1}{4}$	$8\frac{3}{4}$	10	12	$10\frac{1}{2}$	7		$7.50					
23.	Carlson, K.	—	$11\frac{1}{4}$	10	$9\frac{3}{4}$	$8\frac{1}{2}$	9	—		$8.20					
24.	Reese, M.	$8\frac{1}{2}$	7	$9\frac{3}{4}$	—	$10\frac{1}{2}$	12	—		$6.90					

As mentioned in the text, some companies pay overtime for all time worked over 8 hours in a given day. Use this method to complete the following partial payroll ledger. Overtime is paid at time-and-a-half rate.

		Hours Worked							Total Hours		Reg. Rate	O.T. Rate	Gross Earnings		
	Employee	S	M	T	W	Th	F	S	Reg.	O.T.			Reg.	O.T.	Total
25.	Hickman, C.	–	11	8	6	5	10	–			$5.98				
26.	Kelley, R.	–	$9\frac{1}{2}$	$8\frac{1}{4}$	7	$8\frac{3}{4}$	$9\frac{3}{4}$	–			$5.10				
27.	Harris, D.	9	$7\frac{1}{2}$	8	–	$10\frac{3}{4}$	8	–			$6.70				
28.	Clouse, R.	–	9	10	8	6	$9\frac{3}{4}$	–			$8.60				
29.	Fridl, P.	–	$9\frac{1}{2}$	$8\frac{1}{2}$	$7\frac{3}{4}$	8	$9\frac{1}{2}$	–			$10.20				
30.	Linton, E.	6	8	$6\frac{1}{2}$	$8\frac{3}{4}$	–	$10\frac{1}{4}$	–			$7.20				

31. Explain in your own words what premium payment plans are. Select a premium payment plan and describe it. (See Objective 5.)

32. If you were given a choice of overtime pay or compensatory time, which would you choose? Why? (See Objective 5.)

Find the equivalent earnings for each of the following salaries as indicated.

Earnings

	Weekly	Biweekly	Semimonthly	Monthly	Annual
33.	$335	————	————	————	————
34.	————	————	$550	————	————
35.	————	$852	————	————	————
36.	————	————	————	$1150	————
37.	————	————	$620	————	————
38.	$436	————	————	————	————
39.	————	————	————	$2680	————
40.	————	$768	————	————	————
41.	————	————	————	————	$17,880
42.	————	————	————	————	$26,100

Find the weekly gross earnings for the following people who are on salary and are paid time and a half for overtime. (Hint: Round overtime amounts to the nearest cent.)

Employee	Regular Hours per Week	Weekly Salary	Hours Worked	Weekly Gross Earnings
43. Evaldo, F.	40	$380	46	_____
44. Diest, E.	40	$290	42	_____
45. McHugh, C.	45	$418	50	_____
46. Lerner, M.	36	$320	40	_____
47. Russell, G.	32	$450	44	_____
48. Biron, C.	30	$484	45	_____

Solve each of the following word problems.

49. Last week, Melissa Lerner worked 52 hours. Find her gross earnings for the week if she is paid $6.80 per hour and earns time and a half for all hours over 40.

50. An employee is paid $10.36 per hour for straight time, and time and a half for all hours over 40 worked in a week. Find her gross earnings for a week in which she worked 48 hours.

51. Kelly Bell earns $7.80 per hour and is paid time and a half for all time over 8 hours worked on a given day. Find his gross earnings for a week in which he worked the following hours: Monday, $9\frac{1}{2}$; Tuesday, 7; Wednesday, $10\frac{3}{4}$; Thursday, $4\frac{1}{2}$; and Friday, $8\frac{3}{4}$ hours.

52. Glenn Russell worked 10 hours on Monday, $9\frac{3}{4}$ hours on Tuesday, $5\frac{1}{2}$ hours on Wednesday, 12 hours on Thursday, and $7\frac{1}{4}$ hours on Friday. His regular rate of pay is $9.50 an hour, with time and a half paid for all hours over 8 worked on a given day. Find his gross earnings for the week.

53. Chalon Bridges is paid $485 a week as a tax consultant. Her normal work week is 40 hours. She is paid time and a half for overtime. Find her gross earnings for a week in which she worked 42 hours.

54. An employee at Valley Feed Stores is paid $298 for a normal work week of 35 hours. If she is paid time and a half for overtime, find her gross earnings for a week in which she worked 48 hours.

55. Andy Sargent, manager of the local Book House, is paid a salary of $532 per week and has a normal work week of 40 hours. Find his gross earnings in a week in which he worked 56 hours.

56. Arnold Parker, Senior Vice-President of Tours International, worked 50 hours this week. If he is paid a weekly salary of $900 and has a normal work week of 45 hours, find his gross earnings for the week.

57. An employee earns $420 weekly. Find the equivalent earnings if paid (a) biweekly, (b) semimonthly, (c) monthly, and (d) annually.

58. A department supervisor is paid $34,320 annually. Find the equivalent earnings if this amount is paid (a) weekly, (b) biweekly, (c) semimonthly, and (d) monthly.

59. Semimonthly pay periods result in 24 paychecks per year. Biweekly pay periods result in 26 paychecks per year. Which of these pay periods gives three checks in two months of the year? Will it always be the same two months? Explain.

60. Which would you prefer: a monthly pay period or a weekly pay period? What special budgetary considerations might you consider regarding the pay period you choose?

5.2 Gross Earnings (Commission)

OBJECTIVES

1 Find gross earnings using commission rate × sales ($P = R \times B$).

2 Determine commission using a variable commission rate.

3 Use salary and commission rate to find gross earnings.

4 Use a drawing account and quota to find gross earnings.

5 Determine override as part of gross earnings.

Many people in sales and marketing are paid on **commission,** usually a fixed percent of sales. This is an incentive system of compensation and the commissions are designed to produce maximum employee output, since pay is directly dependent on sales. This section discusses all of the common types of sales commissions.

1 With a **straight commission,** the salesperson is paid a fixed percent of sales. Gross earnings are found by the following formula.

$$P \quad = \quad R \quad \times \quad B$$
$$\text{Gross earnings} \ = \ \text{Commission rate} \ \times \ \text{Amount of sales}$$

EXAMPLE 1
Determining Earnings Using Commission

Find the earnings of a real estate broker selling a house for $92,500, if the broker receives a 6% commission.

SOLUTION The broker would receive

$$6\% \times \$92,500 = 0.06 \times \$92,500 = \$5550$$

for selling the house. ∎

EXAMPLE 2
Subtracting Returns When Using Commissions

Karin Sandberg had sales of $8295 with returns and allowances of $950. If her commission rate is 14%, find her gross earnings.

SOLUTION The returns and allowances must first be subtracted from gross sales, and the difference, net sales, multiplied by the commission rate.

$$\text{Gross earnings} = (\$8295 - \$950) \times 14\%$$
$$= \$7345 \times 0.14$$
$$= \$1028.30 \quad ∎$$

CAUTION Before calculating the commission, any **returns** from customers, or any **allowances,** such as discounts, must be subtracted from sales. The company will not pay a commission on sales that are not completed.

2 The **sliding-scale** or **variable commission** plan is a method of pay designed to retain top producing salespeople. With these plans, a higher rate of commission is paid as sales get larger and larger.

EXAMPLE 3

Finding Earnings Using Variable Commission

A salesperson at Kane's Karpets is paid as follows.

Sales	Rate
Up to $10,000	6%
$10,001–$20,000	8%
$20,001 and up	9%

Find the gross earnings of a salesperson selling $32,768 worth of floor coverings.

SOLUTION Use the three commission rates as follows.

	$10,000 at 6% =	$ 600.00	1st $10,000 in sales
	10,000 at 8% =	800.00	next $10,000 in sales
	12,768 at 9% =	1149.12	remaining sales
total sales	$32,768	$2549.12	total commissions

The salesperson earned gross pay of $2549.12. ■

3 With a **salary plus commission,** the salesperson is paid a fixed sum per pay period, plus a commission on all sales. This method of payment is commonly used by large retail stores. Gross earnings with salary plus commission are found by the following formula.

> Gross earnings =
> Fixed amount per pay period + Amount earned on commission

Many salespeople favor this method of determining gross earnings. It is especially attractive to the beginning salesperson who lacks selling experience and personal self-confidence. While providing an incentive, it offers the security of a guaranteed income to cover basic living costs.

EXAMPLE 4

Adding Commission to a Salary

Sherrie Firavich is paid $250 per week by Sanitary Pool Supply, plus 3% on all sales. Find her gross earnings for a week in which her sales were $6848.

SOLUTION   Use the formula in the box.

$$\text{Gross earnings} = \text{Fixed earnings} + \text{Commission}$$
$$= \$250 + (0.03 \times \$6848)$$
$$= \$250 + \$205.44$$
$$= \$455.44 \quad \blacksquare$$

4   The fixed amount of earnings is often a **draw** or loan against future commissions. A **drawing account** is set up with the amounts drawn repaid with future commissions. This is a loan against future commissions but offers the salesperson the assurance of a fixed sum per pay period. The salesperson must repay the drawing account as commissions are earned.

EXAMPLE 5

Subtracting a Draw from Commission

Ben Whitney, a new publisher's representative, has sales of $38,560 for the month and is paid a 7% commission rate. He has had draws of $750 for the month. Find his gross earnings after repaying the drawing account.

SOLUTION

$$\text{Gross earnings} = \text{Commissions} - \text{Draw}$$
$$= (0.07 \times \$38,560) - \$750$$
$$= \$2699.20 - \$750$$
$$= \$1949.20 \quad \blacksquare$$

NOTE Commission earning plans are a strong deterrent to attracting new salespeople. It is for this reason that many companies offer the salary plus commission and the draw plans to help attract new employees.

A *sales quota* is often established for salespeople. The quota is the minimum amount of sales expected from the employee. If the salesperson continually falls short of the sales quota, termination may result. Normally, however, the salesperson is rewarded for passing the sales quota with a bonus or commission. This plan is called a **quota bonus** system.

EXAMPLE 6

Using the Quota Bonus System

Dusty Rainbolt is a sales representative for a mountain bike manufacturer. During a recent week he had sales of $18,780 and was paid a commission of 8% after meeting the sales quota of $5000. Find his gross earnings.

SOLUTION

$$\text{Gross earnings} = \text{Commission rate} \times (\text{Sales} - \text{Quota})$$
$$= 0.08 \times (\$18,780 - \$5000)$$
$$= 0.08 \times \$13,780$$
$$= \$1102.40 \quad \blacksquare$$

5   Sales supervisors and department heads of retail stores are often paid a commission based on the total sales of their staff or department. This payment for the efforts of others rewards the supervisor or department head for doing a good job in training and maintaining a sales staff. This commission is called an **override.** Calculate it like any other commission, but use the total department sales.

EXAMPLE 7
Finding Gross
Earnings with
Commission and
Override

Diver's Den pays their managers a salary plus commission and override. Find the gross earnings for a manager given the following.

Personal sales	$4386	Personal returns	$118
Store sales	$11,865	Store returns	$562
Salary	$375	Personal quota	$2500
Commission rate	4%	Override rate	1%

SOLUTION   First, find the manager's commission on personal sales.

Personal sales − Returns − Quota = Personal commission sales

$4386   − $118 − $2500 = $1768

Personal commission = 0.04 × 1768

= $70.72

Now find the override on store sales.

Store sales − Returns = Override commission sales

$11,865   − $562   = $11,303

Override commission = 0.01 × $11,303

= $113.03

Calculate gross earnings as follows.

Gross earnings = Salary + Commission + Override

= $375 + $70.72   + $113.03

= $558.75   ■

Calculator Approach to Example 7

The manager's commission on personal sales must first be found by sub-tracting returns and quota from personal sales, then multiplying by the commission rate.

$$4386 \boxed{-} 118 \boxed{-} 2500 \boxed{\times} .04 \boxed{M+}$$

This commission is entered in memory to be added to override and salary. Next the override must be determined using store sales, returns, and the override rate. This is also added to memory.

$$11865 \boxed{-} 562 \boxed{\times} .01 \boxed{M+}$$

The final step brings the total of personal commission and override from memory using the $\boxed{MR}$ key, then adds the manager's salary.

$$\boxed{MR} \boxed{+} 375 \boxed{=} 558.75$$

5.2 Exercises

Find the gross earnings for each of the following salespeople.

Employee	Total Sales	Returns and Allowances	Rate of Commission
1. Miller, S.	$4630	$236	8%
2. Biron, C.	$12,636	$790	4%
3. Owen, G.	$3750	$128	15%
4. Spence, R.	$1603	$76	18%
5. Lange, D.	$25,658	$4083	9%
6. Connors, K.	$18,765	$386	8%
7. Dobbins, G.	$45,618	$2281	1%
8. Phares, H.	$34,183	$1169	2%

Bayside Janitorial Supply pays its salespeople the following commission.

First $750 in sales	6%
Next $750 in sales	8%
Sales over $1500	10%

Find the gross earnings for each of the following employees.

Employee	Total Sales	Employee	Total Sales
9. Warrener, G.	$1746	10. Pasco, S.	$1764
11. Prentiss, C.	$1321	12. Maria, P.	$1625
13. Ewing, W.	$974	14. Fisher, L.	$2265
15. Garcia, F.	$1586	16. Manly, C.	$2334

17. Wages and salaries are known as time rates while commissions are called incentive rates of pay. Explain in your own words the difference between these payment methods.

18. A variable commission plan is often referred to as an incentive within an incentive. Explain why this might be an accurate description of a variable commission plan. (See Objective 2.)

Complete the following commission payroll to find gross earnings.

	Employee	Gross Sales	Sales Returns	Net Quota	Commission Sales	Commission Rate	Gross Commission	Salary	Gross Earnings
19.	Davis, J.	$4160	$240	–		6%		$300	
20.	DePalo, T.	$8156	$820	$1000		5%		–	
21.	McKee, J.	$6380	$295	$2000		6%		–	
22.	King, L.	$2975	$682	–		5%		$200	
23.	Chen, C.	$6106	$76	$2500		3%		–	
24.	Ng, B.	$3396	$475	$1500		6%		–	
25.	Lincoln, A.	$4215	$318	$1000		5%		$210	
26.	Tobey, W.	$3570	$220	$1500		7%		$100	

Work each of the following word problems.

27. Esther Saul is a sales representative for Granard Medical Supplies. She is paid a 12% commission rate, and has had a draw of $250 this week. If her sales are $6640 this week, find her gross earnings after repaying the drawing account.

28. Susan Hessney has sales of $70,960 for the month and is paid a 5% commission rate. She has had draws totaling $1200 for the month. Find her gross earnings after repaying the drawing account.

29. Caralee Woods, a real estate broker, has sales of $138,500 this month and is paid a 3% commission by her office. She has had draws of $1600 this month. Find her gross earnings after repaying the drawing account.

30. Bill Bass, an account representative for WAXY-AM radio, is paid a 4% commission rate and has had a draw of $300 this week. If his sales are $24,800 this week, find his gross earnings after repaying the drawing account.

31. Dan Perez is a commission salesperson for an electronics firm which allows him to draw $500 per month. His commission is 6% of the first $3000 in sales, 8% of the next $8000, and 15% of all sales over $11,000. If his sales for the month were $13,850, find (a) his total commission and (b) the earnings due at the end of the month after repaying the drawing account balance of $500.

32. Heidi Squier is a sales representative for Hi Side Greeting Card Company. She is paid a monthly draw of $650. Her commission is 10% of the first $2000 in sales, 12% of the next $4000, and 20% of all sales over $6000. If her sales for the month were $8750, find (a) her total commission and (b) the gross earnings due at the end of the month after repaying the drawing account.

33. The department head in toys is paid a salary plus commission and an override. Find his gross earnings given the following.

Personal sales	$2825	Personal returns	$84
Department sales	$8656	Department returns	$317
Salary	$200	Personal quota	$1000
Commission rate	5%	Override	$1\frac{1}{2}\%$

34. The sales manager for A & A Appliance is paid a salary plus commission and an override. Find her gross earnings given the following.

Personal sales	$5856	Personal returns	$185
Store sales	$19,622	Store returns	$358
Salary	$250	Personal quota	$3000
Commission rate	3%	Override	2%

 5.3 Gross Earnings (Piecework)

OBJECTIVES

1 Find the gross earnings for piecework.

2 Find the gross earnings for differential-piecework.

3 Determine chargebacks and dockings.

4 Find overtime earnings for piecework.

The salaries and wages discussed in Section 5.1 are called **time rates,** since they depend only on the amount of time an employee was actually on the job. Commission earnings in Section 5.2 and the piecework methods discussed in this section are called **incentive rates.** These gross earnings are based on production and pay an employee for actual performance on the job.

1   A **piecework rate** pays an employee so much per item produced. Gross earnings are found using the following formula.

Gross earnings = Number of items × Pay per item

For example, a cabinet finisher who finishes 23 cabinets and is paid a piecework rate of $4 per cabinet would have total gross earnings of

Gross earnings = $4 × 23 = $92.

EXAMPLE 1
Finding Gross Earnings for Piecework

Babette Blanchard was paid $.42 for sewing a jacket collar, $.86 for a sleeve with cuff, and $.94 for a lapel. One week she sewed 318 jacket collars, 112 sleeves with cuffs, and 37 lapels. Find her gross earnings.

SOLUTION   Multiply the rate per item by the number of that type of item.

Item	Number	Rate	Total
Jacket collars	318	$.42	$133.56
Sleeves with cuffs	112	$.86	$ 96.32
Lapels	37	$.94	$ 34.78

The gross earnings can be found by adding the three totals. $133.56 + $96.32 + $34.78 = $264.66 ■

2   A **straight piecework** plan, such as in Example 1, is perhaps the oldest of all incentive payment plans. It is used in many manufacturing and production jobs such as fine jewelry finishing, agricultural and farm work, garment manufacturing, and in the building trades for structural framing, roofing, and floor laying. While many workers prefer working under a piecework plan, there are just as many who dislike it. Labor unions and other employee organizations, senior employees, and others claim that piecework plans result in unsafe work habits and poor quality workmanship.

Companies still using piecework have often made various modifications and changes to the straight piece rate plan. Many of these modified plans incorporate quotas which must be met and then offer an additional **premium rate** for each item produced beyond the quota. These plans offer an added incentive within an incentive. For example, in the **differential-piece rate** plan the rate paid per item depends on the number of items produced.

EXAMPLE 2
Using Differential Piecework

A custom picture frame manufacturer pays as follows.

1–100 items	$1.10 each
101–150 items	$1.25 each
151 or more items	$1.40 each

Find the gross earnings of an employee producing 214 items.

SOLUTION   The gross earnings of a worker producing 214 items would be found as follows.

100	items at $1.10 each	$110.00
50	items at $1.25 each	$62.50
64	items at $1.40 each	$89.60
214	total items	$262.10

The gross earnings are $262.10. ■

3   While companies are often pleased to reward employees with premium rates for surpassing quotas, management is equally concerned with unacceptable quality and unusable production. Ruined items may produce a total loss of material and labor; correctable flaws require additional handling, resulting in added costs and decreased profits. To discourage carelessness and mistakes, many companies require the employee to share in the cost of the spoiled item. These penalties, called **chargebacks** or **dockings,** are normally at a lower rate than the employee receives for producing that piece. This lower rate is used because a small amount of production error is expected.

EXAMPLE 3
Understanding and Using Chargebacks

In Example 2, suppose the company had a chargeback of $.75 per spoiled item and the employee had spoiled 14 items. Find the gross earnings after the chargeback.

SOLUTION   Gross earnings are found by subtracting the chargeback from piece rate earnings.

$$\text{Gross earnings} = \$262.10 - (14 \text{ items} \times \$.75)$$
$$= \$262.10 - \$10.50$$
$$= \$251.60 \quad ■$$

Piecework and differential-piecework rates are frequently modified to include some guaranteed hourly rate of pay. Often this is necessary to meet minimum wage laws. To satisfy the law, the employer may either pay minimum wage or piecework earnings, whichever is higher.

EXAMPLE 4
Finding Earnings with a Guaranteed Hourly Wage

A production worker is paid $8.40 an hour for an 8-hour day, or $.95 per casting, whichever is higher. Find the weekly earnings for an employee having the following production.

Monday	85	castings
Tuesday	70	castings
Wednesday	88	castings
Thursday	68	castings
Friday	82	castings

SOLUTION   The hourly earnings for an 8-hour day are $67.20 (8 × $8.40). If the piecework earnings for the day are less than this amount, the hourly earnings will be paid.

Monday	85 × $.95 =	$80.75	piece rate
Tuesday	70 × $.95 =	$67.20	hourly (piece rate is $66.50)
Wednesday	88 × $.95 =	$83.60	piece rate
Thursday	68 × $.95 =	$67.20	hourly (piece rate is $64.60)
Friday	82 × $.95 =	$77.90	piece rate
		$376.65	weekly earnings ∎

NOTE Since the piecework earnings on Tuesday and Thursday are below the minimum, the hourly rate is paid on those days.

4 Piecework employees, just as other workers, are paid time and a half for overtime. The overtime rate may be computed as $1\frac{1}{2}$ times the hourly rate, but most often, the overtime rate is $1\frac{1}{2}$ times the regular rate per piece.

EXAMPLE 5
Determining Earnings with Overtime Piecework

A worker is paid $.46 per item produced. During one week she produces 530 items on regular time and 110 items during overtime hours. Find her gross earnings for the week if time and a half per piece is paid for overtime.

SOLUTION

$$\text{Gross earnings} = \text{Earnings at regular piece rate}$$
$$+ \text{Earnings at overtime piece rate}$$

$$= 530 \times \$.46 + 110 \times (1\frac{1}{2} \times \$.46)$$

$$= \$243.80 + \$75.90$$

$$= \$319.70 \quad ∎$$

Calculator Approach to Example 5

The regular piece rate earnings are found and then placed in memory.

$$530 \quad \boxed{\times} \quad .46 \quad \boxed{M+}$$

Earnings at the overtime piece rate of time and a half (1.5) are calculated and added to the memory. Gross earnings are then found by pressing the $\boxed{MR}$ key.

$$110 \quad \boxed{\times} \quad .46 \quad \boxed{\times} \quad 1.5 \quad \boxed{M+} \quad \boxed{MR} \quad 319.70$$

5.3 Exercises

*Complete the following payroll ledger for Ecology Recycling. Employees are paid a
straight piece rate. Rates per unit vary depending on worker skills involved.*

	Employee	Units Produced					Total Pieces	Rate Per Unit	Gross Earnings
		M	T	W	T	F			
1.	Young, C.	68	84	61	46	67		$.64	
2.	Plescia, P.	115	103	98	120	83		$.73	
3.	Yost, S.	94	78	105	83	75		$.52	
4.	McIntosh, R.	67	54	72	83	59		$.72	
5.	Todd, R.	118	124	143	132	148		$.68	
6.	Eckern, G.	157	148	169	145	178		$.59	
7.	Anderson, N.	125	118	115	132	98		$.46	
8.	Duerr, D.	56	62	78	58	71		$.95	
9.	Lopes, L.	149	135	118	125	143		$.78	
10.	Lord, J.	87	95	108	92	103		$.63	

Employees at Tickle Time Pickle Factory are paid as follows.

1–100 cases	$.15
101–200 cases	$.16
201–300 cases	$.17
301 cases and up	$.19

Find the gross earnings for each of the following employees.

	Employee	Number of Cases			Employee	Number of Cases
11.	Nutt, C.	495		12.	Thomas, R.	416
13.	Barnum, P. T.	516		14.	Heise, M.	372
15.	Bailey, J.	375		16.	Thumb, T.	589

Suppose that production workers at Classic Tapes are paid as follows for labeling and packaging audio cassette tapes.

1–500 tapes	$.12 each
501–700 tapes	$.14 each
701–1000 tapes	$.16 each
over 1000 tapes	$.18 each

Find the gross earnings for each of the following employees.

	Employee	Number of Tapes			Employee	Number of Tapes
17.	Manly, R.	728		**18.**	Ryan, N.	819
19.	Allen, I.	1104		**20.**	Chin, L.	1215
21.	Waipo, T.	1308		**22.**	Markovich, E.	1439

Find the gross earnings for each of the following employees. Each has an 8-hour workday and is paid $.75 for each unit of production or the hourly rate, whichever is greater.

	Employee	Units Produced					Hourly Rate	Gross Earnings
		M	T	W	T	F		
23.	Foster, B.	66	75	58	72	68	$6.18	
24.	Arcade, A.	62	58	49	60	51	$5.20	
25.	Pieri, Y.	65	60	71	78	64	$5.80	
26.	Dal Porto, J.	72	70	62	88	82	$6.50	
27.	Zurcher, S.	50	56	48	62	45	$4.50	
28.	Frase, E.	63	57	67	75	70	$5.70	
29.	Pantera, A.	73	62	78	64	81	$6.30	
30.	Enos, C.	60	55	59	68	66	$5.40	

Find the gross earnings for each of the following employees. Overtime is $1\frac{1}{2}$ times the normal per piece rate. Rejected units are charged at the chargeback rate.

	Employee	Units Produced		Rejected Units	Rate Per Unit	Chargeback Per Unit	Gross Earnings
		Reg.	O.T.				
31.	Atkins, Q.	460	62	18	$.65	$.40	
32.	Main, F.	340	18	3	$.83	$.70	
33.	Crawford, C.	522	82	38	$.58	$.52	
34.	Londell, L.	410	22	12	$.78	$.72	
35.	Balbi, G.	286	38	4	$.95	$.82	
36.	Fukano, H.	315	64	35	$.74	$.65	
37.	Hughes, G.	403	72	15	$.68	$.45	
38.	Dos Reis, A.	452	12	6	$.59	$.50	

39. Explain in your own words the difference between a piecework rate and a differential piece rate. (See Objective 2.)

40. Describe what a chargeback or docking is for rejected units. Why do you think that the chargeback per unit is usually less than the rate paid per unit? (See Objective 3.)

Solve each of the following word problems.

41. Arnie Muller is paid $1.66 for turning each bowl on a potters wheel, is charged $.95 for each rejection, and is paid time and a half for overtime production. Find his gross earnings for the week when he produces 218 bowls at regular rate, 42 bowls at the overtime rate, and has 18 chargebacks.

42. Larry Sifford decorates cakes at the Cakes To Go Shop, for which he is paid $2.42 each. He is charged $1.40 per rejection and is paid time and a half for all overtime production. Find his gross earnings when production for the week is 128 cakes at regular rate and 19 cakes at overtime rate. He has a total of 5 chargebacks.

43. Darrel Holmes is paid $.83 per videotape duplication, is charged $.52 for each rejection, and is paid time and a half for overtime production. Find his gross earnings for the week when he produces 285 tapes at regular rate, 120 tapes at the overtime rate, and has 12 chargebacks.

44. Cindy Perez sews lace on dance costumes, for which she is paid $1.18 each. She is charged $.90 per rejection and is paid time and a half for all overtime production. Find her gross earnings when production for the week is 138 costumes at regular rate and 28 costumes at overtime rate. She has a total of 9 chargebacks.

45. Danielle Yates inspects and packages competition swimwear. She is paid $.07 per unit and is charged $.05 for each rejected package. Find her gross earnings for the week given the following.

	M	T	W	T	F	Totals
Production	482	563	618	475	520	
Chargebacks	18	21	16	35	26	

46. Kevin McCarthy pumps up basketballs and puts them in a box. He receives $.12 per unit and is charged $.08 for each rejection. Find his gross earnings for the week given the following production.

	M	T	W	T	F	Totals
Production	310	290	328	285	346	
Chargebacks	18	15	23	8	28	

5.4 Social Security, Medicare, and Other Taxes

OBJECTIVES

1 Understand FICA.

2 Find the maximum FICA tax paid by an employee in one year.

3 Understand medicare tax.

4 Find FICA tax and medicare tax.

5 Determine the FICA tax and the medicare tax paid by a self-employed person.

6 Find state disability insurance deductions.

Finding gross earnings is only the first step in preparing a payroll. The employer must then subtract all required deductions from gross earnings. For most employees, these deductions include social security tax, medicare tax, federal income tax withholding, and state tax withholding. Other deductions may include state disability insurance, union dues, retirement, vacation pay, credit union savings or loan payments, purchase of bonds, uniform expenses, group insurance plans, and charitable contributions. Subtracting these deductions from gross earnings results in **net pay,** the amount the employee receives.

1 The **Federal Insurance Contributions Act (FICA)** was passed into law in the 1930s at the middle of the Great Depression. This plan, now called **social security,** was originally designed to give monthly benefits to retired workers and their survivors. Also included today are death benefits and medicare payments. As the numbers of people receiving benefits has increased along with the individual benefit amounts, people paying into social security have had to pay a larger amount of earnings into this fund each year. From 1937 through 1950 an employee paid 1% of income into social security, up to a maximum of $30 per year. This amount has increased over the years until an employee in 1993 paid 7.65% (6.2% FICA + 1.45% medicare) of income, up to more than $4245.75 per year.

For many years both the social security tax rate and the medicare tax rate were combined, however since 1991 these tax rates have been expressed individually. Table 5.2 shows the tax rates and the maximum earnings on which social security and medicare taxes are paid by the employee. The employer pays the same rate as the employee matching dollar for dollar all employee contributions.

Congress sets the tax rates and the maximum employee earnings subject to both social security tax and medicare tax. Because these tax rates change, we will use 6.5% of the first $60,000 that the employee earns in a year for social security tax. For medicare tax, we will use 1.5% of the first $150,000 that the employee earns in a year. These figures are used in all examples and exercises in this chapter.

Each employee must have a social security card. Most post offices have application forms for the cards. All money set aside for an individual is deposited into his or her account according to the social security number. Mistakes are rare, but they do occur. For this reason, every employee should submit a **Request for Earnings and**

TABLE 5.2   Maximum Earnings on which Social Security and Medicare Taxes Are Paid

Year	Social Security Tax		Medicare Tax	
	Social Security Tax Rate	Employee Earnings Subject to the Tax	Medicare Tax Rate	Employee Earnings Subject to the Tax
1991	6.2%	$53,400	1.45%	$125,000
1992	6.2%	$55,500	1.45%	$130,200
1993	6.2%	$57,600	1.45%	$135,000
⋮				
1998	6.2%	$70,000*	1.45%	$165,000*

*Estimated. This will be set by Congress.

Benefit Estimate Statement every 2 years or so, by filling out a form like the one in Figure 5.2. There is a limit of about 3 years, after which errors may not be corrected. To obtain one of the forms and other information about social security you may phone (800) 772-1213.

SOCIAL SECURITY ADMINISTRATION

Form Approved
OMB No. 0960-0466 ☐ SP

Request for Earnings and Benefit Estimate Statement

To receive a free statement of your earnings covered by Social Security and your estimated future benefits, all you need to do is fill out this form. Please print or type your answers. When you have completed the form, fold it and mail it to us.

1. Name shown on your Social Security card:

   _____   _____   _____
   First   Middle Initial   Last

2. Your Social Security number as shown on your card:

   ☐☐☐ - ☐☐ - ☐☐☐☐

3. Your date of birth: _____ _____ _____
                                      Month   Day   Year

4. Other Social Security numbers you have used:

   ☐☐☐ - ☐☐ - ☐☐☐☐
   ☐☐☐ - ☐☐ - ☐☐☐☐

5. Your Sex: ☐ Male   ☐ Female

6. Other names you have used (including a maiden name):

   _____

   _____

7. Show your actual earnings for last year and your estimated earnings for this year. Include only wages and/or net self-employment income covered by Social Security.

   A. Last year's actual earnings:

   $ ☐☐☐ , ☐☐☐ . ☐ ☐
      Dollars only

   B. This year's estimated earnings:

   $ ☐☐☐ , ☐☐☐ . ☐ ☐
      Dollars only

8. Show the age at which you plan to retire: ☐☐
                                                                (Show only one age)

9. Below, show the average yearly amount that you think you will earn between now and when you plan to retire. Your estimate of future earnings will be added to those earnings already on our records to give you the best possible estimate.

   Enter a yearly average, not your total future lifetime earnings. Only show earnings covered by Social Security. Do not add cost-of-living, performance or scheduled pay increases or bonuses. The reason for this is that we estimate retirement benefits in today's dollars, but adjust them to account for average wage growth in the national economy.

   However, if you expect to earn significantly more or less in the future due to promotions, job changes, part-time work, or an absence from the work force, enter the amount in today's dollars that most closely reflects your future average yearly earnings.

   Most people should enter the same amount that they are earning now (the amount shown in 7B).

   Your future average yearly earnings:

   $ ☐☐☐ , ☐☐☐ . ☐ ☐
      Dollars only

10. Address where you want us to send the statement:

    _____
    Name

    _____
    Street Address (Include Apt. No., P.O. Box, or Rural Route)

    _____   _____   _____
    City   State   Zip Code

    I am asking for information about my own Social Security record or the record of a person I am authorized to represent. I understand that if I deliberately request information under false pretenses I may be guilty of a federal crime and could be fined and/or imprisoned. I authorize you to send the statement of earnings and benefit estimates to the person named in item 10 through a contractor.

    ▶

    _____
    Please sign your name (Do not print)

    _____   _____
    Date   (Area Code) Daytime Telephone No.

    ABOUT THE PRIVACY ACT
    Social Security is allowed to collect the facts on this form under Section 205 of the Social Security Act. We need them to quickly identify your record and prepare the earnings statement you asked us for. Giving us these facts is voluntary. However, without them we may not be able to give you an earnings and benefit estimate statement. Neither the Social Security Administration nor its contractor will use the information for any other purpose.

Form SSA-7004-SM-OP3 (9-91) Destroy Prior Editions

FIGURE 5.2

---

2   Remember that social security tax is paid on only the first $60,000 of gross earnings in our examples. An employee earning $60,000 during the first 10 months of a year would pay no more social security tax on additional earnings that year. The maximum social security tax to be paid by an employee is $60,000 × 6.5% = $60,000 × .065 = $3900.

3 Medicare taxes continue to be paid up to $150,000 of earnings in our examples. The maximum medicare tax to be paid by an employee is $150,000 × 1.5% = $150,000 × .015 = $2250.

NOTE Only the highest income earners are affected by the medicare maximum.

4 When finding the amounts to be withheld for social security tax and medicare tax, the employer must use the current rates.

EXAMPLE 1

Finding FICA Tax and Medicare Tax

Find the social security tax and the medicare tax for the following gross earnings.
(a) $291.06   **(b)** $363.34

SOLUTION

(a) The social security tax is found by multiplying gross earnings by 6.5%.

$291.06 × 6.5% = $291.06 × .065 = $18.92 (rounded)

Medicare tax is found by multiplying gross earnings by 1.5%.

$291.06 × 1.5% = $291.06 × .015 = $4.37 (rounded)

(b) Social security tax is

$363.34 × 6.5% = $363.34 × .065 = $23.62 (rounded).

Medicare tax is

$363.34 × 1.5% = $363.34 × .015 = $5.45 (rounded). ∎

EXAMPLE 2

Finding FICA Tax

Nannette Williams has earned $56,791.08 so far this year. Her gross earnings for the current pay period are $4842.08. Find her social security tax.

SOLUTION Social security tax is paid on only the first $60,000 earned in a year. Williams has already earned $56,791.08. Subtract $56,791.08 from $60,000, to find she has to pay social security tax on only $3208.92 of her earnings for the rest of the year.

$60,000.00   maximum earnings subject to tax:
−$56,791.08   earnings to date
$3,208.92   earnings on which tax is due

The social security tax on $3208.92 is $208.58 ($3208.92 x 6.5%). Therefore, Williams pays $208.58 for the current pay period and no additional social security tax for the rest of the year. ∎

5 People who are self-employed pay higher social security tax and higher medicare tax than people who work for others. There is no employer to match the employee contribution so the self-employed person pays a rate that is double that of the employee. In our examples the self-employed person pays 13% of gross earnings for social security tax and 3% of gross earnings for medicare tax.

EXAMPLE 3

Finding FICA and Medicare Tax for the Self-Employed

Find the social security tax and the medicare tax paid by a self-employed person earning $20,680 in a pay period.

SOLUTION

$$\text{Social security tax} = \$20,680 \times 13\% = \$20,680 \times .13$$

$$= \$2688.40$$

$$\text{Medicare tax} = \$20,680 \times 3\% = \$20,680 \times .03$$

$$= \$620.40 \quad \blacksquare$$

CAUTION   All employers and those who are self-employed should have the current tax rates for both social security and medicare. These can always be found in Circular E, Employee's Tax Guide which is available from the Internal Revenue Service.

6   Many states have a state disability insurance program that is paid for by employees. If disabled, the employee would receive weekly benefits. A typical state program defines "disability" as "any illness or injury incurred on or off the job, either physical or mental, including pregnancy, childbirth or related condition, that prevents you from doing your regular work." The employee processes the claim himself or herself after obtaining certification from a doctor or other qualified examiner. Weekly disability benefits, ranging from $50 to $224, are determined by the highest quarter's earnings within the past year of employment.

A typical state program also requires the qualifying employee to pay an **SDI (state disability insurance) deduction** of 1.25% of the first $31,800 earned each year. There are no payments on earnings above this amount. Some states have similar programs, but their insurance is placed with private insurance companies rather than with the state.

EXAMPLE 4

Finding State Disability Insurance Deductions

Find the state disability deduction for an employee with gross earnings of $383 this pay period. Assume an SDI rate of 1.25% and that the employee has not earned $31,800 this year.

SOLUTION   First change 1.25% to the decimal 0.0125. Then multiply.

$$\$383 \times 0.0125 = 4.7875 = \$4.79$$

The state disability deduction is $4.79. $\blacksquare$

EXAMPLE 5

Finding State Disability Insurance Deductions

An employee has earned $30,620 so far this year. Find the SDI deduction if gross earnings this pay period are $3096. Use an SDI rate of 1.25% on the first $31,800.

SOLUTION   The SDI deduction will be taken on $1180 of the current gross earnings.

$$\begin{array}{r} \$31,800 \\ -\ \$30,620 \\ \hline \$\ 1,180 \end{array} \quad \text{earnings this year subject to SDI}$$

The SDI deduction is $14.75 ($1180 × 1.25%). $\blacksquare$

NOTE Always be aware of the current rates and the maximum annual earning amounts against which FICA, Medicare, and SDI payroll deductions may be taken. Those involved in payroll work must always be up to date on federal and state laws and practices.

5.4 Exercises

Find the social security tax and the medicare tax for each of the following amounts of gross earnings. Assume a 6.5% FICA rate and a 1.5% medicare tax rate.

1. $253.86
2. $318.63
3. $840.77
4. $458.21
5. $240.97
6. $372.10
7. $526.15
8. $612.83

Find the social security tax for each of the following employees for the current pay period. Assume a 6.5% FICA rate up to a maximum of $60,000.

	Employee	Prior Gross Earnings This Year	Earnings Current Pay Period
9.	Glovin, P.	$59,915.86	$ 652.18
10.	Connors, K.	$57,622.18	$2700
11.	Straub, R.	$55,721.59	$5780
12.	Albright, W.	$58,018.67	$2162.34
13.	Seniw, J.	$59,819.75	$ 516.92
14.	Owen, G.	$57,992.06	$3273.81

Find the regular earnings, overtime earnings, gross earnings, social security tax, medicare tax, and state disability insurance deduction for each of the following employees. Assume time and a half is paid for any hours over a 40-hour week. Assume a 6.5% FICA rate, a 1.5% medicare rate, a state disability rate of 1.25% and that no one has earned over $31,800 this year.

	Employee	Hours Worked	Regular Rate
15.	Burnside, L.	38	$ 9.75
16.	Clouse, R.	$43\frac{1}{2}$	$10.84
17.	Shehorn, V.	$44\frac{3}{4}$	$ 8.08
18.	Escabl, R.	45	$ 6.58
19.	Cavaliere, C.	45	$ 5.10
20.	Taggart, G.	47	$11.68
21.	Yates, C.	$46\frac{3}{4}$	$ 6.24
22.	Kavanagh, M.	$48\frac{1}{4}$	$ 6.96

Solve each of the following word problems.

23. Sharon Hollowbow worked $49\frac{1}{4}$ hours last week. She received $11.66 per hour, plus time and a half for overtime. Find her (a) social security tax and (b) medicare tax for the week.

24. William Young receives 7% commission on all sales. His sales on Monday of last week were $1412.20, with $1928.42 on Tuesday, $598.14 on Wednesday, $1051.12 on Thursday, and $958.72 on Friday. Find his (a) social security tax and (b) medicare tax for the week.

25. Marja Strutz is paid an 8% commission on sales. During a recent pay period, she had sales of $19,482 and returns and allowances of $193. Find the amount of her (a) social security tax, (b) medicare tax, and (c) state disability for this pay period. (Assume that the FICA rate is 6.5%, the medicare rate is 1.5%, the SDI rate is 1.25%, and earnings will not exceed $31,800.)

26. John Mathews is paid a salary of $300 per week plus a commission of 6% on sales. His sales last week were $1865. Find the amount of his (a) social security tax, (b) medicare tax, and (c) state disability for the pay period. (Assume that the FICA rate is 6.5%, the medicare rate is 1.5%, the SDI rate is 1.25%, and earnings will not exceed $31,800.)

The following problems refer to self-employed individuals. These people pay social security tax of 13% and medicare tax of 3%. Find the taxes on each of the following gross incomes.

27. Robert Andrew, owner of a convenience store, earned $20,473.58.

28. Susanne Sitlington, contractor, earned $16,253.42.

29. Kerry Williams, pharmacist, earned $35,584.18.

30. Richard Stratton, lumber dealer, earned $28,409.13.

31. Marsha Mildred, shop owner, earned $23,384.50.

32. Michelle Washington, commission salesperson, earned $52,748.32.

33. Explain in your own words the importance of an employee sending in a Request for Earnings and Benefit Estimate Statement every two to three years. (See Objective 1.)

34. Describe the difference between the FICA paid by an employee and that paid by a self-employed person. Why does this difference exist? (See Objective 5.)

5.5 Income Tax Withholding

OBJECTIVES

1 Understand the Employee's Withholding Allowance Certificate (Form W-4).

2 Find the federal withholding tax from tables.

3 Find the federal tax using the percentage method.

4 Find the state withholding tax from tables.

5 Find net pay when given gross wages, taxes, and other deductions.

The **personal income tax** is the largest single source of money for the federal government. The law requires that the bulk of this tax owed by an individual be paid periodically, as the income is earned. For this reason, employers must deduct money from the gross earnings of almost every employee. These deductions, called **income tax withholdings**, are sent periodically to the Internal Revenue Service and credited to the accounts of the employees. The amount of money withheld depends on the employee's marital status, the number of withholding allowances claimed, and the amount of gross earnings.

Marital Status. Generally, the withholding tax for a married person is less than the withholding tax for a single person making the same income.

1 **The Number of Withholding Allowances Claimed.** Each employee must file with the employer a W-4 form as shown in Figure 5.3. On this form the employee states the number of **withholding allowances** being claimed along with additional information, so that the employer can withhold the proper amount for income tax.

Form **W-4** Department of the Treasury Internal Revenue Service

Employee's Withholding Allowance Certificate

▶ For Privacy Act and Paperwork Reduction Act Notice, see reverse.

OMB No. 1545-0010 19

1 Type or print your first name and middle initial | Last name | 2 Your social security number

Home address (number and street or rural route)

3 ☐ Single ☐ Married ☐ Married, but withhold at higher Single rate.
Note: *If married, but legally separated, or spouse is a nonresident alien, check the Single box.*

City or town, state, and ZIP code

4 If your last name differs from that on your social security card, check here and call 1-800-772-1213 for more information . ▶ ☐

5 Total number of allowances you are claiming (from line G above or from the Worksheets on back if they apply) | 5

6 Additional amount, if any, you want deducted from each paycheck . . . . | 6 $

7 I claim exemption from withholding and I certify that I meet **ALL** of the following conditions for exemption:
- Last year I had a right to a refund of **ALL** Federal income tax withheld because I had **NO** tax liability; **AND**
- This year I expect a refund of **ALL** Federal income tax withheld because I expect to have **NO** tax liability; **AND**
- This year if my income exceeds $600 and includes nonwage income, another person cannot claim me as a dependent.

If you meet all of the above conditions, enter the year effective and "EXEMPT" here . . . ▶ 7 19

8 Are you a full-time student? (**Note:** *Full-time students are not automatically exempt.*) . . . . | 8 ☐ Yes ☐ No

Under penalties of perjury, I certify that I am entitled to the number of withholding allowances claimed on this certificate or entitled to claim exempt status.

Employee's signature ▶ **Date** ▶ , 19

9 Employer's name and address (Employer: Complete 9 and 11 only if sending to the IRS) | 10 Office code (optional) | 11 Employer identification number

FIGURE 5.3

A W-4 form is usually completed at the beginning of employment. A married person with three children will normally claim five allowances (one each for the employee and spouse, plus one for each child). However, when both spouses are employed, each may claim himself or herself. The number of allowances may be raised if an employee has been receiving a refund of withholding taxes, or the number may be lowered if the employee has had a balance due in previous tax years. The W-4 form has instructions to help determine the proper number of allowances. Some people enjoy receiving a tax refund when filing their income tax return, so they claim fewer allowances, having more withheld from each check. Other individuals would rather receive more of their income each pay period, so they claim the maximum number of allowances to which they are entitled.

2 **Amount of Gross Earnings.**   The withholding tax is found on the basis of the gross earnings per pay period. Income tax withholding is applied to all earnings, unlike social security tax. Generally, the higher a person's gross earnings, the more withholding tax paid. The exact number of allowances *must* be claimed when income tax is filed.

There are two methods that employers use to determine the amount of federal withholding tax to deduct from paychecks: the **wage bracket method** and the **percentage method**.

The Internal Revenue Service supplies withholding tax tables to be used with the wage bracket method. These tables are extensive and cover weekly, biweekly, monthly, and daily pay periods. Figures 5.4 and 5.5 show samples of the withholding tables. Figure 5.4 is for single persons paid weekly, and Figure 5.5 is for married persons paid monthly. Methods of using these tables are shown in the following examples.

SINGLE Persons—WEEKLY Payroll Period

At least	But less than	0	1	2	3	4	5	6	7	8	9	10
440	450	61	53	46	40	33	27	20	13	7	0	0
450	460	63	55	48	41	35	28	21	15	8	1	0
460	470	66	56	49	43	36	30	23	16	10	3	0
470	480	69	58	51	44	38	31	24	18	11	4	0
480	490	72	59	52	46	39	33	26	19	13	6	0
490	500	75	62	54	47	41	34	27	21	14	7	1
500	510	77	65	55	49	42	36	29	22	16	9	2
510	520	80	68	57	50	44	37	30	24	17	10	4
520	530	83	71	58	52	45	39	32	25	19	12	5
530	540	86	73	61	53	47	40	33	27	20	13	7
540	550	89	76	64	55	48	42	35	28	22	15	8
550	560	91	79	67	56	50	43	36	30	23	16	10
560	570	94	82	69	58	51	45	38	31	25	18	11
570	580	97	85	72	60	53	46	39	33	26	19	13
$590	$600	$103	$90	$78	$66	$56	$49	$42	$36	$29	$22	$16
600	610	105	93	81	68	57	51	44	37	31	24	17
610	620	108	96	83	71	59	52	45	39	32	25	19
620	630	111	99	86	74	62	54	47	40	34	27	20
630	640	114	101	89	77	64	55	48	42	35	28	22
640	650	117	104	92	80	67	57	50	43	37	30	23
650	660	119	107	95	82	70	58	51	45	38	31	25
660	670	122	110	97	85	73	60	53	46	40	33	26
670	680	125	113	100	88	76	63	54	48	41	34	28
680	690	128	115	103	91	78	66	56	49	43	36	29
690	700	131	118	106	94	81	69	57	51	44	37	31
700	710	133	121	109	96	84	72	59	52	46	39	32
710	720	136	124	111	99	87	74	62	54	47	40	34
720	730	139	127	114	102	90	77	65	55	49	42	35
730	740	142	129	117	105	92	80	68	57	50	43	37

And the wages are— / And the number of withholding allowances claimed is— / The amount of income tax to be withheld shall be—

FIGURE 5.4

MARRIED Persons—MONTHLY Payroll Period

And the wages are—		And the number of withholding allowances claimed is—										
At least	But less than	0	1	2	3	4	5	6	7	8	9	10
		The amount of income tax to be withheld shall be—										
1,360	1,400	132	103	75	46	17	0	0	0	0	0	0
1,400	1,440	138	109	81	52	23	0	0	0	0	0	0
1,440	1,480	144	115	87	58	29	0	0	0	0	0	0
1,480	1,520	150	121	93	64	35	6	0	0	0	0	0
1,520	1,560	156	127	99	70	41	12	0	0	0	0	0
1,560	1,600	162	133	105	76	47	18	0	0	0	0	0
1,600	1,640	168	139	111	82	53	24	0	0	0	0	0
1,640	1,680	174	145	117	88	59	30	2	0	0	0	0
1,680	1,720	180	151	123	94	65	36	8	0	0	0	0
1,720	1,760	186	157	129	100	71	42	14	0	0	0	0
1,760	1,800	192	163	135	106	77	48	20	0	0	0	0
1,800	1,840	198	169	141	112	83	54	26	0	0	0	0
1,840	1,880	204	175	147	118	89	60	32	3	0	0	0
1,880	1,920	210	181	153	124	95	66	38	9	0	0	0
1,920	1,960	216	187	159	130	101	72	44	15	0	0	0
1,960	2,000	222	193	165	136	107	78	50	21	0	0	0
2,000	2,040	228	199	171	142	113	84	56	27	0	0	0
2,040	2,080	234	205	177	148	119	90	62	33	4	0	0
2,080	2,120	240	211	183	154	125	96	68	39	10	0	0
2,120	2,160	246	217	189	160	131	102	74	45	16	0	0
2,160	2,200	252	223	195	166	137	108	80	51	22	0	0
2,200	2,240	258	229	201	172	143	114	86	57	28	0	0
2,240	2,280	264	235	207	178	149	120	92	63	34	5	0
2,280	2,320	270	241	213	184	155	126	98	69	40	11	0
2,320	2,360	276	247	219	190	161	132	104	75	46	17	0
2,360	2,400	282	253	225	196	167	138	110	81	52	23	0
2,400	2,440	288	259	231	202	173	144	116	87	58	29	1
2,440	2,480	294	265	237	208	179	150	122	93	64	35	7
2,480	2,520	300	271	243	214	185	156	128	99	70	41	13
2,520	2,560	306	277	249	220	191	162	134	105	76	47	19

FIGURE 5.5

EXAMPLE 1

Finding Federal Withholding Using the Wage Bracket Method

Marilyn Moran is single and claims no withholding allowances. (Some employees do this to receive a refund from the government or to avoid owing taxes at the end of the year. The proper number will be used when filing her income tax return.) Use the wage bracket method to find her withholding tax if her weekly gross earnings are $549.63.

SOLUTION   Use the table in Figure 5.4 for single persons—weekly payroll period. The given earnings are found in the row "at least $540 but less than $550." Go across this row to the column headed "0" (for no withholding allowances). From the table, the withholding is $89. ■

EXAMPLE 2

Using the Wage Bracket Method for Federal Withholding

Charles Dawkins is married, claims three withholding allowances, and has monthly gross earnings of $1886.15. Find his withholding tax using the wage bracket method.

SOLUTION   Use the table in Figure 5.5 for married persons-monthly payroll period. Look down the two left columns, and find the range that includes Dawkins's gross earnings: "at least $1880 but less than $1920." Read across the table to the column headed "3" (for the three withholding allowances). The withholding tax is $124. Had Dawkins claimed six withholding allowances, his withholding tax would have been only $38. ■

3   Many companies today prefer to use the *percentage method* to determine federal withholding tax. The percentage method does not require the several pages of tables needed with the wage bracket method and is more easily adapted to computer applications in the processing of payrolls. Instead, the table shown in Figure 5.6 is used.

EXAMPLE 3

Finding Federal Withholding Using the Percentage Method

Bill Cornett is married, claims four withholding allowances, and has weekly gross earnings of $975. Use the percentage method to find his withholding tax.

SOLUTION

Step 1.   Find the withholding allowance for *one* on the weekly payroll period in Figure 5.6. The amount is $44.23. Since Cornett claims four allowances, multiply the one withholding allowance $44.23, by his number of withholding allowances 4.

$$\$44.23 \times 4 = \$176.92.$$

Step 2.   Subtract the amount in step 1 from gross earnings.

$$\$975 - \$176.92 = \$798.08$$

Step 3.   Find the "married person weekly" section of the percentage method withholding table on the next page. Since $798.08 is over $760 but not over $1513, an amount of $96.75 is added to 28% of the excess over $760.

$$\$798.08 - \$760 - \$38.08 \text{ (excess over \$760)}$$

$$\$38.08 \times 28\% = \$38.08 \times .28 = \$10.66$$

$$\$96.75 + \$10.66 = \$107.41 \text{ withholding tax} \quad \blacksquare$$

CAUTION   The amount of withholding tax found using the wage bracket method can vary slightly from the amount of withholding tax found using the percentage method. Any differences would be eliminated when the income tax return is filed.

Percentage Method Income Tax Withholding Table

Payroll Period	One withholding allowance
Weekly	**$44.23**
Biweekly	88.46
Semimonthly	95.83
Monthly	191.67
Quarterly	575.00
Semiannually	1,150.00
Annually	2,300.00
Daily or miscellaneous (each day of the payroll period)	8.85

Tables for Percentage Method of Withholding

TABLE 1—If the Payroll Period With Respect to an Employee is Weekly

(a) SINGLE person—including head of household:

If the amount of wages (after subtracting withholding allowances) is: The amount of income tax to be withheld shall be:

Not over $47 0

Over—	But not over —		of excess over—
$47	—$438	15%	—$47
$438	—$913	$58.65 plus 28%	—$438
$913	. . . .	$191.65 plus 31%	—$913

(b) MARRIED person—

If the amount of wages (after subtracting withholding allowances) is: The amount of income tax to be withheld shall be:

Not over $115 0

Over—	But not over—		of excess over—
$115	—$760	15%	—$115
$760	—$1,513.	$96.75 plus 28%	—$760
$1,513.	. . . .	$307.59 plus 31%	—$1,513

TABLE 2—If the Payroll Period With Respect to an Employee is Biweekly

(a) SINGLE person—including head of household:

If the amount of wages (after subtracting withholding allowances) is: The amount of income tax to be withheld shall be:

Not over $94 0

Over—	But not over —		of excess over—
$94	—$875	15%	—$94
$875	—$1,825.	$117.15 plus 28%	—$875
$1,825.	. . . .	$383.15 plus 31%	—$1,825

(b) MARRIED person—

If the amount of wages (after subtracting withholding allowances) is: The amount of income tax to be withheld shall be:

Not over $231 0

Over—	But not over—		of excess over—
$231	—$1,519.	15%	—$231
$1,519	—$3,027.	$193.20 plus 28%	—$1,519
$3,027.	. . . .	$615.44 plus 31%	—$3,027

TABLE 3—If the Payroll Period With Respect to an Employee is Semimonthly

(a) SINGLE person—including head of household:

If the amount of wages (after subtracting withholding allowances) is: The amount of income tax to be withheld shall be:

Not over $102 0

Over—	But not over —		of excess over—
$102	—$948	15%	—$102
$948	—$1,977.	$126.90 plus 28%	—$948
$1,977.	. . . .	$415.02 plus 31%	—$1,977

(b) MARRIED person—

If the amount of wages (after subtracting withholding allowances) is: The amount of income tax to be withheld shall be:

Not over $250 0

Over—	But not over—		of excess over—
$250	—$1,646.	15%	—$250
$1,646	—$3,279.	$209.40 plus 28%	—$1,646
$3,279.	. . . .	$666.64 plus 31%	—$3,279

TABLE 4—If the Payroll Period With Respect to an Employee is Monthly

(a) SINGLE person—including head of household:

If the amount of wages (after subtracting withholding allowances) is: The amount of income tax to be withheld shall be:

Not over $204 0

Over—	But not over —		of excess over—
$204	—$1,896.	15%	—$204
$1,896	—$3,954.	$253.80 plus 28%	—$1,896
$3,954.	. . . .	$830.04 plus 31%	—$3,954

(b) MARRIED person—

If the amount of wages (after subtracting withholding allowances) is: The amount of income tax to be withheld shall be:

Not over $500 0

Over—	But not over—		of excess over—
$500	—$3,292.	15%	—$500
$3,292	—$6,558.	$418.80 plus 28%	—$3,292
$6,558.	. . . .	$1,333.28 plus 31%	—$6,558

FIGURE 5.6

4 Many states and some cities also have an income tax or **state withholding** tax collected by withholding from the gross earnings of the employee. The state or city supplies tables similar to the one in Figure 5.7.

EXAMPLE 4

Finding State Withholding Tax

James Marshall is single and has weekly gross earnings of $418.50. Find his state withholding tax.

SOLUTION Use the left-hand table of Figure 5.7 for single persons. Earnings of $418.50 are found in the row "over 406 but not over 455." The withholding can be found by multiplying 9% by the amount of earnings and then subtracting $18.84.

$$9\% \times \$418.50 = .09 \times \$418.50 = \$37.67 \text{ (rounded)}$$

$$\$37.67 - \$18.84 = \$18.83 \text{ state withholding tax} \quad \blacksquare$$

```
               STATE WITHHOLDING SCHEDULE
               WEEKLY PAYROLL PERIOD
          ==================================
```

	SINGLE PERSONS				MARRIED PERSONS		
IF THE TAXABLE INCOME IS...		THE COMPUTED TAX IS...		IF THE TAXABLE INCOME IS...		THE COMPUTED TAX IS...	
OVER	BUT NOT OVER	AMOUNT TIMES	MINUS	OVER	BUT NOT OVER	AMOUNT TIMES	MINUS
0	65...	1% –	.00	0	130...	1% –	.00
65	113...	2% –	.65	130	227...	2% –	1.30
113	162...	3% –	1.77	227	324...	3% –	3.57
162	211...	4% –	3.41	324	422...	4% –	6.81
211	260...	5% –	5.51	422	520...	5% –	11.02
280	309...	6% –	8.12	520	618...	6% –	16.23
309	357...	7% –	11.21	618	714...	7% –	22.43
357	406...	8% –	14.77	714	812...	8% –	29.53
406	455...	9% –	18.84	812	909...	9% –	37.68
455	503...	10% –	23.42	909	1,007...	10% –	46.74
503	AND OVER	11% –	28.38	1,007	AND OVER	11% –	56.88

FIGURE 5.7

5 It is common for employees to request additional deductions, such as union dues and credit union payments. The final amount of pay received by the employee, called the **net pay**, is given by the formula

Net pay = Gross earnings − FICA tax (social security) − Medicare tax − Federal withholding tax − State withholding tax − Other deductions

EXAMPLE 5

Determining Net Pay After Deductions

Katherine Steinbacher is married and claims four withholding allowances. Her weekly gross earnings are $418.25. Her union dues are $20. Find her net pay using the percentage method.

SOLUTION First find FICA (social security) tax, which is $27.19, then medicare, $6.27. Federal withholding tax is $18.95 and state withholding is $9.92. Total deductions are

$27.19	FICA tax (6.5%)
$6.27	medicare tax (1.5%)
$18.95	federal withholding
$9.92	state withholding
+ 20.00	union dues
$82.33	total deductions

Find net pay by subtracting total deductions from gross earnings.

$418.25	gross earnings
− $82.33	total deductions
$335.92	net pay

Steinbacher will receive a check for $335.92. ■

An employee's contribution to social security and medicare must be matched by the employer.

5.5 Exercises

Find the federal withholding tax for each of the following employees. Use the wage bracket method.

	Employee	Gross Earnings	Married?	Withholding Allowances
1.	Mildred, M.	$2433.18 monthly	yes	4
2.	Salas, D.	$536.47 weekly	no	1
3.	McLaurin, B.	$449.38 weekly	no	0
4.	Rodrigues, J.	$1875.37 monthly	yes	1
5.	Beckenstein, J.	$2229.83 monthly	yes	6
6.	Yoshi, S.	$1410.42 monthly	yes	4
7.	Lause, C.	$2387.92 monthly	yes	6
8.	Peterson, O.	$532.14 weekly	no	1
9.	Bridges, C.	$2298.14 monthly	yes	3
10.	Buch, P.	$579.08 weekly	no	0

Use the state withholding schedule to find the state withholding tax for each of the following employees.

Employee	Gross Weekly Earnings	Married?
11. Rogers, B.	$285.14	no
12. Sandeford, M.	$382.40	yes
13. Steinbacker, K.	$426.82	no
14. Tubalinal, Y.	$652.15	yes
15. O'Brien, H.	$352.29	yes
16. Stratton, R.	$573.41	no

Use the percentage method of withholding to find federal withholding tax, a 6.5% FICA rate to find FICA tax, and 1.5% to find medicare tax for each of the following employees. Then find the net pay for each employee. The number of withholding allowances and the marital status are listed after each employee's name. Assume that no employee has earned over $60,000 so far this year.

Employee	Gross Earnings
17. Jones, 5, M	$348.12 weekly
18. Biaggi, 3, S	$2418.09 monthly
19. Stahle, 1, S	$1532.18 monthly
20. Adams, 2, M	$347.00 weekly
21. Baumberger, 5, M	$3302.46 monthly
22. Grummitt, 1, S	$496.18 weekly
23. Presleigh, 6, M	$3942.12 monthly
24. Parker, 5, M	$400.00 weekly
25. Barchus, 3, S	$689.16 weekly
26. Hall, 2, S	$4274.08 monthly
27. Mills, 1, S	$389.47 weekly
28. Dunbar, 4, M	$5410.06 monthly
29. Wilson, 3, M	$5312.59 monthly
30. Barr, 2, M	$503.19 weekly
31. Coop, 2, S	$431.25 weekly
32. Strong, 1, S	$3285.20 monthly

33. In your present or past job which deductions were subtracted from gross earnings to arrive at net pay? Which was the largest deduction?

34. Write an explanation of how to determine the federal withholding tax using the wage bracket (tax tables) method. (See Objective 2.)

Use the percentage method of withholding, an FICA rate of 6.5%, a medicare rate of 1.5%, an SDI rate of 1.25%, and the state withholding schedule in the following problems.

35. Richard Wright, a computer programmer, has weekly earnings of $692. He is married and claims five withholding allowances. His deductions include FICA, medicare, federal withholding, state disability insurance, state withholding, union dues of $15.50, and credit union savings of $100. Find his net pay for a week in March.

36. Diane Bolton has earnings of $438 in one week of February. She is single and claims four withholding allowances. Her deductions include FICA, medicare, federal withholding, state disability insurance, state withholding, a United Way contribution of $10, and a savings bond of $50. Find her net pay for the week.

37. The top salesperson for Musser Dental Supplies is paid a salary of $350 per week plus 6% of all sales over $5000. She is single and claims two withholding allowances. Her deductions include FICA, medicare, federal withholding, state disability, state withholding, credit union savings of $25, a Salvation Army contribution of $5, and dues of $10 to the National Association of Professional Saleswomen. Find her net pay for a week in April during which she has sales of $11,284 with returns and allowances of $424.50

38. Gilbert Eckern, a sales representative for a chemical company, is paid on a variable commission, is married, and claims four withholding allowances. He receives 6% of the first $5000 in sales, 8% of the next $3000 in sales, and 10% of all sales over $8000. This week he has sales of $9280 and the following deductions: FICA, medicare, federal withholding, state disability insurance, state withholding, a retirement contribution of $22.83, a savings bond of $37.50, and charitable contributions of $14. Find his net pay after subtracting all of his deductions.

39. Sheri Minkner, a marketing representative for Alternate Heating Company is paid a monthly salary of $3940 plus a bonus of 1.6% on monthly sales. She is married and claims three withholding allowances. Her deductions include FICA, medicare, federal withholding, state disability, credit union savings of $150, charitable contributions of $25, and a savings bond of $50. Find her net pay for a month in which she receives a bonus on sales of $35,820. The state in which Minkner works has no state income tax.

40. River Raft Adventures pays its manager Ron Degler a monthly salary of $2880 plus a commission of .8% based on total monthly sales volume. In the month of May, River Raft Adventures has total sales of $86,280. Degler is married and claims five withholding allowances. His deductions include FICA, medicare, federal withholding, state disability, credit union payment of $300, March of Dimes contributions of $20, and savings bonds of $250. There is no state income tax in the state where Degler works. Find his net pay for May.

▌5.6 Payroll Records and Quarterly Returns

OBJECTIVES

1 Understand payroll records kept by employers.

2 Calculate employer's matching social security and medicare contributions.

3 Find the quarterly amount due the Internal Revenue Service.

4 Identify the form used by employers to file a quarterly tax return.

5 Find the amount of Federal Unemployment Tax due.

Employers keep payroll records for many reasons. Individual payroll records for each employee are used to keep track of social security tax, medicare tax, federal and state withholding, and many other items. The amounts withheld from employee earnings are sent periodically to the proper agency; most are paid entirely by the employee and others are matched by the employer. Usually these records are filed quarterly. These quarters and the filing dates are shown in Table 5.3.

TABLE 5.3   Filing Schedules for Employee Withholding

Quarter	Ending	Due Date
January–February–March	March 31	April 30
April–May–June	June 30	July 31
July–August–September	September 30	October 31
October–November–December	December 31	January 31

1   The payroll ledger, discussed in Section 5.1, was a record of the number of hours worked by all of the employees for a certain time period. The Employee's Earnings Record shown in Figure 5.8 details quarterly totals for an individual employee. This record shows the gross earnings, deduction amounts, and net pay for each pay period during the quarter.

2   The employer must check the earnings of each employee to make sure that the FICA, medicare, and the FUTA (discussed in this section) cutoff points are not passed. Since the employer must also give an end-of-year wage and tax statement (Form W-2) to each employee, the records are also used as the source of this information. In addition, accurate payroll records are important because the employer is required by law to match the employee's social security and medicare contributions.

NAME	Gloria Gibson	CLOCK NUMBER	114	DEPT	Production

STREET _718 Alhambra Blvd._ SOC.SEC. NUMBER _349 - 62 - 0156_

CITY _Glenview, Illinois_ PHONE NO. _482-6319_ DATE STARTED / DATE LEFT

MARITAL STATUS _M_ NO. OF EXEMPT _3_ ☐ M. ☑ F.

RECORD OF PAY CHANGES: _1/1/8___ 7.20 ; _3/19/8___ 8.50

DATE PAY PERIOD ENDING	SUN	M	TU	W	TH	F	SAT	GROSS PAYROLL	F.W.T.	SOC. SEC.	D. INS.	S.W.T.	U.D.	CHECK NO.	DEDUCTION AMOUNTS / NET PAY	
					BROUGHT FORWARD →											
1/7		8	8	7	8	10		298^{80}	18^{00}	22^{44}	18^{00}	13^{80}	5^{00}	1186	221^{56}	1
1/14		8	8	8	8	8		288^{00}	16^{00}	21^{63}	18^{00}	13^{40}	5^{00}	1295	213^{97}	2
1/21		8	10	8	9	8	4	363^{60}	28^{00}	27^{31}	18^{00}	15^{06}	5^{00}	1378	270^{23}	3
1/28		8	8	8	8	8		288^{00}	16^{00}	21^{63}	18^{00}	13^{40}	5^{00}	1498	213^{97}	4
2/4		8	8	6	8	8	2	288^{00}	16^{00}	21^{63}	18^{00}	13^{40}	5^{00}	1601	213^{97}	5
2/11		8	8	8	8	8		288^{00}	16^{00}	21^{63}	18^{00}	13^{40}	5^{00}	1738	213^{97}	6
2/18		8	8	8	8	8		288^{00}	16^{00}	21^{63}	18^{00}	13^{40}	5^{00}	1856	213^{97}	7
2/25		10	8	10	6	6	5	342^{00}	25^{00}	25^{68}	18^{00}	14^{70}	5^{00}	2023	253^{62}	8
3/3		8	8	8	8	8		288^{80}	16^{00}	21^{63}	18^{00}	13^{40}	5^{00}	2186	213^{97}	9
3/10		8	7	8	9	10		309^{60}	19^{00}	23^{25}	18^{00}	13^{90}	5^{00}	2316	230^{45}	10
3/17		8	8	8	8	8		288^{00}	16^{00}	21^{63}	18^{00}	13^{40}	5^{00}	2479	213^{97}	11
3/24		10	8	10	8	8		391^{00}	33^{00}	29^{36}	18^{00}	16^{60}	5^{00}	2632	289^{04}	12
3/31		8	8	8	9	8	4	403^{75}	34^{00}	30^{32}	18^{00}	17^{06}	5^{00}	2801	299^{39}	13
																14
																15
																16
QTR.								4124^{75}	269^{00}	309^{79}	234^{80}	184^{92}	65^{00}		3062^{06}	
TO DATE																

FIGURE 5.8

3   An employee's contribution to social security and medicare must be matched by the employer.

EXAMPLE 1

Finding the Amount of FICA and Medicare Tax Due

If the employees at a company pay a total of $789.10 in social security tax, and $182.10 in medicare tax, how much must the employer send to the Internal Revenue Service?

SOLUTION   The employer must match this and send a total of $971.20 ($789.10 + $182.10 from employees) + $971.20 (from employer) = $1942.40 to the government. ■

NOTE   In addition to the employee's social security tax and a matching amount paid by the employer, the employer must also send the amount withheld for income tax to the Internal Revenue Service on a quarterly basis.

EXAMPLE 2

Finding the
Employers Amount
Due the IRS

Suppose that during a certain quarter a firm has collected $1382.71 from its employees for FICA tax, $319.09 for medicare tax, and $1786.43 in federal withholding tax. Compute the total amount due to the government from the firm.

SOLUTION

$1382.71	collected from employees for FICA tax
1382.71	equal amount paid by employer
319.09	collected from employees for medicare tax
319.09	equal amount paid by employer
1786.43	federal withholding tax
$5190.03	total due to government

The firm must send $5190.03 to the Internal Revenue Service. ■

Calculator Approach to Example 2

The amount withheld for federal income tax is first placed in memory.

$$1786.43 \quad \boxed{M+}$$

Next, the employees' FICA amount is entered into the calculator and then doubled because the employer matches it. This amount is added to the memory using the $\boxed{M+}$ key. The employees' medicare amount is then entered into the calculator and then doubled because the employer matches the medicare amount also. This amount is also added to the memory using the $\boxed{M+}$ key. The $\boxed{MR}$ key is then used to get the total amount paid to the government.

$$1382.71 \quad \boxed{\times} \quad 2 \quad \boxed{M+} \quad 319.09 \quad \boxed{\times} \quad 2 \quad \boxed{M+} \quad \boxed{MR} \quad 5190.03$$

---

4 At the end of each quarter, employers must file **Form 941**, the **Employer's Quarterly Federal Tax Return**. This form reports the amount of income tax withheld by the employer, and the amount of social security taxes and medicare taxes due.

A copy of Form 941 is shown in Figure 5.9. The right column (lines 1 through 18) itemizes total employee wages and earnings, and the income, FICA, and medicare taxes due. The lower portion of Form 941 divides the quarter into its three months, and the amounts of tax liability (employee and employer) are entered on the correct date line of the proper month in that quarter.

The "Net taxes" (line 16) must equal line IV at the bottom, "Total for quarter." The withheld income tax and employee and employer FICA and medicare taxes must be deposited with an authorized financial institution or a Federal Reserve Bank or branch. The amount of taxes owed determines how often these deposits must be made. If the amount of taxes owed by an employer is less than $500 at the end of a quarter, the money does not have to be deposited, but is sent directly to the IRS. Funds can be

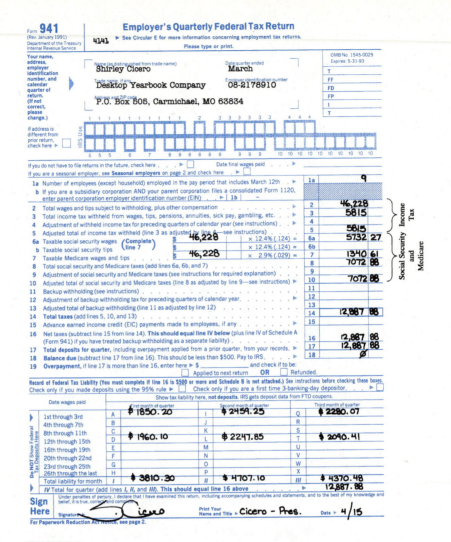

FIGURE 5.9

deposited using the Federal Tax Deposit Coupon Form 8109, shown in Figure 5.10. This form is filed, along with the proper amount of money, at an authorized financial institution, which then forwards the money to the Treasury.

5   The **Federal Unemployment Tax Act (FUTA)** requires employers to pay an additional tax. This **unemployment insurance tax**, paid entirely by employers, is used to pay unemployment benefits to an individual who has become unemployed and is unable to find work.

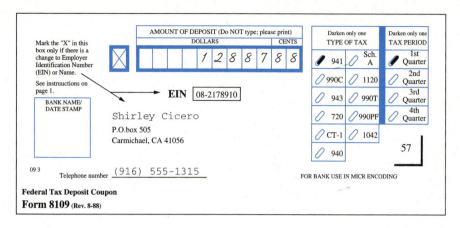

FIGURE 5.10

In general, all employers who paid wages of $1000 or more in a calendar quarter or had one or more employees for some part of a day in any 20 different weeks must file an *Employer's Annual Federal Unemployment (FUTA) Tax Return*. This federal return must be filed each January for the preceding year. The FUTA tax that must be paid by the employer is 6.2% of the first $7000 in earnings for that year for each employee. Most states have unemployment taxes paid by the employer for which the employer is given credit on the FUTA return.

The credit given cannot exceed 5.4%, so the minimum amount due for FUTA is 0.8% (6.2% − 5.4%). States normally require quarterly payment of the unemployment tax. As soon as an employee reaches earnings of $7000, no additional unemployment tax must be paid.

If an employer has a history of few layoffs, an individual state may drop the unemployment tax rate below 5.4%. On the other hand, an employer with high labor turnover may have to pay the higher unemployment tax rate.

EXAMPLE 3

Finding the Amount of Unemployment Tax Due

Joan Spalding earns $2400 each quarter. Find the following amounts: (a) Spalding's earnings in the third quarter of the year that are subject to unemployment tax and (b) the amount of unemployment tax due on third quarter earnings. (Assume a tax rate of 6.2%.)

SOLUTION

(a) Since earnings in the first two quarters are $4800 (2 × $2400), the earnings subject to unemployment taxes in the third quarter are $2200 ($7000 − $4800).

(b) The federal unemployment tax due is $136.40 (0.062 × $2200). ■

5.6 Exercises

*Find the total combined amount of social security and medicare tax (employees' contri-
bution plus employer's contribution) for each of the following firms. Use a FICA rate of
6.5%, a medicare tax rate of 1.5%, and assume no employee has earned over $60,000 so
far this year.*

Firm	Total Employee Earnings
1. Again Books	$3706.36
2. Len's Sporting Goods	$4433.12
3. Village Grain	$17,462.80
4. Leisure Outdoor Furniture	$15,324.15
5. Computers Plus	$28,263.18
6. Owl Drugstore	$42,563.20
7. Teddys and Trains	$62,476.56
8. Crescent Foundry	$122,819.50

*Calculate the total amount due from each of the following firms. Use a FICA rate of 6.5%
and a medicare tax rate of 1.5%.*

Firm	Total Employee Earnings	Total Withholding for Income Tax
9. Biondi Paving	$9890.60	$997.42
10. Sports Memorabilia	$18,769	$4741.12
11. Childlike Publishers	$32,121.85	$8215.08
12. Mart & Bottle	$10,127.80	$2218.40
13. Todd Consultants	$37,271.39	$7128.64
14. Capital Landscape	$10,158.24	$2768.62
15. Sub Shop	$34,547.86	$12,628.19
16. Oaks Hardware	$42,789.54	$11,342.60

17. An employer must file Form 941, Employer's Quarterly Federal Tax Return each
quarter. What kinds of information is included on this form? (See Objective 5.)

18. Describe in your own words four differences between social security and FUTA.
Consider the purpose, amount paid, and who pays in your description.

*Solve the following word problems. Assume no employee has earned over $60,000 so far
this year. Use a FICA rate of 6.5% and a medicare tax rate of 1.5%.*

19. Total employee earnings for one firm are $43,856.20. Find the combined total amount
of FICA and medicare taxes sent to the IRS by the employer.

20. Loomis Foundry has a payroll of $6825.15. How much FICA and medicare taxes
should be sent to the IRS?

21. The AM-PM Mart has an employee payroll of $10,206.52. During the same time
period, $2218.54 was withheld as income tax. Find the total amount due to the
IRS.

22. The payroll at the Oak Furniture Store is $22,607.72. During the same pay period,
$3898.14 was withheld as income tax. Find the total amount that must be sent to the
IRS.

Assume a FUTA rate of 6.2% of the first $7000 in earnings in each of the following.

23. An employee earns $3280 in the first quarter of the year, $2600 in the second quarter, and $3156 in the third quarter. Find (a) the amount of earnings subject to unemployment tax in the third quarter and (b) the amount of unemployment tax due on third quarter earnings.

24. Greg Christofferson earns $720 per month. Find (a) the amount of earnings subject to unemployment tax in the fourth quarter and (b) the amount of unemployment tax due on fourth quarter earnings.

25. Jill Staut is paid $1800 per month. Find (a) the amount of earnings subject to unemployment tax in the second quarter (b) the amount of unemployment tax due on second quarter earnings.

26. Philip Fridl received $4820 in earnings in the first quarter of the year. His earnings in the second quarter are $3815. Find (a) the amount of his earnings subject to FUTA in the second quarter and (b) the amount of tax due in the second quarter.

CHAPTER 5 QUICK REVIEW

TOPIC		APPROACH	EXAMPLE
5.1	Gross earnings	Gross earnings = Hours worked × Rate per hour	40 hours at $6.30 per hour Gross earnings = 40 × $6.30 = $252
5.1	Gross earnings with overtime	First, find regular earnings. Then, determine overtime pay at overtime rate. Finally, add regular and overtime earnings.	40 hours at $6.30 per hour; 8 hours at time and a half. Gross earnings = (40 × $6.30) + (10 × $6.30 × $1\frac{1}{2}$) = $252 + $94.50 = $346.50
5.1	Common pay periods		Find the earnings equivalent of $1400 per month for other pay periods.

Pay Period	Paychecks per Year
Monthly	12
Semimonthly	24
Biweekly	26
Weekly	52

$$\text{Semimonthly} = \frac{1400}{2} = \$700$$

$$\text{Biweekly} = \frac{1400 \times 12}{26} = \$646.15$$

$$\text{Weekly} = \frac{1400 \times 12}{52} = \$323.08$$

TOPIC	APPROACH	EXAMPLE
5.1 Overtime for salaried employees	First, find the equivalent hourly rate. Next, multiply the rate by the overtime hours by $1\frac{1}{2}$. Finally, add overtime earnings to salary.	Salary is $324 per week for 36 hours. Find earnings for 46 hours. $324 \div 36 = \$9.00$ per hour $\$9.00 \times 10 \times 1\frac{1}{2} = \$135$ overtime $\$324 + \$135 = \$459$
5.2 Straight commission	Gross earnings = Commission rate $\times$ Amount of sales	Sales of $25,800; commission rate is 5%. $0.05 \times \$25,800 = \$1290$
5.2 Variable commission	Commission rate varies at different sales levels.	Up to $10,000, 6%; $10,001–$20,000, 8%; $20.001 and up, 9%. Find the commission on sales of $32,768. $0.06 \times \$10,000 = \$\ \ 600.00$ $0.08 \times \$10,000 = \$\ \ 800.00$ $0.09 \times \underline{\$12,768} = \underline{\$1149.12}$ Totals $32,768 $2549.12
5.2 Salary and commission	Gross earnings = Fixed earnings + Commission	Salary, $250 per week; commission rate, 3%. Find gross earnings on sales of $6848. Gross earnings = $\qquad \$250 + (0.03 \times 6848)$ $= \$250 + \$205.44$ $= \$455.44$
5.2 Commissions with a drawing account	Gross earnings = Commission − Draw	Sales for month, $28,560; commission rate, 7%; draw, $750 for month. Find gross earnings. Gross earnings = $\qquad (0.07 \times 28,560) - \$750$ $\qquad = \$1999.20 - \$750$ $\qquad = \$1249.20$
5.3 Gross earnings for piecework	Gross earnings = Number of items $\times$ Payment per item	Items produced, 175; payment per item, $.65. Find gross earnings. $175 \times \$.65 = \$113.75$

TOPIC	APPROACH	EXAMPLE
5.3 Gross earnings for differential piecework	The rate paid per item produced varies with level of production.	1–100 items, \$.75 each; 101-150 items, \$.90; 151 or more items, \$1.04. Find gross earnings for 214 items. $100 \times \$.75 = \$75.00$ $50 \times \$.90 = \$45.00$ $\underline{64 \times \$1.04} = \underline{\$66.56}$ Total 214 \$186.56
5.3 Gross earnings with piece rate and chargebacks	Find piece rate earnings; then calculate chargebacks and subtract them from piece rate earnings to find gross earnings.	Items produced, 318; piece rate, \$.75; spoiled items, 26; chargeback, \$.60. Find gross earnings. $318 \times \$.75 = \$238.50$ $26 \times \$.60 = \$15.60$ $\$238.50 - \$15.60 = \$222.90$
5.3 Overtime earnings on piecework	Gross earnings = Earnings at regular rate + Earnings at overtime rate	Items produced on regular time, 530; items produced on overtime, 110; piece rate, \$.34. Find gross earnings. Gross earnings $= 530 \times \$.34$ $+ 110(1\frac{1}{2} \times \$.34)$ $= \$180.20 + \$56.10$ $= \$236.30$
5.4 FICA; social security tax	The gross earnings are multiplied by the rate. When the maximum earnings are reached, no additional FICA is withheld that year.	Gross earnings, \$458; social security tax rate, 6.5%; find social security tax. $\$458 \times .065 = \$29.77$
5.4 Medicare tax	The gross earnings are multiplied by the tax rate. When the maximum earnings are reached, no additional medicare tax is withheld that year.	Gross earnings, \$458, medicare tax rate, 1.5%, find medicare tax. $\$458 \times .015 = \$6.87$
5.4 State disability insurance deductions	Multiply the gross earnings by the SDI tax rate. When maximum earnings are reached, no additional taxes are paid in that year.	Gross earnings, \$3210; SDI tax rate 1.25%; find SDI tax. $\$3210 \times .0125 = \$40.13$

TOPIC	APPROACH	EXAMPLE
5.5 Federal with-holding tax	Tax is paid on total earnings. No maximum as with FICA.	Single employee with 3 allowances; weekly earnings of $485; find the federal withholding tax. Using wage bracket amount "at least $480, but less than $490," withholding is $46. With the percentage method withholding is $485 − ($44.23 × 3) = $352.31 $352.31 − $47 = $305.31 × .15 = $45.80
5.5 State withholding tax	Tax is paid on total earnings. No maximum as with FICA.	Married employee with weekly earnings of $392; find the state withholding tax. Use the "married" table for earnings "over 324, but not over 422." (4% × $392) − $6.81 $15.68 − $6.81 = $8.87
5.6 Quarterly report, Form 941	Filed each quarter; FICA and federal withholding are sent to the IRS. (FICA + medicare) × 2 (employer) + federal withholding tax	If quarterly FICA withheld from employees is $5269, medicare tax is $1581, and federal withholding tax is $14,780, find the total due the IRS. ($5269 + $1581) × (2) + $14,780 = $28,480
5.6 Federal Unemployment Tax (FUTA)	FUTA is paid by the employer on the first $7000 of earnings each year for each employee.	An employee earned $3850 in the first quarter of a year. Find the amount of unemployment tax using a 6.2% tax rate. $3850 × 6.2% = $238.70

SUMMARY EXERCISE

The manager of a computer service company receives an annual salary of $35,360 which is paid weekly. Her normal work week is 40 hours and she is paid time and a half for all overtime. She is single and claims one withholding allowance. Her deductions include FICA, medicare, federal withholding, state disability insurance, state withholding, credit union payments of $65, retirement deductions of $35, association dues of $12, and a Diabetes Association contribution of $10. Find each of the following for a week in which she works 52 hours.

(a) Regular weekly earnings.

(b) Overtime earnings.

(c) Total gross earnings.

(d) FICA.

(e) Medicare.

(f) Federal withholding.

(g) State disability.

(h) State withholding.

(i) Net pay.

CHAPTER 5 REVIEW EXERCISES

Complete the following partial payroll ledger. Find the total gross earnings for each employee. Time and a half is paid on all hours over 40 in one week. [5.1]

	Employee	Hours Worked	Reg. Hours	O.T. Hours	Reg. Rate	Gross Earnings
1.	Workman, K.	$55\frac{3}{4}$			$6.70	
2.	Stevenson, C.	48			$8.50	
3.	Eriksen, J.	$43\frac{1}{2}$			$7.10	
4.	Dean, K.	$57\frac{1}{4}$			$6.80	

Find the equivalent earnings for each of the following salaries as indicated. [5.1]

	Weekly	Biweekly	Semimonthly	Monthly	Annually
5.	$375	_____	_____	_____	_____
6.	_____	$530	_____	_____	_____
7.	_____	_____	_____	_____	$18,000
8.	_____	_____	$875	_____	_____

Find the weekly gross earnings for the following people who are on salary and are paid time and a half for overtime. [5.1]

	Employee	Regular Hours Per Week	Weekly Salary	Hours Worked	Weekly Gross Earnings
9.	Uldall, E.	40	$420	45	_____
10.	Jung, K.	36	$342	42	_____

Find the gross earnings for each of the following salespeople. [5.2]

	Employee	Total Sales	Returns and Allowances	Rate of Commission
11.	Clark, K.	$22,680	$3176	8%
12.	Spencer, H.	$15,476	$218	6%

Solve each of the following word problems.

13.   Twenty Minute Lube and Oil pays its employees $1.25 for an oil change, $1.50 for each car lubed, and $2.50 if a car gets both an oil change and a lube. This week Andre Herrebout changed the oil in 63 cars, lubed 46 cars, and gave an oil change and lube to 38 cars. Find his gross pay for the week. [5.3]

14.   Floral arrangers at Sherwood Florist are paid as follows: 1-200 arrangements in a week, $1.00 each; 201-300 arrangements, $1.40 each; more than 300 arrangements, $1.70 each. David Garrison completed 325 arrangements in a week. Find his gross earnings. [5.3]

15.   Patrick Kelly receives a commission of 15% for selling advertising. He pays half the commission to his agent and gives half of the remainder to another staff member. Kelly receives the rest. Find the amount he receives personally from the sale of $52,500 in advertising. [5.2]

Use the following information for Exercises 16 and 17. [5.2]
Employees are paid a commission on the following schedule.

First $1500 in sales	8%
Next $1500 in sales	10%
Sales over $3000	12%

16.   Find the gross earnings for an employee with total sales of $4250.

17.   Find the gross earnings for an employee with total sales of $3940.

18.   Pat Rowell ties bows on Christmas wreaths and is paid $.12 for each bow tied. She is charged $.09 for each rejection and is paid time and a half for overtime production. Find her gross earnings for a week when she produces 1850 at regular rate, 285 at overtime rate, and has 92 rejections. [5.3]

Use the following information for Exercises 19 and 20. [5.4]

An employee is paid a salary of $5150 per month. If the FICA rate is 6.5% on the first $60,000 of earnings and the medicare tax rate is 1.5% on the first $150,000 of earnings, how much will the employee pay in (a) FICA tax and (b) medicare tax during the following months?

19. July

20. December

Find the federal withholding tax using the wage bracket method for each of the following employees. [5.5]

21. Quiroz: 6 withholding allowances, single, $698.04 weekly earnings

22. Pieri: 2 withholding allowances, married, $1818.18 monthly earnings

23. Warr: 3 withholding allowances, married, $2450.49 monthly earnings

24. Chang: 1 withholding allowance, single, $506.50 weekly earnings

25. Hartman: 5 withholding allowances, married, $1579.48 monthly earnings

26. Tewell: 2 withholding allowances, single, $482.50 weekly earnings

Find the net pay for each of the following employees after FICA, medicare, federal with-holding tax, state disability, and other deductions have been made. Assume that no one has earned over $60,000 so far this year. Assume a FICA rate of 6.5%, medicare rate of 1.5%, and a state disability rate of 1.25%. Use the percentage method of withholding. [5.5]

27. Precilo: $1364.18 monthly earnings, 1 withholding allowance, single, $27.18 in other deductions

28. Rooke: $356.48 weekly earnings, 3 withholding allowances, married, state withholding of $14.63, credit union savings of $20, educational television contribution of $4.50

29. Talbot: $493.57 weekly earnings, 6 withholding allowances, married, state withholding of $10.14, union dues of $14, charitable contribution of $8

Solve the following word problems. Assume no employee has earned over $60,000 so far this year. Use a FICA rate of 6.5% and a rate of 1.5% for medicare. [5.6]

30. Total employee earnings for Round Table Pizza are $12,720.15. Find the total amount of FICA and medicare taxes sent to the IRS by the employer.

31. Carmichael Plumbing has an employee payroll of $58,370.34. During the same period $9843.15 was withheld as income tax. Find the total amount due the IRS.

Solve the following word problems.

32. A salesperson is paid $452 per week plus a commission of 2% on all sales. The salesperson sold $712 worth of goods on Monday, $523 on Tuesday, $1002 on Wednesday, $391 on Thursday, and $609 on Friday. Returns and allowances for the week were $114. Find the employee's (a) social security tax (6.5%), (b) medicare tax (1.5%), and (c) state disability insurance (1.25%) for the week. [5.3 and 5.4]

33. Sandra Cubelic earned $57,806.13 so far this year until last week. Last week she earned $3279.12. Find her (a) FICA tax and (b) medicare tax. [5.3]

34. The employees of Miracle Floor Covering paid a total of $1496.11 in social security tax last month, $345.30 in medicare tax, and $1768.43 in federal withholding tax. Find the total amount that the employer must send to the Internal Revenue Service.

Assume a FUTA rate of 6.2% on the first $7000 in earnings in each of the following. [5.6]

35. An employee earns $2875 in the first quarter of the year, $3212 in the second quarter, and $2942 in the third quarter. Find (a) the amount of earnings subject to unemployment tax in the third quarter and (b) the amount of unemployment tax due on third quarter earnings.

36. Kara Bererra earns $810 per month. Find (a) the amount of earnings subject to unemployment tax in the third quarter and (b) the amount of unemployment tax due on third quarter earnings.

6

Taxes

There is one thing on which almost everyone agrees. "Taxes are too high." But, taxes are a fact of life. In the early part of this century, Justice Oliver Wendell Holmes, Jr., of the United States Supreme Court said, "taxes are the price we pay to live in a civilized society." Tax dollars pay for education, health services, national defense, streets and highways, parks and recreation facilities, police and fire protection, public assistance for the poor, libraries, and even street lights. As government provides more services, taxes go up.

There are basically three forms of taxation: taxes on sales, property, and income. This chapter examines the basics of taxation and discusses the calculations necessary to work with each type of tax.

6.1 Sales Tax

OBJECTIVES

1 Understand how sales tax is determined.

2 Find the amount of sales tax and the total sale.

3 Find the selling price when the sales tax is known.

4 Find the amount of the sale when the total price is known.

5 Define excise tax.

6 Find the total cost including sales tax and excise tax.

Most states and a large number of counties, parishes, and cities have a tax on sales. This tax, called **sales tax**, is paid on the amount of retail sales. Normally calculated as a percent of the retail price, this tax varies from area to area. For instance, since food is considered a basic necessity, most states do not tax the majority of food items purchased in a grocery store. The same food items, however, may be taxed when

TABLE 6.1
6% Sales Tax

Transaction	Tax
.01– .08	0.00
.09– .24	0.01
.25– .41	0.02
.42– .58	0.03
.59– .74	0.04
.75– .91	0.05
.92–1.08	0.06
1.09–1.24	0.07
1.25–1.41	0.08
1.42–1.58	0.09
1.59–1.74	0.10
1.75–1.91	0.11
1.92–2.08	0.12

purchased in a restaurant. One state recently instituted (but later repealed) a so-called **snack tax**. This was a sales tax charged only on food items that are classified as "snack foods."

The sales tax collected by a specific state is charged only on sales made within the state. For example, the Eddie Bauer Company, outdoor outfitters, says, "Add applicable sales tax for shipments into CA, CO, CT, DC, IL, MA, MD, MI, MN, NJ, OH, PA, VA, WA" on its mail order form. Tax is required in these states because the company has retail stores in each of them. Someone ordering merchandise from a state other than these would pay no sales tax.

1 Many small retail stores use a tax table to compute sales tax. The sales clerk looks up the tax on the sales tax table and enters the amount into the cash register.

Today many stores have cash register systems that keep track of taxable items and automatically calculate the necessary tax. Sales tax tables from a typical state appear in Table 6.1. Table 6.2 on the next page shows the 1992 sales tax rate in each state and the District of Columbia.

The basic percent equation is used to solve sales tax problems. The amount of the sale is the base, the sales tax rate is the rate, and the amount of sales tax is the part.

$$\text{Sales tax} = \text{Amount of Sale} \times \text{Sales tax rate}$$
$$P = B \times R$$

2 A common calculation in business is to find the amount of sales tax and the total amount of the sale including tax.

EXAMPLE 1
Finding Sales Tax and the Total Sale

A customer at Crown Software makes a purchase of $29.49. Sales tax in the state is 4%. Find (a) the amount of sales tax and (b) the total amount collected from the customer.

SOLUTION

(a) The amount of sales tax (part) is found by multiplying the sales tax rate (rate) by the amount of the sale (base). Use the percent equation to find the sales tax.

$$P = BR$$
$$P = \$29.49 \times 4\%$$
$$P = \$29.49 \times 0.04 = \$1.18 \text{ rounded}$$

Sales tax is $1.18.

(b) Add to find the total amount collected from the customer.

$29.49 (amount of sale) + $1.18 (sales tax) =

$30.67 (total sale including tax) ∎

3 If the amount of sales tax and the sales tax rate are known, it is possible to determine the selling price.

TABLE 6.2   1992 Sales Tax Rates

Alabama (plus city and/or county tax where applicable)	4%	Nevada (plus county or local tax where applicable)	$5\frac{3}{4}\%$
Alaska (local tax where applicable)	0%	New Hampshire	0%
		New Jersey	7%
Arizona	5%	New Mexico (plus county or local tax where applicable)	5%
Arkansas (plus local tax where applicable)	$4\frac{1}{2}\%$		
California (plus $\frac{1}{2}\%$ or more local tax where applicable)	7%	New York City (includes 4% state tax)	$8\frac{1}{4}\%$
		New York (State) (plus city or county tax where applicable)	4%
Colorado	3%		
Connecticut	8%	North Carolina	3%
Delaware	0%	North Dakota	5%
District of Columbia	6%	Ohio (plus local tax where applicable)	5%
Florida	6%		
Georgia (plus local tax where applicable)	4%	Oklahoma	$4\frac{1}{2}\%$
Hawaii	4%	Oregon	0%
Idaho	5%	Pennsylvania	6%
Illinois	$6\frac{1}{4}\%$	Rhode Island	7%
Indiana	5%	South Carolina	5%
Iowa (plus local tax where applicable)	4%	South Dakota	4%
		Tennessee	$5\frac{1}{2}\%$
Kansas	$4\frac{1}{4}\%$	Texas (plus local tax where applicable)	$6\frac{1}{4}\%$
Kentucky	6%		
Louisiana	4%	Utah (plus county and local taxes where applicable)	$5\frac{3}{4}\%$
Maine	5%		
Maryland	5%	Vermont	4%
Massachusetts	5%	Virginia	$4\frac{1}{2}\%$
Michigan	4%	Washington (plus county and city taxes where applicable)	$6\frac{1}{2}\%$
Minnesota (plus local tax where applicable)	6%		
Mississippi	6%	West Virginia	6%
Missouri	4.225%	Wisconsin	5%
Montana	0%	Wyoming	3%
Nebraska	5%		

EXAMPLE 2
Finding the Price When Sales Tax Is Known

Sales tax on a pair of cross trainer athletic shoes is $2.30. If the sales tax rate is 5%, find the price of the shoes.

SOLUTION Since sales tax (part) is found by multiplying the sales tax rate (rate) by the amount of the sale (base), the amount of sale is found using the percent equation and solving for base.

$$P = BR$$

$$\$2.30 = B \times 5\%$$

$$\$2.30 = 0.05B$$

$$\frac{\$2.30}{0.05} = \frac{0.05B}{0.05}$$

$$\$46 = B$$

The cross trainers sell for $46 per pair. ∎

NOTE Several states do not have any sales tax. Many counties and cities impose a tax on sales to raise additional revenue which is then used locally.

4 When the total price including sales tax and the sales tax rate are known, the sale amount can be found as shown in the next example.

EXAMPLE 3
Determining the Sale Amount when Total Price Is Known

The total cost of some preschool equipment is $610.56, which includes the sales tax of 6%. Find the price of the equipment before the sales tax.

SOLUTION First, remember that the amount of sale + sales tax = total. Then, use the percent equation to find the amount of the sale (base).

$$B + (6\%)B = \$610.56$$

$$1B + 0.06B = \$610.56$$

$$1.06B = \$610.56$$

$$B = \frac{610.56}{1.06}$$

$$B = \$576$$

The amount of the sale is $576.

To check this answer, multiply the amount of the sale ($576) by the tax rate (6%) to find the tax. Then, add the tax to the amount of the sale to find the total amount.

$$BR = P$$

$$\$576 \times 6\% = P$$

$$\$576 \times 0.06 = \$34.56 \qquad \text{amount of sales tax}$$

Now add.

$$\$576 \text{ (sale)} + \$34.56 \text{ (tax)} = \$610.56 \text{ total sale} \quad ∎$$

TABLE 6.3   Excise Taxes

Product or Service	Rate	Product or Service	Rate
Cigarettes	24¢/pack	Tires (by weight)	
Telephone service	3%	under 40 pounds	No tax
Teletypewriter service	3%	40–69 pounds	15¢/pound over 40
Air transportation	10%	70–89 pounds	$4.50 plus 30¢/pound over 70
International air travel	$6.00/person	90 pounds and more	$10.50 plus 50¢/pound over 90
Air freight	6.25%		
Coal		Truck and trailer, chassis and bodies	12%
underground (lower amount)	$1.10/ton or 4.4%	Inland waterways fuel	15.1¢/gallon
surface (lower amount)	55¢/ton or 4.4%	Fuel used in noncommercial aviation	gasoline: 1¢/gallon; other than gasoline: 17.6¢/gallon
Fishing rods	10%		
Bows and arrows	11%		
Pistols and revolvers	10%	Luxury Tax	
Firearms (other)	11%	cars (amount over $30,000)	10%
Shells and cartridges	11%	boats (amount over $100,000)	10%
Gasoline	14.1¢/gallon		
Gasohol	8.7¢/gallon	furs and jewelry (amount over $10,000)	10%
Alcohol			
beer	32¢/6-pack		
wine	24¢/bottle		

Source: Publication 510, I.R.S., Excise Taxes for 1992

5 An **excise tax** or **luxury tax** is charged on certain items by the federal, state, or local government. The tax is similar to sales tax since it is paid by or passed on to the consumer of goods and services. Excise taxes are charged on firearms, gasoline, tires, tobacco, liquor, and on such services as telephone, entertainment, air transportation, luxury cars, boats, expensive furs and jewelry, and business licenses.

Excise taxes are either a percent of the sales price of an item or a fixed amount for each unit sold. Table 6.3 shows the current federal excise taxes charged on several items.

EXAMPLE 4
Finding the Total Cost with Sales and Excise Taxes

A tire for a John Deere backhoe weighs 76 pounds and sells for $680. Find the total cost of the tire including 7% sales tax and excise tax of $4.50 plus $.30 per each pound over 70 pounds.

SOLUTION   First, find the sales tax using the percent equation.

$$BR = P$$

$$\$680 \times 7\% = P$$

$$\$680 \times 0.07 = \$47.60 \qquad \text{amount of sales tax}$$

Next, find the excise tax.

$$\$4.50 + (76 - 70)(\$.30) = \text{excise tax}$$

$$\$4.50 + (6 \times 0.30) = \text{excise tax}$$

$$\$4.50 + 1.80 = \$6.30 \qquad \text{excise tax}$$

Now find the total cost.

$$\text{Amount of sale} + \text{Sales tax} + \text{Excise tax} = \text{Total cost}$$

$$\$680 \text{ (tire)} + \$47.60 \text{ (sales tax)} + \$6.30 \text{ (excise tax)} = \$733.90 \text{ (total cost)}$$

The total cost of the tire is $733.90. ■

Calculator Approach to Example 4

First, enter the selling price of the tire in memory, and then calculate the sales tax, adding it to memory.

$$680 \;\boxed{M+}\quad \boxed{\times}\; .07 \;\boxed{M+}$$

Next, calculate the excise tax and add it to memory.

$$76 \;\boxed{-}\; 70 \;\boxed{\times}\; .3 \;\boxed{+}\; 4.5 \;\boxed{M+}$$

Finally, press the $\boxed{MR}$ key to see the total cost of the tire including sales tax and excise tax.

$$\boxed{MR}\quad 733.90$$

NOTE Excise taxes are added to the price in addition to sales tax. The excise tax is calculated on the amount of the sale before sales tax is added.

6.1 Exercises

Find (a) the amount of sales tax, (b) the amount of excise tax, and (c) the total sale price including taxes in each of the following problems.

	Sales Price	**Sales Tax Rate**	**Excise Tax Rate**
1.	$5.00	5%	3%
2.	$24.00	6%	8%
3.	$37.80	6%	11%
4.	$21.15	8%	12%
5.	$173.50	5%	9¢/gallon; 165 gallons
6.	$216.75	3%	14¢/gallon; 190 gallons
7.	$736.15	6%	8%
8.	$973.54	7%	12%
9.	$29,400.00	5%	$3.00 per person; 168 people
10.	$57,552.00	4½%	$3.00 per person; 218 people

Find the sales price and total price when given the amount of tax and the sales tax rate.
Round to the nearest cent.

	Amount of Sales Tax	Sales Tax Rate
11.	$1.26	4%
12.	$.80	7%
13.	$8.36	5%
14.	$.84	6%
15.	$9.90	3%

	Amount of Sales Tax	Sales Tax Rate
16.	$55.65	7%
17.	$32.42	6%
18.	$22.32	4%

Find the amount of the sale before sales tax was added and the amount of sales tax in
each of the following. Round to the nearest cent.

	Total Sale	Sales Tax Rate
19.	$21.32	4%
20.	$166.95	6%
21.	$122.91	3%
22.	$311.22	5%
23.	$20.60	4%
24.	$68.48	7%
25.	$671.52	5%
26.	$1043.04	6%
27.	$2945.76	7%
28.	$4469.64	5%

29. What is the sales tax rate where you live? Is there a different tax rate in a county, parish, or city near you? Explain why this difference exists.

30. List three items that you or your family purchased within the last year on which you had to pay an excise tax. (See Objective 5.)

Solve each of the following word problems.

31. The retail price of a fishing rod is $29.95. If sales tax is 3% and the excise tax is 10%, find (a) the amount of the sales tax, (b) the amount of the excise tax, and (c) the total sale including sales tax and excise tax.

32. The selling price of a truck chassis is $18,948.20. If sales tax is 4% and excise tax is 12%, find (a) the amount of the sales tax, (b) the amount of the excise tax, and (c) the total price including sales tax and excise tax.

33. The sales tax on a commercial slicer is $22.08. If the sales tax rate is 6%, find the sales price of the slicer.

34. Sales tax on some wall-to-wall carpet was $62.30. If the tax rate was 7%, find the sales price of the carpet.

35. The price of a laser printer is $2079 including a 5% sales tax. Find the amount of the sales price.

36. K-Ron's Hobbies charges $321.36 including 3% sales tax for a radio controlled glider. Find the price of the glider without tax.

37. Total sales for one day at Club Sunset were $1285.44 including the 4% sales tax charged on all purchases. Find the amount that is sales tax.

38. Pets Incorporated has total receipts for the day of $1134.20. If this includes 7% sales tax on all sales, find the amount that is sales tax.

39. At the close of business one day, Greg Odjakjian a new employee totaled the amount in the cash register and found $1908. He multiplied this sum by the sales tax rate of 6%, and found a "tax" of $1908 $\times$ 0.06 = $114.48. If this amount is sent to the state, the state receives too much money. Find the amount of the overpayment.

40. Santiago Rowland has total daily receipts of $1856. His lounge manager multiplies this total by 5.5%, the tax rate in the area. Is this procedure correct? Find (a) the correct amount of sales tax and (b) the amount of error made by the manager.

41. Auburn Tire offers a 74-pound truck tire for $182 plus tax. If sales tax is $7\frac{1}{2}$% and excise tax is $4.50 plus 30¢ per pound over 70 pounds, find the total cost including tax.

42. Al Gregory purchased a set of six truck tires at a cost of $280 each. Each tire weighs 46 pounds, sales tax is 4%, and excise tax is $.15 per pound over 40 pounds for each tire. Find the total cost to Gregory.

43. The Travel Excellence Group pays $22,550 for a chartered international flight. Sales tax is $4\frac{1}{2}$% and excise tax is $6.00 per person. If 110 people make the flight, find the total cost including tax.

44. Ticket sales for an international flight are $35,964 before taxes. If sales tax is $7\frac{1}{2}$% and excise tax is $6.00 per person, find the total sales including tax if there are 162 passengers.

6.2 Property Tax

OBJECTIVES

1 Use fair market value to find assessed valuation.

2 Use the tax rate formula.

3 Express tax rates in percent, dollars per $100, dollars per $1000, and mills.

4 Find taxes given the assessed valuation and the tax rate.

5 Find the assessed valuation given the tax rate and the tax.

6 Find the tax rate given the assessed valuation and the tax.

In virtually every area of the nation, the owners of **real property** (such as buildings and land) must pay a property tax on their property. In many areas **personal property** (such as mobile homes, furnishings, appliances, motor homes, trailers, boats, and other non-real estate items) is also taxed. Some areas handle these two taxes separately, while others combine them. The money raised by this property tax is used to provide services in the local community, such as police and fire protection, roads, schools, and parks.

1 To find the amount of this tax, each piece of real property in an area must be **assessed**. In this process, a local official, called the assessor, makes an estimate of the **fair market value** of the property, the price for which the property could reasonably be expected to be sold. The **assessed valuation** of the property is then found by multiplying the fair market value by a certain percent called the **assessment rate**. The percent that is used varies drastically from state to state, but normally remains constant within a state.

In some states, assessed valuation is 25% of fair market value, while in other states, the assessed valuation is 40% to 60% or even 100% of fair market value. Occasionally, different rates will be used for homes and for businesses. In theory, this step is unnecessary in calculating property tax. However, using an assessed valuation that is a percent of fair market value has become an accepted practice over the years.

EXAMPLE 1
Determining the Assessed Value of Property

Find the assessed valuation for the following pieces of property.

(a)   fair market value, $28,000; percent used, 25%

(b)   fair market value, $174,500; percent used, 60%

SOLUTION   Multiply the fair market value by the percent used.

(a) $28,000 × 0.25 = $7000 assessed valuation

(b) $174,500 × 0.60 = $104,700 assessed valuation   ■

2 After calculating the assessed valuation of all the taxable property in an area, and determining the amount of money needed to provide the necessary services (the budget), the agency responsible for levying the tax announces the annual **property tax rate**.

This tax rate is determined by the following formula.

$$\text{Tax rate} = \frac{\text{Total tax amount needed}}{\text{Total assessed value}}$$

EXAMPLE 2
Finding the Tax Rate

Find the tax rate for the following areas.

(a)   total tax amount needed, $73,680; total assessed value, $1,228,000

(b)   total tax amount needed, $316,800; total assessed value, $14,400,000

SOLUTION   Divide the total tax amount needed by the total assessed value.

(a) $73,680 ÷ $1,228,000 = 0.06 tax rate

(b) $316,800 ÷ $14,400,000 = 0.022 tax rate   ▪

3   Property tax rates are expressed differently in different parts of the country. The following are several common methods.

Percent.   Some areas express tax rates as a percent of assessed valuation. The tax on a piece of property with an assessed valuation of $74,000 at a tax rate of 9.42% (9.42% = 0.0942) would be

$$\text{Tax} = 0.0942 \times \$74,000 = \$6970.80.$$

Dollars Per $100.   In other areas, the rate is expressed as a number of dollars per $100 of assessed valuation. For example, the rate might be expressed as $11.42 per $100 of assessed valuation. Assuming a tax rate of $11.42 per $100, find the tax on a piece of land having an assessed valuation of $18,000 as follows. First, move the decimal point two places left to find the number of hundreds in $18,000.

$$\$18,000 = 180 \text{ hundreds} \qquad \text{Move the decimal two places to the left.}$$

Then, find the tax.

$$\text{Tax} = \text{Tax rate} \times \text{Number of hundreds of valuation}$$

$$= \$11.42 \times 180$$

$$= \$2055.60$$

Dollars Per $1000.   In other areas, the tax rate is expressed as a number of dollars per $1000 of assessed valuation. If the tax rate is $98.12 per $1000, a piece of property having an assessed valuation of $197,000 would be taxed as follows.

$$\$197,000 = 197 \text{ thousands} \qquad \text{Move the decimal three places to the left.}$$

$$\text{Tax} = \$98.12 \times 197$$

$$= \$19,329.64$$

Mills.   Finally, some areas express tax rates in mills (a **mill** is one-tenth of a cent, or one-thousandth of a dollar). For example, a tax rate might be expressed as 46 mills per dollar (or $.046 per dollar). The tax on a property having an assessed valuation of $81,000, at a tax rate of 46 mills, is

$$\text{Tax} = (0.046) \times \$81,000 \qquad \text{46 mills} = \$.046$$

$$= \$3726.$$

Table 6.4 shows the same tax rates written in the four different systems. Although expressed differently, they are equivalent tax rates.

TABLE 6.4   Writing Tax Rates in Four Systems

Percent	Per $100	Per $1000	In Mills
12.52%	$12.52	$125.20	125.2
3.2%	$3.20	$32.00	32
9.87%	$9.87	$98.70	98.7

NOTE The number of decimal places used and rounding practices in tax rates vary among taxing jurisdictions. A common practice is to round *up* the last digit used. In Table 6.4 rounding 125.2 mills and 98.7 mills to whole mills would result in 126 mills and 99 mills, respectively.

4 Once the assessed valuation and the tax rate are known, find the tax with the following formula.

$$P \quad = \quad R \times B$$
$$\text{Tax} \ = \ \text{Tax rate} \ \times \ \text{Assessed valuation}$$

EXAMPLE 3
Finding the Property Tax

Find the taxes on each of the following pieces of property. Assessed valuations and tax rates are given.

(a) $58,975; 8.4%
(b) $74,500; $7.82 per $100
(c) $129,600; $64.21 per $1000
(d) $221,750; 94 mills

SOLUTION Multiply tax rate by the assessed valuation.

(a) 8.4% = .084

$$\text{Tax} = \text{Tax rate} \ \times \ \text{Assessed valuation}$$
$$\text{Tax} \ = \ 0.084 \times 58,975 = \$4953.90$$

(b) $74,500 = 745 hundreds

$$\text{Tax} \ = \ 745 \times 7.82 = \$5825.90$$

(c) $129,600 = 129.6 thousands

$$\text{Tax} \ = \ 64.21 \times 129.6 = \$8321.62$$

(d) 94 mills = $.094

$$\text{Tax} \ = \ 0.094 \times 221,750 = \$20,844.50 \quad \blacksquare$$

NOTE Some states offer certain tax exemptions which will reduce the amount of property tax due. One type of exemption is the Homeowner's Tax Exemption which allows a specific amount of tax exemption to a person who owns and occupies a home or condominium as a personal residence.

5 The tax formula can also be used to find the assessed valuation when given the amount of tax and the tax rate.

EXAMPLE 4
Finding the Assessed Valuation

The taxes on a car wash in Boden County are $256. If the tax rate is $1.50 per $100, find the assessed valuation.

SOLUTION   Use the formula for finding tax.

$$\text{Tax} = \text{Tax rate} \times \text{Assessed valuation}$$

$$\$256 = \$1.50 \times \text{Assessed valuation}$$

$$\frac{256}{1.5} = \text{Assessed valuation}$$

$$170.67 \text{ hundreds} = \text{Assessed valuation}$$

The assessed valuation is $17,067 (170.67 × 100). ■

6 The tax rate may be found by using the tax formula when the assessed valuation and the amount of tax are given.

EXAMPLE 5
Finding the Tax Rate Given Assessed Valuation and Tax

A commercial property in Suffolk County has an assessed valuation of $46,700 and an annual property tax of $3000.28. Find the tax rate per $1000.

SOLUTION   Use the formula for finding tax.

$$\text{Tax} = \text{Tax rate} \times \text{Assessed valuation}$$

The assessed valuation is 46.7 thousands ($46,700 ÷ 1000).

$$\$3000.28 = \text{Tax rate} \times 46.7$$

$$\frac{\$3000.28}{46.7} = \text{Tax rate}$$

$$\$64.25 = \text{Tax rate per } \$1000$$

The tax rate per $1000 is $64.25. ■

6.2 Exercises

Find the assessed valuation for each of the following pieces of property.

	Fair Market Value	Rate of Assessment
1.	$69,000	45%
2.	$282,500	60%
3.	$52,000	25%
4.	$70,000	38%
5.	$2,300,000	80%
6.	$5,700,000	70%

Find the tax rate for the following. Write the tax rate as a percent rounded to the nearest tenth.

	Total Tax Amount Needed	Total Assessed Value
7.	$312,500	$10,400,000
8.	$4,350,000	$54,375,000
9.	$2,941,500	$81,700,000
10.	$1,290,000	$8,600,000
11.	$1,224,000	$40,800,000
12.	$2,692,520	$35,900,000

Complete the following list comparing tax rates.

	Percent	Per $100	Per $1000	In Mills
13.	(a) _____%	(b) _____	(c) _____	28
14.	(a) _____%	$13.40	(b) _____	(c) _____
15.	2.41%	(a) _____	(b) _____	(c) _____
16.	7.42%	(a) _____	(b) _____	(c) _____
17.	(a) _____%	$3.48	(b) _____	(c) _____
18.	(a) _____%	(b) _____	$39.20	(c) _____

19. Define in your own words fair market value and assessed value. How is the assessment rate used when finding the assessed value? (See Objective 1.)

20. Select any tax rate expressing it as a percent. Write this tax rate in three additional equivalent forms. (See Objective 3.)

Find the tax for each of the following.

	Assessed Valuation	Tax Rate
21.	$428,200	$72.50 per $1000
22.	$289,600	$8.41 per $100
23.	$685,400	6.93%
24.	$386,500	42 mills
25.	$7500	$12.20 per $100
26.	$38,250	$89.70 per $1000

Find the missing quantity.

	Assessed Valuation	Tax Rate	Tax
27.	$111,600	_____ %	$8481.60
28.	_____	$4.26 per $100	$6049.20
29.	$64,100	126 mills	_____
30.	_____	$48.18 per $1000	$1903.11
31.	$152,680	_____ per $100	$8015.70
32.	$375,500	78.6 mills	_____
33.	_____	4.3%	$10,182.40
34.	$96,200	_____ per $1000	$3367

Work each of the following word problems.

35. Henry Burnett's Cactus Farm has property with a fair market value of $198,700. Property in Burnett's area is assessed at 60% of market value. The tax rate is 4.2%. Find the property tax paid.

36. The Consumer's Cooperative owns property with a fair market value of $785,200. The property is located in a county that assesses at 80% of market value. Find the property tax if the tax rate is $14.30 per $1000 of assessed value.

37. Shady Oak Nursery has property with a fair market value of $298,050. Property in the area is assessed at 30% of market value. The tax rate is $2.10 per $100 of assessed valuation. Find the amount of tax paid.

38. Channel 10 broadcasts from a building assessed at $3,875,600. The tax rate is $147.20 per $1000 of assessed valuation. Find the tax.

39. The Videos Now Center has a fair market value of $10,700,000. Property is assessed in the area at 25% of market value. The tax rate is $14.10 per $100 of assessed valuation. Find the tax.

40. In one state, property is assessed at 40% of market value, with a tax rate of 3.21%. In a second state, property is assessed at 24% of market value, with a tax rate of 5.02%. Gerry Baby Products is trying to decide where to place its $295,000 warehouse. (a) Which state would charge the lower property tax? (b) Find the difference in taxes between the two states.

41. Murph The Surf Shop pays $11,634.88 in property taxes. If the tax rate is 70.6 mills, find the assessed valuation.

42. Gilstrap's Five and Dime has property with a fair market value of $148,500. The property is located in an area that is assessed at 25% of market value. The tax rate is $8.26 per $100. Find the property tax paid.

43. Last year the property tax on an executive's estate was $4625, and the tax rate was $12.50 per $1000. After a reassessment this year, the assessed value was increased by $25,000 and the property tax due is $5350. Find the percent of increase in the tax rate. Round to the nearest tenth of a percent. Hint: Do not round until the final answer.

44. Last year the property tax on a warehouse was $3042, and the tax rate was $3.60 per $100. After a reassessment this year, the assessed value was increased by $10,500 and the property tax due is $3705. Find the percent of increase in the tax rate. Round to the nearest tenth of a percent.

45. A prime commercial corner lot was assessed at $45,000, and the tax was $1327.50. The following year the property tax increased to $1353.75 while the tax rate decreased by $.10 per $100. FInd the amount of increase in the assessed value of the commercial lot.

46. An investment property was assessed at $240,000, and the tax was $5400. The following year the property tax increased to $5805, while the tax rate decreased by $1.00 per $1000. Find the amount of increase in the assessed value of the property.

6.3 Personal Income Tax

OBJECTIVES

1 Know the four steps that determine tax liability.

2 Identify information needed to find adjusted gross income.

3 Determine adjusted gross income.

4 Know the standard deductions amounts.

5 Recall the tax rates.

6 List possible deductions to find taxable income.

7 Calculate income tax.

8 Determine a refund or balance due the Internal Revenue Service.

9 Prepare a 1040A and a Schedule 1 Federal Tax Form.

The federal government, most states, many local governments, and some cities use income tax as a source of revenue. However, for most people the federal income tax is the largest tax expense.

As shown in Figure 6.1, the individual income tax provides the largest single source of income to the federal government.

Instructions provided with the tax forms have to cover the situation of every possible taxpayer, from students who earn very little money to professional people, such as lawyers and doctors, who often have complicated financial affairs. For this reason, many people take their tax returns to a professional tax preparer. But even tax preparers do not solve all the problems of the taxpayer—the taxpayer still must supply all the necessary information. Tax preparers only insert the figures in the correct places on the correct forms and then do the necessary calculations.

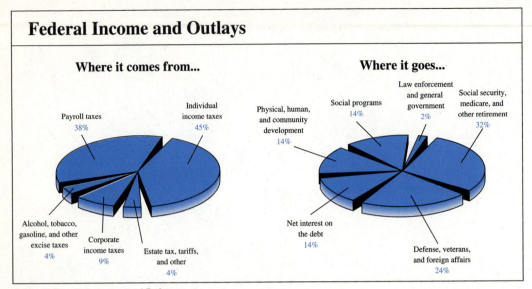

Federal Income and Outlays

Source: Office of Management and Budget

FIGURE 6.1

1 There are four basic steps in finding a person's total tax liability. If a taxpayer understands these steps and does not have involved tax questions, he or she should be able to fill out the federal tax return in a fairly short time.

Step 1	Find the adjusted gross income (AGI) for the year.
Step 2	Find the taxable income.
Step 3	Find the tax.
Step 4	Check to see if a refund is due, or if more money is owed to the government.

2 These steps are explained in order.

To begin, find the **adjusted gross income** for the year by collecting all the **W-2 forms** that were provided by employers during the year. A W-2 form is shown in Figure 6.2. The form shows the total amount of money paid to the employee by the employer, and also shows the total amount that was withheld from the employee's paycheck and sent, in his or her name, to the IRS. Add all the amounts paid to the employee.

1 Control number 22222	For Official Use Only ▶ OMB No. 1545-0008		
2 Employer's name, address, and ZIP code Leisure Travel 1568 Liberty Heights Avenue Baltimore, MD 21233	6 Statutory employee ☐ Deceased ☐ Pension plan ☐ Legal rep. ☐ 942 emp. ☐ Subtotal ☐ Deferred compensation ☐ Void ☐		
	7 Allocated tips		8 Advance EIC payment
	9 Federal income tax withheld $3275.68		10 Wages, tips, other compensation $22,652.62
3 Employer's identification number 94-1287319	4 Employer's state I.D. number 600-5076	11 Social security tax withheld $1404.46	12 Social security wages $22,652.62
5 Employee's social security number 329-15-8825		13 Social security tips	14 Medicare wages and tips $22,652.62
19a Employee's name (first, middle, last) Jo Ann Pychon		15 Medicare tax withheld $328.46	16 Nonqualified plans
		17 See Instrs. for Form W-2	18 Other
5599 Sunrise Blvd. Phoenix, MD 21030			
19b Employee's address and ZIP code			
20	21	22 Dependent care benefits	23 Benefits included in Box 10
24 State income tax	25 State wages, tips, etc. 26 Name of state	27 Local income tax 28 Local wages, tips, etc.	29 Name of locality

Copy A For Social Security Administration   Department of the Treasury—Internal Revenue Service

Form **W-2 Wage and Tax Statement 199**

For Paperwork Reduction Act Notice, see separate Instructions.

FIGURE 6.2

Next, collect any **1099 forms** that may have been received. These informational forms, copies of which go to the IRS, show miscellaneous income received, such as interest on checking or savings accounts, as well as stock dividends. A sample 1099 form is shown in Figure 6.3. Also, include any tips or other employee compensation, and enter the total on the correct line of the income tax form.

3   Using the information from the W-2 and 1099 forms, and adding any dividends, capital gains, unemployment compensation, tips, or other employee compensation, enter the total on the correct line of the income tax form. Subtract any adjustments to income, such as an **Individual Retirement Account (IRA)** or alimony payments. An IRA is a retirement plan which allows contributions to be deducted from income. The result is the **adjusted gross income**.

9292	☐ VOID	☐ CORRECTED		

PAYER'S name, street address, city, state, and ZIP code

Employees Credit Union
2572 Brookhaven Drive
Dundalk, MD 21222

Payer's RTN (optional)

OMB No. 1545-0112

19

Interest Income

PAYER'S Federal identification number | RECIPIENT'S identification number

1 Interest income not included in box 3
$ **923.38**

Copy A
For
**Internal Revenue
Service Center**

RECIPIENT'S name

Jo Ann Pynchon

2 Early withdrawal penalty
$

3 Interest on U.S. Savings
Bonds and Treas. obligations
$

File with Form 1096.

Street address (including apt. no.)
5599 Sunrise Blvd.

4 Federal income tax withheld
$

For Paperwork
Reduction Act
Notice and
instructions for
completing this form,
see **Instructions for
Forms 1099, 1098,
5498, and W-2G.**

City, state, and ZIP code
Phoenix, MD 21030

5 Foreign tax paid

6 Foreign country or U.S.
possession

Account number (optional)

2nd TIN Not.
☐ $

Form **1099-INT**   Cat. No. 14410K   Department of the Treasury - Internal Revenue Service

FIGURE 6.3

EXAMPLE 1
*Finding Adjusted
Gross Income (AGI)*

Jo Ann Pynchon earned $22,652.62 last year from Leisure Travel as a travel consultant and $923.38 in interest from her credit union (see her W-2 and 1099 forms). She had $1500 in IRA contributions. Find her adjusted gross income.

SOLUTION   Add the income from her job ($22,652.62) and the interest ($923.38). Then subtract the IRA contributions.

$$\$22,652.62 + \$923.38 - \$1500 = \$22,076 \quad ∎$$

NOTE When filing your income tax a copy of all W-2 Forms is sent to the Internal Revenue service along with the completed tax forms. However, the IRS does not require copies of 1099 Forms to be sent to them.

4   Most people are almost finished at this point. If deductions for medical expenses, interest, and so on are not to be itemized, and if there are no further adjustments, then the **standard deduction** amount must be determined and subtracted from the adjusted gross income. The most current standard deduction amounts are shown as follows.

- $3400 for single people
- $5700 for married people filing jointly and qualifying widow(er)s
- $2850 for married people filing separately
- $5000 for head of a household

Additional standard deductions are given for taxpayers and dependents who are blind or 65 years of age or older.

Now, only one step remains before the tax owed is found: determine the number of **personal exemptions**. An exemption is taken for the head of the household and for each of his or her dependents, including spouse and children. For example, a married person with a spouse and three children would be allowed to claim five exemptions. The taxpayer is allowed a $2150 reduction in gross income for each exemption. After subtracting $2150 per exemption from the adjusted gross income, the result, **taxable income**, is multiplied by the proper tax rate to determine taxes due.

5 Most recently individual income tax rates have been either 15%, 28%, or 31%, depending on the amount of taxable income and the taxpayer's filing status. Table 6.5, the tax rate schedule, shows the individual tax rates for each filing status.

EXAMPLE 2

Finding Taxable Income and the Income Tax Amount

Find the taxable income and the tax for each of the following people.

(a) Amy Lewis, single, 1 exemption, adjusted gross income, $19,796

(b) The Stillmans, married, filing jointly, 3 children, adjusted gross income, $56,906

SOLUTION

(a) Taxable income is $14,246 ($19,796 − $3400 standard deduction − $2150 for one exemption). The tax is calculated as follows.

$$15\% \times \$14,246 = \$2136.90$$

The tax is $2136.90.

Table 6.5 Tax Rate Schedule

Single			Married Filing Jointly or Qualifying Widow(er)	
Taxable Income	Tax Rate		Taxable Income	Tax Rate
$0–$20,350	15%		$0–$34,000	15%
$20,351–$49,300	28%		$34,001–$82,150	28%
Over $49,300	31%		Over $82,150	31%

Married Filing Separately			Head of Household	
Taxable Income	Tax Rate		Taxable Income	Tax Rate
$0–$17,000	15%		$0–$27,300	15%
$17,001–$41,075	28%		$27,301–$70,450	28%
Over $41,075	31%		Over $70,450	31%

(b) Taxable income is \$40,456 (\$56,906 − \$5700 standard deduction − \$10,750 for five exemptions). "Married filing jointly" tax is:

$$15\% \times \$34{,}000 = \$5100.00$$

$$28\% \times \$6456(\$40{,}456 - \$34{,}000) = \underline{\$1807.68}$$

$$\text{Total} \quad \$6907.68$$

The tax is \$6907.68. ■

CAUTION When taxable income goes beyond the 15% tax rate amount do not make the mistake of using the 28% tax rate on the entire amount of taxable income. For example, for a single person having a taxable income greater than \$20,350, a tax rate of 15% is used for the first \$20,350 and a tax rate of 28% is used *only* on the amount *over* \$20,350.

6 A **tax deduction** is any expense that the IRS will allow the taxpayer to subtract from adjusted gross income. To be of benefit, itemized deductions must exceed the automatic standard deduction allowed by the IRS. Usually, taxpayers will benefit from itemized deductions when they take out a loan in order to purchase a home—they are allowed to deduct the interest on the loan.

The one-fifth of the American population who do itemize all their deductions must go through one additional step before subtracting exemptions to determine taxable income: all deductions must be listed. The most common deductions are given here.

Medical and Dental Expenses. Not all such expenses may be deductible. In general, only amounts in excess of 7.5% of the adjusted gross income may be deducted. For most people, this restriction limits medical deductions to catastrophic illnesses. Expenses reimbursed by insurance companies cannot be deducted.

Taxes. State and local income taxes, real estate taxes, and personal property taxes may be deducted (but not federal income or gasoline taxes).

Interest. Home mortgage interest on the taxpayer's principle residence and a qualified second home is deductible. Other interest charges (including credit card interest) may not be deducted.

Contributions. Contributions to most charities may be deducted.

Miscellaneous Deductions. Miscellaneous expenses are only deductible to the extent that the total amount of such deductions exceeds 2% of the taxpayer's adjusted gross income. These deductions include income tax preparation fees, tax preparation books or computer software, appraisal fees for tax purposes, and legal fees for tax planning or tax litigation.

NOTE When itemizing deductions, the gain in deductions is not the total of all itemized deductions but the difference between the standard deduction amount and the total itemized deductions.

7 After determining the taxable income, the amount of income tax must be found.

EXAMPLE 3
Using Itemized Deductions to Find Taxable Income and Income Tax

Adam Strong is single, has no dependents, and had an adjusted gross income of $15,353 last year, with deductions of $1352 for other taxes, $2616 for mortgage interest, and $317 for charity. Find his taxable income and his income tax.

SOLUTION First find the total of all deductions.

$$\text{Deductions} = \$1352 + \$2616 + \$317 = \$4285$$

Since Strong is single, and the standard deduction is $3400, the larger itemized deduction amount, $4285, is taken. Now find taxable income.

$$\text{Taxable income} = \$15,353 - \$4285 - \$2150 = \$8918$$

Finally, income tax is determined.

$$15\% \times \$8918 = \$1337.70.$$

His tax is $1337.70. ∎

NOTE In preparing personal income tax, refer to current Internal Revenue Service publications, and always use the current tax rates.

8 After calculating the proper tax, determine whether a refund will come from the government. Look again at the W-2 forms to find out how much already has been paid toward the tax bill. These forms show the total amount the employer has withheld and sent to the government. (Usually, no money is withheld for amounts on 1099 forms.) If the amount withheld is greater than the tax owed, the taxpayer is entitled to a refund. If the amount withheld is less than the tax owed, then the taxpayer must send the difference along with the tax return.

EXAMPLE 4
Determining Tax Due or a Tax Refund

Susan Thompson had $375.20 per month withheld for federal income tax from her checks last year. She is single and has taxable income of $24,056 for the year. Does she get a refund? If so, how much?

SOLUTION Thompson had $375.20 \times 12 = \$4502.40$ withheld from her checks last year. The tax due on taxable income of $24,056 is $4090.18; therefore, she will receive a refund in the amount of

$$\$4502.40 - \$4090.18 = \$412.22 \quad ∎$$

CAUTION Be certain that the proper income tax form is used when filing your individual income tax. The 1040 EZ Form is used by many students but you must be single to use this form. If you have over $400 in interest or any adjustments to income a 1040A Form is used. In order to itemize deductions the taxpayer must use a 1040 Form. There are additional considerations and restrictions that determine whether the 1040 EZ, 1040A, or 1040 forms should be used.

9 The next example shows how to complete an income tax return using Form 1040A and a Schedule 1 (Form 1040).

EXAMPLE 5

Preparing a 1040A and a Schedule 1

Jo Ann Pynchon is single and claims one exemption. Her income appears on the W-2 and 1099 forms on pages 199 and 200. Pynchon contributes $1500 to an IRA. Since she has interest income over $400 but does not itemize her deductions she may use Form 1040A and must also file a Schedule 1 (Form 1040). Complete her income tax return.

Calculator Approach to Example 5

Use of the calculator memory function is very helpful in solving this problem because there are several side calculations involving deductions, tax calculation, and the amount of refund. The first series results in adjusted gross income.

22,653 $\boxed{+}$ 923 $\boxed{-}$ 1500 $\boxed{=}$ 22,076 $\boxed{\text{M+}}$

Adjusted gross income is now stored in a memory. Next, the standard deduction and personal exemption must be totaled and subtracted to arrive at taxable income.

3400 + 2150 $\boxed{=}$ 5550 $\boxed{\text{M}-}$ $\boxed{\text{MR}}$ 16,526

Income tax is now calculated using 15%.

16,526 $\boxed{\times}$ .15 $\boxed{=}$ 2478.9 $\boxed{\text{MC}}$ $\boxed{\text{MR}}$

Tax is rounded to $2479. The refund is then found by subtracting the tax from the amount withheld.

3276 $\boxed{-}$ $\boxed{\text{MR}}$ $\boxed{=}$ 797.1 ($797 rounded)

NOTE When completing income tax forms and calculations, notice that all amounts may be rounded to the nearest dollar.

Form
1040A

Department of the Treasury—Internal Revenue Service

U.S. Individual Income Tax Return (S)

OMB No. 1545-0085

Step 1

Label

(See page 16.)

Use the IRS label. Otherwise, please print or type.

L A B E L   H E R E

Your first name and initial   Last name

Jo Ann   Pynchon

If a joint return, spouse's first name and initial   Last name

Home address (number and street). (If you have a P.O. box, see page 16.)   Apt. no.

5599   Sunrise   Blvd.

City, town or post office, state, and ZIP code. (If you have a foreign address, see page 16.)

Phoenix MD   21030

Your social security no.

329 15 8825

Spouse's social security no.

For Privacy Act and Paperwork Reduction Act Notice, see page 3.

Presidential Election Campaign Fund (see page 17)

Do you want $1 to go to this fund? . . . . ☒ Yes ☐ No

If joint return, does your spouse want $1 to go to this fund? ☐ Yes ☐ No

Note: *Checking "Yes" will not change your tax or reduce your refund.*

Step 2

Check your filing status

(Check only one.)

1 ☒ Single

2 ☐ Married filing joint return (even if only one had income)

3 ☐ Married filing separate return. Enter spouse's social security number above and spouse's full name here ▶

4 ☐ Head of household (with qualifying person). (See page 18.) If the qualifying person is a child but not your dependent, enter this child's name here ▶

5 ☐ Qualifying widow(er) with dependent child (year spouse died ▶ 19____). (See page 19.)

Step 3

Figure your exemptions

(See page 20.)

If more than seven dependents, see page 23.

6a ☒ **Yourself.** If your parent (or someone else) can claim you as a dependent on his or her tax return, do not check box 6a. But be sure to check the box on line 18b on page 2.

b ☐ **Spouse**

No. of boxes checked on 6a and 6b   **1**

c **Dependents:**

(1) Name (first, initial, and last name)	(2) Check if under age 1	(3) If age 1 or older, dependent's social security number	(4) Dependent's relationship to you	(5) No. of months lived in your home in 1991

No. of your children on 6c who:
● lived with you
● didn't live with you due to divorce or separation (see page 23)

No. of other dependents listed on 6c

d If your child didn't live with you but is claimed as your dependent under a pre-1985 agreement, check here . . . ▶ ☐

Add numbers entered on lines above   **1**

e Total number of exemptions claimed.

Step 4

Figure your total income

Attach Copy B of your Forms W-2 and 1099-R here.

Attach check or money order on top of any Forms W-2 or 1099-R.

7 Wages, salaries, tips, etc. This should be shown in Box 10 of your W-2 form(s). (Attach Form(s) W-2.)   7   **22653**

8a Taxable interest income (see page 26). (If over $400, also complete and attach Schedule 1, Part I.)   8a   **923**

b Tax-exempt interest. (DO NOT include on line 8a.) 8b

9 Dividends. (If over $400, also complete and attach Schedule 1, Part II.)   9

10a Total IRA distributions. 10a   10b Taxable amount (see page 27). 10b

11a Total pensions and annuities. 11a   11b Taxable amount (see page 27). 11b

12 Unemployment compensation (insurance) from Form(s) 1099-G.   12

13a Social security benefits. 13a   13b Taxable amount (see page 31). 13b

14 Add lines 7 through 13b (far right column). This is your **total income.** ▶ 14   **23576**

Step 5

Figure your adjusted gross income

15a Your IRA deduction from applicable worksheet. 15a   **1500**

b Spouse's IRA deduction from applicable worksheet. **Note:** *Rules for IRAs begin on page 33.* 15b

c Add lines 15a and 15b. These are your **total adjustments.**   15c   **1500**

16 Subtract line 15c from line 14. This is your **adjusted gross income.** (If less than $21,250, see "Earned income credit" on page 41.) ▶ 16   **22076**

Cat. No. 11327A

FIGURE 6.4

Form 1040A   Page 2

| Step 6 | **17** Enter the amount from line 16. | | 17 | 22076 |

18a Check | ☐ **You** were 65 or older ☐ Blind | **Enter number of** | 18a | 0
if: | ☐ **Spouse** was 65 or older ☐ Blind | **boxes checked ▶** |

b If your parent (or someone else) can claim you as a dependent,
check here . . . . ▶ 18b ☐

c If you are married filing separately and your spouse files Form
1040 and itemizes deductions, see page 37 and check here . ▶ 18c ☐

Figure your standard deduction,

19 Enter the **standard deduction** shown below for your filing status.
But if you checked any box on line 18a or b, go to page 37 to
find your standard deduction. **If you checked box 18c, enter -0-.**

- Single—$3,400   - Head of household—$5,000
- Married filing jointly or Qualifying widow(er)—$5,700
- Married filing separately—$2,850 | 19 | 3400

exemption amount, and taxable income

20 Subtract line 19 from line 17. (If line 19 is more than line 17, enter -0-.) | 20 | 18676

21 Multiply $2,150 by the total number of exemptions claimed on line 6e. | 21 | 2150

22 Subtract line 21 from line 20. (If line 21 is more than line 20, enter -0-.)
This is your **taxable income.** ▶ | 22 | 16526

Step 7

Figure your tax, credits, and payments

23 Find the tax on the amount on line 22. Check if from:
☒ Tax Table (pages 44–49) or ☐ Form 8615 (see page 39) | 23 | 2479

24a Credit for child and dependent care expenses.
Complete and attach Schedule 2. | 24a |

b Credit for the elderly or the disabled.
Complete and attach Schedule 3. | 24b |

c Add lines 24a and 24b. These are your **total credits.** | 24c |

If you want the
IRS to figure
your tax, see
the instructions
for line 22 on
page 38.

25 Subtract line 24c from line 23. (If line 24c is more than line 23, enter -0-.) | 25 | 2479

26 Advance earned income credit payments from Form W-2. | 26 | 2479

27 Add lines 25 and 26. This is your **total tax.** ▶ | 27 |

28a Total Federal income tax withheld. (If any
tax is from Form(s) 1099, check here ▶☐ .) | 28a | 3276

b 1991 estimated tax payments and amount
applied from 1990 return. | 28b |

c **Earned income credit.** Complete and
attach Schedule EIC. | 28c |

d Add lines 28a, 28b, and 28c. These are your **total payments.** ▶ | 28d | 3276

Step 8

Figure your refund or amount you owe

29 If line 28d is more than line 27, subtract line 27 from line 28d.
This is the amount you **overpaid.** | 29 | 797

30 Amount of line 29 you want **refunded to you.** | 30 | 797

Attach check or
money order on
top of Form(s)
W-2, etc., on
page 1.

31 Amount of line 29 you want **applied to your
1992 estimated tax.** | 31 |

32 If line 27 is more than line 28d, subtract line 28d from line 27. This is the
amount you owe. Attach check or money order for full amount payable to
the "Internal Revenue Service." Write your name, address, social security
number, daytime phone number, and "1991 Form 1040A" on it. | 32 |

33 Estimated tax penalty (see page 43). | 33 |

Step 9

Sign your return

Keep a copy of
this return for
your records.

Under penalties of perjury, I declare that I have examined this return and accompanying schedules and statements, and to the best of my knowledge
and belief, they are true, correct, and complete. Declaration of preparer (other than the taxpayer) is based on all information of which the preparer
has any knowledge.

Your signature *Jo Ann Pynchon*   Date 3/12/9–   Your occupation Travel Consultant

Spouse's signature (if joint return) BOTH must sign)   Date   Spouse's occupation

Paid preparer's use only

Preparer's signature ▶   Date   Check if self-employed ☐   Preparer's social security no.

Firm's name (or yours
if self-employed) and ▶
address   E.I. No.   ZIP code

FIGURE 6.5

Schedule 1
(Form 1040A)

Department of the Treasury—Internal Revenue Service

**Interest and Dividend Income
for Form 1040A Filers**   (S)

OMB No. 1545-0085

Name(s) shown on Form 1040A

Jo Ann Pynchon

Your social security number

329 15 8825

Part I

**Interest
Income**

(See pages 26
and 50.)

Complete this part and attach Schedule 1 to Form 1040A if:
• You have over $400 in taxable interest, or
• You are claiming the exclusion of interest from series EE U.S. savings bonds issued after 1989.
If you are claiming the exclusion or you received, as a nominee, interest that actually
belongs to another person, see page 50.
Note: *If you received a Form 1099–INT, Form 1099–OID, or substitute statement, from a
brokerage firm, enter the firm's name and the total interest shown on that form.*

1	List name of payer	Amount
	Employees Credit Union	1	*923*
2	Add the amounts on line 1.	2	*923*
3	Enter the excludable savings bond interest, if any, from Form 8815, line 14. Attach Form 8815 to Form 1040A.	3	
4	Subtract line 3 from line 2. Enter the result here and on Form 1040A, line 8a.	4	*923*

Part II

**Dividend
Income**

(See pages 26
and 51.)

Complete this part and attach Schedule 1 to Form 1040A if you received over $400 in dividends.
If you received, as a nominee, dividends that actually belong to another person, see page 51.
Note: *If you received a Form 1099–DIV, or substitute statement, from a brokerage firm, enter
the firm's name and the total dividends shown on that form.*

5	List name of payer	Amount
		5	
6	Add the amounts on line 5. Enter the total here and on Form 1040A, line 9.	6	

For Paperwork Reduction Act Notice, see Form 1040A instructions.   Cat. No. 12075R   Schedule 1 (Form 1040A)

FIGURE 6.6

6.3 Exercises

Find the adjusted gross income for each of the following.

	Name	Income from Jobs	Interest	Misc. Income	Dividend Income	Adjustments to Income
1.	W. Harcos	$16,308	$56	$2608	$178	$71
2.	J. Herlihy	$29,720	$112	$64	$473	$192
3.	The Jisons	$21,380	$625	$139	$184	$618
4.	The Papoffs	$33,650	$722	$375	$218	$473
5.	The Braggs	$42,840	$108	$95	$65	$0
6.	The Wilsons	$37,832	$1418	$418	$118	$2179

Find the amount of taxable income and the tax for each of the following. Use the tax rate schedule. The letter following the name indicates marital status, and all married people are filing jointly.

	Name	Number of Exemptions	Adjusted Gross Income	Total Deductions
7.	M. Miranda, S	1	$19,400	$2208
8.	R. Elsinore, S	1	$16,108	$2965
9.	The Guttermans, M	3	$24,922	$4228
10.	The Loveridges, M	7	$30,618	$6319
11.	The Resers, M	5	$59,500	$3621
12.	C. Dinsmore, S	1	$27,122	$3408
13.	Kathleen Pratt, S	1	$28,500	$3600
14.	Lynn Butler, S	1	$26,700	$1982
15.	Julie Pearson, S	1	$32,218	$2278
16.	The Printices, M	5	$17,852	$3174
17.	The Sloans, M	2	$49,254	$5211
18.	The Reents, M	8	$59,622	$6354

Find the amount of any refund or tax due for the following people. The letter following the name indicates marital status. Assume a 52-week year and that married people are filing jointly.

	Name	Taxable Income	Federal Income Tax Withheld from Checks
19.	Rowell, L., S	$26,756	$486.20 monthly
20.	Davis, L., S	$13,602	$173.90 monthly
21.	Pender, B., S	$24,773	$ 67.21 weekly
22.	The Fungs, M	$39,283	$142.53 weekly
23.	The Gardeners, M	$18,731	$189.65 monthly
24.	The Mullsoys, M	$36,552	$116.52 weekly

25. List four sources of income for which an individual might receive W-2 and 1099 forms. (See Objective 3.)

26. List four possible tax deductions and explain the effect that a tax deduction will have on taxable income and on income tax due. (See Objective 6.)

Find the tax for each of the following.

27. The Lees had an adjusted gross income of $24,236 last year. They had deductions of $224 for state income tax, $112 for city income tax, $316 for property tax, $1562 in mortgage interest, and $204 in contributions. They filed a joint return and claim 5 exemptions.

28. Diane Bolton had an adjusted gross income of $18,811 last year. She had deductions of $1144 for state income tax, $659 for property tax, $2343 in mortgage interest, and $225 in contributions. Bolton claims 1 exemption and files as a single person.

29. Colleen Anderson, filing as a single person and claiming 1 exemption, had an adjusted gross income of $29,306. Her deductions amounted to $2741.

30. The Slausons had an adjusted gross income of $34,220 last year. They had deductions of $1125 for state income tax, $212 for city income tax, $958 for property tax, $4975 in mortgage interest, and $274 in contributions. They claim 5 exemptions and file a joint return.

31. The Jackers had wages of $56,757, dividends of $315, interest of $568, and adjustments to income of $946 last year. They had deductions of $924 for state income tax, $223 for city income tax, $846 for property tax, $3957 in mortgage interest, and $144 in contributions. They claim 5 exemptions and file a joint return.

32. Dave Jeffers had wages of $25,811, other income of $3208, dividends of $180, interest of $265, and an IRA contribution of $692 last year. He had deductions of $976 for state income tax, $1351 for property tax, $805 in mortgage interest, and $458 in contributions. Jeffers claims 1 exemption and files as a single person.

33. John and Vicki Karsten had combined wages and salaries of $36,824, other income of $4342, dividend income of $236, and interest income of $586. They have adjustments to income of $2224. Their itemized deductions are $6516 in mortgage interest, $623 in state income tax, $1065 in real estate taxes, and $1123 in charitable contributions. The Karstens filed a joint return and claimed 6 exemptions.

34. Judy Lewis has wages and salaries of $33,846, other income of $1682, dividend income of $478, and interest income of $986. She has an adjustment to income of $1452. Her itemized deductions are $4615 in mortgage interest, $1136 in state income tax, $856 in real estate taxes, and $835 in charitable contributions. Lewis claims 1 exemption and is a single person.

CHAPTER 6 QUICK REVIEW

TOPIC	APPROACH	EXAMPLE
6.1 Finding sales tax	Collected by states, and some counties and cities. Use $P = BR$, where P is the sales tax, B is the amount of the sale, and R is the sales tax rate.	Sales tax of 5% is charged on a sale of $173.15. Find the amount of sales tax and the total sale including tax. $$P = \$173.15 \times 0.05 = \$8.66$$ $173.15 sale + $8.66 tax $=$ $181.81 total sale
6.1 Finding selling price when the sales tax is known	Use the basic percent equation. $$P = BR$$	Sales tax is $4.59; sales tax rate is 6%. Find the amount of the sale. $$\$4.59 = B \times 0.06$$ $$\frac{\$4.59}{0.06} = B$$ $76.50 $= B$ selling price
6.1 Finding the amount of the sale when the total price is known	Use the percent equation and remember Amount of sale + Sales tax = Total	Total price including tax, $128.96; sales tax, 4%. Find the amount of the sale. $$B + (0.04)B = 128.96$$ $$1.04B = 128.96$$ $$B = \frac{\$128.96}{1.04} = \$124$$
6.1 Excise tax (luxury tax)	A tax charged on certain items by the federal, state, or local government. It may be either a percent of the sale price or a certain amount per item.	A tire weights 50 pounds and sells for $118; sales tax rate is 7%; excise tax is 15¢ per pound over 40 pounds. Find total cost. $118.00 tire 8.26 sales tax 1.50 excise tax $(.15(50 - 40))$ $127.76 total cost
6.2 Fair market value and assessed valuation	Multiply the market value of the property by the assessment rate (a local assessed percent) to arrive at the assessed valuation.	The assessment rate is 30%; fair market value is $115,000. Find the assessed valuation. $$0.3 \times \$115,000 = \$34,500$$

TOPIC	APPROACH	EXAMPLE
6.2 Tax rate	The tax rate formula is $$\text{Tax rate} = \frac{\substack{\text{Total tax}\\ \text{amount needed}}}{\substack{\text{Total assessed}\\ \text{value}}}$$	Tax amount needed $81,888; total assessed value, $1,023,600. Find the tax rate. $$\frac{81,888}{1,023,600} = 0.08$$
6.2 Expressing tax rates in different forms and finding tax	1. Percent—multiply assessed valuation by rate. 2. Dollars per $100—move decimal 2 places to left in assessed valuation and multiply. 3. Dollars per $1000—move decimal 3 places to left in assessed valuation and multiply. 4. Mills—move decimal 3 places to the left in rate and multiply by assessed valuation.	Assessed value, $90,000; Tax rate, 2.5% $90,000 \times 0.025 = \$2250$ Tax rate, $2.50 per $100 $900 \times \$2.50 = \$2250$ Tax rate, $25 per $1000 $90 \times \$25 = \$2250$ Tax rate, 25 mills $90,000 \times \$.025 = \$2250$
6.3 Adjusted gross income	Adjusted gross income includes wages, salaries, tips, dividends, and interest.	Salary, $32,540; interest income, $875; dividends, $315. Find adjusted gross income. $\$32,540 + \$875 + \$315 = \$33,730$
6.3 Standard deduction amounts	The majority of taxpayers use the standard deduction allowed by the IRS.	$3400 for single people $5700 for married people filing jointly $2850 for married people filing separately $5000 for head of household
6.3 Taxable income	The larger of either the total of itemized deductions or the standard deduction is subtracted from adjusted gross income along with $2150 for each personal exemption.	Adjusted gross income, $16,200; single taxpayer; itemized deductions total $2830; find taxable income. Standard deduction is $3400; larger than $2850 itemized deduction Taxable income = $\$16,200 - \$3400 - \$2150 = \$10,650$

TOPIC	APPROACH	EXAMPLE
6.3 Tax rates	There are 3 tax rates, 15%, 28%, and 31%. All taxpayers pay 15% until income reaches a certain level. Earnings over this amount are taxed at 28%, until they reach the highest level and then all further income is taxed at 31%.	Single 15%; over $23,350, 28%; over $49,300, 31%. Married filing jointly or certain widow(er)s 15%; over $34,000, 28%; over $82,150, 31%. Married filing separately 15%; over $17,000, 28%; over $41,075, 31%. Head of household 15%; over $27,300, 28%; over $70,450, 31%.
6.3 Tax due or refund	If the total amount withheld by employers is greater than the tax owed, a refund results. If the tax owed is the greater amount, a balance is due.	Tax owed, $1253; tax withheld, $113 per month for 12 months. Find balance due or refund. $113 × 12 = $1356 withheld $1356 withheld − $1253 owed = $103 refund

SUMMARY EXERCISE

Jack Armstrong, owner of All American Truck Stop is considering two separate locations along the interstate, Anderson and Bentonville. The two locations are about 200 miles apart, and while offering identical business potential there are differences in land acquisition costs, building costs, and most importantly property taxes. Armstrong feels that he needs 11 acres of land and buildings and improvements that will total 90,000 square feet. The land and building costs and property tax information are as follows.

	Anderson	Bentonville
Land cost (per square foot)	$.40	$.35
Building and improvement cost (per square foot)	$32.80	$36.90
Assessment rate	25%	20%
Tax rate	32 mills	$2.95 per $100

Knowing that there are 43,560 square feet in an acre and that the total cost of land improvements will be used as fair market value in both locations, Jack Armstrong needs to answer the following questions to help him in his decision.

(a)   What is the cost of the land and improvements in each location?

(b)   Find the assessed valuation of the land and improvements in each location.

(c)   Find the annual property tax in each location.

(d)   What is the total cost including land, building, and property taxes over a ten-year period in each location?

C H A P T E R   6   R E V I E W   E X E R C I S E S

Find the amount of the sales tax, the excise tax, and the total sales price including taxes in each of the following problems. [6.1]

	Sales Price	Sales Tax Rate	Excise Tax Rate
1.	$280.50	4%	11%
2.	$49.95	6%	10%
3.	$16,500	5%	$6.00 per person; 110 people
4.	$345.96	7%	14.1¢/gallon; 285 gallons

Find the sales price when given the amount of tax and the sales tax rate. [6.1]

	Amount of Sales Tax	Sales Tax Rate
5.	$ 4.90	7%
6.	$ 7.10	5%
7.	$11.34	6%
8.	$ 5.91	$4\frac{1}{2}\%$

Find the amount of the sale before sales tax was added in each of the following. [6.1]

	Total Sale	Sales Tax Rate
9.	$143.52	4%
10.	$180.20	6%
11.	$292.95	5%
12.	$174.41	7%

Complete the following list comparing tax rates. Do not round. [6.2]

	Percent	Per $100	Per $1000	In Mills
13.	_____%	$1.75	_____	_____
14.	_____%	_____	_____	27
15.	1.27%	_____	_____	_____
16.	_____%	_____	$20.30	_____

Find the missing quantity. [6.2]

	Assessed Valuation	Tax Rate	Tax
17.	$285,000	21 mills	_____
18.	$83,500	_____ per $1000	$1878.75
19.	_____	3.5%	$1627.50
20.	$140,500	_____%	$3934
21.	_____	$3.80 per $100	$3655.60
22.	$71,200	32 mills	_____

Find the taxable income and the tax for each of the following. The letter following the name indicates the marital status. Married people file joint returns. [6.3]

	Name	Number of Exemptions	Adjusted Gross Income	Total Deductions
23.	A. Philips, S	1	$33,283	$1622
24.	The Sparks, M	5	$28,721	$4501
25.	M. Gulley-Pavey, M	3	$52,662	$5382
26.	M. Rosen, S	1	$47,218	$2828

Work each of the following word problems.

27. A recently incorporated city budgets on the basis that it will collect $2,339,000. If the total assessed value of the property in the city is $80,475,000, find the tax rate as a percent rounded to the nearest tenth. [6.1]

28. Total receipts for the day at the Toy Circus are $3442.88. If this includes 6% sales tax, find the amount of the sales tax. [6.1]

29. A mini-storage complex has a fair market value of $1,506,400. Property in the area is assessed at 25% of fair market value, with a tax rate of $31.40 per $1000. Find the annual property tax. [6.2]

Find the tax owed in each of the following problems. [6.3]

30. The Cooks, married and filing a joint return, have an adjusted gross income of $57,978, 6 exemptions, and deductions of $1574.

31. Paul Waechtler had an adjusted gross income of $28,809 last year. He had deductions of $936 for state income tax, $759 for property tax, $824 in mortgage interest, and $252 in contributions. Waechtler claims 1 exemption and files as a single person.

32. Diane and David Bolton had total wages and salaries of $56,318, other income of $677, and interest income of $1215. They are allowed an adjustment to income of $2346. Their itemized deductions are $3815 in mortgage interest, $327 in state income taxes, and $1218 in charitable contributions. The Boltons are filing a joint return and claim 3 exemptions.

Find the amount of any refund or amount due for the following people. The letter following the name indicates marital status. Assume a 52-week year and that married people are filing jointly. [6.3]

	Name	Taxable Income	Federal Income Tax Withheld from Checks
33.	The Todds, M	$48,762	$145.20 weekly
34.	Lagera, T., S	$33,825	$533.20 monthly
35.	Albers, K., S	$19,237	$ 88.08 weekly
36.	The Biondis, M	$24,718	$249.80 monthly

7

Risk Management

People buy insurance to protect against risk. In the event that some undesirable event occurs, **peril insurance** provides financial compensation. Perils which are insurable include illness, death, fire, flood, theft, automobile collision, property damage, and personal liability. A person or business buying the insurance, the **insured** or **policy-holder**, pays a relatively small amount of money—called the **premium**—to provide protection against a large loss. If the undesirable event occurs, the insurance company, the **insurer** or **carrier**, pays the insured for the loss up to the **face value** or stated amount of the policy.

Insurance is based on the idea that many pay into a fund while a few draw out of the fund. For example, a business may pay a fire insurance premium of a few hundred dollars for several years without ever having a fire loss. However, should a fire occur, the loss may result in many thousands of dollars being paid to the business.

This chapter looks first at business insurance, including fire and liability coverage; next, motor vehicle insurance is discussed; then, the many types of life insurance policies are examined. Nonforfeiture options and settlement options are covered in the last section of the chapter.

7.1 Business Insurance

OBJECTIVES

1 Define the terms policy, face value, and premium.

2 Identify the factors that determine the premium.

3 Find the annual premium for fire insurance given rating and property values.

4 Calculate short-term rates and cancellations.

5 Calculate prorated insurance premium cancellations.

6 Use the coinsurance formula to solve problems.

7 Find the insurance liability when there are multiple carriers.

8 Find liability of multiple carriers when coinsurance requirement is not met.

9 List additional risk against which a business may be insured.

There is only a slight chance that any particular building will suffer fire damage during a given year. However, if such fire damage were to occur, the financial loss could be very large. To protect against this small chance of a large loss, people pay an amount equal to a small percent of the value of their property to a fire insurance company. The company collects money from a large number of property owners, then pays for expenses due to fire damage for those few buildings which are damaged.

1 The contract between the owner of a building and a fire insurance company is called a **policy**. The amount of insurance provided by the company is called the **face value of the policy**. The charge for the policy is called the **premium**.

2 The amount of premium charged by the insurance company depends on several factors, such as the type of construction of the building, the contents and use of the building, the location of the building, and the type of available fire protection. Wood frame buildings are generally more likely to be damaged by fire, and thus require a larger premium than masonry buildings. Categories are assigned to building types by insurance company employees called **underwriters**. These categories are usually named by letters, such as A, B, C, and so on. Underwriters also assign ratings, called territorial ratings, to each area served which describe the quality of fire protection in the area. While fire insurance rates vary from state to state, the rates in Table 7.1 are typical.

3 The annual premium for fire insurance is expressed as a certain amount for each one hundred dollars in value.

TABLE 7.1   Annual Rates for Each $100 of Fire Insurance

	Building Rating					
	A		B		C	
Territorial Rating	**Building**	**Contents**	**Building**	**Contents**	**Building**	**Contents**
1	$.25	$.32	$.36	$.49	$.45	$.60
2	$.30	$.44	$.45	$.55	$.54	$.75
3	$.37	$.46	$.54	$.60	$.63	$.80
4	$.50	$.52	$.75	$.77	$.84	$.90
5	$.62	$.58	$.92	$.99	$1.14	$1.05

EXAMPLE 1

Finding the Annual Fire Insurance Premium

Joyce Pierscinski has a building in rating class B. The building's territorial rating is 3. Find the annual premium to insure a building worth $242,000 with contents valued at $62,000.

SOLUTION From Table 7.1, the rates per $100 for a class B building in area 3 are $.54 for the building and $.60 for the contents. The premium for the building is found as follows.

$$\text{Value of building} = \$242,000 = 2420 \text{ hundreds}$$

$$\text{Rate for building (from table)} = \$.54$$

$$\text{Premium for building} = \text{Value (in hundreds)} \times \text{Rate}$$

$$= 2420 \times \$.54$$

$$= \$1306.80$$

The premium for the contents can be found in the same way.

$$\text{Value of contents} = \$62,000 = 620 \text{ hundreds}$$

$$\text{Rate for contents} = \$.60 \text{ (from table)}$$

$$\text{Premium for contents} = \text{Value (in hundreds)} \times \text{Rate}$$

$$= 620 \times \$.60$$

$$= \$372$$

$$\text{Total premium} = \$1306.80 \text{ (building)} + \$372 \text{ (contents)}$$

$$= \$1678.80 \text{ (building and contents)} \quad \blacksquare$$

4 Insurance is sometimes purchased for part of a year, perhaps even for just a few months. Also, if a business is sold or the owner wishes to change insurance carriers during the period of a policy, the existing policy must be canceled. In each of these cases, the insurance company will charge a **short-term** or **cancellation rate**. When the short-term rate is used, a penalty results.

As shown in Table 7.2, one month's insurance costs 18% of an annual premium while one month is only $8\frac{1}{3}$ % of a year ($1 \div 12 = 0.083333$). The premium for a six-month policy or a policy canceled after six months costs 70% of the annual premium.

TABLE 7.2 Short-Term Rate Schedule

Time in Months	Percent of Annual Premium	Time in Months	Percent of Annual Premium
1	18%	7	75%
2	35%	8	80%
3	45%	9	85%
4	55%	10	90%
5	65%	11	95%
6	70%	12	100%

EXAMPLE 2
Determining Short-Term Rates

Erich Means sold a small warehouse. Because of the sale he canceled his fire insurance after five months. If the annual premium is $3896, use the short-term rate schedule (see Table 7.2) to find the amount of refund to the insured.

SOLUTION   The short-term rate for 5 months is 65% of the annual premium.

$3896 (annual premium) $\times$ 0.65 = $2532.40 (premium for five months)

The refund is found by subtracting the five-month premium from the annual premium.

$3896 (annual premium) − $2532.40 (five-month premium)

= $1363.60 (refund)   ∎

5   When the insurance company initiates a policy cancellation, the insured is not penalized as with the short-term or cancellation rate. Instead, the insured is charged only for the exact amount of time that the insurance was in force. It is normal for this proration to be to the exact day. Here, we will prorate on a monthly basis, which results in the insured paying only for the number of months that the insurance was provided.

EXAMPLE 3
Calculating Prorated Insurance Cancellations

Your Creations Art Supplies had a fire insurance policy with an annual premium of $2832. The insurance company canceled the policy after seven months and pro-rated the premium. Find (a) the amount of the premium retained by the company and (b) the amount of refund to the insured.

SOLUTION   Since the cancellation is after seven months, the insured is charged for $\frac{7}{12}$ of the year.

(a) The amount of the premium retained by the company is found by multiplying the annual premium by $\frac{7}{12}$.

$2832 (annual premium) $\times \frac{7}{12}$ = $1652 (premium for seven months)

(b) The refund is found by subtracting the premium for seven months from the annual premium.

$2832 (annual premium) − $1652 (seven-month premium) = $1180 (refund)

The refund is equal to $\frac{5}{12}$ of the annual premium.   ∎

6   Most fires damage only a portion of a building and its contents. Since complete destruction of a building is rare, many owners save money by buying insurance for only a portion of the value of the building and contents. Realizing this, insurance companies place a **coinsurance clause** in almost all fire insurance policies. With coinsurance, part of the risk of fire, under certain conditions, is assumed by the business firm taking out the insurance. For example, an 80% coinsurance clause provides that for full protection, the amount of insurance taken out must be at least 80% of the market value of the building and contents insured.

If the amount of insurance is less than 80% of the market value, the insurance company pays only a portion of any loss. For example, if a business firm took out insurance with a face value of only 40% of the market value of the building insured and then had a loss, the insurance company would pay only half the loss, since 40% is half of 80%.

The following formula gives the portion of a loss that will be paid by the insurance company.

Amount insurance companies will pay (assuming 80% coinsurance)

$$= \text{Amount of loss} \times \frac{\text{Amount of policy}}{80\% \text{ of market value}}$$

NOTE The company will never pay more than the face value of the policy, nor will the company pay more than the amount of the loss.

EXAMPLE 4

Using the Coinsurance Formula

Talaya Turner owns a factory valued at $560,000. Her fire insurance policy (with an 80% coinsurance clause) has a face value of $420,000. The building suffers a fire loss of $112,000. Find the amount of loss that the insurance company will pay.

SOLUTION The policy should have been for at least 80% of the value of the store, or

$$0.80 \times \$560{,}000 = \$448{,}000$$

Since the face value of the policy is less than 80% of the value of the building, the company will pay only a portion of the loss. Use the coinsurance formula.

$$\text{Amount insurance company pays} = \$112{,}000 \times \frac{\$420{,}000}{\$448{,}000} = \$105{,}000$$

The company will pay $105,000 toward the loss, and Turner must pay the additional $7000 ($112,000 − $105,000). ∎

Calculator Approach to Example 4

Determine the 80% coinsurance value first.

.8 $\boxed{\times}$ 560000 $\boxed{=}$ 448000

Since the amount of the policy, $420,000, is less than the 80% coinsurance value, $448,000, the insurance company will pay only part of the loss.

Find the portion of loss paid by the insurance company which is $\frac{420{,}000}{448{,}000}$, then multiply by the amount of loss.

420000 $\boxed{\div}$ 448000 $\boxed{\times}$ 112000 $\boxed{=}$ 105000

The company will pay $105,000 and the insured pays the balance.

112000 $\boxed{-}$ 105000 $\boxed{=}$ 7000

The insured pays $7000.

NOTE   In the calculator approach to Example 4 the amount of loss, $112,000, was not multiplied by the face value of the policy, $420,000, as the first step in the problem because the answer, 47,040,000,000, will not fit in the calculator. It is for this reason that 420,000 was divided by 448,000 to determine the portion of the loss paid by the insurance company.

EXAMPLE 5

Finding the Amount of Loss Paid by the Insurance Company

The building owned by Mike's Auto Parts is valued at $172,500. The company has a fire insurance policy with a face value of $170,000. The policy has an 80% coinsurance feature. If the firm has a fire loss of $116,500, find the part of the loss paid by the company.

SOLUTION   The value of the store is $172,500. Take 80% of this value.

$$0.80 \times \$172,500 = \$138,000$$

The business has a fire insurance policy with a face value of more than 80% of the value of the store. Therefore, the insurance company will pay the entire $116,500 loss.   ■

7   A business may have fire insurance placed with several companies, called **multiple carriers**, at the same time. This may be the result of buying additional insurance coverage over a period of time, perhaps as new additions were made to a factory or building complex. Or, if a building is so large that no one insurance company wants to take the entire risk by itself, several companies may agree to each take a portion of the insurance coverage and thereby share the risk. With multiple carriers, each insurance company pays its fractional portion of any claim.

EXAMPLE 6

Understanding Multiple Carrier Insurance

Paul Gailey Trains has an insured loss of $100,000 while insured beyond their coinsurance requirement. The insurance is divided between Company A with $100,000 coverage, Company B with $75,000 coverage, and Company C with $25,000 coverage. Find the amount of the loss paid by each of the insurance companies.

SOLUTION   Start by finding the total face value of all three policies.

$100,000	Company A
75,000	Company B
+ 25,000	Company C
$200,000	total face value

Since the insured loss is $100,000, the amount paid by each of the multiple carriers is as follows.

$$\frac{100,000}{200,000} \times \$100,000 = \$50,000 \qquad \text{Company A}$$

$$\frac{75,000}{200,000} \times \$100,000 = \$37,500 \qquad \text{Company B}$$

$$\frac{25,000}{200,000} \times \$100,000 = \$12,500 \qquad \text{Company C}$$

$$\$100,000 \qquad \text{total loss} \quad ■$$

8 If the coinsurance requirement is not met, the total amount of the loss paid by the insurance coverage is found, and then the amount that each of the carriers pays is found by the method shown in Example 7.

EXAMPLE 7
Finding Liability of
Multiple Carriers
when Coinsurance
Requirements Are
Not Met

Hermitage Building Products' warehouse is valued at $200,000 and is insured under an 80% coinsurance clause for $120,000. $80,000 of the insurance is placed with Company A and $40,000 with Company B. If the warehouse suffers a loss of $20,000, find (a) the part of any loss that is covered, (b) the amount of the loss the insurance companies will pay, (c) each insurance company's payment after the $20,000 loss, and (d) the amount paid by the insured.

SOLUTION

(a) First, find the amount of insurance needed to satisfy the 80% coinsurance clause.

$$0.80 \times \$200,000 = \$160,000$$

Since the face value of the policy ($120,000) is less than 80% ($160,000), the insurance company will only pay a portion of the loss.

$$\text{Part insurance company pays} = \frac{\$120,000}{\$160,000}$$

(b) Use the coinsurance formula to find the amount of the loss that the insurance companies will pay.

$$\text{Amount insurance companies pay} = 20,000 \times \frac{\$120,000}{\$160,000} = \$15,000.$$

(c) The total face value of the insurance is $120,000. Since the amount of the loss that the insurance companies will pay is $15,000, the amount paid by each of the multiple carriers is as follows.

$$\frac{80,000}{120,000} \times \$15,000 = \$10,000 \qquad \text{Company A}$$

$$\frac{40,000}{120,000} \times \$15,000 = \underline{\$5,000} \qquad \text{Company B}$$

$$\$15,000 \qquad \text{amount of loss paid}$$

(d) Hermitage Building Products must pay $5000, the difference between the loss and the amount paid by the insurance companies. ■

9 There are many types of insurance coverage that a business might want. One of the most common is liability coverage, which protects against monetary awards from personal-injury lawsuits caused by the business; another common coverage protects property against damage caused by windstorm, hail, or fire. Homeowners usually buy a **homeowner's policy**, which protects against these losses and many others, including all credit cards and automated teller cards, business property brought home, and medical costs for guests who are injured. Other policies are designed for condominium owners, rental property owners, and apartment dwellers. Many types of additional coverage are available to give complete and comprehensive insurance coverage.

A **business owner's package policy**, known in the insurance industry as a special multiperils policy or **SMP**, typically includes coverage of the following:

- replacement cost for the building and contents;
- contents, which provides for a 25% peak season increase;
- business property that is in transit or temporarily away from the premises;
- money, securities, accounts receivable, and other valuable papers up to $1000;
- loss of income, which includes rents and interruption of business for up to 12 months;
- liability and medical coverage resulting from personal injury, advertising injury, medical malpractice.

In addition to coverage of these standard risks, a list of optional coverages is also available. The businessperson may select those which he or she feels are necessary. A few of these are:

- replacement cost coverage on exterior signs;
- replacement cost coverage for glass;
- minicomputer coverage;
- coverage for loss of refrigeration;
- professional liability coverage for barbers, beauticians, pharmacists, hearing aid sellers, morticians, optometrists, and veterinarians;
- coverage for non-owned and hired automobiles;
- liquor liability coverage.

In addition to the many coverages for business property and personal liability, the employer may be required to provide **worker's compensation insurance** for employees, which provides payments to an employee who is unable to work due to a job-related injury or illness.

An employer may pay the entire premium or part of the premium for employee health insurance, dental insurance, and group life insurance. Most often these **group insurance plans** offer slightly reduced premiums to those participating in the plan. Participation in group insurance plans is sometimes an incentive for remaining with an employer, since changing jobs may eliminate participation in the group insurance plan.

7.1 Exercises

Find the total annual premium for fire insurance for each of the following. Use Table 7.1.

	Territorial Rating	Building Classification	Building Value	Contents Value
1.	2	B	$100,000	$40,000
2.	3	C	$75,000	$30,600
3.	1	C	$142,500	$76,000
4.	3	A	$198,700	$76,000
5.	5	B	$782,600	$212,000
6.	4	C	$285,700	$129,800
7.	5	C	$583,200	$221,400
8.	4	A	$850,500	$425,800

Find the amount of refund to the insured using the Short-Term Rate Schedule (Table 7.2).

	Annual Premium	Months in Force
9.	$900	3
10.	$560	2
11.	$763	6
12.	$572	1
13.	$1478	9
14.	$1866	10
15.	$4860	11
16.	$2250	5

Find (a) the amount of premium retained by the company and (b) the amount of refund to the insured using proration.

	Annual Premium	Months in Force
17.	$1560	6
18.	$1116	3
19.	$1872	5
20.	$876	11
21.	$3264	7
22.	$4704	10

Find the amount of each of the following losses that will be paid by the insurance company. Assume that each policy includes an 80% coinsurance clause.

	Value of Building	**Face Value of Policy**	**Amount of Loss**
23.	$125,000	$112,500	$9400
24.	$360,000	$340,000	$5200
25.	$59,000	$48,000	$4000
26.	$750,000	$500,000	$56,000
27.	$80,000	$62,000	$34,600
28.	$124,800	$80,000	$25,000
29.	$147,850	$100,000	$14,850
30.	$285,000	$150,000	$18,500

Find the amount paid by each insurance company in the following problems involving multiple carriers. Assume that the coinsurance requirement is met. Round all answers to the nearest dollar.

	Insurance Loss	**Companies and Coverage**	
31.	$48,000	Company A	$120,000
		Company B	$80,000
32.	$110,000	Company 1	$40,000
		Company 2	$100,000
		Company 3	$10,000
33.	$130,000	Company 1	$140,000
		Company 2	$90,000
		Company 3	$70,000
34.	$270,000	Company A	$300,000
		Company B	$50,000
		Company C	$150,000

Find (a) the amount of the loss paid by the insurance companies, (b) each insurance company's payment, and (c) the amount paid by the insured in each of the following problems involving coinsurance and multiple carriers. Assume an 80% coinsurance clause and round all answers to the nearest dollar.

	Property Value	**Insurance Loss**	**Companies and Coverage**	
35.	$200,000	$30,000	Company A	$80,000
			Company B	$40,000
36.	$320,000	$50,000	Company A	$180,000
			Company B	$60,000
37.	$250,000	$20,000	Company 1	$75,000
			Company 2	$50,000
38.	$480,000	$100,000	Company 1	$180,000
			Company 2	$60,000

Find the annual fire insurance premium for each of the following.

39. Daniel Lange owns a class B building worth $164,000. Contents are valued at $284,000. The territorial rating is 3.

40. Dave's Auto Body and Paint owns a class A building worth $143,000. Contents are worth $78,500. The territorial rating is 5.

41. The Rocklin Grill owns a building worth $84,000. The contents are worth $18,500. The building is class B and the territorial rating is 1.

42. Wheelchair Whitney, Numismatist, owns a building rated C with a territorial rating of 4. The building is worth $210,000 and the contents are worth $1,364,000.

Find the amount of refund to the insured using the Short-Term Rate Schedule (Table 7.2) in each of the following.

43. Placer Title Company pays an annual fire insurance premium of $1700. They transfer insurance companies after six months.

44. Teddys and Trains pays an annual fire insurance premium of $1250. The business is sold and insurance canceled after seven months.

45. Minkner Ranch Supply cancels their fire insurance after nine months. Their annual premium is $2750.

46. Martinez Horse Stables pays an annual fire insurance premium of $3960. They change insurance companies after two months.

Find (a) the amount of premium retained by the company and (b) the amount of refund to the insured using proration.

47. Broadly Plumbing Repairs pays an annual fire insurance premium of $1248. The insurance company cancels the policy after four months.

48. Carter paint has had their fire insurance canceled after nine months. Their annual premium is $2460.

49. As the result of a recent claim, Buy-Rite Drug Store has had their fire insurance policy canceled after seven months. Their annual premium is $1944.

50. In-Out Burgers pays an annual fire insurance premium of $2892. The insurance company cancels the policy after ten months.

51. Describe three factors that determine the premium charged for fire insurance. (See Objective 2.)

52. Explain the coinsurance clause and describe how coinsurance works. (See Objective 6.)

In each of the following problems, find the amount of the loss paid by (a) the insurance company and (b) the insured. Assume an 80% coinsurance requirement.

53. Angel Odezma owns a hero sandwich shop worth $168,000. The shop is insured for $132,000. Fire loss is $7500.

54. The Towne Apartments is valued at $270,000 and insured for $154,000. Fire loss is $17,000.

55. Headquarters of the Roseville Police Department suffers a loss from fire of $36,000. The building is valued at $440,000 and insured for $240,000.

56. Philip Harwood owns a duplex valued at $196,000 and insured for $148,000. Fire loss is $18,000.

57. Explain in your own words multiple carrier insurance. Give two reasons for dividing insurance among multiple carriers. (See Objective 7.)

58. Several types of insurance coverage beyond basic fire coverage are included in a homeowner's policy. List and explain three losses that would be covered. (See Objective 9.)

In each of the following, find the amount paid by each of the multiple carriers. Assume that the coinsurance requirement has been met and round to the nearest dollar.

59. Helms Bakery had a fire loss of $38,000. They had insurance coverage as follows: Company A, $50,000; Company B, $100,000; and Company C, $70,000.

60. Camp Curry Stable had a fire loss of $68,500. They had insurance as follows: Company 1, $60,000; Company 2, $40,000; and Company 3, $30,000.

In each of the following problems, find (a) the amount that the insured would receive and (b) the amount that each of the insurance companies would pay.

61. The offices of Magic Mortgage are valued at $400,000, and the fire insurance policies contain an 80% coinsurance clause. The fire policies include $180,000 with Company A and $60,000 with Company B. Magic Mortgage suffers a $50,000 fire loss.

62. The fire insurance policies on the Midtown Warehouse contain an 80% coinsurance clause and the warehouse is valued at $240,000. Fire policies on the warehouse are $90,000 with Company A and $30,000 with Company B. Midtown Warehouse has a fire loss of $80,000.

63. Jack Pritchard's Steak House is valued at $360,000. The fire policies are $100,000 with Company 1, $50,000 with Company 2, and $30,000 with Company 3, while each contains an 80% coinsurance clause. There is a fire at the steakhouse causing a $120,000 loss.

64. The main manufacturing plant of Birmingham Fabrics is appraised at $550,000. Fire insurance policies on the plant are $150,000 with Company 1, $100,000 with Company 2, and $80,000 with Company 3. The policies contain an 80% coinsurance clause and the plant suffers a $120,000 fire loss.

7.2 Motor Vehicle Insurance

OBJECTIVES

1 Describe the factors that affect the cost of motor vehicle insurance.

2 Define liability insurance and determine the premium.

3 Define property damage insurance and determine the premium.

4 Describe comprehensive and collision insurance and determine the premium.

5 Define no-fault insurance and uninsured motorist.

6 Apply youthful operator factors.

7 Calculate a motor vehicle insurance premium.

8 Find the amounts paid by the insurance company and the insured.

1 The cost of repairing a motor vehicle after an accident now averages between $2600 and $2900. Businesses and individuals buy motor vehicle insurance to protect against the possible large cost of an accident. The cost of this insurance, the **premium**, is determined by people called **actuaries**, who classify accidents according to location, age and sex of the drivers, and other factors. Insurance companies use these results to determine the premiums. For example, there are more accidents in heavily populated cities than in rural areas. Certain makes and models of automobiles are stolen more often than others. Young male drivers (16–25 years of age) are involved in many more accidents than they should be, considering their proportion of the population. The more expensive a vehicle and the newer a vehicle, the more it costs to repair. These are several of the factors that determine the cost of insurance.

NOTE The combination of youthful drivers and an expensive car can result in very large premiums for a 21-year-old male driver of a Corvette.

The various types of automobile insurance are discussed in this section.

2 Liability or Bodily Injury Insurance. Liability or **body injury insurance** protects the insured in case he or she injures someone with a car. The amount of liability insurance is expressed as a fraction, such as 15/30. The fraction 15/30 means that the insurance company will pay up to $15,000 for injury to one person, and a total of $30,000 for injury to two or more persons in the same accident. Table 7.3 shows typical premium rates for various amounts of liability coverage.

Medical Insurance. Included in the cost of the liability insurance is **medical insurance** provided to the driver and passengers of a vehicle in case of injury. For example, the column of the table headed "15/30" shows that the insured can also receive reimbursement for up to $1000 of his or her own medical expenses in an accident.

For purposes of setting premiums, insurance companies divide the nation into territories, as many as thirty or more. Four territories are shown in Table 7.3. All tables in this section show annual premiums.

TABLE 7.3   Liability (Bodily Injury) and Medical Insurance

	Annual Premiums for the Indicated Coverage				
Territory	**15/30 $1000**	**25/50 $2000**	**50/100 $2000**	**100/300 $5000**	**250/500 $10,000**
1	$147	$162	$183	$208	$225
2	87	96	108	123	133
3	236	260	294	334	360
4	154	169	191	217	234

EXAMPLE 1
Finding the Liability and Medical Premium

Anita Price lives in territory 2 and wants 100/300 liability coverage. Find the amount of the premium for this coverage and the amount of medical coverage included.

SOLUTION   Look up territory 2 in Table 7.3 and 100/300 coverage to find a premium of $123, which includes $5000 of medical coverage.   ∎

3 **Property Damage Insurance.**   **Property damage insurance** pays for damages caused to the property of others. Table 7.4 shows the premiums for property damage insurance. The coverage amount is the maximum amount that the insurance company will pay. If a claim for damages exceeds this maximum amount, the insured must pay the excess.

EXAMPLE 2
Finding the Premium for Property Damage

Find the premium if Anita Price, living in territory 2, wants property damage coverage of $25,000.

SOLUTION   Property damage coverage of $25,000 in territory 2 requires a premium of $39, as Table 7.4 shows.   ∎

4 **Comprehensive Insurance.**   **Comprehensive insurance** pays for damage to a vehicle caused by fire, theft, vandalism, falling trees, and other such events.

Collision Insurance.   **Collision insurance** pays for repairs to a vehicle in case of an accident. Collision insurance often includes a **deductible**. The deductible is paid by the insured in the event of a claim, with the insurance company paying all amounts

TABLE 7.4   Property Damage Insurance

	Property Damage			
Territory	**$10,000**	**$25,000**	**$50,000**	**$100,000**
1	$58	$63	$67	$73
2	34	39	46	54
3	89	104	115	128
4	56	71	82	94

TABLE 7.5 **Comprehensive and Collision Insurance**

Territory	Age Group	Comprehensive			Collision ($100 Deductible)		
		Symbol			Symbol		
		6	7	8	6	7	8
1	1	$29	$32	$45	$123	$135	$154
	2,3	25	28	41	105	117	141
	4,5	22	26	38	86	98	117
	6	17	22	32	62	80	98
2	1	$13	$14	$20	$59	$65	$74
	2,3	11	12	18	50	56	68
	4,5	10	12	17	41	47	56
	6	8	10	14	30	38	47
3	1	$35	$39	$54	$115	$127	$144
	2,3	30	33	45	98	109	132
	4,5	26	32	46	81	92	109
	6	21	26	39	58	75	92
4	1	$21	$23	$33	$67	$74	$84
	2,3	18	20	29	57	64	77
	4,5	16	19	27	47	54	64
	6	13	16	23	34	44	54

above the deductible. Common deductible amounts are $50, $100, $250, and in some cases $500 or $1000. For example, if the cost of repairing damage caused by an accident is $1045 and the deductible amount is $100, the insured pays $100, and the insurance company pays $945 ($1045 − $100 = $945).

NOTE The higher the deducible amount, the lower the cost of the collision coverage: the insured shares a greater portion of the risk as the deductible amount increases.

Table 7.5 shows some typical rates for comprehensive and collision insurance. Rates are determined not only by territories, but also by Age Group and Symbol. Here, age group refers to the age of the vehicle, not the driver. Age group 1 is a new vehicle to one year of age and age group 6 is a vehicle six years of age or older. The symbol is determined by the cost of the vehicle.

NOTE A Ford Escort might be a symbol 6 and a Lincoln Continental might be a symbol 8. The collision coverage here is for $100 deductible coverage.

EXAMPLE 3
Finding the Comprehensive and Collision Premium

Anita Price, living in territory 2, drives a two-year-old car with a symbol of 8. Use Table 7.5 to find the annual premium for (a) comprehensive coverage and (b) collision coverage.

SOLUTION

(a) The annual premium for comprehensive coverage is $18.

(b) The annual premium for collision coverage is $68. ∎

5   **No-Fault Insurance.**   With **no-fault insurance**, the insured is reimbursed for medical expenses and all costs associated with an accident by his or her own insurance company, no matter who caused the accident, and pain and suffering damages are eliminated except in cases of permanent injury or death. Insurance companies argue that no-fault insurance removes lawyers and the courts, and results in easier and less expensive settlements. On the other hand, some trial lawyers and consumer groups contend that no-fault leaves accident victims unable to recover all of their damages and unprotected from the abuses of some insurance companies.

Uninsured Motorist Insurance.   In the states not having no-fault insurance (about 80%), a driver must be concerned about an accident with an uninsured driver. Drivers in these states need **uninsured motorist insurance**, which protects the vehicle owner in a collision with a vehicle that is not insured. Some insurance companies offer **underinsured motorist insurance**, which provides protection in the event that there is a collision with a vehicle that is underinsured. Typical costs for uninsured motorist insurance are shown in Table 7.6.

EXAMPLE 4

Determining the Premium for Uninsured Motorist Coverage

Anita Price, living in territory 2, wants uninsured motorist coverage. Find the premium in Table 7.6.

SOLUTION   The annual premium for uninsured motorist coverage in territory 2 is $24. ∎

6   Most insurance companies distinguish between **youthful** and **adult operators**. Although the age at which a driver becomes an adult varies from company to company, drivers of age 25 or less are usually considered youthful drivers and drivers over 25 are considered adults. Due to the higher proportion of accidents in the 25-and-under bracket, insurance companies add an additional amount to the insurance premium. In Table 7.7, there are two categories of youthful drivers, age 20 or less, and age 21–25. Consideration is also given to the youthful operator who has had driver's training. Some companies give discounts to youthful drivers who are "good students" (a "B" average or better). To use the youthful operator table, first determine the premium for all coverage desired and then multiply this premium by the appropriate youthful operator factor to find the total premium.

TABLE 7.6   Uninsured Motorist Insurance

Territory	Basic Limit
1	$33
2	24
3	38
4	35

TABLE 7.7   **Youthful Operator Factor**

Age	With Driver's Training	Without Driver's Training
20 or less	1.55	1.75
21–25	1.15	1.40

7   The total annual insurance premium is found by adding the costs of each type of insurance coverage.

EXAMPLE 5
Using the Youthful Operator Factor

Patrick Kelley lives in territory 4, is 22 years old, has had driver's training, and drives a 5-year-old car with a symbol of 7. He wants a 25/50 liability policy, $10,000 property damage coverage, a comprehensive and collision policy, and uninsured motorist coverage. Find his annual insurance premium.

SOLUTION   As shown in Table 7.3, his annual premium for 25/50 liability insurance is $169. In Table 7.4, his annual premium for a $10,000 policy is $56. In Table 7.5, comprehensive insurance costs $19 and the premium for collision is $54. Uninsured motorist insurance from Table 7.6 is $35. The youthful operator factor for a 22-year-old with driver's training from Table 7.7 is 1.15. First add the premiums from the various tables.

$$\$169 + \$56 + \$19 + \$54 + \$35 = \$333$$

Then multiply by the youthful operator factor of 1.15, found in Table 7.7.

$$\text{Total premium} = \$333 \times 1.15 = \$382.95 \quad \blacksquare$$

Calculator Approach to Example 5

Look up the insurance rates for each type of coverage in the proper table and add them in a chain calculation to get the annual insurance premium.

$$169 \;\boxed{+}\; 56 \;\boxed{+}\; 19 \;\boxed{+}\; 54 \;\boxed{+}\; 35 \;\boxed{=}\; 333$$

Since there is a youthful operator factor of 1.15, found in Table 7.7, the premium must be multiplied by 1.15.

$$333 \times 1.15 \;\boxed{=}\; 382.95$$

---

8   The cost of increasing insurance coverage limits is usually quite small. For example, in Table 7.3 the additional cost of increasing liability coverage in territory 1 from 50/100 to 100/300 is only $25 per year ($208 − $183) (Medical coverage would also be increased.)

NOTE   Since the insurance company pays only to the maximum amount of insurance coverage and with the driver liable for all additional amounts, many people pay an additional premium for increased coverage.

EXAMPLE 6

Finding the Amounts Paid by the Insurance Company and the Insured

Richard Davis has 15/30 liability limits, $10,000 property damage limits, and $100 deductible collision insurance. While on vacation he was at fault in an accident which caused $4300 damage to his car, $5850 in damage to another car, and resulted in severe injuries to the other driver and her passenger. A subsequent lawsuit for injuries resulted in a judgement of $25,000 and $20,000, respectively, to the other parties. Find the amounts that the insurance company will pay for (a) repairing Davis' car, (b) repairing the other car, and (c) the court judgement. (d) How much will Davis have to pay to the injured parties?

SOLUTION

(a) The insurance company will pay $4200 ($4300 − $100 deductible) to repair Davis' car.

(b) Repairs on the other car will be paid to the property damage limits; here, the total repairs of $5850 are paid.

(c) Since more than one person was injured, the insurance company pays the limit of $30,000 ($15,000 to each of the two injured parties).

(d) Davis is liable for $15,000 ($45,000 − $30,000), the amount awarded over the insurance limits.   ■

Additional factors may affect the annual premium for motor vehicle insurance, such as whether the vehicle is used for pleasure, as transportation to and from work or for business purposes, how far the vehicle is driven each year, whether the youthful driver is male or female, the marital status of the male youthful driver, the past driving record of the driver, and whether the driver has more than one car insured with the insurance company. Quite often, discounts are given to nonsmokers and good students. There are also discounts for automobiles equipped with air bags and antilock braking systems. Many insurance companies charge an annual **policy fee**, which covers the cost of processing the policy each year.

7.2 Exercises

Find the annual premium for each of the following people.

	Name	Territory	Age	Driver Training	Liability	Property Damage	Comprehensive Collision Age Group	Symbol	Uninsured Motorist
1.	Felton	3	40	—	15/30	$25,000	5	6	no
2.	Arons	2	35	—	15/30	$10,000	6	8	yes
3.	Leon	1	60	—	25/50	$10,000	1	6	yes
4.	Burgis	4	19	no	25/50	$10,000	3	7	yes
5.	Carter	2	21	yes	100/300	$25,000	5	6	no
6.	Tao	3	24	yes	100/300	$50,000	5	7	yes
7.	Remy	1	52	—	250/500	$50,000	2	8	yes
8.	Gualco	4	47	—	250/500	$50,000	none	none	no
9.	Mar	3	28	—	50/100	$25,000	4	8	yes
10.	Orr	1	17	yes	15/30	$10,000	4	8	yes
11.	Sargis	2	43	—	100/300	$100,000	6	6	no
12.	Rodriquez	3	64	—	100/300	$100,000	5	7	yes

13. Describe four factors that determine the premium on an automobile insurance policy. (See Objective 1.)

14. Explain in your own words the difference between comprehensive insurance and collision insurance. (See Objective 4.)

Solve each of the following word problems.

15. Lisa Kamins is 22 years old, has had driver's training, lives in territory 4, and drives a 3-year-old car with a symbol of 6. She wants 100/300 liability limits, $10,000 property damage limits, comprehensive and collision insurance, and uninsured motorist coverage. Find her annual insurance premium.

16. George Duda is 46 years old, lives in territory 1, and drives a 1-year-old car with a symbol of 8. He wants 100/300 liability limits, $100,000 property damage limits, comprehensive and collision insurance, and uninsured motorist coverage. Find his annual insurance premium.

17. Timothy Hamptor is 17 years old, has not had driver's training, lives in territory 4, and just purchased a new pickup truck with a symbol of 6. He wants 50/100 liability limits, $25,000 property damage limits, comprehensive and collision insurance, and uninsured motorist coverage. Find his annual insurance premium.

18. Sadie Simms lives in territory 3 and drives a new car with a symbol of 7. She wants 250/500 liability limits, $50,000 property damage limits, comprehensive and collision insurance, and uninsured motorist coverage. She is 45 years old. Find her annual insurance premium.

19. Suppose your bodily injury policy has limits of 15/30 and you injure a pedestrian. The judge awards damages of $22,000 to the pedestrian. (a) How much will the company pay and (b) how much will you pay?

20. You cause injury to three people and they receive damages of $10,000 each. You have a policy with bodily injury limits of 25/50. (a) How much will the company pay to each person and (b) how much must you pay?

21. A reckless driver caused Leslie Silva to collide with a car in another lane. Silva had 50/100 liability limits, $25,000 property damage limits, and collision coverage with a $100 deductible. Silva's car had damage of $1878, while the other car suffered $6936 in damage. The resulting lawsuit gave injury awards of $60,000 and $55,000, respectively, to the two people in the other car. Find the amount that the insurance company will pay for (a) repairing Silva's car, (b) repairing the other car, and (c) personal injury damages. (d) How much must Silva pay beyond her insurance coverage, including the collision deductible?

22. Poor weather and excessive speed caused the car driven by John Taylor to crash into another car. Taylor had 25/50 liability limits, $10,000 property damage limits, and collision coverage with a $100 deductible. Damage to Taylor's car was $3115 while the other car, with a value of $13,400, was totaled. The results of a lawsuit awarded $50,000 and $35,000, respectively, in damages for personal injury to the two people in the other car. Find the amount that the insurance company will pay for (a) repairing Taylor's car, (b) repairing the other car, and (c) personal injury damages. (d) How much must Taylor pay beyond his insurance coverage?

23. Woolever Tire Company was transporting a heavy equipment tire when it fell from the truck into the path of an oncoming car. Damage to the car was $11,208. Both the driver and the passenger suffered severe injuries and were given court awards of $30,000 and $50,000, respectively. The tire company had 25/50 liability insurance limits and $10,000 property damage limits. (a) Find the total amount paid by the insurance company for both property damage and liability and (b) find the total amount beyond the insurance limits for which the business owner was liable.

24. A trailer-mounted concrete mixer being towed by a contractor broke loose on the beltway and caused a serious accident involving a car and three occupants. Damage to the car was $10,807. The driver and two passengers were given court awards for personal injury of $25,000, $35,000, and $38,000, respectively. The contractor had 25/50 liability insurance limits and $10,000 property damage limits. Find (a) the total amount paid by the insurance company for both property damage and liability, and (b) the total amount beyond the insurance limits for which the contractor was liable.

25. The higher the deductible the lower the premium. Do you agree with this statement? Explain. (See Objective 4.)

26. Explain in your own words why insurance companies charge a higher premium on auto insurance sold to a youthful operator. (See Objective 6.)

7.3 Life Insurance

OBJECTIVES

1 List reasons for purchasing life insurance.

2 Define term, ordinary life, limited payment, and endowment life insurance policies.

3 Understand universal life and variable life policies.

4 Find the annual premium for life insurance.

5 Use premium factors with different modes of premium payment.

6 Describe discounts, conditions, and additional coverage.

7 Understand nonforfeiture options.

8 Determine the net cost of insurance policies.

9 Calculate income under various settlement options.

1 Individuals buy life insurance for a variety of reasons. Most often the insured wants to provide for the needs of others in the event of early death or disability. Parents may want to guarantee that their children will have enough money for college, even if the parents die. Also, some types of life insurance provide paybacks upon retirement, paybacks that allow a retired person to live better than he or she might otherwise live. Insurance money can also be used to pay off mortgages. According to the American Council of Life Insurance, the average amount of life insurance per household in the United States today is $98,400.

Life insurance is perhaps even more important for a person in business, particularly for an owner or partner in a small business. A business often takes a number of years to grow and may be the owner's main asset. The unexpected death of the owner might leave the business without proper guidance and control, so that the business might suffer drastically before it can be sold. Life insurance on the partners in a business supplies the surviving partner with the necessary money to buy out a deceased partner's interest in the partnership.

2   There are several types of life insurance policies available. The most common types are the following.

Term Insurance.   **Term insurance** provides protection for a fixed length of time, such as one year, five years, or ten years. At the end of the fixed period of time, the policy can usually be renewed for an additional period of time at a higher premium. Some term policies provide that on the expiration of the term stated in the policy, the insurance can be converted to one of the following types of insurance. Term insurance, the least expensive of the types of insurance listed, accounts for 22% of all life policies and gives the greatest amount of life insurance coverage for the premium dollar. At the expiration of a term insurance policy, however, the insured receives nothing from the insurance company except a request to buy more insurance.

Decreasing Term Insurance.   **Decreasing term insurance** is a modification of term insurance where the insured pays a fixed premium until age 60 or 65, with the amount of life insurance decreasing periodically. This policy is designed to fit the ages and stages of life as life insurance needs change. For the person just starting out, it gives more protection for less money. A typical such policy, costing $11 per month, is shown in Table 7.8. Decreasing term insurance is commonly available to employees of large companies as a fringe benefit, paid for by either the employee or the employer or both. Most mortgage insurance policies are this type. The amount of life insurance coverage decreases as the amount of the mortgage is reduced.

TABLE 7.8   A Typical Decreasing Term Insurance Policy

Age	Amount of Life Insurance
Under 29	$40,000
30–34	$35,000
35–39	$30,000
40–44	$25,000
45–49	$18,000
50–54	$11,000
55–59	$7000
60–66	$4000
67 and over	$0

Ordinary Life Insurance.   **Ordinary life insurance** (also called **straight life** or **whole life insurance**) combines life insurance protection with savings. The insured pays a constant premium until death or until retirement, whichever occurs sooner. Upon retirement, monthly payments may be made by the company to the insured until his or her death.

Ordinary life insurance builds up **cash value**, or money used to pay retirement benefits to the insured. Cash values can be borrowed by the insured at very favorable interest rates. Cash value accumulation is guaranteed by the company. The rate of interest used to calculate cash values by the company is very conservative. For this reason, many consumer finance experts recommend the purchase of term insurance, with the difference in premiums between term insurance and ordinary life invested in a good no-load mutual fund or money market fund.

NOTE One difficulty with the approach of investing the difference is that it is easy to neglect to save and invest the difference, while the discipline of regular premium payments for ordinary life insurance is required.

Two recent developments in the life insurance industry provide the life insurance coverage of term insurance (high coverage per premium dollar) plus a tax-deferred way to accumulate assets and earn interest at money market rates.

3 **Universal Life Insurance.**   Unlike traditional whole life insurance policies, **universal life insurance** allows the insured to vary the amount of premium depending on the changing needs of the insured. The younger insured with limited funds may want maximum insurance protection for the family. At a later date, the insured may want to begin actively building assets and may increase the premium to build cash value for retirement benefits. Universal life insurance is sensitive to interest rate changes. The portion of the premium going into retirement benefits receives money market interest rates and is usually guaranteed a minimum rate of return regardless of what happens to market rates. The result is that the insured profits from higher interest rates but is also protected if interest rates drop below the guaranteed rate. It is hoped that the returns will be greater than those given to ordinary life policyholders.

Variable Life Insurance.   **Variable life insurance** is the latest attempt to encourage sales in the insurance industry's main product—whole life insurance. With variable life, the policyholder has the freedom to specify that premiums go to one or more separate investment funds, including fixed investments, stocks, bonds, and others. Typical policies available today allow the policyholder to switch investments from one fund to another twice each year.

NOTE The above features coupled with some tax benefits have resulted in the variable life policy accounting for 25% and 35% respectively of the new policies sold by two of the largest life insurance companies.

Limited Payment Life Insurance.   **Limited payment life insurance** is similar to ordinary life, except that premiums are paid for only a certain fixed number of years, such as 20 years. For this reason, this insurance is often called "20-pay life," representing payments of 20 years. The premium for limited payment life is higher than for ordinary life polices. Limited payment life is commonly used by athletes, actors, and others whose income is likely to be high for several years and then decline.

Endowment Policies. **Endowment policies** are the most expensive type of policy. These policies guarantee payment of a fixed amount of money to a given individual, whether or not the insured lives. Endowment policies might be taken out by parents to guarantee a sum of money for their children's college education. Because of the high premiums, this is one of the least popular types of policies today.

It is not always easy to decide on the best type of policy. While term insurance gives the greatest amount of return for each premium dollar, it pays only when the insured dies. Ordinary life insurance provides less coverage for each premium dollar in the event of death, however, it does provide a return to the insured at retirement. The only certain method for determining which policy will give the best return is for the insured to know when he or she will die, and this is not possible.

The Commissioners 1980 Standard Ordinary Table (shown in Table 7.9) shows the number of deaths per 100 and the remaining life expectancy in years for both males and females among the people in the United States having life insurance. Insurance companies use this **mortality table** to evaluate their life insurance reserves, from which benefits are paid.

4 Calculation of life insurance rates and premiums uses fairly involved mathematics and is done by *actuaries*. The results of such calculations are published in the tables of premiums. A typical table is shown in Table 7.10 (on page 240).

NOTE Life expectancy for women is greater than for men, so a woman pays a lower life insurance premium than does a man of the same age. Find the insurance premium for a woman by subtracting 3 years from her age before using the table of premiums.

The premium for a life insurance policy is found with the following formula.

Premium = Number of thousands × Rate per $1000

EXAMPLE 1
Finding the Life Insurance Premium

Byron Hopkins wants to buy a life insurance policy with a face value of $25,000. Assuming that Hopkins is 35 years old, use Table 7.10 to find his annual rate for (a) a 10-year term policy, (b) an ordinary life policy, (c) a 20-pay life plan, and (d) a 20-year endowment.

SOLUTION Use Table 7.10 and the life insurance premium formula. Since the table gives rates per $1000 of face value, first find the number of thousands in $25,000.

$$25,000 = 25 \text{ thousands}$$

TABLE 7.9 Commissioners 1980 Standard Ordinary Showing the Life Expectancy of Men and Women at Various Ages

	Males		Females			Males		Females	
Age	Deaths per 1000	Expectation of Life (Years)	Deaths per 1000	Expectation of Life (Years)	Age	Deaths per 1000	Expectation of Life (Years)	Deaths per 1000	Expectation of Life (Years)
0	4.18	70.83	2.89	75.83	50	6.71	25.36	4.96	29.53
1	1.07	70.13	.87	75.04	51	7.30	24.52	5.31	28.67
2	.99	69.20	.81	74.11	52	7.96	23.70	5.70	27.82
3	.98	68.27	.79	73.17	53	8.71	22.89	6.15	26.98
4	.95	67.34	.77	72.23	54	9.56	22.08	6.61	26.14
5	.90	66.40	.76	71.28	55	10.47	21.29	7.09	25.31
6	.86	65.46	.73	70.34	56	11.46	20.51	7.57	24.49
7	.80	64.52	.72	69.39	57	12.49	19.74	8.03	23.67
8	.76	63.57	.70	68.44	58	13.59	18.99	8.47	22.86
9	.74	62.62	.69	67.48	59	14.77	18.24	8.94	22.05
10	.73	61.66	.68	66.53	60	16.08	17.51	9.47	21.25
11	.77	60.71	.69	65.58	61	17.54	16.79	10.13	20.44
12	.85	59.75	.72	64.62	62	19.19	16.08	10.96	19.65
13	.99	58.80	.75	63.67	63	21.06	15.38	12.02	18.86
14	1.15	57.86	.80	62.71	64	23.14	14.70	13.25	18.08
15	1.33	56.93	.85	61.76	65	25.42	14.04	14.59	17.32
16	1.51	56.00	.90	60.82	66	27.85	13.39	16.00	16.57
17	1.67	55.09	.95	59.87	67	30.44	12.76	17.43	15.83
18	1.78	54.18	.98	58.93	68	33.19	12.14	18.84	15.10
19	1.86	53.27	1.02	57.98	69	36.17	11.54	20.36	14.38
20	1.90	52.37	1.05	57.04	70	39.51	10.96	22.11	13.67
21	1.91	51.47	1.07	56.10	71	43.30	10.39	24.23	12.97
22	1.89	50.57	1.09	55.16	72	47.65	9.84	26.87	12.28
23	1.86	49.66	1.11	54.22	73	52.64	9.30	30.11	11.60
24	1.82	48.75	1.14	53.28	74	58.19	8.79	33.93	10.95
25	1.77	47.84	1.16	52.34	75	64.19	8.31	38.24	10.32
26	1.73	46.93	1.19	51.40	76	70.53	7.84	42.97	9.71
27	1.71	46.01	1.22	50.46	77	77.12	7.40	48.04	9.12
28	1.70	45.09	1.26	49.52	78	83.90	6.97	53.45	8.55
29	1.71	44.16	1.30	48.59	79	91.05	6.57	59.35	8.01
30	1.73	43.24	1.35	47.65	80	98.84	6.18	65.99	7.48
31	1.78	42.31	1.40	46.71	81	107.48	5.80	73.60	6.98
32	1.83	41.38	1.45	45.78	82	117.25	5.44	82.40	6.49
33	1.91	40.46	1.50	44.84	83	128.26	5.09	92.53	6.03
34	2.00	39.54	1.58	43.91	84	140.25	4.77	103.81	5.59
35	2.11	38.61	1.65	42.98	85	152.95	4.46	116.10	5.18
36	2.24	37.69	1.76	42.05	86	166.09	4.18	129.29	4.80
37	2.40	36.78	1.89	41.12	87	179.55	3.91	143.32	4.43
38	2.58	35.87	2.04	40.20	88	193.27	3.66	158.18	4.09
39	2.79	34.96	2.22	39.28	89	207.29	3.41	173.94	3.77
40	3.02	34.05	2.42	38.36	90	221.77	3.18	190.75	3.45
41	3.29	33.16	2.64	37.46	91	236.98	2.94	208.87	3.15
42	3.56	32.26	2.87	36.55	92	253.45	2.70	228.81	2.85
43	3.87	31.38	3.09	35.66	93	272.11	2.44	251.51	2.55
44	4.19	30.50	3.32	34.77	94	295.90	2.17	279.31	2.24
45	4.55	29.62	3.56	33.88	95	329.96	1.87	317.32	1.91
46	4.92	28.76	3.80	33.00	96	384.55	1.54	375.74	1.56
47	5.32	27.90	4.05	32.12	97	480.20	1.20	474.97	1.21
48	5.74	27.04	4.33	31.25	98	657.98	.84	655.85	.84
49	6.21	26.20	4.63	30.39					

Source: American Council of Life Insurance, *Life Insurance Fact Book* (Washington, D.C., 1990)

TABLE 7.10   Annual Premium Rate* per $1000 of Life Insurance

Age	10-Year Term	Ordinary Life	20-Pay Life	20-Year Endowment
20	5.11	12.05	19.18	33.69
21	5.22	12.33	19.55	33.80
22	5.35	12.59	19.89	33.86
23	5.45	12.80	20.24	33.89
24	5.62	13.05	20.60	33.99
25	5.77	13.36	20.97	34.11
30	6.59	14.97	22.60	34.45
35	7.54	17.44	25.26	35.22
40	9.13	20.34	28.29	36.42
45	10.82	23.95	31.38	38.44
50		29.27	36.53	41.04
55		35.45	42.17	44.95
60		44.95	50.74	52.38

* For men. For women, subtract three years from the actual age. For example, rates for 28-year-old woman are shown for age 25 in the table.

Now find the rates from the table.

(a) The rate per $1000 for a 35-year-old male for a 10-year term plan is $7.54. The total annual premium is thus

$$\text{Premium} = 25 \times \$7.54 = \$188.50.$$

(b) For an ordinary life policy, the rate is $17.44 per $1000, for a total annual premium of

$$\text{Premium} = 25 \times \$17.44 = \$436.$$

This premium is higher than for 10-year term insurance, since ordinary life insurance builds up cash values, unlike term insurance.

(c) For 20-pay life, the rate per $1000 is $25.26 for an annual premium of

$$\text{Premium} = 25 \times \$25.26 = \$631.50.$$

Hopkins would pay $631.50 annually for 20 years, at which time the plan is paid up. He then has insurance protection until retirement, with a retirement income thereafter.

(d) For a 20-year endowment, the rate is $35.22 per $1000 for a total premium of

$$\text{Premium} = 25 \times \$35.22 = \$880.50.$$

Hopkins would pay $880.50 annually for 20 years or until his death, whichever comes first. In either event, 20 years after the first payment was made the company would pay $25,000 to an individual named by Hopkins. ∎

5 The annual life insurance premium is not always paid in one single payment. Many companies give the insured the option of paying the premium semiannually, quarterly, or monthly. For this convenience, the policyholder pays an additional amount, determined by a **premium factor**. Table 7.11 shows typical premium factors.

TABLE 7.11   Premium Factors

Mode of Payment	Premium Factor
Semiannually	0.51
Quarterly	0.26
Monthly	0.0908

EXAMPLE 2
Using a Premium Factor

Suzy Roig has an annual insurance premium of $980. Use Table 7.11 to find the amount of the premium and the total annual cost if she pays at the following periods.
(a) semiannually   **(b)** quarterly   **(c)** monthly

SOLUTION

(a) The semiannual premium factor is 0.51. So, her premium is

$$\$980 \times 0.51 = \$499.80. \quad \text{semiannual premium}$$

The total annual cost is $999.60 ($499.80 × 2).

(b) Since the quarterly premium factor is 0.26, her quarterly premium is

$$\$980 \times 0.26 = \$254.80. \quad \text{quarterly premium}$$

The total annual cost is $1019.20 ($254.80 × 4).

(c) The monthly premium factor is 0.0908, making the monthly premium

$$\$980 \times 0.0980 = \$88.98. \quad \text{monthly premium}$$

The total annual cost is $1067.76 ($88.98 × 12). ■

6 Many companies today offer a **nonsmokers discount** because they feel that nonsmokers are better insurance risks. Normally, not having smoked for 12 months qualifies one as a nonsmoker. Most policies contain a **suicide clause**. This clause states that suicide is not covered, usually for the first two years of the policy.

Additional coverage is often available for small increases in the premium. The **accidental death benefit** coverage will pay an additional death benefit if the insured dies as the result of an accident. An optional benefit known as **waiver of premium** allows the life insurance policy to remain in force without payment of premium when the insured becomes disabled. A **guaranteed conversion privilege** lets the insured convert term insurance to any type of ordinary life or universal life insurance without physical examination. **Companion** or **spouse insurance** allows an insured to add a companion or spouse to a policy, and results in both being insured.

7   Most insurance, such as fire, motor vehicle, and even term life insurance, protects against a specific hazardous event. The insured or the heirs of the insured collect only if the event takes place. Life insurance is different; the insured often receives benefits while living. These benefits build over the life of the policy and are available even if the insured stops paying premiums and cancels the policy. The benefits available upon cancellation are called **nonforfeiture options**. The life insurance company invests the premium dollars remaining after death benefits and operating expenses are paid. The invested money plus interest become the cash values of the insurance policyholders.

Cash value which has accrued to the insured may be received in one of several forms when the policy is canceled.

Cash Settlement Option.   The policyholder may decide on a **cash settlement option** when canceling the insurance policy. Often the insured borrows against the cash value, leaving the policy in force as an alternative to canceling the policy.

Paid-up Insurance.   The cash value of the policy may be used to buy **paid-up insurance** for a smaller policy amount. This paid-up insurance remains in force for the life of the insured.

Extended Term Insurance.   With this option, the insured purchases insurance of the same face value for a specific period of time. The duration of this **extended term insurance** depends on the amount of the cash value of the insured's policy.

Typical nonforfeiture options for a policy issued at age 25 appear in Table 7.12.

TABLE 7.12   Nonforfeiture Options per $1000/Policy Issued at Age 25

	Ordinary Life				20-Year Life				20-Year Endowment			
			Ext. Term				Ext. Term				Ext. Term	
Years in Force	Cash Value	Paid-up Ins.	Years	Days	Cash Value	Paid-up Ins.	Years	Days	Cash Value	Paid-up Ins.	Years	Days
3*	$ 5	$ 16	1	192	$ 29	$ 93	11	18	$ 40	108	15	121
5	28	84	10	190	70	228	20	96	92	236	24	218
10	96	258	18	112	187	554	29	115	339	529	31	185
15	169	415	20	312	339	789	33	215	602	813	37	350
20	283	579	23	315	491	1000	Life	Life	1000	1000	Life	Life
30	491	698	26	210	523	1000	–	–	–	–	–	–

* Normally, there is no cash value accrued in the first two years.

EXAMPLE 3

*Determining
Nonforfeiture
Options*

James Northington purchased a $30,000 ordinary life insurance policy when he was 25 years old and has paid on the policy for 15 years. Determine the following values for his policy: (a) cash value, (b) the amount of paid-up insurance which he could receive, and (c) the time period for which he could have extended term insurance.

SOLUTION

(a) The cash value found in Table 7.12 under ordinary life for 15 years is $169 per $1000 of insurance. The cash value of his policy is

$$\$169 \times 30 \text{ (number of \$1000's)} = \$5070 \text{ cash value.}$$

(b) Again, from Table 7.12, the amount of paid-up insurance which he could receive is $415 per $1000, or

$$\$415 \times 30 = \$12,450 \text{ paid-up insurance.}$$

This coverage would remain in force until his death without paying any additional premium.

(c) The time period for which he could have extended term insurance of the same amount, $30,000, is 20 years and 312 days. ■

There are two types of insurance companies—**mutual companies** and **stock companies**. The policyholders are the owners in a mutual company, with the policies called **participating policies**. The owners (policyholders) share in any profits of the company; the profits are paid in the form of dividends. If the company prospers, the policyholders receive a dividend or refund of premium. In a stock company, the stockholders are the owners of the company, with the policies called **nonparticipating policies**. If the company prospers, the stockholders, not the policyholders, receive a dividend. The distinction is important in determining the **net cost of insurance policies**.

8 To determine the net cost of an insurance policy, use one of these formulas.

Participating insurance policies:

$$\text{Net cost} = \text{Premiums} - (\text{Cash value} + \text{Dividends})$$

Nonparticipating insurance policies:

$$\text{Net cost} = \text{Premiums} - \text{Cash value}$$

EXAMPLE 4

*Find the Net Cost
of a Policy*

Harold Levinson is planning to buy a $25,000 ordinary life policy. His age is 35 and he will be paying premiums for 30 years, until he is 65. If the premium is $17.44 per $1000 of coverage, the cash value will be $12,275 and he expects to receive a total of $1280 in dividends. Find the net cost of the policy.

S O L U T I O N   To determine the net cost of a participating insurance policy, use the following formula.

$$\text{Net cost} = \text{Premiums} - (\text{Cash value} + \text{Dividends})$$

$$\text{Net cost} = \$17.44 \times 25 \text{ (number of thousands)} \times 30 \text{ years}$$

$$- (\$12,275 + \$1280)$$

$$\text{Net cost} = \$13,080 - \$13,555$$

$$\text{Net cost} = -\$475 \quad \blacksquare$$

NOTE The net cost of this insurance policy is $-\$475$ over the 30 years of coverage. The minus sign shows that the insured actually gets back more dollars than he paid to the company.

9 At the death of a life insurance policyholder, the **beneficiary**, the individual chosen by the insured to receive benefits upon death, has several **settlement options** when choosing how the death benefits are to be received. In many cases the beneficiary elects to receive a single lump sum payment of the face value of the policy. In other cases, the beneficiary allows the life insurance company to invest the face value and to pay the beneficiary the proceeds and interest over a period of time in the form of an **annuity**. The more common options available follow.

Fixed Amount Annuity.   A **fixed amount annuity** may be paid each month. The monthly payments continue, including interest, until all the proceeds are used up.

Fixed Period Annuity.   The beneficiary may prefer the payments of a **fixed period annuity**. The insurance company determines the amount that may be paid monthly, for example, for ten years. The payment continues for exactly that period of time, even if the beneficiary dies.

Payments for Life.   **Payments for life** is another option. Based upon the age and sex of the beneficiary, the insurance company calculates an amount to be paid to the beneficiary for as long as he or she lives.

Payments for Life with a Guaranteed Number of Years.   A last option is **payments for life with a guaranteed number of years**. Here, if the beneficiary dies before receiving the benefits for the guaranteed time period, the payments continue to the beneficiaries' heirs until the guarantee is satisfied. The guarantees usually range from 5 to 25 years.

Table 7.13 shows the monthly income per $1000 of insurance coverage under various settlement options.

TABLE 7.13   Monthly Payments per $1000 of Face Value

Options 1 and 2: Fixed Amount or Fixed Number of Years		Options 3 and 4: Income for Life				
		Age when Payments Begin			Life with 10 Years Certain	Life with 15 Years Certain
Years	Amount	Male	Female	Life Annuity		
10	$9.78	50	53	$4.63	$4.49	$4.38
12	8.46	55	58	5.36	5.16	4.78
14	7.63	60	63	5.94	5.73	4.91
16	6.91	65	68	6.93	6.51	5.34
18	6.07	70	73	7.86	6.93	6.28
20	5.78					

EXAMPLE 5

Finding Settlement Options

Anne Kelly is the beneficiary of a $40,000 life insurance policy. Find (a) the monthly payment if she decides to receive payments for 18 years and (b) the number of years payments will continue if she selects a monthly payment of $300.

SOLUTION

(a)   The monthly payment from Table 7.13 for 18 years is $6.07 per $1000 of face value. The monthly payment she receives is

$$\$6.07 \times 40 \text{ (thousands)} = \$242.80.$$

(b)   A monthly payment of $300 is equivalent to

$$\frac{\$300}{40 \text{ (thousands)}} = \$7.50 \text{ per } \$1000 \text{ face value.}$$

Reading the amount column under Options 1 and 2, find $7.63 (closest to $7.50). The $300 payment will continue a little over 14 years.   ∎

EXAMPLE 6

Finding Settlement Options

Hall Ross, 60 years of age, is the beneficiary of a $20,000 life insurance policy. Find (a) his monthly payment from a life annuity and (b) his monthly payment from a life annuity with 15 years certain.

SOLUTION

(a)   Under Options 3 and 4, look up male, age 60. Look across to the life annuity column, to find $5.94. His monthly payment for life is

$$\$5.94 \times 20 \text{ (thousands)} = \$118.80.$$

(b)   The monthly payment from a life annuity with 15 years certain is

$$\$4.91 \times 20 \text{ (thousands)} = \$98.20.$$ ∎

7.3 Exercises

Find the annual premium, the semiannual premium, the quarterly premium, and the monthly premium for each of the following. (Note: Subtract three years for females.) Use Tables 7.10 and 7.11.

	Face Value of Policy	Age of Insured	Sex of Insured	Type of Policy
1.	$40,000	43	F	10-year term
2.	$50,000	58	F	20-year endowment
3.	$75,000	21	M	ordinary
4.	$50,000	45	M	20-pay life
5.	$85,000	30	M	20-year endowment
6.	$10,000	25	M	ordinary
7.	$10,000	55	M	ordinary
8.	$25,000	38	F	20-pay life
9.	$50,000	23	F	10-year term
10.	$65,000	60	M	20-pay life
11.	$35,000	63	F	ordinary
12.	$58,000	33	F	ordinary
13.	$90,000	40	M	10-year term
14.	$100,000	48	F	20-year endowment

15. Explain in your own words the advantages and disadvantages of buying term life insurance. Would you buy term life insurance for yourself? Why or why not? Why? (See Objective 1.)

16. Describe premium factors and how they are used. How often do you prefer paying an insurance premium; annually, semiannually, quarterly, or monthly? Why? (See Objective 4.)

Find the nonforfeiture values of the following policies. The policies were issued at age 25. Use Table 7.12.

	Years in Force	Type of Policy	Face Value	Nonforfeiture Option
17.	5	20-year endowment	$40,000	paid-up insurance
18.	10	20-year endowment	$75,000	cash value
19.	30	20-pay life	$30,000	cash value
20.	15	ordinary life	$35,000	extended term
21.	3	20-year endowment	$10,000	cash value
22.	15	20-pay life	$25,000	paid-up insurance
23.	20	ordinary life	$50,000	extended term
24.	10	ordinary life	$80,000	extended term

Find the monthly payment or period of payment under the following policy settlement options. Use Table 7.13.

	Beneficiary		Face Value	Settlement Option	Monthly Payment	
	Age	Sex			Years	Amount
25.	51	M	$20,000	Fixed amount per month	20	_____
26.	63	F	$35,000	Life-10-years certain	10	_____
27.	65	M	$10,000	Fixed number of years	_____	$60.70
28.	60	M	$40,000	Fixed number of years	_____	$338.40
29.	58	F	$30,000	Life-15-years certain	15	_____
30.	70	F	$50,000	Fixed amount per month	10	_____

Work each of the following word problems.

31. Mary Taver buys a $36,000, 20-year endowment policy at age 33. Her son Thomas is the beneficiary, and will collect the face value of the policy. (a) Find the annual premium. (b) How much will Thomas get if his mother dies after making payments for 9 years?

32. Thompson Vending feels that it should protect itself in the event the firm's sales manager dies suddenly. Therefore, the firm takes out a $40,000 policy on the sales manager's life. The sales manager is a 38-year-old woman, and the company buys a 10-year term policy. Find the semiannual premium.

33. Find the total premium paid over 20 years for a 20-year endowment policy with a face value of $10,000. Assume the policy is taken out by a 40-year-old man.

34. Louis Martinez takes out a 20-pay life policy with a face value of $42,500. He is 45 years old. Find the monthly premium.

35. The annual premium for a whole life policy is $872. Using premium factors, find (a) the semiannual premium, (b) the quarterly premium, and (c) the monthly premium.

36. A 20-year endowment policy has an annual premium of $2012. Use premium factors to find (a) the semiannual premium, (b) the quarterly premium, (c) the monthly premium, and (d) the total annual cost of each of the plans.

37. Catherine Konradt purchased a $20,000 ordinary life policy 20 years ago when she was 25 years old. Use the table of nonforfeiture options (Table 7.12) to determine the (a) cash value, (b) the amount of paid-up insurance which she could receive, and (c) the time period for which she could have paid-up term insurance.

38. Eli Spector purchased a 20-year endowment policy 5 years ago when he was 25 years old. The face value of the policy is $40,000. Find the following values using the nonforfeiture options table (Table 7.12): (a) cash value, (b) the amount of paid-up insurance which he could have, and (c) the time period for which he could have paid-up term insurance.

39. The annual premium, at age 40, on a $15,000, participating 20-year endowment policy, is $36.42 per $1000 of coverage. At the end of 20 years, the cash value will be $15,000 and the insured will receive a total of $830 in dividends over the life of the policy. Find the net cost of the policy. A negative cost or return is possible.

40. At age 25, a $30,000, 20-pay life policy has an annual premium of $20.97 per $1000 of coverage. After 20 years, the cash value of the policy will be $14,730 and the dividends received over the life of the policy will be $1838. Find the net cost of the policy.

41. Ryan Polstra is the beneficiary of a $25,000 life insurance policy. Polstra is 50 years of age and is considering the various settlement options available. Use Table 7.13 to find (a) the monthly payment if he selects payments for 12 years, (b) the number of years he will receive payments of $145 per month, (c) the monthly payment from a life annuity, and (d) the amount he would receive monthly if he chooses a life annuity with 15 years certain.

42. Jenn Luan is the beneficiary of a $30,000 life insurance policy. Luan is 63 years of age and is considering the various settlement options available. Use Table 7.13 to find (a) the monthly payment she would receive if she selects a fixed amount for 10 years, (b) the number of years she can receive $225 per month, (c) the amount she can receive per month as a life annuity, and (d) the monthly amount she could receive as a life annuity with 10 years certain.

43. Chuck Manly is the beneficiary of a $50,000 life insurance policy. Manly is 60 years of age and is considering the various settlement options available. Use Table 7.13 to find (a) the monthly payment he would receive if he selects a fixed amount for 16 years, (b) the number of years he can receive $305 per month, (c) the amount he can receive per month as a life annuity, and (d) the monthly amount he could receive as a life annuity with 10 years certain.

44. Meghan Anderson is the beneficiary of a $70,000 life insurance policy. Anderson is 58 years of age and is considering the various settlement options available. Use Table 7.13 to find (a) the monthly payment she would receive if she selects a fixed amount for 18 years, (b) the number of years she can receive $405 per month, (c) the amount she can receive as a life annuity, and (d) the monthly amount she could receive as a life annuity with 10 years certain.

CHAPTER 7 QUICK REVIEW

TOPIC	APPROACH	EXAMPLE
7.1 Annual premium for fire insurance	Use the building and territorial rating in Table 7.1 to find the premiums per $100 for the building and for the contents. Add the two premiums.	Building value, $80,000, contents, $35,000; territorial rating, 4; building rating, B. Find the annual premium. Building: $800 \times \$.75 = \$600$ Contents: $350 \times \$.77 = \$269.50$ Total premium: $\$600 + \$269.50 = \$869.50$
7.1 Short-term rates and cancellations	Annual premium is multiplied by the short-term rate. Use Table 7.2.	Annual premium is $580. Short-term rate for 9 months is 85%. Premium for 9 months is $\$580 \times .85 = \$493.$ $\$580 - \$493 = \$87$ refund.
7.1 Calculate prorated insurance premium cancellations	Multiply annual premium by a fraction with months of insurance in force as numerator and 12 as denominator.	Annual premium, $1620; policy canceled after 4 months. Find refund. Premium for 4 months is $\$1620 \times \dfrac{4}{12} = \$540.$ $\$1620 - \$540 = \$1080$ refund.
7.1 Coinsurance formula	Part of the risk is taken by the insured. An 80% coinsurance clause is common. Loss paid by insurance company = Amount of loss $\times \dfrac{\text{Policy amount}}{80\% \text{ of market value}}$	Building value, $125,000; policy amount, $75,000; loss, $40,000; 80% coinsurance clause. Find the amount of loss paid by insurance company. $\$40,000 \times \dfrac{\$75,000}{\$100,000} = \$30,000$

TOPIC	APPROACH	EXAMPLE
7.1 Multiple carriers	Several companies insure the same property to limit their risk; each company pays its fractional portion of any claim.	Insured loss is $100,000. Company A has $100,000; Company B, $75,000; Company C, $25,000. Find the amount of loss paid by each company.

Total insurance

$$= \$100,000 + \$75,000 + \$25,000$$
$$= \$200,000$$

$$A : \frac{100,000}{200,000} \times \$100,000 = \$50,000$$

$$B : \frac{175,000}{200,000} \times \$100,000 = \$37,500$$

$$C : \frac{25,000}{200,000} \times \$100,000 = \$12,500$$

TOPIC	APPROACH	EXAMPLE
7.2 Annual auto insurance premium	Most drivers are legally required to purchase automobile insurance. The premium is determined by the types of coverage selected, the type of car, geographic territory, past driving record, and other factors.	Determine the premium: territory, 2; liability, 50/100; property damage, $50,000; comprehensive and collision, 3-year-old car with a symbol of 8; uninsured motorist coverage; driver, age 23 with driver's training.

$108 liability (Table 7.3)
  46 property damage (Table 7.4)
  18 comprehensive (Table 7.5)
  68 collision (Table 7.5)
  24 uninsured motorist (Table 7.6)
$264 × 1.15 youthful operator factor

$$= \$303.60$$

TOPIC	APPROACH	EXAMPLE
7.2 Amount paid by insurance company and by insured	Company pays up to maximum amount of insurance coverage; insured pays balance.	Policy terms: Liability, 15/30; property damage, $10,000; collision, $100 deductible. Accident caused $2850 damage to insured's car; $3850 to other car; injury liability of $20,000 and $25,000, respectively. Company pays $2750 ($2850 − $100) to repair insured's car; company pays $3850 to repair other car ($10,000 limit); company pays $30,000 for two injured people ($15,000 each); insured pays $15,000 ($45,000 − $30,000), amount over limit.

TOPIC	APPROACH	EXAMPLE

7.3 Annual life insurance premium	There are several types of life policies. Use Table 7.10 and multiply by the number of $1000's of coverage. Subtract three years from the age of females.
	
	Premium = Number of thousands × Rate per $1000
		Find the premiums on $50,000 policy for a 30-year-old male.
		
		(a) 10-Year Term
		   $50 \times \$6.59 = \$329.50$
		
		(b) Ordinary Life
		   $50 \times \$14.97 = \$748.50$
		
		(c) 20-Pay Life
		   $50 \times \$22.60 = \$1130$
		
		(d) 20-Year Endowment
		   $50 \times \$34.45 = \$1722.50$

7.3 Premium factors	If not paid annually, life insurance premiums may be paid semiannually, quarterly, or monthly. The annual premium is multiplied by the premium factor to determine the premium amount. Use Table 7.11.	The annual life insurance premium is $740. Use Table 7.11 to find the semiannual, quarterly, and monthly premium.
		
		(a) Semiannual
		   $\$740 \times 0.51 = \$377.40$
		
		(b) Quarterly
		   $\$740 \times 0.26 = \$192.40$
		
		(c) Monthly
		   $\$740 \times 0.0908 = \$67.19$

7.3 Nonforfeiture options	Upon cancellation of a policy the insured may receive a cash settlement, paid-up insurance, or extended term insurance as a nonforfeiture option. Use Table 7.12.	Insurance is a $40,000, 20-pay life policy; in force for 10 years; issued at age 25. **(a)** Cash value = $\$187 \times 40 = \$7480$ **(b)** Paid-up insurance = $\$554 \times 40$ $= \$22,160$ **(c)** Extended term insurance period is 29 years, 115 days.

TOPIC	APPROACH	EXAMPLE
7.3 Settlement options	Upon the death of the insured, the beneficiary often has choices as to how the money may be received. These range from all cash to various types of payment arrangements. Use Table 7.13.	$30,000 policy; female beneficiary, age 58. Find monthly payments for: **(a)** 16 years; $\quad$ 30 × $6.91 = $207.30 **(b)** life annuity; $\quad$ 30 × $5.36 = $160.80 **(c)** life with 15 years certain. $\quad$ 30 × $4.78 = $143.40 **(d)** For how many years would $200 a month be paid? $\quad \dfrac{\$200}{30} = \$6.67$ per $1000 $6.67 is closest to $6.91; a little less than 16 years.

SUMMARY EXERCISE

Safetyseat Manufacturing produces children's car seats and other automotive and home children's safety products. Planning ahead, the company set aside $20,500 to pay fire insurance premiums on the company property and a semiannual life insurance premium for the company president which were both due in the same month. Find each of the following.

(a)   The building occupied by the company is a class B building worth $865,000. The contents are worth $1,602,000 and the territorial rating is 4. Find the annual fire insurance premium.

(b)   The president of Safetyseat Manufacturing is a 33-year-old woman and the company is buying a $210,000, 10-year term life insurance policy on the president's life. Find the semiannual premium.

(c)   Find the total amount needed to pay the fire insurance premium and the semiannual life insurance premium.

(d)   How much more than the amount needed had the company set aside to pay these expenses?

CHAPTER 7 REVIEW EXERCISES

Find the total annual premium for fire insurance for each of the following. Use Table 7.1.
[7.1]

	Territorial Rating	Building Classification	Building Value	Contents Value
1.	4	B	$148,000	$115,000
2.	2	C	$376,000	$185,000
3.	3	A	$80,000	$30,000
4.	1	B	$193,000	$68,000

Find the amount of refund to the insured using the Short-Term Rate Schedule (Table 7.2).
[7.1]

	Annual Premium	Months in Force
5.	$780	8
6.	$492	2
7.	$1486	9
8.	$2878	5

Find (a) the amount of premium retained by the company and (b) the amount of refund to the insured using proration. [7.1]

	Annual Premium	Months in Force
9.	$1020	3
10.	$2136	8
11.	$864	11
12.	$2784	2

Find the amount of each of the following losses that will be paid by the insurance company. Assume that each policy includes an 80% coinsurance clause. [7.1]

	Value of Building	Face Value of Policy	Amount of Loss
13.	$228,000	$160,000	$22,500
14.	$92,500	$55,000	$32,600
15.	$186,700	$120,000	$3,400
16.	$325,000	$220,000	$42,200

Find the annual motor vehicle insurance premium for the following people. [7.2]

	Name	Territory	Age	Driver Training	Liability	Property Damage	Comprehensive Collision Age Group	Symbol	Uninsured Motorist
17.	Fuller	2	36	–	100/300	$100,000	3	8	no
18.	Barchus	3	19	yes	50/100	$50,000	6	6	yes
19.	Wynant	4	24	no	25/50	$25,000	2	7	yes
20.	Wilson	1	52	–	250/500	$50,000	1	8	yes

Find the annual premium for each of the following life insurance policies. [7.3]

21. Deliah Salas: 20-pay life; $50,000 face value; age 48

22. Ralph Todd: 10-year term; $80,000 face value; age 30

23. Bill Edgar: ordinary life; $30,000 face value; age 21

24. Ginger Cordoba: 20-year endowment; $20,000 face value; age 26

Solve the following word problems.

25. Foxworthy Forest Products had a fire loss of $21,000. They had insurance coverage as follows: Company A, $30,000; Company B, $20,000; Company C, $10,000. Find the amount paid by each of the multiple carriers assuming that the coinsurance clause had been met. Round to the nearest dollar. [7.1]

26. The headquarters building of Western States Life is valued at $820,000, and the fire insurance policies contain an 80% coinsurance clause. The policies include $350,000 with Company 1 and $200,000 with Company 2. The Western building suffered a $150,000 fire loss. Find (a) the amount that Western would receive after the loss and (b) the amount of the loss paid by each insurance company. Round to the nearest dollar. [7.1]

27. A driver who has a bodily injury policy with limits of 25/50 injures a bicycle rider. The judge awards damages of $34,000 to the injured cyclist. (a) How much will the company pay and (b) how much will the driver pay? [7.2]

28. Three people are injured in an automobile accident and receive $15,000 each in damages. The driver has bodily injury insurance of 50/100. (a) How much will the company pay to each person and (b) how much must the driver pay? [7.2]

29. Some scaffolding falls off a truck and into the path of a car, resulting in serious damage and injury. The car had damage of $16,800, while the driver and passenger of the car were given court awards of $25,000 and $35,000, respectively. The driver of the truck had 15/30 liability insurance limits and $10,000 property damage limits. Find (a) the total amount paid by the insurance company for both property damage and liability and (b) the total amount beyond the insurance limits for which the driver was liable. [7.2]

30. The annual premium for a whole life policy is $1084. Use premium factors to find (a) the semiannual premium, (b) the quarterly premium, (c) the monthly premium, and (d) the total annual cost for each of the plans. [7.3]

31. Find the total premium paid over 20 years for a 20-year endowment policy with a face value of $30,000. Assume the policy is taken out by a 43-year-old woman. [7.3]

32. Glenn Lewis purchased a $40,000 ordinary life policy 20 years ago when he was 25 years old. Use Table 7.12 to determine (a) the cash value, (b) the amount of paid-up insurance he could receive, and (c) the time period for which he could have paid-up term insurance. [7.3]

33. The annual premium, at age 25, on a $60,000, 20-pay life policy is $20.97 per $1000 of coverage. After 20 years, the cash value of the policy will be $29,460, and the dividends received over the life of the policy will be $3676. Find the net cost of the policy. [7.3]

34. Ann-Marie Buesing is the beneficiary of a $40,000 life insurance policy. Buesing is 53 years of age and is considering the various settlement options available. Use Table 7.13 to find (a) the monthly payment she would receive if she selects a fixed payment for 20 years, (b) the number of years she can receive $245 per month, (c) the amount she can receive as a life annuity, and (d) the monthly amount she could receive as a life annuity with 10 years certain. [7.3]

8

Mathematics of Buying

Retail businesses make a profit by purchasing items and then selling them for more than they cost. There are several steps in this process: **manufacturers** buy raw materials and component parts and assemble them into products which can be sold to other manufacturers or wholesalers. The **wholesaler**, often called the "middleman," buys from manufacturers or other wholesalers and sells to the retailer. **Retailers** sell directly to the ultimate user, the **consumer**.

Documents called **invoices** help businesses keep track of sales, while various types of **discounts** help them buy products at lower costs to increase profits. This chapter looks at the mathematics needed for working with invoices and discounts—the **mathematics of buying**.

8.1 Invoices and Trade Discounts

OBJECTIVES

1 Complete an invoice.

2 Understand common shipping terms.

3 Identify invoice abbreviations.

4 Calculate net cost and trade discounts.

5 Differentiate between single and series discounts.

6 Calculate series discounts.

7 Use complements to calculate series discounts.

8 Use a table to find the net cost equivalent of series discounts.

An **invoice** is a printed record of a purchase and sale. For the seller it is a **sales invoice** and records a sale; for the buyer it is a **purchase invoice** and records a purchase. The invoice identifies the seller and the buyer, includes a description of the items purchased, the quantity purchased, the unit price of each item, the **extension**

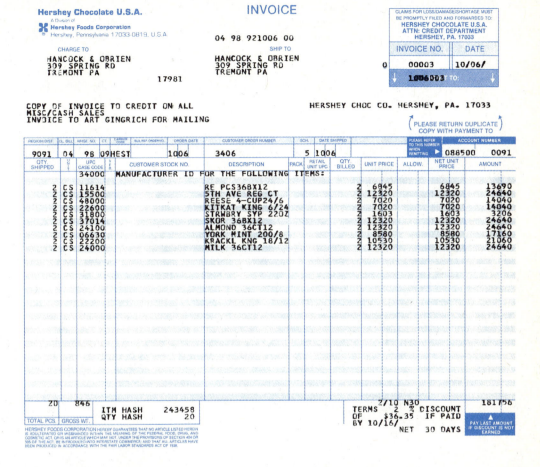

Hershey Chocolate U.S.A.
A Division of
Hershey Foods Corporation
Hershey, Pennsylvania 17033-0819, U.S.A

INVOICE

04 98 921006 00

CLAIMS FOR LOSS/DAMAGE/SHORTAGE MUST
BE PROMPTLY FILED AND FORWARDED TO:
HERSHEY CHOCOLATE U.S.A.
ATTN: CREDIT DEPARTMENT
HERSHEY, PA. 17033

CHARGE TO
HANCOCK & OBRIEN
309 SPRING RD
TREMONT PA
17981

SHIP TO
HANCOCK & OBRIEN
309 SPRING RD
TREMONT PA

INVOICE NO. | DATE
00003 | 10/06/

COPY OF INVOICE TO CREDIT ON ALL
MISC/CASH SALES
INVOICE TO ART GINGRICH FOR MAILING

HERSHEY CHOC CO. HERSHEY, PA. 17033

PLEASE RETURN DUPLICATE
COPY WITH PAYMENT TO

REGION/DIST.	CL. BILL	WHSE. NO.	CT.	CARRIER CODE	BILL/REF.ORDER NO.	ORDER DATE	CUSTOMER ORDER NUMBER	SCH.	DATE SHIPPED		PLEASE REFER TO THIS NUMBER WHEN REMITTING	ACCOUNT NUMBER
9091	04	98	09	HEST		1006	3406	5	1006			088500 0091

QTY. SHIPPED	U/I	UPC CASE CODE	K/R	CUSTOMER STOCK NO.	DESCRIPTION	PACK	RETAIL UNIT UPC	QTY. BILLED	UNIT PRICE	ALLOW.	NET UNIT PRICE	AMOUNT
		34000		MANUFACTURER ID FOR THE FOLLOWING ITEMS:								
2	CS	11614			RE PCS36BX12			2	6845		6845	13690
2	CS	15500			5TH AVE REG CT			2	12320		12320	24640
2	CS	48000			REESE 4-CUP24/6			2	7020		7020	14040
2	CS	22600			KITKAT KING 6/24			2	7020		7020	14040
2	CS	31800			STRWBRY SYP 22OZ			2	1603		1603	3206
2	CS	37014			SKOR 36BX12			2	12320		12320	24640
2	CS	24100			ALMOND 36CT12			2	12320		12320	24640
2	CS	06630			YORK MINT 200/8			2	8580		8580	17160
2	CS	22200			KRACKL KNG 18/12			2	10530		10530	21060
2	CS	24000			MILK 36CT12			2	12320		12320	24640
20	846											181756

TOTAL PCS. | GROSS WT.

ITM HASH 243458
QTY HASH 20

TERMS 2 % DISCOUNT
OF $36.35 IF PAID
BY 10/16/ NET 30 DAYS

2/10 N30

PAY LAST AMOUNT IF DISCOUNT IS NOT EARNED

HERSHEY FOODS CORPORATION HEREBY GUARANTEES THAT NO ARTICLE LISTED HEREIN IS ADULTERATED OR MISBRANDED WITHIN THE MEANING OF THE FEDERAL FOOD, DRUG, AND COSMETIC ACT, OR IS AN ARTICLE WHICH MAY NOT, UNDER THE PROVISIONS OF SECTION 404 OR 505 OF THE ACT, BE INTRODUCED INTO INTERSTATE COMMERCE; AND THAT ALL ARTICLES HAVE BEEN PRODUCED IN ACCORDANCE WITH THE FAIR LABOR STANDARDS ACT OF 1938.

Reprinted by permission of Hershey Chocolate U.S.A., a division of Hershey Foods Corporation.

FIGURE 8.1

total (the number of items purchased times the price per unit), any discounts, the shipping and insurance charges, and the **invoice total** (the sum of all the extension totals).

1 The document in Figure 8.1 is a sales invoice for the Hershey Chocolate Company and a purchase invoice for Hancock and O'Brien. The abbreviation used in the "Unit" column is "CS" for case. Notice that the first item in the "Description" column of the Hershey Chocolate Company invoice is "RE PCS36BX12." The number in the "Quantity Shipped" column, 2, was multiplied by the amount in the "Unit Price" column, 68.45, giving the extension total in the "Amount" column, 136.90. This is done with each item on the invoice until the last item, "MILK 36CT12," with an extension total of 246.40 (2×123.20). The **total invoice amount**, 1817.56, is the sum of all the extension totals.

Trade and cash discounts, discussed later in this section, are never applied to shipping and insurance charges. For this reason shipping and insurance charges are often not included in the invoice total, and the purchaser must add them to the invoice total to find the total amount due.

2 A common shipping term appearing on invoices is **FOB (free on board),** followed by the words **shipping point** or **destination**. The term "FOB—shipping point" means that the *buyer* pays for shipping and that ownership of the merchandise passes to the purchaser when the merchandise is given to the shipper. The term "FOB—destination" means that the *seller* pays the shipping charges and retains ownership until the goods reach the destination. This distinction is important in the event that the merchandise is lost or damaged during shipment.

The shipping term **COD** means **cash on delivery**. Here the shipper makes delivery to the purchaser on the receipt of enough cash to pay for the goods. A shipping term used when goods are moved by ship is "**FAS**," which means **free alongside ship**. Here the goods are delivered to the dock with all freight charges to that point paid by the shipper.

3 A number of abbreviations are used on invoices to identify measurements, quantities of merchandise, shipping terms, and additional discounts. Those most commonly used are shown in Table 8.1. (Some of these measurements are from the metric system. These measurements often appear on invoices for imported goods.)

TABLE 8.1   Common Invoice Abbreviations

ea.	= each	drm.	= drum
doz.	= dozen	cs.	= case
gro.	= gross (144 items)	bx.	= box
gr. gro.	= great gross (12 gross)	sk.	= sack
qt.	= quart	pr.	= pair
gal.	= gallon (4 quarts)	C	= Roman numeral for 100
bbl.	= barrel ($31\frac{1}{2}$ gallons)	M	= Roman numeral for 1000
ml	= milliliter	cwt.	= per hundred weight
cl	= centiliter	cpm.	= cost per thousand
L	= liter	@	= at
in.	= inch	lb.	= pound
ft.	= foot	oz.	= ounce
yd.	= yard	g	= gram
mm	= millimeter	kg	= kilogram
cm	= centimeter	FOB	= free on board
m	= meter	ROG	= receipt of goods
km	= kilometer	EOM	= end of month
ct.	= crate	ex. or x	= extra dating
cart. or ctn.	= carton	COD	= cash on delivery
		FAS	= free alongside ship

4 **Trade discounts** are offered to businesses or individuals who buy an item that is to be sold or used to produce an item that will then be sold. Normally, the seller prices an item at its **list price** (the suggested price at which the item is to be sold to the public). Then the seller gives a trade discount that is subtracted from the list price to get the **net cost** (the amount to be paid by the buyer). Find the net cost by using the following formula.

$$\text{Net cost} = \text{List price} - \text{Trade discount} \qquad \text{or} \qquad \begin{array}{r} \text{List price} \\ -\text{Trade discount} \\ \hline \text{Net cost} \end{array}$$

EXAMPLE 1
Calculating a Single
Trade Discount

The list price of a solar-powered calculator is $12.80, with a trade discount of 25%. Find the net cost.

SOLUTION   First find the amount of the trade discount by taking 25% of $12.80.

$$R \quad \times \quad B \qquad\qquad = \quad P$$

$$25\% \times \$12.80 = 0.25 \times \$12.80 = \$3.20$$

Find the net cost by subtracting $3.20 from the list price of $12.80.

$$\$12.80 \text{ (list price)} - \$3.20 \text{ (trade discount)} = \$9.60 \text{ (net cost)}$$

or

$$\begin{array}{rl} \$12.80 & \text{list price} \\ -\ 3.20 & \text{trade discount} \\ \hline \$\ 9.60 & \text{net cost} \end{array}$$

The net cost of the calculator is $9.60 ∎

5 In Example 1 a **single discount** of 25% was offered. Another type of discount combines two or more discounts into a **series** or **chain discount**. A series discount is written as 20/10, which means that a 20% discount is subtracted from the list price, and *from this difference* another 10% discount is subtracted.

   Discounts are sometimes added to or subtracted from a series discount. For example, another discount of 5% could be added to the series discount 20/10, for a new series discount of 20/10/5.

There are many reasons that might cause discounts to change.

Price changes may cause trade discounts to be raised or lowered.

As the *quantity purchased* increases, the discount offered may increase.

The buyer's position in *marketing channels* may determine the amount of discount offered (a wholesaler would receive a larger discount than the succeeding retailer).

Geographic location may influence the trade discount. An additional discount may be offered to increase sales in one particular area.

Seasonal fluctuations in sales may influence the trade discounts offered.

Competition from other companies may cause raising or lowering of trade discounts.

6 Three methods can be used to calculate a series discount and the net cost. The first of these is by *using discounts separately*.

EXAMPLE 2
Calculating Series Trade Discounts

Suppose a series discount of 20/10 is offered on a circular saw with a list price of $150. Find the net cost after the series discount.

SOLUTION First multiply the decimal equivalent of 20% (0.2) by $150. Then subtract the product ($30) from $150, getting $120. Then multiply the decimal equivalent of the second discount, 10% (0.1), by $120. Subtract the product ($12) from $120, getting $108, the net cost. Write this calculation as

$$
\begin{array}{ll}
\$150 & \text{list price} \qquad \text{Discount: 20/10} \\
-\ \ 30 & (0.2 \times \$150) \\
\hline
\$120 & \\
-\ \ 12 & (0.1 \times \$120) \\
\hline
\$108 & \text{net cost}
\end{array}
$$

After the first discount, each discount is applied to the balance remaining after the preceding discount or discounts have been subtracted. This method demonstrates how trade discounts are applied but is usually *not* the preferred method for finding the invoice amount, because it involves too many steps.

NOTE **Single discounts in a series are never added together**; for example, a series discount of 20/10 is *not the same* as a discount of 30%.

Calculator Approach to Example 2

Using the chain calculation ability of the calculator and the $\boxed{\%}$ is an often-preferred technique for this type of a problem. The list price is entered followed by the $\boxed{-}$ key, the discount is then entered followed by the $\boxed{\%}$. This is repeated for the second discount in the series.

$$150 \ \boxed{-}\ 20 \ \boxed{\%}\ \boxed{-}\ 10 \ \boxed{\%}\ 108$$

If this approach doesn't work, try the following key sequence.

$$150 \ \boxed{\times}\ 20 \ \boxed{\%}\ \boxed{-}\ \boxed{\times}\ 10 \ \boxed{\%}\ \boxed{-}\ 108$$

Remember that calculator operation may vary from one brand to another. Always refer to the operating manual.

---

7 **Using complements.** To use this method of finding the net cost, first find the **complement** (with respect to 1, or 100%) of each single discount. The complement is the number which must be added to a given discount to get 1 or 100%. The complement of 20% is 80% since 20% + 80% = 100%. The complement of 40% is 60%.

Discounts with fractions are occasionally used. The complement (with respect to 1) of $22\frac{1}{2}\%$ is $77\frac{1}{2}\%$ or 0.775 ($22\frac{1}{2}\% = 22.5\%$). When a fractional discount such as $16\frac{2}{3}\%$ is used, the complement (with respect to 1) of $0.166\overline{6}$ is not exact, but a repeating decimal, and if used can cause errors. In this case the fraction $\frac{5}{6}$ is used

TABLE 8.2   Typical Complements with Respect to 1

Discount	Decimal Equivalent	Complement with Respect to 1
10%	0.1	0.9
$12\frac{1}{2}$%	0.125	0.875
15%	0.15	0.85
25%	0.25	0.75
30%	0.3	0.7
$33\frac{1}{3}$%	$0.33\overline{3}\ \left(\frac{1}{3}\right)$	$0.66\overline{6}\ \left(\frac{2}{3}\right)$
35%	0.35	0.65
50%	0.5	0.5

as the complement. Since $16\frac{2}{3}$% equals $\frac{1}{6}$, the complement (with respect to 1) is $\frac{5}{6}$. Use of the fraction equivalents of these repeating decimals will result in fewer errors. Other typical complements (with respect to 1) are shown in Table 8.2.

The complement of the discount is the portion actually paid. For example,

10% discount means 90% paid;

25% discount means 75% paid;

$33\dfrac{1}{3}$% discount means $66\dfrac{2}{3}$% $\left(\dfrac{2}{3}\right)$ paid;

50% discount means 50% paid.

Multiply the complements of the single discounts together to get the **net cost equivalent** or **percent paid**. Then multiply the net cost equivalent (percent paid) by the list price to obtain the net cost, as shown in the formula.

$$\text{Percent paid} \times \text{List price} = \text{Net cost}$$
$$R \qquad \times \qquad B \qquad = \qquad P$$

EXAMPLE 3
Using Complements to Solve Series Discounts

A series discount of 20/10 is offered on a circular saw with a list price of $150. Find the net cost after the series discount.

SOLUTION   For a series discount of 20/10, the complements (with respect to 1) of 20% and 10% are 0.8 and 0.9. Multiplying the complements together gives $0.8 \times 0.9 = 0.72$, the net cost equivalent. (In other words, a series discount of 20/10 is the same as paying 72% of the list price.) To find the net cost, multiply 0.72 by the list price of $150, which gives $108 as the net cost. Write this calculation as follows.

20/10 ← series discount

0.8 × 0.9 = 0.72   net cost equivalent
                    (percent paid)

complements with
respect to 1

Use the formula Percent paid × List price = Net cost.

$$R \times B = P$$

$$0.72 \times \$150 = \$108 \quad \text{net cost}$$

Find the amount of the discount by subtracting the net cost from the list price.

$150 (list price) − $108 (net cost) = $42 (amount of discount) ∎

EXAMPLE 4
*Using Complements
to Solve Series
Discounts*

The list price of some building materials is $250. Find the net cost if a series discount of 20/10/10 is offered.

SOLUTION   Start by finding the complements with respect to 1 of each discount.

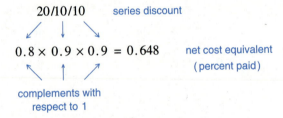

20/10/10   series discount

0.8 × 0.9 × 0.9 = 0.648   net cost equivalent
                           (percent paid)

complements with
respect to 1

Use the formula Percent paid × List price = Net cost.

$$R \times B = P$$

$$0.648 \times \$250 = \$162 \quad \text{net cost} \quad ∎$$

CAUTION Never round the net cost equivalent. If a repeating decimal results, use the fraction equivalent. In Example 4, if the net cost equivalent had been rounded to 0.65, the resulting net cost would have been $162.50 (.65 × $250). This error of $.50 demonstrates the importance of not rounding the net cost equivalent.

Calculator Approach to Example 4

After the complements with respect to 1 are determined, they may be used in a chain calculation with the list price to determine the net cost.

$$.8 \boxed{\times} .9 \boxed{\times} .9 \boxed{=} \boxed{\times} 250 \boxed{=} 162$$

If the net cost equivalent was not needed in the problem, the following alternate approach would work quite well, also.

$$250 \boxed{-} 20 \boxed{\%} \boxed{-} 10 \boxed{\%} \boxed{-} 10 \boxed{\%} 162$$

8 **Using a Table.** People working with series discounts daily often use a *table of net cost equivalents* for various series discounts. For example, to use Table 8.3 for a series discount of 20/10/10, find the number located to the right of 10/10 and below 20%. The number is 0.648, the net cost equivalent for a discount of 20/10/10. Multiply this number by the list price to get the net cost.

The order of the discounts in the series makes no difference. A 10/20 series is the same as a 20/10 series, and a 15/10/20 is identical to a 20/15/10. This is true because changing the order in which numbers are multiplied does not change the answer. The net cost equivalent (percent paid) found using Table 8.3 and the list price are multiplied to find the net cost.

EXAMPLE 5

Using a Table of Net Cost Equivalents

Use Table 8.3 to find the net cost equivalent for the following series discounts.

(a) 10/20   **(b)** 10/10/40   **(c)** 25/20/10

SOLUTION

(a) 0.72   **(b)** 0.486   **(c)** 0.54 ■

TABLE 8.3   **Net Cost Equivalents of Series Discounts**

	5%	10%	15%	20%	25%	30%	35%	40%
5	0.9025	0.855	0.8075	0.76	0.7125	0.665	0.6175	0.57
10	0.855	0.81	0.765	0.72	0.675	0.63	0.585	0.54
10/5	0.81225	0.7695	0.72675	0.684	0.64125	0.5985	0.55575	0.513
10/10	0.7695	0.729	0.6885	0.648	0.6075	0.567	0.5265	0.486
15	0.8075	0.765	0.7225	0.68	0.6375	0.595	0.5525	0.51
15/10	0.72675	0.6885	0.65025	0.612	0.57375	0.5355	0.49725	0.459
20	0.76	0.72	0.68	0.64	0.6	0.56	0.52	0.48
20/15	0.646	0.612	0.578	0.544	0.51	0.476	0.422	0.408
25	0.7125	0.675	0.6375	0.6	0.5625	0.525	0.4875	0.45
25/20	0.57	0.54	0.51	0.48	0.45	0.42	0.39	0.36
25/25	0.534375	0.50625	0.478125	0.45	0.421875	0.39375	0.365625	0.3375
30	0.665	0.63	0.595	0.56	0.525	0.49	0.455	0.42
40	0.57	0.54	0.51	0.48	0.45	0.42	0.39	0.36

NOTE Do not round any of the cost equivalents. Doing so will cause an error in the net cost.

8.1 Exercises

What do each of the following abbreviations stand for?

1. @
2. mm
3. sk.
4. pr.
5. gr. gro.
6. kg
7. cs.
8. gro.
9. drm.
10. doz.
11. cpm.
12. bbl.
13. ea.
14. cwt.
15. cart.
16. ct.

17. Compute each of the following extension totals, find the invoice total, and the total amount due.

J&K'S MUSTANG PARTS
New and Used

Sold to: Dave's Auto Body & Paint
4443-B Auburn Blvd.
Sacramento, CA

Date: July 17
Order No.:   100603
Shipped by: Emery
Terms: Net

Quantity	Order No. / Description	Unit Price	Extension Total
10	filler tube gaskets	$1.25 ea.	_____
8 pr.	taillight lens gaskets	$3.75 pr.	_____
12 pr.	taillight bezels to body	$1.80 pr.	_____
3 gr.	door panel fasteners	$7.20 gr.	_____
20	bumper bolt kits	$6.25 ea.	_____

		Invoice Total	_____
		Shipping and Insurance	$9.90
		Total Amount Due	_____

18. Compute each of the following extension totals, find the invoice total, and the total amount due.

	CALIFORNIA TRUCK SUPPLIERS		
Sold to: Spokane Trucking 66 East Lane Spokane, Washington		Date: February 19 Order No.: 796152 Shipped by: UPS Terms: Net	
Quantity	Order No./ Description	Unit Price	Extension Total
6 doz.	driver log books	$37.80 doz.	_____
3 gro.	imprinted pencils	$12.60 gro.	_____
9 doz.	sets of dispatch forms	$14.04 doz.	_____
8	water pumps	$106.12 ea.	_____
53 pr.	mud guards	$68.12 pr.	_____
		Invoice Total	_____
		Shipping and Insurance	$ 37.45
		Total Amount Due	_____

19. Explain in your own words the difference between "FOB shipping point" and "FOB destination." (See Objective 2.)

20. Name six items that appear on an invoice. Try to do this without looking at an invoice. (See Objective 1.)

Using complements (with respect to 1) of the single discounts, find the net cost equivalent for each of the following discounts. Use Table 8.3 for the first four problems.

21.	$30/20$	**22.**	$15/25$	**23.**	$15/5$
24.	$10/20$	**25.**	$10/16\frac{2}{3}$	**26.**	$40/20/10$
27.	$30/42\frac{1}{2}$	**28.**	$20/20/20$	**29.**	$40/30/20$
30.	$10/10/10/33\frac{1}{3}$	**31.**	$5/10/20$	**32.**	$25/10/20/10$

Find the net cost for each of the following. Round to the nearest cent.

33. $680 less 25/10

34. $80 less 20/10

35. $7.20 less $33\frac{1}{3}$/10

36. $630 less 15/25/10

37. $950 less 30/20

38. $8.80 less 40/10/20

39. $450 less 10/5

40. $15.70 less 5/10/20

41. $25 less 30/$32\frac{1}{2}$

42. $750 less 10/10/10

43. $1500 less 20/$16\frac{2}{3}$

44. $1630 less 10/5/10

45. Explain the difference between a single trade discount and a series or chain trade discount. (See Objectives 4 and 5.)

46. Identify and explain four reasons that might cause series trade discounts to change. (See Objective 5.)

47. Explain in your own words what a complement (with respect to 1 or 100%) is. Give an example. (See Objective 7.)

48. Using complements explain how to find the net cost equivalent of a 25/20 series discount. (See Objective 7.)

Solve each of the following problems in trade discount. Round to the nearest cent.

49. The list price of an aluminum tripod is $65. It is available at either a 15/10/10 discount or a 15/20 discount. (a) Which discount gives the lower price? (b) Find the difference.

50. Chemco Products offers a series discount of 10/10/30 on all bulk purchases. If a 15,000 gallon tank (bulk) of fertilizer is list priced at $57,000, what is the net cost after trade discounts?

51. How much will Teresa Depalo, a retail buyer, pay for three dozen rugby shirts if the list price is $216 per dozen and a series discount of 20/20/15 is offered?

52. Laura Taber, an automotive mechanics student, is offered mechanic's net prices on all purchases at Columbia Auto Supply. If mechanic's net prices mean a 20/10 discount, how much will Taber spend on an alternator list priced at $47?

53. Office-Mart offers a discount of 25/15 to its regular customers. Brett Sullivan, a new man in the billing department, understood the 25/15 terms to mean 40% and computed this trade discount on a list price of $4380. How much difference did this error make in the amount of the invoice?

54. Cynthia Biron has a choice of two suppliers of fiber optics for her business. Syntech Labs offers a 20/10/25 discount on a list price of $5.70 per unit. Video Optics offers a 30/20 series discount on a list price of $5.40 per unit. (a) Which supplier gives her the lower price? (b) How much does she save if she buys 12,500 units from the lower-price supplier?

55. Mary Ellen Heise purchased two dozen National Olympics souvenirs for her employees. The list price of each item was $32, and she received a trade discount of 30/10/5. Find her total net cost for the souvenirs.

56. Oak Furniture Sales purchased an oak serpentine dresser list priced at $550 and two bedside tables list priced at $135 each. If they received a trade discount of 25/$27\frac{1}{2}$, find the net cost of the dresser and two bedside tables.

57. The list price of a neon "OPEN" sign is $125. A retailer has a choice of two suppliers—one offering a 10/10/10 and the other offering a 15/10/5 trade discount. (a) Which discount will give the lower net cost? (b) Find the net cost of one dozen signs at the lower price.

58. The AAA Foto and Copy Shop purchases stickers at a list price of $135 per 1000. If they receive a trade discount of $40/33\frac{1}{3}$, find the net cost of 3500 stickers.

59. One brand of file folders is list priced at $6.60 per dozen. A wholesale stationer offers a trade discount of 10/5/15 on the folders. Find the net cost of $5\frac{1}{2}$ dozen folders.

60. The list price of brass deadbolts is $9.95. A retailer has a choice of two suppliers, one offering a discount of 10/25/15 and the other offering a discount of 20/15/10. If the retailer purchases 4 dozen deadbolts, find (a) the total cost of the less expensive supplier and (b) the amount saved by selecting the lower price.

8.2 Single Discount Equivalents

OBJECTIVES

1 Express a series discount as an equivalent single discount.

2 Find net cost by multiplying list price by the complements of single discounts.

3 Find the list price if given the series discount and the net cost.

4 Determine a single trade discount rate.

5 Find the trade discount that must be added to match a competitor's price.

A series or chain discount must often be expressed as a single discount. Find a **single discount equivalent to a series discount** by multiplying the complements (with respect to 1 or 100%) of the individual discounts. As in the previous section, the result is the net cost equivalent. Then, subtract the net cost equivalent from 1.

1 The result is the single discount that is equivalent to the series discount. The single discount is expressed as a percent.

> Single discount equivalent = 1 − Net cost equivalent

EXAMPLE 1
Finding a Single Discount Equivalent

What is the single discount equivalent of a 20/10 series discount?

SOLUTION   Find the net cost equivalent (percent paid).

20/10

$0.8 \times 0.9 = 0.72$ net cost equivalent

Subtract the net cost equivalent from 1.

$$1.00 \text{ (base) } - 0.72 \text{ (remains) } = 0.28 \text{ or } 28\% \text{ was discounted.}$$

The single discount equivalent of a 20/10 series discount is 28%. ∎

This method may also be used with the table of Net Cost Equivalents of Series Discounts (Table 8.3). For example, the table shows 0.72 as the net cost equivalent for the series discount 20/10. The single discount is therefore 28% (1.00 − 0.72).

2 The net cost can also be found by multiplying the list price by the complements of each of the single discounts in a series, as shown in Example 2.

EXAMPLE 2
Finding the Net Cost Using Complements

The list price of a dishwasher is $450. Find the net price if trade discounts of $20/15/27\frac{1}{2}$ are offered.

SOLUTION

Net Cost = List price × Complements of individual discounts

$$\text{Net cost } = \$450 \times 0.8 \times 0.85 \times 0.725$$

$$20 / 15 / 27\frac{1}{2}$$

$$\text{Net cost } = \$221.85$$ ∎

Calculator Approach to Example 2

The list price may be multiplied in a series calculation without first determining the net cost equivalent.

450 × .8 × .85 × .725 = 221.85

The % key may be used to get the answer with this approach.

450 − 20 % − 15 % − 27.5 % 221.85

---

3 Sometimes the net cost after trade discounts is known along with the series discount, and the list price must be found.

EXAMPLE 3
Solving for List Price

Find the list price if the net cost of an item is $544 after trade discounts of 20/20.

SOLUTION Use a net cost equivalent, along with knowledge of percent. Start by finding the percent paid, using complements.

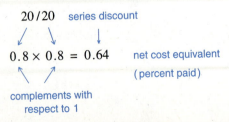

20 / 20   series discount

0.8 × 0.8 = 0.64   net cost equivalent
(percent paid)

complements with
respect to 1

Then, 0.64 or 64% of the list price, or $544, was paid. Use the basic percent equation to find the list price.

$$R \times B = P$$

$$0.64 \times \text{List price} = \$544$$

$$0.64 \times B = \$544$$

$$0.64\,B = \$544$$

$$\frac{0.64\,B}{0.64} = \frac{544}{0.64} = \$850 \quad \text{list price}$$

Check the answer.

$$
\begin{array}{rl}
\$850 & \text{list price} \\
-\ 170 & (0.2 \times \$850) \\
\hline
\$680 & \\
-\ 136 & (0.2 \times \$680) \\
\hline
\$544 & \text{net cost}
\end{array}
$$

The check shows that the list price was $850. ∎

EXAMPLE 4
Solving for List Price

Find the list price of a musical instrument having a net cost of $907.20 and a series discount of 10/30/20.

SOLUTION   Find the percent paid.

$$10 / 30 / 20 \quad \text{series discount}$$

$$0.9 \times 0.7 \times 0.8 = 0.504 \quad \text{percent paid}$$

complements with
respect to 1

Therefore 0.504 of the list price is $907.20. Now use the basic percent equation.

$$R \times B = P$$

$$0.504 \times \text{List price} = \$907.20$$

$$0.504 \times B = \$907.20$$

$$0.504\,B = \$907.20$$

$$\frac{0.504\,B}{0.504} = \frac{907.20}{0.504} = \$1800 \quad \text{list price}$$

The list price of the instrument is $1800. Check this answer as in the previous example. ∎

CAUTION Notice that Examples 3 and 4 are decrease problems similar to those shown in Chapter 3, Section 5. They are still base problems but may look different because the discount is now shown as a series of two or more discounts rather than a single percent decrease as in Chapter 3. If you need help refer to Section 3.5.

EXAMPLE 5
Finding the Single Trade Discount Rate

The list price of a compact disc player is $550. If the wholesaler offers the system at a net cost of $341, find the single trade discount rate being offered.

4 SOLUTION Use the following formula.

$$\text{Percent paid} \times \text{List price} = \text{Net cost}$$

$$P \times L = N$$

$$P \times 550 = 341$$

$$550\,P = 341$$

$$\frac{550\,P}{550} = \frac{341}{550} = 0.62 \text{ or } 62\% \qquad \text{percent paid}$$

Since 62% is paid, the discount offered is 38% ($100\% - 62\% = 38\%$).

For an alternative approach, first find the amount of discount, or $550 - $341 = $209. Next, find the rate of discount by using the basic percent equation

$$R \times B = P$$

$$\underline{\quad}\% \text{ of List price is Discount}$$

$$\underline{\quad}\% \text{ of } \$550 = \$209$$

$$R \times \$550 = \$209$$

$$\$550\,R = \$209$$

$$\frac{550\,R}{550} = \frac{209}{550}$$

to find that

$$R = \frac{209}{550} = 0.38 = 38\%.$$

By either method, the discount is 38%. ∎

EXAMPLE 6
Adding a Discount to Match a Competitor's Price

S and B Distributors offered a 20% trade discount on small compressors list priced at $450. Find the trade discount that must be added to match a competitor's price of $342.

5 SOLUTION First use the formula

$$P \times L = N$$

to find the single discount needed. The percent paid is found by multiplying together the complements of the 20% discount already given and the new, unknown discount, or

$$0.8 \times \text{Complement of discount} \times L = N.$$

$$0.8 \times d \times 450 = 342$$

$$360d = 342$$

$$\frac{360d}{360} = \frac{342}{360}$$

$$d = 0.95 \text{ or } 95\%$$

Therefore, 95% is the complement of the trade discount that must be added. The additional discount needed is 5% (100% − 95%). To match the competition, S and B Distributors must give a 20/5 series discount.   ■

8.2 Exercises

Find the net cost equivalent and the percent form of the single discount equivalent for each of the following series discounts.

1. $15/35$	2. $20/10$	3. $10/33\frac{1}{3}$
4. $40/10$	5. $20/20$	6. $20/20/20$
7. $20/10/20$	8. $5/10/15$	9. $25/10$
10. $30/37\frac{1}{2}$	11. $16\frac{2}{3}/10$	12. $10/15$
13. $10/20/10$	14. $20/20/10$	15. $55/40/10$
16. $30/10/10$	17. $40/25$	18. $5/5/5$
19. $20/12\frac{1}{2}$	20. $30/25$	21. $20/10/20/10$
22. $25/20/10/10$	23. $30/20/5/5$	24. $5/20/30/10$

25. Using complements show that the single discount equivalent of a 20/25/10 series discount is 46%. (See Objective 1.)

26. Suppose that you own a business and are offered a choice of a 10/20 trade discount or a 20/10 trade discount. Which do you prefer? Why? (See Objective 1.)

Find the list price, given the net cost and the series discount.

27. net cost, $324; trade discount, 20/10

28. net cost, $621.35; trade discount, 15/15

29. net cost, $2625; trade discount, $25/33\frac{1}{3}$

30. net cost, $139.65; trade discount, 30/40/5

31. net cost, $1313.28; trade discount, 5/10/20

32. net cost, $1872.72; trade discount, 15/20/10

Solve each of the following problems in trade discount.

33. Judy Lewis' Decorating Den offers a series discount of 20/15/10 while Generic Interiors offers a series discount of 35/4. (a) Which is the higher discount? (b) Find the difference.

34. Jack Rowell is offered oak stair railing by The Turning Point for $1370 less 30/10. Sierra Stair Company offers the same railing for $1220 less 10/10. (a) Which offer is better? (b) How much does Rowell save by taking the better offer?

35. Alcan Industries paid a net cost of $420 for a shipment of brass after discounts of 25% and 20% from the list price. Find the list price.

36. Bill Bauhofer received a shipment of tires which had a net cost of $44 each. If Bauhofer was given a series discount of 25/20, find the list price.

37. On a new jogging shoe, list priced at $92.85, a series discount of 20/10/10 is offered to wholesalers while a series discount of 20/10 is offered to retailers. (a) What is the wholesaler's price? (b) What is the retailer's price? (c) What is the difference between the prices?

38. A satellite dish is list priced at $1995. The manufacturer offers a series discount of 25/20/10 to wholesalers and a 25/20 series discount to retailers. (a) What is the wholesaler's price? (b) What is the retailer's price? (c) What is the difference between the prices?

39. A paper shredder list priced at $719.80 is being sold by a wholesaler at a net cost of $590.24. Find the single trade discount rate being offered. Round to the nearest tenth of a percent.

40. Pisor Industries offers galvanized sheet metal at a net cost of $140 per roll. If the list price of the metal is $250 per roll, find the single trade discount rate.

41. Capitol Alarm purchased a security alarm system at a net cost of $2733.75 and a series discount of $10/10/12\frac{1}{2}$. Find the list price.

42. Find the list price of a set of 15-inch aluminum wire wheels having a net cost of $449.28 and a series discount of 20/20/10.

43. An auto wholesaler offers a 10% trade discount on a case of injector cleaner priced at $27.60. A competitor offers the same oil at $23.60. What additional trade discount must be given to meet the competitor's price? Round to the nearest tenth of a percent.

44. A personal computer distributor has offered a computer system at a $1450 list price less a 30% trade discount. Find the additional trade discount needed to meet a competitor's net price of $933.80.

8.3 Cash Discounts: Ordinary Dating Method

OBJECTIVES

1 Calculate net cost after discounts.

2 Use the ordinary dating methods.

3 Determine whether cash discounts are earned.

4 Use postdating when calculating cash discounts.

5 Determine the amount due when goods are returned.

1   **Cash discounts** are offered by sellers to encourage prompt payment by customers. Since businesses must often borrow money for their operation, the prompt receipt of cash payment from customers increases the efficiency of the business and decreases the need for borrowed money. Saving interest on borrowed funds is a main reason that a cash incentive is often given to customers. In effect, the seller is saying, "Pay me quickly and receive a discount."

To find the net cost when a cash discount is offered, begin with the list price and subtract any trade discounts. From this amount subtract the cash discount. Use the following formula.

> Net cost = (List price − Trade discount) − Cash discount

If an invoice amount includes shipping and insurance charges, subtract these charges before a cash discount is taken. Then add them back to find net cost after the cash discount is subtracted.

The type of cash discount appears on the invoice under "Terms." (See the Scott, Foresman invoice in Figure 8.2.) Many companies using automated billing systems state the exact amount of the cash discount at the bottom of the invoice, to eliminate all calculations on the part of the buyer. However, not all businesses do this, making it important to know how to determine cash discounts.

There are many methods for determining cash discounts, but nearly all of these are based on the "ordinary methods." The ordinary methods discussed in this section, and the methods discussed in the next section, are the ones most commonly used today.

2   The **ordinary dating method** of cash discount, for example, is expressed on an invoice as

2/10, n/30 or 2/10, net/30

and is read "two ten, net thirty." The first digit is the rate of discount (2%), the second digit is the number of days allowed to take the discount (10 days), and n/30 or net/30 is the total number of days given to pay the invoice in full, if the buyer does not use the cash discount. The 2% discount may be subtracted from the amount owed if the invoice is paid within 10 days from the date of the invoice. If payment is made between the 11th and 30th days from the invoice date, the entire amount of the invoice is due. After 30 days from the date of the invoice, the invoice is considered overdue and may be subject to a late charge.

To find the due date of an invoice, use the number of days in each month, given in Table 8.4.

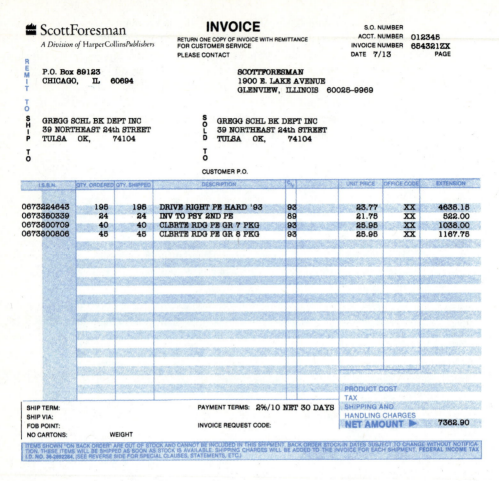

FIGURE 8.2

TABLE 8.4   The Number of Days in Each Month

30-Day Months	31-Day Months		Exception
April	January	August	February
June	March	October	(28 days normally; 29 days in leap year)
September	May	December	
November	July		

NOTE Leap years occur every 4 years. They are the same as Summer Olympic years and presidential election years in the United States. If a year is evenly divisible by the number 4, it is a leap year. The years 1996 and 2000 are both leap years because they are evenly divisible by 4.*

*This is the Gregorian Rule. In fact, all centenary years must be evenly divisible by 400 to be a leap year. The year 1600 was a leap year while 1700, 1800, and 1900 were not.

3 Find the date that an invoice is due by counting from the next day after the date of the invoice. The date of the invoice is never counted. Another way to determine due dates is to add the given number of days to the starting date. For example, to determine 10 days from April 7, add the number of days to the date ($7 + 10 = 17$). The due date, or 10 days from April 7, is April 17.

When the discount date or net payment date falls in the next month, find the number of days remaining in the current month by subtracting the invoice date from the number of days in the month. Then find the number of days in the next month needed to equal the discount period or net payment period. For example, find 15 days from October 20 as follows.

31	days in October
− 20	the beginning date, October 20
11	days remaining in October
+ 4	additional days needed in November to equal 15 days
15	days

Finally, November 4 is 15 days from October 20.

EXAMPLE 1
Finding Cash Discount Dates

If an invoice is dated January 2 and offers terms of 2/10, net 30, find (a) the last date on which the 2% discount may be taken and (b) the net payment date.

SOLUTION

(a) Beginning with the invoice date, January 2, the last date for taking the discount is January 12 ($2 + 10$).

(b) The net payment date is February 1 (29 days remaining in January plus 1 day in February). ■

EXAMPLE 2
Finding the Amount Due on an Invoice

An invoice of $450 is dated July 1 and offers 2/10, n/30. If the invoice is paid on July 8 and the shipping and insurance charges are $23.40, find the total amount due.

SOLUTION   The invoice was paid 7 days after its date ($8 − 1 = 7$); therefore, the 2% cash discount may be taken. The discount is $450 \times 0.02 = \$9$. The cash discount is subtracted from the invoice amount to determine the amount due.

$450 (invoice amount) − $9 (cash discount of 2%) = $441 (amount due)

The shipping and insurance charges are added to find the total amount due.

$441 (amount due) + $23.40 (shipping and insurance) =
$464.40 (total amount due) ■

CAUTION A cash discount is never taken on shipping and insurance charges. Be certain that shipping and insurance charges are excluded from the invoice amount before calculating the cash discount. Shipping and insurance charges must then be added back to find the total amount due.

4 In the ordinary dating method, the cash discount date and net payment date are both counted from the date of the invoice. Occasionally, the seller places a date later than the actual invoice date, sometimes labeling it "as of." This is called **postdating**. Notice that the Levi Strauss invoice in Figure 8.3 is dated "07/25 **AS OF** 08/01." The cash discount period and the net payment date are counted from 08/01 (August 1). This results in giving additional time for the purchaser to pay the invoice and receive the discount.

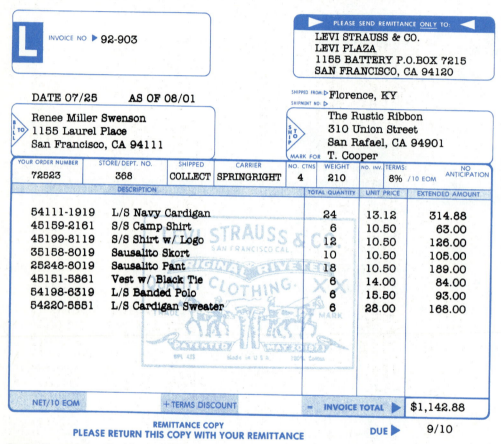

FIGURE 8.3

Reprinted by permission of Levi Strauss & Co.

EXAMPLE 3

Using Postdating "AS OF" with Invoices

An invoice is dated October 21 AS OF November 1 with terms of 3/15, n/30. Find (a) the last date on which the cash discount may be taken and (b) the net payment date.

SOLUTION

(a) Beginning with the postdate (AS OF) of November 1, the last date for taking the discount is November 16 (1 + 15).

(b) The net payment date is December 1 (29 days remaining in November and 1 day in December). ∎

NOTE Sometimes a sliding scale of cash discounts is offered. For example, with terms of 3/10, 2/20. 1/30, n/60, a discount of 3% is given if payment is made within 10 days, 2% if paid from the 11th through the 20th day, and 1% if paid from the 21st through the 30th day. The entire amount (net) must be paid no later than 60 days from the date of the invoice.

EXAMPLE 4
Determining Cash Discount Due Dates

An invoice is dated May 18 and offers terms of 4/10, 3/25, 1/40, n/60. Find (a) the three final dates for cash discounts and (b) the net payment date.

SOLUTION

(a)   The three final cash discount dates are:

4% if paid by May 28 (10 days from May 18)

3% if paid by June 12 (25 days from May 18)

1% if paid by June 27 (40 days from May 18)

(b)   The net payment date is July 17.   ■

NOTE *Never take more than one of the cash discounts. With all methods of giving cash discounts, if the net payment period is not given, the net payment due date is assumed to be 20 days beyond the cash discount period. After that date, the invoice is considered overdue. If either the final discount date or the net payment date is on a Sunday or holiday, the next business day is used. Many companies insist that payment is made when it is received. It is general practice, however, to consider payment made when it is mailed.*

5   A buyer receiving incorrect or damaged merchandise may return the goods to the seller. The value of the **returned goods** must be subtracted from the amount of the invoice before calculating the cash discount.

EXAMPLE 5
Finding the Amount Due when Goods Are Returned

An invoice amounting to $380 is dated March 9 and offers terms of 4/10, net 30. If $75 of goods are returned and the invoice is paid on March 17, what amount is due?

SOLUTION   The invoice was paid 8 days after its date ($17 - 9 = 8$), so the 4% cash discount is taken. The discount is taken on $305.

$380 (invoice amount) $-$ $75 (goods returned) $=$ $305 (goods retained)

The cash discount is subtracted from the $305. Since $305 \times 0.04 = 12.20, the amount due is

$305 (goods retained) $-$ $12.20 (cash discount) $=$ $292.80 (amount due).   ■

8.3 Exercises

Find the final discount date and the net payment date for each of the following problems.

	Invoice Date	As of	Terms
1.	Nov. 23		2/15, net/30
2.	July 3		3/15, n/30
3.	June 30	July 10	3/15, n/60
4.	Nov. 7	Nov. 18	3/10, n/30
5.	Sept. 11		4/20, n/30
6.	April 7		2/10, n/30
7.	Jan. 14		2/10, n/60
8.	Oct. 3		3/10, net 15
9.	Dec. 7	Jan. 5	5/15, n/60
10.	Mar. 1	Mar. 13	2/15, net 30

Solve for the amount of discount and the amount due on each of the following invoices.

	Invoice Amount	Invoice Date	Terms	Shipping and Insurance	Goods Returned	Date Invoice Paid
11.	$38.75	April 2	2/10, net/30			April 11
12.	$40.80	June 17	6/10, n/30			June 22
13.	$78.07	May 5	Net 30	$3.18		June 1
14.	$148	July 19	3/15, 1/25, n/60	$7.45		Aug. 16
15.	$635	Oct. 10	5/10, 2/20, n/30	$53.18		Oct. 23
16.	$1178	March 1	2/8, n/40			March 8
17.	$3403	Sept. 30	1/10, n/60		$125	Oct. 10
18.	$162	Jan. 15	2/15, net 30	$8.18	$12	Jan. 23
19.	$680	Aug. 23	3/20, net 60		$38	Sept. 8
20.	$1623.08	Nov. 12	2/10, n/30	$122.14	$187	Nov. 25

21. Describe the difference between a trade discount and a cash discount. Why are cash discounts offered? (See Objective 1.)

22. Using 2/10, n/30 as an example, explain what an ordinary cash discount means. (See Objective 2.)

Solve each of the following word problems.

23. Stockdale Marine offers cash discounts of 2/10, 1/15, n/30 on all purchases. If an invoice dated May 17 amounting to $1271.60 is paid on June 1, what amount would represent full payment?

24. A submersible pump is list priced at $92.75 with trade discounts of 10/20 and terms of 3/10, n/30. Assuming that a retailer earns the cash discount, find the net cost of this pump.

25. Michigan Supply offers mechanics a trade discount of 10/10/10 on all parts, with terms of net 30. Find the mechanic's price for parts with a total list price of $382 if the invoice was paid within 30 days.

26. Joe Nejad received an invoice for $586.12 for fishing tackle. The invoice was dated February 21, as of March 4, with terms of 4/10, 3/30, n/60. Find the amount necessary to pay the invoice in full on March 22.

27. Dolly Cantrell, a property manager, purchases "For Rent" signs at a list price of $216 per dozen. The supplier offers professional trade discounts of 10/20 and cash terms of 2/10, n/60. Find the net cost per sign if both discounts are earned and taken.

28. An invoice for $3836 from Cynthia Klein-Herring is dated September 8 and has cash terms of 6/20, 4/35, 2/60, n/90. Find the amount necessary to pay in full on November 6.

29. The list price of a popular brand of snowmobile is $5190. If a dealer can obtain trade discounts of 10/20/30 and cash terms of 4/10, n/30, find the lowest possible net cost.

30. The list price of Road Thunder Speakers is $120. If the manufacturer offers trade discounts of 30/10 and terms of 3/15, n/30, find the net cost of the speakers assuming both discounts are taken.

31. An industrial fire extinguisher is list priced at $39.95 with a trade discount of 15/30 and terms of 2/15, n/50. Assuming that both discounts are earned, find the net cost.

32. Sheepskin seat covers are list priced at $79.90 with a trade discount of 10/10/25 and terms of 3/10, n/30. Find the net cost assuming that both discounts are earned.

33. An invoice from Rags Fashions is dated January 18 and offers terms of 6/10, 4/20, 1/30, n/50. Find (a) the three final discount dates and (b) the net payment date.

34. An invoice with terms of 4/15, 3/20, 1/30, n/60 is dated September 4. Find (a) the three final discount dates and (b) the net payment date.

35. Truck Stuff receives an invoice dated March 28 AS OF April 5 with terms of 4/20, n/30. Find (a) the final discount date and (b) the net payment date.

36. The Fireside Shop received an invoice for hardware amounting to $218.80. The invoice is dated July 12 AS OF July 20 and offers terms of 3/20, n/60. Find the amount necessary to pay in full on August 3 if $24.30 worth of goods are returned.

37. An invoice received by Kyotas Nursery for garden supplies amounts to $2386.80. The invoice is dated March 18 AS OF April 8 and offers terms of 4/10, 2/20, n/30. Find the amount necessary to pay in full on April 22 if $172.50 worth of goods are returned.

38. An invoice received by Sydney's Baby Barn amounts to $380.50. The invoice is dated October 25 AS OF November 2 and offers terms of 3/15, n/30. Find the amount necessary to pay in full on November 18 if $56.50 worth of goods are returned.

39. How do you remember the number of days in each month of the year? List the months and the number of days in each.

40. Explain in your own words how "As Of" dating (postdating) works. Why is it used? (See Objective 4.)

8.4 Cash Discounts: Other Dating Methods

OBJECTIVES

1 Solve cash discount problems with end-of-month dating.

2 Use receipt-of-goods dating to solve cash discount problems.

3 Use extra dating to solve cash discount problems.

4 Determine credit for partial payment.

Three other methods of cash discounts are often used in place of the ordinary dating method. Each method is shown here.

1 **End-of-Month and Proximo Dating.** **End-of-month dating** and **proximo dating**, abbreviated **EOM** and **prox.**, are both treated the same way. For example, both

$$3/10 \ \textbf{EOM} \quad \text{and} \quad 3/10 \ \textbf{prox.}$$

mean that a 3% cash discount may be taken if payment is made within 10 days. However, the 10 days are counted from the end of the month in which the invoice is dated. For example, an invoice dated July 14 with terms of 3/10 EOM would have a discount date 10 days from the end of the month, or August 10.

Since this is a method of increasing the length of time during which a discount may be taken, it has become common business practice with EOM and prox. dating to add a month *when the date of an invoice is the twenty-sixth of the month or later.* For example, if an invoice is dated March 25 and the discount offered is 3/10 prox., the last date on which the discount may be taken is April 10. However, if the invoice is dated March 26 (or any later day in March) and the cash discount offered is 3/10 prox., then the last date on which the discount may be taken is May 10.

CAUTION The practice of adding an extra month when the invoice is dated the 26th of a month or after is used *only* with the end-of-month (proximo) dating cash discount. It does *not* apply to any of the other cash discount methods.

EXAMPLE 1
Using End-of-Month Dating

If an invoice is dated October 4, with terms of 2/15 EOM, find (a) the final date on which the cash discount may be taken and (b) the net payment date.

SOLUTION

(a) The discount date is November 15 (15 days after the end of October).

(b) The net payment date is December 5 (20 days after the last discount date since the net payment date is not otherwise given). ■

EXAMPLE 2
Understanding Proximo Dating

Find the amount due on an invoice of $1155 from Oregon Freeze Dried Foods dated August 3 if terms are 1/10 prox., and the invoice is paid on September 4.

SOLUTION   The last date on which the discount may be taken is September 10 (10 days after the end of August). September 4 is within the discount period, so the discount is earned. The 1% cash discount is computed on $1155, the amount of the invoice. Subtract the discount, $11.55 ($1155 × 0.01 = $11.55), from the invoice amount to find the amount due.

$1155 (invoice amount) − $11.55 (cash discount) = $1143.45 (amount due)   ■

NOTE With all methods of cash discounts, if the net payment period is not given, the net payment due date is assumed to be 20 days beyond the cash discount date.

2 **Receipt-of-Goods Dating.**   **Receipt-of-goods dating**, abbreviated **ROG**, offers discounts determined from the date the goods are actually received. This method is often used when shipping time is long. The invoice might arrive overnight by mail, but the goods may take several weeks. Under the ROG method of cash discount, the buyer is given time to receive and inspect the merchandise and then benefit from a cash discount. For example, the discount

3/15 ROG

allows a 3% cash discount if paid within 15 days from receipt of goods. If the invoice was dated March 5 and goods were received on April 7, the last date to take the 3% cash discount is April 22 (April 7 plus 15 days). The net payment date, since it is not stated, is 20 days after the last discount date, or May 12 (April 22 plus 20 days).

EXAMPLE 3
Using Receipt-of-Goods Dating

An invoice is dated December 12, with terms of 2/10 ROG. The goods are received on January 2. Find (a) the final date on which the cash discount may be taken and (b) the net payment date.

SOLUTION

(a)   The discount date is January 12 (10 days after receipt of goods, January 2 + 10 days).

(b)   The net payment date is February 1 (20 days after the last discount date).   ■

EXAMPLE 4
Working with ROG Dating

Find the amount due on an invoice of $170, with terms of 3/10 ROG, if the invoice is dated June 8, goods are received on June 18, and the invoice is paid on June 30.

SOLUTION   The last date to take the 3% cash discount is June 28, 10 days after June 18. Since the invoice is paid on June 30, 2 days after the last discount date, no cash discount may be taken. The entire amount of the invoice must be paid.

$170 (invoice amount) − $0 (no discount) = $170 (amount due)   ■

3 **Extra Dating.**   **Extra dating**, abbreviated **extra, ex.,** or **x**, gives additional time to the buyer to take a cash discount. For example, the discount

2/10-50 extra   or   2/10-50 ex.   or   2/10-50 x

allows a 2% cash discount if paid within (10 + 50) or 60 days from the date of the invoice. The discount is written in this form rather than combining the 10 + 50 and writing 2/60 to show that the 50 days are extra or in addition to the normal 10 days offered.

There are several reasons for using extra dating. The discount period might be extended during a slack season to generate more sales or perhaps to gain a competitive advantage. For example, Christmas merchandise might be offered with extra dating, allowing the buyer to take the cash discount after the holiday selling period.

EXAMPLE 5
Using Extra Dating

An invoice is dated November 23, with terms 2/10-50 ex. Find (a) the final date on which the cash discount may be taken and (b) the net payment date.

SOLUTION

(a)   The discount date is January 22. (7 days remaining in November and 31 days in December total 38. Thus 22 more days are needed in January to total 60.)

(b)   The net payment date is February 11 (20 days after the last discount date).   ∎

EXAMPLE 6
Understanding Extra Dating

An invoice from Rocky Mountaineers is dated August 5, amounts to $750, offers terms of 3/10-30x, and is paid on September 12. Find the net payment.

SOLUTION   The last day to take the 3% cash discount is September 14 (August 5 + 40 days = September 14). Since the invoice is paid on September 12, the 3% discount may be taken. The 3% cash discount is computed on $750, the amount of the invoice.

$$3\% \times \$750 = 0.03 \times \$750 = \$22.50$$

The discount to be taken is $22.50. The cash discount is subtracted from the invoice amount to determine the amount of payment.

$750 (invoice amount) − $22.50 (cash discount)   = $727.50 (amount of payment)   ∎

When customers pay invoices quickly, there is less need for a business to borrow money. In certain industries it is common to deduct interest that would have to be paid on borrowed money from the invoice amount. To do this, the company uses the current rate of interest and calculates the amount of interest over the remaining days on which the cash discount is allowable. This deduction, known as **anticipation**, is taken in addition to the cash discount earned. Anticipation involves the use of simple interest, discussed in Chapter 11.

4   Occasionally, a customer may pay only a portion of the total amount due on an invoice. If this **partial payment** is made within a discount period, the customer is entitled to a discount on the portion of the invoice which is paid.

If the terms of an invoice are 3%, 10 days, then only 97% (100% − 3%) of the invoice amount must be paid during the first 10 days. So, for each $.97 paid, the customer is entitled to $1.00 of credit. When a partial payment is made, the credit given for the partial payment is found by dividing the partial payment by the complement of the cash discount percent. Then, to find the balance due, subtract the credit given from the invoice amount. The cash discount is found by subtracting the partial payment from the credit given.

EXAMPLE 7
Finding Credit for Partial Payment

An invoice of $380, dated March 8, offers terms of 2/10 proximo. A partial payment of $150 is made on April 5. Find (a) the amount credited for the partial payment, (b) the balance due on the invoice, and (c) the cash discount earned.

SOLUTION

(a) The cash discount is earned on the $150 partial payment made on April 5 (April 10 was the last discount date).

$$100\% - 2\% = 98\% = 0.98$$

$$\text{Amount paid} = 0.98 \times \text{Credit given}$$

$$\$150 = 0.98 \times C$$

$$\$150 = 0.98\,C$$

$$\frac{\$150}{0.98} = \frac{0.98\,C}{0.98}$$

$$\frac{\$150}{0.98} = C$$

$$C = \$153.06 \quad \text{credit given (rounded)}$$

(b) Balance due = Invoice amount − Credit given

$$\text{Balance due} = \$380 - \$153.06$$

$$\text{Balance due} = \$226.94$$

(c) Cash discount = Credit given − Partial payment

$$\text{Cash discount} = \$153.06 - \$150$$

$$\text{Cash discount} = \$3.06 \quad \blacksquare$$

NOTE Cash discounts are important, and a business should make the effort to pay invoices early to earn the cash discount. In many cases the money saved through cash discounts has a great effect on the profitability of a business. Often companies will borrow money to enable them to take advantage of cash discounts.

8.4 Exercises

Find the discount date and net payment date for each of the following (the net payment date is 20 days after the final discount date).

	Invoice Date	Terms	Date Goods Received
1.	Jan. 27	2/10-60 ex.	
2.	Oct. 30	1/10 ROG	Dec. 12
3.	Nov. 22	1/10-20x	
4.	May 17	6/30 EOM	
5.	April 11	3/8 EOM	

	Invoice Date	Terms	Date Goods Received
6.	July 12	2/20 ROG	Oct. 3
7.	June 26	2/10 EOM	
8.	Sept. 27	3/15 prox.	
9.	May 12	1/20 prox.	
10.	Jan. 15	3/15 ROG	Feb. 5

Solve for the amount of discount and the amount due on each of the following.

	Invoice Amount	Invoice Date	Terms	Date Goods Received	Date Invoice Paid
11.	$1380	May 28	1/15 EOM		June 10
12.	$23.95	Aug. 2	3/10-20 extra		Sept. 1
13.	$194.04	Aug. 22	5/10-60 ex.		Nov. 5
14.	$9240.40	Nov. 23	1/20 ROG	March 5	March 8
15.	$2960	Oct. 31	2/10 EOM		Dec. 5
16.	$23.80	Jan. 13	4/30 ROG	Jan. 20	Feb. 25
17.	$356.20	May 17	3/15 prox.		June 12
18.	$98	Dec. 17	1/10-10x		Jan. 5
19.	$12.38	March 29	2/15 ROG	April 15	April 30
20.	$5740	March 13	3/10 prox.		March 29
21.	$3250.60	Oct. 17	3/15-20x		Oct. 20
22.	$678.32	May 8	2/20 EOM		June 15
23.	$1708.18	Nov. 13	4/10 prox.		Dec. 10
24.	$13,728.34	April 6	2/10 ROG	April 28	May 6

25. Quite often there is no mention of a net payment date on an invoice. Explain the common business practice when no net payment date is given. (See Objective 1.)

26. Describe in your own words why receipt-of-goods dating (ROG) is offered to customers. Use an example in your description. (See Objective 2.)

Find the credit given and the balance due on the invoice after making the following partial payments.

	Invoice Amount	Invoice Date	Terms	Date Invoice Paid	Partial Payment
27.	$525	Oct. 5	5/15 EOM	Nov. 3	$266
28.	$968	May 2	4/15-20x	June 5	$360
29.	$875	Sept. 19	5/10-30x	Oct. 31	$318
30.	$920	Jan. 11	3/10, 2/15, n/30	Jan. 23	$450.80
31.	$160	Dec. 8	3/10, n/30	Dec. 15	$97
32.	$380	Mar. 20	4/20 prox.	Apr. 18	$240

33. Write a short explanation of partial payment. Why would a company accept a partial payment? Why would a customer make a partial payment? (See Objective 4.)

34. Of all the different types of cash discounts presented in this section, which type is most interesting to you? Explain your reasons.

Solve each of the following problems in cash and trade discounts.

35. An invoice from Leather Plus is dated April 21, with terms of 3/10 EOM. Find (a) the final date on which the discount may be taken and (b) the net payment date.

36. An invoice from Pittsburgh Milling is dated March 4, with terms of 3/20 ROG, and the goods are received on April 8. Find (a) the final date on which the cash discount may be taken and (b) the net payment date.

37. An invoice is dated April 18 with terms of 3/10-15x. Find (a) the final date on which the cash discount may be taken and (b) the net payment date.

38. Find the amount due on an invoice of $1525 with terms of 1/20 ROG. The invoice is dated October 20, goods are received December 1, and the invoice is paid on December 20.

39. What payment should be made on an invoice dated July 30, amounting to $1730 offering terms of 2/10-60x, and paid October 4?

40. Donald Hadd, an outdoor equipment wholesaler, offers terms of 3/15-40x to encourage off-season sales of outdoor equipment. In a recent order, a retailer purchased $1185.30 worth of equipment and was offered the above terms. If the invoice was dated January 10, find (a) the final date on which the cash discount may be taken and (b) the amount paid if the discount was earned.

41. An invoice received from Deluxe Check Printers is dated October 3, with terms of 2/10 prox. Find (a) the final date on which the cash discount may be taken and (b) the net payment date.

42. The invoice of Racine Fabrics totaled $3198.80 was dated July 7, and offered terms of 3/15 ROG. If the shipment was received on August 28 and the invoice was paid on September 11, find the amount due.

43. In a recent purchase of business forms for her employment agency, Joan McKee was offered a cash discount of 3/15 EOM. The invoice amounted to $126.30 and was dated March 21. The supplies were received 5 days later, and the invoice was paid on April 3. Find the amount necessary to pay the invoice in full.

44. The Village Print Shop manufactures and sells posters which are priced at $3.75 each. A recent invoice billed a customer for 835 posters, had cash terms of 6/10-40 ex., and was dated March 12. Find the amount necessary to pay this invoice on May 8.

45. An invoice amounting to $1920 is dated July 23 by Lexington Foot Locker and offers cash terms of 6/30-120x. If a partial payment of $940 is made on November 28, find (a) the credit given for the partial payment and (b) the balance due on the invoice.

46. Mary Gold receives an invoice amounting to $1458, with cash terms of 3/10 prox. and dated January 3. If a partial payment of $833 is made on February 9, find (a) the credit given for the partial payment and (b) the balance due on the invoice.

47. An invoice dated December 8 is received with a shipment of hockey equipment from Canada on April 18 of the following year. The list price of the equipment is $2538, with allowed series discounts of 25/10/10. If cash terms of sale are 3/15 ROG, find the amount necessary to pay in full on April 21.

48. An invoice accompanies an air conditioning compressor and is dated July 28, with terms of 5/10 prox. Find (a) the final date on which the discount may be taken and (b) the net payment date.

49. Michael Anderson Beauty Supplies offers series discounts of 15/10 with terms of 5/15-30x. On an invoice dated June 4 for items list priced at $128, find the amount necessary to pay the invoice in full on June 18.

50. The Copy Corner receives an invoice amounting to $388.20, with terms of 8/10, n/30, and dated August 20 AS OF September 1. If a partial payment of $225 is made on September 8, find (a) the credit given for the partial payment and (b) the balance due on the invoice.

51. Honey Treat Yogurt Shop receives an invoice amounting to $263.40, with terms of 2/20 EOM, and dated September 6. If a partial payment of $150 is made on October 15, find (a) the credit given for the partial payment and (b) the balance due on the invoice.

52. An invoice of $3909.60 with terms of 4/10 prox. is received by Marja Strutz Transmissions Plus and is dated June 13. If partial payment of $3000 is made on July 8, find (a) the credit given for the partial payment and (b) the balance due on the invoice.

53. An invoice received by Chapman Appliance has terms of 3/15-30x and is dated March 18. The amount of the invoice is $792.58, and a partial payment of $580 is made on April 24. Find (a) the credit given for the partial payment and (b) the balance due on the invoice.

54. Auto Detail Plus makes a partial payment of $220 on an invoice of $397.18. If the invoice is dated June 4 with terms of 5/15 prox. and the partial payment is made on July 10, find (a) the credit given for the partial payment and (b) the balance due on the invoice.

CHAPTER 8 QUICK REVIEW

TOPIC	APPROACH	EXAMPLE
8.1 Trade discount and net cost	First find the amount of the trade discount. Then use the formula: Net cost = List price − Trade discount	List price, $28; trade discount, 25%. Find the net cost. $28 × 0.25 = $7 Net cost = $28 − $7 = $21
8.1 Complements with respect to 1	The complement is the number that must be added to a given discount to get 1 or 100%.	Find the complement with respect to 1 for each of the following. (a) 10% 10% + _____ = 100% 100% − 10% = 90% (b) $12\frac{1}{2}\%$; complement = 87.5% (c) 50%; complement = 50%

TOPIC	**APPROACH**	**EXAMPLE**
8.1 Complements and series dis-counts	The complement of a discount is the percent paid. Multiply the comple-ments of the discounts in the series to get the net cost equivalent.	Series discount, 10/20/10. Find the net cost equivalent. 10 / 20 / 10 ↓ ↓ ↓ $0.9 \times 0.8 \times 0.9 = 0.648$
8.1 Net cost equiv-alent (percent paid) and the net cost	Multiply the net cost equivalent (percent paid) by the list price to get the net cost. Percent paid × List price = Net cost	List price, $280; series discount 10/30/20. Find the net cost. 10 / 30 / 20 ↓ ↓ ↓ $0.9 \times 0.7 \times 0.8 = 0.504$ percent paid $0.504 \times \$280 = \$141.12$
8.2 Single discount equivalent to a series discount	Often needed to compare one series discount to another, the single discount equivalent is found by subtracting the net cost equivalent from 1. 1 − Net cost equivalent = Single dis-count equivalent	What single discount is equivalent to a 10/20/20 series discount? 10 / 20 / 20 ↓ ↓ ↓ $0.9 \times 0.8 \times 0.8 = 0.576$ $1 - 0.576 = 0.424 = 42.4\%$
8.2 Finding net cost using comple-ments of indi-vidual discounts	To find the net cost, multiply the list price by the product of the comple-ments of the individual discounts.	List price, $510; series discount, 30/10/5. Find the net cost. 30 / 10 / 5 ↓ ↓ ↓ $\$510 \times 0.7 \times 0.9 \times 0.95 =$ $\$305.24$ (rounded)
8.2 Finding list price if given the series dis-count and the net cost	First, find the net cost equivalent (percent paid), then use the formula to find the list price. $P \times L = N$ Percent paid × List price = Net cost	Net cost, $224; series discount, 20/20. Find list price. 20 / 20 ↓ ↓ $0.8 \times 0.8 = 0.64$ $0.64 \times$ List price $= \$224$ $0.64 L = \$224$ $L = \$340$

TOPIC	APPROACH	EXAMPLE
8.2 Determining the trade discount that must be added to meet a competitor's price	First use the formula $P \times L = N$ to find the single discount needed. The answer is the complement of the discount that must be added; subtract it from 100% to get the discount.	List price $640; trade discount 25%. Find the trade discount that must be added to match the competitor's price of $432. $$P \times L = N$$ $$0.75 \times \text{Complement of discount} \times L = N$$ $$0.75 \times d \times 640 = 432$$ $$480d = 432$$ $$d = 0.9 = 90\%$$ $$100\% - 90\% = 10\% \text{ additional discount}$$
8.3 Determining number of days and dates	30 day months _____ April June September November 31 day months _____ All the rest except February with 28 days	Date, July 24. Find 10 days from date. $$\text{July } 31 - 24 = 7 \text{ remaining in July}$$ $$7 + 3 = 10 \text{ days}$$ $$10 \text{ days} = \text{August 3}$$
8.3 Ordinary dating and cash discounts	With ordinary dating, count days from the date of the invoice. Remember: $$2 \;/\; 10, \quad n \;/\; 30$$ $$\downarrow \quad \downarrow \quad \downarrow \qquad \downarrow$$ $$\% \quad \text{days} \; \text{net} \quad \text{days}$$	Invoice amount $182; terms 2/10, n/30. Find cash discount and amount due. Cash discount: $$\$182 \times 0.02 = \$3.64$$ Amount due: $$\$182 - \$3.64 = \$178.36$$
8.3 Returned goods	Subtract returned goods amount from invoice before calculating the cash discount.	Invoice amount, $95; returned goods, $15; terms, 3/15, n/30. Find amount due if discount is earned. Cash discount: $$(\$95 - \$15) \times 0.03 = \$2.40$$ Amount due: $$\$95 - \$15 - \$2.40 = \$77.60$$
8.4 Cash discounts with end of month dating (EOM or proximo)	Count the final discount date and the net date from the end of the month. If the invoice is dated the 26th or after, add the entire following month when determining the dates. If not stated, the net date is 20 days beyond the discount date.	Terms, 2/10 EOM; invoice date, Oct. 18. Find the final discount date and the net payment date. Final discount date: November 10, which is 10 days from the end of October. Net payment date: November 30, which is 20 days beyond the discount date.

TOPIC	APPROACH	EXAMPLE
8.4 Receipt of goods dating and cash discounts (ROG)	Time is counted from the date goods are received to determine the final cash discount date and the net payment date.	Terms, 3/10 ROG; invoice date, March 8; goods received, May 10. Find the final discount date and the net payment date.
		Final discount date: May 20 (May 10 + 10 days)
		Net payment date: June 9 (May 20 + 20 days)
8.4 Extra dating and cash discounts	Extra dating adds extra days to the usual cash discount period; for example, 3/10-20x means 3/30.	Terms, 3/10-20x; invoice date, January 8. Find the final discount date and the net payment date.
		Final discount date: February 7 (23 days in January + 7 days in February = 30)
		Net payment date: February 27 (February 7 + 20 days)
8.4 Partial payment credit	When only a portion of an invoice amount is paid within the cash discount period, credit is given for the partial payment. Use the formula Amount paid = (1 − Discount rate) × Credit given.	Invoice, $400; terms, 2/10, n/30; invoice date, Oct. 10; partial payment of $200 on Oct. 15. Find credit given for partial payment and the balance due on the invoice.
		$200 = (1 − 0.02) × Credit given
		$200 = 0.98 C
		$204.08 (rounded) = C
		$400 − $204.08 = $195.92 Balance due

SUMMARY EXERCISE

The Plescia Heat and Cool Company specializes in repairs and installation of heating and air conditioning units. In early October they order 15 heater blower motors which have a list price of $180 each, and 18 programmable thermostats which list at $98 per unit. The supplier of these parts offers trade discounts of 20/20 and charges for shipping.

The invoice for this order arrives a few days later, is dated October 20, has terms of 3/10 EOM and shows a shipping charge of $118.80.

Plescia Heat and Cool will need to know all of the following.

(a) The total amount of the invoice excluding shipping.

(b) The final discount date.

(c) The net payment date.

(d) The amount necessary to pay the invoice on Nov. 8 including the shipping.

Find the trade discount and the net cost (invoice amount) for each of the following.
Round to the nearest cent. [8.1]

1. $510 less 20/10

2. $37 less 10/10/12$\frac{1}{2}$

3. $418 less 15/25/5

4. $1620 less 20/25/15

Find the net cost equivalent and the percent form of the single discount equivalent for
each of the following series discounts. [8.2]

5. 25/15

6. 10/10/10

7. 40/33$\frac{1}{3}$

8. 30/20/10/20

Find the list price, given the net cost and the series discount. [8.2]

9. Net cost, $618; trade discount, 15/15

10. Net cost, $120.50; trade discount, 20/10

11. Net cost, $328.70; trade discount, 10/20/15

12. Net cost, $1289.40; trade discount, 5/20/25

Find the discount date and net payment date for each of the following. (The net payment
date is 20 days after the final discount date.) [8.3 and 8.4]

	Invoice Date	Terms	Date Goods Received
13.	Mar. 4	2/10, n/30	
14.	Oct. 12	3/15 ROG	November 6
15.	Jan. 19	2/15 EOM	
16.	June 8	4/10-50 extra	

Solve for the amount of discount and the amount due on each of the following. [8.4]

	Invoice Amount	Invoice Date	Terms	Shipping and Insurance	Date Goods Received	Date Invoice Paid
17.	$74.18	December 1	2/15 proximo			January 10
18.	$118.20	January 7	3/10 ROG	$15.72	February 11	February 15
19.	$875.50	February 20	4/15 EOM	$67.18		March 12
20.	$2210.60	August 5	2/10-60x			October 13

Find the credit given and the balance due on the invoice after making the following partial payments. Round to the nearest cent. [8.4]

	Invoice Amount	Invoice Date	Terms	Date Invoice Paid	Partial Payment
21.	$220	October 20	1/15, n/30	November 2	$100
22.	$1770	May 8	2/20 EOM	June 15	$840
23.	$860	July 23	1/10 prox.	August 5	$500
24.	$3850	September 17	3/10-40x	November 2	$2050

Solve each of the following word problems.

25. The following invoice was paid on April 6. Find (a) the invoice total and (b) the amount that should be paid. [8.1 and 8.3]

Terms: 2/10, 1/15, n/30				March 24
Quantity	**Description**		**Unit Price**	**Extension Total**
10 ctn.	Envelopes, plain size E		@ $ 2.30 ea.	_____
6 pr.	Rollers, print		@ $ 38.15 pr.	_____
12 cases	Paper, bond 8½ × 11		@ $ 7.90	_____
4 gal.	Solvent		@ $ 3.85 gal.	_____
			Invoice Total	_____
			Cash Discount	_____
			Due after Cash Discount	_____
			Shipping and Insurance	$ 15.34
			Total Amount Due	_____

26. Red Baron Aviation offers series discounts of 20/20 to its regular customers. Hap Pischke, a new employee in the billing department, thought that the 20/20 terms meant a 40% discount and computed this trade discount on a list price of $8720. How much difference did this error make in the amount of the invoice? [8.1]

27. Find the list price of a food processor having a net cost of $209.79 and a series discount of 10/10/30. [8.2]

28. Restaurant Distributing offers a commercial pasta maker for $980 with a trade discount of 25%. Find the trade discount that must be added to match a competitor's price of $661.50. [8.2]

29. An invoice amounting to $2018 is dated September 18 and offers terms of 3/20 EOM. If $183 of goods are returned and the invoice is paid on October 18, what amount is due?

30. An invoice from Round Table Pizza Products amounts to $5280, was dated November 1, and offers terms of 4/15 proximo. A partial payment of $1800 is made on December 12. Find (a) the amount credited for the partial payment, (b) the balance due on the invoice, and (c) the cash discount earned.

9

Markup

The success of a business depends on many things. One of the most important is the price that the business charges for its goods and services. Prices must be low enough to attract customers, yet high enough to cover all operating expenses and provide a profit.

The difference between the price a business pays for an item and the price at which the item is sold is called **markup**. For example, if a store buys a package of blank videotapes for $11 and sells it for $15, the markup is $4. There are two standard methods of calculating markup—as a percent of cost and as a percent of selling price. This chapter discusses these two methods, along with how to convert markups from one method to the other, and how to use markup to allow for spoilage.

9.1 Markup on Cost

OBJECTIVES

1 Identify the terms used in selling.

2 Use the basic markup formula.

3 Calculate markup based on cost.

4 Apply percent to markup problems.

1 The terms used in markup are summarized here.

Cost is the price paid to the manufacturer or supplier after trade and cash discounts have been taken. Shipping and insurance charges are included in the cost.

Selling price is the price at which merchandise is offered for sale to the public.

Markup or **margin** or **gross profit** is the difference between the cost and the selling price. These three terms are often used interchangeably.

Operating expenses (or **overhead**) include the many expenses of business operation, such as wages and salaries of employees, rent for buildings and equipment, utilities, insurance, and advertising.

Net profit (net earnings) is the amount, if any, remaining for the business after the cost of goods and operating expenses have been paid. (Income tax for the business is computed on net profit.)

Most manufacturers, many wholesalers, and some retailers calculate markup as a percent of cost, called **markup on cost**. Manufacturers, who usually evaluate their inventories on the basis of cost, find this method to be most consistent with their business operations. Retailers, on the other hand, usually compute **markup on selling price** since retailers compare most areas of their business operations to sales revenue. Such items as sales commissions, sales taxes, advertising, and other items of expense are expressed as a percent of sales. It is reasonable, then, for the retailer to express markup as percent of sales. Wholesalers, however, use either cost or selling price, so be sure to find out which is being used.

2 Whether markup is based on cost or on selling price, the same basic **markup formula** is always used. This formula is as follows.

$$\text{Cost } + \text{ Markup } = \text{ Selling price}$$
$$C + M = S$$

The markup formula is illustrated in Figure 9.1.

Selling price

| $ Cost | $ Operating expenses | $ Net profit |

Markup/Margin/Gross profit

FIGURE 9.1

For example, if the cost of an item is $2 and the markup is $1, the selling price is the sum of these, or $3.

$$\text{Cost } + \text{ Markup } = \text{ Selling price}$$
$$\$2 \ + \quad \$1 \quad = \quad\quad \$3$$

If the cost of an item is $2 and the selling price is $3, the markup is the difference between these, or $1.

$$C + M = S$$
$$\$2 + M = \$3$$
$$M = \$3 - \$2$$
$$M = \$1$$

If the markup is $1 and the selling price is $3, the cost is the difference between these, or $2.

$$C + M = S$$
$$C + \$1 = \$3$$
$$C = \$3 - \$1$$
$$C = \$2$$

Most problems in markup give two of the items in the formula and ask for the third.

EXAMPLE 1   Solve for the missing quantity using the markup formula.

Using the Basic Markup Formula

(a)   Cost = $4

Markup = $2

Selling price = _____

(b)   Cost = $4

Selling price = $6

Markup = _____

(c)   Markup = $2

Selling price = $6

Cost = _____

SOLUTION

(a) $C + M = S$

$\$4 + \$2 = S$

$\$6 = S$

(b) $C + M = S$

$\$4 + M = \$6$

$M = \$6 - \$4$

$M = \$2$

(c) $C + M = S$

$C + \$2 = \$6$

$C = \$6 - \$2$

$C = \$4$ ∎

3 *Markup based on cost* is expressed as a percent of cost. As shown in the work with percent, *the base (that to which a number is being compared) is always 100%, so cost will have a value of 100%.* Markup and selling price will also have percent values found by comparing their dollar values to the dollar value of cost. Solve markup problems with the basic markup formula $C + M = S$.

EXAMPLE 2

Calculating Markup on Cost

Find the percent of markup on cost for an item costing $10 and selling for $15 if markup is based on cost.

SOLUTION   Use the markup formula

$$C + M = S$$

with $C = \$10$ and $S = \$15$.

$$\$10 + M = \$15$$

$$M = \$15 - \$10$$

$$M = \$5$$

4   The markup is $5. Now, find the percent of markup based on cost with the basic percent equation, $R \times B = P$. The base is the cost, or $10, and the markup is the part, or $5. Substituting these values into $R \times B = P$ gives

$$R \times B = P$$

$$R \times \$10 = \$5$$

$$10R = 5$$

$$\frac{10R}{10} = \frac{5}{10}$$

$$R = 0.5 = 50\%$$

An item costing $10 and selling for $15 has a 50% markup based on cost.   ∎

EXAMPLE 3

Finding the Percent of Markup

Find the percent of markup based on cost if a washing machine costing $350 is sold for $420.

SOLUTION   Use the formula to find the markup.

$$C + M = S$$

$$\$350 + M = \$420$$

$$M = \$420 - \$350$$

$$M = \$70$$

The markup is $70. Now use the basic percent equation, $R \times B = P$, with the base equal to $350 (the cost) and the part equal to $70 (the markup), to find the percent of markup.

$$R \times B = P$$

$$R \times \$350 = \$70$$

$$350R = 70$$

$$\frac{350R}{350} = \frac{70}{350}$$

$$R = 0.2 = 20\%$$

The markup based on cost is 20%.   ∎

NOTE The markup formula and the basic percent equation can be used for solving various types of problems involving markup, as shown in the next examples.

EXAMPLE 4
Finding Cost When Cost Is Base

If the markup on a basketball is $14, which is 50% based on cost, find the cost and the selling price.

SOLUTION The markup is 50% of the cost.

$$P = R \times B$$

$$M = 50\% \times C$$

$$M = 0.50C.$$

Since the markup is $14, substitute 14 for M.

$$14 = 0.50C$$

$$\frac{14}{0.50} = \frac{0.50C}{0.50}$$

$$28 = C$$

The cost of the basketball is $28.
   Now use the basic markup formula to find the selling price.

$$C + M = S$$

$$\$28 + \$14 = S$$

$$\$42 = S$$

The selling price of the basketball is $42. ∎

EXAMPLE 5
Finding the Markup and the Selling Price

Find the markup and selling price for a calculator if the cost is $18 and the markup is 25% of cost.

SOLUTION Since the markup is 25% of cost,

$$M = 0.25(\$18)$$

$$M = \$4.50.$$

The markup is $4.50. Now use the markup formula, with $C = \$18$ and $M = \$4.50$.

$$C + M = S$$

$$\$18 + \$4.50 = S$$

$$\$22.50 = S$$

The selling price of the calculator is $22.50. ∎

EXAMPLE 6

Finding Cost When Cost Is Base

Find the cost of a bracelet if the selling price is $112, which is 140% of the cost.

SOLUTION If the selling price is 140% of cost, then the markup must be 40% of cost. (The cost is always 100% when markup is based on cost.) This means

$$M = 0.4C.$$

Now use the basic formula.

$$C + M = S$$
$$C + 0.4C = \$112$$
$$1.4C = \$112$$
$$\frac{1.4C}{1.4} = \frac{\$112}{1.4}$$
$$C = \$80$$

The cost of the bracelet is $80. Check this: 0.40($80) = $32, and $80 + $32 = $112. ■

EXAMPLE 7

Finding the Cost and the Markup

The retail price of a 40-gallon gas water heater is $195.75. If the markup is 35% of cost, find the cost and the markup.

SOLUTION Use the formula, with $M = 0.35C$.

$$C + M = S$$
$$C + 0.35C = \$195.75$$
$$1\,C + 0.35C = \$195.75$$
$$1.35C = \$195.75$$
$$\frac{1.35C}{1.35} = \frac{\$195.75}{1.35}$$
$$C = \$145$$

The cost of the water heater is $145.
Now find markup.

$$C + M = S$$
$$\$145 + M = \$195.75$$
$$M = \$195.75 - \$145$$
$$M = \$50.75$$

The markup is $50.75. ■

NOTE Remember, when calculating markup on cost, cost is always the base, 100%.

9.1 Exercises

Find the missing quantities. Round rates to the nearest tenth of a percent and money to the nearest cent.

	Cost Price	Markup	% Markup on Cost	Selling Price
1.	$3	_____	40%	_____
2.	_____	$9	_____	$45
3.	$12	$7.20	_____	_____
4.	_____	_____	100%	$68.98
5.	$158.70	_____	_____	$198.50
6.	_____	$54.38	50%	_____
7.	_____	$13.50	_____	$81
8.	$7.75	_____	28%	_____
9.	$210	_____	_____	$328
10.	_____	$25.25	_____	$73.80
11.	$165	_____	27%	_____
12.	_____	_____	32%	$11.48

13. Markup may be calculated on cost or on selling price. Explain why most retailers use selling price as base when calculating markup. (See Objective 1.)

14. Write the basic markup formula. Define each term. (See Objective 2.)

Solve each of the following word problems using cost as base. Round rates to the nearest tenth of a percent and money to the nearest cent.

15. A wholesaler pays $16.32 for a box of highlighter pens and the markup is 40% of cost. Find the markup.

16. The cost of a dentist's handpiece is $560 and the markup is 25% of cost. Find the markup.

17. Find the cost if the selling price of a table is $166.40 and the markup is 30% of cost.

18. Thermal Insulation Supplies sells bulk insulation at a price of $9.18 per bag. If the markup is 35% of cost, find the cost.

19. The cost of a contractor's 8-inch drain pipe is $6.48 each. The contractor decides that a markup of 40% on cost would produce adequate profit. Find the selling price.

20. Water Sports purchases jet skis at a cost of $2880 each. If its operating expenses are 25% of its cost, and it wishes to make a net profit of 15% of its cost, find the selling price.

21. A weight clinic sells revised diet books for $7.80 a copy. If this includes a markup of 50% on cost, find the cost.

22. A yard and garden shop sells charcoal lighter fluid for $1.69 per quart. If the shop pays $1.30 per quart, find the markup percent on cost.

23. What percent of markup on cost must be used if a freezer costing $435 is sold for $512.30?

24. Fleet Feet had a markup of $11.66 on some shoes that they sold for $55.66. Find (a) the cost, (b) the markup percent on cost, and (c) the selling price as a percent of cost.

25. Bismark Tool put a markup of 26% on cost on some parts for which they paid $4.50. Find (a) the selling price as a percent of cost, (b) the selling price, and (c) the markup.

26. A jewelry dealer sold custom necklaces at a selling price that was 250% of her cost. If the markup is $135, find (a) the markup percent on cost, (b) the cost, and (c) the selling price.

27. Marvin Levinson determines that the melted butter for which he receives $.20 extra when selling a bag of popcorn costs him $.04. Find his rate of markup on cost.

28. Nature Trails, a manufacturer of hiking equipment, prices lightweight hiking boots at $44.52, which is $127.2% of their cost. Find (a) the cost, (b) the markup as a percent of cost, and (c) the markup.

29. North Area Coins priced a proof coin at $868, which was 112% of cost. Find (a) the cost, (b) the markup as a percent of cost, and (c) the markup.

30. Delta Supply sells plumbing displays for $920. If their operating expenses are 18% of their cost and their net profit is 7% of their cost, find the cost.

31. Bell Hardware has operating expenses of 18% of cost and desires a 17% net profit on cost. If the selling price of a tube of 20-year silicone caulk is $8.95, find the cost.

32. American Glass Company sells eight-foot sliding patio doors for $299.90. If their operating expenses are 15% of cost and their net profit is 15% of cost, find the cost.

9.2 Markup on Selling Price

OBJECTIVES

1 Calculate markup based on selling price.

2 Solve markup problems when selling price is base.

3 Use the markup formula to solve markup problems.

4 Determine percent markup on cost and the equivalent percent markup on selling price.

5 Convert markup percent on cost to selling price.

6 Convert markup percent on selling price to cost.

As mentioned in the previous section, wholesalers sometimes calculate markup based on cost and other times calculate markup based on selling price. Retailers use sales figures in almost all aspects of their business. Almost all expense and income amounts are calculated as a percent of sales. Therefore it is common for retailers to calculate markup based on selling price. In each case, markup will be given as "on cost" or "on selling price." Remember that if markup is based on selling price, then selling price is the base. Since the base is 100%, selling price will have a value of 100%. This section discusses markup on selling price.

1 The same basic markup formula is used with **markup on selling price.**

> Cost + Markup = Selling price
>
> $$C + M = S$$

EXAMPLE 1
Solving for Markup on Selling Price

An item costs $2, sells for $3, and markup is *based on selling price*. Solve for markup and percent of markup on selling price.

2 **SOLUTION**   First, solve for markup.

$$C + M = S$$
$$\$2 + M = \$3$$
$$M = \$3 - \$2$$
$$M = \$1$$

Now solve for percent of markup on selling price. Use the basic percent equation, $R \times B = P$. In this example, P is the markup, or $1, and the base B is the selling price, or $3. Substitute these values into $R \times B = P$, and solve the equation.

$$R \times \$3 = \$1$$

$$R = \frac{\$1}{\$3}$$

$$R = \frac{1}{3} = 0.333\ldots = 33\frac{1}{3}\%$$

The rate of markup on selling price is $33\frac{1}{3}\%$. ∎

3 As with problems where markup is based on cost, the basic formula $C + M = S$ may be used for all variations of markup problems when selling price is the base.

EXAMPLE 2
Finding Markup when Selling Price Is Given

Find the markup if the selling price is $3.43 and the markup is 30% of selling price.

SOLUTION   Since the markup is 30% of the selling price,

$$M = 0.3S$$

or

$$M = 0.3(\$3.43) = \$1.03 \qquad \text{(rounded)}.$$

The markup is $1.03. ∎

EXAMPLE 3
Finding Cost when Selling Price Is Base

If the markup is $1.72, which is 35% based on selling price, find the cost.

SOLUTION Start by finding selling price and then subtract markup to find cost. Here $R = 35\%$ (the rate of markup) and $P = \$1.72$ (the markup). Use $R \times B = P$ as follows.

$$R \times B = P$$

$$35\% \times S = \$1.72$$

$$0.35S = \$1.72$$

$$S = \frac{\$1.72}{0.35}$$

$$S = \$4.91 \qquad \text{(rounded)}$$

The selling price is $4.91. Now solve for cost.

$$C + M = S$$

$$C + \$1.72 = \$4.91$$

$$C = \$4.91 - \$1.72$$

$$C = \$3.19$$

The cost is $3.19. ∎

EXAMPLE 4
Finding the Selling Price and the Markup when Cost Is Given

Find the selling price and the markup if the cost is $1.50 and the markup is 25% of selling price.

SOLUTION Use the formula $C + M = S$. Since the markup is 25% of the selling price, $M = 0.25S$.

$$\$1.50 + 0.25S = S$$

$$\$1.50 = 1S - 0.25S$$

$$\$1.50 = 0.75S$$

$$\frac{1.50}{0.75} = \frac{0.75S}{0.75}$$

$$\$2 = S$$

The selling price is $2.
Now find the markup using the markup formula.

$$C + M = S$$

$$\$1.50 + M = \$2$$

$$M = \$2.00 - \$1.50$$

$$M = \$.50$$

The markup is $.50. ∎

Table 9.1 gives average markups for retail stores.

**TABLE 9.1   Average Markups for Retail Stores
(Markup on Selling Price)**

Type of Store	Markup	Type of Store	Markup
General merchandise stores	29.97%	Furniture and home furnishings	35.75%
Grocery stores	22.05%	Drinking places	52.49%
Other food stores	27.31%	Eating places	56.35%
Motor vehicle dealers (new)	12.83%	Drug and proprietary stores	30.81%
Gasoline service stations	14.47%	Liquor stores	20.19%
Other automotive dealers	29.57%	Sporting goods and bicycle shops	29.72%
Apparel and accessories	37.64%	Gift, novelty, and souvenir shops	41.86%

Source: Sole Proprietorship Income Tax Returns, U.S. Treasury Dept., Internal Revenue Service, Statistics Division

4   Sometimes a markup based on cost must be compared to a markup based on selling price. Such a conversion might be necessary for a manufacturer who thinks in terms of cost, and who wants to understand a wholesaler or retail customer. Or perhaps a retailer or wholesaler might convert markup on selling price to markup on cost to better understand the manufacturer. Make these comparisons by computing first the markup on cost, then computing the markup on selling price.

EXAMPLE 5

*Determining
Equivalent Markups*

A picnic cooler costing $8.40 is sold for $10.50. Find the percent of markup on cost. Also, find the percent of markup on selling price.

SOLUTION   To solve for the percent markup on cost, use the formula $C + M = S$, with $C = \$8.40$ and $S = \$10.50$.

$$C + M = S$$
$$\$8.40 + M = \$10.50$$
$$M = \$10.50 - \$8.40$$
$$M = \$2.10$$

The markup is $2.10.

Next, use the percent equation, $R \times B = P$, with $B = \$8.40$ (the cost, since markup is on cost) and $P = \$2.10$ (the markup).

$$R \times B = P$$
$$R \times \$8.40 = \$2.10$$
$$8.4R = 2.1$$
$$R = \frac{2.1}{8.4}$$
$$R = 0.25 = 25\%$$

The markup on cost is 25%.

To find the percent of markup on selling price, use the percent equation again. While P is still $2.10, *B* changes to $10.50 since the markup on selling price must be found. Substitute into the equation as follows.

$$R \times B = P$$

$$R \times \$10.50 = \$2.10$$

$$10.5R = 2.1$$

$$R = \frac{2.1}{10.5}$$

$$R = 0.2 = 20\%$$

The markup on selling price is 20%. This example shows that a 25% markup on cost is equivalent to a 20% markup on selling price. ∎

NOTE In Example 5 the markup on cost was determined first (25%). The problem was then reworked with the same dollar amounts but with the selling price as base. The result was 20%. This shows that a markup of 25% on cost is the same as a markup of 20% on selling price.

5 Another method for making markup comparisons is to use conversion formulas. Convert markup percent on cost to markup percent on selling price with the following formula.

$$\frac{\% \text{ of markup on}}{\text{selling price}} = \frac{\% \text{ of markup on cost}}{100\% + \% \text{ of markup on cost}}$$

Or, if M_c represents markup on cost and M_s represents markup on selling price,

$$M_s = \frac{M_c}{100\% + M_c}.$$

EXAMPLE 6

Converting Markup on Cost to Markup on Selling Price

Convert a markup of 25% on cost to its equivalent markup on selling price.

SOLUTION Use the formula for converting markup on cost to markup on selling price:

$$\frac{M_c}{100\% + M_c} = M_s,$$

with $M_c = 25\%$.

$$\frac{25\%}{100\% + 25\%} = \frac{25\%}{125\%} = \frac{0.25}{1.25} = \frac{1}{5} = 20\%$$

As in Example 1, a markup of 25% on cost is equivalent to a markup of 20% on selling price. ∎

Calculator Approach to Example 6

First, set up the problem.

$$\frac{25\%}{100\% + 25\%}$$

Next, calculate the denominator and use the $\boxed{\text{M+}}$ key. Finally, divide the numerator by the denominator.

$$100 \quad \boxed{+} \quad 25 \quad \boxed{\text{M+}} \quad 25 \quad \boxed{\div} \quad \boxed{\text{MR}} \quad \boxed{=} \quad 0.2$$

6 Convert markup percent on selling price to markup percent on cost with the following formula.

$$\frac{\% \text{ of markup}}{\text{on cost}} = \frac{\% \text{ of markup on selling price}}{100\% - \% \text{ of markup on selling price}}$$

Or, if M_c represents markup on cost and M_s represents markup on selling price,

$$M_c = \frac{M_s}{100\% - M_s}.$$

EXAMPLE 7

Converting Markup on Selling Price to Markup on Cost

Convert a markup of 20% on selling price to its equivalent markup on cost.

SOLUTION Use the formula for converting markup on selling price to markup on cost:

$$\frac{M_s}{100\% - M_s} = M_c,$$

with $M_s = 20\%$.

$$\frac{20\%}{100\% - 20\%} = \frac{20\%}{80\%} = \frac{0.2}{0.8} = \frac{1}{4} = 25\%$$

A markup of 20% on selling price is equivalent to a markup of 25% on cost. ∎

Table 9.2 shows common markup equivalents expressed as percents on cost and also on selling price.

TABLE 9.2   Markup Equivalents

Markup on Cost	Markup on Selling Price
20%	$16\frac{2}{3}\%$
25%	20%
$33\frac{1}{3}\%$	25%
50%	$33\frac{1}{3}\%$
$66\frac{2}{3}\%$	40%
75%	$42\frac{6}{7}\%$
100%	50%

9.2 Exercises

Find the missing quantities. Round rates to the nearest tenth of a percent and money to the nearest cent.

	Cost Price	Markup	% Markup on Cost	Selling Price
1.	$23.18	_____	35%	_____
2.	$40.00	_____	_____	$58.50
3.	_____	$112	46%	_____
4.	_____	$134	_____	$334
5.	$.78	_____	22%	_____
6.	$17.28	_____	_____	$29.95
7.	_____	_____	25%	$10.95
8.	$53.14	_____	$33\frac{1}{3}\%$	_____
9.	_____	$42.18	_____	$120
10.	$193.15	_____	42.5%	_____

Find the missing quantities by first computing the markup on one base and then computing the markup on the other. Round rates to the nearest tenth of a percent and money to the nearest cent.

	Cost	Markup	Selling Price	% Markup on Cost	% Markup on Selling Price
11.	_____	$115	_____	25%	20%
12.	_____	$.23	$.73	_____	_____
13.	$6.90	_____	_____	_____	38%
14.	$22.80	_____	$45.60	_____	_____
15.	_____	$150	_____	40%	_____
16.	$5.15	_____	$15.45	_____	_____
17.	_____	$39.24	$218	_____	18%
18.	_____	$480	_____	25%	_____

Find the equivalent markups on either cost or selling price using the appropriate formula.
Round to the nearest tenth of a percent.

	Markup on Cost	Markup on Selling Price
19.	25%	_____
20.	$33\frac{1}{3}\%$	_____
21.	_____	26%
22.	_____	$42\frac{6}{7}\%$
23.	50%	_____
24.	85%	_____
25.	_____	40%
26.	_____	$16\frac{2}{3}\%$

27. Use one of the markup conversion formulas to show that a markup of 50% on selling price is equivalent to a markup of 100% on cost.

28. To have a markup of 100% or greater the markup must be calculated on cost. Show why this is always true.

Solve each of the following word problems. Round rates to the nearest tenth of a percent and money to the nearest cent.

29. The cost of a mountain bike is $440 and the markup is 20% of the selling price. Find the selling price.

30. A stationer pays $12 per dozen bottles for typewriter correction fluid and the markup is 50% on selling price. Find the selling price per bottle.

31. Field and Stream Sports pays $20.80 for a fly rod and sells it for $32. Find the percent of markup on selling price.

32. Lawn and Garden sells a lawn mower for $448 and maintains a markup of 40% on selling price. Find the cost.

33. If the cost of steel-belted tires, size P205/70R15, is $71.25 each and the markup is 35% on selling price, find the selling price.

34. Best Furniture pays $356 for a recliner chair. If the retailer wants a 42% markup on selling price, find (a) the selling price and (b) the percent of markup on cost.

35. Lamps For Less sells a lampshade at a markup of 36% on the selling price. If the lampshade has a markup of $4.86, find (a) the selling price, (b) the cost, and (c) the cost as a percent of the selling price.

36. Audio Plus pays $55 for automotive cassette AM-FM radios. If the markup is 32.5% on selling price, find (a) the cost as a percent of selling price, (b) the selling price, and (c) the markup.

37. One dozen shower curtains cost a retailer $144, and the gross profit is $6 per shower curtain. Find the percent of gross profit based on selling price.

38. A retailer pays $87.36 per dozen for baseball hats and has a gross profit of $1.68 per hat. Find the percent of gross profit based on selling price.

39. The Workem's Store placed a selling price of $27.50 on slacks that cost 68% of the selling price. Find (a) the cost, (b) the markup, and (c) the markup as a percent of selling price.

40. Recyclable aluminum can be sold for $2880 per ton (1 ton = 2000 pounds). If Alcan Recycling Plant wants a 50% markup on selling price, (a) how much per pound can it pay local residents for their recycled aluminum? (b) What is the equivalent markup percent on cost?

41. White Water Supply purchased a job lot of 380 river rafts for $7600. If they sold 158 of the rafts at $45 each, 74 at $35 each, 56 at $30 each, and the remainder at $25 each, find (a) the total amount received for the rafts, (b) the total markup, and (c) the markup percent on selling price.

42. Hubs and Wheels purchased 100 sets of Indy wire wheels (1 set = 4 wheels) for $54,000. If they sold 160 wheels at $185 each, 120 wheels at $165 each, 52 wheels at $150 each, and the remainder at $140 each, find (a) the total amount received for the wheels, (b) the total markup, and (c) the markup percent on selling price.

43. A retailer purchases silk flowers for $31.56 per dozen and sells them for $4.78 each. (a) Find his percent of markup on selling price. (b) What is the equivalent markup on cost?

44. Big Boys Auto sells gasket kits for $18.60 each, which reflects a markup of 25% on selling price. Find (a) the cost and (b) the percent of markup on cost.

45. The Tinder Box Smoke Shop buys a special blend of pipe tobacco in ten-pound tins at a cost of $24 per tin. If the shop sells the tobacco for $1.20 per ounce, find (a) the markup on selling price, and (b) the equivalent markup on cost. (Hint: 1 pound = 16 ounces.)

46. A grocer finds that she can sell fireplace logs for $1.29 each. If this gives a 38% markup on selling price, find the grocer's cost for three dozen logs. Find the equivalent percent of markup on cost.

47. A restaurant supplier sells coffee filters for $6.90 per box. If the cost of the filters is $4.80, find (a) the percent of markup on cost and (b) the equivalent percent of markup on selling price.

48. Tiechert Rock Supply sells crushed red lava rock for $14.50 per cubic yard. If the cost of the rock is $8.25 per cubic yard, find (a) the percent of markup on cost and (b) the equivalent percent of markup on selling price.

49. A discount store purchased touch-tone wall phones at a cost of $288 per dozen. If they need 20% of cost to cover operating expenses and 15% of cost for net profit, find (a) the selling price per phone and (b) the percent of markup on selling price.

50. A retailer determines her operating expenses to be 18% of selling price and desires a net profit of 8% on selling price. If the cost of a woodstove is $285, find (a) the selling price and (b) the percent of markup on cost.

51. Cycle City advertises mountain bikes for $199.90. If their cost is $2100 per dozen, find (a) the markup per bicycle, (b) the percent of markup on selling price, and (c) the percent of markup on cost.

52. The Tool Shed advertises standard/metric socket sets (manufactured in the U.S.A.) for $39. If their cost is $351 per dozen sets, find (a) the markup per set, (b) the percent of markup on selling price, and (c) the percent of markup on cost.

9.3 Markup with Spoilage

OBJECTIVES

1 Solve markup problems when items are unfit for sale.

2 Solve markup problems when a certain percent of items are unsaleable.

3 Calculate markup when a percent of the merchandise must be sold at a reduced price.

1   Merchandise that spoils, becomes damaged or soiled, or is manufactured with a blemish, causes problems for many businesses. To a nursery or garden center, produce buyer, food processor, and clothing manufacturer, such problems are a common occurrence. These items that cannot be sold at the regular price, called **irregulars**, are often sold at a reduced price. In fact, such items may be **unsaleable** and represent a total loss. In either case, the markup applied to the items sold at regular price must allow for **spoilage** and damaged items. The result is that perfect items are sold at a higher price to make up for the unsold items, in a process called **markup with spoilage**.

EXAMPLE 1
Finding Selling Price with Spoilage

Planters Nursery purchases 210 pony packs of plants for $175.50. If a markup of 40% on selling price is necessary and 15 of the pony packs will be unfit for sale, find the selling price per pony pack.

SOLUTION   First, find the total selling price of the plants using a 40% markup on selling price and a cost of $175.50.

$$C + M = S$$

$$C + 40\%S = S$$

$$\$175.50 + 0.4S = S$$

$$\$175.50 = 1S - 0.4S$$

$$\$175.50 = 0.6S$$

$$\frac{\$175.50}{0.6} = S$$

$$\$292.50 = S$$

The total selling price is $292.50. Now, divide the total selling price by the number of saleable pony packs to find the selling price per pony pack.

$$\frac{\$292.50}{210 - 15} = \frac{292.5}{195} = \$1.50 \qquad \text{selling price per pony pack}$$

The pony packs must be priced at $1.50 to realize a markup of 40% on selling price and to allow for 15 packs that cannot be sold. ∎

NOTE Controlling loss due to spoilage is critical in business. As spoilage increases, profits will fall. These additional costs due to spoilage may be added to the price of the products sold but the resulting higher price may be too high and no longer competitive.

EXAMPLE 2

Finding Selling Price when a Percent of Items Is Unsaleable

The Pretzel Bender bakes 60 dozen jumbo pretzels. Experience shows that 5% of the pretzels will not be sold and must be thrown away. If the pretzels cost $2.16 per dozen to bake and a markup of 50% on selling price is desired, find the selling price per dozen pretzels.

2 SOLUTION To begin, find the total cost of the pretzels.

$$\text{Cost} = 60 \text{ dozen} \times 2.16 = \$129.60$$

Now find the selling price, using a markup of 50% of selling price.

$$C + M = S$$

$$C + 50\%S = S$$

$$\$129.60 + 0.5S = S$$

$$\$129.60 = 1S - 0.5S$$

$$\$129.60 = 0.5S$$

$$\frac{\$129.60}{0.5} = S$$

$$\$259.20 = S$$

The total selling price is $259.20.

Next, find the number of dozen pretzels that will be sold. Since 5% will not be sold, 95% (100% − 5%) will be sold.

$$95\% \times 60 \text{ dozen} = 57 \qquad \text{dozen pretzels sold}$$

The total selling price of $259.20 must be received from 57 dozen pretzels.

Find the selling price per dozen pretzels by dividing the total selling price by the number of pretzels sold.

$$\frac{259.20}{57} = \$4.55 \qquad \text{selling price per dozen (rounded)}$$

A selling price of $4.55 per dozen gives the desired markup of 50% on selling price while allowing for 5% of the pretzels to be unsold. ■

3 Sometimes part of the merchandise must be sold at a reduced price.

EXAMPLE 3

Finding Selling Price when Some Items Are Sold at a Reduced Price

An athletic shoe manufacturer makes a walking shoe at a cost of $16.80 per pair. Based on past experience, 10% of the shoes will be defective and must be sold as irregulars for $24 per pair. If the manufacturer produces 1000 pairs of shoes and desires a markup of 100% on cost, find the selling price per pair.

SOLUTION First, find the cost of the total production.

$$1000 \text{ pairs} \times \$16.80 = \$16{,}800 \qquad \text{total production cost}$$

The total selling price is

$$C + M = S$$
$$C + 100\%C = S$$
$$2C = S.$$

Since $C = \$16,800$ and $2C = S$, $2 \times \$16,800 = \$33,600$ is the total selling price of all shoes.

If 10% of the shoes will sell for $24 per pair, then the sales of irregulars will be

$$(0.10 \times 1000) \times \$24 = 100 \times \$24$$
$$= \$2400.$$

Calculate the selling price per pair of the regular priced shoe as shown.

$$\$33,600 - \$2400 = \$31,200 \qquad \text{total sales of regulars}$$

$$\frac{\$31,200}{1000 - 100} = \frac{31,200}{900} = \$34.67 \qquad \text{(rounded)}$$

A regular selling price of $34.67 will give the manufacturer a 100% markup on cost while allowing for 10% of the production to sell at $24 per pair. ■

Calculator Approach to Example 3

First, find the total selling price of all the shoes and place it in memory. Since the markup is 100% of cost, the cost must be doubled to obtain the selling price.

$$1000 \;\boxed{\times}\; 16.8 \;\boxed{\times}\; 2 \;\boxed{\text{M+}}$$

Next, find the amount of money coming from the sale of irregulars. Subtract this amount from memory to get the sales from regulars, then divide by 900 (1000 − (10% of 1000)).

$$.1 \;\boxed{\times}\; 1000 \;\boxed{\times}\; 24 \;\boxed{\text{M−}} \quad \boxed{\text{MR}} \quad \boxed{\div}\; 900 \;\boxed{=}\; 34.67 \text{ (rounded)}$$

9.3 Exercises

Find the selling price per item.

	Total Cost	Quantity Purchased	Number Unsaleable	% Markup on Selling Price	Selling Price Per Item
1.	$36	10	1	20%	_____
2.	$27	30	3	10%	_____
3.	$195	1 gr.	14	25%	_____
4.	$144	3 doz.	4	40%	_____
5.	$120	25 pr.	5 pr.	$33\frac{1}{3}\%$	_____
6.	$1071	100	15	50%	_____
7.	$126	8 doz.	6	15%	_____
8.	$2025	250 pr.	25 pr.	25%	_____

Find the missing quantities.

	Total Cost	Quantity Purchased	Percent Unsaleable	% Markup on Selling Price	Number to Sell	Selling Price Per Item
9.	$76	20	5%	20%	_____	_____
10.	$105	50	10%	25%	_____	_____
11.	$198	2 doz.	25%	50%	_____	_____
12.	$105	40	25%	40%	_____	_____
13.	$190	80 pr.	5%	$33\frac{1}{3}\%$	_____	_____
14.	$8750	100	30%	15%	_____	_____
15.	$25,200	2000 gal.	5%	20%	_____	_____
16.	$3600	50 bbl.	10%	60%	_____	_____

Find the missing quantities. Markup is based on total cost.

	Total Cost	Quantity Purchased	Percent Sold at Reduced Price	% Markup on Total Cost	Number at Regular Price	Number at Reduced Price	Reduced Price	Regular Selling Price
17.	$125	50	10%	20%	_____	_____	$2.00	_____
18.	$360	120	20%	25%	_____	_____	$3.00	_____
19.	$1500	20 drm.	5%	30%	_____	_____	$90.00	_____
20.	$270	90 pr.	20%	40%	_____	_____	$4.00	_____
21.	$432	1 gr.	25%	25%	_____	_____	$2.50	_____
22.	$1000	200	10%	$33\frac{1}{3}\%$	_____	_____	$6.00	_____
23.	$1400	500 pr.	30%	50%	_____	_____	$3.00	_____
24.	$7500	1000	50%	25%	_____	_____	$5.00	_____

25. When merchandise is unsaleable it is as if the items were not received. Explain how the price of the saleable items must be adjusted to offset this loss. (See Objective 1.)

26. Explain in your own words how the selling price is determined when part of the merchandise must be sold at a reduced price. (See Objective 3.)

Solve each of the following word problems.

27. The Aztec Pottery Shop finds that 15% of their production cannot be sold. If they produce 100 items at a cost of $2.15 each and desire a markup of 40% on selling price, find the selling price per item.

28. The Bagel Factory baked 200 dozen bagels at a cost of $108. If 20 dozen bagels cannot be sold and the bakery needs a markup of $66\frac{2}{3}\%$ on selling price, find the selling price per dozen bagels.

29. Fowler Nursery purchases 75 mature palm trees for $511. If 2 of the palms are judged unfit for resale and the nursery desires to maintain a $33\frac{1}{3}\%$ markup on selling price, find the selling price for each palm.

30. A produce buyer purchased 15 crates of lettuce containing 3 dozen heads each at a total cost of $118.80. If 2 crates of the lettuce are sold at the reduced price of $.25 per head and the buyer wants a markup of 100% on cost, find the regular price per head of lettuce.

31. Flower Sack purchased twelve gross of carnations at a cost of $128.60. If 25% of the carnations must be sold at $1.50 per dozen and a markup of 200% on cost is needed, find the regular selling price per dozen carnations.

32. Sports Specialty buys 1000 T-shirts at $10 per shirt. If markup of 50% on selling price is needed and 8% of the shirts are unsaleable, find the selling price per shirt.

33. Bethel Metals finds that 20% of its stove shell castings are unsaleable. If the cost of manufacturing 55 stoves is $10,450 and they need a markup of 30% on cost, find the selling price per stove.

34. Rodriquez Jewelry Manufacturing knows that 3% of their ring castings cannot be sold. If the cost of manufacturing 24 dozen rings is $4704 and they need a markup of 38% on cost, find the selling price per dozen rings.

35. Woolever Tire recaps tires at a cost of $11.50 per tire. Past experience shows that 12% of the recaps must be sold as blems for $15. If they recap 500 tires and a markup of 110% on cost is desired, find the regular selling price per tire.

36. Solano Tile manufactures roof tile at a cost of $42 per square. Past experience shows that 8% of a production run are irregulars and must be sold for $45 per square. If a production run of 10,000 squares is completed and they desire a markup of 80% on cost, find the selling price per square.

37. U.S. Publishing Company prints a book on sports memorabilia at a production cost of $10.80 per copy. They know that 20% of the production will be sold for $11.50 per copy. If they print 50,000 books and they want a markup of 50% on selling price, find the selling price per book. Round to the nearest cent.

38. Del Paso Heights Fabric Shop purchased 14,000 yards of fabric at a cost of $4.20 per yard. Past experience shows that 24% of the fabric will have to be sold for $4.50 per yard. Find the selling price per yard if the store wants a markup of 35% on selling price.

CHAPTER 9 QUICK REVIEW

TOPIC	APPROACH	EXAMPLE
9.1 Markup on cost	Use Rate × Base = Part ($R \times B = P$) with Cost as Base (100%), Markup % as Rate, and Markup as Part.	Cost, $160; markup, 25% on cost. Find the markup. $R \times B = P$ $0.25 \times \$160 = \$40$

TOPIC	APPROACH	EXAMPLE
9.1 Calculating the percent of markup	Use Cost + Markup = Selling price $(C + M = S)$ and the basic percent equation $R \times B = P$.	Cost, \$420; selling price, \$546. Find the percent of markup based on cost. $C + M = S$ $\$420 + M = \$546$ $M = \$126$ $R \times B = P$ $R \times 420 = 126$ $R = \dfrac{126}{420} = 0.3 = 30\%$
9.1 Finding the cost and selling price	Use $P = R \times B$ to solve for cost; then use $C + M = S$ to find selling price.	Markup, \$56; markup on cost, 50%. Find cost and selling price. $P = R \times B$ $\$56 = 0.5C$ $C = \dfrac{56}{0.5} = \$112$ cost $C + M = S$ $\$112 + \$56 = \$168$ selling price
9.2 Markup on selling price	Use Rate $\times$ Base = Part $(R \times B = P)$ with Selling Price as Base (100%), Markup % as Rate, and Markup as Part.	Selling price, \$6.00; markup, 25% on selling price. Find the markup. $P = R \times B$ Markup = 25% $\times$ Selling price $M = 0.25(6.00) = \$1.50$
9.2 Finding the cost	Use the formulas $R \times B = P$ and $C + M = S$.	Markup, \$87.50; markup on selling price, 35%. Find the cost. First, use $R \times B = P$ to find selling price. 35% $\times$ Selling price = \$87.50 $0.35S = \$87.50$ $S = \$250$ Now find cost. $C + M = S$ $C + \$87.50 = \$250$ $C = \$250 - \$87.50 = \$162.50$ cost

TOPIC	APPROACH	EXAMPLE
9.2 Calculating the selling price and the markup	Use the formula $C + M = S$.	Cost, \$150; markup, 25% of selling price. Find the selling price and the markup. $C + M = S$ $\$150 + 0.25S = S$ $\$150 = 0.75S$ $\$200 = S$ selling price $C + M = S$ $\$150 + M = \$200$ $M = \$200 - \$150 = \$50$
9.2 Converting markup on cost to markup on selling price	Use the formula $M_s = \dfrac{M_c}{100\% + M_c}.$	Markup on cost, 25%. Convert to markup on selling price. $M_s = \dfrac{25\%}{100\% + 25\%}$ $= \dfrac{0.25}{1.25} = 0.2 = 20\%$
9.2 Converting markup on selling price to markup on cost	Use the formula $M_c = \dfrac{M_s}{100\% - M_s}.$	Markup on selling price, 20%. Convert to markup on cost. $M_c = \dfrac{20\%}{100\% - 20\%}$ $= \dfrac{.2}{.8} = 0.25 = 25\%$
9.3 Solving markup with spoilage or unsaleable items	1. Find total cost and selling price. 2. Subtract total sales at reduced prices from total sales. 3. Divide the remaining sales by the number of saleable units to get selling price per unit.	60 doughnuts cost 15¢ each; 10 are not sold; 50% markup on selling price. Find selling price per doughnut. Cost $= 60 \times \$.15 = \$9$ $C + M = S$ $\$9 + 0.5S = S$ $\$9 = 0.5S$ $\$18 = S$ $\$18 \div 50 = \$.36$ per doughnut

SUMMARY EXERCISE

Price Less Drugs buys 3400 boxes of holiday greeting cards directly from the manufacturer. The list price of the cards is $4.95 per box and there is a trade discount of 30/10/20 and a cash discount of 5/10-40x. Price Less earns and receives both discounts.

The cards were sold as follows: 1080 boxes at $3.95, 1250 boxes at $2.95, 660 boxes at $2.50, 230 boxes at $2.00, and the remaining boxes were unsaleable.

To better manage greeting card sales next year, each of the following must be determined.

(a) The net cost of the greeting cards after trade and cash discounts.

(b) The total sales amount received from all the holiday greeting cards.

(c) The amount of net profit from the sales of the cards.

(d) The markup as a percent of selling price to the nearest whole percent.

(e) The equivalent percent of markup on cost to the nearest whole percent.

CHAPTER 9 REVIEW EXERCISES

Find the missing quantities. Round rates to the nearest tenth of a percent and money to the nearest cent. [9.1]

	Cost Price	Markup	% Markup on Cost	Selling Price
1.	$12	_____	30%	_____
2.	_____	$4	25%	_____
3.	_____	$50.50	_____	$147.60
4.	$105.00	_____	_____	$164

Find the missing quantities. Round rates to the nearest tenth of a percent and money to the nearest cent. [9.2]

	Cost Price	Markup	% Markup on Selling Price	Selling Price
5.	$72.90	_____	35%	_____
6.	_____	$33.50	_____	$83.50
7.	_____	$17.35	$33\frac{1}{3}$%	_____
8.	$386.30	$186	_____	_____

Find the missing quantities by first computing the markup on one base and then computing the markup on the other. Round rates to the nearest tenth of a percent and money to the nearest cent. [9.2]

	Cost Price	Markup	Selling Price	% Markup on Cost	% Markup on Selling Price
9.	_____	$35.20	_____	100%	50%
10.	$22.80	_____	$45.60	_____	_____
11.	_____	$.46	$1.46	_____	_____
12.	_____	$128.16	_____	25%	_____

Find the equivalent markups on either cost or selling price using the appropriate formula. Round to the nearest tenth of a percent. [9.2]

	% Markup on Cost	% Markup on Selling Price
13.	_____	20%
14.	100%	_____
15.	_____	$33\frac{1}{3}\%$
16.	85%	_____

Find the selling price per item. [9.3]

	Total Cost	Quantity Purchased	Number Unsaleable	% Markup on Selling Price	Selling Price Per Item
17.	$81	90	9	10%	_____
18.	$108	20	2	20%	_____
19.	$630	8 doz.	6	15%	_____
20.	$6075	750 pr.	75 pr.	25%	_____

Find the missing quantities. Markup is based on total cost. [9.3]

	Total Cost	Quantity Purchased	Percent Sold at Reduced Price	% Markup on Total Cost	Number at Regular Price	Number at Reduced Price	Reduced Price	Regular Selling Price Each
21.	$250	50	10%	20%	_____	_____	$2.00	_____
22.	$135	90 pr.	20%	40%	_____	_____	$1.00	_____
23.	$864	2 gr.	25%	25%	_____	_____	$2.50	_____
24.	$2800	1000 pr.	30%	50%	_____	_____	$3.00	_____

Solve each of the following word problems on markup.

25. Medico Distributors buys protective glasses for $84 per dozen pairs. If Medico uses a markup of 50% on selling price, find the selling price per pair. [9.2]

26. Fabulous Kitchens sells a self-cleaning oven for $665.60. If the cost of the oven is $512, find the markup as a percent of cost. [9.2]

27. A wholesaler purchased a carton of toothpaste at a cost of $25.65 per carton. If the markup is 15% on cost, find the markup. [9.1]

28. Hal's Auto Air Conditioning installs an auto air conditioner at a cost of $538 including parts and labor. If the markup is based on cost and the retail price to the customer is $712.85, find the percent of markup. What is the equivalent markup on selling price? Round to the nearest tenth of a percent. [9.1]

29. Raleys Superstore bought 1820 swimming pool, blow-up toys at a cost of $10,010. The toys were sold as follows: 580 at $13.95 each, 635 at $9.95 each, 318 at $8.95 each, 122 at $7.95 each, and the balance at $5.00 each. Find (a) the total selling price of all the toys and (b) the markup as a percent of selling price (to the nearest whole percent). [9.2]

30. Fan Fever purchased 200 posters at a cost of $360. If 20% of the posters must be sold at $2 each and a markup of 100% on cost is needed, find the regular selling price of each poster. [9.3]

31. A wholesale stationery supply house pays $4.32 for a box of file folders and sells them for $5.76. Find (a) the percent of markup on selling price and (b) the percent of markup on cost. [9.2]

32. Fosters Doughnuts bakes lemon squares at a cost of $1.93 per dozen. Markup on cost is 100% and 15% of the lemon squares will have to be sold at $2.40 per dozen. If Fosters bakes 180 dozen lemon squares, find the regular selling price per dozen. Round to the nearest cent. [9.3]

10

Markdown and Inventory Control

Management spends a great deal of time controlling inventory. While on one hand the inventory must include the correct kinds and quantities of products to satisfy customers, it is equally important to control inventory to minimize any unsaleable or surplus merchandise. This chapter discusses some of the main ideas of inventory control.

10.1 Markdown

OBJECTIVES

1 Calculate markdown and reduced price.

2 Calculate percent of markdown.

3 Find original selling price.

4 Identify the terms associated with loss.

5 Determine the breakeven point.

6 Calculate operating loss.

7 Determine the amount of a gross or absolute loss.

8 Calculate the percent of absolute loss.

Merchandise often does not sell at its marked price, for any of several reasons. The retailer may have ordered too much, or the merchandise may have become soiled or damaged, or perhaps only odd sizes and colors are left. Also, merchandise may not sell because of lower prices at other stores, seasonal changes, economic fluctuations, or changes in fashion.

1 When merchandise does not sell at its marked price, its price is often reduced. The difference between the original selling price and the reduced selling price is

called the **markdown**, with the selling price after the markdown called **reduced price, sale price**, or **actual selling price**. The basic formula for markdown is as follows.

Reduced price = Original price − Markdown

EXAMPLE 1
Finding the Reduced Price

Sun Leisure has marked down an outdoor patio lounge. Find the reduced price if the original price was $58 and the markdown is 30%.

SOLUTION The markdown is 30% of $58, or 0.3 × $58 = $17.40. The reduced price is

$58.00 (original price) − $17.40 (markdown) = $40.60 (reduced price). ∎

Calculator Approach to Example 1

Use of the $\boxed{\%}$ key is favored by many with this type of problem.

58 $\boxed{-}$ 30 $\boxed{\%}$ 40.6

2 The next example shows how to find a **percent** or **rate of markdown**.

NOTE The percent of markdown is always based on the original selling price.

EXAMPLE 2
Calculating the Percent of Markdown

The total inventory of Mother's Day cards has a retail value of $785. If the cards were sold at reduced prices that totaled $530, what is the percent of markdown on the original price?

SOLUTION First find the amount of the markdown.

$785 (original price) − $530 (reduced price) = $255 (markdown)

To solve for percent of markdown on original price, use the percent equation: Rate × Base = Part. The base is the original price of $785, the rate is unknown, and the part is the amount of markdown or $255.

$$R \times B = P$$

% × $785 = $255

$$R \times \$785 = \$255$$

$$785R = 255$$

$$R = \frac{255}{785}$$

$$R = 0.3248 = 32\%$$ rounded to the nearest whole percent

The cards were sold at a markdown of 32%. ∎

EXAMPLE 3

Finding the Original Price

Find the original price if a backyard swing set is offered at the reduced price of $108 after a 40% markdown.

3   **SOLUTION**   After the 40% markdown, the reduced price represents 60% of the original price. Find the original price, which is the base.

$$R \times B = P$$

$$60\% \times B = \$108$$

$$0.6B = 108$$

$$B = \frac{108}{0.6} = \$180$$

The original price of the swing set was $180. ∎

4   The amount of markdown must be large enough to sell the merchandise while providing as much profit as possible. Merchandise which is marked down will result in either a *reduced net profit, breaking even*, an *operating loss*, or an *absolute* or *gross loss*. Figure 10.1 illustrates the meanings of these terms.

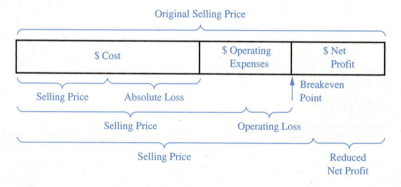

FIGURE 10.1

Reduced net profit results when the reduced price is still within the net profit range; that is, when it is greater than the total cost plus operating expenses.

The **breakeven point** is the point at which the reduced price just covers cost plus overhead (operating expenses).

An **operating loss** occurs when the reduced price is less than the breakeven point. The operating loss is the difference between the breakeven point and the reduced selling price.

An **absolute loss** or **gross loss** is the result of a reduced price that is below the cost of the merchandise alone. The absolute loss (gross loss) is the difference between the cost and reduced selling price.

REDUCED PRICE = ORIG ← (MARKDOWN PRICE)
ORIG. = RED. PRICE + MARKDOWN

The following formulas are helpful when working with markdowns.

C + OPER EXPENSES + PROFIT = S

> Breakeven point = Cost + Operating expenses
>
> Operating loss = Breakeven point − Reduced selling price
>
> Absolute loss = Cost − Reduced selling price

EXAMPLE 4
Determining a
Profit or a Loss

Cordova Appliance paid $40 for a garbage disposal. If operating expenses are 30% of cost and the garbage disposal is sold for $50, find the breakeven point and the amount of loss.

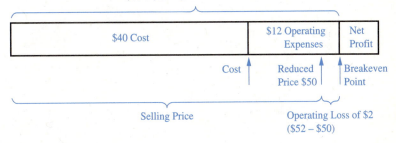

$40 + $12 = $52 Breakeven Point

FIGURE 10.2

5 **SOLUTION** Use the following formula to find the breakeven point.

Cost + Operating expenses = Breakeven point

$40 + (0.3 × $40) = $40 + $12 = $52 breakeven point

Since the breakeven point is $52 and the selling price is $50, there is a loss of

$52 − $50 = $2.

This $2 loss is an operating loss since the selling price is less than the breakeven point but greater than the cost. See Figure 10.2. ■

Calculator Approach to Example 4

Operating expenses of 30% may be added to cost with the use of the $\boxed{\%}$ key to get the breakeven point. The reduced selling price is then subtracted from the breakeven point to find the operating loss.

40 $\boxed{+}$ 30 $\boxed{\%}$ $\boxed{-}$ 50 $\boxed{=}$ 2

EXAMPLE 5

Determining the Operating Loss and the Absolute Loss

A lawn mower normally selling for $360 is marked down 30%. If the cost of the lawn mower is $260 and the operating expenses are 20% of the cost, find (a) the operating loss, (b) the absolute loss, and (c) the percent of absolute loss based on cost (round to the nearest percent).

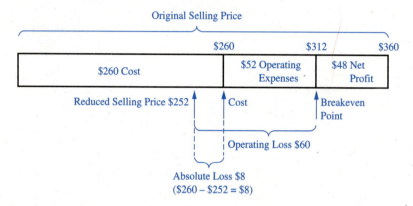

FIGURE 10.3

SOLUTION

6 **(a)** The breakeven point (cost + operating expenses) is $312 ($260 + 0.2 × $260 = $260 + $52). The reduced price is

$$\$360 - (0.3 \times \$360) = \$360 - \$108 = \$252.$$

The operating loss is

$$\$312 \text{ (breakeven point)} - \$252 \text{ (reduced price)} = \$60 \text{ (operating loss)}.$$

7 **(b)** The absolute or gross loss is the difference between the cost and the reduced price.

$$\$260 \text{ (cost)} - \$252 \text{ (reduced price)} = \$8 \text{ (absolute loss)}.$$

8 **(c)** The percent of absolute loss is always expressed as a percent of cost, so find the percent of cost that is the absolute loss using the percent equation.

$$R \times B = P$$

$$\underline{\quad}\% \times \$260 = 8$$

$$260R = 8$$

$$R = \frac{8}{260}$$

$$R = 0.0308 = 3\% \text{ (rounded)}$$

The rate of absolute loss is approximately 3%. See Figure 10.3. ■

EXAMPLE 6

Finding the Original Price and Maximum Percent of Markdown to Be Given

A wood burning stove cost a retailer $210. If the store's operating expenses are 25% of cost, and net profit is 15% of cost, find (a) the original selling price of the stove and (b) the maximum percent of markdown which may be given without taking an operating loss (round to the nearest percent).

SOLUTION

(a) The markup is 40% (25% + 15%) on cost. The selling price is found from the basic markup formula.

$$C + M = S$$

$$\$210 + (0.4 \times \$210) = S$$

$$\$210 + \$84 = S$$

$$\$294 = S$$

The original selling price is $294.

(b) The breakeven point is the sum of cost and operating expenses.

$$\$210 + (0.25 \times 210) = \$210 + \$52.50$$

$$= \$262.50$$

The breakeven point is $262.50.

The maximum amount of markdown which may be taken without an operating loss is

$$\$294 \,\text{(selling price)} \;-\; \$262.50 \,\text{(breakeven point)} \;=\; \$31.50 \,\text{(markdown)}.$$

Since the maximum markdown is $31.50, the maximum percent of markdown can be found by asking this question:

What % of selling price is markdown?

$$R \quad \times \quad B \quad = P$$

$$\underline{}\% \text{ of } \$294 = \$31.50$$

$$\$294\,R = \$31.50$$

$$R = \frac{31.5}{294}$$

$$R = 0.1071 = 11\% \,\text{(rounded)}$$

A maximum of 11% may be taken as markdown without an operating loss. ∎

10.1 Exercises

Find the missing quantities. Round rates to the nearest whole percent and money to the nearest cent.

	Original Price	% Markdown	$ Markdown	Reduced Price
1.	$740		$370	
2.	$19.50		$3.90	
3.	$.77			$.50
4.	$1170			$644
5.		30%		$84
6.		$66\frac{2}{3}\%$		$6.20
7.		40%	$1.08	
8.		20%	$.77	
9.	$36.60	50%		
10.	$122.50	56%		
11.			$175	$682
12.			$12.50	$78

Complete the following. If there is no operating loss or absolute loss write none. *Use Figure 10.1 as a guide.*

	Cost	Operating Expense	Breakeven Point	Reduced Price	Operating Loss	Absolute Loss
13.	$5	$1.25		$5.50		
14.	$20	$5		$22		
15.	$50		$66	$44		
16.	$12.50		$16.50	$11		
17.	$156	$44			$60	
18.	$39	$11			$15	
19.				$25	$14	$4
20.				$100	$56	$16

21. Describe in your own words five reasons why a store will reduce the price (markdown) of merchandise to get it sold.

22. As a result of a markdown, there are three possible results, reduced net profit, operating loss, and absolute loss. As a business owner, which would concern you the most? Explain.

Solve each of the following word problems. Round rates to the nearest whole percent and money to the nearest cent.

23. A banker's lamp is marked down $11.80, a reduction of 40%. Find the original price.

24. At the end of the model year, a Ford Explorer is marked down 15% to $15,725. Find the original price.

25. After water damage, A and A Builders prices their entire stock of carpeting at $37,180. If the original price of the carpet was $68,500, find the percent of markdown on the original price.

26. A television set originally priced at $675 is reduced to $425. Find the percent of markdown on the original price.

27. The Soccer Shop has an end-of-season sale at which they sell a competition soccer ball for $15. If their cost was $12 and their operating expenses were 20% of cost, find the amount of profit or loss.

28. World Lighting paid $150 for a lighting panel. Their operating expenses are $33\frac{1}{3}\%$ of cost. If they sell the lighting panel at a clearance price of $180, find the amount of profit or loss.

29. American Antique paid $153.49 for a fern stand. Their original selling price was $208.78 but this was marked down 46% in order to make room for incoming merchandise. If operating expenses are 14.9% of cost, find (a) the operating loss, (b) the absolute loss, and (c) the percent of absolute loss based on cost.

30. An electronic ignition system normally selling for $58.50 is marked down 37%. If the cost was $41.96 and the operating expenses are 11.5% of the cost, find (a) the operating loss, (b) the absolute loss, and (c) the percent of absolute loss based on cost.

31. Photo Supply, a retailer, pays $190 for an enlarger. The store's operating expenses are 20% of cost and net profit is 15% of cost. Find (a) the selling price of the enlarger and (b) the maximum percent of markdown which may be given without taking an operating loss (round to the nearest whole percent).

32. A room air conditioner cost a retailer $278. The store's operating expenses are 30% of cost and net profit is 10% of cost. Find (a) the selling price of the air conditioner and (b) the maximum percent of markdown that may be given without taking an operating loss.

10.2 Average Inventory and Inventory Turnover

OBJECTIVES

1 Determine average inventory.

2 Calculate stock turnover at retail.

3 Calculate stock turnover at cost.

4 Identify considerations in stock turnover.

The average time needed for merchandise to sell is a common measure of the efficiency of a business. The number of times that the merchandise sells during a certain period of time is called the **inventory turnover** or the **stock turnover**. Businesses such as florist shops or produce departments have a very fast turnover of merchandise, perhaps just a few days. On the other hand, a furniture store will normally have a much slower turnover, perhaps several months.

If inventory is kept at a minimum level, less capital is needed to operate the business and the speed of selling the inventory is increased. In addition, the risk of having old and unsaleable merchandise is decreased. On the other hand, if the inventory is kept low, sales may be lost due to poor selection and inadequate quantities of merchandise offered to the customer.

1   Find stock turnover by first calculating the **average inventory**. The average inventory for a certain time period is found by adding the inventories taken during the time period and then dividing the total by the number of times that the inventory was taken.

EXAMPLE 1
Determining Average Inventory

Inventory at retail value was $16,852 on April 1 and $14,324 on April 30. What was the average inventory?

SOLUTION   First, add the inventory values.

$$
\begin{array}{ll}
\$16,852 & \text{(April 1)} \\
+\,\$14,324 & \text{(April 30)} \\
\hline
\$31,176 &
\end{array}
$$

Then divide by the number of times inventory was taken.

$$\frac{\$31,176}{2} = \$15,588$$

The average inventory is $15,588.   ■

EXAMPLE 2
Finding Average Inventory for the Quarter

Inventory at retail value at Federal Drug was $22,615 on January 1, $18,321 on February 1, $26,718 on March 1, and $16,228 on March 31. Find the average inventory for the first quarter of the year.

SOLUTION   First add the inventories and then divide by the number of inventories taken.

$$\frac{\$22,615 + \$18,321 + \$26,718 + \$16,228}{4} = \$20,970.50$$

The average inventory for the first quarter of the year is $20,970.50.   ■

NOTE   In Example 2, inventory was taken four times to find the average inventory for the first quarter of the year. To find the average inventory for a period of time, an inventory must be taken at the beginning of the period and one final time at the end of the period. To find average inventory for a full year, it is common to find inventory on the first day of each month and on the last day of the last month. Average inventory is found by adding all these inventory amounts (13 of them) and then dividing by 13, the number of inventories taken. Methods of taking inventory and inventory valuation are discussed in the next section.

2 While inventories are most often taken at retail value, many businesses value inventory at cost. For this reason, **stock turnover** is found by either of these formulas.

$$\text{Turnover at retail} = \frac{\text{Retail sales}}{\text{Average inventory at retail}}$$

$$\text{Turnover at cost} = \frac{\text{Cost of goods sold}}{\text{Average inventory at cost}}$$

3 Stock turnover may be identical by either method. The variation that often exists is caused by stolen merchandise (called *inventory shrinkage*) or merchandise which has been marked down or has become unsaleable. Normally, **turnover at retail** is slightly lower than **turnover at cost**. For this reason, many businesses prefer this more conservative figure.

EXAMPLE 3
Finding Stock Turnover at Retail

During a certain month, a feed store has sales of $32,032 and an average retail inventory of $9856. Find the stock turnover at retail.

SOLUTION

$$\text{Turnover at retail} = \frac{\text{Retail sales}}{\text{Average inventory at retail}} = \frac{\$32,032}{\$9856} = 3.25$$

On the average, the store turned over its entire inventory 3.25 times during the month. ■

EXAMPLE 4
Finding Stock Turnover at Cost

If the feed store in Example 3 used a markup of 40% on selling price and if the cost of goods sold was $19,396, find the stock turnover on cost.

SOLUTION Inventory at retail in the feed store was $9856. Since markup is 40% on selling price, the cost is 60% of the inventory.

$$C = 0.6 \times \$9856$$

$$C = \$5913.60$$

Inventory value at cost is $5913.60.

$$\text{Turnover at cost} = \frac{\text{Cost of goods sold}}{\text{Average inventory at cost}} = \frac{\$19,396}{\$5913.60} = 3.28 \text{ at cost (rounded)}.$$

The turnover on cost is 3.28. ■

NOTE In Example 4, the average inventory at cost needed to be calculated. To do this the average markup was used along with the cost of goods sold. Since the markup was 40% on selling price, the cost of goods sold was 60% of the selling price.

4 Stock turnover is useful for comparison purposes only. Many trade organizations publish such operating statistics to permit businesses to compare their operation with the industry as a whole. In addition to this, management will compare turnover from period to period and from department to department.

A fast stock turnover is usually given high priority by management. Some of the benefits are:

- capital invested in inventory is kept at a minimum. This allows additional funds to take advantage of special purchases and discounts;

- items in inventory are up to date, fresher, and are therefore less likely to be sold at a reduced price or loss;

- costly storage space and the other expenses of handling inventory can be minimized.

On the other hand, a high inventory turnover may cause problems which result in reducing profits:

- orders for smaller quantities of goods from wholesalers may result in losses of quantity discounts and additional processing, handling and bookkeeping expenses;

- fewer items limit customer selection, often resulting in fewer sales.

Both inventory selection and inventory turnover are very important management decisions, with much attention given to this part of the business.

10.2 Exercises

Find the average inventory in each of the following.

Date	Inventory Amount at Retail
1. April 1	$6752
April 30	$9670
2. January 1	$24,880
July 1	$32,750
December 31	$28,620
3. April 1	$17,020
May 1	$22,780
June 1	$19,218
4. January 31	$46,320
April 30	$37,240
July 31	$53,810
October 31	$58,700
January 31	$42,650

Date	Inventory Amount at Retail
5. January 1	$16,250
March 1	$20,780
May 1	$28,720
July 1	$24,630
September 1	$23,550
November 1	$34,800
December 31	$22,770
6. January 1	$75,200
April 1	$60,750
July 1	$42,620
October 1	$98,300
December 31	$78,400

Find the stock turnover at retail and at cost in each of the following. Round to the nearest hundredth.

	Average Inventory at Cost	Average Inventory at Retail	Cost of Goods	Retail Sales
7.	$8915	$17,695	$25,197	$49,725
8.	$28,555	$36,410	$195,316	$247,545
9.	$22,390	$32,730	$178,687	$259,876
10.	$30,280	$48,160	$134,816	$212,386
11.	$52,800	$85,320	$541,200	$874,530
12.	$72,120	$138,460	$259,123	$487,379
13.	$180,600	$256,700	$846,336	$1,196,222
14.	$205,790	$390,300	$952,834	$1,779,768

15. A friend who is also a business associate would like to determine average inventory for a full year. Describe to your friend how this could be done. (See Objective 1.)

16. Which departments in a grocery store do you think have the highest turnover? Which ones have the lowest turnover?

Solve each of the following word problems. Round stock turnover to the nearest hundredth.

17. Computer Electronics took inventory at the first of each month for the full year. The sum of these inventories was $518,722. On December 31, inventory was again taken and amounted to $184,318. Find the average inventory for the year.

18. Inventory at retail at Dial One Air Conditioning was $4618 on April 1, $5230 on May 1, and $3950 on June 1. Find the average inventory.

19. Coast Printing has an average inventory at cost of $12,300 and cost of goods sold for the same period is $68,142. Find the stock turnover at cost.

20. The Jumbo Market has an average canned fruit inventory of $2320 at retail. Sales of canned fruit for the year were $98,669. Find the stock turnover at retail.

21. Capital Plating had an average inventory of $27,250 at retail. The cost of goods sold for the year was $103,400 and a markup of 40% on selling price was used. What was the turnover at cost?

22. The Associated Divers uses a markup of 30% on selling price. If their average inventory is $15,650 at retail and the cost of goods sold is $53,023, find the stock turnover at cost.

23. The cost of goods sold at a building supply company was $1,048,320. The following inventories were taken at cost: $105,390, $122,750, and $110,430. Find the stock turnover at cost.

24. Inventory at Harbortown Hobby and Sports was taken at retail value four times and found to be at $53,820, $49,510, $60,820, and $56,380. Sales during the same period were $252,077. Find the stock turnover at retail.

25. The following inventories were taken at retail: $56,280, $76,420, $43,380, $62,400, and $58,900. If this business uses a 40% markup on cost and the cost of goods sold during this period was $154,800, find the turnover at cost.

26. Inventory at Clinton Floor Covering was taken at cost four times and found to be $98,500, $135,820, $107,420, and $124,300. If the company uses a markup of 25% on retail and the sales for this period were $382,400, find the inventory turnover at retail.

10.3 Valuation of Inventory

OBJECTIVES

1 Define perpetual inventory.

2 Read uniform product codes (UPC).

3 Use specific identification to value inventory.

4 Use the weighted average method to value inventory.

5 Use the FIFO method to value inventory.

6 Use the LIFO method to value inventory.

7 Use the gross profit method to estimate inventory.

8 Use the retail method to estimate inventory.

1   Placing a value on the merchandise that a firm has in stock is called **inventory valuation**. It is not always easy to place this value on each of the items in inventory. Many large companies keep a **perpetual inventory** by using a computer. As new items are received, the quantity, size, and cost of each are placed in the computer. Sales clerks enter product codes into the cash register (or uniform product codes are entered automatically with an optical scanner), and the computer processes the information.

2   **Uniform product codes (UPC)** are the black and white stripes known as "bar codes" with numbers printed below them that appear on many items sold in stores. Each product and product size is assigned its own code number. These UPCs are a great help in keeping track of inventory.

A portion of a Cracker Jack box is reproduced here to show its product code. The UPC number on the wrapper is 41257 23255. The check-out clerk in a retail store passes the coded lines over an optical scanner. The numbers are picked up by a computer, which recognizes the product by its code. The computer tells the cash register the price of the item. After all the items being purchased have passed over the scanner, the customer receives a detailed cash register receipt that gives a description of each item, the price of each item, and a total purchase price. This system provides more accurate inventory control and lower labor costs for the store.

Most businesses take a **physical inventory** (an actual count of each item in stock at a given time) at regular intervals. For example, inventory may be taken monthly, quarterly, semiannually, or just once a year. An inventory taken at regular time intervals is called a **periodic inventory**.

There are four major methods used for **inventory valuation**.

3 The **specific identification method** of inventory valuation is useful where items are easily identified and costs do not fluctuate. If the number of items is large and the exact cost of each unit is not known, then it may be difficult or impossible to use this method of inventory. With specific identification, each item is cost-coded, either with numerals or a letter code. The cost may be included in a group of numbers written on the item or in a 10-letter code (where each letter is different).

For example, if a store uses the code SMALPROFIT, or

$$1 \quad 2 \quad 3 \quad 4 \quad 5 \quad 6 \quad 7 \quad 8 \quad 9 \quad 0$$

$$S \quad M \quad A \quad L \quad P \quad R \quad O \quad F \quad I \quad T,$$

then an item bearing the cost code ARF would have a cost of

$$\begin{array}{ccc} A & R & F \\ \downarrow & \downarrow & \downarrow \\ 3 & 6 & 8, \end{array}$$

or $3.68. An item coded PMITT would have a cost of $529.00.

EXAMPLE 1
Finding the Value of Inventory

A camping outfitter has four camp trailers in stock. Cost codes indicate the following costs to the store.

Model A	$1628
Model B	$1983
Model C	$2297
Model D	$2952

Find the value of the camp trailer inventory.

SOLUTION   The value of the inventory is found by adding the costs of the four camp trailers.

Model A	$1628
Model B	1983
Model C	2297
Model D	+ 2952
	$8860 total value of inventory ∎

4 Since the cost of many items changes over time, there may be several of the same items that were purchased at different costs. Because of this variation, there are several common methods used to value an inventory. One method, the **weighted average method**, values the items in an inventory at the average cost of buying them.

EXAMPLE 2
Using Weighted Average (Average Cost) Inventory Valuation

Suppose Shasta Office Products made the following purchases of the same model of file cabinets during the year.

January	50 file cabinets at $80 each
March	60 file cabinets at $85 each
July	40 file cabinets at $75 each
October	100 file cabinets at $90 each

At the end of the year there are 125 file cabinets in inventory. Use the weighted average method to find the inventory value.

SOLUTION Find the average cost of each file cabinet by finding the total cost of all the file cabinets and dividing by the number purchased. (This average, the weighted average, will be discussed in more detail in Section 19.2.)

January	$50 \times \$80 =$	$4000
March	$60 \times \$85 =$	$5100
July	$40 \times \$75 =$	$3000
October	$100 \times \$90 =$	$9000
Total	250	$21,100

Since 250 file cabinets were purchased for a total cost of $21,100, the average cost of each is found by dividing.

$$\frac{\$21,100}{250} = \$84.40 \qquad \text{average cost}$$

The inventory value of the remaining 125 file cabinets is $\$84.40 \times 125 = \$10,550$. So, using the weighted average method gives an inventory value of $10,550. ∎

Calculator Approach to Example 2

First, find the total number of file cabinets.

$$50 \boxed{+} 60 \boxed{+} 40 \boxed{+} 100 \boxed{=} 250$$

Write down this total for later use. Next, find the total cost of all the file cabinets, using the $\boxed{M+}$ key.

$$50 \boxed{\times} 80 \boxed{M+} 60 \boxed{\times} 85 \boxed{M+} 40 \boxed{\times} 75 \boxed{M+} 100 \boxed{\times} 90 \boxed{M+}$$

Then, divide by the total number of file cabinets to find the average cost and finally multiply by the remaining number in inventory.

$$\boxed{MR} \boxed{\div} 250 \boxed{\times} 125 \boxed{=} 10,550$$

---

5 The **first-in, first-out (FIFO) method** of inventory valuation assumes a natural flow of goods through the inventory: the first goods to arrive are the first goods to be sold, so, the last items purchased are the items remaining in inventory.

EXAMPLE 3
Using FIFO
Inventory Valuation

Use the FIFO method to value the inventory of Shasta Office Products in Example 2.

SOLUTION With the FIFO method, the 125 remaining file cabinets are assumed to be made up of the 100 file cabinets purchased in October and $25(125 - 100 = 25)$ file cabinets from the previous purchase in July. The value of the inventory would be found as follows.

October	100 file cabinets at $90 =	$9000 (value of last 100)
July	25 file cabinets at $75 =	$1875 (value of previous 25)
	125 file cabinets	$10,875

The value of the file cabinet inventory is $10,875 using the FIFO method. ∎

6 The **last-in, first-out (LIFO) method** of inventory valuation also assumes a flow of goods through the inventory that is just the opposite of the FIFO method. With LIFO, the goods remaining in inventory are the first goods purchased.

EXAMPLE 4
Using LIFO
Inventory Valuation

Use the LIFO method to value the inventory of Shasta Office Products in Example 2.

SOLUTION The January and March purchases came to 110 file cabinets, so the cost of 15 more $(125 - 110 = 15)$ file cabinets from the July purchase is needed.

January	50 file cabinets at $80 =	$4000 (value of first 50)
March	60 file cabinets at $85 =	$5100 (value of next 60)
July	15 file cabinets at $75 =	$1125 (value of last 15)
	125 file cabinets	$10,225

The value of the file cabinet inventory is $10,225 using the LIFO method. With LIFO, the inventory of 125 file cabinets is assumed to come from the first items purchased.

Depending on the method of valuing inventories that is used, Shasta Office Products may show the inventory value of the 125 file cabinets as follows.

Average cost method	$10,550
FIFO	$10,875
LIFO	$10,225

The preferred inventory valuation method would be determined by Shasta Office Products, perhaps on the advice of an accountant. ∎

NOTE Accepted accounting practice insists that the method used to evaluate inventory be stated on the company financial statements.

The large quantities and varied types of items that are often in inventory make it time-consuming and expensive to take an actual physical inventory. Where this is the case, a physical inventory may be taken only once or twice a year. However, the need to monitor the performance of the business throughout the year is extremely important. To do this, methods of approximating inventory value have been developed. Two common methods for doing this are the *gross profit method* and the *retail method*.

7 An estimate of inventory using the **gross profit method** is found as follows.

> Beginning inventory (at cost)
> + Purchase (at cost)
> ———————————————
> Merchandise available for sale (at cost)
> − Cost of goods sold
> ———————————————
> Ending inventory (at cost)

The beginning inventory and amount of purchases are taken from company records and the cost of goods sold is normally determined by applying the rate of markup to the amount of net sales.

EXAMPLE 5

Estimating Inventory Value Using the Gross Profit Method

Inventory on June 30 was $242,000. During the next 3 months, the company had purchases of $425,000 and net sales of $528,000. Use the gross profit method to estimate the value of the inventory on September 30 if the company uses a markup of 25% on selling price.

SOLUTION   First, find the cost of goods sold. Since markup is 25% of selling price, find cost.

$$C + M = S$$

$$C + 0.25S = S$$

$$C + 0.25S - 0.25S = S - 0.25S$$

$$C = S - 0.25S$$

$$C = 0.75S$$

$$C = 0.75 \times \$528,000 = \$396,000$$

The cost of goods sold is $396,000. Now use the gross profit method.

$242,000	beginning inventory (June 30)
+ 425,000	purchases
$667,000	merchandise available for sale
− 396,000	cost of good sold
$271,000	ending inventory (September 30)

The estimated value of the inventory on September 30 is $271,000. ∎

8 The **retail method** of estimating inventory requires that a business keep records of all purchases at both cost and retail prices. The format for estimating inventory value at retail is the same as that used in estimating inventory using the gross profit method. The difference however, is that all amounts used are at retail. Inventory at retail is estimated as follows.

Beginning inventory (at retail)
+ Purchases (at retail)
Merchandise available for sale (at retail)
− Net sales
Ending inventory (at retail)

Notice that net sales are used in this method instead of cost of goods sold. Also, ending inventory value at retail must now be changed to an estimated value at cost. This is done by multiplying the ending inventory value at retail by a ratio determined by comparing the merchandise available for sale at cost to the merchandise available for sale at retail.

EXAMPLE 6
Estimating Inventory Value Using the Retail Method

At one store, inventory on March 31 was valued at $9000 at cost and $15,000 at retail. During the next 3 months, the company made purchases of $36,000 at cost, or $60,000 at retail, and had total sales of $54,000. Use the retail method to estimate the value of inventory at cost on June 30.

SOLUTION

At Cost	*At Retail*	
$9,000	$15,000	beginning inventory
+ 36,000	+ 60,000	purchases
$45,000	$75,000	merchandise available for sale
	− 54,000	net sales
	$21,000	June 30 inventory (at retail)

Now find the ratio of merchandise available for sale at cost to merchandise available for sale at retail.

$$\frac{\$45,000}{\$75,000} \quad \text{merchandise available for sale at cost} \atop \text{merchandise available for sale at retail}$$

Finally, the estimated inventory value at cost on June 30 is found by multiplying inventory at retail on June 30 by this ratio.

$$\$21,000 \times \frac{45,000}{75,000} = \$12,600 \text{ June 30 inventory (at cost)}$$

The retail method of estimating inventory value assumes that the ratio of the merchandise available for sale at cost to the merchandise available for sale at retail is the same as the ratio of the ending inventory at cost to ending inventory at retail. Both the gross profit method and the retail method of estimating inventories must be updated from time to time with physical inventories to assure accurate record keeping. ∎

10.3 Exercises

Find the inventory value in each of the following using the specific identification method.

Description	Cost
1. good	$178
better	$158
best	$198
3. small	$118
medium	$295
large	$306

Description	Cost
2. economy	$58
standard	$68
luxury	$96
deluxe	$122
4. incomplete	$450
cheap	$575
improved	$690
tolerable	$925

Find the inventory values using (a) the weighted average method, (b) the FIFO method, and (c) the LIFO method for each of the following. Round to the nearest dollar.

Purchases		Now in Inventory
5. March	20 units at $5.20	
May	30 units at $5.50	
July	25 units at $5.30	30 units
6. April	100 units at $36.30	
October	150 units at $39.60	
December	200 units at $43.50	210 units
7. January	50 units at $30.50	
March	70 units at $31.50	
June	30 units at $33.25	
August	40 units at $30.75	75 units
8. February	700 units at $1.25	
May	400 units at $1.75	
August	500 units at $2.25	
October	600 units at $3.00	720 units

Solve each of the following word problems. Round to the nearest dollar.

9.   Sentry Safe Company had the following home safes in stock.

Serial Number	Cost
380612	$190
793562	$129
618751	$259
245532	$678
112079	$351

Find the inventory value using the specific identification method.

10. A manufacturer of gasoline power generators had the following generators in stock.

Model Number	Cost
K335	$798
322 AC	$618
312	$430
342AC	$415
21100	$390

Use the specific identification method to find the inventory value.

11. A law office made the following purchases of envelopes.

March	24 units at $1.50
June	40 units at $1.35
August	48 units at $1.25
November	18 units at $1.60

Inventory at the end of the year shows that 35 units remain. (a) Find the inventory value using the weighted average method. (b) Find the inventory value using the FIFO method. (c) Find the inventory value using the LIFO method.

12. The Iron Horse had purchases of model railroad track during the year as follows.

January	400 sections at 16¢
April	300 sections at 20¢
July	200 sections at 25¢
September	900 sections at 15¢
October	400 sections at 20¢

At the end of the year they had 700 sections of track in stock. (a) Find the inventory value using the weighted average method. (b) Find the inventory value using the FIFO method. (c) Find the inventory value using the LIFO method.

13. B & B Appliance Repair made the following purchases of dishwasher pumps.

April	200 units at $3.10
July	250 units at $3.50
August	300 units at $4.25
October	280 units at $4.50

Inventory at the end of October shows that 320 units remain. (a) Find the inventory value using the weighted average method. (b) Find the inventory value using the FIFO method. (c) Find the inventory value using the LIFO method.

14. Purchases of square-dancing dresses by Dance World were as follows.

February	300 dresses at $7.20
May	400 dresses at $8.00
October	450 dresses at $8.10
November	350 dresses at $7.50

Inventory at the end of November shows that 530 dresses remain. (a) Find the inventory value using the weighted average method. (b) Find the inventory value using the FIFO method. (c) Find the inventory value using the LIFO method.

15. Central States Auto Wholesalers made the following purchases of antifreeze.

September	350 cases at $8.25
October	300 cases at $9.50
November	360 cases at $11.45
December	240 cases at $10.10

The January inventory found that there were 625 cases remaining. (a) Find the inventory value using the weighted average method. (b) Find the inventory value using the FIFO method. (c) Find the inventory value using the LIFO method.

16. Industrial Linen Supply made the following purchases of shop towels.

March	650 towels at $3.80
June	500 towels at $4.20
September	450 towels at $3.95
December	600 towels at $4.05

In January an inventory found that there were 775 towels remaining. (a) Find the inventory value using the weighted average method. (b) Find the inventory value using the FIFO method. (c) Find the inventory value using the LIFO method.

17. The inventory on December 31 at Weather-Tite Roofing was $68,000 at cost. During the next 3 months, the company made purchases of $74,000 (cost) and had net sales of $118,000. Use the gross profit method to estimate the value of the inventory at cost on March 31 if the company uses a markup of 35% on selling price.

18. Happy Toys has an inventory of $52,000 at cost on June 30. Purchases during the next 3 months were $68,000 (cost) and net sales were $126,000. If the company uses a 40% markup on selling price, use the gross profit method to estimate the value of the inventory at cost on September 30.

19. The September 30 inventory at Liverpool Piano Repair was $43,750 at cost and $62,500 at retail. Purchases during the next 3 months were $51,600 at cost, $73,800 at retail, and net sales were $92,500. Use the retail method to estimate the value of inventory at cost on December 31.

20. Uptown Sound had an inventory of $27,000 at cost and $45,000 at retail on March 31. During the next 3 months, they made purchases of $108,000 at cost, $180,000 at retail, and had net sales of $162,000. Use the retail method to estimate the value of inventory at cost on June 30.

21. In your opinion, what are the benefits to a merchant who is using uniform product codes (UPC)? (See Objective 2.)

22. Which of the three inventory valuation methods discussed in this section was most interesting to you? Explain how this method determines inventory value.

CHAPTER 10 QUICK REVIEW

TOPIC	APPROACH	EXAMPLE
10.1 Percent of markdown	Markdown is always a percent of the original price. Use the formula $$\frac{\text{Markdown}}{\text{percent}} = \frac{\text{Markdown amount}}{\text{Original price}}.$$	Original price, $76; markdown, $19. Find the percent of markdown. $$\frac{\text{Markdown}}{\text{percent}} = \frac{19}{76} = 0.25 = 25\%$$
10.1 Breakeven point	Add cost to operating expenses to find the breakeven point.	Cost, $54; operating expenses, $16. Find the breakeven point. $54 + $16 = $70 breakeven point
10.1 Operating loss	When the reduced price is below the breakeven point, subtract the reduced price from the breakeven point to find the operating loss.	Breakeven point, $70; reduced price, $58. Find the operating loss. $70 − $58 = $12 operating loss
10.1 Absolute loss (Gross loss)	When the reduced price is below cost, subtract the reduced price from the cost to find the absolute loss.	Cost, $54; reduced price, $48. Find the absolute loss. $54 − $48 = $6 absolute loss
10.2 Average inventory	Take inventory two or more times; add the totals and divide by the number of inventories to get the average.	Inventories: $22,635, $24,692, and $18,796. Find the average inventory. $$\frac{\$22,635 + \$24,692 + \$18,796}{3}$$ $$= \frac{\$66,123}{3} = \$22,041 \text{ average inventory}$$
10.2 Turnover at retail	Use the formula $$\text{Turnover} = \frac{\text{Retail sales}}{\text{Average inventory at retail}}.$$	Sales, $78,496; average inventory at retail, $18,076. Find turnover at retail. $$\frac{\$78,496}{\$18,076} = 4.34 \text{ at retail (rounded)}$$

TOPIC	APPROACH	EXAMPLE
10.2 Turnover at cost	Use the formula $$\text{Turnover} = \frac{\text{Cost of goods sold}}{\substack{\text{Average inventory} \\ \text{at cost}}}.$$	Cost of goods sold, $26,542; average inventory at cost, $6592. Find turnover at cost. $$\frac{\$26,542}{\$6592} = 4.03 \text{ at cost (rounded)}$$
10.3 Specific identification to value inventory	Cost code each item; add the costs to find total inventory.	Costs: item 1, $593; item 2, $614; item 3, $498. Find total value of inventory. $$\$593 + \$614 + \$498 = \$1705$$
10.3 Weighted average method of inventory valuation	This method values items in an inventory at the average cost of buying them.	Purchases of an item: 20 at $75; 15 at $80; 25 at $65; 18 at $70. Find the value of the 22 remaining in inventory. $$20 \times \$75 = \$1500$$ $$15 \times \$80 = \$1200$$ $$25 \times \$65 = \$1625$$ $$\underline{18 \times \$70 = \$1260}$$ Totals 78 $5585 $$\frac{\$5585}{78} = \$71.60 \text{ average cost}$$ $$\$71.60 \times 22 = \$1575.20$$
10.3 First-in, first-out (FIFO) method of inventory valuation.	First items in are first sold. Inventory is based on cost of last items purchased.	Purchases of an item: July 5, 25 items at $40; Aug. 7, 30 items at $35. Find the value of the 35 remaining in inventory. $$30 \times \$35 = \$1050 \quad \text{(value of last 30)}$$ $$\underline{5 \times \$40 = \ \ \$200} \quad \text{(value of previous 5)}$$ Totals 35 $1250 value of inventory

TOPIC	APPROACH	EXAMPLE
10.3 Last-in, first-out (LIFO) method of inventory valuation	The goods remaining in inventory are the first goods purchased.	Purchases of an item: Feb. 15, 48 items at $20 each; May 9, 40 items at $25 each. Find the value of the 55 remaining in inventory.

$$48 \times \$20 = \$960 \quad \text{(value of first 48)}$$

$$7 \times \$25 = \$175 \quad \text{(value of last 7)}$$

$$\text{Totals } 55 \qquad \$1135 \quad \text{value of inventory}$$

SUMMARY EXERCISE

McIntosh Pet Center purchased two dozen pet travel cages at a cost of $780. Operating expenses for the store are 25% of selling price while total markup on this type of product is 35% of selling price. Only 6 of the cages sell at the original price and the owner decides to markdown the remaining cages. The price is reduced 25% and 6 more cages sell. The remaining 12 cages are marked down 50% of the original selling price and are finally sold.

(a) Find the original selling price of each cage.

(b) Find the total of the selling prices of all the cages.

(c) Find the operating loss.

(d) Find the absolute loss.

CHAPTER 10 REVIEW EXERCISES

Find the missing quantities. Round rates to the nearest whole percent and money to the nearest cent. [10.1]

	Original Price	% Markdown	$ Markdown	Reduced Price
1.	$18.30	50%	————	————
2.	————	30%	————	$21
3.	————	40%	$4.32	————
4.	$1170	————	————	$760.50

Complete the following. If there is no operating loss or absolute loss, write none. *Use Figure 10.1 as a guide.* [10.1]

	Cost	Operating Expense	Breakeven Point	Reduced Price	Operating Loss	Absolute Loss
5.	$10	_____	$13.20	$8.80	_____	_____
6.	$15	$3.75	_____	$16.50	_____	_____
7.	$78	$22	_____	_____	$30	_____
8.	$5	$1.25	_____	$5.50	_____	_____

Find the average inventory in each of the following. [10.2]

	Date	Inventory Amount at Retail
9.	January 1	$16,446
	January 31	$19,234
11.	January 1	$77,159
	April 1	$67,305
	July 1	$80,664
	October 1	$95,229
	December 31	$61,702

	Date	Inventory Amount at Retail
10.	January 1	$112,014
	July 1	$144,762
	December 31	$126,816
12.	January 1	$36,502
	April 1	$27,331
	July 1	$28,709
	October 1	$32,153
	December 31	$39,604

Find the stock turnover at retail and at cost in each of the following. Round to the nearest hundredth. [10.2]

	Average Inventory at Cost	Average Inventory at Retail	Cost of Goods	Sales
13.	$35,660	$70,780	$100,788	$198,900
14.	$44,780	$65,460	$357,374	$519,752
15.	$90,300	$128,350	$423,168	$598,111
16.	$102,895	$195,150	$476,417	$889,884

Find the inventory value in each of the following using the specific identification method.
[10.2]

Description	Cost		Description	Cost
17. large	$175		**18.** good	$78
giant	$218		better	$110
colossal	$320		best	$163
19. economy	$795		**20.** fair	$1080
standard	$850		good	$1175
luxury	$915		very good	$1286
deluxe	$1080		excellent	$1428

Solve the following word problems.

21. At a sidewalk sale a 30-inch color television originally priced at $807 is marked down to $537. Find the percent of markdown on the original price. (Round to the nearest whole percent.) [10.1]

22. A portable telephone cost a retailer $56. The store's operating expenses are 30% of cost and net profit is 10% of cost. Find (a) the selling price of the portable telephone and (b) the maximum percent of markdown that may be given without taking an operating loss. (Round to the nearest whole percent.) [10.1]

23. Inventory at the Pro-Shop was $12,648 on January 1, $9724 on July 1, and $10,874 on December 31. Find the average inventory. [10.2]

24. Price Less Drug Store has an average inventory of $328,320 at cost. If the cost of goods sold for the year was $4,785,562, find the stock turnover at cost. (Round to the nearest hundredth.) [10.2]

25. A retailer had an average inventory at cost of $26,720.60 and an average markup of 32% on selling price during the last quarter. Sales during this period were $135,568. Find the stock turnover at retail. (Round to the nearest hundredth.) [10.3]

26. American River Raft Rentals made the following purchases of life jackets.

January	70 units at $12.50
March	40 units at $17.75
July	50 units at $22.50
October	60 units at $30.00

At the end of the year they had 72 units in stock. (a) Find the inventory value using the weighted average method. (b) Find the inventory value using the FIFO method. (c) Find the value of the inventory using the LIFO method. [10.3]

27. The inventory on December 31 at Modern Clothiers was $118,000 at cost. During the next 3 months, the company made purchases of $186,000 (cost) and had net sales of $378,000. Use the gross profit method to estimate the value of the inventory at cost on March 31 if the company uses a markup of 50% on selling price. [10.3]

28. Tap Plastics had an inventory of $54,000 at cost and $90,000 at retail on June 30. During the next 3 months, they made purchases of $216,000 at cost, $360,000 at retail, and had net sales of $324,000. Use the retail method to estimate the value of the inventory at cost on September 30. [10.3]

11

Simple Interest

Some of the oldest documents in existence—clay tablets going back almost 5000 years—involve the calculation of interest charges. **Interest**—a fee for borrowing money—is about as old as civilization itself. Today, interest rates fluctuate up and down. Prime rates (the interest rate charged to the largest and most secure corporations) of 6% and more are not unusual. Because of the cost of interest, it is very important that business people have a good understanding of interest and how it is calculated.

Two basic types of interest are in common use today: *simple interest* and *compound interest.* **Simple interest,** normally used for short-term loans, is interest computed only on the principal. **Compound interest** is interest computed on both principal and interest. This chapter discusses simple interest and Chapter 13 covers compound interest.

11.1 Basics of Simple Interest

OBJECTIVES

1 Find simple interest.

2 Find interest for less than a year.

3 Find principal if given rate and time.

4 Find rate if given principal and time.

5 Find time if given principal and rate.

Interest is the price paid for borrowing money. Interest rates are usually expressed as a percent of the amount borrowed. For example, in some states, Sears, Wards, and Penney's charge 18% interest per year on money owed to them. The amount borrowed is called the **principal.** The percent of interest charged is called the **rate of interest.** The number of years or fraction of a year for which the loan is made is called the **time.**

1 Simple interest, interest charged on the entire principal for the entire length of the loan, is found by the following formula, a modification of the basic percent formula.

> The *simple interest, I,* on a principal of *P* dollars at a rate of interest *R* percent per year for *T* years is given by
>
> $$I = PRT.$$
>
> The rate, *R*, is expressed as a decimal or fraction.

EXAMPLE 1
Finding Simple Interest

Find the simple interest on $4000 at 12% for $1\frac{1}{2}$ years.

SOLUTION   Use the formula $I = PRT$. Substitute $4000 for *P*, 0.12 (the decimal form of 12%) for *R*, and $1\frac{1}{2}$ for *T*.

$$I = PRT$$

$$I = \$4000 \times 0.12 \times 1\frac{1}{2}$$

$$I = \$720$$

The simple interest is $720. ■

NOTE Simple interest is usually used for short-term loans, such as those for less than a year. This makes it important to remember that in the formula for simple interest, time is expressed *in years* or *parts of years.*

2 Notice in the next example how 9 months is written as $\frac{9}{12}$ of a year before using the formula.

EXAMPLE 2
Finding Simple Interest for Less Than a Year

Find the interest of $960 for 9 months at 5%.

SOLUTION   Since there are 12 months in a year, 9 months is $\frac{9}{12}$ of a year. Find the interest by the formula $I = PRT$.

$$I = PRT$$

$$I = \$960 \times 0.05 \times \frac{9}{12}$$

Now use a calculator or cancel where possible.

$$I = \$36 ■$$

Calculator Approach to Example 2

Use the formula $I = PRT$ multiplying and dividing in a chain calculation to find the interest.

$$960 \boxed{\times} .05 \boxed{\times} 9 \boxed{\div} 12 \boxed{=} 36$$

3 Sometimes the amount of interest is known, but the principal, rate or time must be found. Do this with the following modifications of the formula for simple interest, $I = PRT$. Dividing both sides by RT gives the formula for P.

$$P = \frac{I}{RT}$$

Dividing both sides of $I = PRT$ by PT gives the formula for R.

$$R = \frac{I}{PT}$$

And dividing both sides of $I = PRT$ by PR gives the formula for T.

$$T = \frac{I}{PR}$$

CAUTION Don't forget, for an annual rate the time is always *in years*.

EXAMPLE 3
Finding the Principal

Find the principal that would produce interest of $110 in 6 months at a 4% rate of interest.

SOLUTION As discussed, find the formula for principal by dividing both sides of $I = PRT$ by RT.

$$P = \frac{I}{RT}$$

Now substitute $110 for I, 0.04 for R, and $\frac{6}{12}$ for T (since 6 months is $\frac{6}{12}$ of a year).

$$P = \frac{\$100}{0.04 \times \frac{6}{12}}$$

Simplify the denominator completely as a first step.

$$P = \frac{\$110}{0.04 \times 0.5}$$

$$P = \frac{\$110}{0.02}$$

$$P = \$5500$$

The principal is $5500. ∎

4 The next example shows how to find the interest rate if the principal and time are given.

EXAMPLE 4
Finding the Rate

A loan of $9000 for 9 months had an interest charge of $540. Find the rate.

SOLUTION Divide both sides of $I = PRT$ by PT to get

$$R = \frac{I}{PT}.$$

Then substitute $540 for I, $9000 for P, and $\frac{9}{12}$ for T.

$$R = \frac{\$540}{\$9000 \times \frac{9}{12}}$$

$$R = \frac{\$540}{\$9000 \times 0.75}$$

$$R = \frac{\$540}{\$6750}$$

$$R = 0.08$$

The rate is 8%. ■

Calculator Approach to Example 4

First calculate the denominator and place it in memory.

9000 $\boxed{\times}$ 9 $\boxed{\div}$ 12 $\boxed{\text{M+}}$ 6750

Now enter the numerator and divide by the stored value.

540 $\boxed{\div}$ $\boxed{\text{MR}}$ $\boxed{=}$ 0.08

---

5 The simple interest formula can also be used to find the time of a loan.

EXAMPLE 5

Finding the Time

Find the time in months needed for a loan of $4800 at 10% to produce $280 in interest.

SOLUTION Use $I = PRT$ and divide both sides by PR to get

$$T \text{ (in years)} = \frac{I}{PR}.$$

We included "(in years)" to emphasize this important point—time is measured in years. Now substitute $280 for I, $4800 for P, and 0.10 for R.

$$T \text{ (in years)} = \frac{\$280}{\$4800 \times 0.10}$$

$$T \text{ (in years)} = \frac{\$280}{\$480}$$

Writing $\frac{\$280}{\$480}$ in lowest terms gives

$$T \text{ (in years)} = \frac{7}{12} \text{ year,}$$

or 7 months. ■

NOTE In all the examples of this section the time has been expressed in years or months. Section 11.2 will deal with interest problems in which the time is expressed in days.

11.1 Exercises

Find the simple interest for each of the following. Round to the nearest cent.

1. $1800 at 8% for 1 year
2. $2400 at 8% for 2 years
3. $900 at 14% for $1\frac{1}{2}$ years
4. $600 at 10% for $1\frac{1}{4}$ years
5. $278 at 7% for 6 months
6. $324 at 12% for 9 months
7. $412 at 9% for 8 months
8. $7630 at 6% for 10 months
9. $16,500 at 5% for 3 months
10. $19,000 at 12% for 7 months
11. $5200 at $11\frac{3}{4}$% for 5 months
12. $7500 at $12\frac{1}{2}$% for 7 months
13. $9874 at $7\frac{1}{8}$% for 11 months
14. $10,745 at $4\frac{5}{8}$% for 9 months
15. $74,986.15 at 12.23% for 5 months
16. $39,072.76 at 11.23% for 7 months

Complete this chart. Round money to the nearest cent, rate to the nearest tenth of a percent, and time to the nearest month.

	Principal	Interest	Rate	Time in Months
17.	$5000	_____	9%	8
18.	$7000	_____	11%	9
19.	_____	$162.50	8%	6
20.	_____	$84	10%	7
21.	$6300	$294	_____	8
22.	$3500	$157.50	_____	9
23.	$10,000	$700	12%	_____
24.	$18,000	$1485	9%	_____

Solve each word problem. Round money to the nearest cent, rate to the nearest tenth of a percent, and time to the nearest month.

25. A loan produces interest of $225 in 6 months at 9%. Find the principal.
26. Suppose the interest due on a 3 month, 12% loan is $1350. Find the principal.
27. Find the principal if $245 in interest is due after 10 months at 7%.
28. What amount of principal produces $55 in interest after 1 month at 11%?
29. What time (in months) is necessary for a principal of $840 to produce $77 in interest at 10%?
30. How many months are necessary for $4800 to produce $44 in interest at 11%?
31. Find the rate if a principal of $1890 produces $138.60 in interest after 11 months.

32. What rate would produce interest of $260 from a principal of $16,000 after 3 months?

33. How many years would be needed for a $5000 loan to produce $5000 in interest at 5%?

34. In Exercise 33, how many years would be needed at 8%?

35. Doug Minder misses a payment on a loan. The payment is 4 months late. The penalty is 9% simple interest on a balance of $7600. Find the penalty.

36. Trisha Martin bought a new car. To pay for the car, which was priced at $12,250, she gave $4000 as a down payment and agreed to pay the balance in 5 months. Find the amount of interest charged if the interest rate is $10\frac{1}{4}$%.

37. The Green Care Company needs to borrow $7000 to buy new lawn mowers. The firm wants to pay no more than $560 in interest. If the interest rate is 12%, what is the longest time for which the money may be borrowed?

38. The Mall Frame Shop wants to borrow $9300 to remodel the front of the store. The least expensive interest rate they can find is 14%. Find the longest time for which the money may be borrowed if the firm can pay only $1193.50 in interest.

39. Sam Casio deposits $5400 in a savings account at the Friendly Savings and Loan Bank. When he withdraws his money 8 months later, he receives a check for $5544. What rate of interest does the bank pay?

40. Dorothy Duerr invested $7800 in an account that pays dividends monthly, based on simple interest. If Duerr has received a total of $276.25 over the past ten months what rate of interest does the account pay?

41. A $2000 loan was made for 3 months at 7% simple interest. A student calculates the interest due on the loan as follows:

$$I = \$2000 \times 0.07 \times 3 = \$420.$$

Is this correct? If not, explain why not and state the correct answer. (See Objective 1.)

42. Explain the difference between simple interest and compound interest.

11.2 Simple Interest For a Given Number of Days

OBJECTIVES

1 Find the number of days from one date to another using a table.

2 Find the number of days from one date to another using the actual number of days.

3 Find exact and ordinary interest.

The previous section showed how to find simple interest for loans of a given number of months or years. In this section, loans for a given number of *days* are discussed. In business, it is common for loans to be for a given number of days, such as "due in 90 days," or else to be due at some fixed date in the future, such as "due on April 17."

1 When dealing with days, there are two ways to find the number of days from one date to another. One way is by the use of Table 11.1. This table assigns a number to each day of the year. For example, the number for June 11 is found by locating 11 at the left, and June across the top. You should find that June 11 is day 162. Also, December 29 is day 363. The number of days from June 11 to December 29 is found by subtracting.

$$\begin{array}{rl} \text{December 29 is day} & 363 \\ \text{June 11 is day} & -\,162 \qquad \text{Subtract.} \\ \hline & 201 \end{array}$$

There are 201 days from June 11 to December 29. (Throughout this book, ignore leap years unless otherwise stated.)

TABLE 11.1   The Number of Each of the Days of the Year
(Add 1 to each date after February 29 for a leap year)

Day of Month	Jan.	Feb.	March	April	May	June	July	Aug.	Sept.	Oct.	Nov.	Dec.	Day of Month
1	1	32	60	91	121	152	182	213	244	274	305	335	1
2	2	33	61	92	122	153	183	214	245	275	306	336	2
3	3	34	62	93	123	154	184	215	246	276	307	337	3
4	4	35	63	94	124	155	185	216	247	277	308	338	4
5	5	36	64	95	125	156	186	217	248	278	309	339	5
6	6	37	65	96	126	157	187	218	249	279	310	340	6
7	7	38	66	97	127	158	188	219	250	280	311	341	7
8	8	39	67	98	128	159	189	220	251	281	312	342	8
9	9	40	68	99	129	160	190	221	252	282	313	343	9
10	10	41	69	100	130	161	191	222	253	283	314	344	10
11	11	42	70	101	131	162	192	223	254	284	315	345	11
12	12	43	71	102	132	163	193	224	255	285	316	346	12
13	13	44	72	103	133	164	194	225	256	286	317	347	13
14	14	45	73	104	134	165	195	226	257	287	318	348	14
15	15	46	74	105	135	166	196	227	258	288	319	349	15
16	16	47	75	106	136	167	197	228	259	289	320	350	16
17	17	48	76	107	137	168	198	229	260	290	321	351	17
18	18	49	77	108	138	169	199	230	261	291	322	352	18
19	19	50	78	109	139	170	200	231	262	292	323	353	19
20	20	51	79	110	140	171	201	232	263	293	324	354	20
21	21	52	80	111	141	172	202	233	264	294	325	355	21
22	22	53	81	112	142	173	203	234	265	295	326	356	22
23	23	54	82	113	143	174	204	235	266	296	327	357	23
24	24	55	83	114	144	175	205	236	267	297	328	358	24
25	25	56	84	115	145	176	206	237	268	298	329	359	25
26	26	57	85	116	146	177	207	238	269	299	330	360	26
27	27	58	86	117	147	178	208	239	270	300	331	361	27
28	28	59	87	118	148	179	209	240	271	301	332	362	28
29	29		88	119	149	180	210	241	272	302	333	363	29
30	30		89	120	150	181	211	242	273	303	334	364	30
31	31		90		151		212	243		304		365	31

EXAMPLE 1

Finding the Number
of Days In a Loan
Using a Table

Find the number of days from (a) February 24 to June 24 and (b) November 8 to March 17.

SOLUTION

(a)   February 24 is day 55, and June 24 is day 175.

$$
\begin{array}{lr}
\text{June 24 is day} & 175 \\
\text{February 24 is day} & -\ 55 \\ \hline
& 120
\end{array}
$$

There are 120 days from February 24 to June 24.

(b)   Since November 8 is in one year, and March 17 is in the next year, proceed as follows. First, find the number of days from November 8 to the end of the year.

$$
\begin{array}{lr}
\text{last day of the year is number} & 365 \\
\text{November 8 is day} & -\ 312 \\ \hline
& 53
\end{array}
$$

There are 53 days from November 8 to the end of the year.

Then, find the number of days from the beginning of the next year to March 17. From the chart, March 17 is the 76th day of the year. Add to get the *total* number of days.

$$
\begin{array}{lr}
\text{November 8 to end of year} & 53 \\
\text{first of year to March 17} & +\ 76 \\ \hline
& 129
\end{array}
$$

There are 129 days from November 8 to March 17.   ■

NOTE Using this method, you are not counting the day the loan was made, but you are counting the day the money was returned as a full day.

2   An alternate way of finding the number of days, useful when Table 11.1 is not available, is to use the actual number of days in each month, as shown in Table 11.2.

TABLE 11.2   The Number of Days in Each Month

31 Days		30 Days	28 Days
January	August	April	February
March	October	June	(29 days in leap year)
May	December	September	
July		November	

EXAMPLE 2

*Finding the Number
of Days in a Loan
Using Actual Days*

Find the number of days from (a) March 6 to June 17 and (b) November 2 to February 25.

SOLUTION

(a)   Since March has 31 days, there are $31 - 6 = 25$ days left in March, then 30 days in April, 31 in May, and an additional 17 days in June for a total of

25	remaining in March
30	April
31	May
+ 17	June
103	

days from March 6 to June 17.

(b)   Add.

28	remaining in November
31	December
31	January
+ 25	February
115	

There are 115 days from November 2 to February 25. ■

EXAMPLE 3

*Finding Specific
Dates*

Find the date that is 90 days from (a) March 25 and (b) November 7.

SOLUTION

(a)   From the chart, March 25 is day 84. Add 90.

March 25 is day	84
	+ 90 days
	174

As shown in Table 11.1, day 174 is June 23, so 90 days from March 25 is June 23. Alternatively, work as follows.

March 25 to end of month	6
April	30
May	+ 31
	67

Since $90 - 67 = 23$, an additional 23 days in June are needed, giving June 23.

(b)   November 7 is day 311. Add 90 days to get

$$\begin{array}{r} 311 \\ + 90 \\ \hline 401. \end{array}$$

since there are only 365 days in a year, subtract 365.

$$\begin{array}{r} 401 \\ -\ 365 \\ \hline 36 \end{array}$$ day of the following year

Day 36 of the following year is February 5, so that 90 days from November 7 is February 5 of the following year. ∎

In the formula for simple interest, time is always measured in years or parts of years. In the examples of the previous section, time was in months, with T in the formula $I = PRT$ written as

$$T = \frac{\text{Given number of months}}{12}.$$

3 Things are not so simple when the loan is given in days—there are two common methods for calculating simple interest for a given number of days: **exact interest,** and **ordinary** or **banker's interest.**

In the formula $I = PRT$, the fraction for time is found as follows.

Exact interest	$T = \dfrac{\text{Exact number of days in the loan}}{365}$
Ordinary or banker's interest	$T = \dfrac{\text{Exact number of days in the loan}}{360}$

Government agencies and the Federal Reserve Bank use exact interest, as do many credit unions, while most banks and other financial institutions use ordinary interest. Ordinary interest may have been used originally because it is easier to calculate than exact interest. With the modern use of calculators and computers, however, ordinary interest is probably used today out of tradition and because it produces more interest, as shown in the next example.

EXAMPLE 4
Finding Exact and Ordinary Interest

A loan of $12,000 is for 175 days at 9%. Find the interest on the loan, using (a) exact interest and (b) ordinary interest.

SOLUTION

(a) With exact interest, 175 days is assumed to be $\frac{175}{365}$ of a year. Find the interest with the formula $I = PRT$, with $P = \$12,000, R = 0.09,$ and $T = \frac{175}{365}$.

$$I = PRT$$

$$I = \$12,000 \times 0.09 \times \frac{175}{365}$$

$$I = \$517.81$$

(Throughout our work with interest, round to the nearest cent unless otherwise specified.)

(b) For ordinary interest, 175 days is assumed to be $\frac{175}{360}$ of a year. Use the same formula and numbers as in part (a), except that $T = \frac{175}{360}$.

$$I = PRT$$

$$I = \$12,000 \times 0.09 \times \frac{175}{360}$$

$$I = \$525$$

The amount of ordinary interest is larger than the amount of exact interest; ordinary interest is

$$\$525 - \$517.81 = \$7.19$$

more than exact interest. ∎

The next examples review the work done earlier, with days instead of months used in the time fraction.

With either exact interest or ordinary interest, use the exact number of days of the loan as the numerator when finding T, and either 365 or 360, as specified, as the denominator. See the next example.

EXAMPLE 5

Finding the Exact and Ordinary Interest

A loan of \$17,650 is made on May 12. The loan, at an interest rate of 13.5%, is due on August 27. Find the interest on the loan using (a) exact interest and (b) ordinary interest.

SOLUTION   Using Table 11.1, or calculating from the number of days in each month, there are 107 days from May 12 to August 27.

(a) The exact interest is found from $I = PRT$ with $P = \$17,650$, $R = 0.135$, and $T = \frac{107}{365}$ (remember to use 365 as denominator with exact interest).

$$I = PRT$$

$$I = \$17,650 \times 0.135 \times \frac{107}{365}$$

$$I = \$698.50$$

(b) For ordinary interest, use the same formula and values, except that $T = \frac{107}{360}$.

$$I = PRT$$

$$I = \$17,650 \times 0.135 \times \frac{107}{360}$$

$$I = \$708.21$$

In this example, the ordinary interest is $\$708.21 - \$698.50 = \$9.71$ more than the exact interest. ∎

The method for forming the *time fraction* used for *T* in the formula $I = PRT$ is summarized as follows.

The *numerator* is the *exact number* of days of the loan.

The *denominator* is one of the following:
  exact interest assumes 365 days in a year and uses 365 as denominator.
  ordinary, or *banker's, interest* assumes 360 days in a year and uses 360 as denominator.

NOTE Throughout the balance of this book, assume ordinary, or banker's, interest unless stated otherwise.

11.2 Exercises

Find the exact number of days from the first date to the second. (In Exercises 5–6, assume that the second month given is in the following year.)

1. May 15 to December 15

2. April 14 to July 11

3. August 31 to November 10

4. October 7 to December 25

5. September 2 to March 17

6. July 24 to March 30

Find the date that is the indicated number of days from the given date.

7. 60 days from June 12

8. 90 days from September 19

9. 150 days from February 28

10. 120 days from May 30

11. 45 days from December 29

12. 90 days from March 30

Find the ordinary interest for each of the following. Round to the nearest cent.

13. $8500 at 7% for 50 days

14. $9720 at 10% for 60 days

15. $2580 at 11% for 90 days

16. $7285 at 9% for 240 days

17. $9843 at $12\frac{1}{4}$% for 220 days

18. $12,502 at $7\frac{1}{8}$% for 270 days

19. A loan of $1250 at 11% made on May 9 and due August 25

20. A loan of $680.40 at 12% made on June 20 and due December 26

21. A loan of $1520 at 10% made on February 27 and due August 5

22. A loan of $3600 at 11% made on December 2 and due February 20

Find the exact interest for each of the following. Round to the nearest cent.

23. $1000 at 8% for 73 days

24. $1800 at 9% for 82 days

25. $4680 at 10% for 146 days

26. $5810 at 11% for 219 days

27. $11,684 at $11\frac{1}{4}$% for 158 days

28. $40,968 at $12\frac{3}{4}$% for 204 days

29. A loan of $6500 at 7% made on July 12 and due on October 12

30. A loan of $8120 at 9% made on January 30 and due May 20

31. A loan of $2050 at 12% made on June 24 and due November 17

32. A loan of $14,000 at 8% made on August 12 and due March 19 of the next year

33. Explain the difference between exact and ordinary interest. (See Objective 3.)

34. A loan is made on May 15 and due on November 15. In calculating interest, would you use 6 months as the value for time or would you use 184 days (the exact number of days from May 15 to November 15)? Justify your answer.

Solve each of the following word problems using exact interest. Round to the nearest cent.

35. Oscar Torres' property tax is due April 10. He doesn't pay until June 22. The county adds a penalty of 11% simple interest on his unpaid tax of $946.50. Find the penalty.

36. Bella Steinem misses an income tax payment. The payment was due June 15 and paid September 7. The penalty is 14% simple interest on the unpaid tax of $4600. Find the penalty.

Work each word problem using ordinary interest.

37. Ann Land borrows $6500 on January 15 and agrees to repay the loan on May 30 at $9\frac{3}{4}$% interest. Find the interest she must pay.

38. On May 18, the Wilson Dude Ranch bought a supply of cowboy outfits for $11,270. The ranch agreed to pay for them on August 30, with $10\frac{1}{2}$% interest. Find the interest owed.

39. Lisa Brink opened a security service. To pay for the building the firm uses, Brink borrowed $134,500 at the bank on March 3, agreeing to repay the money on December 12, at $11\frac{3}{8}$% interest. Find the interest she must pay.

40. Laurie Thomas bought a new car. To pay for the car, she gave $7000 as a down payment, and agreed to pay an additional $6950 in 115 days. Find the interest owed, if the rate is $11\frac{3}{4}$%.

In Exercises 41–44 find the (a) exact interest and (b) ordinary interest for each of the following. Then (c) find the amount by which the ordinary interest is larger.

41. $72,000 at 11% for 100 days

42. $61,000 at 12% for 150 days

43. $108,952 at $9\frac{5}{8}$% for 225 days

44. $372,812 at $8\frac{1}{4}$% for 294 days

Work each of the following word problems.

45. Western Sound needs to borrow $160,000 to finance an inventory of cassette players for Christmas sales. The loan will be for 95 days at $9\frac{5}{8}$%. How much more would the interest be at a bank using ordinary interest than at one using exact interest?

46. Life Foods wants to borrow $120,000 to take advantage of a manufacturer's overstock and buy a large inventory of granola. The firm can sell off the granola in 120 days, when it will pay off the loan. The interest rate is $13\frac{1}{2}$%. How much more would the firm pay at a bank using ordinary interest than at a bank using exact interest?

11.3 Finding Principal, Rate, and Time

OBJECTIVES

1 Find principal.

2 Find rate.

3 Find time.

4 Decide when borrowing is beneficial.

Section 1 of this chapter showed how to modify the formula $I = PRT$ to solve for either P, R, or T.

$$P = \frac{I}{RT}$$

$$R = \frac{I}{PT}$$

$$T \text{ (in years)} = \frac{I}{PR}$$

CAUTION Be sure to express the rate as a decimal in these formulas.

As before, it is important to remember that time is always measured in years.

NOTE In the examples in this section, ordinary interest is used for simplicity, although only a small change would be needed for exact interest.

1 In the first example, the principal is found with time given in days.

EXAMPLE 1
Finding Principal

Find the principal that would produce interest of $18 at 10% in 54 days.

SOLUTION Find principal with the formula

$$P = \frac{I}{RT}.$$

Substitute $18 for I, 0.10 for R, and $\frac{54}{360}$ for T.

$$P = \frac{\$18}{0.10 \times \frac{54}{360}}$$

Simplify the denominator first. Since $0.10 \times \frac{54}{360} = 0.015$,

$$P = \frac{\$18}{0.015}.$$

Divide to get

$$P = \$1200.$$

The principal is $1200.

    Check this answer with the formula for simple interest, $I = PRT$. Use $1200 for P, 0.10 for R, and $\frac{54}{360}$ for T.

$$I = PRT$$

$$\$18 = \$1200 \times 0.10 \times \frac{54}{360} \quad \blacksquare$$

Calculator Approach to Example 1

Calculate the denominator and place it in memory.

$$.1 \;\boxed{\times}\; 54 \;\boxed{\div}\; 360 \;\boxed{M+}\; 0.015$$

Divide the value in the numerator by the stored value.

$$18 \;\boxed{\div}\; \boxed{MR} \;\boxed{=}\; 1200$$

---

2 The next example illustrates how to find the rate.

EXAMPLE 2 Suppose $3400 is invested for 135 days and earns $89.25 interest. Find the rate of
Finding the Rate interest.

SOLUTION The rate of interest can be found as follows. Start with

$$R = \frac{I}{PT}$$

and substitute to get

$$R = \frac{\$89.25}{\$3400 \times \frac{135}{360}}$$

Simplify the denominator.

$$R = \frac{\$89.25}{\$1275}$$

Divide.

$$R = 0.07$$

Convert 0.07 to a percent; the rate is 7%. ■

Calculator Approach to Example 2

Calculate the denominator and place it in memory.

$$3400 \; \boxed{\times} \; 135 \; \boxed{\div} \; 360 \; \boxed{M+} \; 1275$$

Divide the value in the numerator by the stored value.

$$89.25 \; \boxed{\div} \; \boxed{MR} \; \boxed{=} \; 0.07$$

---

3 The last variable in the formula $I = PRT$ is T; to find T (the time) in years, divide both sides by PR, getting

$$T = \frac{I}{PR}.$$

Using this formula would give the time *in years*. In most problems, however, the time *in days* is needed. To convert time *in years* to time *in days*, multiply the time in years by 360. (For example, $\frac{1}{2}$ year is $\frac{1}{2} \times 360 = 180$ days.) With this change, the formula for time in days follows.

$$\text{Time in days} \; = \; \frac{I}{PR} \times 360$$

EXAMPLE 3

Finding the Time in Days

Suppose $960 is deposited at 11% and earns $79.20 interest. Find the time in days.

SOLUTION

$$\text{Time in days} \; = \; \frac{\$79.20}{\$960 \times 0.11} \times 360 = \frac{\$79.20}{\$960 \times 0.11} \times \frac{360}{1}$$

Multiply 79.20 and 360 in the numerator, and multiply 960 and 0.11 in the denominator.

$$\text{Time in days} \; = \; \frac{\$28,512}{\$105.60}$$

Divide to get

$$\text{Time in days} = 270 \text{ days.}$$

The money was deposited for 270 days. ∎

Calculator Approach to Example 3

Calculate the denominator and place it in memory.

960 ☒ .11 M+ 105.6

Multiply the two values in the numerator and divide by the stored value.

79.20 ☒ 360 ÷ MR = 270

We can now summarize the various formulas for finding interest, principal, rate, and time.

NOTE All these formulas are just modifications of the formula $I = PRT$.

Find

Interest	$I = PRT$
Principal	$P = \dfrac{I}{RT}$
Rate	$R = \dfrac{I}{PT}$
Time	$\text{Time in years} = \dfrac{I}{PR}$
	$\text{Time in days} = \dfrac{I}{PR} \times 360$

---

4 As mentioned in Chapter 8, it is often a good idea to borrow money to take advantage of a cash discount. The next example shows why.

EXAMPLE 4

Applying the Rate Formula

An invoice for $3000 offers terms of 2/30, n/90. Find the maximum rate of interest that could be paid on borrowed money to make the cash discount beneficial.

SOLUTION   Start with the cash discount: find 2% of $3000.

$$2\% \times \$3000 = 0.02 \times \$3000 = \$60$$

Paying the invoice within 30 days permits a cash discount of $60 to be taken, so that only $3000 − $60 = $2940 need be paid. For the maximum benefit from the cash discount, the $2940 should be borrowed on day 30 (because of 2/30) and repaid 60 days later, when the full amount would have been due (n/90).

Find the rate of interest for a 60-day loan of $2940, with interest of $60 using the rate formula as shown.

$$R = \frac{I}{PT}$$

$$R = \frac{\$60}{\$2940 \times \frac{60}{360}}$$

$$R = 0.122 = 12.2\% \text{ (rounded)}$$

It will be beneficial to borrow money to pay the invoice if the money can be borrowed at any rate less than 12.2%. ■

11.3 Exercises

Find the principal in each of the following. Round to the nearest cent.

	Rate	Time (in Days)	Interest
1.	9%	180	$360
2.	12%	75	$9
3.	14%	80	$11.20
4.	10%	25	$6.40
5.	15%	30	$5
6.	12%	72	$72
7.	7.8%	92	$904.12
8.	6.2%	114	$549.25

Find the rate in each of the following. Round to the nearest tenth of a percent.

	Principal	Time (in Days)	Interest
9.	$6000	90	$120
10.	$9000	72	$162
11.	$300	60	$5.75
12.	$2000	90	$62.50
13.	$1742.46	13	$4.56
14.	$31,974.82	209	$1995.54

Find the time in each of the following. Round to the nearest day.

	Principal	Rate	Interest
15.	$4000	10%	$80
16.	$600	9%	$6
17.	$5000	10%	$180
18.	$20,000	8%	$1200
19.	$2798.54	11.5%	$146.69
20.	$17,474.96	6.5%	$2287.52

In each of the following word problems, find principal to the nearest dollar, rate to the nearest tenth of a percent, or time to the nearest day.

21. Find the length of time that Crown Furniture must invest $7000 of spare cash at 6% to earn $315 interest.

22. Morris Young invested money for 120 days at 8%. The interest earned was $336. Find the principal.

23. Bell Alzug invested $1250 for 90 days, earning $21.35 interest. Find the rate of interest paid.

24. Thomasine Handlery deposited money for 72 days at 9% earning $280 interest. Find the principal.

25. Find the amount that must be deposited by Lucille McGillicuddy at 12% interest for 120 days in order to make $840 interest.

26. Franklin Furniture lets a $1360 mortgage payment go 54 days overdue. The firm is charged a penalty of $26. Find the rate of interest charged as a penalty.

27. Nonesuch Produce charges a penalty of 18% simple interest for past due accounts. On one account, for $1500, the penalty was $33.75. Find how long the account was overdue.

28. The county charges $11\frac{1}{2}$% simple interest on delinquent taxes. Woodland Farms' penalty, for being 38 days late, was $30.35. Find the amount of the original tax bill.

29. Myron Winick bought an air conditioner from Wards. He paid off the item after 60 days, with a finance charge of $6. If Wards charges 9% interest, find the cost of the air conditioner.

30. Amlings loans $6400 cash to Forest Nursery for 75 days and earns $87 interest. Find the rate of interest on the loan.

31. A loan of $260 made to Singer Sewing Goods at $10\frac{1}{2}$% requires interest of $4.17. Find the length of time the loan was outstanding.

32. The Frampton Chamber of Commerce invests its building fund in an account paying 13.5%. The money is on deposit for 100 days, and earns $599.40. Find the amount of deposit.

33. Harry Medovy, an investor, makes $78 on a deposit of $12,500 for 25 days. Find his rate of interest.

34. Siragusa's Train Shop deposits $9850 at $5\frac{1}{4}$% and makes $117.79 interest. Find the length of time the money was deposited.

The following exercises are for students who have studied cash discounts. In Exercises 35–38, an invoice amount and cash discount terms are given. Find the maximum interest rate that could be paid so that borrowing money to take advantage of the cash discount would be beneficial. Round to the nearest tenth of a percent.

35. $5000, 2/10, n/45

36. $8110, 2/15, n/60

Solve the following word problems.

37. Gladys' Dress Shop received an invoice for $2543, with terms of 2/15, n/60. The store can borrow money at the bank at 12%. How much would be saved by borrowing money to take advantage of the cash discount?

38. Westside Pet Supplies received an invoice of $1796, with terms 1/10, n/30. The store can borrow money at 14.5%. How much would the store save by borrowing money to take advantage of the cash discount?

39. If you had your own business, would you ever consider borrowing money to take advantage of cash discounts? Why or why not?

40. Explain how to find principal in Example 1 if exact interest is used instead of ordinary interest.

11.4 Maturity Value

OBJECTIVES

1 Find maturity value.

2 Find principal if given maturity value, time, and rate.

3 Find rate if given principal, maturity value, and time.

4 Find time if given maturity value, principal, and rate.

Suppose $8000 is borrowed at 11% interest for 9 months. The interest owed on the loan would be calculated as follows.

$$I = PRT$$

$$I = \$8000 \times 0.11 \times \frac{9}{12}$$

$$I = \$660$$

1 The total amount that must be repaid in 9 months is made up of the principal and the interest, or

$$\text{Principal} + \text{Interest} = \$8000 + \$660 = \$8660.$$

This amount, $8660, is called the **maturity value** of the loan, and the date the loan is paid off is the **maturity date.** The formula for maturity value is as follows.

> A loan with a principal of *P* dollars and interest of *I* dollars has a maturity value *M* given by
>
> $$M = P + I.$$

EXAMPLE 1
Finding Interest and
Maturity Value

A loan for $2000 is made for one year at 9% interest. Find the interest due on the loan and the maturity value of the loan.

SOLUTION   Find the interest with $I = PRT$; here $P = \$2000, R = 0.09$, and $T = 1$.

$$I = PRT$$

$$I = \$2000 \times 0.09 \times 1$$

$$I = \$180$$

The borrower must repay the principal of $2000 plus interest of $180.
   The maturity value is found with the following formula.

$$M = P + I$$

$$M = \$2000 + \$180$$

$$M = \$2180$$

One year after receiving the $2000, the borrower must repay $2180 to the lender.   ■

   The formula for maturity value, $M = P + I$, can be written in a different way if *I* is replaced with *PRT* (since $I = PRT$).

$$M = P + I$$

$$M = P + PRT \qquad \text{Substitute } PRT \text{ for } I.$$

$$M = P(1 + RT) \qquad \text{Use the distributive property.}$$

Now there are two formulas for maturity value.

> The *maturity value, M,* of a principal of *P* dollars at a rate of interest *R* for *T* years is either
>
> $$M = P + I,$$
>
> or, since $I = PRT$,
>
> $$M = P(1 + RT). \qquad \leftarrow \text{(NO INT. IS KNOWN)}$$

EXAMPLE 2
Finding
Maturity Value

Use the formula $M = P(1 + RT)$ to find the maturity value for a loan of $6000 for 9 months at 4% interest.

SOLUTION   Substitute $6000 for P, 0.04 for R, and $\frac{9}{12}$ for T (since 9 months is $\frac{9}{12}$ of a year). The maturity value is

$$M = P(1 + RT)$$

$$M = \$6000 \times \left[1 + \left(0.04 \times \frac{9}{12} \right) \right].$$

NOTE Parentheses were placed around 0.04 and $\frac{9}{12}$ to show that these numbers are multiplied as a first step.

After multiplying 0.04 and $\frac{9}{12}$, add 1.

$$M = \$6000 \times (1 + 0.03)$$

$$M = \$6000 \times 1.03$$

$$M = \$6180$$

The interest could be found by subtracting the principal from the maturity value.

$$I = \$6180 - \$6000 = \$180 \quad \blacksquare$$

Calculator Approach to Example 2

Start the calculation with the innermost parentheses. Add 1 to this value and place it in memory.

$$.04 \; \boxed{\times} \; 9 \; \boxed{\div} \; 12 \; \boxed{+} \; 1 \; \boxed{M+} \; 1.03$$

Multiply 6000 by the stored value.

$$6000 \; \boxed{\times} \; \boxed{MR} \; \boxed{=} \; 6180$$

---

2 In Example 2, the principal, rate, and time were given and the maturity value was found. Sometimes the maturity value is given, and either the principal, rate, or time must be found, as shown in the following examples.

EXAMPLE 3
Finding Principal
Given Time, Rate,
and Maturity Value

Find the principal that would produce a maturity value of $1530 in 4 months at 6% interest.

SOLUTION   The formula for maturity value, $M = P(1 + RT)$, can be used to find P. Since P is unknown, solve the formula for P by dividing both sides by $1 + RT$. This gives

$$M = P(1 + RT)$$

$$\frac{M}{1 + RT} = \frac{P(1 + RT)}{1 + RT}$$

$$\frac{M}{1 + RT} = P.$$

Use this formula, substituting $1530 for M, 0.06 for R, and $\frac{4}{12}$ for T.

$$P = \frac{M}{1 + RT}$$

$$P = \frac{\$1530}{1 + \left(0.06 \times \frac{4}{12}\right)}$$

As shown by the parentheses, first multiply 0.06 and $\frac{4}{12}$, and then add 1.

$$P = \frac{\$1530}{1 + 0.02}$$

$$P = \frac{\$1530}{1.02}$$

$$P = \$1500$$

The principal is $1500; the interest is $1530 − $1500 = $30. ■

Calculator Approach to Example 3

Calculate the denominator and place it in memory. To do this, first calculate the quantity in the parentheses and then add 1.

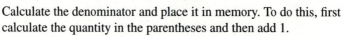
.06 $\boxed{\times}$ 4 $\boxed{\div}$ 12 $\boxed{+}$ 1 $\boxed{\text{M+}}$ 1.02

Now enter the numerator and divide by the stored value.

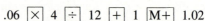
1530 $\boxed{\div}$ $\boxed{\text{MR}}$ $\boxed{=}$ 1500

---

3 If the principal, maturity value, and time are given, the rate can be found.

EXAMPLE 4

Finding Rate Given Principal, Maturity Value, and Time

A principal of $8400 produces a maturity value of $9100 in 200 days. Find the rate of interest.

SOLUTION   Both principal and maturity value are given, so first find the interest by subtracting.

$$I = \text{Maturity value} - \text{Principal}$$

$$I = \$9100 - \$8400$$

$$I = \$700$$

Now the interest, principal, and time are known. Find the rate, as explained in the previous section.

$$R = \frac{I}{PT}$$

$$R = \frac{\$700}{\$8400 \times \frac{200}{360}}$$

$$R = 0.15$$

The rate was 15%. ∎

4 In a similar manner, the time can be determined.

EXAMPLE 5
Finding the Time in Days

A loan with a maturity value of $12,675 had a principal of $12,500 and a rate of 7%. Find the time of the loan in days.

SOLUTION   First, find the amount of interest.

$$I = \$12,675 - \$12,500 = \$175$$

Now the interest, principal, and rate are known. Find the time in days using the formula.

$$\text{Time in days} = \frac{I}{PR} \times 360$$

$$\text{Time in days} = \frac{\$175}{\$12,500 \times 0.07} \times 360$$

$$\text{Time in days} = 72$$

The loan was for 72 days. ∎

11.4 Exercises

Find the interest and the maturity value for each of the following loans. Round to the nearest cent.

1. $4000 at 8% for $1\frac{1}{2}$ years
2. $8000 at 7% for $1\frac{3}{4}$ years
3. $7400 at 11% for 9 months
4. $6300 at 9% for 8 months
5. $2580 at $10\frac{1}{2}$% for 225 days
6. $5420 at $6\frac{3}{4}$% for 170 days

Complete this chart. Round money to the nearest cent, rate to the nearest tenth of a percent, and time to the nearest day.

	Principal	Interest	Rate	Time in Days	Maturity Value
7.	$3900	————	9%	270	————
8.	$74,500	————	7%	200	————
9.	$8400	$224	8%	————	————
10.	$9500	$598.50	6%	————	————
11.	$11,700	$438.75	————	150	————
12.	$16,500	$605	————	120	————
13.	————	————	6%	90	$21,315
14.	————	————	14%	205	$38,870
15.	$4217.19	————	12.4%	150	————
16.	$13,509.76	————	13.5%	172	————
17.	$1800	————	14%	————	$1926
18.	$11,250	————	————	115	$11,710
19.	————	$3272.92	————	185	$45,732.36
20.	————	$1963.33	————	76	$76,963.33
21.	————	$1311.01	13.7%	————	$33,811.01
22.	————	$8086.05	9.1%	————	$89,086.05

Solve the following word problems.

23. Find the maturity value of a loan at 11% for 7 months, if the principal is $7000. Use both the formula $M = P + I$ and $M = P(1 + RT)$.

24. Find the maturity value of a loan of $9250 at 10% for 5 months. Use both the formula $M = P + I$ and $M = P(1 + RT)$.

25. Outer Banks Oil Drilling bought $108,000 of new equipment. The firm agreed to borrow the necessary money at $12\frac{1}{4}$% and to pay the loan off in 110 days. Find the maturity value of the loan.

26. Jola Manchester borrowed $14,000 to finance an investment. The money was repaid in 78 days at $7\frac{1}{4}$% interest. Find the maturity value of the loan.

27. Walt Wilson borrows $60,000 at 9% interest to expand his car dealership. He agrees to repay $61,800. Find the time in days and the amount of interest paid.

28. Jenny Cronin borrows $46,000 to open her medical office. She agrees to repay $49,105 in 270 days. Find the interest rate and the amount of interest.

29. Pat Lutz borrows some money to buy a new car. The loan is made at 10% interest for 270 days. She pays $1200 in interest. Find the principal and the maturity value of her loan.

30. Jim Sell borrowed some money at his credit union. After 300 days he paid a maturity value of $8220, which included interest of $1020. Find the principal and the rate of interest on this loan.

31. Explain in words how to calculate the time of a loan in days if the maturity value, principal, and interest rate are known. (See Objective 4.)

32. There are two formulas for finding maturity value. Explain when each formula should be used.

11.5 Present Value

OBJECTIVES

1 Determine present value of money at simple interest.

2 Define the time value of money.

3 Find present value for a given maturity value.

4 Find present value after a loan is made.

Most of the problems so far in this chapter have concerned the interest or maturity value for a loan. In many problems, however, the amount of money that is needed at some time in the future is known and the amount that could be invested today to produce the future amount must be found.

1 The principal that can be invested today to produce a given future amount is called the **present value** of the future amount. To find a formula for present value, start with the formula for maturity value.

$$M = P(1 + RT).$$

In this formula, M is now the amount needed in the future (future value), and P is the amount to be invested today (present value). As shown earlier, solve for P by dividing both sides by $1 + RT$, getting the following result.

> The *present value at simple interest, P,* of a future value M at a rate of interest R for a time T is
> $$P = \frac{M}{1 + RT}.$$

$$\frac{M}{1+RT} = P\frac{(1+RT)}{1+RT}$$

$$\frac{M}{1+RT} = P$$

CAUTION In this formula, P is used for present value, while earlier P was used for *principal.* Don't be confused by this—P is the principal (or present value) that could be deposited today and produce some maturity value (or future value) at a later date.

EXAMPLE 1
Finding
Present Value

A business must pay a debt of $6000 in 4 months. Find the amount that could be deposited today, at 9% simple interest, so that enough money would be available to pay the debt.

SOLUTION Find the present value of $6000 in 4 months at 9% interest, using present value formula with $M = \$6000$, $R = 9\%$, and $T = \frac{4}{12}$ year.

$$P = \frac{M}{1 + RT}$$

$$P = \frac{\$6000}{1 + \left(0.09 \times \frac{4}{12}\right)}$$

Multiply 0.09 and $\frac{4}{12}$, and then add 1.

$$P = \frac{\$6000}{1 + 0.03}$$

$$P = \frac{\$6000}{1.03}$$

Divide.

$$P = \$5825.24$$

A deposit of $5825.24 today, at 9% interest, will produce $6000 in 4 months.

$$\$6000 - \$5825.24 = \$174.76$$

represents interest. ■

Calculator Approach to Example 1

Calculate the denominator and place it in memory. To do this, first calculate the quantity in parentheses and then add 1.

.09 $\boxed{\times}$ 4 $\boxed{\div}$ 12 $\boxed{+}$ 1 $\boxed{\text{M+}}$ 1.03

Now enter the numerator and divide by the stored value.

6000 $\boxed{\div}$ $\boxed{\text{MR}}$ $\boxed{=}$ 5825.24

---

2   As this example shows, $5825.24 today is the same as $6000 in 4 months, assuming an interest rate of 9%. The average interest rate that money is loaned for at a given time is sometimes called the **time value of money,** or sometimes just the **value of money**.

NOTE   The time value of money is not necessarily the same as the interest rate on a given loan. A loan may well be at a fixed rate of interest for 90 days, for example. During this 90 days, the interest rate of the loan will not change, but the time value of money could change many times.

EXAMPLE 2
Finding the Time
Value of Money

Ben Whitney owes $5000 to Arnold Parker. The debt is payable in 10 months. Suppose Whitney decides to pay off the debt today. If Parker is willing to accept an early payoff, what amount should he be willing to accept? Assume money has a value of 6%.

SOLUTION   The amount that Parker should be willing to accept is given by the present value of $5000.

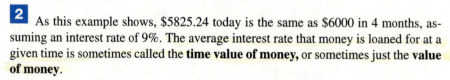

$$P = \frac{5000}{1 + \left(0.06 \times \frac{10}{12}\right)} = \frac{5000}{1 + 0.05} = \frac{5000}{1.05} = \$4761.90$$

Parker should be willing to accept $4761.90 today in settlement of his debt. ■

3 Example 2 discussed the present value of the principal on a loan. More realistic problems would consider the present value of the *maturity value* (principal plus interest).

EXAMPLE 3

Finding Present Value on Date Loan Is Made

A loan of $450 is due in 9 months, with an interest rate of 12%. Find the present value of the loan on the day it is made, if money has a time value of 10%.

SOLUTION   First find the maturity value for the loan, as explained earlier in this chapter.

$$M = P(1 + RT)$$

$$M = \$450\left[1 + \left(0.12 \times \frac{9}{12}\right)\right]$$

$$M = \$450(1 + 0.09)$$

$$M = \$450(1.09)$$

$$M = \$490.50$$

Now find the present value of this maturity value. The time, 9 months, is the same, but the interest rate is now 10%, instead of 12%. Use the present value formula.

$$P = \frac{M}{1 + RT}$$

$$P = \frac{490.50}{1 + \left(0.10 \times \frac{9}{12}\right)} = \frac{490.50}{1 + 0.075} = \frac{490.50}{1.075} = \$456.28$$

On the day the loan is made, the person to whom the money is owed should be willing to accept $456.28 in settlement of the debt. ■

Figure 11.1 summarizes Example 3.

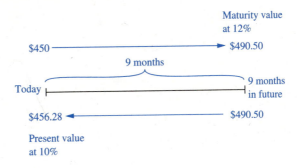

FIGURE 11.1

NOTE   In Example 3, an agreement was made to loan money at 12%. A sudden change in interest rates caused the time value of money to change to 10%. If the time value of money was also 12%, then the present value and the principal would have been the same, or $450.

4 It is sometimes necessary to find the present value on some date after a loan is made, but before it is due. Such a step might be necessary, for example, in preparing a balance sheet—this would give the exact value of the loan on the date the balance sheet was prepared. (Balance sheets are explained in Chapter 17.) Also, a present value might be found before deciding to convert the loan to cash by discounting it at the bank (see Section 12.3).

EXAMPLE 4

Finding Present Value on a Date After Loan Is Made

A loan of $6500 is made on May 13, for 90 days. The interest rate on the loan is 8%. After the loan is made, the general level of interest rates rises quickly so that the time value of money is 12%. Find the present value of the loan on June 26.

SOLUTION First find the maturity value of the loan. The principal is $6500, the rate is 8%, and the time is 90 days, or $\frac{90}{360}$ year.

$$M = P(1 + RT)$$

$$M = \$6500\left[1 + \left(0.08 \times \frac{90}{360}\right)\right]$$

$$M = \$6500(1 + 0.02)$$

$$M = \$6500(1.02)$$

$$M = \$6630$$

The loan was made on May 13, for 90 days. The loan is due on August 11. As shown in Figure 11.2, the number of days from June 26 (the day for which the present value is desired) to August 11 is

4	days in June
31	days in July
+ 11	days in August
46	total days.

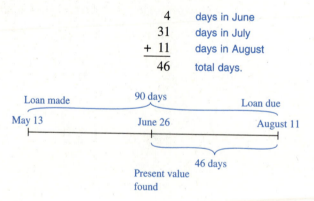

FIGURE 11.2

The total number of days could also be found by using Table 11.1.

To find the present value 46 days before the loan is paid off, use the formula for present value, with $M = \$6630$, $R = 12\%$, and $T = \frac{46}{360}$ year.

$$P = \frac{M}{1 + RT}$$

$$P = \frac{6630}{1 + \left(0.12 \times \frac{46}{360}\right)} \quad \textit{REMAINING TIME}$$

$$P = \$6529.88 \quad \text{(rounded)} \quad \textit{WORTH 46 DAYS BEFORE IT IS DUE.}$$

NOTE When time value of money and interest rate are different and when present value is found on a date after a loan is made, both the rate and the time fraction are different.

The person to whom the money is owed should be willing to accept $6529.88 on June 26 in full payment of the loan, both principal and interest. ■

CAUTION Since $\frac{46}{360}$ does not produce a terminating decimal, it is important that it not be rounded at an intermediate step. The calculation should be done in one step and the final answer rounded.

Calculator Approach to Example 4

Calculate the denominator and place it in memory. To do this, first calculate the quantity in parentheses and then add 1.

.12 $\boxed{\times}$ 46 $\boxed{\div}$ 360 $\boxed{+}$ 1 $\boxed{\text{M+}}$ 1.0153333

Now enter the numerator and divide by the stored value.

6630 $\boxed{\div}$ $\boxed{\text{MR}}$ $\boxed{=}$ 6529.8752

The answer, rounded to the nearest cent, is $6529.88.

11.5 Exercises

Find the present value of the following. Round to the nearest cent.

	Maturity Value	Value of Money	Time	
1.	$1000	10%	180 days	**$952.38**
2.	$850	8%	60 days	**$838.82**
3.	$4200	9%	100 days	**$4097.56**
4.	$1900	11%	80 days	**$1854.66**
5.	$9384.72	7.4%	146 days	**$9111.28**
6.	$21,802.43	11.5%	201 days	**$20,486.99**

Find the present value of the following loans on the day they are made. Round to the nearest cent.

Principal Amount	Interest Rate on Loan	Length of Loan	Time Value of Money
7. $8000	8%	60 days	7%
8. $390	12%	90 days	10%
9. $3159.72	8%	132 days	14.9%
10. $7680.54	9.6%	159 days	15.8%

Find the present value for the following loans on the indicated date. Assume the time value of money is 12%. Round to the nearest cent.

Amount	Interest Rate on Loan	Length of Loan	Loan Made	Find Present Value on
11. $600	10%	60 days	Apr. 7	May 20
12. $4500	9%	90 days	Sept. 12	Nov. 5
13. $1542.73	12.2%	120 days	May 7	June 21
14. $9483.71	15.7%	90 days	Jan. 29	March 4

15. Explain in your own words the difference between the interest rate on a loan and the time value of money.

16. Outline the procedure for determining the present value of a loan on a date that is after the loan is made but before it is due. (See Objective 4.)

Work the following word problems.

17. Find the present value of $8640 in 120 days at 8%.

18. What amount should a lender accept today in payment for a 210-day loan with a maturity value of $8200 if money has a value of 10%?

19. A loan of $1200 was made for 120 days at 9%. Find the present value of the loan on the day it was made if money is worth 6%.

20. Find the present value on the date it was made of a loan of $14,700 at 12% for 210 days if money is worth 10%.

21. A loan of $6980 was made on May 24, for 214 days, at 11%. Find the present value of the loan on July 9, if the value of money is 10%.

22. On February 24, an 89-day loan of $980, at 12% is made. Find the present value of the loan on March 10, if the value of money is 10%.

23. On April 7, Plank Lumber Company borrowed $14,000 from a wholesaler. The loan was for 153 days at 12%. The firm came up with some extra cash, and decided to pay the loan off on July 20. If the value of money is 10%, find the amount it would take to pay off the loan.

24. McKeague Dairy has borrowed $7600. The loan, made on September 11, is for 91 days at 10%. Find the amount necessary to pay off the loan on October 30, if the value of money is 12%.

In the following exercises, three different bids for a single item are given. Find the lowest bid by calculating the present value of each. Assume money has a value of 12%.

25. $5600 today, $5800 in 150 days, $6000 in 210 days

26. $41,250 today, $43,500 in 210 days, $45,000 in 300 days

CHAPTER 11 QUICK REVIEW

TOPIC	APPROACH	EXAMPLE
11.1 Finding simple interest given time expressed in years	Use formula $I = PRT$ with R in decimal form and time in years.	Find the simple interest on $4000 for $2\frac{1}{2}$ years at 8% per year. $I = PRT$ $I = \$4000 \times 0.08 \times 2.5$ $= \$800$
11.1 Finding simple interest given time expressed in months	Use $I = PRT$. Express time in years by dividing time in months by 12.	Find the simple interest on $1200 for 15 months at 7% per year. $I = PRT$ $I = \$1200 \times 0.07 \times \dfrac{15}{12}$ $= \$1200 \times 0.07 \times 1.25$ $= \$105$
11.1 Determining principal given interest, rate, and time	Use formula $P = \dfrac{I}{RT}$ with R in decimal form and time in years.	Find the principal that would produce an interest of $150 in 8 months at 6%. $P = \dfrac{I}{RT}$ $P = \dfrac{\$150}{0.06 \times \frac{8}{12}} = \$3750$

TOPIC	APPROACH	EXAMPLE
11.1 Finding rate given interest, principal, and time	Use formula $R = \dfrac{I}{PT}$ with T in years.	Find the rate on a $15,000 loan for 60 months if the interest was $6750. $R = \dfrac{I}{PT}$ $R = \dfrac{\$6750}{\$15,000 \times \frac{60}{12}} = 0.09$ $= 9\%$
11.1 Determining time given interest, principal, and rate	Use formula $T = \dfrac{I}{PR}$ with R in decimal form.	Find the time for a loan of $4000 at 11% to produce $1320 in interest. $T = \dfrac{I}{PR}$ $T = \dfrac{\$1320}{\$4000 \times 0.11} = 3$ yrs.
11.2 Finding the number of days from one date to another using a table	Find the day corresponding to each date and subtract.	Find the number of days from February 15th to July 28th. July 28 is day $\qquad$ 209 Feb. 15 is day $-$ 46 $\qquad\qquad\qquad\quad$ 163
11.2 Determining the number of days from one date to another using the actual number of days in a month	Add the actual number of days in each month or partial month from one date to the next.	Find the number of days from January 17th to April 15th. 14 remaining in January 28 February 31 March + 15 April $\qquad$ 88
11.2 Exact interest	Use formula $I = PRT$ with $T = \dfrac{\text{Time in days}}{365}$	Find the exact interest on $600 at 8% for 120 days. $I = PRT$ $I = \$600 \times 0.08 \times \dfrac{120}{365}$ $= \$15.78$

TOPIC	APPROACH	EXAMPLE
11.2 Ordinary interest	Use formula $I = PRT$ with $$T = \frac{\text{Time in days}}{360}$$	Find the ordinary interest on $1100 at 7% for 90 days. $$I = PRT$$ $$I = \$1100 \times 0.07 \times \frac{90}{360}$$ $$= \$19.25$$
11.3 Finding time in days when principal, rate, and interest are known	Use formula $$T = \frac{I}{PR} \times 360 \text{ with } R \text{ in decimal form.}$$	Find the time in days that $1500 was invested at 8% if $25 interest was earned. $$T = \frac{I}{PR} \times 360$$ $$T = \frac{\$25}{\$1500 \times 0.08} \times 360$$ $$= 75 \text{ days}$$
11.3 Determining principal when interest, rate, and time in days are known	Use formula $$P = \frac{I}{RT} \text{ with } R \text{ in decimal form}$$ and T in years.	Find the principal that would produce an interest of $24 in 60 days at 8%. $$P = \frac{I}{RT}$$ $$P = \frac{\$24}{0.08 \times \frac{60}{360}} = \$1800$$
11.3 Finding rate when principal, interest, and time in days are known	Use formula $$R = \frac{I}{PT} \text{ with } T \text{ in years.}$$	Find the rate when a principal of $8000 is deposited for 30 days and earns interest of $40. $$R = \frac{I}{PT}$$ $$R = \frac{\$40}{\$8000 \times \frac{30}{360}} = 0.06$$ $$= 6\%$$

TOPIC	APPROACH	EXAMPLE
11.4 Determining the maturity value of a loan, when principal, rate, and time are known	Use formula $M = P(1 + RT)$ with R in decimal form and T in years.	Find the maturity value of a $2500 loan that is made for 2 years at 6%. $$M = P(1 + RT)$$ $$M = \$2500[1 + (0.06 \times 2)]$$ $$M = \$2800$$
11.4 Finding the principal when maturity value, rate, and time are known	Use formula $$P = \frac{M}{1 + RT}$$ with R in decimal form and T in years.	Find the principal that would produce a maturity value of $1500 in 9 months at 4%. $$P = \frac{M}{1 + RT}$$ $$P = \frac{\$1500}{1 + \left(0.04 \times \frac{9}{12}\right)}$$ $$= \$1456.31 \text{ (rounded)}$$
11.4 Determining the time in days when maturity value, rate, and principal are known	Use formula $I = M - P$ to find interest. Then use formula $T = \dfrac{I}{PR} \times 360$ with R in decimal form.	A principal of $12,000 produces a maturity value of $12,540 at a 6% rate. Find the time of the loan in days. $$I = M - P$$ $$I = \$12,540 - \$12,000$$ $$= \$540$$ $$T = \frac{I}{PR}$$ $$T = \frac{\$540}{\$12,000 \times 0.06} \times 360$$ $$= 270 \text{ days}$$

TOPIC	APPROACH	EXAMPLE
11.4 Finding rate given principal, maturity value, and time	Use formula $I = M - P$ to find interest. Then use formula $R = \dfrac{I}{PT}$ with time expressed in years.	A principal of \$8400 produces a maturity value of \$8596 in 210 days. Find the rate of interest. $$I = M - P$$ $$I = \$8596 - \$8400$$ $$= \$196$$ $$R = \frac{I}{PT}$$ $$R = \frac{\$196}{\$8400 \times \frac{210}{360}} = 0.04$$ $$= 4\%$$
11.5 Determining present value given maturity value, rate, and time	Use formula $P = \dfrac{M}{1 + RT}$ with R in decimal form and T in years.	A debt of \$8000 must be paid in 9 months. Find the amount that could be deposited today at 9% interest so that enough money will be available. $$P = \frac{M}{1 + RT}$$ $$P = \frac{\$8000}{1 + \left(0.09 \times \frac{9}{12}\right)}$$ $$= \$7494.15$$
11.5 Finding present value given rate and time value of money	Use the formula $M = P(1 + RT)$ with R in decimal form and time in years. Then use the formula $P = \dfrac{M}{1 + RT}$ with R = time value of money and T in years.	A loan of \$750 at 12% is due in 15 months. Find the present value of the loan if the time value of money is 9%. $$M = P(1 + RT)$$ $$M = \$750\left[1 + \left(0.12 \times \frac{15}{12}\right)\right]$$ $$= \$862.50$$ $$P = \frac{M}{1 + RT}$$ $$R = \frac{\$862.50}{1 + \left(0.09 \times \frac{15}{12}\right)}$$ $$= \$775.28$$

TOPIC	APPROACH	EXAMPLE
11.5 Finding present value after a loan is made	Use formula $M = P(1 + RT)$ with R in decimal form and T in years. Next, use the formula $P = \dfrac{M}{1 + RT}$ with $R = $ time value of money, $T = $ number of days from present value date to due date.	An $8000 loan is made on June 5 for 90 days at 9%. The time value of money is 11%. Find the present value of the loan on August 10. $M = P(1 + RT)$ $M = \$8000\left[1 + \left(0.09 \times \dfrac{90}{360}\right)\right]$ $= \$8180$ Now, find time in days.

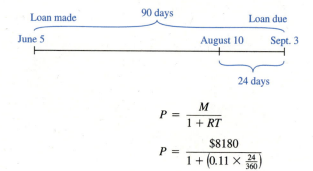

$$P = \frac{M}{1 + RT}$$

$$P = \frac{\$8180}{1 + \left(0.11 \times \frac{24}{360}\right)}$$

$$= \$8120.45$$

SUMMARY EXERCISE

Oscar Torres took out a bank loan of $9000 on September 6. The loan was due on March 15 of the following year. The interest rate was 8%.

(a) Find the interest due on the loan. **$380**

(b) Find the maturity value of the loan. **$9380**

(c) If the time value of money becomes 12% on the day the loan was made, find the present value. **$8821.32**

(d) How much should the bank be willing to accept in payment of the loan on December 15 if the time value of money on that date is 10%? **$9151.22**

CHAPTER 11 REVIEW EXERCISES

Complete this table. Round money to the nearest cent, rate to the nearest tenth of a percent, and time to the nearest month. [11.1]

	Interest	Principal	Rate	Time
1.	**$216**	$800	9%	3 years
2.	**$371.25**	$1500	8.25%	36 months
3.	$150	**$3333.33**	9%	6 months
4.	$350	**$1538.46**	7%	$3\frac{1}{4}$ years
5.	$810	$12,000	**9%**	9 months
6.	$750	$8000	**7.5%**	15 months
7.	$540	$12,000	6%	**9 months**
8.	$1600	$8000	8%	**30 months**

OVER 12 MTHS (NOT 360!)

11.2

Find the number of days from the first date to the second. [11.1]

9. April 15 to August 7 **114 days**

10. October 31 to January 5 **66 days**

Find the exact interest in each of the following. Round to the nearest cent. [11.2]

	Interest	Principal	Rate	Time
11.	**$18.00**	$1000	9%	73 days
12.	**$187.20**	$4680	10%	146 days
13.	**$222.51**	$7200	8%	From July 12 to November 30

73/365

$I = P \times R \times T$

Find the ordinary interest in each of the following. Round to the nearest cent. [11.2]

	Interest	Principal	Rate	Time
14.	**$43.17**	$7400	7%	30 days
15.	**$70.95**	$2580	11%	90 days

$I = P \times R \times T$

Complete the following table. Round money to the nearest cent, rate to the nearest tenth of a percent, and time to the nearest day. [11.3]

	Principal	Rate	Time (in days)	Interest
16.	_____	12%	75	$9
17.	_____	11%	180	$340
18.	$6000	_____	60	$70
19.	$7500	_____	120	$150
20.	$6000	8%	_____	$160
21.	$15,000	9%	_____	$1800

Complete the following table. Round money to the nearest cent and rate to the nearest tenth of a percent. [11.4]

	Maturity Value	Principal	Rate	Time
22.	_____	$1200	7%	3 years
23.	_____	$1800	8%	15 months
24.	_____	$12,000	9%	60 days
25.	$1500	_____	11%	6 months
26.	$25,000	_____	10%	2 years
27.	$8120	$8,000	_____	60 days
28.	$17,537.50	$15,250	_____	15 months

Find the present value of each of the following. Round to the nearest cent. [11.5]

	Present Value	Maturity Value	Rate	Time
29.	_____	$2000	9%	150 days
30.	_____	$12,000	12%	100 days

Find the present value of the following loans on the day they are made. Round to the nearest cent. [11.5]

	Present Value	Principal Amount	Interest Rate of Loan	Length of Loan	Value of Money
31.	_____	$5000	10%	9 months	8%
32.	_____	$20,000	7%	15 months	9%

Find the present value for the following loans on the indicated dates. Assume the value of money is 9%. Round to the nearest cent. [11.5]

	Present Value	Amount	Interest Rate of Loan	Length of Loan	Loan Made	Find Present Value on
33.	_____	$800	10%	60 days	Feb. 1	March 15
34.	_____	$20,000	12%	120 days	Sept. 5	Nov. 10

Work the following word problems. Round money to the nearest cent, rate to the nearest tenth of a percent, and time to the nearest day.

35. Find the simple interest on $4560 at $7\frac{1}{2}$% for 250 days. [11.1]

36. Suppose a loan of $8400 for 240 days has a maturity value of $8904. Find the rate of interest. [11.4]

37. A loan of $12,900 has a maturity value of $13,652.50. The rate on the loan is 12%. Find the time. [11.4]

38. Tom Tower borrows $32,400 from the bank to start a new business. He repays the loan with a single payment of $36,720 in 320 days. Find the rate of the loan. [11.4]

39. Collins Dairy has just bought new milking machines. The machines must be paid for with a single payment of $12,000 in 270 days. The firm has $11,200 that it can invest today. What rate of interest (to the nearest tenth of a percent), must it earn on this deposit to have the necessary $12,000? [11.5]

40. Quik Print is ordering a new $27,500 printing press. The seller of the press wants payment in 120 days. The print shop has $26,000 available for investment today. What rate of interest (to the nearest tenth of a percent) must it earn on this deposit to have the needed $27,500? [11.5]

41. How many days will it take for $17,600 to become $18,348 at 17% interest? [11.3]

42. Find the present value of a loan on the day it was made if the loan is for $9100 at 11% for 85 days. Assume that money has a time value of 9.7%. [11.5]

43. A loan of $19,250 is made on October 15, at 12%. The loan is for 75 days. Find the present value of the loan on November 27 if money has a time value of 11.7%. [11.5]

44. Suppose a loan of $11,800 is made on July 12, for 153 days, at 9%. Find the present value of the loan on September 20, if money has a time value of 11%. [11.5]

12

Notes and Bank Discount

When an individual or business borrows money, written proof of the loan often takes the form of a **promissory note**—a document in which one person or firm agrees to pay a stated amount of money, at a stated time and interest rate, to another. Such notes are discussed in this chapter.

12.1 Simple Interest Notes

OBJECTIVES

1 Identify the parts of a simple interest promissory note.

2 Find the due date of a note.

3 Find the face value, time, and rate of a note.

An example of a promissory note is shown in Figure 12.1.

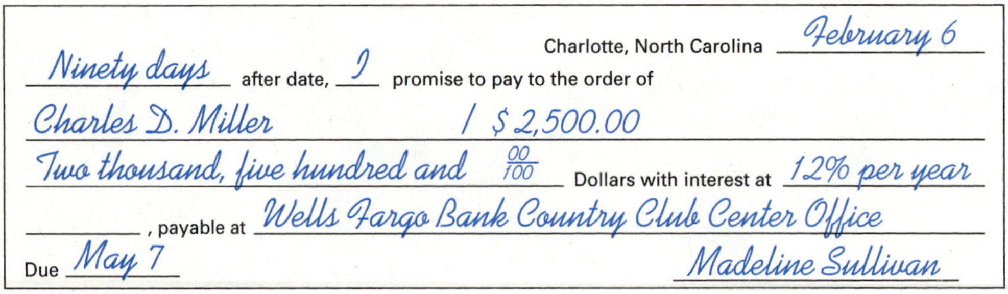

Charlotte, North Carolina ___*February 6*___

Ninety days after date, *I* promise to pay to the order of

Charles D. Miller / $ *2,500.00*

Two thousand, five hundred and ⁰⁰/₁₀₀ Dollars with interest at *12% per year*

___, payable at *Wells Fargo Bank Country Club Center Office*

Due *May 7* *Madeline Sullivan*

FIGURE 12.1

1 The person borrowing the money is called the **maker** or **payer** of the note. The maker in the note in Figure 12.1 is Madeline Sullivan. The person who loaned the money, and who will receive the repayment, is called the **payee.** The payee in the note in Figure 12.1 is Charles D. Miller. The length of time until the note is due

is the **term of the note.** The **face value** of the note is the amount written on the line in front of "Dollars." The face value of the note is $2500. The interest rate on the note in Figure 12.1 is 12% per year. The phrase "per year" is very important—inclusion of the phrase eliminates arguments over the period for which the interest applies. The **maturity value** of the loan is the face value plus any interest that is due. Since the interest for this note is found by formulas for simple interest, this note is a **simple interest note.** Find the interest due on the loan in Figure 12.1 as follows.

$$\text{Interest} = \$2500 \times 0.12 \times \frac{90}{360} = \$75$$

The maturity value of the loan is

$$\begin{aligned}\text{Maturity value} &= \text{Face value} + \text{Interest} \\ &= \$2500 + \$75 \\ &= \$2575.\end{aligned}$$

Madeline Sullivan must pay $2575 to Charles D. Miller at the note's maturity, that is, 90 days after February 6.

The promissory note shown in Figure 12.1 contains all the information needed to calculate interest owed and maturity value. However, banks and other financial institutions use a more comprehensive note containing very detailed listings of necessary payment dates and amounts, as well as paragraphs giving the bank's rights in case of nonpayment of the note. A typical promissory note from a large bank is shown in Figure 12.2 on the next page.

Many notes written by banks are secured by **collateral.** That is, the person borrowing the money must pledge assets that the bank can take in the event of nonpayment of the note. Typical collateral includes automobiles, stocks and bonds, real estate, or savings accounts. The collateral for the note in Figure 12.2 is real estate—in the event of nonpayment, the bank has the right to take a particular piece of property owned by the maker of the note, sell the property, and use the proceeds to pay off the note. (Any excess proceeds would be returned to the maker.)

2 When the time on a promissory note is given in months, the loan is due on the same day of the month, after the given number of months has passed. For example, a four-month note made on May 25 would be due on the 25th, four months in the future. Since four months from May is September, the note would be due September 25. Other examples are shown in the following table.

Date Made	Length of Loan	Due Date
March 12	5 months	August 12
April 24	7 months	November 24
October 7	9 months	July 7
January 31	3 months	April 30

FIXED RATE CONSUMER NOTE, DISCLOSURE AND SECURITY AGREEMENT

OFFICER INITIALS	BORROWER					
	ADDRESS					
	TELEPHONE NO.	IDENTIFICATION NO.				
			CUSTOMER NUMBER		LOAN NUMBER	

INTEREST RATE	PRINCIPAL AMOUNT	FUNDING DATE	MATURITY DATE		

** ANNUAL PERCENTAGE RATE ** THE COST OF THE CREDIT AS A YEARLY RATE.	** FINANCE CHARGE ** THE DOLLAR AMOUNT THE CREDIT WILL COST.	AMOUNT FINANCED THE AMOUNT OF CREDIT PROVIDED TO THE BORROWER OR ON BORROWER'S BEHALF.	TOTAL OF PAYMENTS THE AMOUNT BORROWER WILL HAVE PAID AFTER PAYMENTS HAVE BEEN MADE AS SCHEDULED.
12%	$ 1957.04	$ 10,000	$ 11,957.04

NUMBER OF PAYMENTS	AMOUNT OF PAYMENTS	WHEN PAYMENTS ARE DUE
36	$ 332.14 monthly	beginning April 11

DEMAND FEATURE: ☐ This Note has a demand feature.

REQUIRED DEPOSIT ACCOUNT: ☐ If checked, the Lender requires that Borrower maintain a deposit balance with Lender. The Annual Percentage Rate does not take into account required deposits.

SECURITY: A security interest has been granted in: ☐ Collateral securing other loans with Lender may also secure this loan; ☐ Any deposit accounts of Borrower with Lender; ☒ The goods or property being purchased; ☐ Other (describe):

FILING FEES: $ ___NONE___ in fees are being paid to public officials in order to research, perfect or release a security interest in the Collateral.

PREPAYMENT: If Borrower pays off early, Borrower ☐ may ☐ will not have to pay a penalty; ☐ may ☐ will not be charged a minimum finance charge; ☐ may ☐ will not be entitled to a refund of part of the finance charge.

ITEMIZATION: Borrower has the right to receive at this time an itemization of the Amount Financed. Borrower ☐ does ☐ does not want an itemization.

LATE CHARGES: If an installment is received more than _____ days late, Borrower will be charged a late payment charge of: ☐ _____ % of the unpaid late installment; ☐ _____ % of the unpaid late installment or $ _____ , whichever is ☐ greater ☐ less; as permitted by law.

ASSUMPTION: ☐ This loan may not be assumed on its original terms. ☐ This loan may be assumed on its original terms, subject to certain conditions.

See your contract documents for additional information about nonpayment, default, prepayment penalties and refunds and acceleration. ℯ means an estimate

FIGURE 12.2

FACE VALUE = PRIN.

NOTE A loan made on January 31, for 3 months, would normally be due on April 31. However, there are only 30 days in April, so that the loan is due on April 30. Whenever a due date does not exist, such as February 30 or November 31, use the last day of the month (February 28 or November 30 in these examples).

EXAMPLE 1

Finding Due Date, Interest, and Maturity Value

Find the due date, the interest, and the maturity value for each of the following loans.

(a) a loan made May 15 for 6 months at 8%, with a face value of $750   PRINC.

(b) a loan made September 30 for 5 months at 9.5% with a face value of $2380

SOLUTION

(a) Since 6 months from May 15 is November 15, the loan is due on November 15. Find the interest owed with the formula $I = PRT$. Substitute $750 for P, 0.08 for R, and $\frac{6}{12}$ for T.

$$I = PRT$$

$$I = \$750 \times 0.08 \times \frac{6}{12}$$

$$I = \$30$$

The interest on the loan is $30. Find the maturity value by adding principal and interest, with the formula $M = P + I$.

$$M = P + I$$

$$M = \$750 + \$30$$

$$M = \$780$$

The maturity value is $780; this amount must be paid on November 15.

(b) Counting 5 months from September 30 produces February 30. Since February has only 28 days (if not a leap year), the note would be due on the last day of February, or February 28. Interest for five months is

$$I = \$2380 \times 0.095 \times \frac{5}{12} = \$94.21 \text{ (rounded)}$$

with maturity value

$$M = \$2380 + \$94.21 = \$2474.21.$$

A total of $2474.21, representing both principal and interest, must be paid on February 28. ■

It is very common for the term of a promissory note to be expressed in days instead of months. For example, a loan might be signed on March 12, and be due in 90 days. To find the date due, use the exact number of days in a month. This can be done in either of two ways, as shown in Chapter 11.

One way is to look back at Table 11.1 which shows the number of each day. From the table, March 12 is the 71st day of the year. The loan is due 90 days after March 12. The number of the day on which the loan is due is

71	number of day loan is made
+ 90	number of day until due
161	number of day loan is due

From Table 11.1, day 161 is June 10. A 90-day loan made on March 12 is due on June 10.

As an alternate method, use the actual number of days in each month. The loan is made on March 12. Since March has 31 days, there are

$$\begin{array}{r} 31 \\ -\ 12 \\ \hline 19 \end{array}$$

or 19 more days in March. There are 30 days in April, and 31 in May. Find the total as follows.

19	rest of days in March
30	days in April
+ 31	days in May
80	

The loan is for 90 days, which is 10 more than 80, making the loan due on June 10. The following table shows several more examples.

Date Made	Length of Loan	Due Date
January 9	60 days	March 10
May 28	120 days	September 25
November 21	100 days	March 1
October 9	180 days	April 7

3   The next examples show how to find the face value, time, or rate for a note. Each of these examples uses formulas from Chapter 11.

NOTE   Face value for simple interest notes is the same as the principal *P*, that was used in Chapter 11.

EXAMPLE 2
Finding Face Value and Interest

A note has an interest rate of 12% and is for 120 days. A single payment of $1248 paid the note when it was due. Find the face value and interest for the note.

SOLUTION   The payment of $1248 is the maturity value of the note. The maturity value is found with the following formula from Chapter 11.

$$M = P(1 + RT)$$

Since P is not known in this example, get a formula for P by dividing both sides by $1 + RT$.

$$P = \frac{M}{1 + RT}$$

Now substitute $1248 for M, 0.12 for R, and $\frac{120}{360}$ for T.

$$P = \frac{\$1248}{1 + \left(0.12 \times \frac{120}{360}\right)}$$

$$P = \frac{\$1248}{1 + 0.04}$$

$$P = \frac{\$1248}{1.04}$$

$$P = \$1200$$

The face value of the note was $1200; the interest charge was $1248 − $1200 = $48. ■

EXAMPLE 3

Finding the Time of a Note

A note is signed with a face value of $820. The interest rate is 10%, with a maturity value of $830.25. Find the time of the note, in days.

SOLUTION   The interest on the note is

$$\$830.25 - \$820 = \$10.25$$

Recall the formula for time in days from Chapter 11.

$$T \text{ (in days)} = \frac{I}{PR} \times 360$$

Find the time by substituting $10.25 for I, $820 for P, and 0.10 for R.

$$T \text{ (in days)} = \frac{\$10.25}{\$820 \times 0.10} \times 360$$

$$T \text{ (in days)} = \frac{\$10.25}{\$82} \times 360$$

$$T \text{ (in days)} = 0.125 \times 360$$

$$T \text{ (in days)} = 45 \text{ days}$$

The loan was for 45 days. ■

NOTE A common error when solving for time (T) is forgetting to multiply by 360. When solving for time in Example 3, the number 0.125 $\left(\frac{1}{8}\right)$ is the time in years. Multiplying by 360 gives the time in days.

EXAMPLE 4
Finding the Rate of a Note

A note with a face value of $9200 is signed on March 27. On July 10, a maturity value of $9522 is paid. Find the rate on the note.

SOLUTION   The interest on the loan is

$$\$9522 - \$9200 = \$322.$$

Find the rate by starting with the formula for simple interest, $I = PRT$, and dividing both sides by PT.

$$R = \frac{I}{PT}$$

Now use $322 for I, $9200 for P, and $\frac{105}{360}$ for T, since there are 105 days from March 27 to July 10.

$$R = \frac{\$322}{\$9200 \times \frac{105}{360}}$$

$$R = 0.12$$

The rate was 12%. ■

On test — round to near 100th percent. .12567 would be 12.57%.

12.1 Exercises

Jackson, Mississippi __October 27__

__Ninety days__ after date, __I__ promise to pay to the order of

__Donna Sharp__ / $ 750.00

__Seven hundred fifty and__ $\frac{00}{100}$ _____ Dollars with interest at __8% per year__

_____, payable at __Crocker-Citizens Bank, Oak Park Branch__

Due __January 25__   __Helen Spence__

Identify each of the following from the note above.

1. maker
2. payer
3. payee
4. face value
5. term of loan
6. day loan made
7. day loan due
8. maturity value

Find the due date for each of the following.

Date Made	Term of Loan
9. February 24	7 months
10. July 10	8 months
11. May 31	4 months
12. August 31	3 months
13. January 6	70 days
14. September 14	125 days
15. November 24	150 days
16. December 8	160 days

Find the date due and the maturity value for each of the following. Use Table 11.1 on page 350 in your textbook. Round money to the nearest cent.

Date Made	Face Value	Term of Loan	Rate
17. June 12	$6000	150 days	9%
18. February 28	$3500	240 days	10%
19. April 24	$6800	180 days	7%
20. July 14	$680	90 days	11%
21. August 30	$390.74	115 days	8.6%
22. January 17	$908.56	104 days	13.9%

$I = PRT$
THEN
$M = P + I$

Complete the following table. Round money to the nearest cent, time to the nearest day, and rate to the nearest tenth of a percent.

Principal	Rate	Time	Maturity Value
23. _____	9%	150 days	$16,600
24. _____	6%	80 days	$1216
25. $3600	8%	_____	$3696
26. $9000	11%	_____	$9660
27. $10,000	_____	90 days	$10,300
28. $4000	_____	150 days	$4250
29. $8725.50	9.6%	66 days	_____
30. $13,743.52	8.2%	123 days	_____

31. State and explain the different parts of a simple interest promissory note. (See Objective 1.)

32. A simple interest promissory note is written on March 31st. It is due in 3 months. A student states that the due date is July 1. Is this correct? If not, state the correct due date and justify your answer. (See Objective 2.)

Work each of the following word problems. Use Table 11.1 on page 350 in your textbook.

33. In order to take advantage of a cash discount, Amy's Veterinary Supply borrowed $8100 on October 29. A note was signed for 150 days at 9%. Find (a) the due date and (b) the maturity value of the loan.

34. Ms. Martinella borrowed $987.63 on September 12, signing a 72-day, 10% note. Find (a) the due date and (b) the maturity value of the loan.

35. Krapen Auto Supply signed a note with a face value of $17,500 on September 10. The note is for 90 days and carries an interest rate of 9%. Find (a) the due date and (b) the maturity value of the note.

36. Susan Eisenhammer and Pam Carlson manage the Nelison Real Estate Office. They bought a supply of "for sale" and "sold" signs by signing a 100-day, $8\frac{1}{4}$% note for $1125 on October 1. Find (a) the due date and (b) the maturity value of the note.

37. Jill Sample's Ski House bought $15,900 worth of skis from Head on September 19. The firm signed a 200-day, $11\frac{1}{2}$% note for the skis. Find (a) the due date and (b) the maturity value of the note.

38. Clare Lynch bought a new office typewriter for $1040. She signed a 10%, 150-day note on April 12. Find (a) the due date and (b) the maturity value of the note.

39. A 100-day note with an interest rate of 12% has a maturity value of $15,500. Find the face value.

40. A tire company gives a supplier a 72-day note, with interest of 9%. The maturity value of the note is $9671. Find the face value of the note.

41. West Stationery is getting ready to pay a note that is due. The interest rate is 12%, the face value is $4000, and the interest is $120. Find the time (in days) of the note.

42. Lewin Skin Diving Equipment just paid the $7536 maturity value on a note with a face value of $7200. The interest rate was 8%. Find the time (in days) of the note.

43. The manager of the local electronics plant bought a security system for $12,000, paying for it with a 120-day note with a maturity value of $12,320. Find the interest rate she paid on the note.

44. A coffee merchant signed a $17,000, 90-day note for a shipment of coffee. The maturity value of the note was $17,382.50. Find the interest rate paid.

12.2 Simple Discount Notes

OBJECTIVES

1 Define simple discount notes.

2 Find bank discount and proceeds.

3 Calculate proceeds if given face value, discount rate, and time.

4 Distinguish between discount rates and interest rates.

5 Find effective interest rates.

6 Find the face value that produces the desired proceeds.

7 Find discount rate, face value, or time.

FACE VALUE ~ MAT. VALUE
DISCT = I

With the simple interest notes of the previous section, interest is found on the face value. The sum of the face value and the interest is the maturity value of the note.

1 Another common type of note, called a **simple discount note,** has the interest deducted in advance from the face value, with only the difference given to the borrower. Such notes are sometimes called **interest-in-advance notes** since the interest is subtracted before any money is given to the borrower.

For a simple discount note, the face value and the maturity value of the note are the same. The amount of interest charged is called the **bank discount,** or just the **discount.** The borrower receives a sum of money called the **proceeds,** which is the difference between the discount and the face value of the note. (As this discussion shows, a discount is just interest deducted in advance.)

For example, suppose a borrower signs a note for $2000, and the bank charges a discount of $150. The proceeds, the amount the borrower actually receives, is

$$\$2000 - \$150 = \$1850.$$

NOTE In this example, the maturity value of the note is $2000, which is also the face value. This shows a key feature of simple discount notes—the face value and maturity value are the same.

It is important to understand the difference between simple interest notes and simple discount notes.

> Simple *interest* is calculated on the *principal*, while simple *discount* is calculated on the *maturity value*.

2 The formula for finding bank discount is very similar to the formula for simple interest.

> The *discount B*, on a simple discount note with a maturity value (or face value) M, for T years at a discount rate D is
>
> $$B = M \cdot D \cdot T.$$
>
> The *proceeds, P,* are
>
> $$P = M - B.$$

NOTE Actually, the formula for simple interest, $I = PRT$, could be used with simple discount. However, the formula is written $B = M \cdot D \cdot T$ to emphasize that the loan is a *discount* loan.

EXAMPLE 1
Finding Discount and Proceeds

Elizabeth Thornton signs an $8800, 8-month note at the bank. The banker discounts the note at 12%. Find the amount of the discount and the proceeds.

SOLUTION   To find the discount, use the formula $B = M \cdot D \cdot T$. Here, $M = \$8800$, $D = 12\%$, and $T = \frac{8}{12}$ year.

$$B = M \cdot D \cdot T$$

$$B = \$8800 \times 0.12 \times \frac{8}{12}$$

$$B = \$704$$

The discount of $704 represents the interest charge on the loan. The proceeds are found by subtracting the discount from the face value, using the formula $P = M - B$.

$$\text{Proceeds} = \$8800 - \$704 = \$8096$$

Upon signing the note for $8800, Thornton will be given $8096. Then 8 months later, she must make a single payment of $8800. ■

In Example 1, the proceeds of $8096 could be thought of as the present value at simple interest of $8800 at 12% for 8 months.

3   As given by the discount formula, the discount is $B = M \cdot D \cdot T$. If P represents the proceeds, then P is found by subtracting the bank discount from the face value, or

$$P = M - (M \cdot D \cdot T).$$

The distributive property gives the formula for proceeds shown in the next box.

The *proceeds, P*, for a simple discount note with a maturity value (or face value) M for *T* years at a discount rate *D* is

$$P = M - B$$

or

$$P = M(1 - DT).$$

EXAMPLE 2
Finding Proceeds

Wes Blake borrows $6000 for 90 days at a discount rate of 12%. Find the proceeds.

SOLUTION   There are two ways to find the proceeds. One way would be to first use the formula $B = M \cdot D \cdot T$, find the discount, and then subtract the discount from the face value to find the proceeds. Doing this,

$$B = M \cdot D \cdot T$$

$$B = \$6000 \times 0.12 \times \frac{90}{360} = \$180.$$

The proceeds are then

$$P = M - D = \$6000 - \$180 = \$5820.$$

As a second method for finding the proceeds, use the formula $P = M(1 - DT)$. Here, $M = \$6000$, $D = 12\%$, and $T = \frac{90}{360}$.

$$P = M(1 - DT)$$

$$P = \$6000\left[1 - \left(0.12 \times \frac{90}{360}\right)\right]$$

Inside the brackets, be sure to first multiply 0.12 and $\frac{90}{360}$, and then subtract.

$$P = \$6000(1 - 0.03)$$

$$P = \$6000\,(0.97)$$

$$P = \$5820$$

By this method, it is not necessary to find the bank discount. ∎

Calculator Approach to Example 2

Calculate the quantity in parentheses and place it in memory.

.12 $\boxed{\times}$ 90 $\boxed{\div}$ 360 $\boxed{\text{M+}}$ 0.03

Now enter 1 and subtract the stored value and multiply by 6000.

1 $-$ $\boxed{\text{MR}}$ $\boxed{=}$ $\boxed{\times}$ 6000 $\boxed{=}$ 5820

---

4 A discount rate of 12% is not the same as an interest rate of 12%. The next example shows why.

EXAMPLE 3
Comparing Discount Rates and Interest Rates

Two different notes each have a face value of $7500 and a time of 90 days. One has a simple interest rate of 12%, and the other has a discount rate of 12%.

(a) Find the interest owed on each.

SOLUTION

For the Simple Interest Note	For the Simple Discount Note
$I = PRT$	$B = M \cdot D \cdot T$
$I = \$7500 \times 0.12 \times \dfrac{90}{360}$	$B = \$7500 \times 0.12 \times \dfrac{90}{360}$
$I = \$225$	$B = \$225$

In each case, the interest is $225.

(b) Find the amount actually received by the borrower in each case.

For the Simple Interest Note	For the Simple Discount Note
Principal = Face value = \$7500	Proceeds = $M - B$ = \$7500 − \$225 = \$7275

With the simple interest note, the borrower has the use of \$7500, but only \$7275 is available with the simple discount note. In each case, the interest charge is the same, \$225, but more money is available with the simple interest note.

(c) Find the maturity value of each note.

For the Simple Interest Note	For the Simple Discount Note
$M = P + I$ = \$7500 + \$225 = \$7725	Maturity value = Face Value = \$7500

The differences between these two notes can be summarized as follows.

	Simple Interest	Simple Discount
Face value	\$7500	\$7500
Interest	\$225	\$225
Amount available to borrower	\$7500	\$7275
Maturity value	\$7725	\$7500

5 Because of the possible confusion resulting from the different ways of calculating interest charges, the **Federal Truth in Lending Act** was passed in 1969. This act requires that all interest rates be given as comparable percents. While this law is discussed in more detail in Chapter 13, the next example shows how to get the simple interest rate corresponding to the given discount rate of Example 3.

EXAMPLE 4

Finding Rate of
Interest for
Discount Notes

Find the rate of interest for the simple discount note in Example 3.

SOLUTION   The discount rate of 12% given in Example 3 is not the rate of interest, since the 12% applies to the maturity value of \$7500 and not to the proceeds of \$7275. Since the borrower received only \$7275, the interest rate must be found from this amount. Do this with the formula for simple interest, $I = PRT$. Here $I = \$225$ (the discount), $P = \$7275$ (the proceeds), $T = \frac{90}{360}$ year, and R must be found.

Start with $I = PRT$, and divide both sides by PT.

$$R = \frac{I}{PT}$$

Then substitute the given numbers.

$$R = \frac{\$225}{\$7275 \times \frac{90}{360}}$$

PROCEEDS BORROWER REC'D →

$$R = \frac{\$225}{\$1818.75}$$

$$R = 0.1237 \quad \text{(rounded)}$$

The rate of interest is 12.37% rounded to the nearest hundredth of a percent. This rate is called the **effective rate of interest,** or the **true rate of interest.** By federal regulations, a person borrowing $7500 for 90 days at a discount rate of 12% would have to be told that the **annual percentage rate** on the loan is 12.5% (instead of 12.37%, since the regulations require rounding up to the nearest quarter of a percent). ∎

6 Normally a borrower wants to borrow a certain amount of money. The next example shows how to find the face value of a simple discount note so that the proceeds will be the amount needed by the borrower.

EXAMPLE 5

Finding Face Value that Produces Desired Proceeds

Mike Collins needs $4000 to repair his roof. Find the value of a note that will provide the $4000 in proceeds if he plans to repay the note in 180 days and the bank charges a 15% discount rate.

SOLUTION Start with the formula $P = M(1 - DT)$. Since M is not known, find a formula for M by dividing both sides by $1 - DT$.

$$M = \frac{P}{1 - DT}$$

Replace P with $4000, D with 0.15, and T with $\frac{180}{360}$.

$$M = \frac{\$4000}{1 - \left(0.15 \times \frac{180}{360}\right)}$$

$$M = \frac{\$4000}{1 - 0.075}$$

$$M = \frac{\$4000}{0.925}$$

$$M = \$4324.32 \quad \text{(rounded)}$$

Collins must sign a note with a face value of $4324.32 (to the nearest cent) to get the $4000 that he needs. ∎

7 Just as the formula for simple interest, $I = PRT$, can be solved for $P, R,$ or T, the formula for discount, $B = M \cdot D \cdot T$, can be solved for $M, D,$ or T. Do this as shown in the next example.

EXAMPLE 6
Finding Discount

A simple discount note has a face value of $12,000 and proceeds of $11,275. Find the discount rate if the note is for 150 days.

SOLUTION To find the discount rate, start with the formula $B = M \cdot D \cdot T$ and divide both sides by $M \cdot T$.

$$D = \frac{B}{M \cdot T}$$

The discount is

$$B = \$12,000 - \$11,275 = \$725;$$

also $M = \$12,000$ and $T = \frac{150}{360}$. Now find D.

$$D = \frac{\$725}{\$12,000 \times \frac{150}{360}}$$

$$D = \frac{\$725}{\$5000}$$

$$D = 0.145$$

The discount rate is 14.5%. ∎

One very common use of discount interest comes when buying **U.S. Treasury bills** (often called just **T-bills**). These T-bills are one way the federal government borrows money. They are currently available with 13-week, 26-week, or 52-week maturities. Investors buy T-bills for a price equal to the proceeds after the discount is subtracted. Then, at maturity, the investor receives the full face value on the T-bill. Since T-bills are a loan to the federal government, they are considered one of the safest of all possible investments.

12.2 Exercises

Find the discount and the proceeds. Round money to the nearest cent.

	Maturity Value	Discount Rate	Time in Days
1.	$12,000	9%	120
2.	$850	7%	150
3.	$1525	6%	240
4.	$5400	10%	30
5.	$11,710	12%	75
6.	$21,175	8%	70

Find the due date and the proceeds for the following.

	Maturity Value	Discount Rate	Date Made	Time in Days
7.	$975	8%	Aug. 10	99
8.	$820	10%	May 3	110
9.	$5800	9%	Sept. 14	160
10.	$3200	11%	Nov. 4	165

Complete this table.

	Maturity Value	Discount Rate	Date Made	Due Date	Time in Days	Discount	Proceeds
11.	$16,000	9%	5/11	_____	90	_____	_____
12.	$8275	7%	_____	9/10	120	_____	_____
13.	$14,400	_____	_____	1/4	150	$660	_____
14.	$8200	_____	2/9	5/10	_____	$205	_____
15.	_____	_____	11/12	_____	90	$108	$7092
16.	_____	_____	11/4	6/2	_____	$1176	$24,024

Solve each of the following word problems. Round rate to the nearest tenth of a percent and money to the nearest cent.

17. A $5000 note is signed for 120 days at a discount rate of 8%. Find the discount and the proceeds.

18. The First National Bank is currently charging a 12% discount rate. Find the discount and the proceeds on a $6240 note for 30 days.

19. A note having a face value of $8000 was discounted 12%. If the discount was $320, find the length of the loan in days.

20. Suppose a borrower signs a $14,600 note at a discount rate of 9% with proceeds of $13,724. Find the length of the loan in days.

21. Bob Jensen signs a $2000, 90-day note at the bank, receiving proceeds of $1925. Find the discount rate.

22. Philippa Gordon has received proceeds of $4576 after signing a 210-day note for $4800. Find the discount rate.

23. Paula Gibb needs $5196 to pay for remodeling work on her house. Her bank loans money at a discount rate of 13%, and the loan is for 240 days. Find the face value of the loan so she will have $5196.

24. Mary Johnson decides to go back to college. To get to school she buys a small car for $8200. She decides to borrow the money at the bank, for 8 months, at a 12% discount rate. Find the face value of the loan so she will have $8200.

25. Marge Prullage signs a $4200 note at the bank. The bank charges an 11% discount rate. Find the proceeds if the note is for 10 months. Find the effective interest rate charged by the bank.

26. Ed Foust goes to the bank and signs a note for $8400. The bank charges a 7% discount rate. Find the proceeds and the effective rate charged by the bank if the note is for 8 months.

27. Suppose an $83,544 note is signed at a bank that charges a 13.7% discount rate. If the loan is for 175 days, find the proceeds and the effective rate charged by the bank.

28. A note for $108,720 with an 11.8% discount rate is signed. The note is for 234 days. Find the proceeds and the effective rate charged by the bank.

Exercises 29 and 30 involve present value at simple interest, discussed in Section 11.5.

29. Find the proceeds of a $4000, 90-day note at an 8% discount rate. Find the present value of $4000 in 90 days at 8% interest.

30. Find the proceeds of a $700 note for 180 days at a 10% discount rate. Find the present value of $700 in 180 days at 10% interest.

The following exercises apply to U.S. Treasury bills, discussed at the end of this section. (Assume 52 weeks per year for each exercise, and round to the nearest hundredth of a percent.)

31. An investor buys a $5000 T-bill at a 4% discount for 13 weeks. Find each of the following: (a) the purchase price of the T-bill, (b) the maturity value, (c) the interest earned, and (d) the effective rate of interest.

32. Melissa Wilson buys a $100,000 T-bill at a 3.2% discount for 26 weeks. Find each of the following: (a) the purchase price of the T-bill, (b) the maturity value, (c) the interest earned, and (d) the effective rate of interest.

33. Explain in your own words, the difference between simple interest notes and simple discount notes.

34. Describe in detail the procedure for finding the effective annual interest rate on a discount note. (See Objective 5.)

12.3 Comparing Simple Interest and Simple Discount

OBJECTIVES

1 Compare simple interest and simple discount notes.

2 Convert between simple interest and simple discount rates.

Simple interest notes and simple discount notes have many similarities and many differences. In this section, we first compare and contrast these two important types of notes, and then discuss ways of comparing simple interest rates and simple discount rates.

First, let us list the key similarities between these two types of notes.

> Both types of notes are repaid with a single payment at the end of a stated period of time.
> This length of time is generally one year or less.

1 Table 12.1 compares these two types of notes.

TABLE 12.1   A Comparison of Simple Interest and Simple Discount Notes

	Variables Used for Simple Interest	**Variables Used for Simple Discount**
	I = Interest	B = Discount
	P = Principal (Face value)	P = Proceeds
	R = Rate of interest	D = Discount rate
	T = Time in years, or Fraction of a year	T = Time in years, or Fraction of a year
	M = Maturity value	M = Maturity value (FACE VALUE)

	Simple Interest	**Simple Discount**
Face value	Stated on note, or $P = \dfrac{M}{1 + RT}$	Same as Maturity value, or $M = \dfrac{P}{1 - DT}$
Interest charge	$I = PRT$	$B = M \cdot D \cdot T$
Maturity value	$M = P + I$ or $M = P(1 + RT)$	Same as face value, or $M = \dfrac{P}{1 - DT}$
Amount received by borrower	Face value or principal	Proceeds: $P = M - B$ or $P = M(1 - DT)$
Identifying phrases	Interest at a certain rate Maturity value greater than face value	Discounted at a certain rate Proceeds Maturity value equal to face value
True annual interest rate	Same as stated rate, R	Greater than stated rate, D

2   As shown earlier, a 15% simple interest rate is not the same as a 15% simple discount rate. The rest of this section shows formulas for conversion back and forth between simple interest rates and simple discount rates.

To find these formulas, start with the key formulas for simple interest and for simple discount. *SIMPLE INT.*   *SIMPLE DISCT*

$$M = P(1 + RT) \quad \text{and} \quad P = M(1 - DT)$$

Solve each of these formulas for *P*.

$$P = \frac{M}{1 + RT} \qquad P = M(1 - DT)$$

Since each right hand side is equal to P, the two right-hand sides must be equal to each other, or

$$\frac{M}{1 + RT} = M(1 - DT).$$

Divide both sides by *M* to get

$$\frac{1}{1 + RT} = 1 - DT.$$

By going through several more algebraic steps, this equation can be solved first for *R* and then for *D*, giving the results in the box.

The simple interest rate *R* and the simple discount rate *D* are calculated by the formulas   *SIMPLE INTR*   *SIMPLE DISCT*

$$R = \frac{D}{1 - DT} \quad \text{and} \quad D = \frac{R}{1 + RT}$$

where *T* is time in years.

NOTE The simple interest rate corresponding to a simple discount rate is also called the **effective rate of interest**. As these formulas show, the maturity value plays no part in converting between rates—only the rate and the time matter.

EXAMPLE 1

Converting Interest and Discount Rates

Convert as indicated.

(a) Find the simple interest rate corresponding to a simple discount rate of 9% for 270 days.

SOLUTION   Find *R* with the following formula.

$$R = \frac{D}{1 - DT}$$

Here $D = 0.09$ and $T = \frac{270}{360}$.

$$R = \frac{0.09}{1 - \left(0.09 \times \frac{270}{360}\right)} = \frac{0.09}{1 - 0.0675} = \frac{0.09}{0.9325} = 0.0965$$

↑ SIMPLE INT RATE

rounding to the nearest hundredth of a percent. The corresponding simple interest rate is 9.65%.

(b) Find the simple discount rate that corresponds to a simple interest rate of 7% for 90 days. Use the following formula.

$$D = \frac{R}{1 + RT}$$

Replace R with 0.07 and T with $\frac{90}{360}$. Then

$$D = \frac{0.07}{1 + \left(0.07 \times \frac{90}{360}\right)} = \frac{0.07}{1 + .0175} = \frac{0.07}{1.0175} = 0.0688$$

or 6.88%, rounded to the nearest hundredth of a percent. ■

12.3 Exercises

$R = \frac{P}{1 - DT}$

Find the simple interest rate that corresponds to the given discount rate for the given time. Round to the nearest hundredth of a percent.

1. 7%, 1 year

2. 10%, 1 year

3. 11%, 90 days

4. 8%, 180 days

5. 9%, 90 days

6. 9%, 210 days

Find the simple discount rate that corresponds to the given simple interest rate for the given time. Round to the nearest hundredth of a percent.

7. 6%, 1 year

8. 10%, 1 year

9. 14%, 180 days

10. 9%, 120 days

11. 15%, 120 days

12. 16%, 180 days

13. Is the rate associated with simple discount notes the true annual interest rate? If not, explain why not and show how to calculate the true rate.

14. List some advantages of using a simple discount note instead of a simple interest note.

*Solve each of the following word problems. Round to the nearest hundredth of a percent
in Exercises 17 and 18.*

15. Sherri Johnson needs to borrow money for her college expenses. She can borrow at a
13% simple interest rate or at a 12.8% simple discount rate. If she needs the money
for 90 days, where should she borrow?

16. Bill Walsh wants to borrow money to expand his business. One bank charges a 17%
simple interest rate and a second bank charges a 16.4% simple discount rate. If he
needs the money for 120 days, where should he borrow?

17. Marla Trump wants to borrow money for 20 days to take advantage of a cash
discount. One bank will loan her the money at 16% simple interest. A second bank
also wants to loan her the money, but the second bank uses a simple discount rate.
What is the maximum discount rate that Trump should accept at the second bank so
that she does not pay more interest than at the first bank?

18. Jim Worthington has been offered a substantial cash discount if he pays an invoice 60
days early. One bank will loan him the needed money at an 11% simple interest rate.
A second bank will also loan him the money, but at a simple discount rate. What is
the maximum discount rate that Worthington can accept at the second bank so that he
does not pay more interest than at the first bank?

12.4 Discounting a Note

OBJECTIVES

1 Find the discount and the proceeds of a note.

2 Find the proceeds of a rediscounted note.

Businesses often accept notes, either simple interest notes or simple discount notes,
in place of immediate payment for goods or services. For example, a manufacturer of
ski equipment may deliver goods for ski shops in October and may agree not to collect from the shops until April. To secure its payment, the manufacturer may request
promissory notes from the ski shops receiving the goods.

As a result, the manufacturer may have a considerable amount of cash tied up in
promissory notes that will not be paid until April. To get cash earlier, the manufacturer
can sell the promissory notes to a bank. The bank will give the manufacturer the
maturity value of the notes, less a fee charged by the bank for this service. This fee
is called the **bank discount**, and the process of receiving cash for a note is called
discounting a note.

The amount of cash actually received by the manufacturer is called the **proceeds**.
The bank then collects the maturity value from the maker of the note when it becomes
due. Normally, such notes are sold with **recourse**, so that if the maker of the note does
not pay for some reason, the bank collects from the seller of the note. This protects
the bank against loss.

1 Use the following procedure to **discount a note.**

---

1. Find the maturity value of the original note (if necessary). $M = P(1 + RT)$
2. Find the discount period.
3. Find the discount using the formula $B = M \cdot D \cdot T$.
4. The proceeds are found by $P = M - B$.

This method is shown in the next examples.

EXAMPLE 1

Finding the
Discount and
Proceeds of a Note

A firm holds a 90-day note dated July 9, with a face value of $1850 and interest of 12%. The firm holding the note wishes to convert the note to cash on August 19. Assume a discount rate of 14%. Find the proceeds to the firm holding the note.

SOLUTION   Go through the four steps in discounting a note given in the box.

Step 1.   First find the interest on the note.

OCT 7 – DUE

$$\text{Interest} = \$1850 \times 0.12 \times \frac{90}{360} = \$55.50$$

Find the maturity value.

$$\text{Maturity value} = \$1850 + \$55.50 = \$1905.50$$

Step 2.   Find the **discount period**, the number of days remaining before the note is due. The discount period is often found by a diagram as shown in Figure 12.3.

FIGURE 12.3

In this example, the date of the note is July 9, the note is discounted on August 19, and the due date is October 7 (July 9 + 90 days = October 7). August 19 to October 7 is 49 days, found as follows.

12	days left in August
30	days in September
+ 7	days until note is due in October
49	days discount period

Step 3.   Find the discount, using the formula

$$B = M \cdot D \cdot T.$$

Use the numbers of the example, including a discount rate of 16%.

$$B = \$1905.50 \times 0.14 \times \frac{49}{360} = \$36.31$$

The discount is $36.31.

Step 4.   Find the proceeds, using the formula $P = M - B$.

$$P = M - B$$

$$P = \$1905.50 - \$36.31 = \$1869.19$$

The bank will take the note on August 19 and pay $1869.19 in cash to the firm holding the note. The bank will then collect $1905.50 from the maker of the note on October 7. In summary,

Date	Transaction	
August 19	Bank pays out $1869.19	Bank makes the difference of these amounts, or $36.31 which is the discount. ∎
October 7	Bank receives $1905.50	

EXAMPLE 2
Finding Proceeds and Discount

On February 27, Andrews Lincoln-Mercury receives a 150-day note with a face value of $3500 at 8% interest per year. On March 27, the firm discounts the note at the bank. Find the proceeds if the discount rate is 12%.

SOLUTION   Again, go through the four steps in discounting a note.

Step 1.   Find the interest and maturity value. Find the interest with the formula $I = PRT$.

$$\text{Interest} = \$3500 \times 0.08 \times \frac{150}{360} = \$116.67$$

The interest on the note is $116.67. The maturity value is found with the formula $M = P + I$.

$$\text{Maturity value} = \$3500 + \$116.67 = \$3616.67$$

Step 2.   Find the discount period using the diagram in Figure 12.4.

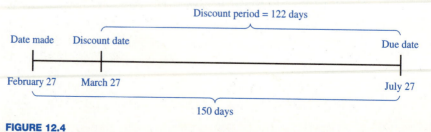

FIGURE 12.4

CAUTION Remember: the discount period is calculated from the *due date* of the loan, and not from the date the loan was made.

The discount period is 122 days.

Step 3. Find the bank discount, using the discount rate of 12%. Use the formula $B = M \cdot D \cdot T$.

$$\text{Discount} = \$3616.67 \times 0.12 \times \frac{122}{360} = \$147.08$$

The discount is $147.08.

Step 4. Find the proceeds.

$$P = M - B$$

$$P = \$3616.67 - \$147.08 = \$3469.59$$

Andrews receives $3469.59 from the bank on March 27. ■

2 In the next example, a company borrows money from a bank by signing a simple discount note. The bank making the loan then sells the note to another bank. In this case, with the same note being discounted twice, the note is said to have been **rediscounted**. Notice in the example that the rate charged by the second bank to the first bank is lower than the rate charged to the public. This is very common in transactions between banks, with the lower rate a sort of "wholesale" rate.

Even though the note in Example 3 is rediscounted, the steps used are basically the same as those used in earlier examples. The only difference is that since the original note was a simple discount note instead of a simple interest note, it is not necessary to solve for maturity value. The face value *is* the maturity value.

EXAMPLE 3
Finding Proceeds of a Rediscounted Note

The River Raft Company signed a $4000, 90-day note at the bank. (That is, the company agreed to pay a total of $4000 to the bank after 90 days.) The bank discounted the note at 12%. Then, 54 days after the note was signed, the bank rediscounted the note at a second bank, which charged an 8% discount rate. Find the proceeds to the first bank.

SOLUTION Go through the steps given for discounting a note.

Step 1. The maturity value of the note is $4000.

NOTE The fact that the first bank charged a 12% discount rate plays no part in the problem since only the maturity value of the note is needed.

Step 2. The discount period is $90 - 54 = 36$ days.

Step 3.   The discount (at the second bank) is

$$\text{Discount} = \$4000 \times 0.08 \times \frac{36}{360} = \$32.$$

Step 4.   The proceeds are

$$\$4000 - \$32 = \$3968.$$

This example can be summarized as follows: The River Raft Company signs a note with a maturity value of $4000. Then, 54 days after the note is signed, the first bank rediscounts the note at a second bank, receiving proceeds of $3968. Finally, 90 days after signing the note and 54 days after the note was discounted, River Raft Company pays $4000 to the second bank. ∎

Not only notes are discounted. It is very common for a business to sell part of its accounts receivable (money owed to the business—see Section 17.3) to a financial institution. This process is called **factoring**, and the people who buy the accounts receivable are called **factors**. The calculations involved with factoring are just the ones discussed in this section.

12.4 Exercises

Find the discount period for each of the following.

	Loan Made	Length of Loan	Date of Discount
1.	January 30	210 days	April 30
2.	April 7	150 days	June 25
3.	May 28	74 days	June 18
4.	September 17	130 days	January 13
5.	June 4	63 days	July 15
6.	March 30	91 days	April 28

Find the proceeds when each of the following simple discount notes are discounted.

	Maturity Value	Discount Period	Discount Rate
7.	$6000	120 days	8%
8.	$12,000	150 days	7%
9.	$3600	40 days	10%
10.	$3000	60 days	9%
11.	$5798.46	163 days	6.54%
12.	$11,715.28	113 days	11.02%

Each of the following simple interest notes was discounted at 15%. Find the discount period, the discount, and the proceeds for each.

	Loan Made	Face Value	Length of Loan	Rate	Discounted
13.	January 9	$3500	120 days	9%	March 9
14.	April 23	$4000	150 days	7%	June 11
15.	July 10	$2000	72 days	12%	August 2
16.	May 29	$4500	80 days	8%	July 8
17.	September 18	$10,000	120 days	10%	December 10
18.	October 11	$17,500	100 days	11%	January 2
19.	April 8	$12,504.20	78 days	13.8%	May 17
20.	December 4	$7958.46	125 days	14.7%	February 23

Work each of the following word problems.

21. Bob's Carriage House, Inc., accepts a $6000 note on June 5. The note is for 94 days at 8% interest. The note is discounted on July 9 at a 10% discount rate. Find (a) the discount period, (b) the discount, and (c) the proceeds.

22. Better-Buy Wholesale Grocery Supply accepted a $2800 note on October 17. The note is for 96 days at 14% interest. The note is discounted on November 1 at a 16% discount rate. Find (a) the discount period, (b) the discount, and (c) the proceeds.

23. The holder of a $1000, 14%, 90-day note dated November 5 decides to sell the note at a discount. If the note is sold on December 20 at a discount of 18%, find (a) the discount and (b) the proceeds.

24. On April 18, Moline Foundry accepts a $2475 note in settlement of a bill for goods purchased by a customer. The note is for 120 days at 7% interest. If Moline sells the note at a 10% discount rate 30 days after receipt, find (a) the discount and (b) the proceeds.

25. Eastside Bank accepted a $2000 simple discount note from one of its customers. The note was for 90 days and was discounted at 16%. The bank then rediscounted the note at 12% to a second bank, 30 days before the maturity date of the note. Find each of the following: (a) the proceeds to the customer of Eastside Bank, (b) the proceeds to Eastside Bank when it sold the note, and (c) the actual amount of interest earned by Eastside Bank on the note.

26. Farmer's Bank accepted a $17,000 simple discount note from a customer. The note was for 120 days at an 11% discount rate. The bank then rediscounted the note at a second bank, at 8%, 15 days before the maturity date of the note. Find each of the following: (a) the proceeds to the customer of Farmer's Bank, (b) the proceeds to Farmer's Bank when it rediscounted the note, and (c) the actual amount of interest earned by Farmer's Bank on the note.

27. The Third National Bank owns a $2400 simple discount note at 17%, made on November 9 and due on March 9 of the following year. On January 23, the bank rediscounts the note at 13%. Find each of the following: (a) the proceeds to the maker of the note, (b) the proceeds to the Third National Bank when it rediscounted the note, and (c) the actual amount of interest earned by the Third National Bank on the note.

28. On December 9, the Sunrise Bank accepted a $27,000 simple discount note from a customer. The note is at a discount rate of 16% and is due on March 9. On February 12, the bank rediscounted the note at 10%. Find each of the following: (a) the proceeds to the customer of Sunrise Bank, (b) the proceeds to Sunrise Bank when it rediscounted the note, and (c) the actual amount of interest earned by Sunrise Bank on the note.

29. Explain how the discount period is calculated if the time of the note, original date of the note, and discount date are known. (See Objective 1.)

30. Explain the purpose of discounting a note. What does the discounting procedure cost the original holder of the note?

CHAPTER 12 QUICK REVIEW

TOPIC	APPROACH	EXAMPLE
12.1 Maturity value of a loan	Use $I = PRT$ to find interest; then use $M = P + I$ to find maturity value.	A note with a face value of $1200 is due in 60 days. The rate is 8%. Find the maturity value. $$I = PRT$$ $$I = \$1200 \times 0.08 \times \frac{60}{360}$$ $$= \$16$$ $$M = P + I$$ $$M = \$1200 + \$16 = \$1216$$
12.1 Finding the due date, interest, and maturity value of a note with the term in months	1. Add the number of months to date of note to find due date. 2. Use $I = PRT$ to find interest. 3. Use $M = P + I$ to find maturity value.	Find due date, interest, and maturity value of a $1500 loan made on February 15 for 7 months at 8%. Due date is 7 months from February 15 which is September 15. $$I = PRT$$ $$I = \$1500 \times 0.08 \times \frac{7}{12} = \$70$$ $$M = P + I$$ $$M = \$1500 + \$70 = \$1570$$
12.1 Determining the face value of a note, given rate, time, and maturity value	Use the formula $$P = \frac{M}{1 + RT}.$$	A 90-day note has an interest rate of 9% and a maturity value of $1431.50. Find the face value. $$P = \frac{M}{1 + RT}$$ $$P = \frac{\$1431.50}{1 + \left(0.09 \times \frac{90}{360}\right)}$$ $$= \$1400$$

TOPIC	APPROACH	EXAMPLE
12.1 Finding the time of a note in days given maturity value, face value, and interest rate.	Use $I = M - P$ to find interest (I); then use $T = \dfrac{I}{PR} \times 360$ to find days.	A note has a face value of $4800, interest rate of 6%, and a maturity value of $5000. Find the time of the note in days. $I = \$5000 - \$4800 = \$200$ $T = \dfrac{\$200}{\$4800 \times 0.06} \times 360$ $= 250$ days
12.1 Determining the rate of a note given the face value, time, and maturity value	First, find the interest on the note by using the formula $I = M - P$; then, use $R = \dfrac{I}{PT}$ to find the rate.	A 240-day note has a face value of $9000 and a maturity value of $9300. Find the interest rate. $I = M - P$ $= \$9300 - \$9000 = \$300$ $I = \dfrac{I}{PT} = \dfrac{\$300}{\$9000 \times \frac{240}{360}} = 0.05$ The rate is 5%.
12.2 Finding the discount and proceeds of a simple discount note	1. Calculate bank discount (B) using the formula $B = M \cdot D \cdot T$ with $D =$ discount rate. 2. Calculate proceeds using the formula $P = M - B$.	Tom Jones borrows $5000 for 60 days at a discount rate of 9%. Find the bank discount and proceeds. $B = M \cdot D \cdot T$ $= \$5000 \times 0.09 \times \dfrac{60}{360} = \$75$ $P = M - B$ $= \$5000 - \$75 = \$4925$
12.2 Determining the effective rate or true rate of interest given face value, time, and discount rate	First, find the discount (B) using the formula $B = M \cdot D \cdot T$. Find the proceeds using the formula $P = M - B$. Calculate the true rate of interest from the formula $R = \dfrac{I}{PT}$.	A note has a face value of $9000, a time of 120 days, and a discount rate of 12%. Find the true rate of interest. $B = M \cdot D \cdot T$ $= \$9000 \times 0.12 \times \dfrac{120}{360} = \$360$ $P = M - B$ $= \$9000 - \$360 = \$8640$ $R = \dfrac{I}{PT} = \dfrac{\$360}{\$8640 \times \frac{120}{360}} = 0.125$ The effective rate is 12.5%.

TOPIC	APPROACH	EXAMPLE
12.2 Finding the face value of a simple discount note	Use the formula $M = \dfrac{P}{1 - DT}$ to find the face value M.	Find the face value of a note that will provide \$15,000 in proceeds if the note is repaid in 180 days and the bank charges a 7% discount rate.$$M = \frac{P}{1 - DT} = \frac{\$15,000}{1 - \left(0.07 \times \frac{180}{360}\right)}$$$$= \$15,544.04$$
12.2 Determining the discount rate of a note given face value and proceeds	Find the discount (B) from the formula $B = M - P$. Find the rate from the formula $D = \dfrac{B}{M \cdot T}$.	A 90-day note has a face value of \$15,000 and proceeds of \$14,568.75. Find the discount rate.$$B = M - P$$$$B = \$15,000 - \$14,568.75$$$$= \$431.25$$$$D = \frac{B}{M \cdot T}$$$$= \frac{\$431.25}{\$15,000 \times \frac{90}{360}} = 0.115$$The discount rate is 11.5%.
12.4 Finding the proceeds to an individual or firm which discounts a note	**1.** Find I, the interest on the note, and add it to the face value to find the maturity value, M. **2.** Find the discount period. **3.** Find the bank discount using $B = M \cdot D \cdot T$. **4.** Find the proceeds by using $P = M - B$.	Moe's Ice Cream converts a 9% 150-day note dated March 1 with a face value of \$1500 to cash on June 1. Assume a discount rate of 11% and find the proceeds.$$I = \$1500 \times 0.09 \times \frac{150}{360} = \$56.25;$$$$M = \$1500 + \$56.25 = \$1556.25.$$Find the discount period.

$$B = \$1556.25 \times 0.11 \times \frac{58}{360}$$

$$= \$27.58$$

$$P = \$1556.25 - \$27.58 = \$1528.67$$

The bank will pay \$1528.67 to Moe on June 1 and collect \$1556.25 on July 29 from the maker of the note.

SUMMARY EXERCISE

On October 15, Glenn Russell signs a $15,000 note for a loan from the credit union. The credit union charges a 9% discount rate. The note is for 120 days.

(a) Find the proceeds of the note.

(b) If the credit union discounts the note at 12% at a bank on December 15, find the amount the credit union receives from the bank.

(c) What is the value of the note at maturity?

(d) What is the effective rate of interest paid by Russell?

CHAPTER 12 REVIEW EXERCISES

Complete the following table for simple interest notes. [12.1]

	Face Value	Rate	Time	Interest	Maturity Value
1.	$3000	8%	120 days	_____	_____
2.	$8000	_____	180 days	$440	_____
3.	$15,000	_____	60 days	_____	$15,225

In the following, find the due date and the maturity value. [12.1]

	Date Made	Face Value	Term of Loan	Interest Rate	Date Due	Maturity Value
4.	April 11	$1200	150 days	7%	_____	_____
5.	Jan. 15	$3000	270 days	11%	_____	_____

Find the discount and the proceeds for the following discounted notes. [12.2]

	Face Value	Discount Rate	Time	Discount	Proceeds
6.	$12,000	9%	90 days	_____	_____
7.	$11,710	$12\frac{1}{2}\%$	75 days	_____	_____

[handwritten notes in right margin:]

$I = PRT$

THEN $M = P(1+RT)$

$I = M - P$, THEN $R = \dfrac{I}{PT}$

$M = P(1+RT)$

[handwritten notes near exercises 6–7:]

TO FIND DISCT $= (B = MDT)$ — THEN DEDUCT DISCT FROM FACE VALUE TO GET PROCEEDS

MAT. VAL. *[above "Face Value"]*

Each of the following simple interest notes was discounted 15%. Find the (a) discount period, (b) discount, and (c) proceeds for the following discounted notes. [12.4]

	Loan Made	Face Value	Length of Loan	Rate	Date of Discount
8.	August 10	$970	85 days	10%	October 15
9.	October 11	$16,500	100 days	11%	January 2

$m = p(1+RT)$

THEN

$B = mDT$

$P = M - B$

Find the true simple interest rate corresponding to each of the following simple discount rates. Round to the nearest hundredth of a percent.

	Time	Discount Rate
10.	90 days	12%
11.	170 days	9%

$R = \dfrac{D}{1 - DT}$

Solve the following problems. Round rates to the nearest hundredth of a percent, time to the nearest day, and money to the nearest cent.

12. A 120-day note with an interest rate of 8% has a maturity value of $9856. Find the face value. [12.1]

13. On June 15, a firm accepts a $7000, 90-day note with an interest rate of 9%. The firm discounts the note at 12% on August 25. Find (a) the discount and (b) the proceeds. [12.4]

14. Sam Mode accepted a 180-day, $12,000 note on April 15. The interest rate on the note was 10%. The note was then discounted at 13% on September 10. Find the proceeds. [12.4]

15. Find the rate of interest that will produce a maturity value of $6655.70 in 270 days from a principal of $6200. [12.1]

$R = \dfrac{I}{PT} \quad \dfrac{(455.70)}{6200 \times \frac{270}{360}}$

16. A $9750 note is signed for 80 days at a discount rate of 9%. Find the proceeds. [12.2]

17. A 150-day note with an interest rate of 8% has a maturity value of $6200. Find the face value. [12.1]

$P = \dfrac{m}{1+RT}$

18. A note with a face value of $5700 was discounted at 15%. If the discount was $641.25, find the length of the loan in days. [12.2]

19. A $7964 note is signed for 100 days at a discount rate of 14%. Find the proceeds. [12.2]

$P = m(1 - DT)$

20. A 144-day note with an interest rate of 16% has a maturity value of $15,428. Find the face value. [12.1]

21. Sarah Leeds needs $11,200 to buy a truck. She signs a simple discount note at the bank, which charges a 12% discount rate. If the note is for 270 days, find the face value of the note. [12.2]

$M = \dfrac{P}{1 - DT}$

22. West Stables must pay a note given to one of its suppliers. The interest rate on the note is 8%, the face value is $12,300, and the interest is $410. Find the time of the note. [12.1]

23. Wilson Design must pay a note given to Capital Wholesale Yard Goods. Find the time of the note if the interest rate is 15%, the face value is $9500, and the maturity value is $9816.67. [12.1]

24. A company signed a $79,000, 120-day note for a shipment of goods. The maturity value of the note is $83,187. Find the rate of interest paid on the note. [12.1]

25. Mary Knabe borrowed $5600 at an 11% discount rate for 120 days. Find the effective rate. [12.2]

26. Tom Watson Insurance accepted a 270-day, $8000 note on May 25. The interest rate on the note is 15%. The note was then discounted at 12% on August 7. Find the proceeds. [12.4]

27. A note with a face value of $6570 was discounted at 16%. If the discount was $788.40, find the length of the loan in days. [12.4]

28. Find the simple interest rate that corresponds to a simple discount rate of 17% for 45 days. [12.3]

29. A company signed an $81,000, 150-day note for a shipment of goods. The maturity value of the note is $86,062.50. Find the rate of interest paid on the note. [12.1]

30. On November 19, a firm accepts a $21,000, 150-day note with an interest rate of 15%. The firm discounts the note at 18% on February 2. Find the proceeds. [12.4]

31. Linda Youngman accepted a $16,000, 120-day note from a customer. The note had an interest rate of 9% and was accepted on May 12. The note was then discounted at 11% on July 20. Find the proceeds to Youngman. [12.4]

32. Colleen Elledge borrowed $17,500 at a 16% discount rate for 150 days. Find the equivalent simple interest rate. [12.2]

33. Diane Thompson needs $7580 to buy a computer. She signs a simple discount note at the bank, which charges a 14% discount rate. If the note is for 120 days, find the face value of the note. [12.2]

34. The Florist Wholesale Shop accepted a 210-day, $6420 note on December 12. Find the proceeds if the interest rate on the note is 12% and the note was discounted at 15% on January 19. [12.4]

35. Find the simple discount rate that corresponds to a simple interest rate of 15% on a 270-day note. [12.3]

36. What simple interest rate corresponds to a simple discount rate of 11% on a 100-day note? [12.3]

13

Compound Interest

With simple interest, the interest is calculated only on the principal, and not on any past interest. Simple interest is common for loans of one year or less. For most bank deposits, it is more common to use **compound interest**. With compound interest, the interest is found on past interest, as well as the principal. (For reference, a summary of all the formulas for compound interest is given at the end of Chapter 15, as well as inside the cover of this book.)

13.1 Compound Interest

OBJECTIVES

1 Find compound interest and compound amount from the definition.

2 Determine the number of periods and rate per period.

3 Find values in the interest table.

4 Use the formula for compound interest to find the compound amount.

5 Find the effective rate of interest.

1 With **compound interest**, the interest is found by calculating the interest on all past interest as well as on the original principal. For example, suppose $1000 is deposited in an account paying 10% interest, with interest calculated at the end of each year. Let us find the amount of compound interest that will be earned in three years. At the end of the first year, interest is paid on the original deposit of $1000.

$$\text{Interest} = \$1000 \times 0.10 \times 1 = \$100$$

At the end of the first year, the account contains

$$\text{Principal} + \text{Interest} = \$1000 + \$100 = \$1100.$$

The interest for the second year is paid on the original deposit plus the first year's interest.

$$\text{Interest} = \$1100 \times 0.10 \times 1 = \$110$$

$$\text{Amount at end of second year} = \$1100 + \$110 = \$1210$$

The interest for the third year is paid on the amount at the end of the second year.

$$\text{Interest} = \$1200 \times 0.10 \times 1 = \$121$$

$$\text{Amount at end of third year} = \$1210 + \$121 = \$1331$$

This amount, $1331, the final amount on deposit at the end of the three year investment period, is called the **compound amount**, and symbolized with the letter, *M*.

NOTE The compound amount can also be referred to as maturity value.

The interest earned during the time of the investment is found by the following formula.

$$\text{Interest} = \text{Compound amount} - \text{Original principal}$$

In our example,

$$\text{Interest} = \$1331 - \$1000 = \$331.$$

NOTE As a comparison, the *simple* interest on $1000 at 10% for 3 years is $300. The compound interest, therefore, is $31 more than the simple interest ($331 − $300). The advantage of compound interest over simple interest increases greatly as the number of years increases.

The process used for finding the compound amount could be simplified by multiplying the principal by the expression

$$1 + \textbf{Rate} \text{ (rate expressed as a decimal).}$$

This multiplication should be done as many times as the number of years in the problem. In the example above, the rate was 10%, or the decimal 0.10. The principal at the beginning of a year should be multiplied by 1 + 0.10 = 1.10. Multiply by 1.10 three times to find the compound amount after three years. Work as follows.

$1000	original principal
× 1.10	1 + rate as a decimal
$1100	amount after 1 year
× 1.10	
$1210	amount after 2 years
×1.10	
$1331	amount after 3 years

The total amount after 3 years is $1331; as mentioned earlier, this sum is the compound amount.

The compound amount has been found by multiplying the principle of $1000 by 1.10 a total of three times or

$$\$1000 \times 1.10 \times 1.10 \times 1.10 = \$1331.$$

The product of 1.10 three times can be expressed in a simpler fashion. In algebra, this type of repeated product is written with exponents. An **exponent** tells how many times a number is used as a product. Since 1.10 is used three times to find a product, it is written with an exponent of 3, which is placed to the upper right of 1.10.

$$1.10 \times 1.10 \times 1.10 = (1.10)^3$$

CAUTION   In the expression $(1.10)^3$, the 3 does not mean $3 \cdot 1.10$ but 1.10 times itself 3 times.

So the compound amount can be written as

$$\$1000(1.10)^3.$$

NOTE   The number 3 is the exponent and represents the number of years that the interest is calculated on an initial deposit of $1000.

2   Compound interest is often calculated more often than once a year. Banks may calculate compound interest every 6 months (compounded semiannually), every 3 months (compounded quarterly), every month (compounded monthly), or every day (compounded daily).

EXAMPLE 1
Finding Number of Periods and Rate Per Period

(a)   A bank pays interest of 8%, compounded semiannually. This means that semi-annually, or twice a year, interest of $8\% \div 2 = 4\%$ is added to all money that has been on deposit for 6 months or more.

(b)   An interest rate of 12% per year, compounded quarterly, means that every 3 months (quarterly), interest of $12\% \div 4 = 3\%$ is added to all money that has been on deposit for at least a quarter.   ■

NOTE   In Example 1(a), the **period of compounding** is semiannual (every six months), while it is quarterly (every 3 months) in Example 1(b).

The number of times interest is compounded changes as the period of compounding changes. For example, if interest is compounded annually for 5 years, then interest will be added to the account five times—at the end of each year for 5 years. Semiannual compounding would have interest added to the account

$$5 \times 2 = 10 \text{ times}$$

in the 5 years—at the end of each 6-month period. Also, quarterly compounding would have interest added

$$5 \times 4 = 20 \text{ times}$$

during the 5 years. (Finally, monthly compounding would have interest added 60 times during the 5 years.)

EXAMPLE 2
Finding Interest on Semiannual Deposits

Find the interest earned on $800 at 8% per year, compounded semiannually for $2\frac{1}{2}$ years.

SOLUTION Interest is 8% per year, compounded semiannually, with 8% ÷ 2 = 4% paid every six months. In $2\frac{1}{2}$ years, there are $2\frac{1}{2} \times 2 = 5$ semiannual compounding periods. To find the compound amount, multiply $800 by 1 + 0.04 = 1.04 a total of five times.

$800	original principal
× 1.04	
832.00	amount after one period
× 1.04	
865.28	amount after two periods
× 1.04	
899.89	amount after three periods (to the nearest cent)
× 1.04	
935.89	amount after four periods
× 1.04	
$973.33	amount after five periods

Using exponents, the compound amount can be written as follows.

$$\$800(1 + .04)^5 \text{ or}$$

$$\$800(1.04)^5.$$

The compound amount is $973.33. The amount of interest earned is

$$\text{Interest} = \text{Compound amount} - \text{Original principal}$$

$$= \$973.33 - \$800$$

$$= \$173.33. \quad \blacksquare$$

The formula for compound interest is expressed using exponents.

If P dollars are deposited at a rate of interest i per period for n periods, then the *compound amount M*, or the final amount on deposit, is

$$M = P(1 + i)^n.$$

Interest earned is

$$I = M - P.$$

NOTE It is important to keep in mind that the interest rate for the formula is *per compounding period*, and not per year, and n is the number of *periods*, not the number of years.

3 The value of $(1 + i)^n$ can be found by direct calculation (which is usually impractical), by scientific calculators, or from tables. One such table is given in the compound interest column (column A) of the interest table in Appendix C.

EXAMPLE 3

Using the Interest Table

Find the following values in the compound interest table in Appendix C.

(a) $(1 + 5\%)^{12}$ or $(1 + 0.05)^{12} = (1.05)^{12}$

Find the 5% page of the interest table. Look in column A, for compound interest, and find 12 (or 12 periods) at the left side. You should find 1.79585633.

(b) $(1 + 8\%)^{27} = (1.08)^{27} = 7.98806147$

Find the 8% page. Then look in column A and find 27 at the left. ∎

Calculator Approach to Example 3

Many scientific calculators have a key $\boxed{y^x}$ which evaluates exponential expressions like the one in the compound interest formula.

(a) The value of $(1.05)^{12}$ can be found using this key as follows.

$$1.05 \quad \boxed{y^x} \quad 12 \quad \boxed{=} \quad 1.79585633$$

(b) The value of $(1.08)^{27}$ is found as follows.

$$1.08 \quad \boxed{y^x} \quad 27 \quad \boxed{=} \quad 7.98806147$$

NOTE Some calculators have an $\boxed{a^x}$ key instead of a $\boxed{y^x}$ key. Both keys are used in the same way.

4 The evaluation of $(1 + i)^n$ using tables or calculators can now be used to find the compound amount and interest.

EXAMPLE 4

Using the Formula to Find Compound Amount

Find the compound amount if $5000 is deposited at 8% compounded annually for 4 years. Find the amount of interest earned.

SOLUTION By the formula above, the compound amount is

$$P(1 + i)^n = \$5000(1 + .08)^4 = \$5000(1.08)^4.$$

From column A of the interest table, $(1.08)^4 = 1.36048896$, and the compound amount is

$$\$5000(1.36048896) = \$6802.44,$$

the same result found by direct calculation at the very beginning of this section.
The amount of interest earned is

$$\$6802.44 - \$5000 = \$1802.44 \quad ∎$$

EXAMPLE 5
*Finding Interest
for Quarterly
Compounding*

Find the amount of interest earned by a deposit of $1000 for 6 years at 8% compounded quarterly.

SOLUTION   Interest compounded quarterly is compounded four times a year. In 6 years, there are $4 \times 6 = 24$ quarters or 24 periods. Interest of 8% per year is 2% per quarter. The compound amount is thus

$$\$1000(1 + 2\%)^{24} = \$1000(1 + 0.02)^{24} = \$1000(1.02)^{24}.$$

The value of $(1.02)^{24}$ can be found in column A of the interest table; locate the 2% page and find 24 periods at the left. It should show the number 1.60843725.

$$M = \$1000(1.60843725) = \$1608.44 \text{ (rounded to the nearest cent)}$$

The compound amount is $1608.44 and the interest earned is

$$\$1608.44 - \$1000 = \$608.44. \quad \blacksquare$$

EXAMPLE 6
*Finding Compound
Amount for Monthly
Compounding*

Find the compound amount if $900 is deposited at 9% compounded monthly for 3 years.

SOLUTION   In 3 years there are $3 \times 12 = 36$ monthly periods. Interest of 9% per year is $9\% \div 12 = \frac{3}{4}\%$ per month. Look in column A of the interest table for $\frac{3}{4}\%$ and 36 periods, finding the number 1.30864537. The compound amount is*

$$A = \$900(1.30864537) = \$1177.78 \quad \blacksquare$$

Calculator Approach to Example 6

Find the value of $(1 + 0.0075)^{36}$ and then multiply by 900.

$$1.0075 \quad \boxed{y^x} \quad 36 \quad \boxed{\times} \quad 900 \quad \boxed{=} \quad \$1177.78$$

The more often interest is compounded, the more interest that is earned. Use a financial calculator or a compound interest table more complete than the one in this text and use the compound interest formula to get the results shown in Table 13.1. (Leap years were ignored in finding daily interest.)

TABLE 13.1   Interest on $1000 at 12% per Year for 10 Years

Compounded	Interest
Not at all (simple interest)	$1200.00
Annually	$2105.85
Semiannually	$2207.14
Quarterly	$2262.04
Monthly	$2300.39
Daily	$2319.46

*Some calculators will not take all these digits. With these, round to as many digits as will fit. This procedure may make answers vary by a few cents, especially on large sums of money.

As suggested by Table 13.1, it makes a big difference whether interest is compounded or not. Interest differs by $905.85 when simple interest is compared to interest compounded annually. However, increasing the frequency of compounding makes smaller and smaller differences in the amount of interest earned.

5 As with simple interest in Chapter 11, the rate of interest stated with compound interest is an annual rate. This rate is called the **nominal** or **stated rate**. If interest is compounded more often than annually, the actual rate of interest is more than the nominal rate. For example, depositing $1000 for 1 year at 12% compounded quarterly produces a compound amount of

$$M = \$1000(1.12550881) \qquad \text{from the table}$$

$$M = \$1125.51 \qquad \text{(to the nearest cent)}$$

The interest earned on this deposit is $125.51, which is 12.551% of the original deposit of $1000. This amount of interest is the same as if the $1000 were invested at simple interest of 12.551% for one year. Although the stated rate of interest was 12%, the actual increase in the investment was 12.551%, the **effective rate of interest**.

NOTE The effective rate of interest is sometimes called the effective annual yield.

EXAMPLE 7

Finding the Effective Rate of Interest

Find the effective rate corresponding to a nominal rate of 8% compounded semiannually.

SOLUTION Look in Column A of the interest table for 4% and 2 periods (corresponding to 8% ÷ 2 = 4% per period and 2 semiannual periods in a year). You should find the number 1.08160000. This number means that $1 will increase to $1.08160000, an actual increase of 8.16%. The effective rate is 8.16%. ∎

Find the effective rate of interest as follows.

1. Find the entry in column A of the interest table that corresponds to the proper rate per period and the proper number of periods.
2. Subtract 1 from the number.
3. Round to the nearest hundredth of a percent.

CAUTION In Step 2, be sure to subtract 1 from the digits to the *left* of the decimal point.

EXAMPLE 8

Finding the Effective Rate of Interest

Find the effective rate corresponding to a stated rate of 18% compounded monthly.

SOLUTION Since 18% per year is 18% ÷ 12 = $1\frac{1}{2}$% per month, look in column A of the interest table for $1\frac{1}{2}$% and 12 periods, finding 1.19561817. Then subtract 1.

$$
\begin{array}{ll}
1.19561817 & \text{number from the table} \\
-1.00000000 & \text{subtract 1} \\
\hline
0.19561817 &
\end{array}
$$

Rounding to the nearest hundredth of a percent gives an effective rate of 19.56%. ∎

13.1 Exercises

Find the compound amount and the amount of interest earned for each of the following. Round to the nearest cent. Do not use tables in Exercises 1–4.

1. $1000 at 7% compounded annually for 4 years
2. $4500 at 8% compounded semiannually for 5 years
3. $15,000 at 6% compounded quarterly for $1\frac{1}{2}$ years
4. $20,000 at 12% compounded quarterly for $\frac{1}{2}$ year

Find the compound amount when the following deposits are made. Round to the nearest cent.

5. $1000 at 6% compounded annually for 8 years
6. $1000 at 9% compounded annually for 10 years
7. $4500 at 10% compounded annually for 20 years
8. $925 at 5% compounded annually for 12 years
9. $470 at 12% compounded semiannually for 9 years
10. $15,000 at 8% compounded semiannually for 11 years
11. $46,000 at 12% compounded semiannually for 5 years
12. $1050 at 11% compounded semiannually for 13 years
13. $7429.11 at 8% compounded quarterly for 9 years
14. $8765.72 at 12% compounded monthly for 4 years

Find the amount of interest earned by the following deposits.

15. $8000 at 7% compounded annually for 10 years
16. $21,000 at 9% compounded annually for 5 years
17. $43,000 at 10% compounded semiannually for 9 years
18. $10,500 at 8% compounded semiannually for 5 years
19. $8235.40 at 5% compounded quarterly for 6 years
20. $4275.89 at 12% compounded quarterly for 3 years

Use column A of the interest table to find the simple interest and the interest compounded annually. Find the amount by which the compound interest is larger. Round to the nearest cent.

	Principal	Rate	Number of Years
21.	$1000	6%	5
22.	$800	7%	6
23.	$7908.42	5%	8
24.	$9854.76	8%	11

Find the effective rate corresponding to each of the following nominal rates. Round to the nearest hundredth of a percent.

25. 10% compounded semiannually

26. 12% compounded semiannually

27. 12% compounded monthly

28. 9% compounded monthly

Work each of the following problems. Round to the nearest cent.

29. Find the interest earned on $10,000 for 4 years at 6% compounded (a) yearly, (b) semiannually, (c) quarterly, and (d) monthly. (e) Find the simple interest.

30. Suppose $32,000 is deposited for 2 years at 10% interest. Find the interest earned on the deposit if the interest is compounded (a) yearly, (b) semiannually, (c) quarterly, and (d) monthly. (e) Find the simple interest.

31. Benjamin Moore loans $8800 to the owner of a new restaurant. He will be repaid at the end of 4 years, with interest at 8% compounded semiannually. Find how much he will be repaid.

32. Glenda Wong deposits $8270 in a bank that pays 12% interest, compounded semiannually. Find the amount she will have at the end of 5 years.

33. There are two banks in Citrus Heights. One pays interest of 4% compounded annually, and the other pays 4% compounded quarterly. If Stan deposits $10,000 in each bank, (a) how much will he have in each bank at the end of 3 years? (b) How much more would he have in the bank that paid more interest?

34. (a) Which yields more interest for Barker aluminum: $5000 at 12% simple interest for 7 years, or $4000 at 12% interest compounded semiannually for 7 years? (b) How much more interest?

35. In order to guarantee a certain pension income, Mr. Watkins must have $125,000 in the bank 3 years from now. Suppose he deposits $80,000 today at 12% compounded monthly and leaves it there for 3 years. How much additional money would he then have to add to have the required amount?

36. To settle a government claim about the company's pension plan, West Hardware must have $275,000 in an account $2\frac{1}{2}$ years from now. Suppose $200,000 is deposited today at 12% interest compounded quarterly. How much additional money would have to be added in $2\frac{1}{2}$ years to have the necessary amount?

Use a financial calculator or a calculator with a $\boxed{y^x}$ key to find the compound amount for the following.

37. $7689.11 at 12.29% compounded annually for 7 years

38. $9054.27 at 15.48% compounded semiannually for $5\frac{1}{2}$ years

39. $28,907.58 at 19.42% compounded quarterly for $3\frac{3}{4}$ years

40. $51,978.76 at 16.82% compounded monthly for $2\frac{5}{6}$ years

41. **(a)** Explain in words the basic difference between simple interest and compound interest.

    (b) Explain in words the basic process of calculating interest on $10,000 invested at 4% compounded annually for 4 years.

42. Define the term effective rate of interest and the process used to calculate it. (See Objective 5.)

◾13.2 Daily and Continuous Compounding

OBJECTIVES

1 Calculate interest compounded daily.

2 Find compound interest for time deposit accounts.

3 Determine the penalty for early withdrawal.

4 Find compound amount with continuous compounding.

A savings account is one of the safest places for money. Money deposited in these accounts at a bank or at a savings and loan is guaranteed up to a certain amount by an agency of the federal government. A credit union normally offers similar guarantees.

These institutions offer several different types of accounts.

1 **Passbook Accounts.** **Passbook accounts** meet the daily money needs of a person or business. Money may be deposited in or withdrawn from a passbook account anytime, with no penalty. In recent years, interest rates have ranged from $2\frac{1}{2}$% to 6% per year.

Interest in a passbook account is compound interest. It is common for banks to pay interest **compounded daily**—in this way, interest is paid for every day that the money is on deposit.

The formula for daily compounding is exactly the same as the formula of the last section. However, because the annual interest rate must be divided by 365 (for daily compounding), the arithmetic can be very tedious. To avoid this, use a special table, such as Table 13.2, which gives the values of $(1 + i)^n$ for 1 to 90 days, as well as for 1 to 4 quarters, assuming $5\frac{1}{4}$% interest, compounded daily. The table goes only to 90 days since, even though interest is compounded daily, it is normally credited to the depositor's account only quarterly. The four quarters in a year begin on January 1, April 1, July 1, and October 1. It is a common practice to assume 30 days per month, and to assume that money deposited on the 31st day of the month was deposited on the 30th.

EXAMPLE 1
Finding Interest Using Daily Compounding

Paul Joseph deposited $1746 in a passbook account paying $5\frac{1}{4}$% interest, compounded daily, on July 9. He withdrew the money on August 17. Find the amount of interest he earned.

SOLUTION Assume 30 days per month. There are an additional 21 days in July (from the 9th), and 17 days in August, so that the money was on deposit for

TABLE 13.2   Values of $(1 + i)^n$ for $5\frac{1}{4}\%$

Interest Compounded Quarterly		Interest Compounded Daily					
Number of Quarters	Value of $(1 + i)^n$	Number of Days n	Value of $(1 + i)^n$	n	Value of $(1 + i)^n$	n	Value of $(1 + i)^n$
1	1.013028415	1	1.000143836	31	1.004468538	61	1.008811940
2	1.026226569	2	1.000287692	32	1.004613016	62	1.008957043
3	1.039596674	3	1.000431569	33	1.004757515	63	1.009102167
4	1.053140970	4	1.000575467	34	1.004902035	64	1.009247312
		5	1.000719385	35	1.005046576	65	1.009392478
		6	1.000863324	36	1.005191137	66	1.009537665
		7	1.001007284	37	1.005335720	67	1.009682872
		8	1.001151264	38	1.005480323	68	1.009828100
		9	1.001295266	39	1.005624947	69	1.009973350
		10	1.001439288	40	1.005769591	70	1.010118620
		11	1.001583330	41	1.005914257	71	1.010263911
		12	1.001727394	42	1.006058943	72	1.010409223
		13	1.001871478	43	1.006203650	73	1.010554556
		14	1.002015582	44	1.006348378	74	1.010699909
		15	1.002159708	45	1.006493127	75	1.010845284
		16	1.002303854	46	1.006637896	76	1.010990679
		17	1.002448021	47	1.006782687	77	1.011136096
		18	1.002592209	48	1.006927498	78	1.011281533
		19	1.002736417	49	1.007072330	79	1.011426992
		20	1.002880647	50	1.007217183	80	1.011711971
		21	1.003024897	51	1.007362057	81	1.011717971
		22	1.003169167	52	1.007506951	82	1.011863492
		23	1.003313459	53	1.007651867	83	1.012009034
		24	1.003457771	54	1.007968030	84	1.012154597
		25	1.003602104	55	1.007941760	85	1.012300181
		26	1.003746458	56	1.008086738	86	1.012445786
		27	1.003890832	57	1.008231737	87	1.012591412
		28	1.004035227	58	1.008376756	88	1.012737058
		29	1.004179643	59	1.008521797	89	1.012882726
		30	1.004324080	60	1.008666858	90	1.013028415

$21 + 17 = 38$ days. From Table 13.2, 38 days gives the number 1.005480323, so that the compound amount is

$$\$1746(1.005480323) = \$1755.57.$$

The interest earned is

$$\$1755.57 - \$1746 = \$9.57. \quad \blacksquare$$

Calculator Approach to Example 1

First calculate the daily interest, i, by dividing $5\frac{1}{4}\%$ by 365.

$$.0525 \;\boxed{\div}\; 365$$

Now add 1 to this value and raise it to the 38 power to evaluate $(1 + i)^n$.

$$\boxed{+}\; 1 \;\boxed{=}\; \boxed{y^x}\; 38$$

Multiply this value by $1746.

$$\boxed{\times}\; 1746 \;\boxed{=}\; \$1755.57$$

EXAMPLE 2
Finding Interest on Multiple Deposits

Jane Gunton had $2463 in her savings account on January 1. She deposited an additional $1320 on February 18, with $804 deposited on March 3. Find the total interest she earned during the quarter.

SOLUTION   Treat each of the three amounts separately. The $2463 was in the account for the entire quarter. From Table 13.2, use either 90 days or 1 quarter to get the number 1.013028415. The compound amount is

$$\$2463(1.013028415) = \$2495.09.$$

A deposit of $1320 was made on February 18. Assume 12 additional days in February, with 30 days in March, for a total of $12 + 30 = 42$ days. From Table 13.2, the compound amount is

$$\$1320(1.006058943) = \$1328.$$

Finally, $804 was deposited for $30 - 3 = 27$ days, giving a compound amount of

$$\$804(1.003890832) = \$807.13.$$

The total of the compound amounts is

$$\$2495.09 + \$1328 + \$807.13 = \$4630.22.$$

The total of the deposits is

$$\$2463 + \$1320 + \$804 = \$4587.00.$$

The interest earned during the quarter is

$$\$4630.22 - \$4587 = \$43.22. \quad\blacksquare$$

EXAMPLE 3
Finding Quarterly Interest

Rich Cairns had $11,094 in his savings account on July 1. He withdrew $4280 on August 25. How much interest did he earn for the quarter?

SOLUTION   Of his original $11,094, a total of

$$\$11,094 - \$4280 = \$6814$$

earned interest for the entire quarter. From Table 13.2, the compound amount for this sum is

$$\$6814(1.013028415) = \$6902.78.$$

The interest earned is

$$\$6902.78 - \$6814 = \$88.78.$$

The withdrawn \$4280 earned interest for 30 days in July and 25 days in August, for a total of 55 days. Here, the compound amount is

$$\$4280(1.007941760) = \$4313.99.$$

The interest earned is

$$\$4313.99 - \$4280 = \$33.99.$$

The total interest earned by the account is

$$\$88.78 + \$33.99 = \$122.77.$$

The balance in the account at the end of the quarter is as follows.

	$11,094.00	original balance
−	4280.00	withdrawal
	6814.00	
+	122.77	interest
	$6936.77	final balance

2   **Time Deposit Accounts.**   While passbook savings accounts are very useful for money needed for day-to-day living, the low interest rate paid by these accounts makes them undesirable for larger amounts of money, such as money being saved for retirement. These larger amounts are better off in a **time deposit account** where money must be left for a fixed period of time. For example, one local savings and loan pays $3\frac{1}{4}\%$ on money in a day-in and day-out passbook account, but pays $5\frac{1}{2}\%$ on money left with a **certificate of deposit** for 2 years. With a certificate of deposit (abbreviated CD), money must be left for some minimum time period, and a minimum amount of money must be deposited. Another popular certificate of deposit currently available pays interest depending on the interest rate paid by the U.S. government. While these CDs pay higher interest (as high as 6% or 8% at times) and require that money be left for only 6 months, a large minimum deposit (perhaps \$10,000) may be required. A typical certificate of deposit is shown in Figure 13.1.

It is probably not a good idea to invest all of one's money in a certificate of deposit, since a penalty is charged for early withdrawal. At least some cash should be left in a passbook savings account (or perhaps in the money market accounts discussed later) for daily needs.

NEW ENGLAND FEDERAL
— *Savings Bank* —

Certificate of Deposit

1. Account Summary

Accountholder(s)   JOHN DOE

Account Number   123-45670
Date of Issuance   JANUARY 23
Maturity Date   JULY 23

Principal Amount	Term	Nominal Rate / APR	Additional Deposits
$ 6,400.00	30 MONTHS	4.08/4.50%	None

2. General

This is a Certificate of Deposit in the amount set forth above issued to the Accountholder(s) named above, by New England Federal Savings Bank.

3. Account Renewal

Unless the Accountholder(s) has instructed the Bank not to renew this certificate of deposit, it will automatically and repeatedly be renewed at its maturity for an identical term and at the interest rate the Bank is then offering. Notice of maturity will be mailed to the Accountholder(s) at least 15 days prior to each maturity. The Bank reserves the right not to renew this certificate of deposit, but it must mail notice of such intention to the Accountholder(s) at least 15 days prior to maturity.

4. Interest

This certificate of deposit shall earn interest at the rate set forth above. Such interest shall be compounded daily and credited monthly. During renewal terms, this certificate of deposit will earn interest at the rate the Bank is then offering. Interest earned during any term may be withdrawn during that term without penalty. Upon renewal, principal shall include interest earned (but not paid) during the prior term.

5. Interest Checks   N/A

The Accountholder(s) has authorized the Bank to pay interest on the following basis:
☐ Monthly   ☐ Quarterly   ☐ Semi Annually

6. Withdrawal Penalty

In the event of any withdrawal of principal at any time prior to the maturity of this or any renewal term, the Accountholder(s) shall pay a penalty equal to three months' interest, (if the term of this certificate of deposit is equal to or less than one year), or six months' interest, (if the term of this certificate of deposit is greater than one year), on the amount withdrawn, at the rate being paid on this certificate of deposit at the time of withdrawal. If the Accountholder withdraws part or all of the balance of this certificate of deposit during the seven calendar days subsequent to the maturity of this or any renewal term, there will be no withdrawal penalty.

Any withdrawal which reduces the balance of this certificate of deposit below $1,000 will be treated as a withdrawal of the remaining balance.

No penalty will be charged for withdrawal following the death or adjudicated incompetence of the Accountholder.

NEW ENGLAND FEDERAL SAVINGS BANK

By   *Sue Smith*
———————————————————
Authorized Representative

FIGURE 13.1

The higher interest paid by some certificates of deposit can be found using Table 13.3. (This table assumes daily compounding and 365 days per year.)

TABLE 13.3   Compound Interest for Time Deposit Accounts

Number of Years	Interest Rate			
	8%	9%	10%	12%
1	1.08327757	1.09416214	1.10515578	1.12747462
2	1.17349030	1.19719080	1.22136930	1.27119901
3	1.27121572	1.30992085	1.34980334	1.43324461
4	1.37707948	1.43326581	1.49174297	1.61594692
5	1.49175931	1.56822519	1.64860837	1.82193913
10	2.22534585	2.45933025	2.71790955	3.31946220

EXAMPLE 4

Finding Compound Amount and Interest on Time Deposits

David Herren invests $20,000 in a certificate of deposit paying 8%. Find the compound amount after 5 years. Also, find the interest earned.

SOLUTION   Look in Table 13.3 for 8% and 5 years, finding 1.49175931. Then

$$\text{Compound amount} = \$20,000(1.49175931)$$

$$= \$29,835.19.$$

Of this amount,

$$\$29,835.19 - \$20,000 = \$9835.19$$

is interest. ∎

3 A depositor who agrees to leave money in an account for a certain period of time, but then withdraws it early, must pay a penalty. While it is not possible for the depositor to lose any of the *principal* involved, it is very possible that all or part of the *interest* may be lost. The procedure for calculating this early withdrawal penalty is not standard. Many financial institutions use the following rules for calculating the **early withdrawal penalty**.

1. If money is withdrawn within 3 months of the deposit, no interest will be paid at all on the money withdrawn.

2. If the money is withdrawn after 3 months, then only the regular passbook interest will be paid on the account, after deducting 3 months from the time that the account has been open.

EXAMPLE 5
Finding Interest
When Early
Withdrawal Occurs

Use the rules listed in the box to find the amount of interest earned on each of the following.

SOLUTION

(a)   On January 5, Raymond Hoyle deposited $5000 in a 1-year certificate of deposit paying 9%. He withdrew the money on March 12 of the same year.

Since March 12 is within 3 months of January 5, no interest at all is earned. The bank will simply return the $5000.

(b)   Bob Kashir deposited $6000 in a 4-year certificate of deposit paying 10%. He withdrew the money 15 months later. The passbook rate at his bank is $5\frac{1}{4}\%$ compounded daily.

The money is withdrawn early, so 3 months interest is lost. The money was on deposit for 15 months, but only $15 - 3 = 12$ months interest will be paid. Also, interest will be paid at the passbook rates, $5\frac{1}{4}\%$, instead of the more generous 10%. From Table 13.2 under 12 months (or 4 quarters) at $5\frac{1}{4}\%$, find the number 1.053140970. Since $6000 was deposited, a total of

$$\$6000(1.053140970) = \$6318.85$$

will be in the account. To find the amount of interest, subtract the initial deposit of $6000 from $6318.85.

$$\text{Interest } = \$6318.85 - \$6000 = \$318.85 \quad \blacksquare$$

Insured Money Market Accounts.   Many savings institutions offer **insured money market accounts** (often called **IMMAs**). These accounts offer interest rates almost as high as those of certificates of deposit, while permitting funds to be withdrawn at any time. A typical IMMA account is insured by the federal government (up to a certain maximum), allows for balances as low as $2500, pays interest rates within 1% or so of CDs, and allows for three checks per month to be written without charge. Unlike certificates of deposit, however, the interest rate may change weekly or even daily. As an example, Table 13.4 lists the interest rates paid during one 30-day period by a local bank on an IMMA account. Notice how often the rates changed.

TABLE 13.4   Sample IMMA Account Interest Rates

Effective Date of Rate	Interest Rate
11/24	8.50%
11/30	8.25%
12/17	8.15%
12/18	8.00%
12/21	7.75%

Insured money market accounts were set up to compete with the money market funds offered by many stock brokerage firms—IMMAs offer competitive interest rates with the benefit of federal insurance.

4   In the first section of this chapter, we discussed annual, semiannual, quarterly, and monthly compounding. Then we saw daily compounding. There is no reason that interest could not be compounded more frequently, such as every hour or even every minute. Table 13.5, an extension of Table 13.1, shows the interest earned on $1000 at 12% per year for 10 years, assuming various frequencies of compounding. (The results in this table were found with the formula $P(1 + i)^n$ and a financial calculator.)

TABLE 13.5   Interest on $1000 at 12% per Year for 10 Years

Frequency of Compounding	Number of Periods	Interest
Annually	10	$2105.85
Semiannually	20	$2207.14
Quarterly	40	$2262.04
Monthly	120	$2300.39
Daily	3650	$2319.46
Hourly	87,600	$2320.09
Every Minute	5,256,000	$2320.11

Increasing the frequency of compounding makes less and less difference—for example, going from compounding daily to compounding every minute produces only 65 cents additional interest on $1000 after 10 years.

It would be possible to extend Table 13.5 to include compounding every second, every half-second, or any desired small time interval. It would even be possible to think of compounding *every instant*. Compounding every instant is called **continuous compounding**. The formula for continuous compounding, given in the next box, uses the number *e*. The number *e* is approximately equal to 2.7182818. Some calculators have an e^x button for working with this number.

> If P dollars is deposited at a rate of interest i per year *compounded continuously* for n years, the compound interest M is
>
> $$M = Pe^{ni}.$$

Continuous compounding is useful in more advanced courses when discussing such things as inflation. With high inflation, prices are increasing all the time, so that continuous compounding is more useful than, say, monthly compounding, which would assume that prices increase only at the end of a month (in one big jump).

EXAMPLE 6

Finding the Compound Amount for Continuous Compounding

Find the compound amount for the following deposits.

SOLUTION

(a) $1000 at 12% compounded continuously for 10 years

Use the formula in the box with $P = 1000$, $i = 0.12$, and $n = 10$. The compound amount is

$$M = Pe^{ni}$$

$$M = 1000e^{10(0.12)}$$

$$= 1000e^{1.2}.$$

The value of $e^{1.2}$ is found in the table in Appendix B. Find 1.2 in the column labeled x and read across to the number 3.32011692 in the column labeled e^x. Then

$$M = 1000(3.32011692) = \$3320.12.$$

Of this amount,

$$\$3320.12 - \$1000 = \$2320.12$$

is interest, only 1 cent more than when interest is compounded every minute, as shown in Table 13.5 in this section.

(b) $48,906.11 at 15% compounded continuously for 6 years (use Appendix B)

$$= \$48,906.11e^{6(0.15)}$$

$$= \$48,906.11e^{0.90}$$

$$= \$48,906.11(2.45960311)$$

$$= \$120,289.62.$$

The compound amount is $120,289.62, which includes $71,383.51 of interest. ∎

13.2 Exercises

Find the interest earned by the following. Assume $5\frac{1}{4}\%$ interest compounded daily.

	Amount	Date Deposited	Date Withdrawn
1.	$1000	Oct. 23	Dec. 15
2.	$1000	July 30	Oct. 4
3.	$6500	Feb. 21	Mar. 11
4.	$2830	May 4	June 23
5.	$15,635.51	Sept. 15	Nov. 5
6.	$32,754.58	Mar. 24	May 23
7.	$4600	Dec. 12	Feb. 4
8.	$3250	Aug. 28	Nov. 3

Find the amount on deposit at the end of the quarter when the following sums are deposited as indicated. Assume $5\frac{1}{4}$% interest compounded daily.

	Amount	Date Deposited
9.	$7235.82	Feb. 14
10.	$1125.40	April 7
11.	$2965.72	July 1
12.	$4031.46	April 1

Find the compound amount for each of the following certificates of deposit. Assume daily compounding.

	Amount Deposited	Interest Rate	Time in Years
13.	$3500	9%	5
14.	$3800	8%	2
15.	$7000	10%	5
16.	$16,000	8%	4

Find the amount of interest earned by the following certificates of deposit. Assume daily compounding.

	Amount Deposited	Interest Rate	Time in Years
17.	$6000	10%	10
18.	$9000	10%	5
19.	$62,500	9%	4
20.	$36,540	8%	3

21. List some applications where continuous compounding is useful. Explain why this type of interest calculation is preferred over other applications. (See Objective 4.)

22. Explain the difference between passbook accounts, time deposit accounts, certificates of deposit, and insured money market accounts.

Solve each of the following word problems. Assume $5\frac{1}{4}\%$ interest compounded daily. Round to the nearest cent.

23. Pat Kutsch had $6134 in her savings account on October 1. On November 25, she deposited an additional $654, with $212 deposited on December 26. Find the interest earned during the quarter and the balance at the end of the quarter.

24. Scott Hardy had $14,702 in his savings account on January 1. On January 12 he deposited a check for $1464, with a $976 tax refund check deposited on March 15. Find the interest earned during the quarter and the balance at the end of the quarter.

25. Ace Tire Service has a savings account for spare cash. On the first day of a quarter the account contained $17,500. A withdrawal of $5000 was made 21 days later, with a further withdrawal of $980 made 12 days before the end of the quarter. Find the interest earned during the quarter and the balance at the end of the quarter.

26. Fred's Stationery maintains a savings account for the money it uses to pay income tax. On April 1, the account contained $61,200. A withdrawal of $9616 was made on April 15, with an additional $20,000 withdrawn on June 15. Find the interest earned during the quarter and the balance at the end of the quarter.

For the following word problems on certificates of deposit, use the rules for finding the early withdrawal penalty as given in the text.

27. Robin Wilson deposited $3500 in a 5-year account paying 7% interest. She withdrew her money 74 days later. How much interest did she receive?

28. Laura Garcia deposited $7200 in a 4-year account paying 6%. She took the money out $1\frac{3}{4}$ months later. How much interest did she receive?

29. Frank Bella deposited $5000 in a 5-year account paying 9% in a bank whose passbook rate is $5\frac{1}{8}\%$. He withdrew the money 17 months later. (a) For how many months would he be paid interest? (b) What rate of interest would he be paid for these months?

30. Mark Bonilla placed $6000 in a 4-year account at 12% in a savings and loan whose passbook rate is $5\frac{1}{4}\%$. He took the money out after 10 months. (a) For how many months would he be paid interest? (b) At what rate?

31. Emma Gilger placed $20,000 in a 10-year account paying 11% interest. The savings and loan where she placed her money pays a passbook rate of $5\frac{1}{4}\%$ compounded daily. She withdrew $5000 of her money after 15 months. Find the interest that she earned on the $5000.

32. Trish Hardison deposited $18,680 in a 4-year account paying 10% interest. The bank where she put the money pays a passbook rate of $5\frac{1}{4}\%$ compounded annually. She withdrew $2000 after 15 months. Find the interest that she earned on the $2000.

Find the compound amount and the interest for the following deposits. Assume continuous compounding.

	Amount	Interest Rate	Time	
33.	$1000	10%	5 years	**$1648.72; $648.72**
34.	$1000	12%	4 years	**$1616.07; $616.07**
35.	$3850	8%	11 years	**$9281.96; $5431.96**
36.	$4710	9%	3 years	**$6169.93; $1459.93**
37.	$8119.54	8%	9 months	**$8621.62; $502.08**
38.	$2508.76	9%	8 months	**$2663.89; $155.13**

Work the following word problems.

39. Juanita Metzger can choose between two investments: one pays 10% compounded semiannually, and the other pays $9\frac{1}{2}$% compounded continuously. If she wants to deposit $17,000 for $1\frac{1}{2}$ years, which investment should she choose? How much extra interest will she earn by making the correct choice? (Hint: $e^{0.1425} = 1.15315308$.) **10% compounded semiannually; $76.03**

40. Gary Orr wishes to invest $62,904 from his company's pension plan. One investment offers 12% compounded quarterly, while another offers 11.75% compounded continuously. Which investment should he choose, if the money will be invested for 2 years? How much extra interest will he earn by making the proper choice? (Hint: $e^{0.235} = 1.26490877$.) **12% compounded quarterly; $117.08**

13.3 Finding Time and Rate

OBJECTIVES

1 Determine time given compound interest.

2 Determine rate.

3 Use more than one table to solve interest problems.

We saw in the previous chapter how to use the formula for simple interest, $I = PRT$, and find the value of any of the four variables when given the value of the other three. A similar thing can be done with the formula for compound interest, $M = P(1 + i)^n$.

While algebra was used to solve $I = PRT$, a different procedure is needed for $M = P(1 + i)^n$. This different procedure is required because of the exponent n in the formula.

1 The first two examples show how to find time for an investment.

EXAMPLE 1
Finding Time Given
Compound Interest

Suppose $1500 is deposited at 10% compounded annually. How long will it take to have a compound amount of $2415.77?

SOLUTION   Use the formula $M = P(1 + i)^n$, with $M = \$2415.77$, $P = \$1500$, and $i = 0.10$. The value of n is unknown.

$$M = P(1 + i)^n$$

$$\$2415.77 = \$1500(1 + 0.10)^n$$

$$\$2415.77 = \$1500(1.10)^n$$

Divide both sides by $1500.

$$\frac{\$2415.77}{\$1500} = (1.10)^n$$

Use a calculator to divide on the left side.

$$1.61051333 = (1.10)^n$$

Actually solving this equation would require advanced mathematics. However, a good approximation can be found by looking down column A of the 10% page of the interest table in Appendix C. The number 1.61051000 in row 5 is very close to the number on the left side of the equation above. Since interest is compounded annually, the deposit was for 5 years. ∎

EXAMPLE 2
Finding Time

How long would it take for $28,500 at 8% interest compounded quarterly to become $34,741.34?

SOLUTION   Interest of 8% per year is $8\% \div 4 = 2\%$ per quarter. Use the formula $M = P(1 + i)^n$ with $M = \$34,741.34$, $P = \$28,500$, and $i = 0.02$.

$$\$34,741.34 = \$28,500(1.02)^n$$

Use a calculator to divide both sides by $28,500.

$$1.21899439 = (1.02)^n$$

Now look in column A of the 2% page of the interest table to find the number closest to 1.21899439. The closest number is 1.21899442, which corresponds to 10 quarters, or $2\frac{1}{2}$ years. ∎

EXAMPLE 3
Finding Time
to Double

Suppose the general level of inflation in the economy averages 4% per year. Find the number of years it would take for the general level of prices to double.

SOLUTION   To find the number of years it will take for $1 worth of goods and services to cost $2, solve for n in the equation

$$2 = 1(1 + 4\%)^n$$

or

$$2 = 1(1 + 0.04)^n,$$

where $M = 2$, $P = 1$, and $i = 4\%$. This equation simplifies as

$$2 = (1.04)^n.$$

As in the previous examples, look down column A of the 4% page of the interest table to find the number closest to 2. The closest number is 2.02581652. This number corresponds to 18 periods, so to the nearest year the general level of prices would double is 18 years. ∎

2   The same method used for finding time can be used to find rate. Find rate by first looking in column A for the proper number of periods. Then look through several pages corresponding to different rates, as necessary.

EXAMPLE 4
Finding Rate Given Compound Amount

A principal of $5500 is deposited for 15 months, with interest compounded monthly. Find the rate if the compound amount is $6876.28.

SOLUTION   Use the equation $M = P(1 + i)^n$, with i unknown.

$$\$6876.28 = \$5500(1 + i)^{15}$$

Divide both sides by $5500.

$$1.25023273 = (1 + i)^{15}$$

Find the row for 15 periods in column A of the interest table. Check this number in row 15 of column A as necessary until you find the number closest to 1.25023273. The closest number is 1.25023207, for an interest rate of $1\frac{1}{2}$% per month, or

$$1\frac{1}{2} \times 12 = 18\% \quad \text{per year} \quad ∎$$

3   Some problems require the use of more than one table, as in the next example.

EXAMPLE 5
Using More than One Table

George Fredricks has deposited $21,000 in an account paying 10% per year, compounded semiannually. After $3\frac{1}{2}$ years, he removes all the money in the account and buys a 5-year certificate of deposit paying 12%. Find the final amount on deposit at the end of the $8\frac{1}{2}$-year period.

SOLUTION   Start with $21,000 deposited for 10% per year, compounded semiannually for $3\frac{1}{2}$ years, or 7 semiannual periods. Look in Column A of the interest table for 7 periods and 10% ÷ 2 = 5% interest, finding 1.40710042. The compound amount is

$$\$21,000(1.40710042) = \$29,549.11.$$

This amount is used to purchase a certificate of deposit. Look in Table 13.3 for 12% and 5 years, finding 1.82193913. The final amount is

$$\$29,549.11(1.82193913) = \$53,836.68.$$

After $3\frac{1}{2} + 5 = 8\frac{1}{2}$ years, the original $21,100 has become $53,836.68. Of this amount,

$$\$53,836.68 - \$21,000 = \$32,836.68$$

represents interest. ∎

13.3 Exercises

Complete this table. Round time to the nearest period, interest to the nearest whole per-cent per year, and money to the nearest cent. (As review, some of these problems do not require the methods of this section.)

	Principal	Compound Amount	Interest	Compounded	Time in Years
1.	$6000	$9519.76	8%	annually	_____
2.	$5000	$8811.71	12%	annually	_____
3.	$2950	$3736.97	12%	quarterly	_____
4.	$5320	$7302.85	8%	quarterly	_____
5.	$15,711.42	$23,323.69	5%	semiannually	_____
6.	$28,904.76	$36,679.72	12%	monthly	_____
7.	_____	$4331.91	10%	semiannually	9
8.	_____	$8084.11	5%	quarterly	6
9.	$7000	$12,869.21	_____	annually	9
10.	$2500	$7846.07	_____	annually	12
11.	$15,000	$23,369.51	_____	semiannually	$7\frac{1}{2}$
12.	$14,000	$29,104.99	_____	semiannually	$7\frac{1}{2}$
13.	$28,110	$41,280.48	_____	quarterly	$3\frac{1}{4}$
14.	$37,440	$57,881.48	_____	quarterly	$5\frac{1}{2}$

15. Describe some situations that would require the use of more than one interest table. (See Objective 3.)

16. Explain how to determine the number of years it will take for an investment to double. Does the time depend on the amount of the investment? (See Objective 1.)

Work the following word problems. Round as in Exercises 1–14.

17. Jack Taylor invests $15,000 in an account paying 6% per year compounded annually. In how many years will the compound amount become $18,937.15?

18. Bob Allgood places a $27,000 inheritance in an account paying 16% per year compounded quarterly. In how many years will the account contain $41,565.26?

19. Roy Bledsoe deposits $46,000 in an account that has interest compounded semiannually. In $2\frac{1}{2}$ years the account contains $58,708.95. Find the interest rate paid.

20. Find the interest rate paid if a deposit of $35,200 becomes $61,723.41 in $4\frac{3}{4}$ years, with interest compounded quarterly.

Use the ideas of Example 3 in the text to answer the following questions. Find the time it would take for the general level of prices in the economy to double if the average annual inflation rate is

21. 3%

22. 4%

23. 5%

24. 6%

25. The consumption of electricity has increased historically at 6% per year. If it continued to increase at this rate indefinitely, find the number of years before the electric utilities would need to double the amount of generating capacity.

26. Suppose a conservation campaign coupled with higher rates caused the demand for electricity to increase at only 2% per year, as it has recently. (See Exercise 25.) Find the number of years before the utilities would need to double generating capacity.

The remainder of these exercises may require the use of any of the tables presented so far in this chapter.

27. Dawn Young deposits $10,000 at 8% compounded quarterly. Two years after she makes the first deposit, she adds another $20,000, also at 8%, compounded quarterly. What total amount will she have five years after her first deposit?

28. Jenny Toms deposits $10,000 in a bank account paying 8% compounded quarterly. After three years she deposits another $7500, just when the bank changes its rate to 6% compounded semiannually. Find the total amount in her account after an additional two years.

For exercises 29–32 use Table 13.3 for the certificates of deposit.

29. Robert Jay deposits $4200 in an account paying 8% per year compounded quarterly. After $3\frac{3}{4}$ years, the compound amount is used to buy a 3-year certificate of deposit paying 12%. What is the final amount, principal and interest, that Jay will have at the end of the $6\frac{3}{4}$-year period?

30. Daniel Jones buys a 10-year $24,000 certificate of deposit paying 12%. After 10 years, the compound amount is placed in an account paying 16% per year, compounded quarterly. If the money is left in this account for an additional 15 months, find the final amount, principal and interest, that Jones will have.

31. Jean Sides has $11,000 in an account paying 10% compounded semiannually. After the money has been on deposit for 4 years, $5000 is removed to buy a certificate of deposit paying 12% per year for 3 years. (The remaining money stays at 10% compounded semiannually.) Find the total amount on deposit in both accounts, both principal and interest, after the 7 years.

32. Frank Sabas has $45,000 in an account paying 8% compounded quarterly. After $2\frac{1}{4}$ years, Sabas removes $20,000 and buys a 5-year certificate of deposit paying 10%. (The remaining money continues to earn 8% compounded quarterly.) Find the total amount on deposit in both accounts (both principal and interest) after the $7\frac{1}{4}$ years.

13.4 Present Value at Compound Interest

OBJECTIVE

1 Find the present value of a future amount.

The formula for compound interest, $M = P(1 + i)^n$, has been used to find the compound amount, M, when the principal, P, the interest rate per period, i, and the number of periods, n, are known. This section discusses how to find P, the amount of money that can be deposited today that will amount to A dollars after n periods.

1 Earlier, P was called the **principal**, that amount that is deposited today. When the amount to be deposited today is unknown, it is often called the **present value**. Present value is the amount that can be deposited today that will become A dollars after n periods at a rate of interest i per period. Since principal and present value are really just the sum that can be deposited today, no confusion will be caused by using the letter P for both.

To find a formula for P, start with $M = P(1+i)^n$ and divide both sides by $(1+i)^n$.

$$M = P(1 + i)^n$$

$$\frac{M}{(1 + i)^n} = \frac{P(1 + i)^n}{(1 + i)^n}$$

$$P = \frac{M}{(1 + i)^n}$$

The present value, P, is found by dividing the compound amount, M, by $(1 + i)^n$. The values of $(1 + i)^n$, given in column A of the interest table, are usually long decimals, making the division very tedious without a calculator. To avoid this difficulty, rewrite

$$\frac{M}{(1 + i)^n} \quad \text{as} \quad M \cdot \frac{1}{(1 + i)^n}$$

In summary,

---

the **present value**, P, of the future amount, M, at an interest rate of i per period for n periods is

FACTOR FOUND IN APP. C

$$P = \frac{M}{(1 + i)^n} = M \cdot \frac{1}{(1 + i)^n}$$

(Use Column B of the interest table for value of $\frac{1}{(1 + i)^n}$).

EXAMPLE 1
Finding
Present Value

Joan Trestrail must pay a lump sum of $6000 in 5 years. What lump sum deposited today at 8% compounded annually will produce the needed $6000?

SOLUTION   Use the formula in the box with $M = \$6000$, $i = 8\%$, and $n = 5$.

$$P = M \cdot \frac{1}{(1 + i)^n}$$

$$P = \$6000 \cdot \frac{1}{(1 + 0.08)^5}$$

$$P = \$6000 \cdot \frac{1}{(1.08)^5}$$

Look on the 8% page of the interest table, in row 5, and the present value column to find that $\dfrac{1}{(1.08)^5} = 0.68058320$, and

$$P = \$6000\,(0.68058320) = \$4083.50.$$

A deposit of $4083.50 today at 8% compounded annually will produce $6000 in 5 years. Of this $6000,

$$\$6000 - \$4083.50 = \$1916.50$$

represents interest earned on the initial deposit of $4083.50. ■

The same result could have been found by using the compound interest table, column A, and *dividing*. Looking up 8% and 5 periods in column A gives 1.46932808. Now divide

$$P = \frac{\$6000}{1.46932808} = \$4083.50.$$

Here both methods gave the same answer. Sometimes the answers may differ by a few cents because of rounding error.

NOTE For extremely large amounts of money, the method of *dividing* with a number from column A can be slightly more accurate.

EXAMPLE 2
Finding
Present Value

Find the present value of $16,000 in 9 years if money can be deposited at 6% compounded semiannually.

SOLUTION   In 9 years there are $2 \times 9 = 18$ semiannual periods. A rate of 6% per year is 3% each semiannual period. Look at the 3% page of the interest table, and find 18 periods in column B. You should see the number 0.58739461. The present value is

$$\$16,000(0.58739461) = \$9398.31.$$

A deposit of $9398.31 today, at 6% compounded semiannually, will produce $16,000 in 9 years. ■

EXAMPLE 3
Finding Value of a Business

Tom Fredrickson has a business worth $125,000. The business is doing well, with Fredrickson sure that the value of the business will increase at the rate of 16% per year, compounded semiannually, for the next four years. If he sells the business, he will invest the proceeds at 8% compounded quarterly. What sale price should he insist on?

SOLUTION This problem requires two steps. First decide on the future value of the business. This is done with the formula for compound amount, $M = P(1 + i)^n$. Here, $P = \$125,000$, $i = 16\% \div 2 = 8\%$, and $n = 4 \times 2 = 8$ periods.

FIND FUTURE VALUE

$$M = \$125,000(1 + 8\%)^8$$

$$M = \$125,000(1.85093021) \qquad \text{Use column A.}$$

$$M = \$231,366.28$$

Now find the present value of this sum, assuming that money can be invested at 8% compounded quarterly. Use the formula

THEN PRESENT VALUE

$$P = M \cdot \frac{1}{(1 + i)^n}$$

with $M = \$231,366.28$, $i = 8\% \div 4 = 2\%$, and $n = 4 \times 4 = 16$ periods.

$$P = \$231,366.28 \cdot \frac{1}{(1 + 0.02)^{16}}$$

$$P = \$231,366.28(0.72844581) \qquad \text{Use column B.}$$

$$P = \$168,537.80$$

Fredrickson should not sell the business for less than $168,537.80—an investment of this amount at 8% compounded quarterly for 4 years will produce the same future amount as the growth in value of the business. ∎

13.4 Exercises

Find the present value and the amount of interest earned for each of the following. Round to the nearest cent.

	Amount Needed	Time	Interest	Compounded
1.	$1000	6 years	7%	annually
2.	$19,000	9 years	5%	annually
3.	$2700	6 years	8%	annually
4.	$2500	5 years	9%	annually
5.	$11,500	8 years	10%	semiannually
6.	$25,400	7 years	6%	semiannually
7.	$44,796	11 years	12%	semiannually
8.	$20,984	9 years	10%	quarterly

9. Explain how an individual should determine the sale price of a business based on the rate of growth of the business and the current interest rates.

 10. Outline the procedure for finding the present value of an investment using (a) Column A of the interest table and (b) Column B of the interest table.

Work each of the following word problems.

11. David Fontana Backpackers will need to buy some new pack mules in 5 years. These mules will cost a total of $5000. What lump sum should the firm invest today at 7%, compounded annually, in order to be able to buy the mules? How much interest will be earned? **$3564.93; $1435.07**

12. Thomasina's Yarn Shop feels that business conditions will require that it move into a larger store in 4 years. Moving will cost $46,200. What lump sum should be invested today at 15%, compounded semiannually, to yield $46,200? How much interest will be earned? **$25,904.44; $20,295.56**

13. The retail meat industry is gradually becoming more automated. Halmost Meat Market feels that it will need to invest $37,500 in 4 years for new machinery. What lump sum must be invested today at 12%, compounded quarterly, so that the firm will have the necessary money? **$23,368.76**

14. A new *Encyclopedia of World Business* is being prepared that will cost $3675 for all volumes. The encyclopedia will be available in 2 years. What lump sum should be invested by the Manhattan Business Library at 8%, compounded quarterly, so that the library will have enough to buy the new books? **$3136.58**

15. If money can be invested at 8% compounded quarterly, which is larger, $1000 now or $1520 in 5 years? (Hint: find the present value of the $1520.) **$1520 in 5 years**

16. If money can be invested at 11% compounded annually, which is larger, $6000 now or $15,000 in 10 years? **$6000 now**

17. An investment of $30,000 earns interest of 10% compounded semiannually for $2\frac{1}{2}$ years. Find the future value of the investment. If money can be deposited at 8% compounded quarterly, find the present value of the investment. **$38,288.45; $31,409.86**

18. Suppose $50,000 was invested in a business, with the value of the investment growing at 12% per year, compounded quarterly. Find the value of the investment in 5 years. Find the minimum sales price of the investment if money earns 9% per year, compounded annually. **$90,305.56; $58,692.42**

19. A note is due in 3 years, with simple interest of 8%. The face value of the note is $35,000. Find the maturity value of the note. Find the minimum sale price of the note if money can be deposited at 10% compounded annually. **$43,400; $32,607.06**

20. In 6 years, Susan Hessney must pay off a note with a face value of $12,000, and simple interest of 9% per year. Find the maturity value of the note. What should the holder of the note be willing to accept in complete payment today, if money can be invested at 6% per year compounded quarterly? **$18,480; $12,927.57**

21. A partnership agreement says that on the death of a partner, the remaining partner may buy complete control of the company by paying half the value of the company (as of the day of death) 5 years after the death. Simple interest will be paid at 10% per year. Suppose half the value of the company is $430,000, and the husband of the dead partner wishes to receive the money immediately. If money can be invested at 8%, compounded quarterly, what lump sum should he receive? **$434,066.51**

22. In Exercise 21, suppose the husband wants to receive the money 3 years after the death. What lump sum would he receive? **$550,501.29**

CHAPTER 13 QUICK REVIEW

TOPIC	APPROACH	EXAMPLE
13.1 Find the compound amount and the interest	Determine the interest rate per period and the number of compounding periods. Use the formula $M = P(1 + i)^n$ and the interest table to calculate the compound amount. Then subtract the principal from the compound amount to obtain interest.	Find the compound amount and the interest if $1200 is deposited at 12% compounded monthly for 4 years. $$i = \frac{0.12}{12} = 0.01; n = 4 \times 12 = 48.$$ $$M = P(1 + i)^n$$ $$= \$1200(1.01)^{48}$$ $$= \$1200(1.61222608)$$ $$= \$1934.67$$ $$I = M - P$$ $$= \$1934.67 - \$1200 = \$734.67$$
13.1 Determining the effective rate of interest	Determine the value from Column A of the interest table that corresponds to the rate and number of periods. Subtract 1 from this value and round as required.	Find the effective rate of interest to the nearest hundredth, if the annual rate is 8% compounded quarterly. $$i = \frac{0.08}{4} = 0.02; n = 4$$ 1.08243216 table value for $i = 2\%$, $n = 4$ $$1.08243216 - 1.00000000$$ $$= 0.08243216$$ The effective rate is 8.24%.

TOPIC	APPROACH	EXAMPLE
13.2 Interest compounded daily	Determine the number of days and then find the value of $(1 + i)^n$ from a table or calculator. Multiply this value by the principal to obtain compound amount. Subtract principal from compound amount to obtain interest.	$1535 was deposited on September 5 in an account paying $5\frac{1}{4}\%$ and withdrawn on December 5. How much interest was earned? Assume 30 days in a month; there are 25 additional days in September and 5 in December. $25 + 30 + 30 + 5 = 90$ days Table value $= 1.013028415$ Compound amount $\quad = \$1535(1.013028415) = \$1555$ Interest $= \$1555 - \$1535 = \$20$
13.2 Finding the interest and balance when withdrawals are made	Find amount which earns interest for entire quarter and determine compound amount and interest on this sum. Then, find compound amount and interest for amount withdrawn. Find the final balance by adding the total interest to the original balance and subtracting the withdrawal.	Tom had $1500 in his $5\frac{1}{4}\%$ savings account on September 1. He withdrew $450 on October 15. How much interest did he earn in the quarter and what was his final balance? $\$1500 - \$450 = \$1050$ earns interest for the entire quarter. Compound amount $\quad = \$1050 (1.013028415) = \$1063.68$ Interest $= \$1063.68 - \$1050 = \$13.68$ The withdrawn $450 earns interest for 45 days. Compound amount $\quad = \$450(1.006493127) = \$452.92$ Interest $= \$452.92 - \$450 = \$2.92$ Total interest $\quad = \$13.68 + \$2.92 = \$16.60$ Final balance $\quad = \$1500 + \$16.60 - \$450$ $\quad = \$1066.60$

TOPIC	APPROACH	EXAMPLE
13.2 Finding the compound amount and interest earned on time deposits	Use Table 13.3 to find the value corresponding to the rate and number of years. Next multiply table value by initial amount to obtain amount. Then subtract initial investment from compound amount to obtain interest.	Mike invests $15,000 in a certificate of deposit paying 10%. Find the compound amount and interest after 4 years. Table value = 1.49174297 Compound amount = $15,000(1.49174297) = $22,376.14 Interest = $22,376.14 − $15,000 = $7376.14
13.2 Finding the penalty for early withdrawal of funds from a time deposit account	Determine the number of months for which interest will be paid. Find value in table for rate and time. Then multiply this by initial deposit to obtain compound amount. Find the interest by subtracting initial deposit from compound amount.	Tom deposited $5000 in a 3-year CD paying 9%. He withdrew the money 15 months later. The passbook rate at his bank is $5\frac{1}{4}\%$ compounded daily. Find the amount of interest earned. Tom will get the passbook rate for $15 - 3 = 12$ months. Passbook rate of $5\frac{1}{4}\%$ for 12 months (4 quarters) gives a table value of 1.05314097. Interest = $5265.70 − $5000 = $265.70
13.2 Determining the interest and compound amount for continuous compounding	Use the formula $M = Pe^{ni}$. Use table in Appendix C to find value of e^{ni}. Find interest from the formula $I = M - P$.	Find the interest and compound amount for $2000 at 9% compounded continuously for 8 years. $M = Pe^{ni}$ $M = \$2000e^{(8)(0.09)} = \$2000e^{0.72}$ $= \$2000(2.05443321) = \$4108.87$ $I = M - P$ $I = \$4108.87 - \$2000 = \$2108.87$

TOPIC	APPROACH	EXAMPLE
13.3 Finding time given interest rate, compound amount, and principal	Substitute values for M, P, and i in the formula $M = P(1 + i)^n$; then divide both sides by the value of P. Find the value in column A of the interest table (Appendix C) closest to the left-hand side of the equation for the correct value of i. The corresponding value of n is the number of periods required to obtain the compound amount.	How long would it take for $1800 at 9% compounded semiannually to become $7361.97? $i = 9\% \div 2 = 4.5\%$ $M = P(1 + i)^n$ $\$7361.97 = \$1800(1.045)^n$ $4.0899833 = (1.045)^n$ In column A of the 4.5% page the number 4.08998104 is *very close* to 4.0899833, so $n = 32$ and it would take 32 6-month periods or 16 years.
13.3 Finding the rate, given principal, compound amount, and time	Divide the compound amount by the principal. Use the row of the interest table that corresponds to the number of interest periods and find the value in Column A closest to the quotient obtained above. Then find the interest rate per year.	A principal of $7000 is deposited for 18 months with interest compounded monthly. Find the rate if the compound amount is $8373.03. $M = P(1 + i)^n$ $\$8373.03 = \$7000(1 + i)^{18}$ $1.196147 = (1 + i)^{18}$ Find the row for 18 periods in the interest table. Check the table until an entry closest to 1.196147 is found. The closest number is 1.19614748 per month or $1\% \times 12 = 12\%$ per year.
13.4 Finding the present value of a future amount	Use the formula $$P = \frac{M}{(1 + i)^n} \text{ with}$$ $M =$ Future amount; $i =$ interest rate per period; and $n =$ number of periods. Substitute values for i, n, and M and find the value of $\dfrac{1}{(1 + i)^n}$ from Column B of the interest table.	What amount deposited today at 9% compounded monthly will produce $8000 in 3 years? $M = \$8000$ $i = \dfrac{9\%}{12} = .75\%$ $n = 3 \times 12 = 36$ $P = \dfrac{M}{(1 + i)^n} = M \cdot \dfrac{1}{(1 + i)^n}$ $P = \$8000 \cdot \dfrac{1}{(1 + 0.0075)^{36}}$ $P = \$8000 \cdot \dfrac{1}{(1.0075)^{36}}$ $P = \$8000(0.76414896)$ $P = \$6113.19$

SUMMARY EXERCISE

Bill Heaslip invests $5000 at 8%. Find the amount he would have at the end of 5 years if the money was compounded (a) annually, (b) semiannually, (c) quarterly, and (d) continuously.

Bill needs $8000 in 4 years. How much should he deposit today, at 8%, if the money is compounded (e) annually, (f) semiannually, and (g) quarterly.

CHAPTER 13 REVIEW EXERCISES

Find the compound amount and the interest earned for each of the following. Round to the nearest cent. [13.1]

1. $6000 at 6% compounded annually for 7 years

2. $15,000 at 12% compounded annually for 2 years

3. $10,000 at 9% compounded semiannually for 3 years

4. $12,000 at 6% compounded quarterly for 5 years

5. $12,000 at 12% compounded monthly for 3 years

6. $8000 at 9% compounded monthly for 4 years

Find the effective rate of interest corresponding to the following nominal rates. Round to the nearest hundredth of a percent. [13.1]

7. 8% compounded monthly

8. 8% compounded quarterly

9. 7% compounded semiannually

10. 10% compounded monthly

Find the interest earned by the following. Assume $5\frac{1}{4}\%$ interest compounded daily. Round to the nearest cent. [13.2]

	Interest	Amount	Date Deposited	Date Withdrawn
11.	_____	$1000	October 3	December 18
12.	_____	$7500	September 1	November 15
13.	_____	$8200.53	March 17	May 10

Find the amount on deposit at the end of the quarter when the following sums are deposited as indicated. Assume $5\frac{1}{4}$% compounded daily. Round to the nearest cent. [13.2]

	Amount at End of Quarter	Amount	Date Deposited
14.	_____	$3500	January 22
15.	_____	$7200.35	April 22
16.	_____	$7178.75	September 3

Find the compound amount for each of the following certificates of deposit. Assume daily compounding. Round to the nearest cent. [13.2]

	Compound Amount	Amount Deposited	Interest Rate	Time in Years
17.	_____	$2500	10%	5
18.	_____	$7300	9%	2
19.	_____	$3900.25	8%	4

Find the compound amount and the interest for the following deposits. Assume continuous compounding. [13.2]

	Compound Amount	Interest	Amount	Interest Rate	Time
20.	_____	_____	$1000	8%	4 years
21.	_____	_____	$1800	9%	5 years

Complete the following table. Round time to the nearest period, interest to the nearest whole percent per year, and money to the nearest cent. [13.3]

	Principal	Compound Amount	Interest Rate	Compounded	Time in Years
22.	$7500	$10,203.50	_____	annually	4
23.	$8600	$11,566.04	_____	quarterly	3
24.	$7500	$9914.25	_____	quarterly	$3\frac{1}{2}$
25.	$6000	$7986.00	10%	annually	_____
26.	$8400	$10,357.20	6%	monthly	_____

Find the present value for each of the following. Round to the nearest cent. Also find the interest earned. [13.4]

	Amount Needed	Time	Interest Rate	Compounded	Present Value
27.	$1000	7 years	8%	annually	_____
28.	$4700	5 years	11%	semiannually	_____
29.	$8300	3 years	10%	quarterly	_____
30.	$9600	3 years	12%	quarterly	_____

Solve the following word problems.

31. Tom Thumb deposits $1500 in his $5\frac{1}{4}$% passbook account on July 1. On August 13 he adds $865 and then deposits $1150 on September 15. Find the interest earned during the quarter and the balance at the end of the quarter. [13.2]

32. Sam Cracker deposits $18,000 in an 8% certificate of deposit for 10 years. Find the compound amount and the interest earned. [13.2]

33. Melissa Smith deposited $7350 in an 8%, 1-year certificate of deposit. She took out the money 9 months later. What was the interest Melissa received if her bank has a passbook rate of $5\frac{1}{4}$%? (Use the rules for finding the early withdrawal penalty as given in the text.) [13.2]

34. Wooden Desk Company will need $47,500 in 4 years for capital improvements. What lump sum should be invested today at 12% compounded monthly to yield $47,500? [13.4]

14

Multiple-Payment Plans

It is almost impossible to pay cash for everything. Using the telephone, turning on the lights, or using running water involves credit. Many people buy on credit at the department store, use a credit card at the gas station, or buy cars or furniture on the installment plan. In addition, it is often necessary to borrow to pay taxes, medical expenses, or educational costs. Almost everyone borrows when buying a home.

Years ago, consumer credit was offered as an additional service to attract more customers and increase total sales. Today, consumer credit is not merely a service to the customer; for many retail stores the interest or finance charge represents a large portion of company profit. This chapter examines the various methods used in determining interest charges on installment purchases. (Real estate loans are discussed in the next chapter.)

There is a fundamental difference between the notes discussed in earlier sections and those discussed in this chapter. In the earlier situations, a sum of money was paid back, with interest, with a lump sum payment at some future date. In this chapter, the principal and interest are paid back in periodic payments. This type of loan is called an **installment loan.**

Before discussing installment buying, we look at the **United States Rule,** which is a commonly used method for handling partial loan payoffs. This rule is used with several of the methods of handling installment sales.

14.1 The United States Rule

OBJECTIVES

1 Find the amount due on the maturity date, using the United States Rule.

2 Find the total interest paid.

It is fairly common for a loan, or part of a loan, to be paid off before it is due. There are several reasons for this—a person might come into some extra money, or might be able to borrow money at a cheaper rate and pay off a more expensive loan. This section discusses methods of handling these prepayments of a loan.

1   The first method is called the **United States Rule,** since it is the method used by the U.S. Government, as well as most states. With the United States Rule, any payment is first applied to any interest owed, with the balance used to reduce the principal amount of the loan. The Untied States Rule is applied as follows.

> *Step 1.*   Find the interest due from the date the loan was made until the date the partial payment is made.
>
> *Step 2.*   Subtract this interest from the amount of the payment.
>
> *Step 3.*   Any difference is used to reduce the principal.
>
> *Step 4.*   Additional partial payments are treated in the same way, always applying interest only to the balance after the last partial payment.
>
> *Step 5.*   On the date the loan is due, any additional principal, together with interest on this unpaid principal, is due.

NOTE   If the partial payment is not large enough to pay the interest due, the payment is simply held until enough money is available to pay the interest due. This means that a partial payment smaller than the interest due offers no advantage to the borrower—the lender just holds the partial payment until enough money is available to pay the interest owed.

EXAMPLE 1

Finding Amount Due Using the United States Rule

A 120-day note is made on May 9, has a face value of $4000, and carries interest of 10%. On June 17, a payment of $1500 is made. Find the balance owed on the principal. If no additional payments are made, find the amount that will be due on the maturity date of the loan.

SOLUTION   First find the interest due from May 9 until June 17. There are $22 + 17 = 39$ days from May 9 until June 17. The interest due is found from the formula $I = PRT$.

$$I = \$4000\,(0.10)\left(\frac{39}{360}\right) = \$43.33. \qquad \text{interest due}$$

The payment made on June 17 was $1500. Of this amount, $43.33 is applied to interest. The difference,

$$
\begin{array}{rl}
\$1500.00 & \text{payment} \\
-\quad 43.33 & \text{interest due} \\
\hline
\$1456.67 & \text{applied to reduction of principal}
\end{array}
$$

is applied to the reduction of the amount owed. The amount owed was $4000; after June 17, it is

$$
\begin{array}{rl}
\$4000.00 & \text{amount owed} \\
-\quad 1456.67 & \text{principal reduction} \\
\hline
\$2543.33 & \text{balance owed}
\end{array}
$$

The balance owed on the note is $2543.33.

The note was originally for 120 days, with the partial payment paid after 39 days. This means that interest on the $2543.33 will be charged only for $120 - 39 = 81$ days. The interest, still at 10%, is

$$I = \$2543.33 \, (0.10) \left(\frac{81}{360} \right) = \$57.22.$$

If no additional partial payments are made,

$2543.33	principal owed
+ 57.22	interest
$2600.55	total owed

will be due on the maturity date of the note. ∎

2 In order to find the total interest paid when partial payments are made, the individual interest payments are added.

EXAMPLE 2
Finding Total Interest Paid

A lawn furniture manufacturer signs a 140-day note on February 5. The note, for $45,600, is to a supplier of aluminum tubing for the furniture, and carries an interest rate of 12%. On March 19, the manufacturer receives an unexpected payment from one of its customers, and applies $16,000 toward the note. A further early payment permits a second $13,250 partial payment on April 23. Find the interest paid on the note and the amount paid on the due date of the note.

SOLUTION   The first partial payment was made on March 19, which is $23 + 19 = 42$ days after the loan is made. In 42 days, the interest on the note is

$$I = PRT$$

$$I = \$45,600 \, (0.12) \left(\frac{42}{360} \right) = \$638.40.$$

A partial payment of $16,000 was made on March 19. Of this amount, $638.40 is applied to interest.

$16,000.00	amount of payment
− 638.40	interest owed
$15,361.60	applied to principal

After March 19, the balance on the loan is as follows.

$45,600.00	original amount of loan
− 15,361.60	applied to principal
$30,238.40	new amount owed

After March 19, the balance on the note is $30,238.40. A second partial payment is made on April 23, which is $12 + 23 = 35$ days later. Interest on $30,238.40 for 35 days is

$$I = \$30{,}238.40 \,(0.12)\left(\frac{35}{360}\right) = \$352.78.$$

A payment of $13,250 is made on April 23. Of this, $352.78 applies to interest, leaving

$$\$13{,}250 - \$352.78 = \$12{,}897.22$$

to reduce the principal. After April 23, the principal is as follows.

$$
\begin{array}{ll}
\$30{,}238.40 & \text{previous balance} \\
-\;\;12{,}897.22 & \text{applied to principal} \\
\hline
\$17{,}341.18 & \text{new principal}
\end{array}
$$

The first partial payment was made 42 days after the note was signed, with the second payment made 35 days after that. The second payment was made $42 + 35 = 77$ days after the note was signed. Since the note was for 140 days, the note is due

$$140 - 77 = 63$$

days after the second partial payment. Interest on the new balance of $17,341.18 for 63 days is

$$I = \$17{,}341.18 \,(0.12)\left(\frac{63}{360}\right) = \$364.16.$$

On the date the loan matures, a total of

$$\$17{,}341.18 + \$364.16 = \$17{,}705.34$$

must be paid. The total interest paid over the life of the loan is

$$\$638.40 + \$352.78 + \$364.16 = \$1355.34.$$

All this work can be summarized in the following table.

Date Payment Made	Amount of Payment	Applied to Interest	Applied to Principal	Remaining Balance
March 19	$16,000	$638.40	$15,361.60	$30,238.40
April 23	$13,250	$352.78	$12,897.22	$17,341.18
Date of maturity (June 25)	$17,705.34	$364.16	$17,341.18	$0
Totals		$1355.34	$45,600	

14.1 Exercises

Find the balance due on the maturity date of the following notes. Find the total amount of interest paid on the note. Use the United States Rule.

	Principal	Interest	Time in Days	Partial Payments
1.	$6000	8%	60	$2000 on day 40
2.	$15,000	7%	90	$6500 on day 50
3.	$29,800	12%	150	$14,000 on day 120
4.	$68,500	9%	180	$242,750 on day 75
5.	$18,457	12%	120	$5978 on day 34 $3124 on day 55
6.	$39,864	7%	105	$8458 on day 43 $11,354 on day 88

7. Explain the concept of the United States Rule. (See Objective 1.)

8. Why is it of no advantage to the borrower to make a partial payment smaller than the amount of interest due? What would the lender do with this payment?

Work the following word problems.

9. Carmen's Packaging borrowed $63,000 on May 7, signing a note due in 90 days and carrying 9.5% interest. On June 24, the company made a partial payment of $17,275. Find the amount due on the maturity date of the note and the amount of interest paid on the note.

10. The Main Street Frostee finances a remodeling program by giving the builder a note for $37,500. The note was made on September 14 and is due in 120 days. Interest on the note is 14.5%. On December 9, the firm makes a partial payment of $12,000. Find the amount due on the maturity date of the note and the amount of interest paid on the note.

11. To save on freight charges, Wholesale Paper orders large quantities of basic paper goods every 4 months. For their last order, the firm signed a note on February 18 that will mature on May 15. The face value of the note was $104,500, with interest of 11%. The firm made a partial payment of $38,000 on March 20, with a second partial payment of $27,200 on April 16. Find the amount due on the maturity date of the note and the amount of interest paid on the note.

12. Mid-City Electronics bought new testing equipment, paying for it with a note for $32,000. The note was made on July 26 and is due on November 20. The interest rate is 13%. The firm made a partial payment of $6000 on August 31, with a second partial payment of $11,700 on October 4. Find the amount due on the maturity date of the note and the amount of interest paid on the note.

13. Tom Johnson owes $12,000 with interest of 8%. He borrowed the money for 120 days on February 24. He made a partial payment of $800 on May 24. Find the amount due on the maturity date of the note and the amount of interest paid on the note.

14. Patti Wilson borrowed $27,500 on August 7. The loan was for 150 days with interest of 12%. She made a partial payment of $1500 on December 6. Find the amount due on the maturity date of the note and the amount of interest paid on the note.

14.2 Open-End Credit

OBJECTIVES

1. Define open-end credit.
2. Understand revolving charge accounts.
3. Use the unpaid balance method to calculate finance charges.
4. Use the average daily balance method.

There are two common ways of buying items on credit. In one method, the consumer agrees to pay a fixed amount of money per time period until the loan is paid off. An example would be paying $250 per month for 48 months to pay off a car loan. This type of installment buying is discussed in the next section.

1 As we'll discuss in this section, the other common way of buying on credit, called **open-end credit,** has no fixed number of payments—the consumer continues making payments until no outstanding balance is owed. With open-end credit, additional credit is often extended before the initial amount is paid off. Examples of open-end credit include most department store charge accounts and bank charge cards, such as MasterCard, VISA, and Discover.

2 With a typical department store account or bank card, a customer might make several small purchases during a month. Such accounts are often never paid off and new purchases are continually being made, although a minimum amount must be paid each month. Since the account is perhaps never paid off, it is called a **revolving charge account.**

VISA, MasterCard, Discover, and some oil company charge cards use this method of extending credit. Sometimes there is an annual membership fee or a minimum monthly charge for the use of this service. A sample copy of a receipt signed by a customer using a credit card is shown in Figure 14.1.

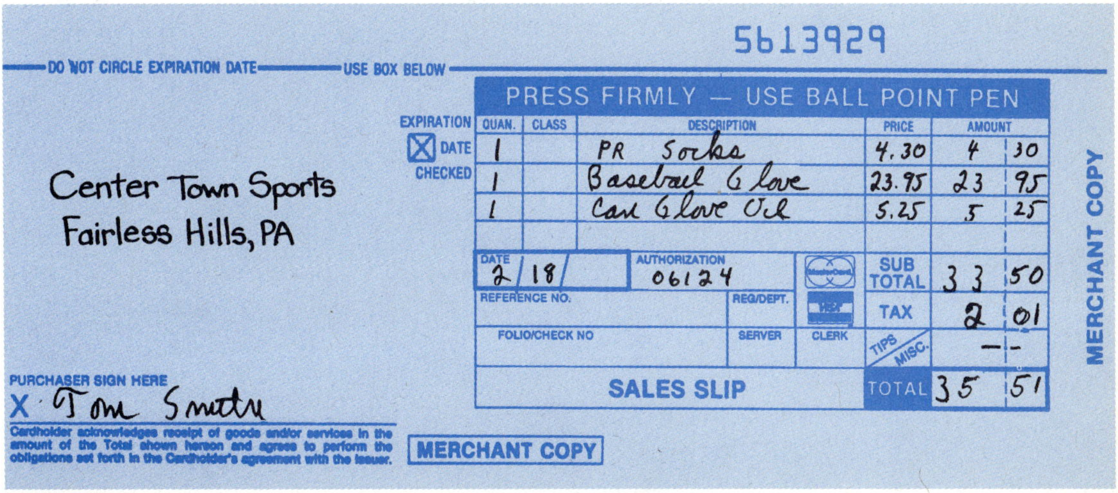
5613929

DO NOT CIRCLE EXPIRATION DATE — USE BOX BELOW

PRESS FIRMLY — USE BALL POINT PEN

EXPIRATION DATE CHECKED

QUAN.	CLASS	DESCRIPTION	PRICE	AMOUNT
1		PR Socks	4.30	4 30
1		Baseball Glove	23.95	23 95
1		Can Glove Oil	5.25	5 25
			SUB TOTAL	33 50
			TAX	2 01
			TIPS MISC.	—
			TOTAL	35 51

DATE 2/18 AUTHORIZATION 06124

REFERENCE NO. REG/DEPT.

FOLIO/CHECK NO SERVER CLERK

SALES SLIP

Center Town Sports
Fairless Hills, PA

PURCHASER SIGN HERE
X Tom Smith

Cardholder acknowledges receipt of goods and/or services in the amount of the Total shown hereon and agrees to perform the obligations set forth in the Cardholder's agreement with the issuer.

MERCHANT COPY

MERCHANT COPY

FIGURE 14.1

At the end of a billing period the customer receives a statement of payments and purchases made. This statement typically takes one of two forms: **country club billing** provides a carbon copy of all original charge receipts, while **itemized billing,** becoming more and more common because of its lower cost to the credit card companies, provides an itemized listing of all charges, without copies of each individual charge. A typical itemized statement is shown in Figure 14.2.

Any charges beyond the cash price of an item are called **finance charges.** Finance charges include interest, credit life insurance, a time payment differential, or carrying charges.

Finance charges on open-end credit accounts are usually calculated with one of two methods: the *unpaid balance method,* or the *average daily balance method.* The explanation for each of these methods follows.

3   When a store or financial institution uses the **unpaid balance method** to calculate the finance charge, it is common to use the *unpaid balance* at the end of the previous month to determine the finance charge. Any purchases or returns during the current month are *not* used in calculating the finance charge. Payments and finance charges are calculated using the United States Rule. The next example shows how the unpaid balance method works.

EXAMPLE 1

Finding Finance Charges and Balance Using the Unpaid Balance Method

(a) Marian Porath's VISA account had an unpaid balance of $179.82 on July 1. During July she made a $30 payment and purchases totaling $101.58. Find the finance charge and the unpaid balance on August 1, if the bank charges 1.6% per month on the unpaid balance.

SOLUTION   A finance charge of 1.6% per month on the unpaid balance would be

$$\$179.82\,(0.016) = \$2.88,$$

so the **unpaid balance** on August 1 is calculated as follows.

Previous balance		Finance charge		Purchases during month		Payment		New balance
↓		↓		↓		↓		↓
$179.82	+	$2.88	+	$101.58	−	$30	=	$254.28

Porath's unpaid balance on August 1 is $254.28.

(b) During August, Porath made a payment of $85, returned $42.95 of items, and took a client to lunch for $19.84. Find her unpaid balance on September 1. The finance charge calculated on the unpaid balance is

$$\$254.28\,(0.016) = \$4.07.$$

NOTE   The finance charge is calculated on the unpaid balance at the end of July.

The unpaid balance on September 1 is

$$\$254.28 + \$4.07 + \$19.84 - \$42.95 - \$85 = \$150.24.$$

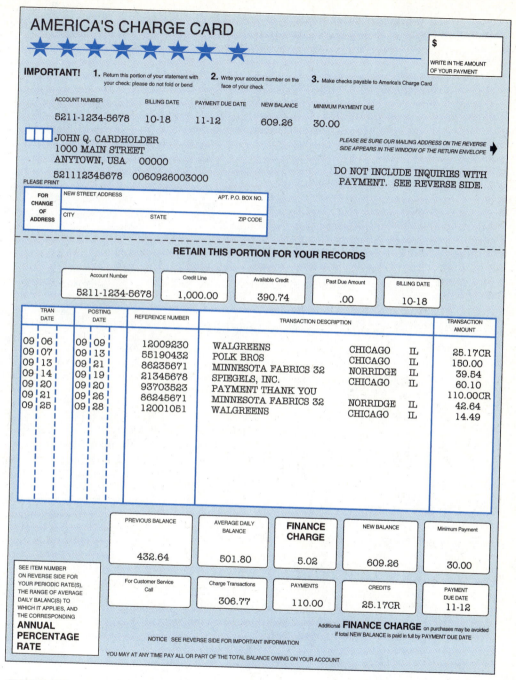

(c) In September, Porath made a payment of $70, and made purchases of $25.97. Find her unpaid balance on October 1. The finance charge for the month is

$$\$150.24 \,(0.016) = \$2.40,$$

with the unpaid balance on October 1 equal to

$$\$150.24 + \$2.40 + \$25.97 - \$70 = \$108.61.$$

These 3 months of Porath's VISA account can be summarized as follows.

Month	Unpaid Balance at Beginning of Month	Finance Charge	Purchases During Month	Returns	Payment	Unpaid Balance at End of Month
July	$179.82	$2.88	$101.58	–	$30	$254.28
August	254.28	4.07	19.84	$42.95	85	150.24
September	150.24	2.40	25.97	–	70	108.61

The total finance charge during the 3-month period was

$$\$2.88 + \$4.07 + \$2.40 = \$9.35. \quad \blacksquare$$

NOTE The monthly finance charge was calculated on the unpaid balance at the beginning of each month.

4 Most revolving charge plans now calculate finance charges using the **average daily balance method.** First, the balance owed on the account is found at the end of each day during a month or billing period. All of these amounts are added and the total divided by the number of days during the billing period. The result is the average daily balance of the account. The finance charge is then calculated on this amount.

EXAMPLE 2
Finding Average Daily Balance

The activity in the MasterCard account of Kay Chamberlin for one billing period is shown in the following table. Find the average daily balance on the next billing date of April 3, if the previous balance was $209.46.

SOLUTION

Transaction Description		Transaction Amount
Previous balance, $209.46		
March 3	Billing date	
March 12	Payment	$50.00 CR*
March 17	Clothes	$28.46
March 20	Mail order	$31.22
April 1	Auto parts	$59.10

*CR represents "credit."

At the close of business on March 3, the unpaid balance was $209.46. This balance was the same for 9 days until March 12, when it changed to

$$209.46 - \$50 = \$159.46.$$

This balance was the same for 5 days until March 17 when it became

$$159.46 + \$28.46 = \$187.92.$$

In 3 days, on March 20, the balance became

$$187.92 + \$31.22 = \$219.14,$$

which remained unchanged for 12 days, becoming

$$219.14 + \$59.10 = \$278.24$$

on April 1. The new billing date is April 3, so the unpaid balance was $278.24 for 2 days. These results are summarized in the following table.

Date	Unpaid Balance	Number of Days Until Balance Changes
March 3	$209.46	9
March 12	$159.46	5
March 17	$187.92	3
March 20	$219.14	12
April 1	$278.24	2
		31 total number of days in billing period

To find the average daily balance, weight each unpaid balance according to the number of days for that balance, total the products, and then divide by the 31 days of the billing cycle. Do all this with the following shortcut procedure.

$$
\begin{array}{r}
\$209.46 \times 9 = \$1885.14 \\
\$159.46 \times 5 = 797.30 \\
\$187.92 \times 3 = 563.76 \\
\$219.14 \times 12 = 2629.68 \\
\$278.24 \times 2 = 556.48 \\
\hline
\$6432.36
\end{array}
$$

(For example, $209.46 \times 9 = \$1885.14$ represents the sum of the average daily balances at the end of the day from March 3 through March 11.) Now divide the total by 31.

$$\frac{\$6432.36}{31} = \$207.50 \text{ average daily balance}$$

Chamberlin will pay a finance charge based on the average daily balance of $207.50.   ∎

CAUTION The billing period in Example 2 is 31 days. Some billing periods are 30 days. Be sure to use the correct number of days.

If finance charges are expressed on a per month basis, find the **annual percentage rate** by multiplying the monthly rate by 12, the number of months in a year. The following table shows typical monthly rates and the corresponding annual percentage rates.

Monthly Finance Charges and Corresponding Annual Percentage Rates

Quoted Monthly Finance Charge	Annual Percentage Rate
$\frac{1}{2}$ of 1%	6%
$\frac{2}{3}$ of 1%	8%
$\frac{3}{4}$ of 1%	9%
$\frac{5}{6}$ of 1%	10%
1%	12%
$1\frac{1}{4}$%	15%
$1\frac{1}{2}$%	18%
$1\frac{2}{3}$%	20%
$1\frac{3}{4}$%	21%
2%	24%

14.2 Exercises

Find the finance charge on each of the following revolving charge accounts. Assume interest is calculated on the unpaid balance of the account. Round to the nearest cent.

	Unpaid Balance	Monthly Interest Rate
1.	$244.88	1.3%
2.	$600.36	1.5%
3.	$167.99	$1\frac{5}{8}$%
4.	$655.18	$1\frac{1}{4}$%
5.	$746.92	1.608%
6.	$997.30	1.771%

Complete each of the following tables, showing the unpaid balance at the end of each month. Assume an interest rate of 1.7% per month on the unpaid balance.

7.

Month	Unpaid Balance at Beginning of Month	Finance Charge	Purchases During Month	Returns	Payment	Unpaid Balance at End of Month
February	$297.11	_____	$86.14	—	$50	_____
March	_____	_____	$109.83	$15.75	$60	_____
April	_____	_____	$39.74	—	$72	_____
May	_____	_____	$56.29	$18.09	$50	_____

8.

Month	Unpaid Balance at Beginning of Month	Finance Charge	Purchases During Month	Returns	Payment	Unpaid Balance at End of Month
October	$554.19	_____	$128.72	$23.15	$125	_____
November	_____	_____	$291.64	—	$170	_____
December	_____	_____	$147.11	$17.15	$150	_____
January	_____	_____	$27.84	$139.82	$200	_____

9.

Month	Unpaid Balance at Beginning of Month	Finance Charge	Purchases During Month	Returns	Payment	Unpaid Balance at End of Month
August	$822.91	_____	$155.01	$38.11	$100	_____
September	_____	_____	$208.75	—	$75	_____
October	_____	_____	$56.30	—	$90	_____
November	_____	_____	$190	$83.57	$150	_____

10.

Month	Unpaid Balance at Beginning of Month	Finance Charge	Purchases During Month	Returns	Payment	Unpaid Balance at End of Month
March	$1522.83	_____	$308.13	$74.88	$250	_____
April	_____	_____	$488.35	—	$350	_____
May	_____	_____	$134.99	$18.12	$175	_____
June	_____	_____	$157.72	—	$190	_____

Find the finance charge for each of the following revolving charge accounts. Assume interest is calculated on the average daily balance of the account.

	Average Daily Balance	**Monthly Interest Rate**
11.	$225.00	$1\frac{1}{4}\%$
12.	$65.80	$1\frac{1}{2}\%$
13.	$108.17	$1\frac{1}{4}\%$
14.	$415.75	$\frac{5}{6}\%$
15.	$138.20	$1\frac{1}{2}\%$
16.	$425.37	$1\frac{2}{3}\%$

Find the average daily balance for each of the following credit card accounts. Assume one month between billing dates (using the proper number of days in the month). Then find the finance charge, if interest is $1\frac{1}{2}\%$ per month on the average daily balance.

17. Previous balance, $810.25

May 9	Billing date	
May 17	Payment	$300.00
May 30	Dinner	$56.14

18. Previous balance, $119.74

September 12	Billing date	
September 20	Payment	$32.00
September 21	Athletic shoes	$25.15

19. Previous balance, $228.95

January 27	Billing date	
February 9	Cheese	$11.08
February 13	Returns	$26.54
February 20	Payment	$29.00
February 25	Repairs	$71.19

20. Previous balance, $415.63

June 11	Billing date	
June 15	Returns	$94.57
June 20	Jewelry	$110.85
June 24	Car rental	$46.15
July 3	Payment	$125.00

21. Previous balance, $714.58

August 17	Billing date	
August 21	Mail order	$14.92
August 23	Returns	$25.41
August 27	Beverages	$31.82
August 31	Payment	$108.00
September 9	Returns	$71.14
September 11	Plane ticket	$110.00
September 14	Cash advance	$100.00

22. Previous balance, $355.72

March 29	Billing date	
March 31	Returns	$209.53
April 2	Auto parts	$28.76
April 10	Gasoline	$14.80
April 12	Returns	$63.54
April 13	Returns	$11.71
April 20	Payment	$72.00
April 21	Flowers	$29.72

23. Explain the difference between the unpaid balance method and the average daily balance method of calculating interest. (See Objectives 3 and 4.)

24. Which method of calculating interest (unpaid balance or average daily balance) produces higher interest? Justify your answer with a specific example.

14.3 Installment Buying

OBJECTIVES

1 Find the amount financed.

2 Find the annual percentage rate, total installment cost, and finance charge.

3 Use the formula for approximate annual percentage rate (APR).

4 Use a table to find the APR.

In this section we discuss installment plans. With installment plans, the amount of money to be paid back, the rate per time period, and the number of periods are all fixed. Car loans are a good example—the purchase of a car is often financed at a fixed amount per month for a fixed number of months, such as 36, 48, or 60 months.

1 Installment plans almost always require a **down payment**—a portion of the cash price paid at the time of purchase. (With a car, the trade-in often makes most or all of the down payment.) The **amount financed** is found by subtracting the down payment from the cash price.

$$\text{Amount financed} \ = \ \text{Cash price} \ - \ \text{Down payment}$$

For example, a $12,000 car with a $4000 down payment would have an amount financed of

$$\$12,000 - \$4000 = \$8000.$$

(Any additional items purchased, such as insurance, must be included in the amount financed.) The **deferred payment price** is found by adding the cash price and the finance charge.

> Deferred payment price = Cash price + Finance charge

2 Since the enactment of the **Federal Truth-in-Lending Law in 1969 (Regulation Z),** lenders must report their **finance charges** (the charge for credit) and their **annual percentage rate (APR).** The Truth-in-Lending Law does not regulate the interest rates or credit charges but merely requires a standardized and truthful report of what they are. The individual states set the allowable interest rates and charges.

Lenders normally give borrowers a document, such as the one in Figure 14.3, showing all credit charges.

Since interest rates and credit charges now must be shown to the borrower, there is less need to learn to calculate finance charges and greater need to be aware of their significance. The charge for borrowing money or obtaining credit varies from source to source, just as the price for any other product or service varies. Although the amount of credit charges paid by the borrower depends on the borrower's past credit record, present financial standing, amount of down payment, and other factors, some lenders follow an "all that the traffic will bear" policy. This means that the more a person knows about credit, the less it might cost to use it.

To find the annual percentage rate, it is necessary to find the **total installment cost** (or the **deferred payment price**) and the **finance charge** on the loan. Do this with the following steps.

> *Step 1.* Find the total installment cost.
>
> Total installment = Down payment
> + (Amount of each payment × Number of payments)
>
> *Step 2.* Find the finance charge.
>
> Finance charge = Total installment − Cash price
>
> *Step 3.* Finally, find the amount financed.
>
> Amount financed = Cash price − Down payment

Note and Disclosure Statement

BORROWER NAME (Last – First – Middle Initial) AND ADDRESS (Street – City – State – Zip Code)	DATE	MEMBER NUMBER	NOTE NUMBER

Smith, John Q.
10123 Fair Oaks Blvd.
Fair Oaks, CA 95628

CONTRACT NUMBER	REFERENCE NUMBER	MATURITY DATE
012-2719-6	XXXXXXXXX	XXXXXXX

In this agreement "you" and "your" mean each person who signs this agreement. The "credit union" means the credit union whose name appears above and anyone to whom the credit union transfers its rights under this agreement. The terms on the reverse side are part of this agreement. Boxes checked below apply to this agreement.

TRUTH IN LENDING DISCLOSURE

ANNUAL PERCENTAGE RATE The cost of your credit as a yearly rate.	**FINANCE CHARGE** The dollar amount the credit will cost you.	**Amount Financed** The amount of credit provided to you or on your behalf.	**Total of Payments** The amount you will have paid when you have made all payments as scheduled.	**Prepayment:** If you pay off early you will not have to pay a penalty. e means an estimate
13.99%	$ 1,605.64	$ 6,800.00	$ 8,405.64	

	Number of Payments	**Amount of Payments**	**When Payments Are Due**	**Property Insurance:** You may obtain property insurance from anyone you want that is acceptable to the credit union.
Your Payment Schedule will be:	36	$233.49	monthly beginning May 15	XXXXXXXXXXXXXXXXXXXXXXXXXXXXXXXXXXXXXX $

Security: Collateral securing other loans with the credit union will also secure this loan. You are giving a security interest in your shares and/or deposits in the credit union; and [X] the goods/property being purchased; [ ] Other (Describe)

Late Charge: N/A

	Filing Fees	Non-Filing Insurance
	$ N/A	$ N/A

See your contract documents for any additional information about nonpayment, default, and any required repayment in full before the scheduled date.

ITEMIZATION OF THE AMOUNT FINANCED

ITEMIZATION OF AMOUNT FINANCED OF $	AMOUNT GIVEN TO YOU DIRECTLY $	AMOUNT PAID ON YOUR ACCOUNT $	PREPAID FINANCE CHARGE $
AMOUNT PAID TO OTHERS ON YOUR BEHALF $	To	$	To
	To	$	To

NOTE AND SECURITY AGREEMENT   CONTINUED ON REVERSE SIDE

Promise to Pay: You promise to pay $ _____ to the credit union plus interest on the unpaid balance at _____ % per year until what you owe has been repaid.

Collection Costs: You promise to pay all costs of collecting the amount you owe under this agreement including court costs and reasonable attorney fees.

Security Offered:

	MODEL	YEAR	I.D. NUMBER	TYPE	VALUE
	Chevrolet Caprice		1NA1G1H96XE6811		

Other (Describe):

You Pledge Shares and/or Deposits of $ _____ in account number _____ Key No. _____ This Note is governed by the laws of Illinois

SIGNATURE: If you agree to make and be bound by the terms of this Note and Security Agreement sign below. *If you are not a borrower but an owner of the collateral for this loan, sign below and check the box for "Owner of Collateral". By doing so you agree only to the terms of the Security Agreement.*

CAUTION: IT IS IMPORTANT THAT YOU THOROUGHLY READ THIS CONTRACT BEFORE YOU SIGN IT.

Borrower X (SEAL)	Date	Borrower [ ] Owner of Collateral (other than a Borrower) X (SEAL)	Date
Borrower [ ] Owner of Collateral (other than a Borrower) X (SEAL)	Date	Witness X (SEAL)	Date

CREDIT INSURANCE APPLICATION

"You" or "Your" means the member and the joint insured (if applicable).

Credit insurance **is voluntary and not required in order to obtain this loan.** You may select any insurer of your choice. You can get this insurance only if you check the "yes" box below and sign your name and write in the date. The rate you are charged for the insurance is subject to change. You will receive written notice before any increase goes into effect. You have the right to stop this insurance by notifying your credit union in writing. Your signature below means you agree that:

- If you elect insurance, you authorize the credit union to add the charges for insurance to your loan each month.
- You are eligible for disability insurance only if you are working for wages or profit for 25 hours a

week or more on the date of any advance. If you are not, that particular advance will not be insured until you return to work. If you are off work because of temporary layoff, strike or vacation, but soon to resume, you will be considered at work. Are you working for wages or profit for 25 hours a week or more? [ ] Yes [ ] No

- You are eligible for insurance up to the Maximum Age for Insurance. Insurance will stop when you reach that age.

NOTE: THE LIFE AND DISABILITY INSURANCE CONTAINS CERTAIN BENEFIT EXCLUSIONS, INCLUDING A PRE-EXISTING CONDITION EXCLUSION. PLEASE REFER TO YOUR CERTIFICATE FOR DETAILS.

YOU ELECT THE FOLLOWING INSURANCE COVERAGE(S)	YES	NO	PREMIUM SCHEDULE	INSURANCE MAXIMUMS	DISABILITY	LIFE
CREDIT DISABILITY		X	$ e	MONTHLY TOTAL BENEFIT	$ 600	N/A
				INSURABLE BALANCE PER LOAN ACCOUNT	$50,000	N/A
				MAXIMUM AGE FOR INSURANCE	66	N/A

If you are totally disabled for more than **30** days, then the Disability Benefit will begin with the **31st** day of disability.

SECONDARY (If you desire to name one) BENEFICIARY

DATE April 3	DATE OF BIRTH	DATE	DATE OF BIRTH

SIGNATURE OF BORROWER ELIGIBLE TO BE INSURED (Be sure to check the boxes above.)

X *John Q. Smith*

SIGNATURE OF JOINT INSURED (CO-BORROWER) (Only required if JOINT CREDIT LIFE coverage is selected)

X _____ N/A

FIGURE 14.3

EXAMPLE 1
*Finding Total
Installment Cost,
Amount Financed,
and Finance
Charge*

Diane Phillips bought a motorcycle for $980. She paid $200 down and then made 24 payments of $39.60 each. Find the (a) total installment cost, (b) finance charge, and (c) amount financed.

SOLUTION

(a) The total installment cost is found by multiplying the amount of each payment by the number of payments, and adding the down payment.

$$\text{Total installment cost} = \$200 + (\$39.60 \times 24)$$

$$= \$200 + \$950.40$$

$$= \$1150.40$$

(b) The finance charge is the difference between the total installment cost and the cash price.

$$\text{Finance charge} = \$1150.40 - \$980$$

$$= \$170.40$$

Phillips pays an additional $170.40 for the motorcycle because it is bought on credit.

(c) The amount financed is

$$\$980 - \$200 = \$780. \quad \blacksquare$$

NOTE In determining the total installment cost, the down payment is added to the total cost of the monthly payments.

3 The *approximate* annual percentage rate (approximate APR) can be found with the formula in the next box.

This formula gives only an *approximate* APR. The results with the formula are *not* accurate enough for the purposes of the Federal Truth-in-Lending Act. The formula is included here since it can be used to get a reasonably approximate rate when the lengthy federal tables are not available.

The *approximate* annual percentage rate (APR) for a loan paid off in monthly payments is given by

$$\text{Approximate APR} = \frac{24 \times \text{Finance charge}}{\text{Amount financed} \times (1 + \text{Total number of payments})}.$$

EXAMPLE 2
Finding
Approximate APR

Ed Chamski decides to buy a used car for $6400. He has a down payment of $1200 and pays monthly payments of $179 for 36 months. Find the approximate annual percentage rate.

SOLUTION   Use the steps given in the first APR box.

Step 1.   Total installment cost = Down payment + (Amount of payment × Number of payments)

$$= \$1200 + (\$179 \times 36 \text{ months})$$

$$= \$1200 + \$6444$$

$$= \$7644 \text{ total installment cost}$$

Step 2.   Finance charge = Total installment cost − Cash price

$$= \$7644 - \$6400$$

$$= \$1244 \text{ finance charge (time-price differential)}$$

Step 3.   Amount of loan = Cash price − Down payment

$$= \$6400 - \$1200$$

$$= \$5200$$

Use the formula for approximate APR given in the box. Replace the finance charge with $1244, the amount financed with $5200, and the number of payments with 36.

$$\text{Approximate APR} = \frac{24 \times \text{Finance charge}}{\text{Amount financed} \times (1 + \text{Total number of payments})}$$

$$= \frac{24 \times \$1244}{\$5200 \times (1 + 36)}$$

$$= \frac{\$29{,}856}{\$192{,}400}$$

$$= 0.155, \text{ or } 15.5\% \qquad \text{approximate APR}$$

The approximate annual percentage rate on this loan is 15.5%. ∎

Calculator Approach to Example 2

First, calculate the value of the denominator and place it in memory.

5200 ☒ 37 M+ 192400

Now calculate the value of the numerator and divide it by the value in memory.

24 ☒ 1244 ÷ MR = 0.155

4 As noted, this formula for APR is only approximate and does not satisfy federal law. For APR rates that do satisfy federal law, use the *Annual Percentage Rate Tables,* available from the nearest Federal Reserve Bank or the Board of Governors of the Federal Reserve System, Washington, DC 20551. The complete set of tables consists of two volumes. Volume I provides four tables for varying interest rates and time periods and Volume II includes irregular transactions and is used with Volume I. A portion of such a table is shown in Table 14.1 on page 472.

Find the annual percentage rate as follows.

---

1. Divide the finance charge by the amount financed, and multiply by $100, that is,

$$\frac{\text{Finance charge}}{\text{Amount financed}} \times \$100$$

The result is the finance charge per $100 of the amount financed.

2. Read down the left column of Table 14.1 to the proper number of payments. Go across to the number closest to the number found in Step 1. Read up the column to find the annual percentage rate.

The annual percentage rate found with this method is accurate to the nearest quarter of a percent, as required by federal law.

The next example shows how to use Table 14.1 to find an annual percentage rate that does satisfy the requirements of federal law.

EXAMPLE 3
Finding Annual Percentage Rate

In Example 2, a used car costing $6400 was financed at $179 per month for 36 months after a down payment of $1200. The total finance charge was $1244, and the amount financed was $5200. Find the annual percentage rate.

SOLUTION Divide the finance charge ($1244) by the total amount financed ($5200) and multiply by $100.

$$\frac{\$1244}{\$5200} \times \$100 = \$23.92$$

This gives the finance charge per $100 of amount financed.

Read down the left column of Table 14.1 to the line for 36 months (the actual number of monthly payments). Follow across to the right to find the number closest to $23.92. Here, find exactly $23.92. Read up this column of figures to find the annual percentage rate, 14.5%.

In this example, 14.5% is the annual percentage rate that must be disclosed to the buyer of the car. The formula for the approximate annual percentage rate gave an answer of 15.5%, which is not accurate enough to meet the requirements of the law. ▪

EXAMPLE 4

Constructing a
Payment Schedule

Suppose a loan of $500 is repaid in 6 monthly payments of $87.27 each. The total amount repaid is

$$6 \times \$87.27 = \$523.62,$$

and the finance charge is

$$\$523.62 - \$500 = \$23.62.$$

Find the annual percentage rate.

SOLUTION $\dfrac{\text{Finance charge}}{\text{Amount financed}} \times 100 = \dfrac{\$23.62}{\$500} \times \$100 = \$4.72$

From the "6 payment," row of Table 14.1, the annual percentage rate is 16%.

By the United States Rule, the first portion of the $87.27 payment is applied to interest. The interest for the first month is

$$\$500 \times 0.16 \times \frac{1}{12} = \$6.67.$$

Of the $87.27 payment, $6.67 pays interest, and $87.27 - \$6.67 = \$80.60$ is applied to the reduction of principal. After the first month, the balance owed is

$$\$500 - \$80.60 = \$419.40.$$

Continuing this process gives the results shown in the following table.

Month	Balance Owed	Payment	Interest for Month	Applied to Balance	New Balance
1	$500	$87.27	$6.67	$80.60	$419.40
2	419.40	87.27	5.59	81.68	337.72
3	337.72	87.27	4.50	82.77	254.95
4	254.95	87.27	3.40	83.87	171.08
5	171.08	87.27	2.28	84.99	86.09
6	86.09	87.24	1.15	86.09	0

As this chart shows, if interest of 16% is calculated on the balance owed each month, and if the United States Rule is used for applying interest, then the 6 payments will pay off both the $500 principal and the finance charge of $23.62. ■

NOTE   In Example 4, the final payment is adjusted by 3 cents due to rounding error. It is a common practice to make an adjustment to the final payment in an installment loan.

TABLE 14.1 Annual Percentage Rate Table for Monthly Payment Plans

Number of Payments	Annual Percentage Rate (Finance Charge per $100 of Amount Financed)													
	14%	$14\frac{1}{2}$%	$14\frac{3}{4}$%	15%	$15\frac{1}{4}$%	$15\frac{1}{2}$%	$15\frac{3}{4}$%	16%	$16\frac{1}{4}$%	$16\frac{1}{2}$%	17%	$17\frac{1}{2}$%	18%	$18\frac{1}{2}$%
1	1.17	1.21	1.23	1.25	1.27	1.29	1.31	1.33	1.35	1.37	1.42	1.46	1.50	1.54
2	1.75	1.82	1.85	1.88	1.91	1.94	1.97	2.00	2.04	2.07	2.13	2.19	2.26	2.32
3	2.34	2.43	2.47	2.51	2.55	2.59	2.64	2.68	2.72	2.76	2.85	2.93	3.01	3.10
4	2.93	3.04	3.09	3.14	3.20	3.25	3.30	3.36	3.41	3.46	3.57	3.67	3.78	3.88
5	3.53	3.65	3.72	3.78	3.84	3.91	3.97	4.04	4.10	4.16	4.29	4.42	4.54	4.67
6	4.12	4.27	4.35	4.42	4.49	4.57	4.64	4.72	4.79	4.87	5.02	5.17	5.32	5.46
7	4.72	4.89	4.98	5.06	5.15	5.23	5.32	5.40	5.49	5.58	5.75	5.92	6.09	6.26
8	5.32	5.51	5.61	5.71	5.80	5.90	6.00	6.09	6.19	6.29	6.48	6.67	6.87	7.06
9	5.92	6.14	6.25	6.35	6.46	6.57	6.68	6.78	6.89	7.00	7.22	7.43	7.65	7.87
10	6.53	6.77	6.88	7.00	7.12	7.24	7.36	7.48	7.60	7.72	7.96	8.19	8.43	8.67
11	7.14	7.40	7.53	7.66	7.79	7.92	8.05	8.18	8.31	8.44	8.70	8.96	9.22	9.49
12	7.74	8.03	8.17	8.31	8.45	8.59	8.74	8.88	9.02	9.16	9.45	9.73	10.02	10.30
13	8.36	8.66	8.81	8.97	9.12	9.27	9.43	9.58	9.73	9.89	10.20	10.50	10.81	11.12
14	8.97	9.30	9.46	9.63	9.79	9.96	10.12	10.79	10.45	10.62	10.95	11.28	11.61	11.95
15	9.59	9.94	10.11	10.29	10.47	10.64	10.82	11.00	11.17	11.35	11.71	12.06	12.42	12.77
16	10.20	10.58	10.77	10.95	11.14	11.33	11.52	11.71	11.90	12.09	12.46	12.84	13.22	13.60
17	10.82	11.22	11.42	11.62	11.82	12.02	12.22	12.42	12.62	12.83	13.23	13.63	14.04	14.44
18	11.45	11.87	12.08	12.29	12.50	12.72	12.93	13.14	13.35	13.57	13.99	14.42	14.85	15.28
19	12.07	12.52	12.74	12.97	13.19	13.41	13.64	13.86	14.09	14.31	14.76	15.22	15.67	16.12
20	12.70	13.17	13.41	13.64	13.88	14.11	14.35	14.59	14.82	15.06	15.54	16.01	16.49	16.97
21	13.33	13.82	14.07	14.32	14.57	14.82	15.06	15.31	15.56	15.81	16.31	16.81	17.32	17.82
22	13.96	14.48	14.74	15.00	15.26	15.52	15.78	16.04	16.30	16.57	17.09	17.62	18.15	18.68
23	14.59	15.14	15.41	15.68	15.96	16.23	16.50	16.78	17.05	17.32	17.88	18.43	18.98	19.54
24	15.23	15.80	16.08	16.37	16.65	16.94	17.22	17.51	17.80	18.09	18.66	19.24	19.82	20.40
25	15.87	16.46	16.76	17.06	17.35	17.65	17.95	18.25	18.55	18.85	19.45	20.05	20.66	21.27
26	16.51	17.13	17.44	17.75	18.06	18.37	18.68	18.99	19.30	19.62	20.24	20.87	21.50	22.14
27	17.15	17.80	18.12	18.44	18.76	19.09	19.41	19.74	20.06	20.39	21.04	21.69	22.35	23.01
28	17.80	18.47	18.80	19.14	19.47	19.81	20.15	20.48	20.82	21.16	21.84	22.52	23.20	23.89
29	18.45	19.14	19.49	19.83	20.18	20.53	20.88	21.23	21.58	21.94	22.64	23.35	24.06	24.77
30	19.10	19.81	20.17	20.54	20.90	21.26	21.62	21.99	22.35	22.72	23.45	24.18	24.92	25.66
31	19.75	20.49	20.87	21.24	21.61	21.99	22.37	22.74	23.12	23.50	24.26	25.02	25.78	26.55
32	20.40	21.17	21.56	21.95	22.33	22.72	23.11	23.50	23.89	24.28	25.07	25.86	26.65	27.44
33	21.06	21.85	22.25	22.65	23.06	23.46	23.86	24.26	24.67	25.07	25.88	26.70	27.52	28.34
34	21.72	22.54	22.95	23.37	23.78	24.19	24.61	25.03	25.44	25.86	26.70	27.54	28.39	29.24
35	22.38	23.23	23.65	24.08	24.51	24.94	25.36	25.79	26.23	26.66	27.52	28.39	29.27	30.14
36	23.04	23.92	24.35	24.80	25.24	25.68	26.12	26.57	27.01	27.46	28.35	29.25	30.15	31.05
48	31.17	32.37	32.98	33.59	34.20	34.81	35.52	36.03	36.65	37.27	38.50	39.75	41.00	42.26
60	39.61	41.17	41.95	42.74	43.53	44.32	45.11	45.91	46.71	47.51	49.12	50.73	52.36	54.00

14.3 Exercises

Find the total cost and the finance charge for each of the following.

	Amount Financed	Down Payment	Cash Price	Number of Payments	Amount of Payment	Total Installment Cost	Finance Charge
1.	$860	$120	$980	24	$45	_____	_____
2.	$1115	$215	$1330	36	$37	_____	_____
3.	$275	none	$275	9	$35	_____	_____
4.	$28	none	$28	3	$10	_____	_____
5.	$2450.79	$450	$2900.79	18	$156.94	_____	_____
6.	$6388.46	$380	$6768.46	60	$136.82	_____	_____

Find the approximate annual percentage rate using the approximate annual percentage rate formula. Round to the nearest tenth of a percent.

	Amount Financed	Finance Charge	Number of Monthly Payments	Approximate Annual Percentage Rate
7.	$1750	$500	48	_____
8.	$350	$38	24	_____
9.	$2000	$375	36	_____
10.	$4500	$800	48	_____

Find the annual percentage rate using the Annual Percentage Rate Table.

	Amount Financed	Finance Charge	Number of Monthly Payments	Annual Percentage Rate
11.	$1476	$88.52	8	_____
12.	$720	$165.89	36	_____
13.	$400	$30.96	12	_____
14.	$3780	$1292.80	48	_____

15. Explain the process used to calculate the annual percentage rate using tables. Assume the amount of each payment, the number of payments, and the down payment are given. (See Objective 4.)

16. Explain why the approximate APR is not sufficient for use on documents detailing credit charges. What is the value of calculating the approximate APR? (See Objective 3.)

Work each of the following word problems.

17. At a recent appliance sale, Gil Eckern purchased a portable color television set for $450. He decided to charge the set, paying nothing down and agreeing to payments of $27.98 per month for 18 months. Find the annual percentage rate for this loan.

18. On a 12-month loan of $1000 payable in equal monthly installments, the Mouse House advertises only $92 interest. What is the annual percentage rate?

19. To help in her lawn business, Ellen McCall decides to purchase a small truck. The purchase price is $6300. She puts $800 down and will pay $190 per month for 36 months. Find (a) the total purchase price including the down payment and (b) the annual percentage rate.

20. If $16,800 is borrowed to construct a swimming pool and the interest paid over a 5-year period is $8012, find the annual percentage rate if the loan is repaid in equal monthly payments.

21. House Television and Appliance wants to advertise a table model color television for $400, with 25% down and monthly payments of only $39.75 per month for 8 months. They must also include the annual percentage rate in the ad. Find the annual percentage rate.

22. A department store has a sofa on sale for $900. A buyer paying 20% down may finance the balance by paying $34.75 per month for 2 years. Find the annual percentage rate that the store must include in its advertising.

23. A refrigerator sells for $850. Suppose a customer pays $200 down, and finances the balance by paying $113.12 per month for 6 months. (a) Find the finance charge. (b) Find the annual percentage rate. (c) Complete this table.

Month	Balance Owed	Payment	Interest for Month	Applied to Balance	New Balance
1	$650.00	$113.12	$8.13	$104.99	$545.01
2	$545.01	$113.12	_____	_____	_____
3	_____	$113.12	_____	_____	_____
4	_____	$113.12	_____	_____	_____
5	_____	$113.12	_____	_____	_____
6	_____	_____	_____	_____	_____

24. A used motorcycle sells for $900. Suppose a down payment of $300 is made, with the balance financed with monthly payments of $104.72 each for 6 months. (a) Find the finance charge. (b) Find the annual percentage rate. (c) Complete this table.

Month	Balance Owed	Payment	Interest for Month	Applied to Balance	New Balance
1	$600.00	$104.72	$8.00	$96.72	$503.28
2	$503.28	$104.72	_____	_____	_____
3	_____	$104.72	_____	_____	_____
4	_____	$104.72	_____	_____	_____
5	_____	$104.72	_____	_____	_____
6	_____	_____	_____	_____	_____

14.4 The Rule of 78

OBJECTIVES

1 Understand the Rule of 78.

2 Use the Rule of 78 to calculate unearned interest.

If a consumer agrees to repay a loan by making a fixed number of payments for a fixed number of months, then the amount of each payment should be set to pay the principal and interest. Each payment goes partially to the principal and partially to interest. If the loan is paid off early, then not all the scheduled interest is owed.

1 Lenders must disclose to the borrower the method that will be used to calculate the reduction in interest if the loan is paid off early. One standard method (but a method not legal in all states) is based on the United States Rule and is called the **Rule of 78.** The interest not owed is called the **unearned interest,** or the unearned finance charge, since it is money not earned by the lender.

Under the Rule of 78, the numbers of the periods in an installment loan contract are totaled. In a 12-month contract, the numbers 1 through 12 add up to 78. (This is how the method derived its name.) In a 6-month contract, the digits 1 through 6 add to 21.

The Rule of 78 assumes that the finance charge for the use of credit is allocated among the months as follows. If the loan is for 12 months, the finance charge for the first month would be $\frac{12}{78}$ of the total finance charge, with $\frac{11}{78}$ in the second month, $\frac{10}{78}$ in the third month, and $\frac{1}{78}$ in the final month. The refund is calculated by multiplying the total finance charge by a fraction whose denominator is the sum of the total number of payments and whose numerator is the sum of the number of payments remaining.

2 As a shortcut, use the following formula to find the amount of unearned interest by the Rule of 78.

The *unearned interest* is given by

(REBATE)

$$\text{Unearned interest} = \frac{\text{Finance charge} \times \text{No. of payments remaining}}{\text{Total no. of payments}}$$

$$\times \frac{(1 + \text{No. of payments remaining})}{(1 + \text{Total no. of payments})}$$

EXAMPLE 1

Finding Unearned Interest

A loan payable in 12 equal monthly installments has a finance charge of $312. Find the amount of unearned interest if the loan is paid in full with 3 payments remaining.

SOLUTION The finance charge is $312, the loan was scheduled to run for 12 months, and the loan is paid off with 3 payments remaining. Use the formula to find the amount of unearned interest.

$$\text{Unearned interest} = \frac{\$312 \times 3 \times (1 + 3)}{12 \times (1 + 12)}$$

$$= \frac{\$312 \times 3 \times 4}{12 \times 13}$$

$$= \$24$$

The unearned interest is $24. By paying off the loan 3 months early, the borrower saves $24 in interest. ■

NOTE In Example 1, the loan was paid off with $\frac{3}{12} = \frac{1}{4} = 25\%$ of its life left, but only $\frac{\$24}{\$312} = 0.076$, or about 8%, of the interest is saved. Since the early payment on a loan involves more interest and less principal, the savings from paying off a loan early are often surprisingly small.

EXAMPLE 2

Finding Payoff Value

Adrian Ortega borrowed $600, which he is paying back in 24 monthly payments of $29.50 each. With 9 payments remaining, he decides to repay the loan in full. Find (a) the amount of unearned finance charge and (b) the amount necessary to repay the loan in full.

SOLUTION

(a) Ortega is scheduled to make 24 payments of $29.50 each, for a total repayment of

$$24 \times \$29.50 = \$708$$

His finance charge is

$$\$708 - \$600 = \$108.$$

Find the amount of unearned interest as follows. The finance charge is $108, the scheduled number of payments is 24, and the loan is paid off with 9 payments left. Use the formula.

$$\text{Unearned interest} = \frac{\$108 \times 9 \times (1 + 9)}{24 \times (1 + 24)}$$

$$= \frac{\$108 \times 9 \times 10}{24 \times 25}$$

$$= \$16.20$$

Paying off the loan 9 months early produces a savings of $16.20 in interest.

(b) When Ortega decides to pay off the loan, he has 9 payments of $29.50 left. These payments total

$$9 \times 29.50 = \$265.50.$$

By paying the loan early, Ortega saves the unearned interest of $16.20, so

$$\$265.50 - \$16.20 = \$249.30$$

is needed to pay the loan in full. ∎

Calculator Approach to Example 2

(a) Calculate the value of the denominator and place it in memory.

$$24 \; \boxed{\times} \; 25 \; \boxed{M+} \; 600$$

Then calculate the value of the numerator and divide it by the stored value.

$$108 \; \boxed{\times} \; 9 \; \boxed{\times} \; 10 \; \boxed{\div} \; \boxed{MR} \; \boxed{=} \; 16.2$$

(b) Calculate the amount of the loan that must be paid and subtract the unearned interest.

$$9 \; \boxed{\times} \; 29.5 \; \boxed{-} \; 16.2 \; \boxed{=} \; 249.3$$

14.4 Exercises

Each of the following loans is paid in full before their date of maturity. Find the amount of unearned interest. Use the Rule of 78.

Finance Charge	Total Number of Payments	Remaining Number of Payments when Paid in Full
1. $975	48	30
2. $325	36	6
3. $174	18	5
4. $325	24	22
5. $3653.82	48	9
6. $3085.54	60	15

7. Explain the purpose of the Rule of 78. What is the basic assumption of this rule? (See Objective 1.)

8. Outline the process used to calculate the payoff figure for a loan if the monthly payment, payments remaining, and total number of payments in the original loan are known. (See Objective 2.)

Work the following word problems.

9. The finance charge (time-price differential) for a certain loan is $276.75. If the total number of equal monthly installments to repay the loan is 24 and the loan is paid in full with 6 months remaining, find the amount of unearned interest.

10. Sheila Goshorn decides to use her income tax refund to pay her travel agency loan in full. She finds that her 36-month loan includes $240 interest and that she will be paying the loan in full with 21 months remaining. Calculate the amount of unearned interest.

11. George Duda has decided that making the small monthly payment on a 6-month loan is a nuisance. The total finance charge is only $6.80, and the loan is paid in full with 3 months remaining. Find the unearned interest.

12. Anne Kelly purchased a 21-speed speed mountain bike, payable in 8 monthly installments. If the finance charge was $30 and she pays the loan in full with 3 months remaining, find the amount of unearned interest.

13. Ralph Todd purchased a refrigerator on the "easy payment plan" with only $100 down and 18 equal monthly payments of $45.20. The total cash price of the refrigerator was $800. After making 6 monthly payments, he decided to pay the loan in full. Find (a) the amount of unearned interest and (b) the amount necessary to pay the loan in full.

14. A car costs $8850. After a down payment of $2000, the balance is financed with 48 payments of $194.25 each. Suppose the loan is paid off with 15 payments left. Find (a) the amount of unearned interest, and (b) the amount necessary to pay the loan in full.

CHAPTER 14 QUICK REVIEW

TOPIC	APPROACH	EXAMPLE
14.1 United States Rule for repayment of loans	First find interest from date of loan to date of partial payment. Then subtract interest from partial payment. Next reduce principal by any difference. Find additional interest from date of partial payment to next partial payment or maturity date and add this interest to unpaid principal.	Sam Spade signed a 120-day note for $3000 at 11% on February 1. Sam made a partial payment of $1200 on March 18. What is the amount due at maturity? There are 27 + 18 = 45 days from February 1 to March 18. $I = PRT$ $I = \$3000\,(0.11)\left(\dfrac{45}{360}\right) = \$41.25$ $1200.00 - \$41.25 = \$1158.75$ is applied to reduction of principal. $3000.00 - \$1158.75 = \$1841.25$ is balance owed. There are 120 − 45 = 75 days until maturity, so additional interest is $I = \$1841.25\,(0.11)\left(\dfrac{75}{360}\right)$ $= \$42.20$ Then $1841.25 + \$42.20 = \$1883.45$ is due at maturity.
14.2 Finding the finance charge on a revolving charge account using the unpaid balance method	Calculate the finance charge on the previous month's unpaid balance. Then add the finance charge and purchases to the previous balance. Next subtract any payments made.	Pat Moyer's VISA account had an unpaid balance of $182.50 on June 1. During June she made a $30 payment and purchases totaling $114.35. Find the finance charge and the unpaid balance on July 1 if the bank charges 1.4% per month on the unpaid balance. Finance charge = ($182.50)(0.014) = $2.56 Unpaid balance = $182.50 + $2.56 + $114.35 − $30 = $269.41

TOPIC	APPROACH	EXAMPLE

14.2 Finding the finance charge on a revolving charge account using the average daily balance method

First find the unpaid balance on each day. Then add the daily unpaid balances and divide by the number of days in the billing period.

Finally, calculate the finance charge by multiplying the average daily balance by the interest rate.

Previous balance, $115.45; November 1, Billing date; November 15, Payment of $35; November 22, Jacket $45. Find the finance charge if interest is 1% per month on the average daily balance.

14 days at $115.45 = $1616.30

7 days at ($115.45 − $35 = $80.45)

$$= \$563.15$$

9 days at ($80.45 + $45 = $125.45)

$$= \$1129.05$$

$14 + 7 + 9 = 30$ days

$1616.30 + $563.15 + $1129.05

$$= \$3308.50$$

Average daily balance $= \dfrac{\$3308.50}{30}$

$$= \$110.28$$

Finance charge $= \$110.28 \times 0.01$

$$= \$1.10$$

14.3 Finding the total installment cost, finance charge, and amount financed

Total installment cost = Down payment + (Amount of each payment × Number of payments)

Finance charge = Total installment cost − Cash price

Amount financed = Cash price − Down payment

Joan Taylor bought a fur coat for $1580. She put $350 down and then made 12 payments of $115 each. Find the total installment cost, the finance charge, and the amount financed.

Total installment cost =
$350 + (12 × $115) = $1730

Finance charge = $1730 − $1580

$$= \$150$$

Amount financed = $1580 − $350

$$= \$1230$$

TOPIC	APPROACH	EXAMPLE
14.3 Determining the approximate APR using a formula	**1.** Determine the finance charge. **2.** Find the amount financed. **3.** To calculate approximate APR, divide (24 × Finance charge) by Amount financed × (1 + Number of payments)	Nick Palmer buys a motorcycle for $7500. He makes a down payment of $1800 and monthly payments of $200 for 36 months. Find the approximate APR. Total installment cost = $1800 + ($200 × 36) = $9000 Finance charge = $9000 − $7500 = $1500 Amount financed = $7500 − $1800 = $5700 Approximate APR = $$\frac{24 \times \$1500}{\$5700 \times (1 + 36)} = 17.07\%$$
14.3 Finding APR using a table	**1.** Determine the finance charge per $100: $$\frac{\text{Finance charge}}{\text{Amount financed}} \times \$100.$$ **2.** Find the number of payments in the leftmost column of Table 14.1; then go across to the number closest to the number found in Step 1 and read up to find APR.	Use the table to find the APR for Nick Palmer in the previous example Finance charge = $1500 Amount financed = $5700 Finance charge per $100 $$= \frac{\$1500}{\$5700} \times \$100 = 26.32$$ Number of payments = 36; table value closest to $26.32 is $26.12; APR = 15.75%.

TOPIC	APPROACH	EXAMPLE

14.4 Finding the un-earned interest using the Rule of 78

Find the unearned interest:

$$\frac{\left(\begin{array}{c}\text{Finance}\\\text{charge}\end{array}\right) \times \left(\begin{array}{c}\text{No. of payments}\\\text{remaining}\end{array}\right)}{\text{Total no. of payments}}$$

$$\times \frac{\left(\begin{array}{c}1 + \text{ No. of payments}\\\text{remaining}\end{array}\right)}{\left(\begin{array}{c}1 + \text{Total no.}\\\text{of payments}\end{array}\right)}$$

Then find the amount left to pay and subtract the unearned interest to find balance remaining.

Tom Fish borrows $1500 which he is paying back in 36 monthly install-ments of $52.75 each. With 10 pay-ments remaining he decides to pay the loan in full. Find the amount of unearned interest and the amount necessary to pay the loan in full.

Installment cost = 36 × $52.75
= $1899

Finance charge = $1899 − $1500
= $399

Unearned Interest =

$$\frac{\$399 \times 10}{36} \times \frac{(1 + 10)}{(1 + 36)} = \$32.95$$

The 10 payments of $52.75 that are left amount to $52.75 × 10 = $527.50.

Balance = $527.50 − $32.95
= $494.55

SUMMARY EXERCISE

Trish Decker has a 120-day, 9% note for $3000 that she signed on September 15. She inherits $5000 and makes a payment of $1250 on November 10.

(a) What is the balance due on the maturity date of the note?

(b) What amount of interest does Decker pay on the note?

(c) Decker also wishes to use some of her inheritance to pay off her charge account. The account charges $1\frac{1}{2}\%$ on the average daily balance to determine interest charges. Her most recent statement contains the following information.

Previous balance		$460.85
October 3	Billing Date	
October 10	Returns	$37.15
October 15	Baby clothes	$48.96
October 20	Payment	$40.00
October 30	Baby stroller	$89.65

How much is due on the bill in order to pay it off?

(d) Finally, Decker has a loan on which she is paying $51.46 per month. The original loan was for 48 months and had a finance charge of $470. She wants to pay it off with 12 payments remaining. Using the rule of 78, find the payoff value.

(e) Will Decker have enough money left to pay off the note in part (a) after paying off the charge account and the loan? If so, how much money remains from her $5000 inheritance?

CHAPTER 14 REVIEW EXERCISES

Find the balance due on the maturity date and the total amount of interest on the following notes. Use the United States Rule. [14.1]

	Principal	Interest	Time in Days	Partial Payments
1.	$8000	8%	90 days	$1500 on day 24
2.	$9000	12%	120 days	$2000 on day 40
3.	$6000	11%	120 days	$3200 on day 30 $2000 on day 90
4.	$9000	9%	90 days	$3000 on day 30 $1500 on day 45

Find the finance charge on each of the following revolving charge accounts. Assume the interest is calculated on the unpaid balance of the account. Round to the nearest cent. [14.2]

	Unpaid Balance	Monthly Interest Rate
5.	$428.93	$1\frac{1}{2}\%$
6.	$915.38	$1\frac{1}{8}\%$
7.	$1231.25	1.123%

Complete the following table, showing the unpaid balance at the end of each month. Assume an interest rate of 1.5% on the unpaid balance. [14.2]

	Month	Unpaid Balance at Beginning of Month	Finance Charge	Purchase During Month	Returns	Payments	Unpaid Balance at End of Month
8.	June	$316.53	_____	$73.25	—	$50	_____
	July	_____	_____	$123.17	$14.36	$75	_____
	August	_____	_____	$86.14	$35.43	$100	_____
	September	_____	_____	$93.12	$75.51	$125	_____

Find the finance charge for each of the following revolving charge accounts. Assume interest is calculated on the average daily balance of the account. [14.2]

	Average Daily Balance	Monthly Interest Rate
9.	$135	$1\frac{1}{4}\%$
10.	$216.48	$1\frac{1}{2}\%$
11.	$348.53	1.531%

Find the average daily balance for each of the following credit card accounts. Assume one month between billing dates (using the proper number of days in the month). Then find the finance charge if interest is $1\frac{1}{2}\%$ per month on the average daily balance. [14.2]

12. Previous balance $634.25
  March 9   Billing date
  March 17   Payment $125
  March 30   Lunch $34.26

13. Previous balance $236.26
  July 10   Billing date   — AUG 10
  July 15   Athletic shoes $28.25
  July 20   Payment $75.00
  July 31   Pillow cases $35.00
  August 5   Returns $24.36

Find the total installment cost and the finance charge for each of the following. [14.3]

	Amount Financed	Down Payment	Cash Price	Number of Payments	Amount of Payment	Total Installment Cost	Finance Charge
14.	$900	$75	$925	15	$75	————	————
15.	$2600	$300	$2900	18	$160	————	————
16.	$10,000	$1000	$11,000	36	$285	————	————

Find the approximate annual percentage rate using the approximate APR formula. Round to the nearest tenth of a percent. [14.3]

	Amount Financed	Finance Charge	Number of Monthly Payments
17.	$7000	$325	12
18.	$1800	$255	24
19.	$1925	$450	48

Find the annual percentage rate using the Annual Percentage Rate Table. [14.3]

	Amount Financed	Finance Charge	Number of Monthly Payments
20.	$1800	$160	12
21.	$3650	$576.70	24
22.	$4225	$1047.80	36
23.	$7600	$1816.92	36

Each of the following loans is paid in full before the date of maturity. Find the amount of unearned interest. Use the Rule of 78. [14.4]

	Finance Charge	Total Number of Payments	Remaining Number of Payments when Paid in Full
24.	$225	24	9
25.	$375	18	6
26.	$160	20	6
27.	$68	12	4

Work each of the following word problems.

28. Sandmeyer Concrete Company was the maker of an 11% note for $5600 dated June 20 for 150 days. The firm made partial payments of $1330 on July 20 and $1655 on September 3. (a) What payment is required when the note is due? (b) What was the total interest paid on the note? [14.1]

29. Debbie Blaisdell has a revolving charge at a department store. Her monthly statement contained the following information: [14.2]

6–10	Billing date; previous balance	$52.45
6–20	Payment	$15.00 CR
6–25	Craft department	$17.40
7–2	Shoe department	$23.00

Find the average daily balance on the next billing date of July 10. Then, find the finance charge if the interest is 1.5% per month on the average daily balance.

30. To purchase a new car Chris Papa puts $500 down and agrees to pay $322 a month for 36 months. The purchase price is $9800. Find the total purchase price including down payment and the annual percentage rate. Use Table 14.1 on page 472. [14.3]

15

Annuities, Sinking Funds, and Amortization

The earlier work with simple and compound interest involved *lump sums:* a lump sum of money would be borrowed or deposited today, with the appropriate formulas used to find the maturity value or future value, respectively. However, in practical, day-to-day life, such lump sum payments are not as common as sequences of *periodic payments*. For example, few people prepare for their children's college education, or their own retirement, by making a lump sum deposit—most people must save for these events by periodic deposits.

Also, most loans are not paid back with a single payment, but rather in a series of periodic payments. These periodic payments are discussed in this chapter. (Please note that a summary of all the formulas in the chapter is given at the end of the chapter.)

15.1 Amount of an Annuity

OBJECTIVES

1. Identify the types of annuities.
2. Find the amount of an annuity.
3. Find the amount of an annuity payment.
4. Find the number of payments.
5. Find the amount of an annuity due.

Suppose a small firm decides to accumulate money to buy a new truck. To do so, they make deposits of $1500 at the end of each year for 6 years in an account paying 8% per year, compounded annually. Such a sequence of equal payments is called an annuity. (Many people think of an annuity only as a sequence of payments made by a life insurance company when a person retires, but this is only one special kind of annuity.)

The time between the payments of an annuity is the **payment period,** with the time from the beginning of the first payment period to the end of the last called the **term of the annuity**. The **amount of the annuity,** the final sum on deposit, is defined as the sum of the compound amounts of all the payments, compounded to the end of the term.

1 There are many kinds of annuities. An **annuity certain** has a specified beginning date and a specified ending date. The example of payments for 6 years is an annuity certain. Other examples would include the 48 monthly payments needed to pay off a car loan, or 18 annual payments into a college fund beginning at the birth of a child.

A **contingent annuity** has variable beginning or ending dates. For example, an insurance policy that pays a fixed amount per month beginning when a person is age 65 and lasting until that person's death has a variable ending date and is a contingent annuity. A person might prepare a will leaving a fixed annual sum to the surviving spouse for a fixed number of years, an example of a contingent annuity with a variable beginning date (because the annual payments do not start until the death of the person making the will).

Because of the variation in the beginning or ending dates of contingent annuities, their study requires a knowledge of probability theory not given in this book. Therefore, we will only discuss annuities certain.

With an **ordinary annuity,** payments are made at the *end* of each period of time, while an **annuity due** has payments made at the *beginning* of each period.

Finally, a **simple annuity** has payment dates matching the compounding period. For example, an annuity with payments made quarterly and having interest compounded quarterly is a simple annuity, while an annuity with payments made quarterly and interest compounded daily is not a simple annuity.

While there are formulas available for annuities that are not simple (see a textbook on mathematics of finance), we discuss only simple annuities in this book.

Let us return to the annuity mentioned at the beginning of this section—payments of $1500 at the end of each year for 6 years in an account paying 8% per year compounded annually. By the definitions, this annuity is certain, ordinary, and simple. To find the amount of the annuity, or the final sum on deposit, find the sum of the compound amounts of all the payments compounded to the end of the term.

The first deposit of $1500 will produce a compound amount of

$$1500 \, (1 + 0.08)^5 = 1500 \, (1.08)^5.$$

Use 5 as the exponent instead of 6 since the money is deposited at the *end* of the first year, and earns interest for only 5 years. The second payment of $1500 will produce a compound amount of $1500(1.08)^4$. Continuing in this way, the amount of the annuity is $1500(1.08)^5 + 1500(1.08)^4 + 1500(1.08)^3 + 1500(1.08)^2 + 1500(1.08)^1 + 1500$. (The last payment earns no interest at all.) From column A of the interest table in Appendix C, this sum is

$$\$1500 \, (1.46932808) + \$1500 \, (1.36048896) + \$1500 \, (1.25971200)$$
$$+ \, \$1500 \, (1.16640000) + \$1500 \, (1.08000000) + \$1500$$
$$= \$2203.99 + \$2040.73 + \$1889.57 + \$1749.60 + \$1620$$
$$+ \, \$1500$$
$$= \$11,003.89.$$

The amount of the annuity is $11,003.89. Since 6 deposits of $1500 each were made, the interest earned is

$$\$11,003.89 - (6 \times \$1500) = \$2003.89.$$

Figure 15.1 shows each payment into the annuity and the compound amount of each payment.

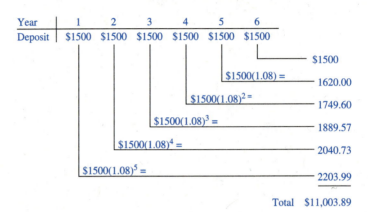

FIGURE 15.1

2 This method for finding the amount of the annuity of $1500 at the end of each year for 6 years was tedious. Using algebra, a formula for the amount of an annuity can be derived. This formula follows.

> If a simple annuity is made up of payments of R dollars at the end of each period for n periods, at a rate of interest i per period, then the amount of the annuity, S, is
>
> $$S = R\left[\frac{(1 + i)^n - 1}{i}\right]$$
>
> The quantity in brackets is commonly written $s_{\overline{n}|i}$ (read "s-angle-n-at-i") so that
>
> $$S = R \cdot s_{\overline{n}|i}.$$

For our annuity, $R = \$1500$, $n = 6$, and $i = 0.08$. By the formula, the amount of the annuity is

$$S = R \cdot s_{\overline{n}|i}$$

$$S = \$1500 \cdot s_{\overline{6}|0.08}.$$

By the definition of the symbol $s_{\overline{6}|0.08}$,

$$S = \$1500 \left[\frac{(1 + 0.08)^6 - 1}{0.08} \right].$$

$$S = \$1500 \left[\frac{(1.08)^6 - 1}{0.08} \right].$$

The value of $(1.08)^6$ can be found in column A of the interest table in Appendix C or by using a calculator. By either method,

$$S = \$1500 \left(\frac{1.58687432 - 1}{0.08} \right)$$

$$S = \$1500 \, (7.33592900)$$

$$S = \$11,003.89,$$

exactly the same result found earlier.

To save time, tables of values of $s_{\overline{n}|i}$ have been calculated. They appear in column C of the interest table in Appendix C. Look in this table for 8% and 6 periods to find

$$s_{\overline{6}|0.08} = 7.33592904.$$

NOTE The number from the table is slightly different from the result found by using the formula. This variation is due to rounding.

EXAMPLE 1
Finding the Amount of an Annuity

Tom Bleser is an athlete who feels that his playing career will last 7 years. To prepare for his future, he deposits $22,000 at the end of each year for 7 years in an account paying 10% compounded annually. How much will he have on deposit after 7 years?

SOLUTION His payments form an ordinary annuity with $R = \$22,000$, $n = 7$, and $i = 0.10$. The amount of this annuity is from the formula

$$S = \$22,000 \left[\frac{(1.10)^7 - 1}{0.10} \right].$$

From column C of the interest table, the number in brackets, $s_{\overline{7}|0.10}$, is 9.48717100, so

$$S = \$22,000 \, (9.48717100) = \$208,717.76.$$

Bleser deposited $22,000 per year for 7 years, for a total deposit of

$$7 \times \$22,000 = \$154,000.$$

Of the $208,717.76, which was the amount of his annuity, the difference

$$\$208,717.76 - \$154,000 = \$54,717.76$$

represents interest earned. ∎

EXAMPLE 2
Finding the Amount of an Annuity

Suppose $100 is deposited at the end of each month for 3 years in an account paying 12% compounded monthly. Find the amount of the annuity.

SOLUTION   Interest of $12\% \div 12 = 1\%$ is earned monthly. In 3 years there are $3 \times 12 = 36$ monthly periods. Find $s_{\overline{36}|0.01}$ in column C of the interest table. Look on the 1% page and down 36 periods, to see $s_{\overline{36}|0.01} = 43.07687836$. The $100 deposits will lead to

$$S = \$100 \, (43.07687836) = \$4307.69.$$

Since deposits of $100 at the end of each month for 3 years represent $3 \times 12 = 36$ payments of $100 each, the total deposit is $36 \times \$100 = \$3600$. Of the amount of the annuity, $4307.69, this means

$$\$4307.69 - (36 \times \$100) = \$4307.69 - \$3600 = \$707.69$$

represents interest. ∎

3   Sometimes the lump sum that will be needed at some time in the future is known, and the amount of each payment into an annuity that will guarantee the availability of the necessary amount must be found.

EXAMPLE 3
Finding the Amount of an Annuity Payment

Wolf Films needs to buy a new model video camera 3 years from now. The firm wants to deposit an equal amount at the end of each quarter for 3 years in order to accumulate enough money to pay for the camera. The camera will cost $2400, and the bank pays 8% interest compounded quarterly. Find the amount of each of the 12 deposits to be made.

SOLUTION   This example describes an ordinary annuity with $S = \$2400$, $i = 2\%$ ($8\% \div 4 = 2\%$), and $n = 3 \times 4 = 12$ periods. The unknown here is the amount of each payment, R. Use the formula for the amount of an annuity.

$$2400 = R \cdot s_{\overline{12}|0.02}$$

From column C of the interest table, with $n = 12$ and $i = 2\%$, find $s_{\overline{12}|0.02} = 13.41208973$, and

$$\$2400 = R \, (13.41208973).$$

Dividing both sides by 13.41208973 gives

$$\$178.94 = R.$$

Each payment must be $178.94. (As we shall see in Section 3 of this chapter, these payments form a sinking fund.) ∎

CAUTION The value of n is the number of compounding periods (not years) and i is the interest per compounding period (not interest per year). So $n = 12$ and $i = 0.02$.

4   The next example shows how to find the number of periods necessary to accumulate a certain amount of money.

FIND AMT. OF DEPOSITS TO BE MADE
OR
DIVIDE →

EXAMPLE 4

Finding the
Number of
Payments

The Minknas want to go on a "dream" vacation, costing $4000. They can save $275 per quarter. If they deposit this amount in an account paying 3% interest compounded quarterly, how long will it be before they can go on the vacation?

SOLUTION   Here the amount of the annuity is known, S, and R is known, the amount of each payment, as is i, the interest rate per period. The unknown is n, the number of quarters for which deposits must be made. Start with the formula for the amount of an annuity.

$$S = R \cdot s_{\overline{n}|i}$$

Replace S with 4000, R with 275, and i with $3\% \div 4 = \frac{3}{4}\%$.

$$S = R \cdot s_{\overline{n}|i}$$

$$\$4000 = \$275 \cdot s_{\overline{n}|0.0075}$$

Divide both sides by $275 to get the following.

$$14.54545455 = s_{\overline{n}|0.0075}$$

Go to the $\frac{3}{4}\%$ page in the interest table. Look down column C for the first number *larger* than 14.54545455. The first number that is larger is 14.70340370 which corresponds to 14 quarters. The family must save for 14 quarters; at the end of this period of time they will have

$$\$275 \,(14.70340370) = \$4043.44. \quad \blacksquare$$

NOTE The table value used is the one *larger* than the calculated value not closest to it.

5   As mentioned earlier, with ordinary annuities payments are made at the *end* of each time period. With **annuities due** the payments are made at the *beginning* of the time period.

> To find the amount of an annuity due, treat each payment as if it were made at the *end* of the *preceding* period. Then use column C of the interest table to find $s_{\overline{n}|i}$ for *one additional* period; to compensate for this, subtract the amount of one payment.

EXAMPLE 5

Finding the Amount
of an Annuity Due

Find the amount of an annuity due if payments of $500 are made at the beginning of each quarter for 7 years, in an account paying 4% compounded quarterly.

SOLUTION   In 7 years, there are $4 \times 7 = 28$ quarterly periods. Use the $4\% \div 4 = 1\%$ page of the interest table. Look in row 29 $(28 + 1)$ of column C of the table and find the number 33.45038766. Multiply this number by 500, the amount of each payment.

$$\$500 \,(33.45038766) = \$16,725.19$$

Subtract the amount of one payment from this result.

$$\$16,725.19 - \$500 = \$16,225.19$$

The account will contain a total of $16,225.19 after 7 years. ∎

CAUTION Be sure to add one *period* to the total number of annuity periods and then subtract one *payment* to find the total in the account.

15.1 Exercises

Find each of the following values. Use column C of the interest table.

1. $s_{\overline{15}|0.03}$ **2.** $s_{\overline{18}|0.08}$

3. $s_{\overline{16}|0.04}$ **4.** $s_{\overline{40}|0.02}$

5. $s_{\overline{20}|0.01}$ **6.** $s_{\overline{18}|0.015}$

7. $s_{\overline{36}|0.10}$ **8.** $s_{\overline{20}|0.025}$

9. $s_{\overline{36}|0.0125}$ **10.** $s_{\overline{12}|0.10}$

Find the value of the following ordinary annuities. Interest is compounded annually. Find the total amount of interest earned.

11. $R = \$100,$
$i = 0.04,\ n = 20$

12. $R = \$1000,$
$i = 0.08,\ n = 12$

13. $R = \$10,000,$
$i = 0.09,\ n = 8$

14. $R = \$100,000$
$i = 0.05,\ n = 11$

15. $R = \$46,299.44,$
$i = 0.06,\ n = 7$

16. $R = \$74,388.99,$
$i = 0.08,\ n = 9$

Find the value of each of the following ordinary annuities. Payments are made and interest is compounded as given. Find the total amount of interest earned.

17. $R = \$800$, 8% per year compounded semiannually for 8 years

18. $R = \$5300$, 6% per year compounded quarterly for 5 years

19. $R = \$19,805$, 12% per year compounded quarterly for 3 years

20. $R = \$37,644$, 10% per year compounded semiannually for 9 years

Find the amount of each of the following annuities due. Assume that interest is compounded annually. Find the amount of interest earned.

21. $R = \$900,$
$i = 0.07,\ n = 10$

22. $R = \$1400,$
$i = 0.08,\ n = 10$

23. $R = \$17,544,$
$i = 0.08,\ n = 6$

24. $R = \$64,715,$
$i = 0.06,\ n = 12$

25. Explain the procedure used to calculate the amount of an annuity if the deposit is made at the beginning of each period. (See Objective 5.)

26. Explain the difference between an annuity certain and a contingent annuity.

Find the amounts of each of the following annuities due. Find the amount of interest earned.

27. payments of $200 made at the beginning of each quarter for 11 years at 6% compounded quarterly

28. $50 deposited at the beginning of each month for 4 years at 6% compounded monthly

29. $100 deposited at the beginning of each quarter for 9 years at 8% compounded quarterly

30. $1500 deposited at the beginning of each semiannual period for 11 years at 14% compounded semiannually

Find the periodic payment that will amount to the following sums under the given conditions.

31. $S = \$10,000$, interest is 8% compounded annually, payments made at the end of each year for 12 years

32. $S = \$50,000$, interest is 7% compounded semiannually, payments made at the end of each semiannual period for 8 years

33. $S = \$50,000$, interest is 12% compounded quarterly, payments made at the end of each quarter for 8 years

34. $S = \$24,000$, interest is 9% compounded monthly, payments are made at the end of each month for $3\frac{1}{4}$ years

Find the minimum number of payments that must be made to accumulate the given amount of money at the stated interest rate. Also, find the amount of the annuity.

35. $9500 needed, payments of $250 are made at the end of each quarter at 8% compounded quarterly

36. $21,000 needed, payments of $1500 are made at the end of each 6-month period at 10% compounded semiannually

37. $40,000 needed, payments of $750 are made at the end of each month at 10% compounded monthly

38. $37,500 needed, payments of $1250 are made at the end of each month at 12% compounded monthly

Solve each word problem.

39. At the end of each quarter, the Tomlinsons deposit $1000 in a certificate of deposit paying 6% compounded quarterly. At maturity, both principal and interest are renewed. Find the amount of this annuity after $2\frac{3}{4}$ years. How much interest have the Tomlinsons earned?

40. Pat Dillon deposits $12,000 at the end of each year for 9 years in an account paying 8% interest compounded annually. Find the final amount she will have on deposit. Find the amount of interest she will earn.

41. Dillon's brother-in-law works in a bank which pays 6% compounded annually. If she deposits her money in this bank, instead of the one in Exercise 40, how much would she have in her account? Find the amount of interest she would earn in this bank.

42. How much would Dillon lose over 9 years by using her brother-in-law's bank? (See Exercises 40 and 41.)

43. Pam Parker deposits $2435 at the beginning of each year for 8 years in an account paying 6% compounded annually. She then leaves that money alone, with no further deposits, for an additional 5 years. Find the final amount on deposit after the entire 13-year period. Find the total amount of interest earned.

44. Ray Berkowitz needs $10,000 in 8 years. What amount can he deposit at the end of each quarter at 14% compounded quarterly so that he will have his $10,000?

45. Find Berkowitz's quarterly deposit (see Exercise 44) if the money is deposited at 12% compounded quarterly.

46. Barb Silverman wants to buy an $18,000 car in 6 years. How much money must she deposit at the end of each quarter in an account paying 3% compounded quarterly, so that she will have enough to pay for her car?

47. Tom and Sandra Kip are trying to save $4000 as the down payment on a new motor home. If they can deposit $125 at the end of each month in an account paying 4% compounded monthly, how long will it take them to accumulate the necessary amount? How much will they actually accumulate?

48. Western Motors needs $120,000 as a down payment on a new showroom. If the company deposits $10,000 at the end of each quarter at 5% compounded quarterly, how long will it take them to get the needed money? How much will the company actually have?

15.2 Present Value of an Annuity

OBJECTIVES

1 Calculate the present value of an annuity from the definition.

2 Use the formula for the present value of an annuity.

3 Find the equivalent cash price.

The previous section discussed how to find the amount of an annuity after a series of equal, periodic payments. This section considers the present value of such an annuity. There are two ways to think of the **present value of an annuity**.

> 1. The *present value of an annuity* is a lump sum that can be deposited today that will amount to the same final total as would the periodic *payments* of an annuity, or
>
> 2. The present value of an annuity is a lump sum that could be deposited today so that equal periodic *withdrawals* could be made.

1 As an example of this second way of looking at the present value of an annuity, let us find the amount that must be deposited today, at 10% compounded annually, so that $1500 could be removed at the end of each year for 6 years.

The amount that must be deposited today is the sum of the present values of each of the separate withdrawals. In other words, today's deposit must include the present value of the withdrawal to be made at the end of the first year. The present value in 1 year of $1500 at 10% compounded annually is found by looking in column B of the interest table in Appendix C for 10% and 1 period, finding 0.90909091. The present value is

$$\$1500\,(0.90909091) = \$1363.64.$$

It is also necessary to deposit today the present value of the $1500 to be withdrawn at the end of the second year. Again use column B of the interest table, this time with 10% and 2 periods, finding 0.82644628. The present value for the withdrawal at the end of the second year is

$$\$1500\,(0.82644628) = \$1239.67.$$

Continuing in this way for all six withdrawals gives the result shown in Figure 15.2.

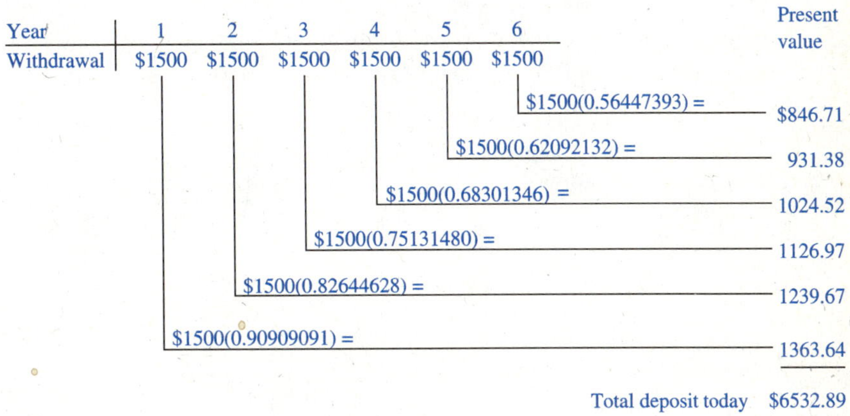

Year	1	2	3	4	5	6		Present value
Withdrawal	$1500	$1500	$1500	$1500	$1500	$1500		

$1500(0.56447393) = $846.71
$1500(0.62092132) = 931.38
$1500(0.68301346) = 1024.52
$1500(0.75131480) = 1126.97
$1500(0.82644628) = 1239.67
$1500(0.90909091) = 1363.64

Total deposit today $6532.89

FIGURE 15.2

A lump sum deposit today of $6532.89 at 10% compounded annually would permit withdrawals of $1500 at the end of each year for 6 years. Also, a lump sum deposit today of $6532.89 left in an account for 6 years would produce the same final total as deposits of $1500 at the end of each year for 6 years, with all deposits at 10% compounded annually.

2 The formula for the present value of an annuity is as follows.

> The present value of an annuity, A, of R dollars at the end of each period for n periods, at a rate of interest i per period, is
>
> $$A = R\left[\frac{(1+i)^n - 1}{i(1+i)^n}\right].$$
>
> The expression in brackets is abbreviated $a_{\overline{n}|i}$, making the formula
>
> $$A = R \cdot a_{\overline{n}|i}.$$

Values of $a_{\overline{n}|i}$ are given in column D of the interest table. We can use the table to check the problem given above. Look on the 10% page, for 6 payments at 10%, finding the number 4.35526070. Then multiply, which gives

$$A = \$1500\,(4.35526070) = \$6532.89,$$

the same answer found earlier.

EXAMPLE 1

Finding the Present Value

What lump sum deposited today at 5% compounded annually will yield the same total amount as payments of $4200 at the end of each year for 7 years, also at 5% compounded annually?

SOLUTION Find the present value of an annuity of $4200 per year for 7 years at 5% compounded annually, using the formula given above. Column D of the interest table shows that $a_{\overline{7}|0.05} = 5.78637340$.

 COL. "D"

$$A = R \cdot a_{\overline{n}|i}$$

$$A = \$4200 \cdot a_{\overline{7}|0.05}$$

$$A = \$4200\,(5.78637340)$$

$$A = \$24{,}302.77$$

A lump sum deposit of $24,302.77 today at 5% compounded annually will yield the same total after 7 years as deposits of $4200 at the end of each year for 7 years at 5% compounded annually.

Check this result. The compound amount in 7 years of a deposit of $24,302.77 today at 5% compounded annually can be found by the formula $M = P(1+i)^n$. From column A of the interest table, $24,302.77 will produce a total of

CHECK RESULT

$$\$24{,}302.77\,(1.40710042) = \$34{,}196.44.$$

On the other hand, from column C of the interest table deposits of $4200 at the end of each year for 7 years, at 5% compounded annually, give an amount of

$$\$4200\,(8.14200845) = \$34{,}196.44$$

the same result. ■

In summary, there are two ways to produce $34,196.44 in 7 years at 5% compounded annually—a single deposit of $24,302.77 today, or payments of $4200 at the end of each year for 7 years.

This result can also be thought of as follows: if $24,302.77 is borrowed today, at 5% compounded annually, the principal and interest may be repaid with payments of $4200 at the end of each year for 7 years.

EXAMPLE 2
Finding Lump Sum Deposits

Ms. Gonzalez agrees to pay $500 at the end of each year for 9 years to settle a business obligation. If money can be deposited at 10% compounded annually, find the lump sum she could deposit today to have enough money, with principal and interest, to make the payments.

SOLUTION The necessary amount is the present value of an annuity of $500 per year for 9 years, at 10% compounded annually. Use the formula

$$A = R \cdot a_{\overline{n}|i},$$

with $R = 500$, $n = 9$, and $i = 10\%$. From column D of the interest table, $a_{\overline{9}|0.10} = 5.75902382$, so

$$A = \$500\,(5.75902382) = \$2879.51.$$

A deposit of $2879.51 today, at 10% compounded annually, will permit withdrawals of $500 at the end of each year for 9 years. Since the withdrawals total $9 \times \$500 = \$4500$, the interest earned is

$$\$4500 - \$2879.51 = \$1620.49. \quad \blacksquare$$

EXAMPLE 3
Finding Lump Sum Payments

To hire a new president, the Texas Machine Company agrees to pay to the person selected a retirement benefit of $40,000 at the end of each semiannual period for 8 years, starting in 5 years. If money can be invested at 4% compounded semiannually, find the lump sum that the company could deposit today to take care of this retirement contract.

SOLUTION Two steps are necessary here. First, find the amount of money necessary to pay the retirement annuity to the president—the present value of an annuity having payments of $40,000 at the end of each 6-month period for 8 years, with interest of 4% compounded semiannually. Find this amount with the formula of this section. Using column D of the interest table for $8 \times 2 = 16$ periods and $4\% \div 2 = 2\%$ per period.

$$A = \$40,000 \cdot a_{\overline{16}|0.02}$$

$$= \$40,000\,(13.57770931) \quad \text{from column D}$$

$$= \$543,108.37$$

A deposit of $543,108.37 will permit the payments of $40,000 at the end of each semiannual period for 8 years.

The retirement payments do not begin for 5 years. This means that the company can deposit a lump sum today that will produce the lump sum $543,108.37 in 5 years. Find the lump sum today with the present value formula from Chapter 13.

Using column B of the interest table for 10 periods and 2% per period, the present value today is

$$A = \$543,108.37 \,(0.82034830) \quad \text{from column B}$$

$$= \$445,538.03$$

A lump sum deposit today of $445,538.03 will grow to $543,108.37 in 5 years and permit the payment of $40,000 at the end of each 6-month period for 8 years. See Figure 15.3.

FIGURE 15.3

Interest is 4% per year, compounded semiannually. ▪

3 As we have seen, two sums of money can look quite different and yet be equivalent because the sums of money are available at different periods of time. As in the next example, the present value of a future sum must be calculated to permit meaningful comparisons.

EXAMPLE 4
Finding Equivalent Cash Price

Julia Smithers is an attorney trying to settle an estate. The estate owns a piece of property which is desired by two different developers. Developer A offers $140,000 in cash, today, for the land. Developer B offers $50,000 now as a down payment, with payments of $8000 at the end of each quarter for 4 years. Money may be invested at 12% compounded quarterly. If Developer B offers a bank guarantee that the payment will be made, making each offer equally safe, which bid should the attorney accept?

SOLUTION   The bids can be compared only by finding the present value of the offer of Developer B. This offer is a down payment and an annuity of $8000 at the end of each quarter for 4 years. The present value of this annuity is found with column D of the interest table, with $n = 4 \times 4 = 16$ periods, and, since money may be invested at 12% compounded quarterly, $i = 12\% \div 4 = 3\%$. The value of R is $8000.

$$A = R \cdot a_{\overline{n}|i}$$

$$= \$8000 \cdot a_{\overline{16}|.03}$$

$$= \$8000 \,(12.56110203)$$

$$= \$100,488.82.$$

The present value of the annuity is $100,488.82. Since Developer B also offers a down payment of $50,000, the total cash price today of Developer B's offer is

$$\$50,000 + \$100,488.82 = \$150,488.82.$$

This amount, $150,488.82, is called the **equivalent cash price**. This exceeds the $140,000 offered by Developer A, so the attorney should accept the bid of Developer B. ▪

15.2 Exercises

Find each of the following values.

1. $a_{\overline{20}|0.06}$

2. $a_{\overline{10}|0.03}$

3. $a_{\overline{18}|0.04}$

4. $a_{\overline{30}|0.015}$

5. $a_{\overline{16}|0.01}$

6. $a_{\overline{32}|0.02}$

Find the present value of each of the following annuities. Round to the nearest cent.

	Amount per Payment	Payment at End of Each	No. of Years	Money Invested at
7.	$1000	year	5	10%, compounded annually
8.	$6000	year	7	9%, compounded annually
9.	$740	year	8	6%, compounded annually
10.	$2700	year	4	7%, compounded annually
11.	$1700	6 months	4	9%, compounded semiannually
12.	$34,000	6 months	6	8%, compounded semiannually
13.	$2746.15	quarter	9	8%, compounded quarterly
14.	$894.73	quarter	8	6%, compounded quarterly
15.	$19,854	quarter	4	10%, compounded quarterly
16.	$32,172	quarter	8	7%, compounded quarterly

17. John Needham needs a certain amount of money in 8 years for college tuition. Describe two different ways Needham could accumulate the necessary funds.

18. An individual wins a state lottery that pays $50,000 a year for 20 years. Must the state have one million dollars to pay for this prize? If not, how can the state ensure that it has the necessary funds?

Work each of the following word problems. Round to the nearest cent.

19. Find the present value of an annuity of $8691 at the end of each quarter for 9 years. Assume money can be invested at 8% compounded quarterly.

20. Find the present value of an annuity of $2150 at the end of each 6-month period for the next 9 years. Assume money can be invested at 10% compounded semiannually.

21. Tom Frederickson wants to buy a piece of property for a service station. The seller wants to receive $5000 at the end of each year for the next 9 years. If Frederickson can invest money at 6% compounded annually, find the lump sum that he should deposit today so he will be able to make the annual payments.

22. "The Million Dollar Lottery" offers a first prize of $1,000,000 paid at the rate of $25,000 at the end of each 6-month period for 20 years. If the lottery officials can invest money at 10% compounded semiannually, find the lump sum they must deposit today so they will be able to make the semiannual payments.

23. What lump sum deposited today at 8% compounded semiannually would permit withdrawals of $1200 at the end of each 6-month period for 7 years? How much interest is earned?

24. Find the amount that could be placed in a bank account today, at 8% compounded quarterly, to permit withdrawals of $1000 at the end of each quarter for 5 years.

25. Tracey Cook wants to deposit a lump sum today so that she can withdraw $800 at the end of each 6-month period during her 4 years in college. If money earns 7% compounded semiannually, find the amount she must deposit. Find the total of all her withdrawals. How much interest did she earn?

26. At retirement, a baseball player wishes to make a lump sum deposit so that he can withdraw $12,000 at the end of each year for 10 years. Find this lump sum, if money earns 11% compounded annually. Find the total of all the withdrawals. How much interest was earned?

27. To hire a new sales manager, Ace Ford Sales must guarantee her an annual retirement bonus of $7000 at the end of each year for 8 years, starting in 6 years. The firm can invest money at 12% compounded annually. Find the lump sum that will be necessary to guarantee the retirement payments. Find the amount that can be deposited today that will produce that lump sum.

28. The Smith's daughter will enter college in 5 years. At that time, they want her to be able to withdraw $2000 at the end of each 6-month period for 4 years. The Smith's can invest money at 7% compounded semiannually. Find the lump sum that will be necessary to guarantee the payments while in college. Find the amount that can be deposited today that will produce that lump sum.

29. A small commercial building sells for a down payment of $11,000, and payments of $4000 at the end of each semiannual period for 20 years. Find the equivalent cash price of the building, if money may be invested at 10% compounded semiannually.

30. A fishing boat is sold with a down payment of $21,000 and payments of $3500 at the end of each quarter for $7\frac{1}{2}$ years. Find the equivalent cash price of the boat if money may be invested at 12% compounded quarterly.

Based only on present value, which of the following bids should be accepted?

31. $100,000 today, or $51,000 down and $8000 at the end of each year for 12 years; money may be invested at 10% compounded annually

32. $140,000 today, or $86,000 down and $2000 at the end of each month for 3 years; money may be invested at 12% compounded monthly

33. $2,500,000 today, or $1,250,000 down and $50,000 at the end of each quarter for 10 years; money may be invested at 16% compounded quarterly

34. $4,000,000 today, or $600,000 down and $300,000 at the end of each 6-month period for 8 years; money may be invested at 10% compounded semiannually

OBJECTIVES

1. Find the amount of a sinking fund payment.
2. Set up a sinking fund table.

Section 1 of this chapter showed how to find the amount of an annuity—the sum of money that will be in an account after making a series of equal periodic payments. Businesses often have a need to raise a certain amount of money at some fixed time in the future. In such a case, the problem is turned around. The businessperson knows how much money is needed in the future, and must find the amount of each periodic payment.

A **sinking fund** is a fund that is set up to receive these periodic payments. The periodic payments plus the interest on them produce the necessary lump sum needed in the future.

Sinking funds are set up to provide money to build new factories, buy equipment, and so on. Also, many corporations and governmental agencies set up sinking funds to cover the face value of **bonds** that must be paid off at some time in the future.

A bond has many similarities to a promissory note—a bond is a promise to pay a fixed amount of money at some stated time in the future. Bonds and notes both pay simple, and not compound, interest. However, interest on a bond is often paid periodically, while interest on a note is usually paid only on the maturity date of the note. Bonds are normally issued only by large corporations and by governments, including cities, states, and the federal government. A typical U.S. government bond is shown in Figure 15.4.

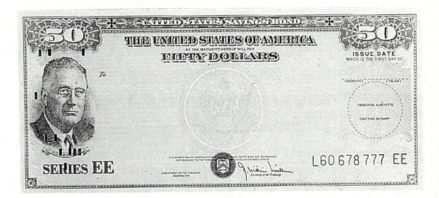

FIGURE 15.4

This section discusses only the mechanics of setting up a sinking fund to pay off a bond when it is due. In Chapter 18 the investment aspect of bonds is discussed in detail.

1 The payments into a sinking fund are just the payments of an annuity. If S is the amount that must be accumulated, R is the amount of each periodic payment, n is the number of periods, and i is the interest rate per period, then

$$S = R \cdot s_{\overline{n}|i}.$$

For sinking fund, S, the amount needed, is known, and R, the amount of each periodic payment, is unknown. Divide both sides of the formula for S by $s_{\overline{n}|i}$ to get

$$R = \frac{S}{s_{\overline{n}|i}}.$$

The amount of each payment, R, into a *sinking fund* that must contain S dollars after n payments, with interest of i per period, is

$$R = S \cdot \left(\frac{1}{s_{\overline{n}|i}} \right).$$

Values of $1 \div s_{\overline{n}|i}$ are given in column E of the interest table. (These values also can be found by dividing the corresponding numbers from column C into 1.)

EXAMPLE 1
Finding the Amount of a Sinking Fund Payment

A small corporation has sold $100,000 worth of bonds that must be paid off in 8 years. The corporation now must set up a sinking fund to accumulate the necessary $100,000. Find the amount of each payment into a sinking fund if the payments are made at the end of each year and the fund earns 10% compounded annually.

SOLUTION Look in column E of the interest table for 10% and 8 payments, finding 0.08744402. The amount of each payment is

$$R = S \cdot \left(\frac{1}{s_{\overline{n}|i}} \right)$$

$$R = \$100,000 \left(\frac{1}{s_{\overline{8}|0.10}} \right)$$

$$R = \$100,000 \, (0.08744402)$$

$$R = \$8744.40.$$

If the corporation deposits $8744.40 at the end of each year for 8 years in an account paying 10% compounded annually, it will have the necessary $100,000.

NOTE The 10% interest rate in Example 1 is what the corporation earns on money it has deposited. The interest that the corporation pays to the people who bought the $100,000 in bonds plays no part in this calculation. ■

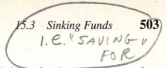

i.e. "SAVING FOR

2 To keep track of the various payments into a sinking fund, accountants often make up a sinking fund table, as shown in Example 2.

EXAMPLE 2

Set Up a Sinking Fund Table

The corporation in Example 1 deposited $8744.40 at the end of each year in a sinking fund that earned 10% compounded annually. Set up a sinking fund table for these deposits.

SOLUTION The sinking fund account contains no money until the end of the first year, when a single deposit of $8744.40 is made. Since the deposit is made at the end of the year, no interest is earned.

At the end of the second year, the account contains the original $8744.40, plus the interest earned by this money. This interest is found by the formula for simple interest.

$$I = P \times R \times T$$

$$I = \$8744.40 \, (0.10) \, (1) = \$874.44$$

An additional deposit is also made at the end of the second year, so that the sinking fund then contains a total of

$$\$8744.40 + \$874.44 + \$8744.40 = \$18{,}363.24.$$

Continue this work to get the following sinking fund table.

Sinking Fund Table

	Beginning of Period		End of Period	
Period	Accumulated Amount	Periodic Deposit	Interest Earned	Accumulated Amount
1	$0	$8744.40	$0	$8744.40
2	8744.40	8744.40	874.44	18,363.24
3	18,363.24	8744.40	1836.32	28,943.96
4	28,943.96	8744.40	2894.40	40,582.76
5	40,582.76	8744.40	4058.28	53,385.44
6	53,385.44	8744.40	5338.54	67,468.38
7	67,468.38	8744.40	6746.84	82,959.62
8	82,959.62	8744.42	8295.96	100,000.00 ■

NOTE In Example 2, the last payment differs by 2 cents due to rounding error. The accumulated amount must equal $100,000.

In Example 1 a sinking fund was set up to pay off the *principal* due on some bonds. However, in the next example a sinking fund is set up to pay off both *principal* and *interest* on a loan.

EXAMPLE 3

Finding the Payment into a Sinking Fund

A business owes $6000, with interest at 12% per year, compounded semiannually. The face value and interest must be paid in 4 years. The business decides to set up a sinking fund so that the note may be paid off. Find the amount of each payment into the fund, if the money in the fund earns 8% compounded annually and annual payments are made into the fund.

SOLUTION   First find the maturity value of the note, which is given by the formula for a compound amount.

$$\text{Maturity value} = \$6000(1 + 6\%)^8$$
$$= \$6000\,(1.59384807) \qquad \text{from column A}$$
$$= \$9563.09$$

The sinking fund must produce enough to pay off this total. Now use the formula for sinking fund.

$$R = S \cdot \left(\frac{1}{s_{\overline{n}|i}}\right)$$

Here, $S = \$9563.09$, $n = 4$ periods, and $i = 8\%$.

$$R = \$9563.09 \left(\frac{1}{s_{\overline{4}|0.08}}\right)$$

$$R = \$9563.09\,(0.22192080)$$

$$R = \$2122.25$$

Payment of $2122.25 at the end of each year into a sinking fund paying 8% per year compounded annually will produce enough to pay off the debt. In Exercise 21, which follows, the sinking fund table for this example is completed. ∎

NOTE In Example 3, two different interest rates are involved—the company agreed to pay 12% per year compounded semiannually on the money it borrowed, but received only 8% compounded annually on its deposits into a sinking fund. Such an **interest rate spread** is very common. The spread between what banks charge for loans and what they pay for deposits is used to pay the bank's operating expenses and accounts for any profits that are made.

15.3 Exercises

Find each of the following values.

1. $1/s_{\overline{20}|0.03}$

2. $1/s_{\overline{5}|0.08}$

3. $1/s_{\overline{25}|0.04}$

4. $1/s_{\overline{16}|0.01}$

Find the amount of each payment to be made into a sinking fund so that the indicated amount will be present. Round to the nearest cent.

$R = S\left(\dfrac{i}{s_{\overline{n}|i}}\right)$

5. $4000, money earns 4% compounded annually, 8 annual payments

6. $8500, money earns 8% compounded annually, 7 annual payments

7. $15,000, money earns 5% compounded semiannually, 12 semiannual payments

8. $75,000, money earns 6% compounded semiannually, 9 semiannual payments

9. $40,000 money earns 8% compounded quarterly, 18 quarterly payments

10. $25,000, money earns 12% compounded quarterly, 11 quarterly payments

11. Explain the purpose of a sinking fund.

12. Define the term *interest rate spread*.

Work each of the following word problems. Round to the nearest cent.

13. Find the amount of each payment into a sinking fund if $100,000 must be accumulated. Assume payments are made at the end of each quarter for 4 years, with interest at 12% per year compounded quarterly. Find the total amount of interest earned by the deposits.

14. Suppose $472,500 must be available in 3 years to pay for a new fishing boat. Find the amount of each payment into a sinking fund if payments are made at the end of each month and money earns 12% compounded monthly. Find the total amount of interest earned by the deposits.

15. Smith Dry Cleaning must buy a new cleaning machine in 9 years for $110,000. The firm desires to set up a sinking fund for this purpose. Find the payment into the fund at the end of each year if money in the fund earns 6% compounded annually.

16. Catriona Kaplan's Baby Beautiful Talent Agency needs $79,000 in 6 years. To accumulate the necessary funds, the company sets up a sinking fund with payments made into the fund quarterly. Find the payment into this fund if money in the fund earns 5% compounded quarterly.

17. The Carmichael Ford Agency wants to build a new showroom in 4 years. The agency sets up a sinking fund to accumulate the necessary $750,000. How much should be deposited semiannually in this fund if the money in the fund earns 10% compounded semiannually?

18. Cronkite Sheet Metal will need $157,000 in 5 years for new machinery. Find the quarterly deposit into a sinking fund if money in the fund earns 12% compounded quarterly.

19. A city sold $4,000,000 worth of bonds to pay for a new jail. To pay off the bonds when they mature in 8 years the city sets up a sinking fund. Find the amount of each payment into the fund if the city makes annual payments, and the money earns 6% compounded annually. Find the amount of interest earned by the deposits.

20. A small church-related college sold $1,480,000 in bonds to pay for an addition to the administration building. The bonds must be paid off in 15 years. To accumulate the money to pay off the bonds, the college sets up a sinking fund. If the college makes payments at the end of each 6 months and the money earns 10% compounded semiannually, find the amount of each payment into the fund. Find the amount of interest earned by the deposits.

21. Complete this sinking fund table for Example 3.

| | Beginning of Period | End of Period | | |
Period	Accumulated Amount	Periodic Deposit	Interest Earned	Accumulated Amount
1	$0	$2122.25	$0	$2122.25
2	2122.25	2122.25	_____	_____
3	_____	2122.25	_____	_____
4	_____	_____	_____	_____

22. Complete this sinking fund table for Exercise 19 above.

| | Beginning of Period | End of Period | | |
Period	Accumulated Amount	Periodic Deposit	Interest Earned	Accumulated Amount
1	$0	$404,143.76	0	$404,143.76
2	$404,143.76	$404,143.76	_____	_____
3	_____	$404,143.76	_____	_____
4	_____	$404,143.76	_____	_____
5	_____	$404,143.76	_____	_____
6	_____	$404,143.76	_____	_____
7	_____	$404,143.76	_____	_____
8	_____	_____	_____	_____

23. Cindy Drew sells some land in Nevada. She will be paid a lump sum of $60,000 in 4 years. Until then, the buyer pays 8% simple interest. (a) Find the amount of each interest payment if they are made quarterly. (b) The buyer sets up a sinking fund so that enough money will be present to pay off the $60,000. The buyer wants to make payments into the sinking fund at the end of each semiannual period; the account pays 8% compounded semiannually. Find the amount of each payment into the fund. (c) Prepare a table showing the amount in the sinking fund after each deposit.

24. Jeff Reschke bought a rare stamp for his collection. He agreed to pay a lump sum of $4000 after 5 years. Until then, he pays 6% simple interest. (a) Find the amount of each interest payment if they are made semiannually. (b) Reschke sets up a sinking fund so that money will be present to pay off the $4000. He wants to make annual payments into the fund. The account pays 8% compounded annually. Find the amount of each payment into the fund. (c) Prepare a table showing the amount in the sinking fund after each deposit.

15.4 Amortization

OBJECTIVES

1 Find the amount of a loan amortization payment.

2 Set up an amortization schedule.

3 Determine monthly payments.

4 Find monthly home payments.

5 Define impound accounts.

6 Define fixed and variable rate loans.

7 Compare sinking funds and amortization.

A loan is **amortized** if both the principal and interest are paid off by a sequence of equal periodic payments. This is different from many of the loans discussed earlier in the book, for which it was assumed that a loan was paid with a single payment for both principal and interest.

A car loan paid off over a period of 48 months is an example of a loan that is amortized. Paying for a house in monthly payments for 30 years is another example.

1   When an item is purchased with cash, there is no need to make any payments; there would be no loan to amortize. This means that the amount of any loan used to buy an item (cash price minus down payment) is the present value of an annuity. To find the periodic payment for the annuity, use the formula from Section 15.2. The present value of an annuity is given by

$$A = R \cdot a_{\overline{n}|i}$$

where A is the present value, R is the amount of each payment, and $a_{\overline{n}|i}$ comes from column D of the interest table. To find R, divide both sides of the formula for A by $a_{\overline{n}|i}$:

$$R = \frac{A}{a_{\overline{n}|i}}$$

or

$$R = A\left(\frac{1}{a_{\overline{n}|i}}\right)$$

In summary,

the periodic payment, R, needed to amortize a loan of A dollars, with interest of i per period for n periods, is

$$R = A\left(\frac{1}{a_{\overline{n}|i}}\right).$$

Values of $1 \div a_{\overline{n}|i}$ are given in column F of the interest table. (These values can also be found by dividing the corresponding numbers from column D into 1.)

EXAMPLE 1
Finding Monthly Payments

A delivery truck costs $12,000. After a down payment of $4000, the balance is financed with monthly payments at $\frac{3}{4}\%$ interest per month for 3 years. Find the amount of each monthly payment.

SOLUTION   The loan is figured as follows.

$$
\begin{array}{ll}
\$12,000 & \text{cash price} \\
-\quad 4,000 & \text{down payment} \\
\hline
\$8,000 & \text{amount financed}
\end{array}
$$

Since 3 years have $3 \times 12 = 36$ months, look in column F of the interest table for $\frac{3}{4}\%$ and 36 periods, finding 0.03179973. The monthly payment is

$$R = A\left(\frac{1}{a_{\overline{n}|i}}\right)$$

$$R = \$8000\left(\frac{1}{a_{\overline{36}|0.0075}}\right)$$

$$R = \$8000\,(0.03179973) \qquad \text{from column F}$$

$$R = \$254.40$$

The finance charge paid by the business can be found by subtracting the cash price from the total of all the monthly payments, or

$$(36 \times \$254.40) - \$8000 = \$9158.40 - \$8000 = \$1158.40.$$

Of the total of $9158.40 paid back in the 36 payments, $1158.40 represents interest (the finance charge).   ∎

EXAMPLE 2
Finding Payments, Interest, and Balances

A speculator agrees to pay $15,000 for a parcel of land; this amount will be paid in 3 years with semiannual payments at an interest rate of 8%.

(a)   Find the amount of each payment.

SOLUTION   If the speculator paid $15,000 immediately, their would be no need for any payments at all. This means that $15,000 is the present value of an annuity of R dollars, $2 \times 3 = 6$ periods, and $i = 8\% \div 2 = 4\%$. To find R, use the formula

$$R = A\left(\frac{1}{a_{\overline{n}|i}}\right).$$

In this example, $A = \$15,000$, with

$$R = \$15,000\left(\frac{1}{a_{\overline{6}|0.04}}\right).$$

From column F of the interest table, $1 \div a_{\overline{6}|0.04} = 0.19076190$, with the semi-annual payment given by

$$R = \$15{,}000 \,(0.19076190) = \$2861.43.$$

Each payment is $2861.43.

(b) Find the portion of the first payment that represents interest. Interest is 8% per year. During the first period, the entire $15,000 is owed. Interest on this amount for 6 months ($\frac{1}{2}$ year) is found by the formula for simple interest.

$$I = PRT$$

$$I = \$15{,}000 \,(0.08)\left(\frac{1}{2}\right)$$

$$= \$600$$

At the end of 6 months, the speculator makes a payment of $2861.43; since $600 of this represents interest, a total of

$$\$2861.43 - \$600 = \$2261.43$$

is applied to the reduction of the original debt.

(c) Find the balance due after 6 months.
The original balance due is $15,000. After 6 months, $2261.43 is applied to the reduction of the debt. The debt after 6 months is

$$\$15{,}000 - \$2261.43 = \$12{,}738.57.$$

(d) How much interest is owed for the second 6-month period?
A total of $12,738.57 is owed for the second 6 months. Interest on this amount is

$$I = (\$12{,}738.57)\,(0.08)\left(\frac{1}{2}\right) = \$509.54.$$

A payment of $2861.43 is made at the end of this period with

$$\$2861.43 - \$509.54 = \$2351.89$$

applied to the debt. ■

2 Continue this process to get the **amortization schedule** shown in Table 15.1. This table shows the equal payments needed to pay off the loan (principal and interest) in a specified time period. Notice that the payment is always the same in these amortization schedules, except perhaps for a small adjustment in the final one. Payment 0 represents the original amount of the loan.

TABLE 15.1   Amortization Schedule

PRINC X INT

Loan of $15,000 repaid in semiannual payments of 8%.

Payment Number	Amount of Payment	Interest for Period	Portion of Principal	Balance at End of Period
0	—	—	—	$15,000.00
1	$2861.43	$600.00	$2261.43	12,738.57
2	2861.43	509.54	2351.89	10,386.68
3	2861.43	415.47	2445.96	7940.72
4	2861.43	317.63	2543.80	5396.92
5	2861.43	215.88	2645.55	2751.37
6	2861.42	110.05	2751.37	0

3 Tables of values of $1 \div a_{\overline{n}|i}$ may be used to decide on the payment that will amortize a loan. It is more common, however, to use a special **loan payoff table,** a portion of which is shown in Table 15.2. To find the monthly payment, the number from the table is multiplied by the amount to be financed.

EXAMPLE 3

Finding Monthly Payments

After a down payment, Linda Dean owes $8700 on a Ford Taurus. She wishes to pay the loan off in 60 monthly payments. Find the amount of each payment and the finance charge, if the APR on her loan is 18%.

SOLUTION   Multiply the amount to be financed, $8700, and the number from Table 15.2 for 60 months and 18%, 0.025393.

$$\text{Payment} = (\$8700) (0.25393) = \$220.92$$

The total amount repaid in 60 months is

$$60 (\$220.92) = \$13,255.20.$$

The finance charge is

$$\$13,255.20 - \$8700 = \$4555.20. \quad \blacksquare$$

4 A house is perhaps the most expensive single item purchased by the average person. Finding monthly house payments is done just as shown in Example 3, except that the number of periods involved ($12 \times 25 = 300$ periods for a typical 25 year loan, for example), and the great variety of different interest rates involved, require a special table. A portion of such a table is shown in Table 15.3. This table shows the monthly payment necessary to repay a $1000 loan for different interest rates and repayment periods.

TABLE 15.2   Loan Payoff Table

Months APR	18	24	30	36	42	48	54	60
8%	0.059138	0.045229	0.036887	0.031335	0.027376	0.024413	0.022113	0.020277
9%	0.0596	0.045683	0.037347	0.0318	0.027845	0.024885	0.022589	0.020758
10%	0.060056	0.046146	0.03781	0.032267	0.028317	0.025363	0.023072	0.021247
11%	0.061516	0.046608	0.038277	0.032739	0.028793	0.025846	0.023561	0.021742
12%	0.060984	0.047075	0.038847	0.033214	0.029276	0.026333	0.024057	0.022245
13%	0.06145	0.047542	0.03922	0.033694	0.029762	0.026827	0.024557	0.022753
14%	0.061917	0.048013	0.0397	0.034178	0.030252	0.027327	0.025065	0.023268
15%	0.062383	0.048488	0.04018	0.034667	0.03075	0.027831	0.025578	0.02379
16%	0.062885	0.048963	0.040663	0.035159	0.03125	0.02834	0.026096	0.024318
17%	0.063328	0.049442	0.04115	0.035653	0.031755	0.028854	0.026620	0.024853
18%	0.063806	0.049925	0.04164	0.036153	0.032264	0.029369	0.027152	0.025393
19%	0.064283	0.050408	0.042133	0.036656	0.032779	0.0299	0.027687	0.02594
20%	0.064761	0.050896	0.04263	0.037164	0.033298	0.030431	0.02823	0.026493
21%	0.065244	0.051388	0.04313	0.037675	0.033821	0.030967	0.028776	0.027053

TABLE 15.3   Amortization (Principal and Interest per Thousand Dollars)

Term in Years	7%	$7\frac{1}{4}\%$	$7\frac{1}{2}\%$	$7\frac{3}{4}\%$	8%	$8\frac{1}{4}\%$	$8\frac{1}{2}\%$	$8\frac{3}{4}\%$	9%	$9\frac{1}{4}\%$	$9\frac{1}{2}\%$	$9\frac{3}{4}\%$
10	11.62	11.75	11.88	12.01	12.14	12.27	12.40	12.54	12.67	12.81	12.94	13.08
15	8.99	9.13	9.28	9.42	9.56	9.71	9.85	10.00	10.15	10.30	10.45	10.60
20	7.76	7.91	8.06	8.21	8.37	8.53	8.68	8.84	9.00	9.16	9.33	9.49
25	7.07	7.23	7.39	7.56	7.72	7.89	8.06	8.23	8.40	8.57	8.74	8.92
30	6.66	6.83	7.00	7.17	7.34	7.52	7.69	7.87	8.05	8.23	8.41	8.60

EXAMPLE 4
*Finding Monthly
Home Payments*

Use Table 15.3 to find the monthly payment necessary to amortize a 9% loan of $56,280 over a 30-year term.

SOLUTION   Locate 30 years in the left-hand column and look to the right, to find $8.05 in the column labeled 9%. This is the amount necessary to amortize $1000 at 9% interest in 30 years. Find the number of thousands in 56,280. To do this, move the decimal point 3 places to the left. The result is 56.28. Multiply the amount per thousand by the number of thousands to find the monthly payment necessary to amortize $56,280 at 9% interest in 30 years.

$$\$8.05 \times 56.28 = \$453.05 \qquad \text{monthly payment} \quad \blacksquare$$

CAUTION Be sure to divide the loan amount by $1000 before calculating the monthly payment.

The interest on real estate loans is computed on the decreasing balance of the loan. Each equal monthly payment is first applied toward interest for the previous month. The balance is then applied toward reduction of the amount owed. Payments in the early years of a real estate loan are mostly interest; only a small amount goes toward reducing the principal. The amount of interest decreases each month, so that larger and larger amounts of the payment will apply to the principal. During the last years of the loan, most of the monthly payment is applied toward the principal.

Many lenders supply an **amortization schedule** or a **repayment schedule** showing the amount of payments for interest, the amount for principal, and the principal balance for each month over the entire life of the loan. The calculations can also be done by hand as follows.

Step 1.   Balance of loan × Interest rate = Interest for 1 year

Step 2. $\dfrac{\text{Interest for 1 year}}{12}$ = Interest for 1 month

Step 3.   Monthly payment − Interest for 1 month = Payment on principal

Step 4.   Amount of loan − Payment on principal = Balance of principal

---

EXAMPLE 5
*Preparing
Repayment
Schedules*

(a) Prepare a repayment schedule for the first month on a loan of $60,000 at 8% interest for 30 years. The monthly payment on this loan is $440.40.

SOLUTION   Find the interest for 1 year.

$60,000	amount of the loan
× .08	interest rate
$4800	interest for 1 year

To find the interest for 1 month, divide the interest for a year by 12.

$$\frac{\$4800}{12} = \$400 \qquad \text{interest for 1 month}$$

Find the amount of the payment that applies to the principal.

$$
\begin{array}{rl}
\$440.40 & \text{monthly payment} \\
-\$400.00 & \text{interest for 1 month} \\
\hline
\$40.40 & \text{applies to principal in first month}
\end{array}
$$

Now find the balance due on the principal.

$$
\begin{array}{rl}
\$60,000.00 & \text{amount of loan} \\
-\$40.40 & \text{applies to principal in first month} \\
\hline
\$59,959.60 & \text{balance due after first month}
\end{array}
$$

These results have been used to make the following repayment schedule for the first month.

Repayment Schedule

Payment Number	Interest Payment	Principal Payment	Balance of Principal
1	$400	$40.40	$59,959.6(∎

(b) Prepare a repayment schedule for the second month of the loan of Example 5 (a).

SOLUTION Find the interest for 1 year on the balance of the principal (not the original principal).

$$
\begin{array}{rl}
\$59,959.60 & \text{balance on loan} \\
\times \quad\ .08 & \text{interest rate} \\
\hline
\$4796.77 & \text{interest for 1 year (rounded)}
\end{array}
$$

Find the interest for 1 month by dividing this result by 12.

$$\frac{\$4796.77}{12} = \$399.73 \qquad \text{interest for 1 month}$$

Find the payment on the principal.

$$
\begin{array}{rl}
\$440.40 & \text{monthly payment} \\
-\$399.73 & \text{interest for 1 month} \\
\hline
\$40.67 & \text{payment on principal in second month}
\end{array}
$$

Now find the balance due on the principal.

$59,959.60	previous balance of loan
− $40.67	payment on principal in second month
$59,918.93	new balance on principal

The following repayment schedule shows the first and second months of this loan.

Repayment Schedule

Payment Number	Interest Payment	Principal Payment	Balance of Principal
1	$400	$40.40	$59,959.60
2	$399.73	$40.67	$59,918.93 ■

The remaining schedule of payments can be completed using the same steps for each succeeding month. However, computing the entire repayment schedule for this 30-year loan (30 years × 12 months = 360 payments) would be very time-consuming. The loan reduction schedule in Table 15.4 shows the interest and principal payments and the balance of the loan for the first 24 months and the last 6 months of the loan discussed in Example 5. Also included is information for the 256th through the 270th payments.

During the first 12 months of this loan, a total of $4781.83 has been paid to interest while the principal balance of the loan has been reduced by $502.97. During the next 12 months $4740.09 will be paid to interest; the principal will be reduced by $544.71. The 257th payment is the first payment in which a larger amount goes to principal than to interest. After the 269th payment (22 years, 5 months), the principal will be reduced to $29,858.98 slightly less than one half of the original $60,000 borrowed. The final payment (360th) will be $230.21.

It is often enlightening for a borrower to calculate the total cost of a home including interest. Multiplying the total number of payments by the monthly payment (359 × $440.40 + $230.21 final payment) shows that the home will cost $158,333.81 plus any down payment. In addition to this the buyer will have paid property taxes and insurance each year.

5   Many lenders require **escrow accounts** (also called **impound accounts**) for people taking out a mortgage from them. With an escrow account, buyers pay $\frac{1}{12}$ of total estimated property tax and insurance each month. The lender holds these funds until the taxes and insurance fall due, and then pays the bills for the borrower. Many consumer groups oppose this practice, since the lender earns interest on the money while waiting for payments to come due. Because of these complaints, these accounts are not as common as they once were, and when they are required, lenders usually pay interest on them.

TABLE 15.4 **Loan Reduction Schedule**

Interest rate: 8%
Loan amount: $60,000.00
Monthly principal and interest payment: $440.40

Term in years: 30
Total number of payments: 360

Payment Number	Interest Payment	Principal Payment	Remaining Balance	Payment Number	Interest Payment	Principal Payment	Remaining Balance
1	400.00	40.40	59,959.60	256	220.50	219.90	32,854.74
2	399.73	40.67	59,918.93	257	219.03	221.37	32,633.37
3	399.46	40.94	59,877.99	258	217.55	222.85	32,410.53
4	399.19	41.21	59,836.78	259	216.07	224.33	32,186.20
5	398.91	41.49	59,795.29	260	214.57	225.83	31,960.37
6	398.64	41.76	59,753.53	261	213.07	227.33	31,733.04
7	398.36	42.04	59,711.49	262	211.55	228.85	31,504.19
8	398.08	42.32	59,669.17	263	210.03	230.37	31,273.82
9	397.79	42.61	59,626.56	264	208.49	231.91	31,041.91
10	397.51	42.89	59,583.67	265	206.95	233.45	30,808.46
11	397.22	43.18	59,540.49	266	205.39	235.01	30,573.45
12	396.94	43.46	59,497.03	267	203.82	236.58	30,336.87
13	396.65	43.75	59,453.28	268	202.24	238.16	30,098.72
14	396.36	44.04	59,409.24	269	200.66	239.74	29,858.98
15	396.06	44.34	59,364.90	270	199.06	241.34	29,617.64
16	395.77	44.63	59,320.27	⋮	⋮	⋮	⋮
17	395.47	44.93	59,275.34				
18	395.17	45.23	59,230.11	355	15.87	424.53	1,955.31
19	394.87	45.53	59,184.58	356	13.04	427.36	1,527.95
20	394.56	45.84	59,138.74	357	10.19	430.21	1,097.74
21	394.26	46.14	59,092.60	358	7.32	433.08	664.66
22	393.95	46.45	59,046.15	359	4.43	435.97	228.69
23	393.64	46.76	58,999.39	360	1.52	228.69	0.00
24	393.33	47.07	58,952.32		$98,331.96	$60,000	

6 The home loans discussed here are called **fixed rate loans**—they are made at a fixed, stated rate of interest. In a time of high inflation, lenders do not like to make such loans, since the dollars repaid by borrowers can be worth far less than the dollars lent out. To protect themselves against inflation, many lenders now make **variable interest rate** loans, in which the interest rate can vary, up or down, at stated periods over the life of the loan. It is not unlikely that such loans will someday be the only ones available for home purchases.

When filing an annual income tax return, a person with a real estate loan must decide whether to take the standard deduction or to itemize deductions. Both the interest paid on the loan and the property taxes may currently be used in itemizing deductions. If interest and taxes are itemized, the result is usually more than the standard deduction. The resulting tax savings are often a major reason to by instead of rent. However, because of the standard deduction given to everyone, these deductions do not usually result in a dollar-for-dollar gain. While the tax advantages of owning are often praised greatly by zealous real estate sales people, don't forget that because of the standard deduction the savings are often not as great as claimed and, in any event, the savings may not show up until a refund is received next April, while the house payments begin immediately.

7 Students often have difficulty remembering the differences between the sinking funds of Section 15.3 and the amortization of this section. Table 15.5 compares these two types of periodic payments.

TABLE 15.5   Sinking Funds Versus Amortization

Sinking Funds	**Amortization**
Accumulates money to pay off an obligation in the future (such as the principal on a bond)	Pays off an obligation today (such as a car or house)
Formula: $R = S \cdot \left(\dfrac{1}{s_{\overline{n}\,i}} \right)$	Formula: $R = A \cdot \left(\dfrac{1}{a_{\overline{n}\,i}} \right)$
Column E from the interest table	Column F from the interest table

15.4 Exercises

Find each of the following.

1. $\dfrac{1}{a_{\overline{24}\,0.03}}$

2. $\dfrac{1}{a_{\overline{9}\,0.08}}$

3. $\dfrac{1}{a_{\overline{12}\,0.015}}$

4. $\dfrac{1}{a_{\overline{48}\,0.035}}$

Find the payment necessary to amortize each of the following loans. Use column F of the interest table in Appendix C and the formula of this section.

5. $1000, 6%, 7 annual payments

6. $3500, 8%, 10 quarterly payments

7. $41,000, 8%, 10 semiannual payments

8. $90,000, 9%, 12 annual payments

9. $110,000, 10%, 25 quarterly payments

10. $7400, 10%, 18 semiannual payments

11. $4876.11, 12%, 24 monthly payments

12. $48,631.56, 9%, 48 monthly payments

13. Explain how to construct a repayment schedule. (See Objective 2.)

14. Explain the process used to determine the amount of each monthly payment that is going toward interest and the amount going toward principal.

Work each of the following word problems.

15. The Taylors opened a new delicatessen. The store represented a total investment of $420,000. They paid $50,000 of their own money and agreed to pay off the rest in quarterly payments, over 9 years at 10%. Find the quarterly payment necessary to amortize the loan. Find the total amount of interest paid over 9 years.

16. Midtown Limousine Service bought a new Cadillac limousine for $57,000. They agreed to pay 10% down and pay off the rest with monthly payments for 36 months, at 18%. Find the amount of each monthly payment necessary to amortize the loan. Find the total amount of interest paid over 3 years.

17. An insurance firm pays $4000 for a new printer for its computer. It amortizes the loan for the printer in 4 annual payments at 8%. Prepare an amortization schedule for this machine.

18. Large semitrailer trucks cost $72,000 each. Ace Trucking buys such a truck and agrees to pay for it by a loan which will be amortized with 9 annual payments at 8%. Prepare an amortization schedule for this truck.

19. Zenith charges $1048 for a word processor. A firm of tax accountants buys 8 of these machines. They make a down payment of $1200 and agree to amortize the balance with monthly payments at 18% for 4 years. Prepare an amortization schedule showing the first six payments.

20. When Denise Sullivan opened her law office, she bought $14,000 worth of law books and $7200 worth of office furniture. She paid $1200 down and agreed to amortize the balance with semiannual payments for 5 years at 12%. Prepare an amortization schedule for this purpose.

Use Table 15.2 and find the monthly payment and finance charge for each loan.

	Amount Financed	Number of Months	APR
21.	$3500	24	8%
22.	$4800	30	9%
23.	$7284	36	11%
24.	$8102	48	16%

Use Table 15.3 to find the monthly payments needed to amortize each home loan.

	Amount of Loan	Number of Years	Interest Rate
25.	$45,000	25	9%
26.	$182,000	15	$8\frac{1}{4}\%$
27.	$97,500	30	$7\frac{1}{2}\%$
28.	$167,500	20	$9\frac{1}{2}\%$

Prepare a repayment schedule for each of the following.

29. Loan: $56,750
    Interest rate: $9\frac{3}{4}\%$
    Term of loan: 30 years

Repayment Schedule

Payment Number	Total Payment	Interest Payment	Principal Payment	Balance of Principal
1	(a)	(b)	(c)	(d)

30. Loan: $51,000
    Interest rate: 9%
    Term of loan: 30 years

Repayment Schedule

Payment Number	Total Payment	Interest Payment	Principal Payment	Balance of Principal
1	(a)	(b)	(c)	(d)

31. Loan: $58,500
Interest rate: $8\frac{1}{2}\%$
Term of loan: 25 years

Repayment Schedule

Payment Number	Total Payment	Interest Payment	Principal Payment	Balance of Principal
1	(a)	(b)	(c)	(d)
2	(e)	(f)	(g)	(h)

32. Loan: $72,900
Interest rate: $7\frac{1}{4}\%$
Term of loan: 20 years

Repayment Schedule

Payment Number	Total Payment	Interest Payment	Principal Payment	Balance of Principal
1	(a)	(b)	(c)	(d)
2	(e)	(f)	(g)	(h)

CHAPTER 15 QUICK REVIEW

TOPIC	APPROACH	EXAMPLE
15.1 Finding the amount of an annuity	Use n, the number of periods, and i, the interest rate per period, to find $s_{\overline{n}|i}$ in column C of the interest table in Appendix C. Find the amount S from the formula $S = R \cdot s_{\overline{n}|i}$ with R the periodic payment into the annuity.	Nick Pinto deposits $1500 at the end of each year at 4% compounded annually. How much will Nick have at the end of 20 years? $n = 20; i = 4\%$. From the table $s_{\overline{20}|0.04} = 29.77807858$ $S = (\$1500)(29.77807858)$ $= \$44,667.12$

TOPIC	APPROACH	EXAMPLE

15.1 Finding the amount of each payment into an annuity

Determine the amount needed in the future, S, the interest rate per period, i, and the number of periods, n. Use the interest table in Appendix C to find $s_{\overline{n}|i}$, then find R from the formula $S = R \cdot s_{\overline{n}|i}$

Find the amount of the periodic payment that will produce $18,000 if the interest is 6% compounded monthly and monthly payments are made for 4 years.

$$S = \$18,000;$$

$$n = 4 \times 12 = 48;$$

$$i = 0.06 \div 12 = 0.005$$

$$s_{\overline{48}|\,0.005} = 54.09783222$$

$$S = R \cdot s_{\overline{n}|i}$$

DIVIDE

$$\$18,000 = R(54.09783222)$$

$\dfrac{\$18,000}{54.09783222} =$

$$\$332.73 = R$$

15.1 Finding the number of payments

Divide S, the amount of the annuity, by R, the amount of the payment. Find the page in Appendix C corresponding to the interest rate i. Look in column C for S/R (or the first number larger) and find n for this number.

George Gleine needs $5000. He can put $210 per quarter into an account paying 4% compounded quarterly. How long will take to accumulate the money?

$$s_{\overline{n}|\,0.01} = \frac{S}{R} = \frac{\$5000}{\$210}$$

$$= 23.80952381$$

Closest table value is 24.47158599 so $n = 22$ quarters; $22 \div 4 = 5\frac{1}{2}$ years.

15.1 Finding the amount of an annuity due

Add 1 to the number of periods and use this as the value of n. Use n and i, the interest rate per period, to find $s_{\overline{n}|i}$ in the interest table. To find the amount, use the formula $S = R \cdot s_{\overline{n}|i} - $ One payment.

Find the amount of an annuity due if payments of $700 are made at the beginning of each month for 3 years into an account paying 5% compounding monthly.

$$n = (12 \times 3) + 1 = 37;$$

$$i = 5\% \div 12 = \frac{5}{12}\%$$

$$s_{\overline{37}|\,0.467} = 39.91480775$$

$$S = \$7000\,(39.91480775)$$
$$-\$700$$

$$= \$27,240.37$$

ADD 1 TO FACTOR! THEN SUBTRACT ONE PYMT.

TOPIC	APPROACH	EXAMPLE
15.2 Finding the present value of an annuity	Use the number of periods, n, interest rate per period, i, and column D of the interest table to find $a_{\overline{n}|i}$. Find the present value of the annuity, A, using the formula $$A = R \cdot a_{\overline{n}|i}$$ with R the payment per period.	What lump sum deposited today at 8% compounded annually will yield the same total as payments of $160 at the end of each year for 10 years? $$R = \$160; n = 10; i = 8\%.$$ $$a_{\overline{10}|0.08} = 6.71008140$$ $$A = \$160\,(6.71008140)$$ $$= \$1073.61$$
15.2 Finding equivalent cash price	Use the number of periods, n, interest rate per period, i, and column D of the interest table to find $a_{\overline{n}|i}$. Find the present value using the formula $$A = R \cdot a_{\overline{n}|i}.$$ Add the value of A to the down payment to obtain the equivalent cash value.	A buyer offers to purchase a business for $75,000 down and quarterly payments of $4000 for 5 years. If money may be invested at 8% compounded quarterly, how much is the buyer actually offering? $$R = \$4000;$$ $$n = 4 \times 5 = 20;$$ $$i = 8\% \div 4 = 2\%.$$ $$a_{\overline{20}|0.02} = 16.3514334$$ $$A = \$4000 \times 16.3514334$$ $$= \$65,405.73$$ Equivalent cash value $= \$75,000$ $+ \$65,405.73 = \$140,405.73$
15.3 Determining the payment into a sinking fund	Use the number of payments, n, the interest rate per period, i, and column E of the interest table to find the value of $1 \div s_{\overline{n}|i}$. Use the formula $R = P \cdot \dfrac{1}{s_{\overline{n}|i}}$ to calculate payment.	A company must set up a sinking fund to accumulate $50,000 in five years. Find the amount of the payments if they are made at the end of each year and the fund earns 8%. $$n = 5; i = 0.05.$$ $$\frac{1}{s_{\overline{n}|i}} = 0.17045645$$ $$R = \$50,000(0.17045645)$$ $$= \$8522.82$$

TOPIC	APPROACH	EXAMPLE

15.3 Setting up a sinking fund table

Determine the payment R and the interest at the end of each payment. Then add the previous total, next payment, and interest to find the accumulated amount. Repeat for each period.

A company wants to set up a sinking fund to accumulate $10,000 in four years. It wishes to make annual payments into the account, which pays 8% compounded annually. Set up a table.

$n = 4; i = 0.08.$

$s_{\overline{4}|0.08} = 0.22192080$

$R = \$10,000(0.22192080)$
$= \$2219.21$ (rounded)

	Beginning of Period		End of Period	
Period	Accumulated Amount	Periodic Deposit	Interest Earned	Accumulated Amount
1	$0	$2219.21	0	$2219.21
2	$2219.21	$2219.21	$177.54	$4616.96
3	$4615.96	$2219.21	$369.28	$7204.45
4	$7204.45	$2219.19	$576.36	$10,000.00

15.4 Finding the periodic payment to amortize a loan

Use the number of periods for the loan, n, interest rate per period, i, and column F of the interest table to find $1 \div a_{\overline{n}|i}$. Then use the formula

$$R = A \cdot \frac{1}{a_{\overline{n}|i}}$$

to calculate the payment.

Bob agrees to pay $12,000 for a car. The amount will be repaid in monthly payments over 3 years at an interest rate of 6%. Find the amount of each payment.

$n = 12 \times 3 = 36;$

$i = \dfrac{6\%}{12} = \dfrac{1}{2}\%.$

$\dfrac{1}{a_{\overline{36}|0.005}} = 0.03042194$

$R = \$12,000 \times 0.03042194$
$R = \$365.06$

TOPIC	APPROACH	EXAMPLE
15.4 Setting up an amortization schedule	Find the periodic payment R; then find the interest for the first period using $I = PRT$. Subtract I from R and reduce the original debt by this amount, D. Find the balance by subtracting the debt reduction D from the original amount A. Repeat until original debt is amortized.	Terry Meyer borrows $1800 for 2 years at 10%. She will repay this amount with semiannual payments. Set up an amortization schedule.

$$n = 4; i = \frac{10\%}{2} = 5\%.$$

$$\frac{1}{a_{\overline{4}|0.05}} = 0.28201183$$

$$R = \$1800 \times 0.28201183$$
$$= \$507.62$$

$$I = PRT$$
$$= \$1800 \times 0.10 \times \frac{1}{2}$$
$$= \$90$$

$$D = R - I = \$507.62 - \$90$$
$$= \$417.62$$

$$A - D = \$1800 - \$417.62$$
$$= \$1382.38$$

Continue to get table shown below.

Payment Number	Amount of Payment	Interest for Period	Portion to Principal	Principal at End of Period
0	—	—	—	$1800.00
1	$507.62	$90.00	$417.62	$1382.38
2	$507.62	$69.12	$438.50	$943.88
3	$507.62	$47.19	$460.43	$483.45
4	$507.62	$24.17	$483.45	$0

TOPIC	APPROACH	EXAMPLE
15.4 Finding monthly payments, total amount paid, and finance charge	Multiply the amount to be financed by the number from Table 15.2 This is the periodic payment. Find the total amount repaid by multiplying the periodic payment by the number of payments. Subtract the amount financed from the total amount repaid to obtain the finance charge.	Nick owes $9600 on a Ford Taurus. He wishes to pay the car off in 48 monthly payments. Find the amount of each payment and the finance charge if the APR on his loan is 12%. $9600 =$ amount financed Table value (Table 15.2) for 48 payments and 12% is 0.026333 Payment $= \$9600 \times 0.026333$ $\qquad = \$252.80$ Total amount repaid $= \$252.80 \times 48$ $\qquad\qquad\qquad = \$12,134.40$ Finance charge $= \$12,134.40 - \$9600$ $\qquad\qquad\qquad = \$2534.40$
15.4 Finding the amount of monthly mortgage payments and total interest charges over the life of a mortgage	Use the number of years and the interest rate to find the amortization value per thousand dollars from Table 15.3. Then multiply the table value by the number of thousands in the principal to obtain monthly payment. Find total amount of payment and subtract original amount owed from total payment to obtain interest paid.	Lou and Rose buy a house at the shore. After a down payment, they owe $75,000. Find the monthly payment at $7\frac{3}{4}\%$ and the total charges over the life of a 25-year mortgage. $n = 25; i = 7\frac{3}{4}\%;$ Table Value (Table 15.3) $= 7.56$ There are $\dfrac{\$75,000}{1000} = 75$ thousands in $75,000 Monthly payment $= 75 \times 7.56$ $\qquad\qquad\qquad = \$567$ There are $25 \times 12 = 300$ payments. So total payments $= 300 \times \$567$ $\qquad\qquad\qquad\qquad = \$170,100$ Interest Paid $= \$170,100 - \$75,000$ $\qquad\qquad\quad = \$95,100$

SUMMARY EXERCISE

Tom Fister deposits $200 at the end of each month for 4 years in an account that pays 6% compounded monthly.

(a) Find the final amount of money on deposit at the end of 4 years.

(b) How much interest did Fister earn?

(c) What lump sum could Fister deposit today at 6% compounded monthly to produce the same yield as the payments in (a)?

(d) If Fister actually needed $15,000 at the end of 4 years, how much should his monthly deposit have been?

CHAPTER 15 REVIEW EXERCISES

Find the amount of each of the following annuities. Round to the nearest cent. [15.1]

1. $1000 is deposited at the end of each year for 15 years, money earns 8% compounded annually

$$S = R \left(s\,\overline{\underset{n}{}}\,|_i \right)$$

2. $2500 is deposited at the end of each semiannual period for $5\frac{1}{2}$ years, money earns 12% compounded semiannually

3. $250 is deposited at the end of each quarter for $7\frac{1}{4}$ years, money earns 12% compounded quarterly

4. $600 is deposited at the end of each month for $2\frac{3}{4}$ years, money earns 9% compounded monthly

5. $100 is deposited at the beginning of each year for 5 years, money earns 6% compounded annually

6. $4800 is deposited at the beginning of each quarter for $3\frac{3}{4}$ years, money earns 8% compounded quarterly

7. Willa Burke deposits $803.47 at the end of each quarter for $3\frac{3}{4}$ years, in an account paying 12% compounded quarterly. Find the final amount in the account. Find the amount of interest earned.

8. A firm of attorneys deposits $7500 of profit sharing money at the end of each semiannual period for $7\frac{1}{2}$ years. Find the final amount in the account if the deposit earns 5% compounded semiannually. Find the amount of interest earned.

Find the present value of each of the following ordinary annuities. Round to the nearest cent. [15.2]

9. payments of $1500 are made annually for 9 years at 8% compounded annually

10. payments of $500 are made semiannually at 10% compounded semiannually for $3\frac{1}{2}$ years

$$A = R \left(a\,\overline{\underset{n}{}}\,|_i \right)$$

11. payments of $800 are made quarterly for $6\frac{3}{4}$ years at 6% compounded quarterly

12. payments of $615.34 are made monthly for $2\frac{11}{12}$ years at 10% compounded monthly

Find the amount of each payment to be made to a sinking fund so that enough money will be available to pay off the indicated loan. Round to the nearest cent. [15.3]

$$R = S\left(\frac{1}{s_{\overline{n}|i}}\right)$$

13. $10,000 loan, money earns 10% compounded annually, 7 annual payments

14. $42,000 loan, money earns 6% compounded quarterly, 26 quarterly payments

15. $100,000 loan, money earns 12% compounded semiannually, 9 semiannual payments

16. $35,000 loan, money earns 9% compounded monthly, 47 monthly payments

Find the amount of each payment necessary to amortize each of the following loans. Round to the nearest cent. [15.4]

$$R = A\left(\frac{1}{a_{\overline{n}|i}}\right)$$

17. $35,000 loan, repaid at 11% in 8 semiannual payments

18. $43,000 loan, repaid at 10% in 12 quarterly payments

Find the monthly payment and finance charge for each of the following loans. Round to the nearest cent. [15.4]

19. $2500 financed for 24 months at an APR of 8%

20. $4800 financed for 36 months at an APR of 12%

21. $12,000 financed for 48 months at an APR of 10%

22. $14,000 financed for 60 months at an APR of 9%

Table 15.2 for APR

$2500 (TABLE FIG) = 113.07

(113.07) ÷ 2500

FIN. CHRG = 24(113.07)
= $213.68

Work each of the following word problems.

23. The owner of Eastside Hallmark borrows $54,000 to expand the business. The money will be repaid in equal payments at the end of each year for 9 years. Interest is 8%. Find the amount of each payment. [15.4]

24. A small resort must add a swimming pool to compete with a new resort built nearby. The pool will cost $28,000. The resort borrows the money and agrees to repay it with equal payments at the end of each quarter for $6\frac{1}{2}$ years, at an interest rate of 12%. Find the amount of each payment. [15.4]

25. In 3 years Ms. Thompson must pay a pledge of $7500 to her college's building fund. What lump sum can she deposit today, at 10% compounded semiannually, so that she will have enough to pay the pledge? [15.2]

26. According to the terms of a divorce settlement, one spouse must pay the other a lump sum of $2800 in 17 months. What lump sum can be invested today, at 6% compounded monthly, so that enough will be available for the payment? [15.2]

Prepare an amortization schedule for each of the following loans. [15.4]

27. $8500 repaid at 12% in semiannual payments for $3\frac{1}{2}$ years.

28. $40,000 repaid at 16% in quarterly payments for $1\frac{3}{4}$ years

A business finds its net income (profit) by subtracting all expenses from the amount of money received by the business (revenues). Major expenses include the cost of goods sold, salaries, rent, and utilities. Other expenses include the cost of assets such as machines, buildings, and fixtures. These assets usually last several years, so it would not show the true income of the business if the entire cost of an asset were considered an expense in the year of purchase. Instead, a method called **depreciation** is used to spread the value of the asset over the several years of its life. Depreciation is used with assets having a useful life of more than one year. The asset to be depreciated must have a predictable life: a computer can be depreciated because its useful life can be estimated, but land cannot be depreciated because its life is indefinite.

Physical assets such as machinery, cars, or typewriters are *tangible assets*. A tangible asset may be depreciated, as long as its life can be estimated.

The key terms used in depreciation are summarized as follows.

Cost, the basis for determining depreciation, is the total amount paid for the asset.

Useful life is the period of time for which the asset is expected to last in the business. The Internal Revenue Service (IRS) has guidelines as to the estimated life of assets used in a particular trade or business. However, useful life depends on the use of the asset, repair policy, replacement policy, obsolescence, and other factors.

Salvage value or **scrap value** (sometimes called **residual value**) is the estimated value of an asset when it is retired from service, traded in, disposed of, or exhausted. The term *scrap value* is sometimes used in place of *salvage value*, since an asset's value at the end of its useful life is often only its value as scrap. An asset may have a salvage value of zero or **no salvage value**.

Accumulated depreciation is the amount of depreciation taken so far, a running balance of depreciation to date.

Book value is the cost of an asset minus the total depreciation to date (cost minus accumulated depreciation). The book value at the end of an asset's life will be equal to the salvage value. Book value can never be less than salvage value.

Over the years, several methods of computing depreciation have been used, including *straight-line, declining-balance, sum-of-the-years'-digits*, and *units-of-production*. These methods are used in keeping company accounting records, and, in most states, preparing state income tax returns. Assets purchased after 1981 are depreciated for federal tax returns with the accelerated cost recovery system or the modified accelerated cost recovery system, discussed later.

A company need not use the same method of depreciation for all of its various assets. For example, the straight-line method of depreciation might be used on some assets and the declining-balance method on other assets. Furthermore, the depreciation method used in preparing a company's financial statement may be different from the method used in preparing income tax returns.

This chapter discusses each of these methods in detail and also examines the newest system of depreciation as introduced by the Tax Reform Act of 1986.

16.1 Straight-Line Method

OBJECTIVES

1 Use the straight-line method to find the annual depreciation.

2 Use the straight-line method to find the book value of an asset.

3 Determine the book value of an asset after several years.

4 Calculate the accumulated depreciation.

5 Use the straight-line method to prepare a depreciation schedule.

The simplest method of depreciation, **straight-line depreciation**, assumes that assets lose an equal amount of value during each year of life.

1   For example, suppose an industrial sewing machine costs $4700, has an estimated useful life of 8 years, and has a salvage value of $700. Find the amount to be depreciated (the **depreciable amount**) using the following formula.

Amount to be depreciated = Cost − Salvage value

Here the amount to be depreciated over the 8-year period is figured as follows.

$4700	cost
− 700	salvage value
$4000	amount to be depreciated

With the straight-line method, an equal amount of depreciation is taken each year of the 8-year life of the machine. The annual depreciation for this machine is

$$\$4000 \div 8 = \$500.$$

Or, use the following formula.

> The annual depreciation by the *straight-line method* for an item having a cost
> of c, a salvage value s, and a life of n years, is d, where
>
> $$d = \frac{c - s}{n}.$$

Use the formula for the example by substituting \$4700 for c, \$700 for s, and 8 for n.

$$d = \frac{\$4700 - \$700}{8} = \frac{\$4000}{8} = \$500$$

The annual straight-line depreciation is \$500. Each year during the 8-year life of the
machine, \$500 will be treated as an expense by the company owning the machine.
The annual depreciation of \$500 is $\frac{1}{8}$ of the depreciable amount. The annual rate of
depreciation is often given as a percent, in this case, $12\frac{1}{2}\%$ $\left(\frac{1}{8} = 12\frac{1}{2}\%\right)$.

2   The **book value**, or remaining value of an asset at the end of a year, is the original
cost minus the depreciation up to and including that year (the **accumulated depreciation**). In the example, the book value at the end of the first year is \$4200.

\$4700	cost
− 500	first-year's depreciation
\$4200	book value

Book value is found with the following formula.

> Book value = Cost − Depreciation

EXAMPLE 1
*Finding First Year
Depreciation and
Book Value*

A word processor costs \$850. The estimated life of the word processor is 5 years, with
a salvage value of \$250. Find the (a) annual rate of depreciation, (b) annual amount
of depreciation, and (c) book value at the end of the first year.

SOLUTION

(a) The annual rate of depreciation is 20%, since a 5-year life means $\frac{1}{5}$ or 20%
per year.

(b) First find the depreciable amount.

\$850	cost
− 250	salvage value
\$600	depreciable amount

This $600 will be depreciated evenly over the 5-year life for an annual depreciation of $120 ($600 × 20% = $120 or $600 ÷ 5 = $120). The annual depreciation can also be found by the formula

$$d = \frac{c - s}{n}.$$

Substitute $850 for c, $250 for s, and 5 for n.

$$d = \frac{\$850 - \$250}{5} = \frac{\$600}{5} = \$120$$

The annual depreciation by the straight-line method is $120.

(c) Since the annual depreciation is $120, the book value at the end of the first year will be found as follows.

$850   cost
− 120   first-year's depreciation
─────
$730   book value after 1 year

The book value of the word processor after 1 year is $730. ∎

Calculator Approach to Example 1

The annual rate of depreciation is $\frac{1}{5}$ or 20%. Cost is first placed in memory so that it can be used later to find the book value. The annual depreciation is then calculated.

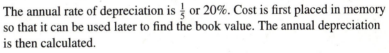

850 $\boxed{\text{M+}}$ $\boxed{-}$ 250 $\boxed{÷}$ 5 $\boxed{=}$ 120

The annual depreciation ($120) is now subtracted from memory to get the book value at the end of the first year.

$\boxed{\text{M−}}$ $\boxed{\text{MR}}$ 730

If an asset has **no salvage value** at the end of the expected life, then the entire cost will be depreciated over the life of the asset. In Example 1, if the word processor was expected to have no salvage value at the end of 5 years, the annual amount of depreciation would have been $170 (since $850 × 20% = $170).

NOTE Find the book value at the end of any year by multiplying the annual amount of straight-line depreciation by the number of years and subtract this result, the depreciation to date, from the cost.

FINDING
BOOK
VALUE

EXAMPLE 2
Finding the Book Value at the End of Any Year

A lighted display case costs $3400 and has an estimated life of 10 years and a salvage value of $800. Find the book value at the end of 6 years.

3 **SOLUTION**   The annual rate of depreciation is 10% (10-year life leads to $\frac{1}{10}$ or 10%).

$3400	cost
− 800	salvage value
$2600	depreciable amount

Since $2600 is depreciated evenly over the 10-year life of the case, the annual depreciation is $260 ($2600 × 10% = $260).

4   The accumulated depreciation over the 6-year period is

$260 × 6 (years) = $1560 accumulated depreciation (6 years).

Find the book value at the end of 6 years by subtracting the accumulated depreciation from the cost.

$3400	cost
− 1560	accumulated depreciation (6 years)
$1840	book value at the end of 6 years

After 6 years, this display case would be carried "on the books" with a value of $1840. ∎

NOTE This book value helps the owner of a business estimate the value of the business, which is especially important when the owner is borrowing money or trying to sell the business.

5   A **depreciation schedule** is often used to show the annual depreciation, accumulated depreciation, and book value over the useful life of an asset. As an aid in comparing the three methods of depreciation, the depreciation schedule of Example 3 and the schedules shown in the double-declining-balance method (see Section 16.2) and the sum-of-the-years'-digits method (see Section 16.3) use the same asset.

EXAMPLE 3
Preparing a Depreciation Schedule

Community Cable bought a new pickup truck for $14,000. The truck has a useful life of 5 years, when it will have a salvage value (trade-in value) of $2000. Prepare a depreciation schedule using the straight-line method of depreciation.

SOLUTION   The annual rate of depreciation is 20% (5-year life $= \frac{1}{5}$ per year $=$ 20%). Find the depreciable amount as follows.

$14,000	cost
− 2,000	salvage value
$12,000	depreciable amount

This $12,000 will be depreciated evenly over the 5-year life, giving an annual depreciation of $2400 ($12,000 × 20% = $2400).

This depreciation schedule includes a year zero to show the initial cost of the truck.

Year	Computation	Amount of Depreciation	Accumulated Depreciation	Book Value
0	—	—	—	$14,000
1	(20% × $12,000)	$2400	$2400	$11,600
2	(20% × $12,000)	$2400	$4800	$9200
3	(20% × $12,000)	$2400	$7200	$6800
4	(20% × $12,000)	$2400	$9600	$4400
5	(20% × $12,000)	$2400	$12,000	$2000

The depreciation is $2400 each year, the accumulated depreciation at the end of 5 years is equal to the depreciable amount, and the book value at the end of 5 years is equal to the salvage value. ▪

CAUTION If the rate is a repeating decimal, use the fraction that is equivalent to the decimal. Instead of 33.3%, use the fraction $\frac{1}{3}$; instead of 16.7%, use the fraction $\frac{1}{6}$.

16.1 Exercises

Find the annual straight-line rate of depreciation, given each of the following estimated lives.

$R = \dfrac{1}{n}$

1. 5 years

2. 4 years

3. 8 years

4. 10 years

5. 16 years $= 6.25\%$

6. 20 years

7. 25 years

8. 30 years

9. $\left(33\frac{1}{3}\text{ years} \dfrac{1}{33\frac{1}{3}} = \dfrac{1}{1003} = \dfrac{3}{100} = 3\% \right)$

10. 40 years

11. 50 years

12. 100 years

Round to the nearest dollar in the remainder of this exercise set.

Find the annual amount of depreciation for each of the following, using the straight-line method.

$d = \dfrac{C - S}{n}$

13. Cost: $35,000
Estimated life: 25 years
Estimated scrap value: none

14. Cost: $2300
Estimated life: 5 years
Estimated scrap value: $500

15. Cost: $120
Estimated life: 3 years
Estimated scrap value: $30

16. Cost: $8100
Estimated life: 6 years
Estimated scrap value: $750

17. Cost: $1500
Estimated life: 10 years
Estimated scrap value: none

18. Cost: $7000
Estimated life: 8 years
Estimated scrap value: $600

Find the book value at the end of the first year for each of the following, using the straight-line method.

$$d = \frac{c-s}{n}$$

$$b = c - d$$

19. Cost: $5400
  Estimated life: 12 years
  Estimated scrap value: $600

20. Cost: $4500
  Estimated life: 5 years
  Estimated scrap value: none

21. Cost: $1600
  Estimated life: 10 years
  Estimated scrap value: $400

22. Cost: $17,000
  Estimated life: 15 years
  Estimated scrap value: $1700

Find the book value at the end of 5 years for each of the following, using the straight-line method.

$$d = \frac{c-s}{n}$$

$$b = c - 5d$$

23. Cost: $1200
  Estimated life: 10 years
  Estimated scrap value: $150

24. Cost: $1800
  Estimated life: 20 years
  Estimated scrap value: $300

25. Cost: $80,000
  Estimated life: 50 years
  Estimated scrap value: $10,000

26. Cost: $660
  Estimated life: 8 years
  Estimated scrap value: $100

27. Develop a single formula that will show how to find annual depreciation using the straight-line method of depreciation. (See Objective 1.)

28. Explain in your own words why the accumulated depreciation plus the book value equals the total cost in each year of an asset's life.

Work each of the following word problems.

29. Bridgeport Construction selects the straight-line method of depreciation for an earth tamper costing $8000 and having a 3-year life and an expected scrap value of $2000. Prepare a depreciation schedule using the straight-line method of depreciation.

Year	Computation	Amount of Depreciation	Accumulated Depreciation	Book Value
0	—	—	—	$8000
1	_____	_____	_____	_____
2	_____	_____	_____	_____
3	_____	_____	_____	_____

30. Sewage System has purchased a laboratory clay crusher costing $18,000 and having an estimated life of 4 years and a salvage value of $1600. Prepare a depreciation schedule using the straight-line method of depreciation.

Year	Computation	Amount of Depreciation	Accumulated Depreciation	Book Value
0	—	—	—	$18,000
1				
2				
3				
4				

31. Shippers' Express paid $9400 for office equipment with an estimated life of 6 years and a salvage value of $2200. Prepare a depreciation schedule using the straight-line method of depreciation.

32. Dorothy Sargent buys fixtures for her shop at a cost of $7800 and estimates that the life of the fixtures is 10 years, at which time they will have no salvage value. Prepare a depreciation schedule calculating depreciation by the straight-line method.

33. Off Shore Drilling purchased a splicing rig at a cost of $25,000. The estimated life is 10 years at which time it will have a salvage value of $2500. Use the straight-line method of depreciation to find the annual amount of depreciation. Find the book value at the end of 4 years.

34. A scaffold has a cost of $7250, an estimated life of 8 years, and scrap value of $1050. Find the annual depreciation and the book value at the end of 4 years using the straight-line method of depreciation.

35. A freshwater barge has an estimated life of 15 years and no scrap value. If the barge cost $37,900 and the straight-line method is used, find the annual depreciation and the book value after 7 years.

36. A broadcasting tower has a cost of $258,900, an estimated life of 10 years and a salvage value of $25,000. Find the book value of the tower after 8 years using the straight-line method of depreciation.

37. A bookcase costs $880, has an estimated life of 8 years, and has a scrap value of $160. Use the straight-line method of depreciation to find (a) the annual rate of depreciation, (b) the annual amount of depreciation, and (c) the book value at the end of the first year.

38. Levinson Supply purchased a new forklift for $12,500. The estimated life is 10 years, with a salvage value of $2500. Use the straight-line method of depreciation and find (a) the annual rate of depreciation, (b) the annual amount of depreciation, (c) the book value at the end of 5 years, and (d) the accumulated depreciation at the end of 8 years.

16.2 Declining-Balance Method

OBJECTIVES

1 Compare the declining-balance methods.

2 Find the declining-balance rate.

3 Find depreciation and book value using the double-declining-balance method.

4 Use the formula to find depreciation by the declining-balance method.

5 Prepare a depreciation schedule using the declining-balance method.

The straight-line method of depreciation assumes that the cost of an asset is spread equally and evenly over each year of its life. This assumption is not realistic for many assets. For example, a new car loses much more value during its first year of life than during its fifth year. Using straight-line depreciation for such assets would give a book value higher than the actual value of the asset.

Methods of accelerated depreciation are used to more accurately reflect the rate at which most assets actually lose value. **Accelerated depreciation** produces larger amounts of depreciation in the earlier years of the life of an asset and smaller amounts in the later years. The total amount of depreciation taken over the life of an asset is the same as with the straight-line method (the difference of cost and salvage value), but the distribution of the annual amounts is different.

One of the more common accelerated methods of depreciation is called the **declining-balance method;** with this method a *declining-balance rate* is first established. This rate is multiplied by the previous year's book value to get the current year's depreciation. *Since the book value declines from year to year, the annual depreciation will also decline;* this explains the method's name.

1   There are three common declining-balance methods:

> **200% declining-balance method** or **double-declining-balance method**. With this method, 200% of the straight-line rate, or twice the straight-line rate, is used.
> **150% declining-balance method**. With this method, $1\frac{1}{2}$ times the straight-line rate is used.
> **125% declining-balance method**. With this method, $1\frac{1}{4}$ times the straight-line rate is used.

2   Calculate depreciation using the declining-balance method by first finding the straight-line rate of depreciation. Then adjust the straight-line rate to the desired declining-balance rate (200%, 150%, or 125% as desired). The following examples of declining-balance depreciation show the *200%* or *double-declining-balance method.*

EXAMPLE 1
Finding the 200% Declining-Balance Rate

Find the straight-line rate and the double-declining-balance (200%) rate for each of the following years of life.

SOLUTION

Years of Life	Straight-Line Rate	Double-Declining-Balance Rate
3	33.33% $\left(\frac{1}{3}\right)$	66.67% $\left(\frac{2}{3}\right)$
4	25%	50%
5	20%	40%
10	10%	20%
20	5%	10%
25	4%	8%
30	3.33% $\left(\frac{1}{30}\right)$	6.67% $\left(\frac{1}{15}\right)$
50	2%	4%

ROUND TO NEAREST DOLLAR

NOTE Throughout the remainder of this chapter, money amounts will be rounded to the nearest dollar, a common practice when dealing with depreciation. The rounded value is then used in further calculations.

EXAMPLE 2
Finding Depreciation and Book Value Using Double-Declining-Balance

A produce scale costs $650 and has an estimated life of 4 years and an estimated salvage value of $50. Find the depreciation for the first and second years and the book value at the end of the first and second years using the double-declining-balance method of depreciation.

3 **SOLUTION** Start by finding the double-declining-balance rate: find this rate by doubling the straight-line rate. The straight-line rate for a life of 4 years is $\frac{1}{4}$, or 25%, and 25% doubled is 50%. The double-declining-balance rate (50%) is then multiplied by the book value, or in year 1 the *original cost (not the depreciable amount)*. The depreciation in year 1 is

Original cost × Double-declining rate

or

$$\$650 \times 0.50 = \$325.$$

Depreciation in year 1 is $325. Therefore, the book value at the end of the first year is as follows.

$650	cost
− 325	depreciation to date
$325	book value at the end of the first year

The second year's depreciation is 50% of $325 (last year's book value or declining balance), or

$325 (declining balance) × 0.50 = $163 (depreciation in second year, rounded).

The book value at the end of the second year is figured as follows.

$650	cost
− 488	depreciation to date ($325 + $163 = $488)
$162	book value at the end of the second year ∎

4 Declining-balance depreciation can also be found with the following formula.

> The annual depreciation, *d*, by the declining-balance method, is given by
>
> $$d = r \times b,$$
>
> where *r* is the declining-balance rate and *b* is the book value in the previous year. (In year 1, *b* is the original cost of the asset.)

EXAMPLE 3
Using a Formula to Find Depreciation and Book Value

A portable tool shed costs $2700 and is expected to have a life of 10 years, at which time it will have no salvage value. Using the double-declining-balance method of depreciation, find the first and second years' depreciation and the book value at the end of the first and second year.

SOLUTION The straight-line depreciation rate for a 10-year life is 10%. The double-declining rate is 10% times 2, or 20%. The first year's depreciation is 20% of the declining balance or, in the first year, 20% of the cost. Use the formula, substituting 0.20 for *r* and $2700 for *b*.

$$d = r \times b$$

$$= 0.20 \times \$2700 = \$540$$

The depreciation in the first year is $540. The book value at the end of the first year is as follows.

$2700	cost
− 540	depreciation to date
$2160	book value at the end of the first year

The second year's depreciation is 20% of $2160 (last year's book value or declining balance) or, again with the formula,

$$d = r \times b$$

$$= 0.20 \times \$2160 = \$432.$$

The depreciation in the second year is $432. At the end of the second year the book value is figured as shown.

$$\begin{array}{ll} \$2700 & \text{cost} \\ -\quad 972 & \text{depreciation to date (\$540 + \$432 = \$972)} \\ \hline \$1728 & \text{book value at the end of the second year } \blacksquare \end{array}$$

NOTE The total amount of depreciation taken over the life of the asset is the same using either the straight-line or the double-declining-balance methods of depreciation, but the distribution of the annual amounts is different.

5 The next example shows a depreciation schedule for the same pickup truck used in Example 3 of Section 16.1. Here, the declining-balance method is used, where the same rate is used each year, and the rate is multiplied by the declining balance (last year's book value). This example shows that the amount of depreciation in a given year may have to be adjusted so that book value is never less than salvage value.

EXAMPLE 4
Preparing a
Depreciation
Schedule

Community Cable bought a new pickup truck for $14,000. It is estimated that the truck will have a useful life of 5 years, at which time it will have a salvage value (trade-in value) of $2000. Prepare a depreciation schedule using the double-declining-balance method of depreciation.

SOLUTION The annual rate of depreciation is 40% (20% straight-line × 2 = 40%). *Do not subtract salvage value from cost before calculating depreciation. In year 1, the full cost is used to calculate depreciation.*

Year	Computation	Amount of Depreciation	Accumulated Depreciation	Book Value
0	—	—	—	$14,000
1	(40% × $14,000)	$5600	$5600	$8400
2	(40% × $8400)	$3360	$8960	$5040
3	(40% × $5040)	$2016	$10,976	$3024
4	(40% × $3024)	$1024	$12,000	$2000
5		0	$12,000	$2000

Notice that in year 4, 40% of $3024 is $1210. If this amount were subtracted from $3024, the book value would drop below the salvage value of $2000. Since book value may never be less than salvage value, only $1024 of depreciation is taken in year 4, resulting in a book value equal to the salvage value. No further depreciation remains for year 5. ■

NOTE The declining-balance method of depreciation allows rapid depreciation in early years but little or no depreciation in the later years of an asset's life. As mentioned, the total depreciation over the life of the asset is the same by all methods of depreciation.

16.2 Exercises

Find the annual double-declining-balance (200% method) rate of depreciation, given each of the following estimated lives.

1. 5 years
2. 6 years
3. 8 years
4. 10 years
5. 15 years
6. 20 years
7. 25 years
8. 30 years
9. $33\frac{1}{3}$ years
10. 40 years
11. 50 years
12. 100 years

Round to the nearest dollar in the rest of this exercise set.

Find the first year's depreciation for each of the following, using the double-declining-balance method of depreciation.

13. Cost: $185
    Estimated life: 10 years
    Estimated scrap value: none

14. Cost: $120
    Estimated life: 3 years
    Estimated scrap value: $30

15. Cost: $10,500
    Estimated life: 5 years
    Estimated scrap value: $500

16. Cost: $38,000
    Estimated life: 40 years
    Estimated scrap value: $5000

17. Cost: $4800
    Estimated life: 4 years
    Estimated scrap value: $500

18. Cost: $1850
    Estimated life: 20 years
    Estimated scrap value: none

Find the book value at the end of the first year for each of the following, using the double-declining-balance method of depreciation.

19. Cost: $2800
    Estimated life: 5 years
    Estimated scrap value: $500

20. Cost: $2500
    Estimated life: 6 years
    Estimated scrap value: $400

21. Cost: $170
    Estimated life: 4 years
    Estimated scrap value: none

22. Cost: $580
    Estimated life: 20 years
    Estimated scrap value: $150

Find the book value at the end of 3 years for each of the following, using the double-declining-balance method of depreciation.

23. Cost: $8100
    Estimated life: 8 years
    Estimated scrap value: $700

24. Cost: $250
    Estimated life: 10 years
    Estimated scrap value: $50

25. Cost: $6000
    Estimated life: 3 years
    Estimated scrap value: $750

26. Cost: $75,000
    Estimated life: 50 years
    Estimated scrap value: none

27. Another name for the double-declining-balance method of depreciation is the 200% method. Explain why the straight-line method of depreciation is often called the 100% method.

28. Explain in your own words why the book value of an asset may never be less than the salvage value.

Work each of the following word problems.

29. A pneumatic tire changer costing $1680 has a 3-year life and a scrap value of $200. Prepare a depreciation schedule using the double-declining-balance method of depreciation.

Year	Computation	Amount of Depreciation	Accumulated Depreciation	Book Value
0	—	—	—	$1680
1				
2				
3				

30. The Stockdale Marine selects the double-declining-balance method of depreciation for a piece of equipment costing $2400. If the estimated life of the equipment is 4 years and the salvage value is zero, prepare a depreciation schedule.

Year	Computation	Amount of Depreciation	Accumulated Depreciation	Book Value
0	—	—	—	$2400
1				
2				
3				
4				

31. Rusch Park District decides to use the double-declining-balance method of depreciation on a tractor which was acquired at a cost of $8500. If the estimated life of the tractor is 8 years and the estimated scrap value is $1500, prepare a depreciation schedule.

32. Prepare a depreciation schedule for the installation of a conveyor system using the double-declining-balance method of depreciation. Cost = $14,000; estimated life = 5 years; estimated scrap value = $2500.

33. True Value Hardware purchased some new parts bins at a cost of $8200. The estimated life of the bins is 8 years and the expected salvage value is $1250. Use the double-declining-balance method of depreciation to find the depreciation in the third year.

34. A commercial fishing boat cost $326,800 and has an estimated life of 10 years and a salvage value of $45,000. Find the depreciation in the second year using the double-declining-balance method of depreciation.

35. Nature's Products purchased a new juice extractor. The cost of the extractor is $1090 and it has an estimated life of 5 years with no salvage value. Use the double-declining-balance method of depreciation to find the book value at the end of the third year.

36. Lens Craft bought some optical equipment at a cost of $9850. They estimate the life of the equipment to be 10 years at which time the value will be $500. Use the double-declining-balance method of depreciation to find the book value at the end of 5 years.

37. West Construction purchased a truck tool chest for $580. It has a life of 8 years and a scrap value of $100. Use the double-declining-balance method of depreciation to find (a) the annual rate of depreciation, (b) the amount of depreciation in the first year, (c) the accumulated depreciation at the end of the fifth year, and (d) the book value at the end of the fifth year.

38. Kay Schrudder bought some white boards for her spelling clinic at a cost of $3620. The estimated life of the white boards is 5 years, with a salvage value of $400. Use the double-declining-balance method of depreciation to find (a) the annual rate of depreciation, (b) the amount of depreciation in the first year, (c) the accumulated depreciation at the end of the third year, and (d) the book value at the end of the third year.

16.3 Sum-of-the-Years'-Digits Method

OBJECTIVES

1 Understand the sum-of-the-years'-digits method.

2 Find the depreciation fractions for the sum-of-the-years'-digits method.

3 Use the formula to calculate the sum-of-the-years'-digits depreciation.

4 Prepare a depreciation schedule using the sum-of-the-years'-digits method.

1 The double-declining-balance method produces more depreciation than the straight-line method in the early years of an asset's life, and less in the later years. An alternate accelerated method, called the **sum-of-the-years'-digits method,** produces results in-between; more than straight-line at the beginning and more than double-declining-balance at the end.

The use of the sum-of-the-years'-digits method requires a **depreciation fraction,** instead of the depreciation rate used earlier. If this depreciation fraction, which decreases annually, is multiplied by the depreciable amount (cost minus salvage value) the result is the annual depreciation.

2 To find the **depreciation fraction,** first find the denominator, which remains constant for every year of the life of the asset. The denominator is the sum of all the years of the estimated life of the asset (sum-of-the-years'-digits). For example, if the life is 6 years, the denominator is 21 (since $1 + 2 + 3 + 4 + 5 + 6 = 21$). The numerator of the fraction changes each year, and represents the years of life remaining at the beginning of that year.

EXAMPLE 1

Finding the Depreciation Fraction

Find the depreciation fraction for each year if the sum-of-the-years'-digits method of depreciation is to be used for an asset with a useful life of 6 years.

SOLUTION   First determine the denominator of the depreciation fraction. The denominator is $21 (1 + 2 + 3 + 4 + 5 + 6 = 21)$. Next determine the numerator for each year. The number of years of life remaining at the beginning of any year is the numerator.

Year	Depreciation Fraction
1	$\frac{6}{21}$
2	$\frac{5}{21}$
3	$\frac{4}{21}$
4	$\frac{3}{21}$
5	$\frac{2}{21}$
6	$\frac{1}{21}$
21 sum of the years' digits	$\frac{21}{21}$

As this table shows, by the sum-of-the-years'-digits method an asset having a life of 6 years is assumed to lose $\frac{6}{21}$ of its value the first year, $\frac{5}{21}$ the second year, and so on. The sum of the six fractions in the table is $\frac{21}{21}$, or 1, so that the entire depreciable amount is used over the 6-year life. ■

NOTE It is common not to write these fractions in lowest terms, so that the year in question can be seen.

A fast method of finding the sum-of-the-years'-digits is to use the formula

> Sum-of-the-years'-digits $= \dfrac{n(n+1)}{2}$,
>
> where n is the estimated life of the asset.

For example, if the life is 6 years, 6 is multiplied by 6 plus 1, resulting in 6×7, or 42. Then 42 is divided by 2, giving 21, the same denominator used in Example 1. This method eliminates adding digits and is especially useful when the life of an asset is long.

3 The depreciation fraction in any year is multiplied by the amount to be depreciated (as in the straight-line method) to calculate the amount of depreciation in any one year.

> The formula for sum-of-the-years'-digits depreciation is
>
> $$d = r \times (c - s),$$
>
> where r is the depreciation fraction, c is the cost of the asset, and s is the salvage value.

EXAMPLE 2
Finding Depreciation Using the Sum-of-the-Years'-Digits Method

Suppose an asset costs $3600 and has a useful life of 5 years and an estimated salvage value of $600. Find the first and second years' depreciation using the sum-of-the-years'-digits method.

SOLUTION The depreciation fraction has a denominator of 15 (or $1+2+3+4+5$). The numerator in the first year is 5.

The first year fraction $\frac{5}{15}$ is multiplied by the depreciable amount, $3000 ($3600 cost $-$ $600 salvage value). Substitute the proper numbers into the formula

$$d = r \times (c - s)$$

$$= \frac{5}{15} \times (\$3600 - \$600)$$

$$= \frac{5}{15} \times \$3000 = \$1000$$

The first year's depreciation is $1000.

The book value at the end of the first year is $3600 (original cost) − $1000 (first year's depreciation) = $2600. For the second and succeeding years, always go back to the *original* depreciable amount and not to book value, as in the declining-balance method. The depreciation fraction for the second year, $\frac{4}{15}$, is multiplied by the original depreciable amount, $3000 ($3600 cost − $600 salvage value). This gives

$$\frac{4}{15} \times \$3000 = \$800.$$

The second year's depreciation is $800. (In this example the depreciation for any year is always found by multiplying the appropriate fraction by $3000.) ∎

Calculator Approach to Example 2

Start by finding the depreciable amount, then divide it by the denominator of the depreciation fraction (sum-of-the-years'-digits). This gives a constant multiplier which should be placed in memory.

3600 $\boxed{-}$ 600 $\boxed{\div}$ 15 = 200 $\boxed{\text{M+}}$

The depreciation in any year may be found by recalling the constant $\left(\frac{1}{15}\right.$ of the depreciable amount here$\left.\right)$ and multiplying by the numerator for that year. Find the depreciation in the first year as follows.

$\boxed{\text{MR}}$ $\boxed{\times}$ 5 $\boxed{=}$ 1000

Now find the depreciation in the second year.

$\boxed{\text{MR}}$ $\boxed{\times}$ 4 $\boxed{=}$ 800

EXAMPLE 3

Finding Depreciation When There Is No Salvage Value

Using the sum-of-the-years'-digits method of depreciation, find the first and second years' depreciation for an asset which has a cost of $2000 and has an estimated life of 4 years and no salvage value.

SOLUTION   The depreciation fraction has a denominator of 10 (or $4 + 3 + 2 + 1$). The numerator in the first year is 4. The first year depreciation fraction is $\frac{4}{10}$, which is multiplied by the amount to be depreciated, or $2000 ($2000 cost − no salvage value). Use the formula as follows.

$$d = r \times (c - s)$$

$$= \frac{4}{10} \times (\$2000 - \$0)$$

$$= \frac{4}{10} \times \$2000$$

$$= \$800$$

The first year's depreciation is $800.

The fraction for finding the depreciation in the second year is $\frac{3}{10}$, which is multiplied by the depreciable amount, or $2000.

$$\frac{3}{10} \times \$2000 = \$600$$

The second year's depreciation is $600. ■

4   For comparison, the next example uses the same pickup truck discussed in Sections 16.1 and 16.2.

EXAMPLE 4   Community Cable bought a new pickup truck for $14,000. It is estimated that the
Preparing a   truck will have a useful life of 5 years, at which time it will have a salvage value of
Depreciation $2000. Prepare a depreciation schedule using the sum-of-the-years'-digits method of
Schedule   depreciation.

SOLUTION   The depreciation fraction has a denominator of $(5 \times 6) \div 2$, or 15.

Year	Computation	Amount of Depreciation	Accumulated Depreciation	Book Value
0	—	—	—	$14,000
1	$\left(\frac{5}{15} \times \$12,000\right)$	$4000	$4000	$10,000
2	$\left(\frac{4}{15} \times \$12,000\right)$	$3200	$7200	$6800
3	$\left(\frac{3}{15} \times \$12,000\right)$	$2400	$9600	$4400
4	$\left(\frac{2}{15} \times \$12,000\right)$	$1600	$11,200	$2800
5	$\left(\frac{1}{15} \times \$12,000\right)$	$800	$12,000	$2000 ■

NOTE   The sum-of-the-years'-digits method of depreciation allows rapid depreciation in the early years of the asset's life and also provides some depreciation during the last years.

The sum-of-the-years'-digits method of depreciation allows rapid depreciation in the early years of the asset's life while still providing some depreciation during later years. With each of the depreciation methods, the total depreciation over the life of the asset is the same, but the distribution of the amount is different.

The three methods of depreciation can be compared visually by graphing the amounts of depreciation in each year and the book values at the end of each year. Figures 16.1 and 16.2 show the annual depreciation and book value for the pickup truck owned by Community Cable.

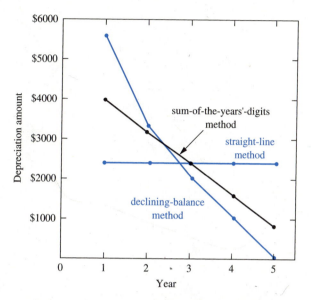

FIGURE 16.1   **Comparison of depreciation on Community Cable pickup truck using three depreciation methods**

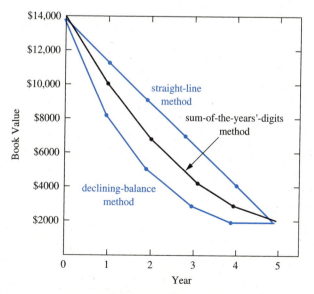

FIGURE 16.2   **Comparison of book value on Community Cable pickup truck using three depreciation methods**

While there is no simple way to decide which method of depreciation is preferable in a given case, the following considerations may help to arrive at an answer.

- Will a larger deduction in the first year or years help pay for the asset with the tax dollars saved?

- Is it expected that earnings during the first years will be larger than in the following years? Larger depreciation deductions help to reduce taxes.

- Will a steady deduction over the life of the asset be advantageous?

- Accelerated deductions in early years mean little or no deductions in later years.

- Is profit expected to increase in the coming years during the life of the asset? If this is the case, a steady deduction over the life of the asset will allow depreciation in later years.

- Will repair bills be more in later years? Since these are also deductions, they might offset lower depreciation amounts in later years.

16.3 Exercises

Find the sum-of-the-years'-digits depreciation fraction for the first year given each of the following estimated lives.

1. 3 years	**2.** 4 years	**3.** 5 years	**4.** 6 years
5. 7 years	**6.** 8 years	**7.** 10 years	**8.** 20 years

Round to the nearest dollar in the rest of this exercise set.

Find the first year's depreciation for each of the following, using the sum-of-the-years'-digits method of depreciation.

9. Cost: $1400
   Estimated life: 3 years
   Estimated scrap value: $500

10. Cost: $2500
    Estimated life: 6 years
    Estimated scrap value: $400

11. Cost: $60,000
    Estimated life: 10 years
    Estimated scrap value: $5000

12. Cost: $1440
    Estimated life: 8 years
    Estimated scrap value: none

13. Cost: $450
    Estimated life: 5 years
    Estimated scrap value: $75

14. Cost: $275,000
    Estimated life: 20 years
    Estimated scrap value: $25,000

Find the book value at the end of the first year for each of the following, using the sum-of-the-years'-digits method of depreciation.

15. Cost: $3800
    Estimated life: 5 years
    Estimated scrap value: $500

16. Cost: $4000
    Estimated life: 3 years
    Estimated scrap value: $400

17. Cost: $5000
    Estimated life: 6 years
    Estimated scrap value: $1000

18. Cost: $25,000
    Estimated life: 10 years
    Estimated scrap value: none

Find the book value at the end of 3 years for each of the following, using the sum-of-the-years'-digits method of depreciation.

19. Cost: $4500
    Estimated life: 8years
    Estimated scrap value: $900

20. Cost: $600
    Estimated life: 5 years
    Estimated scrap value: $150

21. Cost: $3800
    Estimated life: 4years
    Estimated scrap value: $300

22. Cost: $27,500
    Estimated life: 10 years
    Estimated scrap value: none

23. Write a description of how the depreciation fraction is determined in any year of an asset's life when using the sum-of-the-years'-digits method of depreciation. (See Objective 2.)

24. Of the three depreciation methods, straight-line, double-declining-balance, and sum-of-the-years'-digits, which do you find most interesting? Why?

Work each of the following word problems.

25. Using the sum-of-the-years'-digits method of depreciation, prepare a depreciation schedule for a copier that costs $3900, has an expected life of 3 years, and an estimated salvage value of $480.

Year	Computation	Amount of Depreciation	Accumulated Depreciation	Book Value
0	—	—	—	$3900
1				
2				
3				

26. Old South Restaurant has purchased a new steam table for $7200. The expected life of the unit is 4 years, at which time the salvage value is estimated to be $1200. Complete a depreciation schedule using the sum-of-the-years'-digits method of depreciation.

Year	Computation	Amount of Depreciation	Accumulated Depreciation	Book Value
0	—	—	—	$7200
1				
2				
3				
4				

27. Sunset Real Estate Company has purchased office furniture at a cost of $2700. The estimated life of the furniture is 6 years, at which time the salvage value is estimated to be $600. Complete a depreciation schedule using the sum-of-the-years'-digits method of depreciation.

28. Prepare a depreciation schedule for the following fork lift, using the sum-of-the-years'-digits method of depreciation. Cost is $15,000, estimated life is 10 years, and estimated scrap value is $4000.

29. Tropical Fish "Я" Us purchased a new display tank at a cost of $2800. The expected life of the tank is 5 years and the scrap value is estimated to be $400. Use the sum-of-the-years'-digits method of depreciation to determine the first year's depreciation.

30. Orangevale Rents uses the sum-of-the-years'-digits method of depreciation on all hospital rental equipment. If they purchase new hospital beds at a cost of $12,800 and estimate the life of the beds to be 10 years with no scrap value, find the book value at the end of the fourth year.

31. Find the book value at the end of the third year using the sum-of-the-years'-digits method of depreciation for an automobile frame straightener which costs $15,400 and has an expected life of 20 years and an estimated salvage value of $2000.

32. Find the depreciation in the third year for a solar collector, using the sum-of-the-years'-digits method of depreciation. Cost is $23,000, estimated life is 8 years, and estimated scrap value is $5000.

33. The cost of a depreciable asset is $2650. It has a useful life of 7 years and no salvage value. Find (a) the first and (b) the second year's depreciation using the sum-of-the-years'-digits method.

34. Using the sum-of-the-years'-digits method of depreciation, find (a) the first and (b) the second year's depreciation for an asset that has a cost of $3375 and an estimated life of 5 years and no salvage value.

35. LA Workout purchased some weight training equipment for $14,780. The expected life of the equipment is 8 years, with a scrap value of $2000. Use the sum-of-the-years'-digits method of depreciation to find (a) the first year's depreciation fraction, (b) the amount of depreciation in the first year, (c) the accumulated depreciation at the end of the eighth year, and (d) the book value at the end of the fourth year.

36. Blue Ribbon Septic Service bought some new equipment for $12,800. The life of the equipment is 10 years and the scrap value is $2400. Use the sum-of-the-years'-digits method of depreciation to find (a) the first year's depreciation fraction, (b) the amount of depreciation in the first year, (c) the accumulated depreciation at the end of the tenth year, and (d) the book value at the end of the sixth year.

16.4 Units-of-Production Method and Partial-Year Depreciation

OBJECTIVES

1 Describe the units-of-production method of depreciation.

2 Find the depreciation per unit.

3 Calculate annual depreciation by the units-of-production method.

4 Prepare a depreciation schedule using the units-of-production method.

5 Calculate partial-year depreciation by the straight-line method.

6 Calculate partial-year depreciation by the double-declining-balance method.

7 Calculate partial-year depreciation by the sum-of-the-years'-digits method.

1 An asset often has a useful life given in terms of *units of production*, such as hours of use or miles of service. For example, an airliner or truck may have a useful life given as hours of air time or miles of travel. A steel press or stamping machine may have a life given as the total number of units that it can produce. With these assets, the **units-of-production method** of depreciation is used. Just as with the straight-line method of depreciation, a constant amount of depreciation is taken with the units-of-production method. With the straight-line method a constant amount of depreciation is taken each year, while the units-of-production method depreciates a constant amount per unit of use or production.

2 With the units-of-production method, find the depreciation per unit with the following formula.

$$\text{Depreciation per unit} = \frac{\text{Depreciable amount}}{\text{Units of life}}$$

For example, suppose a machine costs $15,000 and has a salvage value of $3000 and a useful life of 25,000 units. The depreciable amount is $15,000 − $3000 = $12,000. Use the formula to find the depreciation per unit.

$$\frac{\$12,000 \text{ depreciable amount}}{25,000 \text{ units of life}} = \$.48 \quad \text{depreciation per unit}$$

3 Then multiply the depreciation per unit by the number of units produced during the year to find the annual depreciation.

EXAMPLE 1

Using Units-of-Production Depreciation

A Stokes Tablet Machine costs $9200 and has a scrap value of $1500 and an estimated life of 5000 hours. Find the depreciation for a year in which the machine was in operation 2000 hours.

SOLUTION First, find the depreciable amount.

$$
\begin{array}{ll}
\$9200 & \text{cost} \\
-\ 1500 & \text{scrap value} \\
\hline
\$7700 & \text{depreciable amount}
\end{array}
$$

Next, find the depreciation per unit.

$$\frac{\$7700 \text{ depreciable amount}}{5000 \text{ units of life}} = \$1.54 \qquad \text{depreciation per hour}$$

Multiply to find the depreciation for the year.

$$2000 \text{ hours} \times \$1.54 = \$3080 \qquad \text{depreciation for the year} \quad \blacksquare$$

Calculator Approach to Example 1

Find the depreciation per hour and then multiply it by the number of hours of operation.

9200 $\boxed{-}$ 1500 $\boxed{\div}$ 5000 $\boxed{\times}$ 2000 $\boxed{=}$ 3080

EXAMPLE 2

Preparing a Depreciation Schedule

A machine costs $52,300, has an estimated salvage value of $4000, and an expected life of 230,000 units. Prepare a depreciation schedule using the units-of-production method of depreciation. Use the following production schedule.

Year 1	80,000 units
Year 2	50,000 units
Year 3	30,000 units
Year 4	40,000 units
Year 5	30,000 units

SOLUTION The depreciable amount is $48,300 (or $52,300 − $4000). The depreciation per unit is

$$\frac{\$48,300}{230,000 \text{ units}} = \$.21 \text{ per unit.}$$

The annual depreciation is found by multiplying the number of units produced each year by the depreciation per unit.

Year 1	80,000 units × 0.21	=	$16,800
Year 2	50,000 units × 0.21	=	$10,500
Year 3	30,000 units × 0.21	=	$6300
Year 4	40,000 units × 0.21	=	$8400
Year 5	30,000 units × 0.21	=	$6300
Total	230,000 units		$48,300 depreciable amount

These results were used to help prepare the following depreciation schedule.

Year	Computation	Depreciation	Accumulated Depreciation	Book Value
0	—	—	—	$52,300
1	(80,000 × $.21)	$16,800	$16,800	$35,500
2	(50,000 × $.21)	$10,500	$27,300	$25,000
3	(30,000 × $.21)	$6300	$33,600	$18,700
4	(40,000 × $.21)	$8400	$42,000	$10,300
5	(30,000 × $.21)	$6300	$48,300	$4000

NOTE In Example 2, the book value at the end of year 5 ($4000) is the amount of the salvage value. This is true because the total number of units of life (230,000) have been produced by the machine during the 5 years. The machine may continue in use producing more units, however, no additional depreciation may be taken.

5 So far, each of the examples in depreciation assumed that the depreciable asset was purchased at the beginning of a year. If the asset is purchased during the year, only a fraction of the first year's depreciation may be taken. For example, if an asset is acquired on June 1, only $\frac{7}{12}$ (since 7 months remain) of the first year's depreciation may be taken. For an asset acquired on April 1, only $\frac{9}{12}$ or $\frac{3}{4}$ of the first year's depreciation may be taken. If the asset is purchased at other than the beginning of the month, then count that month for depreciation if purchased on or before the 15th of the month. This **partial-year depreciation** is explained in the following examples.

Each of the methods of depreciation studied so far (except the units-of-production method) is affected differently by a partial year. The units-of-production method is not affected by the partial first year since actual use determines depreciation.

EXAMPLE 3
Finding Partial-Year Depreciation with Straight-Line

A machine purchased on October 1 at a cost of $4500 has an estimated salvage value of $500 and an expected life of 5 years. Using the straight-line method of depreciation, find the depreciation in the year of purchase.

SOLUTION   The depreciation for a full year is

$$\frac{\$4500 - \$500}{5 \text{ years}} = \frac{\$4000}{5} = \$800.$$

Since the purchase date is October 1, 3 months remain in the year. This means that only $\frac{3}{12}$ or $\frac{1}{4}$ of the $800 may be taken in the year of purchase.

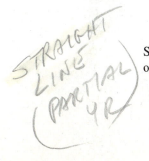

$$\$800 \times \frac{1}{4} = \$200$$ depreciation allowed in the year of purchase

The next 4 years are depreciated at the full $800 per year and the last 9 months $\left(\frac{3}{4}\right)$ of the fifth year has depreciation figured as follows.

$$\$800 \times \frac{3}{4} = \$600$$ partial-year depreciation

As before, the total depreciation over all the years is the depreciable amount, or $4000. ∎

EXAMPLE 4

Finding Partial-Year Depreciation with Double-Declining-Balance

An asset with a life of 10 years is purchased on April 1 at a cost of $12,000. If the double-declining-balance method is used, find the depreciation for the first partial year and the next full year.

SOLUTION The double-declining-balance rate is 20% $\left(\frac{1}{10} \times 2 = \frac{2}{10} = \frac{1}{5}\right.$ = 20%$\left.\right)$. Calculate the first year's depreciation.

$$\$12,000 \times 0.2 = \$2400$$ depreciation first full year

Now find the depreciation for 9 months or $\frac{3}{4}$ year.

$$\$2400 \times \frac{3}{4} = \$1800$$ partial-year depreciation

The book value (declining balance) is $10,200 ($12,000 − $1800). Use this book value to find the first full year depreciation.

$$\$10,200 \text{ declining balance} \times 0.2 = \$2040$$

The depreciation for the first full year is $2040. Depreciation for the following years would be calculated as usual. (Make sure that book value does not go below any scrap value.) ∎

EXAMPLE 5

Finding Partial-Year Depreciation with Sum-of-the-Years'-Digits

A new compressor is purchased on July 1 at a cost of $3800. It is estimated that the compressor will have a life of 4 years and a scrap value of $600. Use the sum-of-the-years'-digits method to find the depreciation for each year of the life of the asset.

SOLUTION The partial year here is $\frac{1}{2}$ (6 months). The depreciation fraction in year 1 is $\frac{4}{10}$ and the depreciable amount is $3200 ($3800 − $600).

$$\frac{4}{10} \times \$3200 = \$1280$$ depreciation year 1

$$\$1280 \times \frac{1}{2} = \$640$$ partial-year depreciation

Partial-year depreciation in the sum-of-the-year's-digits method requires depreciation in the first full year (year 2) to be the sum of the second half of depreciation in year 1 and the first half of depreciation in year 2. Depreciation in year 3 will be the sum of the second half of year two and the first half of year three and so on for the remaining life. See Figure 16.3.

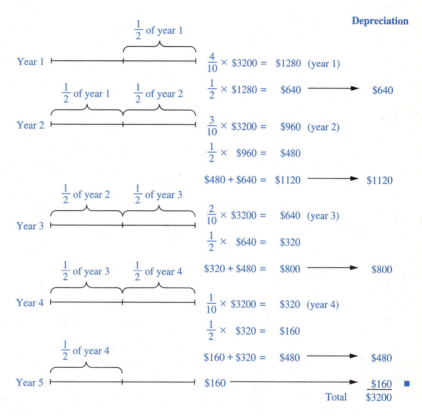

FIGURE 16.3

16.4 Exercises

Find the depreciation per unit in each of the following. Round to the nearest thousandth of a dollar.

	Cost	Salvage Value	Estimated Life
1.	$3750	$250	120,000 units
2.	$22,000	$2000	200,000 miles
3.	$2500	$200	10,000 units
4.	$1850	$350	20,000 units
5.	$75,000	$15,000	250,000 miles
6.	$600,000	$50,000	2000 hours
7.	$175,000	$25,000	5000 hours
8.	$115,000	$15,000	1,000,000 units

(handwritten notes in right margin)

FIND DEPRE. AMT

① C − S =

② FIND DEPRE. PER UNIT

$$\frac{C-S}{n} =$$

Find the annual amount of depreciation in each of the following.

	Depreciation per Unit	Units Produced			Depreciation per Unit	Units Produced
9.	$.54	32,000		10.	$.73	16,500
11.	$.07	85,000		12.	$.01	750,000
13.	$.185	15,000		14.	$.36	24,000
15.	$.04	16,000		16.	$.015	180,000

17. Describe in your own words the conditions under which the units-of-production method of depreciation is most applicable. (See Objective 1.)

18. Explain in your own words how the annual depreciation amount is found using the units-of-production method of depreciation. (See Objective 3.)

Find the depreciation in the first partial year for each of the following. Round to the nearest dollar.

	Cost	Salvage Value	Life	Depreciation Method	Date Acquired	Units Produced
✓ 19.	$1450	$250	8000 hours	Units-of-production	March 1	1800 hours
20.	$17,000	$2000	25,000 units	Units-of-production	April 1	4000 units
✓ 21.	$4850	$350	5 years	Straight-line	June 1	
22.	$2800	$500	20 years	Straight-line	Oct. 1	
✓ 23.	$20,000	$1000	20 years	Double-declining	March 1	
24.	$5250	$550	10 years	Double-declining	May 1	
✓ 25.	$1800	none	6 years	Sum-of-years'-digits	July 1	
26.	$8100	$600	5 years	Sum-of-years'-digits	Sept. 1	

Solve each of the following word problems. Round to the nearest dollar.

27. Mama's Pies purchased a new oven at a cost of $6800. The expected life is 5000 hours of production, at which time it will have a salvage value of $500. Prepare a depreciation schedule using the units-of-production method given the following production.

Year 1	1350 hours
Year 2	1820 hours
Year 3	730 hours
Year 4	1100 hours

Year	Computation	Amount of Depreciation	Accumulated Depreciation	Book Value
0	—	—	—	$6800
1				
2				
3				
4				

28. Norma Foust purchased a Kenworth Truck at a cost of $85,000. She estimates that it is good for 250,000 miles and will have a salvage value of $20,000. Use the units-of-production method to prepare a depreciation schedule given the following production.

Year 1	125,000 miles
Year 2	70,000 miles
Year 3	55,000 miles

Year	Computation	Amount of Depreciation	Accumulated Depreciation	Book Value
0	—	—	—	$85,000
1				
2				
3				

29. A bubble pack machine costs $22,000, has a scrap value of $5000, and has an estimated life of 10,000 hours. Find the depreciation for a year in which the machine was in operation 1800 hours.

30. A cardboard crusher costs $13,800, has an estimated salvage value of $2400, and has an expected life of 300,000 units. Find (a) the amount of depreciation each year and (b) the book value at the end of each year. Use the units-of-production method of depreciation given the following production schedule.

Year 1	36,000 units
Year 2	42,000 units
Year 3	39,000 units

31. A new irrigation system costs $78,000, has an estimated life of 10 years, and a scrap value of $5000. If the straight-line method of depreciation is used and the system is purchased on October 1, find the first partial-year depreciation.

32. A new roof is purchased on April 1 at a cost of $4800. The estimated life is 15 years and there is no scrap value. Use the sum-of-the-years'-digits to find the first partial year's depreciation and the following full year's depreciation.

33. Action Answering Service purchased a $14,200 switching system on July 1. The estimated life of the system is 8 years and the salvage value is $3000. Use the double-declining-balance method of depreciation to find the first partial-year's depreciation and the following full year's depreciation.

34. The Diet Center bought new office furniture on September 1. The cost of the furniture is $3800, the salvage value is $300, and expected life is 4 years. Use the sum-of-the-years'-digits to find the first partial-year's depreciation and the following full year's depreciation.

16.5 Modified Accelerated Cost Recovery System

OBJECTIVES

1 Understand the modified accelerated recovery system (MACRS).

2 Determine the recovery period of different types of property.

3 Find the depreciation rate given the recovery period and recovery year.

4 Use the MACRS method to find the amount of depreciation.

5 Prepare a depreciation schedule using the MACRS.

1 A depreciation method known as the **accelerated cost recovery system (ACRS)** originated as part of the Economic Recovery Tax Act of 1981. It was later modified by the Tax Equity and Fiscal Responsibility Act of 1982 and again by the Tax Reform Act of 1984. The Tax Reform Act of 1986 brought the most recent and significant overhaul to the accelerated cost recovery system (ACRS), and applies to all property placed in service after 1986. This new method is known as the **modified accelerated cost recovery system (MACRS)**. The result is that there are now three systems for computing depreciation for federal tax purposes.

1. The MACRS method of depreciation is used for all property placed in service after 1986.

2. The ACRS method of depreciation will continue to be used for all property placed in service from 1981 through 1986.

3. The straight-line, declining-balance, and sum-of-the-years'-digits methods continue to be used if the property was placed in service before 1981.

NOTE The units-of-production method of depreciation is still allowed under the MACRS.

Keep two things in mind about MACRS: First, the system is designed, really, for tax purposes (it is sometimes called the **income tax method**), and businesses often use some alternate method of depreciation (in addition to MACRS) for financial accounting purposes. Second, most states do not allow the modified accelerated cost recovery system of depreciation for finding state income tax liability. This means businesses must use the MACRS on the federal tax return and one of the previous methods on the state tax return.

2 Under the modified accelerated cost recovery system, assets are placed in one of eight **recovery classes**, depending on whether the law assumes a 3-, 5-, 7-, 10-, 15-, 20-, 27.5-, or 31.5-year life for the asset. These lives, or **recovery periods**, are determined as follows.

3-year property	Tractor units for over-the-road use, any race horse that is over 2 years old, or any other horse that is over 12 years old
5-year property	Automobiles, trucks, buses, computers and peripheral equipment, office machinery (typewriters, calculators), copiers, and research equipment
7-year property	Office furniture and fixtures (desks, files), and any property not designated by law to be in any other class
10-year property	Vessels, barges, tugs, and similar water transportation equipment
15-year property	Wharves, roads, fences, and any municipal waste-water treatment plant
20-year property	Certain farm buildings and municipal sewers
27.5-year property	Residential rental real estate such as rental houses and apartments
31.5-year property	Nonresidential rental real estate such as office buildings, stores, and warehouses

EXAMPLE 1

Finding the Recovery Period for Property

Determine the recovery period for each of the following properties.

(**a**) an electric typewriter

(**b**) an industrial warehouse

(**c**) an automobile

(**d**) office furniture

(**e**) a farm building

SOLUTION Use the list just given.

(a) 5 years

(b) 31.5 years

(c) 5 years

(d) 7 years

(e) 20 years ■

3 With MACRS, salvage value is ignored, so that depreciation is based on the entire orginal cost of the asset. The depreciation rates are determined by applying the double-declining-balance (200%) method to the 3-, 5-, 7-, and 10-year class properties, the 150% declining-balance method to the 15- and 20-year class properties, and the straight-line (100%) method to the 27.5- and 31.5-year class properties. Since these calculations are repetitive and require additional knowledge, the Internal Revenue Service provides tables that show the depreciation rates expressed as percents. The rates are shown in Table 16.1. To determine the rate of depreciation for any year of life, find the recovery year in the left-hand column, and then read across to the allowable recovery period.

Notice that the number of recovery years is one greater than the class life of the property. This is because only a half year of depreciation is allowed for the first year that property is placed in service, regardless of when the property is placed in service during the year. This is known as the **half-year convention** and is used by most tax payers. A complete coverage of depreciation, including all depreciation tables, is included in the **Internal Revenue Service, Publication 534, Depreciation**, and may be obtained by contacting the IRS Forms Distribution Center.

CAUTION MACRS is the income tax method of depreciation and several important points should be remembered.
1. No salvage value is used.
2. The life of the asset is determined by using the recovery periods assigned to different types of property.
3. A depreciation rate is usually found for each year by referring to a MACRS Table of Depreciation Rates.

EXAMPLE 2
Finding the Rate of Depreciation with MACRS

Find the rate of depreciation given the following recovery year and recovery period.

Recovery Year	Recovery Period	Recovery Year	Recovery Period
(a) 4	5-year	(c) 3	10-year
(b) 2	3-year	(d) 9	27.5-year

SOLUTION

(a) 11.52%   (b) 44.45%   (c) 14.40%   (d) 3.637% ■

TABLE 16.1   MACRS Depreciation Rates

Recovery Year	Applicable Percent for the Class of Property							
	3-year	5-year	7-year	10-year	15-year	20-year	27.5-year	31.5-year
1	33.33	20.00	14.29	10.00	5.00	3.750	1.818	1.587
2	44.45	32.00	24.49	18.00	9.50	7.219	3.636	3.175
3	14.81	19.20	17.49	14.40	8.55	6.677	3.636	3.175
4	7.41	11.52	12.49	11.52	7.70	6.177	3.636	3.175
5		11.52	8.93	9.22	6.93	5.713	3.636	3.175
6		5.76	8.92	7.37	6.23	5.285	3.636	3.175
7			8.93	6.55	5.90	4.888	3.636	3.175
8			4.46	6.55	5.90	4.522	3.636	3.175
9				6.56	5.91	4.462	3.637	3.175
10				6.55	5.90	4.461	3.636	3.174
11				3.28	5.91	4.462	3.637	3.175
12					5.90	4.461	3.636	3.174
13					5.91	4.462	3.637	3.175
14					5.90	4.461	3.636	3.174
15					5.91	4.462	3.637	3.175
16					2.95	4.461	3.636	3.174
17						4.462	3.637	3.175
18						4.461	3.636	3.174
19						4.462	3.637	3.175
20						4.461	3.636	3.174
21						2.231	3.637	3.175
22							3.636	3.174
23							3.637	3.175
24							3.636	3.174
25							3.637	3.175
26							3.636	3.174
27							3.637	3.175
28							3.636	3.174
29								3.175
30								3.174
31								3.175
32								3.174

4   No salvage value is subtracted from the cost of property. Under the MACRS method, the depreciation rate multiplied by the full cost determines the depreciation amount.

Depreciation by the MACRS method is given by

$$d = r \times c$$

where d is the depreciation for a rate r (from Table 16.1) and an original cost c.

EXAMPLE 3

Finding the Amount of Depreciation with MACRS

Find the amount of depreciation in the third year for an offset printer costing $6450.

SOLUTION   Since a printer is equipment, the recovery period is 5 years. From Table 16.1, the depreciation rate in the third year of recovery of 5-year property is 19.20%. Multiply this rate by the full cost of the property to determine the amount of depreciation.

$$19.20\% \times \$6450 = \$1238.40$$

The amount of depreciation is $1238 (rounded to the nearest dollar).   ∎

EXAMPLE 4

Preparing a Depreciation Schedule with MACRS

Omaha Insurance Company has purchased desks and chairs at a cost of $24,160. Prepare a depreciation schedule using the modified accelerated cost recovery system.

5   SOLUTION   No salvage value is used with MACRS. Office desks and chairs have a 7-year recovery period. The annual depreciation rates for 7-year property are as follows.

Recovery Year	Recovery Percent (Rate)
1	14.29%
2	24.49%
3	17.49%
4	12.49%
5	8.93%
6	8.92%
7	8.93%
8	4.46%

Multiply the appropriate percents by $24,160 to get the results shown in the following depreciation schedule.

Year	Computation	Amount of Depreciation	Accumulated Depreciation	Book Value
0	—	—	—	$24,160
1	(14.29% × $24,160)	$3452	$3452	$20,708
2	(24.49% × $24,160)	$5917	$9369	$14,791
3	(17.49% × $24,160)	$4226	$13,595	$10,565
4	(12.49% × $24,160)	$3018	$16,613	$7547
5	(8.93% × $24,160)	$2157	$18,770	$5390
6	(8.92% × $24,160)	$2155	$20,925	$3235
7	(8.93% × $24,160)	$2157	$23,082	$1078
8	(4.46% × $24,160)	$1078	$24,160	$0

The MACRS method of depreciation allows a rapid rate of investment recovery and at the same time results in a less complicated computation. By eliminating the necessity of estimating the life of an asset and the need for using a salvage value, the tables provide a more direct method of calculating depreciation.

Current tax law allows a business to elect to treat some of the cost of depreciable property as an expense in the year of purchase. The maximum dollar amount that may be taken is currently $10,000. There are several limitations to this deduction, making it important for the taxpayer to check with the Internal Revenue Service or a tax expert.

16.5 Exercises

Use Table 16.1 to find the recovery percent (rate) given the following recovery year and recovery period.

	Recovery Year	Recovery Period			Recovery Year	Recovery Period
1.	1	3-year		**2.**	1	5-year
3.	1	10-year		**4.**	1	20-year
5.	3	7-year		**6.**	2	3-year
7.	14	27.5-year		**8.**	6	31.5-year
9.	4	3-year		**10.**	4	27.5-year
11.	7	20-year		**12.**	4	31.5-year

Round to the nearest dollar in all these exercises.

Find the first year's depreciation for each of the following, using the MACRS method of depreciation.

13. Cost: $44,780
Recovery period: 10 years

14. Cost: $22,600
Recovery period: 20 years

15. Cost: $9680
Recovery period: 3 years

16. Cost: $640
Recovery period: 5 years

17. Cost: $430,500
Recovery period: 27.5 years

18. Cost: $786,400
Recovery period: 31.5 years

Find the book value at the end of the first year for each of the following, using the MACRS method of depreciation.

19. Cost: $32,750
Recovery period: 10 years

20. Cost: $10,820
Recovery period: 15 years

21. Cost: $137,000
Recovery period: 27.5 years

22. Cost: $370,500
Recovery period: 31.5 years

Find the book value at the end of 3 years for each of the following, using the MACRS method of depreciation.

23. Cost: $8850
   Recovery period: 3 years

24. Cost: $26,200
   Recovery period: 10 years

25. Cost: $87,300
   Recovery period: 27.5 years

26. Cost: $390,800
   Recovery period: 31.5 years

27. The same business asset may be depreciated using two or more different methods. Explain why a business would do this. (See Objective 1.)

28. After learning about MACRS, what three features stand out to you as being unique to this method? (See Objective 3.)

Solve the following word problems.

29. Foothill Backhoe purchased a tractor for $10,980. Prepare a depreciation schedule using the MACRS method of depreciation. Round to the nearest dollar.

Year	Computation	Amount of Depreciation	Accumulated Depreciation	Book Value
0	—	—	—	$10,980
1				
2				
3				
4				

30. Inventory Plus purchased new research equipment for $6240. Prepare a depreciation schedule using the MACRS method of depreciation. Round to the nearest dollar.

Year	Computation	Amount of Depreciation	Accumulated Depreciation	Book Value
0	—	—	—	$6240
1				
2				
3				
4				
5				
6				

31. Gulf Drilling purchased a tugboat for $122,700. Prepare a depreciation schedule using the MACRS method of depreciation.

32. Ken Albers purchased a desktop computer for his office for $5800. Prepare a depreciation schedule using the MACRS method of depreciation.

33. Shirley Cicero purchased an apartment building for $285,000. Find the book value at the end of the tenth year using the MACRS method of depreciation.

34. Delta Dental purchased new office furniture at a cost of $13,800. Find the book value at the end of the fifth year using the MACRS method of depreciation.

35. Bralley's Bookkeeping purchased a new office building at a cost of $225,000. Find the amount of depreciation each year for the first five years using the MACRS method of depreciation.

36. Dick and Jeanne Hill bought a new building for their business, Oaks Hardware, at a cost of $450,000. Find the amount of depreciation each year for the first five years using the MACRS method of depreciation.

CHAPTER 16 QUICK REVIEW

TOPIC	APPROACH	EXAMPLE
16.1 Straight-line method of depreciation	The depreciation is the same each year. Use the formula $$d = \frac{c - s}{n}$$ with $c = $ cost, $s = $ salvage value, and $n = $ life (in years)	Cost, $500; salvage value, $100; life, 8 years. Find the annual depreciation. $$d = \frac{\$500 - \$100}{8} = \frac{\$400}{8} = \$50$$
16.1 Book value	Book value is the value remaining at the end of the year. Cost minus accumulated depreciation equals book value.	Cost, $400; salvage value, $100; life, 3 years. Find the book value at the end of the first year. $$d = \frac{\$400 - \$100}{3} = \frac{\$300}{3} = \$100$$ Book value $= \$400 - \$100 = \$300$
16.2 Double-declining-balance rate	First, find the straight-line rate, then adjust it as follows: 200%: multiply by 2 150%: multiply by $1\frac{1}{2}$ 125%: multiply by $1\frac{1}{4}$	Life of an asset is 10 years. Find the double-declining-balance (200%) rate. $$10 \text{ year} = 10\%\left(\frac{1}{10}\right) \text{ straight-line}$$ $$2 \times 10\% = 20\%$$

TOPIC	APPROACH	EXAMPLE
16.2 Double-declining-balance depreciation method	First, find the double-declining-balance rate; then use the formula $d = r \times b$ where b is total cost in the first year and the declining-balance in the following years.	Cost, $1400; life, 5 years. Find depreciation in years 1 and 2. $2 \times 20\%$ (straight-line rate) $= 40\%$ Year 1: Depreciation $= 40\% \times \$1400 = \$560$ Book Value $= \$1400 - \$560 = \$840$ Year 2: Depreciation $= 40\% \times \$840 = \$336$

16.3 Sum-of-the-years'-digits depreciation fraction

Add the years' digits together to get the denominator. The numerator is the number of years of life remaining. The denominator shortcut is

$$\text{Sum-of-the-years'-digits} = \frac{n(n + 1)}{2}$$

Useful life is 4 years. Find the depreciation fraction for each year.

$1 + 2 + 3 + 4 = 10$

Year	Depreciation Fraction
1	$\dfrac{4}{10}$
2	$\dfrac{3}{10}$
3	$\dfrac{2}{10}$
4	$\dfrac{1}{10}$

16.3 Sum-of-the-years'-digits depreciation method

First find the depreciation fraction, and then use the formula

$$d = r \times (c - s).$$

Cost, $2500; salvage value, $400; life, 6 years. Find depreciation in year 1.

$$\text{Depreciation fraction} = \frac{6}{21}$$

$$d = \frac{6}{21} \times (\$2500 - \$400)$$

$$= \frac{6}{21} \times \$2100 = \$600$$

16.4 Units-of-production depreciation amount per unit

Use the formula

$$\text{Depreciation per unit} = \frac{\text{Depreciable amount}}{\text{Units of life}}.$$

Cost $10,000; salvage value, $2500; useful life, 15,000 units. Find depreciation per unit.

$$\text{Depreciation per unit} =$$
$$\frac{\$7500 \text{ depreciable amount}}{15,000 \text{ units of life}} = \$.50$$

16.4 Units-of-production depreciation method

Multiply the depreciation per unit (hour) by the number of units (hours) of production.

In the preceding example: first year's production, 3800 units. Find depreciation in year 1.

$3800 \times \$.50 = \$1900$

TOPIC	APPROACH	EXAMPLE
16.4 Partial-year depreciation	If an asset is purchased during the year, take only a fraction of the year's depreciation.	Depreciable amount, \$4500; life, 5 years; date purchased, June 1. Find first partial-year depreciation by straight-line method. $7 \text{ months} = \dfrac{7}{12} \text{ year}$ $\dfrac{\$4500}{5} \times \dfrac{7}{12} = \$525$
16.5 Modified accelerated cost recovery system (MACRS)	Established in 1986 for federal tax. No salvage value. Recovery periods are: 3-year 15-year 5-year 20-year 7-year 27.5-year 10-year 31.5-year Use the formula $$d = r \times c$$ with rate from Table 16.1.	Cost, \$4850; recovery period, 5 years; recovery year, 3. Find the depreciation. Find 5-year recovery period column at top of Table 16.1, and recovery year 3 in leftmost column; rate is 19.20% $d = 19.20\% \times \$4850 = \$931.20$

SUMMARY EXERCISE

Miller's Markets purchased fixtures at a cost of \$165,000. The estimated life of the fixtures is 5 years, at which time they will have no salvage value. The company would like to compare allowable depreciation methods and decides to prepare depreciation schedules for the fixtures using the straight-line, double-declining-balance, and the sum-of-the-years'-digits methods of depreciation. Using the depreciation schedules, the company wants to answer the following questions. Find the answers to these questions for Miller's Markets.

(a) What is the book value at the end of 3 years using the straight-line depreciation method?

(b) With the sum-of-the-year's-digits method of depreciation, what is the accumulated depreciation at the end of 3 years?

(c) Using the declining-balance method of depreciation, what is the book value at the end of the third year?

(d) What amount of depreciation will be taken in year 4 with each of the methods.

CHAPTER 16 REVIEW EXERCISES

Find the annual straight-line and double-declining-balance rates (percents) of deprecia-tion and the sum-of-the-years'-digits fractions in the first year for each of the following estimated lives. [16.1–16.3]

1. 5 years   **2.** 4 years   **3.** 3 years

4. 10 years   **5.** 6 years   **6.** 8 years

Use Table 16.1 to find the recovery percent (rate) given the following recovery year and recovery period. [16.5]

Recovery Year	Recovery Period		Recovery Year	Recovery Period
7. 2	3-year	**8.**	4	5-year
9. 11	15-year	**10.**	3	7-year
11. 15	27.5-year	**12.**	20	31.5-year

Work the following word problems. Round to the nearest dollar if necessary.

13. Use the straight-line method of depreciation to find the amount of depreciation that should be charged off each year for an industrial freezer that cost $4884, has an estimated life of 4 years, and a scrap value of $800. [16.1]

14. The machinery in a small dry-cleaning plant cost $86,000, has an estimated life of 50 years and an estimated scrap value of $9000. Use the straight-line method of depreciation to find the book value of the machinery at the end of 8 years. [16.2]

15. A landscape contractor purchased a scraper at a cost of $22,000. If the estimated life of the scraper is 10 years, find the book value at the end of 3 years using the double-declining-balance method of depreciation. [16.2]

16. Mardi Gras Barbers bought several chairs at a total cost of $6500. The estimated life of the chairs is 6 years and there is no scrap value. Find the depreciation in the first year using the double-declining-balance method of depreciation. [16.2]

17. Better Home Real Estate purchased cellular phone units and all accessories for its 16-person sales staff. The equipment has a total cost of $2700, an estimated life of 6 years, and a salvage value of $450. Use the sum-of-the-years'-digits method of depreciation to find the book value for all cellular phone equipment at the end of the third year. [16.3]

18. Murray's Delicatessen purchased a new display case for $7375. It has an estimated life of 10 years, and salvage value of $500. Use the sum-of-the-year's-digits method of depreciation to find the book value at the end of the third year. [16.3]

19. A grape press costs $11,000, has a scrap value of $2500, and an estimated life of 5000 hours. Use the units-of-production method to find the depreciation for a year in which the machine was in operation 900 hours. [16.4]

20. A canning machine costs $27,600, has an estimated salvage value of $4800, and an expected life of 150,000 units. Find (a) the amount of depreciation each year and (b) the book value at the end of each year. Use the units-of-production method of depreciation given the following production schedule.

    Year 1   18,000 units
    Year 2   21,000 units
    Year 3   39,000 units   [16.4]

21. Dave's Auto Body and Paint purchased a prefabricated warehouse at a cost of $30,000. The estimated life of the warehouse is 15 years and the scrap value is $4500. Find the book value at the end of 10 years, using the straight-line method of depreciation. [16.1]

22. Using the sum-of-the-years'-digits method of depreciation, find the amount of depreciation to be charged off *each year* on an earth mover that cost $124,800, has an estimated life of 5 years, and a scrap value of $24,500. [16.3]

23. A recycled glass crusher costs $48,000, has an estimated life of 5 years, and a scrap value of $4500. If the straight-line method of depreciation is used and the system is purchased on September 1, find the first partial-year depreciation. [16.4]

24. A parking lot is resurfaced on June 1 at a cost of $9720. The estimated life is 8 years and there is no scrap value. Use the sum-of-the-years'-digits method to find the first year's depreciation and the following full year's depreciation. [16.4]

25. Instant Copy Service purchased a new copy system at a cost of $28,400 on July 1. The estimated life of the system is 10 years and the salvage value is $6000. Use the double-declining-balance method of depreciation to find the first partial-year's depreciation and the following full year's depreciation. [16.4]

26. An automatic car wash machine that cost $9250 has a scrap value of $1000 and an estimated life of 6 years. Use the sum-of-the-years'-digits method of depreciation to find the book value at the end of the third year. [16.3]

27. A job printer purchased an automatic composer at a cost of $15,000. If the estimated life of the composer is 8 years, find the book value at the end of 4 years, using the double-declining-balance method of depreciation. Assume no scrap value. [16.2]

28. Century Sales purchased a new videotape training program for use by its training manager. The total cost of the program was $5400; it has an estimated life of 5 years and a salvage value of $600. Use the sum-of-the-years'-digits method of depreciation to find the book value of the program of the end of the second year. [16.3]

29. King's Table bought new dining room tables at a cost of $14,750. If the estimated life of the tables is 8 years, at which time they will be worthless, and the double-declining-balance method of depreciation is used, find the book value at the end of the third year. [16.2]

30. Use the MACRS method of depreciation to find the amount of depreciation to be taken during each of the 4 years on a $19,600 tractor that is 3-year property. [16.5]

31. Kathy Woodward purchased a new refrigeration system (7-year property) for her flower shop at a cost of $8100. Find the amount of depreciation for each of the first five years using the MACRS method of depreciation. [16.5]

32. An investor purchased a new warehouse (31.5-year property) for $235,000. Find the book value at the end of the fifth year using the MACRS method of depreciation. [16.5]

17

Financial Statements and Ratios

[handwritten annotations: GROSS SALES – RET. TO NET SALES – COST OF GOODS SOLD TO GROSS PROFIT – OPER. TO NET INCOME EXPS.]

A business owner or manager must keep careful records of the expenses and income of the business. Only by paying careful attention to income and expenses will an adequate net income be provided for the firm. Companies use bookkeepers to help keep track of the money coming in and going out, while accountants answer questions like "Why is this year's net income less than last year's?"; "How do our business expenses compare to those of similar firms?"; and "Have our expenses for overhead increased as a percent of sales?" This chapter discusses some of the methods used by accountants to answer these and other questions.

17.1 The Income Statement

OBJECTIVES

1 Learn the terms used with income statements.
2 Calculate net income.
3 Complete an income statement.

1 An **income statement** is prepared for the management and owners of a business to summarize all income and expenses for a given period of time, such as a month or a year. As a first step, find the **gross sales,** the total amount of money received from customers for the goods or services sold by the firm. Then subtract the value of any **returns** from customers to arrive at **net sales,** the value of the goods and services bought and kept by customers. Use the following formula.

$$\text{Net sales} = \text{Gross sales} - \text{Returns}$$

After finding net sales, look at company records to find the **cost of goods sold,** the amount paid by the firm for the items sold to customers during the period of time covered by the income statement. Then subtract the cost of goods sold from the net sales to find the **gross profit.**

Gross profit = Net sales − Cost of goods sold

The gross profit is the amount of money left over after the business pays for the goods it sells. Some of this money is used to pay the operating expenses involved in running the business.

Operating expenses represent the amount paid by the firm in an attempt to sell its goods. Common expenses include rent, salaries and wages, advertising, utilities, losses from uncollectible accounts, and taxes on inventory and payroll. Operating expenses are sometimes called **overhead.**

Finally, **net income,** the actual amount earned by the firm during the given time period, is found with the following formula.

Net Income = Gross profit − Operating expenses

2 The key formulas for use with income statements are summarized as follows.

Net sales
− Cost of goods sold

Gross profit
− Operating expenses

Net income

EXAMPLE 1
Finding Net Income

In one year, Walter's Card Shop had net sales of $186,000; the cost of goods sold was $114,000. The operating expenses totaled $41,000. Find the net income for the year.

SOLUTION   Use the formulas in the box. Start by finding the gross profit.

Gross profit = Net sales − Cost of goods sold

$= \$186{,}000 - \$114{,}000$

$= \$72{,}000$

Walter's had a gross profit of $72,000 left over after paying for the goods it sold. This amount is used to pay all the expenses of running the shop. Now find the net income.

$$\text{Net income} = \text{Gross profit} - \text{Operating expenses}$$

$$= \$72,000 - \$41,000$$

$$= \$31,000$$

After paying for all goods sold and all operating expenses, Walter's had a net income of $31,000. These results can be summarized as in the following income statement. ∎

WALTER'S CARD SHOP INCOME STATEMENT FOR THE YEAR ENDING DECEMBER 31	
Net Sales	$186,000
Cost of Goods Sold	−114,000
Gross Profit	$72,000
Operating Expenses	−41,000
Net Income	$31,000

3 The two basic formulas can be combined into the following single formula.

> Cost of goods sold + Expenses + Net income = Net sales

This formula can be used to check the results shown on the income statement for Walter's Card Shop in Example 1.

Cost of goods + Expenses + Net income = Net sales

$$\$114,000 \ + \ \$41,000 + \ \ \$31,000 \ \ = \$186,000$$

The example for Walter's Card Shop shows the basics of an income statement, but contains far too little information to be of practical use to a business person. In particular, Example 1 gives the value for the cost of goods sold. In a realistic situation, this amount would have to be calculated. Find the cost of goods sold with the following formula, where **inventory** represents the value of all goods on hand for sale, either at the beginning or the end of the time period, as appropriate.

> Cost of goods sold = Initial inventory
> + Cost of goods purchased during time period
> + Freight − Inventory at end of time period

Notice how this formula is used in the following example.

EXAMPLE 2

Preparing an Income Statement

Josie's Clothing had gross sales of $159,000 during the past year, with returns of $9000. Inventory on January 1 of last year was $47,000. A total of $104,000 worth of goods was purchased last year, with freight on the goods totaling $2000. Inventory on December 31 of last year was $56,000. Wages paid to employees totaled $18,000. Rent was $9000, advertising was $1000, utilities totaled $2000, and taxes on inventory and payroll totaled $4000. Miscellaneous expenses totaled $6000. Complete an income statement for the store.

SOLUTION   Go through the steps on the following page, which refer to the income statement in Figure 17.1.

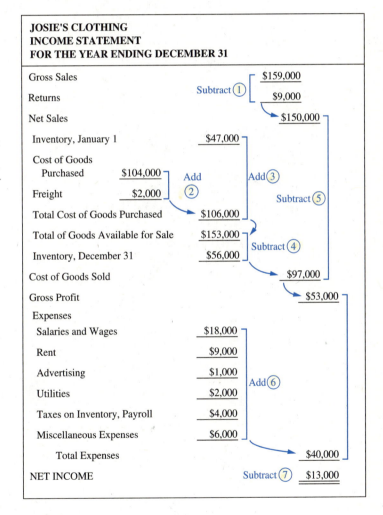

JOSIE'S CLOTHING
INCOME STATEMENT
FOR THE YEAR ENDING DECEMBER 31

Gross Sales		$159,000
Returns	Subtract ①	$9,000
Net Sales		$150,000
Inventory, January 1	$47,000	
Cost of Goods Purchased	$104,000	Add ③
Freight	$2,000	Subtract ⑤
Total Cost of Goods Purchased	$106,000	
Total of Goods Available for Sale	$153,000	
Inventory, December 31	$56,000	Subtract ④
Cost of Goods Sold		$97,000
Gross Profit		$53,000
Expenses		
Salaries and Wages	$18,000	
Rent	$9,000	
Advertising	$1,000	Add ⑥
Utilities	$2,000	
Taxes on Inventory, Payroll	$4,000	
Miscellaneous Expenses	$6,000	
Total Expenses		$40,000
NET INCOME	Subtract ⑦	$13,000

FIGURE 17.1

Step 1.   Enter gross sales and sales returns. Subtract sales returns from gross sales to find net sales. Net sales in this example were $150,000.

Step 2.   Enter the cost of goods purchased and the freight. Add these two numbers.

Step 3.   Add the inventory on January 1 and the total cost of goods purchased.

Step 4.   Subtract the inventory on December 31 from the result of Step 3. This gives the cost of goods sold.

Step 5.   Subtract the cost of goods sold from net sales, which were found in Step 1. The result is the gross profit.

Step 6.   Enter all expenses and add them to get the total expenses.

Step 7.   Subtract total expenses from gross profit. The result is the net income. ■

NOTE Be sure to check the results of your income statement by adding the cost of goods sold, expenses, and net income. This total should equal the net sales.

17.1 Exercises

Find the gross profit and the net income for each firm.

1. Last year Barker's Flowers had a cost of goods sold of $132,000, operating expenses of $64,000, and net sales of $212,000.

2. The Collegiate Bookstore had net sales of $376,000, operating expenses of $36,000, and cost of goods sold of $294,000.

Find the cost of goods sold for the following firms.

3. At Eastside Auto Parts the inventory on January 1 was $423,000, with $174,000 worth of goods purchased during the year. Freight was $3400 and the inventory on December 31 was $372,000.

4. On January 1 the inventory at Wilson Medical Supplies was valued at $504,000. The firm paid freight of $9600 during the year on its purchases of $362,000 worth of goods. The inventory on December 31 was $517,000.

Complete the accompanying income statements for the firms in Exercises 5–7.

5. Carmichael Auto Parts had gross sales of $284,000 last year, with returns of $6000. The inventory on January 1 was $58,000. A total of $232,000 worth of goods was purchased, with freight of $3000. The inventory on December 31 was $69,000. Salaries and wages were $15,000, rent was $6000, advertising was $2000, utilities were $1000, taxes on inventory and payroll totaled $3000, and miscellaneous expenses totaled $4000.

CARMICHAEL AUTO PARTS
INCOME STATEMENT
YEAR ENDING DECEMBER 31

Gross Sales	284,000
Returns	6,000
Net Sales	278,000
Inventory, January 1	58,000
Cost of Goods Purchased	232,000
Freight	3,000
Total Cost of Goods Purchased	235,000
Total of Goods Available for Sale	293,000
Inventory, December 31	69,000
Cost of Goods Sold	224,000
Gross Profit	54,000
Expenses	
Salaries and Wages	15,000
Rent	6,000
Advertising	2,000
Utilities	1,000
Taxes on Inventory, Payroll	3,000
Miscellaneous Expenses	4,000
Total Expenses	31,000
NET INCOME	23,000

6. New England Dental Supply is a regional wholesaler which had gross sales last year of $2,215,000. Returns totaled $26,000. Inventory on January 1 was $215,000. Goods purchased during the year totaled $1,123,000. Freight was $4000. Inventory on December 31 was $265,000. Salaries and wages were $154,000, rent was $59,000, advertising was $11,000, utilities were $12,000, taxes on inventory and payroll totaled $10,000, and miscellaneous expenses were $9000.

NEW ENGLAND DENTAL SUPPLY
INCOME STATEMENT
YEAR ENDING DECEMBER 31

Gross Sales		2,215,000
Returns		26,000
Net Sales		2,189,000
Inventory, January 1	215,000	
Cost of Goods Purchased	1,123,000	
Freight	4000	
Total Cost of Goods Purchased	1,127,000	
Total of Goods Available for Sale	1,342,000	
Inventory, December 31	1,077,000	
Cost of Goods Sold		265,000
Gross Profit		1,924,000
Expenses		
Salaries and Wages	154,000	
Rent	59,000	
Advertising	11,000	
Utilities	12,000	
Taxes on Inventory, Payroll	10,000	
Miscellaneous Expenses	9,000	
Total Expenses		255,000
NET INCOME		1,669,000

7. Norman's Auto Mart had gross sales of $326,000 last year, with returns of $7000. The inventory on January 1 was $22,000. A total of $125,000 worth of goods was purchased during the year, with freight of $5000. The inventory on December 31 was $26,000. Salaries and wages totaled $32,000, advertising was $29,000, rent was $16,000, utilities were $4000, taxes on inventory and payroll were $7000, and miscellaneous expenses totaled $8000.

NORMAN'S AUTO MART
INCOME STATEMENT
FOR THE YEAR ENDING DECEMBER 31

Gross Sales		326,000
Returns		− 7,000
Net Sales		319,000
Inventory, January 1	22,000	
Cost of Goods Purchased	125,000	
Freight	5,000	
Total Cost of Goods Purchased	130,000	
Total of Goods Available for Sale	152,000	
Inventory, December 31	26,000	
Cost of Goods Sold		126000
Gross Profit		193,000
Expenses		
Salaries and Wages	32,000	
Rent	16,000	
Advertising	29,000	
Utilities	4,000	
Taxes on Inventory, Payroll	7,000	
Miscellaneous Expenses	8,000	
Total Expenses		96,000
NET INCOME		97,000

8. Outline the method used to calculate the cost of goods sold.

9. (a) Discuss the purpose of an income statement.
    (b) Outline the basic structure of an income statement. (See Objective 2.)

17.2 Analyzing the Income Statement

OBJECTIVES

1 Compare income statements using vertical analysis.

2 Calculate percents of net sales.

3 Compare an income statement with published charts.

4 Prepare a horizontal analysis.

By going through the steps presented in the previous section, a firm can find its net income for a given period of time. A question which might be asked is, "What happened to each part of the sales dollar?" The first step toward answering this question is to list each of the important items on the income statement as a percent of net sales, in a process called a **vertical analysis** of the income statement.

1 A vertical analysis of an income statement is another application of the fundamental formula for percent from Chapter 3, $P = RB$. Since a percent is needed, the formula must be solved for the rate R, as in the next box.

> In a vertical analysis, each item is found as a percent of net sales.
>
> $$\left(R = \frac{P}{B}\right) \quad \text{or} \quad \left(R = \frac{\text{Particular item}}{\text{Net sales}}\right)$$

EXAMPLE 1
Performing a Vertical Analysis

Perform a vertical analysis of the income statement for Walter's Card Shop from the previous section. The income statement is repeated here for reference.

WALTER'S CARD SHOP INCOME STATEMENT FOR THE YEAR ENDING DECEMBER 31	
Net Sales	$186,000
Cost of Goods Sold	−114,000
Gross Profit	$72,000
Operating Expenses	−41,000
Net Income	$31,000

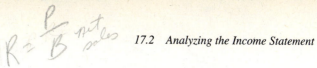

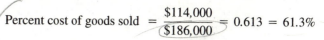

SOLUTION   First, find the cost of goods sold as a percent of net sales.

$$\text{Percent cost of goods sold} = \frac{\$114{,}000}{\$186{,}000} = 0.613 = 61.3\%$$

The cost of goods sold was 61.3% of net sales. Now do the same for gross profit, expenses, and net income.

$$\text{Percent gross profit} = \frac{\$72{,}000}{\$186{,}000} = 0.387 = 38.7\%$$

$$\text{Percent expenses} = \frac{\$41{,}000}{\$186{,}000} = 0.220 = 22.0\%$$

$$\text{Percent net income} = \frac{\$31{,}000}{\$186{,}000} = 0.167 = 16.7\%$$

2   The formula given in the previous section for checking income statements,

Cost of goods sold + Expenses + Net income = Net sales,

is just as valid for percents as for dollar amounts. Use the information from this example.

$$61.3\% + 22.0\% + 16.7\% = 100.0\%$$

Here 100.0% represents net sales. ■

EXAMPLE 2

Finding Percents of Net Sales

Write each of the following items as a percent of net sales.

Gross sales	$209,000	Salaries and wages	$11,000
Returns	$9000	Rent	$6000
Cost of goods sold	$145,000	Advertising	$11,000

SOLUTION   Use the formula for net sales, with gross sales = $209,000 and returns = $9000.

Net sales = Gross sales − Returns

Net sales = $209,000 − $9000 = $200,000

Now find all the desired percents.

$$\text{Percent gross sales} = \frac{\$209{,}000}{\$200{,}000} = 1.045 = 104.5\%$$

NOTE This percent is more than 100% because returns are included in it, but not in net sales.

$$\text{Percent returns} = \frac{\$9000}{\$200,000} = 0.045 = 4.5\%$$

$$\text{Percent cost of goods sold} = \frac{\$145,000}{\$200,000} = 0.725 = 72.5\%$$

$$\text{Percent salaries and wages} = \frac{\$11,000}{\$200,000} = 0.055 = 5.5\%$$

$$\text{Percent rent} = \frac{\$6000}{\$200,000} = 0.03 = 3\%$$

$$\text{Percent advertising} = \frac{\$11,000}{\$200,000} = 0.055 = 5.5\% \quad \blacksquare$$

To compare results for two different years, perform a vertical analysis for each of the two years. This results in a **comparative income statement.** A typical comparative income statement (for the Eastside Taxidermy Shop) is shown in Figure 17.2.

EASTSIDE TAXIDERMY SHOP
COMPARATIVE INCOME STATEMENT

	This Year		Last Year	
	Amount	**Percent**	**Amount**	**Percent**
Gross Sales	$924,000	100.4%	$808,000	101.0%
Returns	4000	0.4%	8000	1.0%
Net Sales	920,000	100.0%	800,000	100.0%
Cost of Goods Sold	723,000	78.6%	621,000	77.6%
Gross Profit	197,000	21.4%	179,000	22.4%
Wages	48,000	5.2%	43,000	5.4%
Rent	6000	0.7%	6000	0.8%
Advertising	18,000	2.0%	15,000	1.9%
Utilities	14,000	1.5%	7000	0.9%
Taxes on Inv., Payroll	13,000	1.4%	11,000	1.4%
Miscellaneous Expenses	35,000	3.8%	30,000	3.8%
Total Expenses	134,000	14.6%	112,000	14.0%
Net Income	63,000	6.8%	67,000	8.4%

FIGURE 17.2

3 Once the percent of net sales for each item on the income statement has been found, they can be compared to the percents for similar businesses. To do this, consult published charts which have the required data. One such chart is shown in Table 17.1. These charts are compiled by averaging statistics from many similar firms.

TABLE 17.1   Typical Percents

Type of Business	Cost of Goods	Gross Profit	Total Operating Expenses*	Net Income	Wages	Rent	Advertising
Supermarkets	82.7%	17.3%	13.9%	3.4%	6.5%	0.8%	1.0%
Men's and women's apparel	67.0%	33.0%	21.2%	11.8%	8.0%	2.5%	1.9%
Women's apparel	64.8%	35.2%	23.4%	11.7%	7.9%	4.9%	1.8%
Shoes	60.3%	39.7%	24.5%	15.2%	10.3%	4.7%	1.6%
Furniture	68.9%	31.2%	21.7%	9.6%	9.5%	1.8%	2.5%
Appliances	66.9%	33.1%	26.0%	7.2%	11.9%	2.4%	2.5%
Drugs	67.9%	32.1%	23.5%	8.6%	12.3%	2.4%	1.4%
Restaurants	48.4%	51.6%	43.7%	7.9%	26.4%	2.8%	1.4%
Service station	76.8%	23.2%	16.9%	6.3%	8.5%	2.3%	0.5%

* This column represents the total of all expenses involved in running the firm. Total operating expenses include, but are not limited to, wages, rent, and advertising.

For example, suppose Burton's Shoes calculates the percents of net sales as shown in the table, and then compares them to the figures given under "Shoes" in Table 17.1, with the following results.

	Cost of Goods	Gross Profit	Total Expenses	Net Income	Wages	Rent	Advertising
Burton's Shoes	58.2%	41.8%	28.3%	13.5%	11.7%	5.6%	2.8%
Shoes (from chart)	60.3%	39.7%	24.5%	15.2%	10.3%	4.7%	1.6%

This comparison shows that Burton's expenses are higher than the average for other shoe stores, while Burton's net income is lower. Wages are higher; this could be because Burton's is located in an area with high wages, or it could be because Burton's is not efficient in utilizing its employees. Burton's also spends a higher percent than the average for advertising. Advertising expenses should be lowered, if possible.

4   Another way to analyze an income statement is to prepare a **horizontal analysis.** A horizontal analysis finds percents of change (either increases or decreases) between the current time period and a previous time period. This comparison helps detect unusual changes, such as expenses that are increasing at a faster than usual rate. To perform a horizontal analysis, find the amount of any change from last year to this year, both in dollars and as a percent. For example, the income statement for the Eastside Taxidermy Shop given in Figure 17.2 shows that net sales increased from $800,000 last year to $920,000 this year, an increase of $920,000 − $800,000 = $120,000. Find the percent of increase by comparing this increase to last year's sales.

$$\frac{\$120,000}{\$800,000} = 0.15 = 15\%$$

> Percent of change = $\dfrac{\text{Change}}{\text{Last year's amount}}$
>
> Always use last year as the base.

The result of a horizontal analysis of a portion of an income statement for Eastside Taxidermy is shown in Figure 17.3.

NOTE Using standard accounting practice, decreases are shown in parentheses.

EASTSIDE TAXIDERMY SHOP
COMPARATIVE INCOME STATEMENT (PORTION)

	This Year	Last Year	Increase or (Decrease) Amount	Percent
Gross Sales	$924,000	$808,000	$116,000	14.4%
Returns	4000	8000	(4000)	(50.0%)
Net Sales	920,000	800,000	120,000	15.0%
Cost of Goods Sold	723,000	621,000	102,000	16.4%
Gross Profit	197,000	179,000	18,000	10.1%

FIGURE 17.3

17.2 Exercises

Prepare a vertical analysis for each of the following firms. Round percents to the nearest tenth of a percent.

1. Last year Barker's Flowers had a cost of goods sold of $94,000, operating expenses of $47,000, and net sales of $164,000.

$\frac{94,000}{164,000} = 57.3\%$

2. The Collegiate Bookstore had net sales of $376,000, operating expenses of $36,000, and cost of goods sold of $294,000.

$\frac{294,000}{376,000}$ 78.2%

NET SALES 376,000

The charts below show some figures from the income statements of several companies. For each firm, prepare a vertical analysis by expressing each item as a percent of net sales. Then write in the appropriate percent from Table 17.1. Round percents to the nearest tenth of a percent.

3.

VERTICAL ANALYSIS

HANDY ANDY APPLIANCES

	Amount	Percent	Percent from Table 17.1
Net Sales	DENOM $750,000	100.0%	100.0%
Cost of Goods Sold	488,000 / 750,000 488,000	65.1	66.9
Gross Profit	262,000	34.9	33.1
Wages	85,000	11.3	11.9
Rent	20,000	2.7	2.4
Advertising	18,000	2.4	2.5
Total Expenses	210,000	28	26.0
Net Income	52,000	6.9	7.2

4.

ELLIS RESTAURANT

	Amount	Percent	Percent from Table 17.1
Net Sales	$600,000	100.0%	100.0%
Cost of Goods Sold	280,000	46.7	————
Gross Profit	320,000	————	————
Wages	160,000	————	————
Rent	15,000	————	————
Advertising	8000	————	————
Total Expenses	255,000	————	————
Net Income	65,000	————	————

Complete the following comparative income statement. Round percents to the nearest tenth of a percent.

5.

HERNANDEZ NURSERY
COMPARATIVE INCOME STATEMENT

	This Year		Last Year	
	Amount	**Percent**	**Amount**	**Percent**
Gross Sales	$1,856,000 *(1,856,000 / 1,850,000)*	100.3	$1,692,000	100.7
Returns	6000	.3	12,000	.7
Net Sales *(DENOM)*	1,850,000	100.0%	1,680,000	100.0%
Cost of Goods Sold	1,202,000	65%	1,050,000	62.5
Gross Profit	648,000	35%	630,000	37.5
Wages	152,000	8.2%	148,000	8.8
Rent	82,000	4.4	78,000	4.6
Advertising	111,000	6%	122,000	7.3
Utilities	32,000	1.7	17,000	1.0
Taxes on Inv., Payroll	17,000	.9	18,000	1.1
Miscellaneous Expenses	62,000	3.4	58,000	3.5
Total Expenses	456,000	24.6	441,000	26.3
Net Income	192,000	10.4	189,000	11.3

Complete the following horizontal analysis for the Hernandez Nursery comparative income statement given above. Round percents to the nearest tenth of a percent.

6.

			Increase or (Decrease)	
	This Year	**Last Year**	**Amount**	**Percent**
Gross Sales	$1,856,000	$1,692,000	_____	_____
Returns	6000	12,000	_____	_____
Net Sales	1,850,000	1,680,000	_____	_____
Cost of Goods Sold	1,202,000	1,050,000	_____	_____
Gross Profit	648,000	630,000	_____	_____
Wages	152,000	148,000	_____	_____
Rent	82,000	78,000	_____	_____
Advertising	111,000	122,000	_____	_____
Utilities	32,000	17,000	_____	_____
Taxes on Inv., Payroll	17,000	18,000	_____	_____
Miscellaneous Expenses	62,000	58,000	_____	_____
Net Income	192,000	189,000	_____	_____

The following tables give the percents for various items from the income statements of firms in various businesses. Complete these tables by including the appropriate percents from Table 17.1. Identify any areas that might require attention by management.

Type of Store	Cost of Goods	Gross Profit	Total Operating Expenses	Net Income	Wages	Rent	Advertising
7. Drug	69.4%	30.6%	27.9%	2.7%	17.4%	2.9%	1.7%
8. Service station	74.2%	25.8%	17.1%	8.7%	9.1%	2.1%	0.7%
9. Furniture	65.4%	34.6%	24.9%	9.7%	10.8%	2.0%	1.6%
10. Restaurant	57.8%	42.2%	38.6%	3.6%	28.1%	2.4%	1.0%

11. Explain how to prepare a vertical analysis of an income statement. (See Objective 1.)

12. Explain the purpose of comparing percent of net sales on an income statement to percents for similar businesses. (See Objective 2.)

17.3 The Balance Sheet

OBJECTIVES

1 Identify the terms used with balance sheets.

2 Prepare a balance sheet.

An income statement summarizes the financial affairs of a business firm for a given period of time, such as a year. On the other hand, a **balance sheet** describes the financial condition of a firm *at one point in time,* such as the last day of a year. A balance sheet shows the worth of a business at a particular time by listing its **assets**— the things it owns, such as property, equipment, and money owed to the business, as well as its **liabilities**—amounts owed by the business to others. The difference of these two amounts gives the **owner's equity** in the business.

Both assets and liabilities are divided into two categories, **long-term** and **current (short-term),** usually depending on whether the time involved is more than a year or less than a year.

1 The following terms appear on a balance sheet.

Current Assets. **Current assets** consist either of cash or items that can be converted into cash within a year. Current assets include:

- *cash.* All cash in checking and savings accounts on the date the balance sheet is made. (As with all items on a balance sheet, this is assumed to be on the date the balance sheet is made.)

- *accounts receivable.* Money owed by customers of the firm, for the purchase of goods and services sold by the firm on credit.

- *notes receivable.* The value of all notes owed to the firm. Normally a note receivable is for a period of less than one year. A firm might require a note from a customer of unknown or unstable financial condition. In the event of bankruptcy of the customer, a note might be paid before an account receivable.

- *inventory.* The cost of the merchandise that the firm has for sale on the date of the balance sheet.

Plant and Equipment. **Plant and equipment,** also called **fixed assets** or **plant assets,** are those assets that are expected to be used for more than one year. Plant and equipment include:

- *land.* The value of any land owned by the firm.
- *buildings.* The value of any buildings owned by the firm.
- *equipment.* The value of equipment, store fixtures, furniture, machinery, and similar items owned by the firm. (As with buildings, "value" refers to book value.)

Items and expenses which must be paid by the firm are called **liabilities.** Liabilities, like assets, are divided into two categories, current and long-term.

Current Liabilities. **Current liabilities** are those expenses which must be paid by the firm within a short period of time, usually one year. Current liabilities include:

- *accounts payable.* Amounts that must be paid to other firms.
- *notes payable.* The value of all notes owed by the firm.

Long-Term Liabilities. **Long-term liabilities** are those expenses which will be paid after one year. Long-term liabilities include:

- *mortgage payable.* The total balance due on all mortgages on which the firm is paying.
- *long-term notes payable.* The total of all other debts of the firm that are not due for more than a year.

The difference between the total of all assets and the total of all liabilities is called the **owner's equity** in the firm. That is,

$$\text{Owner's equity} = \text{Assets} - \text{Liabilities}.$$

Owner's equity is also called **proprietorship, net worth,** or, for a corporation, **stockholders' equity.** The formula for owner's equity is equivalent to the following *fundamental formula for accounting.*

Assets = Liabilities + Owner's equity

2 Now that all the terms have been defined, a balance sheet can be prepared.

EXAMPLE 1

Preparing a Balance Sheet

The Farmersville Market lists its current cash assets as $8000. Notes receivable total $11,000, accounts receivable total $15,000, and inventory is $51,000. Plant assets include land worth $24,000, buildings worth $22,000, and fixtures worth $18,000. Current liabilities include notes payable, which are $8000, and accounts payable, which are $26,000. Mortgages total $39,000 and long-term notes payable total $24,000. ·Owner's equity is $52,000. Complete a balance sheet for the market.

SOLUTION   To prepare a balance sheet, go through the following steps. Refer to the balance sheet in Figure 17.4.

Step 1.   Enter all current assets. On the balance sheet cash is $8000, notes receivable are $11,000, accounts receivable are $15,000, and inventory is $51,000.

Step 2.   Add the current assets. The total in the example is $85,000.

Step 3.   Enter all plant assets. In the example, land is $24,000, buildings are $22,000, and fixtures are $18,000.

Step 4.   Add the plant assets of Step 3. In the example, the total is $64,000.

Step 5.   Add the results from Steps 2 and 4. This gives the total value of all assets owned by the firm. Total assets in the example are $149,000.

Step 6.   Enter all current liabilities. In the example, notes payable are $8000 and accounts payable are $26,000.

Step 7.   Add all current liabilities. The sum in the example is $34,000.

Step 8.   Enter long-term liabilities. In the example, mortgages total $39,000, and long-term notes payable total $24,000.

Step 9.   Add all long-term liabilities. The sum in the example is $63,000.

Step 10.   Add the results of Steps 7 and 9. This gives the total of all liabilities owed by the firm. The total liabilities in the example is $97,000.

Step 11.   Enter owner's equity. In the example, owner's equity is $52,000.

Step 12.   Add owner's equity to total liabilities. The total in the example is $97,000+ $52,000 = $149,000.

Step 13.   Use the fundamental formula for accounting:

Assets = Liabilities + Owner's equity.

In the example, assets = $149,000, liabilities = $97,000, and owner's equity = $52,000. To check, see that

$$149,000 = 97,000 + 52,000,$$

which is correct.   ∎

NOTE Always make sure that total assets equal total liabilities plus owner's equity.

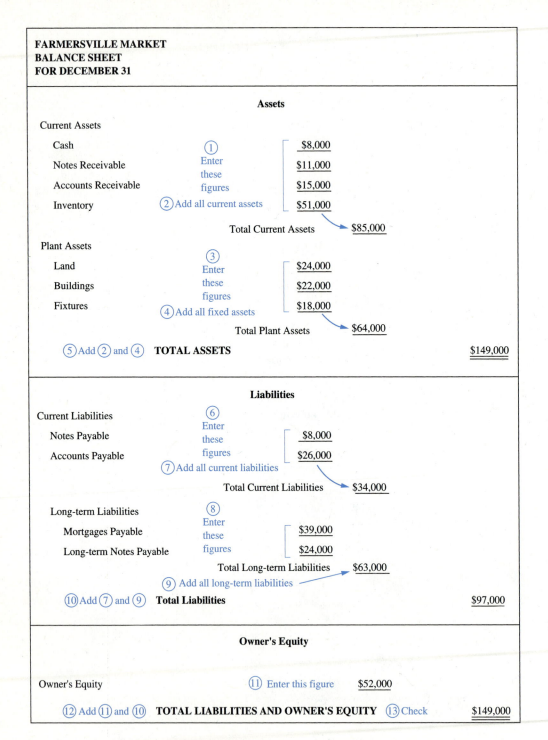

FIGURE 17.4

17.3 Exercises

Complete the corresponding balance sheets for the following business firms.

1. Outdoor Shed Company has mortgages totaling $65,000. Its notes receivable are
    $28,000; land is $42,000; notes payable total $52,000; accounts payable total
    $42,000; buildings are worth $35,000; cash is $21,000; inventory is $54,000;
    long-term notes payable are $9000; owner's equity is $57,000; fixtures are $9000;
    accounts receivable are $36,000.

OUTDOOR SHED COMPANY
BALANCE SHEET FOR DECEMBER 31

Assets

Current Assets

  Cash   _____

  Notes Receivable   _____

  Accounts Receivable   _____

  Inventory   _____

               Total Current Assets   _____

Plant Assets

  Land   _____

  Buildings   _____

  Fixtures   _____

               Total Plant Assets   _____

        TOTAL ASSETS   _____

Liabilities

Current Liabilities

  Notes Payable   _____

  Accounts Payable   _____

               Total Current Liabilities   _____

Long-term Liabilities

  Mortgages Payable   _____

  Long-term Notes Payable   _____

               Total Long-term Liabilities   _____

        Total Liabilities   _____

Owner's Equity

Owner's Equity   _____

      TOTAL LIABILITIES AND OWNER'S EQUITY   _____

2. Ernie Lopez Rent-All has land valued at $8750. Its accounts payable total $49,230; notes receivable are $2600; accounts receivable are $37,820; cash is $14,800; buildings are $21,930; notes payable are $3780; owner's equity is $54,320; long-term notes payable total $18,740; mortgages total $26,330; inventory is $49,680; fixtures are $16,820.

ERNIE LOPEZ RENT-ALL
BALANCE SHEET FOR DECEMBER 31

	Assets	
Current Assets		
Cash		_____
Notes Receivable		_____
Accounts Receivable		_____
Inventory		_____
	Total Current Assets	_____
Plant Assets		
Land		_____
Buildings		_____
Fixtures		_____
	Total Plant Assets	
TOTAL ASSETS		_____

	Liabilities	
Current Liabilities		
Notes Payable		_____
Accounts Payable		_____
	Total Current Liabilities	_____
Long-term Liabilities		
Mortgages Payable		_____
Long-term Notes Payable		_____
	Total Long-term Liabilities	_____
Total Liabilities		_____

	Owner's Equity	
Owner's Equity		_____
TOTAL LIABILITIES AND OWNER'S EQUITY		_____

3. Explain the purpose of a balance sheet. (See Objective 2.)

4. What is the fundamental formula for accounting? Explain how it is used to check a balance sheet. (See Objective 1.)

17.4   Analyzing the Balance Sheet; Financial Ratios

OBJECTIVES

1 Compare balance sheets by vertical analysis.

2 Prepare a horizontal analysis.

3 Find the current ratio.

4 Find the acid-test ratio.

5 Find the ratio of net income after taxes to average owner's equity.

6 Find the accounts receivable turnover.

7 Find the average age of accounts receivable.

8 Find the debt-to-equity ratio.

1 A balance sheet can be analyzed in much the same way as an income statement. In a **vertical analysis**, each item on the balance sheet is expressed as a percent of total assets.

NOTE   In income statements, each item was expressed as a percent of net sales. In a vertical analysis, however, each item on the balance sheet is expressed as a percent of total assets.

An example of such an analysis is shown in Figure 17.5 on page 592. The numbers in the columns headed "Percent" were found by expressing each item in the "Amount" column as a percent of total assets on the balance sheet date. For example, the percent figure for cash was found as follows.

$$\text{Percent} = \frac{\text{Particular item}}{\text{Total assets}} = \frac{\$25,000}{\$200,000} = 0.125 = 12.5\%$$

In the liabilities section, the percent figure for mortgages payable at year's end was found as follows.

$$\text{Percent mortgages payable} = \frac{\$16,000}{\$160,000} = 0.100 = 10.0\%$$

($160,000 was total assets for last year.) Usually, percent calculations are made to the nearest tenth of a percent.

2 To perform a **horizontal analysis**, find the change, both in dollars and percents, for each item on the balance sheet from the previous year to the current year. As before, always use the previous year as a base when computing percents.

EXAMPLE 1
Preparing a
Horizontal Analysis

According to the balance sheet for Conaghan's Sporting Goods, shown in Figure 17.5, cash this year is $25,000, while cash last year was $20,000. This represents an increase of $25,000 − $20,000 = $5000. The percent increase is

$$\frac{\$5000}{\$20,000} = 0.25 = 25\%.$$

In a similar way, complete a horizontal analysis of the current assets portion of Conaghan's Sporting Goods' balance sheet. The result is shown in Figure 17.6. As before, a decrease is enclosed in parentheses. ■

CONAGHAN'S SPORTING GOODS
COMPARATIVE BALANCE SHEET
VERTICAL ANALYSIS

	Amount This Year	Percent This Year	Amount Last Year	Percent Last Year
Assets				
Current Assets				
Cash	$25,000	12.5%	$20,000	12.5%
Notes Receivable	$5,000	2.5%	$8,000	5.0%
Accounts Receivable	$70,000	35.0%	$37,000	23.1%
Inventory	$75,000	37.5%	$70,000	43.8%
Total Current Assets	$175,000	87.5%	$135,000	84.4%
Plant Assets				
Land	$8,000	4.0%	$8,000	5.0%
Buildings	$12,000	6.0%	$12,000	7.5%
Fixtures	$5,000	2.5%	$5,000	3.1%
Total Plant Assets	$25,000	12.5%	$25,000	15.7%
TOTAL ASSETS	$200,000	100.0%	$160,000	100.0%
Liabilities				
Current Liabilities				
Notes Payable	$5,000	2.5%	$5,000	3.1%
Accounts Payable	$75,000	37.5%	$55,000	34.4%
Total Current Liabilities	$80,000	40.0%	$60,000	37.5%
Long-term Liabilities				
Mortgages Payable	$16,000	8.0%	$16,000	10.0%
Long-term Notes Payable	$34,000	17.0%	$24,000	15.0%
Total Long-term Liabilities	$50,000	25.0%	$40,000	25.0%
Total Liabilities	$130,000	65.0%	$100,000	62.5%
Owner's Equity	$70,000	35.0%	$60,000	37.5%
TOTAL LIABILITIES AND OWNER'S EQUITY	$200,000	100.0%	$160,000	100.0%

FIGURE 17.5

After preparing a balance sheet for a business firm, an accountant will often calculate several different *financial ratios* for the firm. These ratios can be compared to financial ratios for other firms in the same industry or of the same size. A ratio that is far out of line when compared to other similar firms or to industry averages might well indicate coming financial difficulties.

The first two ratios we discuss are designed to measure the **liquidity** of a firm; liquidity refers to a firm's ability to raise cash quickly without being forced to sell assets at a big loss.

CONAGHAN'S SPORTING GOODS
HORIZONTAL ANALYSIS (PARTIAL)

Current Assets	Amount This Year	Amount Last Year	Increase or (Decrease) Amount	Increase or (Decrease) Percent
Cash	$25,000	$20,000	$5,000	25%
Notes Receivable	5000	8000	(3000)	(37.5%)
Accounts Receivable	70,000	37,000	33,000	89.2%
Inventory	75,000	70,000	5000	7.1%
Total Current Assets	$175,000	$135,000	$40,000	29.6%

FIGURE 17.6

3   The **current ratio**, also known as **banker's ratio**, is found by dividing current assets by current liabilities.

$$\text{Current ratio} = \frac{\text{Current assets}}{\text{Current liabilities}}$$

EXAMPLE 2
Finding Current Ratio

Find the current ratio for Conaghan's Sporting Goods.

SOLUTION   From the balance sheet for Conaghan's Sporting Goods given in Figure 17.5, find that current assets = $175,000 and current liabilities = $80,000. Now use the formula for the current ratio.

$$\text{Current ratio} = \frac{\$175,000}{\$80,000} = 2.1875 \quad \blacksquare$$

The ratio in Example 2 is often expressed as 2.1875 to 1 or as 2.1875:1. A common rule of thumb, not necessarily applicable to all businesses or at all times, is that the current ratio should be at least 2:1. This ratio, 2:1, is based on past experience—in general, a firm having a current ratio much less than 2:1 has an increased risk of financial difficulty; such a firm might well have a difficult time borrowing money at a bank.

One disadvantage of the current ratio is that inventory is included in current assets. In a period of financial difficulty, a firm might have trouble disposing of the inventory at a reasonable price. Some accountants feel that the "acid test" for a firm's financial health is to consider only **liquid assets**: assets that are either cash or that can be converted to cash quickly, such as securities and accounts and notes receivable.

4 The **acid-test ratio**, also called the **quick ratio**, is defined as follows.

$$\text{Acid-test ratio} = \frac{\text{Liquid assets}}{\text{Current liabilities}}$$

NOTE As a general rule, the acid-test ratio should be at least 1 to 1, with the idea that liquid assets are at least enough to cover current liabilities.

EXAMPLE 3

Finding the Acid-Test Ratio

Find the acid-test ratio for Conaghan's Sporting Goods.

SOLUTION From the balance sheet given in Figure 17.5, liquid assets are made up of $25,000 in cash, $5000 in notes receivable, and $70,000 in accounts receivable, for a total of

$$\$25,000 + \$5000 + \$70,000 = \$100,000.$$

Since current liabilities are $80,000, the acid-test ratio is

$$\frac{\$100,000}{\$80,000} = 1.25,$$

or 1.25 to 1. ∎

5 A company with a large amount of capital invested should have a higher net income than a company that has only a relatively small amount invested. To check on this, accountants often find the **ratio of net income after taxes to average owner's equity**. The average owner's equity is found by adding the owner's equity at the beginning and end of the year and dividing by 2.

$$\frac{\text{Average}}{\text{owner's equity}} = \frac{\text{Owner's equity at beginning} + \text{Owner's equity at end}}{2}$$

Then the ratio of net income after taxes to average owner's equity is found as follows.

$$\frac{\text{Ratio of net income}}{\text{after taxes to average}} = \frac{\text{Net income after taxes}}{\text{Average owner's equity}}$$

NOTE The ratio of net income after taxes to average owner's equity is also called "return on equity."

Net income *after taxes* refers to the net income of a firm after all income taxes have been paid.

EXAMPLE 4

Finding Ratio of Net Income after Taxes to Average Owner's Equity

At the beginning of a year, a firm had owner's equity of $140,000; at the end of the year, the owner's equity was $190,000. The net income after taxes for the firm is $19,000. Find the ratio of net income after taxes to average owner's equity.

SOLUTION   The average owner's equity is

$$\frac{\$140,000 + \$190,000}{2} = \$165,000.$$

Using the net income after taxes for the firm gives the following ratio of net income after taxes to average owner's equity.

$$\frac{\$19,000}{\$165,000} = 0.115 = 11.5\% \qquad \text{rounded} \quad \blacksquare$$

NOTE   The ratio of net income after taxes to average owner's equity should be at least as much as the interest paid on savings accounts by banks—otherwise the capital represented by these assets should be deposited in a bank account. After all, savings accounts are guaranteed by the federal government, while business profits aren't. This increased risk should bring a higher return than that of risk-free savings accounts.

6   The accounts receivable of a firm represent credit sales—goods sold on credit and later billed to the customer. The **accounts receivable turnover** is an indication of how fast the firm is collecting its bills. If this ratio starts to decline, then the firm may well need to be more aggressive in collecting its receivables from customers. By collecting receivables promptly, the firm will need to borrow less money, thus cutting its interest charges.

To find the accounts receivable turnover ratio, first find the average accounts receivable.

$$\text{Average accounts receivable} =$$

$$\frac{\text{Accounts receivable at beginning } + \text{ Accounts receivable at end}}{2}$$

Then,

$$\text{Accounts receivable turnover} = \frac{\text{Net sales}}{\text{Average accounts receivable}}$$

EXAMPLE 5

Finding Accounts Receivable Turnover

Suppose a firm had accounts receivable of $75,000 at the beginning of a year and $90,000 at the end. Then the average accounts receivable are

$$\frac{\$75,000 + \$90,000}{2} = \frac{\$165,000}{2} = \$82,500.$$

If the firm had net sales of $1,050,000, find its accounts receivable turnover.

SOLUTION   Use the formula in the box.

$$\text{Accounts receivable turnover} = \frac{\$1,050,000}{\$82,500} = 12.7. \quad \blacksquare$$

7 As mentioned, a firm must collect its accounts receivable promptly to minimize its own need to borrow money. To tell how well accounts are being collected, the firm can find the **average age of accounts receivable**, or the average number of days needed to collect its receivables. This is found by the formula

$$\frac{\text{Average age of}}{\text{accounts receivable}} = \frac{365}{\text{Accounts receivable turnover}}$$

EXAMPLE 6

Finding Average Age of Accounts

The firm in Example 5 had an accounts receivable turnover of 12.7. The average age of these accounts is

$$\text{Average age of accounts receivable} = \frac{365}{12.7} = 28.7 \text{ days.} \quad \blacksquare$$

NOTE If this average age of accounts receivable is less than the period allowed for paying receivables (often 30 days), then the receivables are probably being collected promptly.

8 Companies borrow money to expand and take advantage of business opportunities. This is fine as long as total debt does not become excessive. One common measure used to see if debt is reasonable is the **debt-to-equity ratio**, the ratio of all liabilities to all owner's equity.

$$\text{Debt-to-equity ratio} = \frac{\text{Current liabilities} + \text{Long-term liabilities}}{\text{Owner's equity}}$$

EXAMPLE 7

Finding Debt-to-Equity Ratio

A firm has current liabilities of $24,000, long term liabilities of $68,000, and owner's equity of $114,000. Find the debt-to-equity ratio for this firm.

SOLUTION   Use the formula given in the box.

$$\text{Debt-to-equity ratio} = \frac{\$24,000 + \$68,000}{\$114,000}$$

$$= \frac{\$92,000}{\$114,000} = 0.807 \text{ or } 80.7\%. \quad \blacksquare$$

NOTE An acceptable level for debt-to-equity ratios varies drastically from industry to industry. For some, a ratio of 100% is reasonable, while for others a 25% ratio might make the firm's bankers get nervous.

17.4 Exercises

Complete the following.

1. Complete the balance sheet for Interstate Rubber Supply. Round to the nearest tenth of a percent.

2. Complete the horizontal analysis for a portion of the balance sheet for Interstate Rubber Supply.

INTERSTATE RUBBER SUPPLY COMPARATIVE BALANCE SHEET	Amount This Year	Percent This Year	Amount Last Year	Percent Last Year
Assets				
Current Assets				
Cash	$52,000	_____	$42,000	_____
Notes Receivable	$8,000	_____	$6,000	_____
Accounts Receivable	$148,000	_____	$120,000	_____
Inventory	$153,000	_____	$120,000	_____
Total Current Assets	_____	_____	_____	_____
Plant Assets				
Land	$10,000	_____	$8,000	_____
Buildings	$14,000	_____	$11,000	_____
Fixtures	$15,000	_____	$13,000	_____
Total Plant Assets	_____	_____	_____	_____
TOTAL ASSETS	_____	100.0%	_____	100.0%
Liabilities				
Current Liabilities				
Accounts Payable	$3,000	_____	$4,000	_____
Notes Payable	$201,000	_____	$152,000	_____
Total Current Liabilities	_____	_____	_____	_____
Long-term Liabilities				
Mortgages Payable	$20,000	_____	$16,000	_____
Long-term Notes Payable	$58,000	_____	$42,000	_____
Total Long-term Liabilities	_____	_____	_____	_____
Total Liabilities	_____	_____	_____	_____
Owner's Equity	$118,000	_____	$106,000	_____
TOTAL LIABILITIES AND OWNER'S EQUITY	_____	_____	_____	_____

	This Year	Last Year	Increase or (Decrease) Amount	Increase or (Decrease) Percent
Assets				
Current Assets				
Cash	$52,000	$42,000		
Notes Receivable	$8,000	$6,000	_____	_____
Accounts Receivable	$148,000	$120,000	_____	_____
Inventory	$153,000	$120,000	_____	_____
Total Current Assets	$361,000	$288,000	_____	_____
Plant Assets				
Land	$10,000	$8,000		
Buildings	$14,000	$11,000	_____	_____
Fixtures	$15,000	$13,000	_____	_____
Total Plant Assets	$39,000	$32,000	_____	_____
TOTAL ASSETS	$400,000	$320,000	_____	_____

In Exercises 3–6, find the current ratio and the acid-test ratio. Round each ratio to the nearest hundredth.

3. Interstate Rubber Supply, having balance sheet given on page 597.

4. Earthworm Tractor Company has current assets of $326,000; current liabilities of $175,000; cash total of $18,000; notes and accounts receivable total of $215,000; inventory of $93,000.

5. Amclack Hose Supply has current assets of $479,000; current liabilities of $275,000; cash total of $21,000; notes and accounts receivable total of $318,000; and inventory of $140,000.

6. Wilson Auto Parts has current assets of $800,000; current liabilities of $425,000; cash total of $55,000; notes and accounts receivable total of $514,000; inventory of $231,000.

A portion of a comparative balance sheet is shown on the opposite page. First complete the chart, and then find the current ratio and the acid-test ratio for the indicated year. Round each ratio to the nearest hundredth.

7. This year

8. Last year

	Amount This Year	Percent This Year	Amount Last Year	Percent Last Year
Current assets				
Cash	$12,000	————	$15,000	————
Notes Receivable	4,000	————	6,000	————
Accounts Receivable	22,000	————	18,000	————
Inventory	26,000	————	24,000	————
Total Current Assets	64,000	80.0%	63,000	84.0%
Total Plant and Equipment	16,000	————	12,000	————
TOTAL ASSETS	————	100.0%	————	100.0%
Total Current Liabilities	$30,000	————	$25,000	————

Find the debt-to-equity ratio for each of the following firms. Give the ratio as a percent, rounded to the nearest tenth of a percent.

9. Interstate Rubber Supply from Exercises 1 and 3

10. Earthworm Tractor Company from Exercise 4: owner's equity of $1,150,000, long-term liabilities of $278,000

11. Amclack Hose Supply from Exercise 5: owner's equity of $2,580,000, long-term liabilities of $748,000

12. Wilson Auto Parts from Exercise 6: owner's equity of $1,806,000, long-term liabilities of $1,150,000

Find the ratio of net income after taxes to average owner's equity for the following firms. Round to the nearest tenth of a percent.

13. Owner's equity at beginning of year $750,000; owner's equity at end of year $825,000; net income after taxes $14,500

14. Owner's equity at beginning of year $4,320,000; owner's equity at end of year $5,500,000; net income after taxes $840,000

Find the accounts receivable turnover rate and the average age of the accounts receivable for the following firms. Round each rate to the nearest tenth.

15. Accounts receivable at beginning of year $32,000; accounts receivable at end of year $45,000; net sales $650,000

16. Accounts receivable at beginning of year $110,000; accounts receivable at end of year $80,000; net sales $875,000

17. Describe the difference between an income statement and a balance sheet.

18. List three ratios that can be used to analyze a balance sheet and the purpose of each ratio.

CHAPTER 17 QUICK REVIEW

TOPIC	APPROACH	EXAMPLE

17.1 Gross profit and net income	Gross profit = Net sales
	    − Cost of goods sold
	
	Net income = Gross profit
	    − Operating expenses
		Cost of goods sold, $156,000; operating expenses, $35,000; net sales, $210,000. Find gross profit and net income.
		Gross profit = $210,000 − $156,000
		    = $54,000
		Net income = $54,000 − $35,000
		    = $19,000

17.2 Finding the percent of net sales of individual items	Subtract returns from gross sales to determine net sales. Then divide the value of an item by net sales to obtain percent of net sales.	Express the following items for Mr. Bill's Appliance Store as percents of net sales: gross sales, $340,000; returns, $15,000; cost of goods sold, $210,000; wages, $19,000; gross profit.
		Net sales = $340,000 − $15,000
		    = $325,000
		Gross profit = $325,000 − $210,000
		    = $115,000
		$\text{Percent gross sales} = \dfrac{\$340,000}{\$325,000}$
		    = 104.6%
		$\text{Percent returns} = \dfrac{\$15,000}{\$325,000}$
		    = 4.6%
		$\text{Percent cost of goods sold} = \dfrac{\$210,000}{\$325,000}$
		    = 65%
		$\text{Percent wages} = \dfrac{\$19,000}{\$325,000} = 5.8\%$
		$\text{Percent gross profit} = \dfrac{\$115,000}{\$325,000}$
		    = 35.4%

TOPIC	APPROACH	EXAMPLE

17.2 Comparing income statements to published charts

In one chart, list the percents of net sales for each item from a published chart and a particular company.

Prepare a vertical analysis of Mr. Bill's Appliance Store.

Cost of Goods	Gross Profit	Wages	
65%	35.4%	5.8%	Mr. Bill's Appliances
66.9%	33.2%	11.9%	(from chart)

17.2 Preparing a horizontal analysis

List last year's and this year's values for each item.
Then calculate the amount of the increase or decrease for each item and express as percents.

The results of a horizontal analysis of the portion of a business is given. Calculate the % increases or decreases in each item.

	This Year	Last Year	Increase Amount	or	Decrease Percentage
Gross Sales	$735,000	$700,000	$35,000		5%
Returns	5,000	10,000	(5,000)		(50%)
Net Sales	730,000	690,000	40,000		5.8%
Cost of Goods Sold	530,000	540,000	(10,000)		(1.9%)
Gross Profit	200,000	150,000	50,000		33.3%

17.4 Current ratio

$$\frac{\text{Current}}{\text{ratio}} = \frac{\text{Current assets}}{\text{Current liabilities}}$$

The Circle Towne Agency has current assets of $250,000, current liabilities of $110,000, cash of $45,000, and accounts receivable of $80,000. The agency had owner's equity of $140,000 at the beginning of the year, and $180,000 at the end of the year. The net income after taxes was $25,000. Calculate the current ratio and ratio of net income after taxes to the average owner's equity.

$$\frac{\text{Current}}{\text{ratio}} = \frac{\$250,000}{\$110,000} = 2.2727$$

Acid test ratio

$$\frac{\text{Acid-test}}{\text{ratio}} = \frac{\text{Liquid assets}}{\text{Current liabilities}}$$

$$\frac{\text{Acid-test}}{\text{ratio}} = \frac{\$45,000 + \$80,000}{\$110,000}$$

$$= 1.136$$

$$\frac{\text{Average owner's equity}}{} = \frac{\$140,000 + \$180,000}{2}$$

$$= \$160,000$$

Ratio of net income after taxes to the average owner's equity

$$\text{Ratio} = \frac{\text{Net income after taxes}}{\text{Average owner's equity}}$$

Ratio of net income after taxes to average owner's equity

$$\frac{\$25,000}{\$160,000} = 0.156 = 15.6\%$$

TOPIC	APPROACH	EXAMPLE
17.4 Accounts receivable turnover	Accounts receivable turnover $$= \frac{\text{Net sales}}{\text{Average accounts receivable}}$$	A firm has net sales of \$793,750; accounts receivable of \$50,000 at the beginning of the year; \$75,000 at the end of the year; current liabilities of \$15,000; long-term liabilities of \$10,000; and owner's equity of \$80,000. Find the accounts receivable turnover, the average age of accounts receivable and the debt-to-equity ratio.
Average age of accounts receivable	Average age of accounts receivable $$= \frac{365}{\text{Accounts receivable turnover}}$$	Average accounts receivable $$= \frac{\$50,000 + \$75,000}{2} = \$62,500$$ Accounts receivable turnover $$= \frac{\$793,750}{\$62,500} = 12.7$$ Average age of accounts receivable $$= \frac{365}{12.7} = 28.7$$
Debt-to-equity ratio	Debt-to-equity ratio $$= \frac{\text{Current liabilities} + \text{Long-term liabilities}}{\text{Owner's equity}}$$	Debt-to-equity ratio $$= \frac{\$15,000 + \$10,000}{\$80,000} = 0.3125$$ or 31.25%

SUMMARY EXERCISE

Carlotta Reyes needs to do a financial analysis of her business. She has collected the following facts for last year.

Gross Sales	\$212,000
Returns	\$12,500
Inventory on January 1	\$44,000
Cost of Goods Purchased	\$75,000
Freight	\$8000
Inventory on December 31	\$26,000
Salaries and Wages	\$37,000
Rent	\$12,000
Advertising	\$2000
Utilities	\$3000
Taxes on Inventory, Payroll	\$7000
Miscellaneous Expenses	\$4500

(a)   Prepare an income statement.

CARLOTTA'S CHINA SHOP
INCOME STATEMENT
YEAR ENDING DECEMBER 31

Gross Sales		*212,000*
Returns		*− 12,500*
Net Sales		*199,500*
Inventory, January 1	*44,000*	
Cost of Goods Purchased	*+ 75,000*	
Freight	*8,000*	
Total Cost of Goods Purchased	*83,000*	
Total of Goods Available for Sale	*127,000*	
Inventory, December 31	*26,000*	
Cost of Goods Sold		*101,000*
Gross Profit		*98,500*
Expenses		
Salaries and Wages	*37,000*	
Rent	*12,000*	
Advertising	*2,000*	
Utilities	*3,000*	
Taxes on Inventory, Payroll	*7,000*	
Miscellaneous Expenses	*4,500*	
Total Expenses		*65,500*
NET INCOME		*33,000*

(b)   Express the following items as a percent of net sales.

Gross sales $\frac{212,000}{199,500} = 106.3$ Salaries and wages $\frac{37,000}{199,500} = 18.5\%$

Returns $\frac{12,500}{199,500} = 6.3\%$ Rent $\frac{12,000}{199,500} = 6\%$

Cost of goods sold $\frac{101,500}{199,500} = 50.6\%$ Utilities $\frac{3,000}{199,500} = 1.5\%$

(c)   After the year is completed, Reyes has $62,000 in cash, $2500 in notes receivable, $8200 in accounts receivable, and $26,000 in inventory. She has land worth $7600, buildings valued at $28,000, and fixtures worth $13,500. She also has $4500 in notes payable, $27,000 in accounts payable, mortgages for $15,000, long-term notes payable of $8000, and owner's equity of $93,300. Prepare a balance sheet.

CARLOTTA'S CHINA SHOP
BALANCE SHEET
DECEMBER 31

	Assets		
Current Assets			
Cash		62,000	
Notes Receivable		2,500	
Accounts Receivable		8,200	
Inventory		26,000	
	Total Current Assets		98,700
Plant Assets			
Land		7,600	
Buildings		28,000	
Fixtures		13,500	
	Total Plant Assets		49,100
TOTAL ASSETS			147,800

	Liabilities		
Current Liabilities			
Notes Payable		4,500	
Accounts Payable		27,000	
	Total Current Liabilities		31,500
Long-term Liabilities			
Mortgages Payable		15,000	
Long-term Notes Payable		8,000	
	Total Long-term Liabilities		23,000
Total Liabilities			54,500

	Owner's Equity		
Owner's Equity		93,300	
TOTAL LIABILITIES AND OWNER'S EQUITY			$ 147,800

(d) Find the current ratio and the acid-test ratio for Reyes' business. Do you think she has a strong operation? Explain your reasoning.

CHAPTER 17 REVIEW EXERCISES

Find the *gross profit* and *net income* in each of the following. [17.1]

[handwritten: NET SALES – COST OF GOODS SOLD THEN GROSS PROFIT – OPER EXP.]

	Cost of Goods	Operating Expenses	Net Sales
1.	$75,000	$34,000	$125,000
2.	$94,000	$46,000	$150,000
3.	$125,000	$75,000	$325,000
4.	$215,000	$80,000	$325,000
5.	$315,000	$100,000	$475,000

[handwritten: 125,000 – 75,000 = $50,000]
[handwritten: 325,000 – 125,000 = $200,000]
[handwritten: 475,000 – 315,000 = $160,000]

Find the *cost of goods sold* for each of the following firms. [17.1]

[handwritten: INITIAL INV. + COST OF GOODS PURCH. + FREIGHT – FINAL INVEN.]

	Initial Inventory	Cost of Goods Purchased	Freight	Final Inventory
6.	$200,000	$125,000	$20,000	$195,000
7.	$150,000	$75,000	$15,000	$185,000
8.	$90,000	$20,000	$5000	$100,000
9.	$86,000	$14,000	$7000	$80,000
10.	$75,000	$15,000	$10,000	$70,000

Complete the accompanying income statements for the following firms. [17.1]

11. Rose's Party Balloons had gross sales of $175,000 last year, with returns of $8000. The inventory on January 1 was $44,000. A total of $126,000 worth of goods was purchased with a freight of $2000. The inventory on December 31 was $52,000. Salaries and wages were $9000, rent was $4000, advertising was $1500, utilities were $1000, taxes on inventory and payroll totaled $2000, and miscellaneous expenses totaled $3000.

ROSE'S PARTY BALLOONS
INCOME STATEMENT
FOR THE YEAR ENDING DECEMBER 31

Gross Sales	175,000
Returns	− 8,000
Net Sales	167,000
Inventory, January 1	44,000
Cost of Goods Purchased	126,000
Freight	2,000 +
Total Cost of Goods Purchased	128,000
Total of Goods Available for Sale	172,000
Inventory, December 31	52,000
Cost of Goods Sold	120,000
Gross Profit	155,000
Expenses	
Salaries and Wages	9,000
Rent	4,000
Advertising	1,500
Utilities	1,000
Taxes on Inventory, Payroll	2,000
Miscellaneous Expenses	3,000
Total Expenses	20,500
NET INCOME	13,450

12. Mike's Computer Store had gross sales of $2,215,000 with returns of $26,000. The inventory on January 1 was $215,000. A total of $1,123,000 worth of goods was purchased with a freight of $4000. The inventory on December 31 was $265,000. Salaries and wages were $154,000, rent was $59,000, advertising was $11,000, utilities were $12,000, taxes on inventory and payroll totaled $10,000, and miscellaneous expenses totaled $9000.

MIKE'S COMPUTER STORE
INCOME STATEMENT
FOR THE YEAR ENDING DECEMBER 31

Gross Sales   _____

Returns   _____

Net Sales   _____

   Inventory, January 1   _____

   Cost of Goods
     Purchased   _____

   Freight   _____

   Total Cost of Goods Purchased   _____

   Total of Goods Available for Sale _____

   Inventory, December 31   _____

Cost of Goods Sold   _____

Gross Profit   _____

   Expenses

    Salaries and Wages   _____

    Rent   _____

    Advertising   _____

    Utilities   _____

    Taxes on Inventory, Payroll _____

    Miscellaneous Expenses   _____

     Total Expenses   _____

NET INCOME   _____

Prepare a vertical analysis for each of the following firms. Round to the nearest tenth of a percent. [17.2]

Cost of Goods Sold	Operating Expenses	Net Sales
13. $105,000	$52,000	$125,000
14. $125,000	$45,000	$250,000

Complete the following chart. Express each item as a percent of net sales and then write in the appropriate average percent from Table 17.1. Round each percent to the nearest tenth of a percent. [17.2]

15. Andy's Steak House

	Amount	Percent	Percent from Table 17
Net Sales	$300,000	100%	100%
Cost of Goods Sold	$125,000	_____	_____
Gross Profit	$175,000	_____	_____
Wages	$72,000	_____	_____
Rent	$12,000	_____	_____
Advertising	$5700	_____	_____
Total Expenses	$123,000	_____	_____
Net Income	$52,000	_____	_____

Complete the following balance sheet. [17.3]

16. The Wooden Boat Company has notes payable of $11,000; accounts receivable of $3000; cash is $9000; long term notes payable of $10,000; building worth of $15,000; inventory of $12,000; fixtures are $8000; owner's equity is $21,000; notes receivable of $4000; accounts receivable of $3000; land is $28,000; accounts payable of $15,000 and mortgages of $22,000.

WOODEN BOAT COMPANY
BALANCE SHEET
FOR DECEMBER 31

Assets

Current Assets

  Cash   _____

  Notes Receivable   _____

  Accounts Receivable   _____

  Inventory   _____

              Total Current Assets   _____

Plant Assets

  Land   _____

  Buildings   _____

  Fixtures   _____

              Total Plant Assets   _____

TOTAL ASSETS   ═══════

Liabilities

Current Liabilities

  Notes Payable   _____

  Accounts Payable   _____

              Total Current Liabilities   _____

Long-term Liabilities

  Mortgages Payable   _____

  Long- term Notes Payable   _____

              Total Long-term Liabilities   _____

Total Liabilities   _____

Owner's Equity

Owner's Equity   _____

TOTAL LIABILITIES AND OWNER'S EQUITY   ═══════

Calculate the current ratio, acid-test ratio, and debt-to-equity ratio for each of the following. Round to the nearest hundredth. [17.4]

	Current Assets	Current Liabilities	Long-Term Liabilities	Owner's Equity	Liquid Assets
17.	$35,000	$15,000	$5000	$25,000	$18,000
18.	$160,000	$60,000	$20,000	$125,000	$90,000
19.	$80,000	$25,000	$10,000	$50,000	$75,000

Find the accounts receivable turnover rate and the average age of the accounts receivable in each of the following firms. Round to the nearest tenth. [17.4]

20. Accounts receivable at beginning of year $120,000
     Accounts receivable at end of year $160,000
     Net sales $1,652,000

21. Accounts receivable at beginning of year $75,000
     Accounts receivable at end of year $50,000
     Net sales $768,750

Securities and Profit Distribution

As shown in the previous chapter, the net profit of a business is the amount left over after all the expenses involved in running the business are paid. Typically, a portion of any net profit is reinvested in the business, for labor-saving machinery, to build new plants, and so on. The rest of the net profit can then be distributed to the owners of the business. This chapter discusses the way the profits are distributed.

The distribution of profits depends on the way a company is formed. If a business is a **sole proprietorship**, that is, if it is owned by one person, then all the profits go to that person. Sole proprietorships are most common among the smallest businesses, such as a small retail store, hair salon, and the like. With a typical sole proprietorship, there is no division of assets between personal assets and business assets, so that personal property could be **attached** (seized under court order) to pay debts associated with the business, while business assets could also be attached to pay personal debts.

A **partnership** is a business formed by two or more parties. Since partnerships involve the resources of several people, they are common for somewhat larger businesses, such as a small factory or perhaps a small chain of retail stores. In a partnership, any profits are divided equally among the partners, unless they have a prior agreement setting up a different method.

Partnerships are often set up by individuals with different interests and abilities—one partner might actually run the business on a day-to-day basis, while the other partner makes a substantial financial investment but does not actively take part in the business. A partner who makes only a financial investment is called a **silent partner**.

The law often says that partners are responsible "jointly and separately" for partnership debts, which means that a partner with money may have to pay all debts of the partnership. The methods of dividing the profits in a partnership are discussed in Section 18.5.

To get around the problem of the lack of protection for personal assets, most larger businesses are set up as **corporations**. The people investing money in a corporation have **limited liability**—they can lose no more money than they have invested in the corporation. Distribution of profits in a corporation is discussed in the first section.

18.1 Distribution of Profits in a Corporation

OBJECTIVES

1 Compare preferred and common stocks.

2 Distribute profits to shareholders and calculate dividend per share.

3 Find earnings per share.

A corporation is set up with money, or **capital**, raised by selling shares of **stock**. A share of stock represents partial ownership in a corporation. If one million shares of stock are sold to establish a new firm, the owner of one share will hold 1/1,000,000 of the corporation. The ownership of stock is shown by **stock certificates**.

In most states, corporations are required to have an **annual meeting**. At this meeting, open to all owners of the stock (or **stockholders**), the management of the firm is open to questions from stockholders. The stockholders also elect a **board of directors**—a group of people who represent the stockholders. The board of directors hires the **executive officers** of the corporation, such as the president, vice presidents, and so on. The board of directors also distributes any profits in the form of dividends. Dividends are covered in more detail later in this section.

1 Corporations normally issue two types of stock, **preferred stock** and **common stock**. As the name implies, preferred stock has certain rights over common stock. Owners of preferred stock must be paid dividends before any dividends can be paid to owners of common stock. In the case of bankruptcy of the corporation, owners of preferred stock must be paid off completely before common stock owners get any money. (Preferred stockholders receive no money, however, until all other debts of the corporation are paid.)

Each share of preferred stock has a **par value**—the amount printed on the stock certificate that must be paid to its owner before common stockholders receive any money. Each share also has a stated **dividend**, often given as a percent of par value. These dividends must be paid by the company to the preferred stockholders before any dividends can be paid to the common stockholders. (However, there is no guarantee that any dividends will be paid at all.)

Sometimes, preferred stock is given additional features to make it more attractive to potential buyers. For example, the stock may be **cumulative preferred stock**, which means that any dividends not paid in the past must be paid before common stockholders receive any money. The stock might also be **convertible preferred stock**, which means that one share is convertible into a stated number of shares of common stock at some future date.

Holders of preferred stock usually are not able to vote at the annual meeting of the corporation. Also, most preferred stock is **nonparticipating**, which means the corporation will never pay dividends above the stated rate. (Holders of **participating** preferred stock could share in any good success of the corporation by an increase in the dividend.)

NOTE   Common stock carries no guarantees—its holders are last in line when profits are distributed or when the corporation is dissolved. However, common stockholders are able to vote at the annual meeting. Common stock may or may not have a par value, but since nothing is guaranteed, par value for common stock is of little importance.

2   The next examples show how the profits of a corporation might be distributed.

EXAMPLE 1
Calculating Dividend per Share

Thornton Electronics had a net income of $1,200,000 last year. The board of directors decides to reinvest $500,000 in the business and distribute the remaining $700,000 to stockholders. The company has 40,000 shares of $100 par value, 6% preferred stock, and 350,000 shares of common stock. Find (a) the amount paid to holders of preferred stock, and (b) the amount per share given to holders of common stock.

SOLUTION

(a)   Each share of preferred stock has a par value of $100, and pays a dividend of 6%. The dividend per share is

$$\text{Dividend per share} = \$100 \times 6\% = \$100 \times 0.06 = \$6$$

A dividend of $6 must be paid for each share of preferred stock. Since there are 40,000 shares of preferred, a total of

$$\$6 \times 40,000 = \$240,000$$

will be paid to owners of preferred shares.

(b)   A total of $700,000 is available for stockholders, with $240,000 going to the owners of preferred shares, leaving

$$
\begin{array}{lr}
\$700,000 & \text{total} \\
-\ \ 240,000 & \text{to preferred} \\
\hline
\$460,000 &
\end{array}
$$

available for the common stockholders. There are 350,000 shares of common stock outstanding, with each share being paid a dividend of

$$\frac{\$460,000}{350,000} = \$1.31 \quad \blacksquare$$

EXAMPLE 2
Finding Dividends

Because of a steep drop in the price of beef last year, Rocky Mountain Land paid no dividend. This year, the board of directors has set aside $175,000 for the payment of dividends. The company has outstanding 12,500 shares of cumulative preferred stock having par value of $50, with an 8% dividend. The company also has 40,000 shares of common stock. What dividend will be paid to the owners of each type of stock?

SOLUTION   The dividend per share of preferred stock is

$$\$50 \text{ par value} \times 8\% \text{ (dividend rate)} = \$4.$$

Dividends have not been paid for 2 years, so that each share of preferred stock must be paid

$$\$4 \text{ per share} \times 2 \text{ years} = \$8$$

before any dividends can be paid to holders of common stock. Since there are 12,500 shares of preferred stock outstanding, a total of

$$\$8 \times 12,500 = \$100,000$$

must be paid to the owners of the preferred stock. This leaves

$$
\begin{array}{ll}
\$175,000 & \text{total} \\
-\ 100,000 & \text{to owners of preferred} \\
\hline
\$75,000 &
\end{array}
$$

to be divided among owners of common stock. Since there are 40,000 shares of common stock, each share will be paid a dividend of

$$\frac{\$75,000}{40,000} = \$1.88 \text{ (rounded).} \quad \blacksquare$$

NOTE In Example 2, the dividend for owners of preferred stock was paid for each of the last two years before any common stock dividends were paid.

3   One way to measure the financial success of a corporation is by finding the **earnings per share** made by the corporation. Earnings per share is found with the following formula.

$$\text{Earnings per share} = \frac{\text{Net income} - \text{Dividends on preferred}}{\text{Number of shares of common outstanding}}$$

EXAMPLE 3
Finding Earnings per Share

(a)   A company made \$650,000 last year. The company has 1,000,000 shares of common stock outstanding and no preferred stock. The earnings per share are

$$\text{Earnings per share} = \frac{\$650,000 - 0}{1,000,000} = \$.65,$$

or 65¢ per share.

(b)   The company in Example 1 had net income of \$1,200,000. Of this, \$240,000 was paid to owners of preferred shares. The earnings per share are

$$\text{Earning per share} = \frac{\$1,200,000 - \$240,000}{350,000}$$

$$= \frac{\$960,000}{350,000} = \$2.74$$

The earnings per share of \$2.74 are more than the dividend of \$1.31 paid to common shareholders. The difference represents the money reinvested in the corporation, plus the dividends paid to preferred shareholders.   ■

18.1 Exercises

Find the dividend that will be paid for each share of stock.

	Common Stock (in Shares)	Preferred Stock (in Shares)	Total Dividends
1.	650,000	none	$1,700,000
2.	850,000	none	$1,232,500
3.	125,000	15,000, $100 par value, 7%	$234,000
4.	3,000,000	500,000, $200 par value 8%	$10,300,000
5.	925,000	80,000, $1000 par value, 6%	$7,500,000
6.	400,000	10,000, $50 par value 8%	$940,000

7. A small factory making brass fittings had a net income of $700,000 last year. If $500,000 was reinvested in the business, find the dividend per share on the 450,000 shares of common stock outstanding.

8. Williams Textiles had a net income of $7,000,000 last year. The board of directors decided to reinvest $4,500,000 in the business. Find the dividend for each of the company's 1,500,000 shares of common stock.

9. Hardy Tool Works has 600,000 shares of $100 par value, 8% preferred stock outstanding, along with 2,000,000 shares of common stock. Find the dividend per share if the board of directors set aside $6,300,000 for dividends.

10. The local Chevrolet dealer is a corporation with 1000 shares of $200 par value, 11% preferred stock, and 5000 common shares. Decide on the dividend per share for a total dividend of $39,500.

11. Northern Main Paper Products has sold 25,000 shares of $40 par value, 4% preferred stock to help remodel its mill. It already had 300,000 shares of common stock. Find the dividend per share if the total profit is $850,000, and 35% was distributed to shareholders.

12. The Harris Furniture Company had a net income of $2,937,500 last year. The company decided to distribute 40% of this money to shareholders. Find the dividend per share if there are 50,000 shares of $100 par value, 10% preferred stock outstanding, and 300,000 shares of common stock.

13. Since the computer business is booming, a small new company has decided to pay no dividend for 3 years, and instead, reinvests the profits in expansion. After 4 years, the board decides to pay a dividend of $2,675,000. Find the dividend per share if the company has outstanding 20,000 cumulative preferred shares of $100 par value, at 5%, and 450,000 common shares.

14. To pay for a new factory, Wilson Rubber Goods has paid no dividend for 2 years. Now, after 3 years, a dividend of $1,200,000 was declared. Find the dividend per share if the company has 10,000 cumulative preferred shares outstanding of $100 par value at 10%, and 400,000 common shares.

15. A corporation had net income of $7,000,000, has 1,200,000 common shares, and no preferred shares. Find the earnings per share.

16. Suppose a corporation with 750,000 common shares outstanding and no preferred shares had net income of $2,350,000 last year. Find the earnings per share.

17. Far East Imports has 300,000 common shares, and 12,500 preferred shares, of $150 par value, 10%. The company last year had net income of $1,500,000, with 45% of this going to shareholders. Find the earnings per share.

18. Boyle Cleaners had net income of $600,000 last year, and distributed 55% to shareholders. The firm has 50,000 common shares, and 10,000 preferred shares, of $100 par value, 12%. Find the earnings per share.

19. Explain the difference between a common stock and preferred stock. (See Objective 1.)

20. Explain the process used to calculate the dividend per share for common stocks. (See Objective 2.)

18.2 Buying Stock

OBJECTIVES

1 Know the basics of stock ownership.

2 Read stock tables.

3 Find the commission for buying or selling stocks.

4 Find the total price of a stock purchase.

5 Find the current yield on a stock.

6 Find the PE ratio of a stock.

1 As mentioned in the previous section, buying stock in a corporation makes the stockholder a part owner of the corporation. In return for the money a person invests in stock, he or she shares in any profits the company makes. Hopefully, the company will do well and prosper. If this happens, many other people will want the company's stock, and they will be willing to pay a good price for its shares. If this happens, the stockholders can sell at a profit.

On the other hand, if the company does not do well, then fewer people will want its stock and the price will fall. The price of a share of stock is set by the law of supply and demand at institutions called *stock exchanges*. The largest stock exchange is the New York Stock Exchange, located on Wall Street in New York City.

The public does not go directly to the exchange to buy and sell stock. Instead, members of the public buy their stock through **stockbrokers**, people who do have access to the exchange. Stockbrokers charge a fee for buying or selling stock, as discussed below.

Most people buy stock in hopes of making a profit. Obviously, there is no way to know for sure which stocks will increase in value and which will decrease. Stockbrokers can give advice, but this advice is in no way guaranteed to produce a profit.

2 Find the current price of a stock by looking in many daily newspapers, or in *The Wall Street Journal*. A portion of the stock market page from *The Journal* is shown in Figure 18.1.

	52 Weeks Hi	52 Weeks Lo	Stock	Sym	Div	Yld %	PE	Vol 100s	Hi	Lo	Close	Net Chg.
			-A-A-A-									
	15⅞	10⅝	AAR	AIR	.48	4.1	19	75	11¾	11⅝	11¾	...
	11⅝	10⅛	ACM Gvt Fd	ACG	.96	8.5	...	479	11⅜	11¼	11¼	...
	10⅜	9	ACM OppFd	AOF	.80	8.2	...	321	9⅞	9¾	9¾	+ ⅛
	11⅞	10	ACM SecFd	GSF	.96	8.5	...	867	11⅜	11¼	11¼	...
	9¾	8¼	ACM SpctmFd	SI	.79	8.3	...	546	9⅝	9½	9½	− ⅛
	10⅝	8¼	ACM MgdIncFd	AMF	1.08	10.2	...	762	10⅝	10½	10⅝	...
	12⅞	9⅞	ACM MgdMultFd	MMF	1.08	10.7	...	355	10¼	10	10⅛	+ ⅛
	2½	1	ADT wt			...	...	932	1⅛	1	1⅛	+ ⅛
	9½	5	ADT	ADT		...	...	922	7	6⅝	7	...
	34	23¼	AFLAC	AFL	.44	1.4	15	1631	31½	30⅝	31½	+ ⅞
	26	17⅝	AL Labs A	BMD	.18	.8	91	632	23¾	22¾	23¾	+ ¾
	2⅛	½	AM Int	AM		...	...	406	⅝	9/16	9/16	...
	10¾	1⅝	AM Int pf			...	...	119	2	2	2	...
	11⅞	10⅞	AMEV Sec	AMV	1.02	8.7	...	35	11¾	11⅝	11¾	...
	80¼	54½	AMR	AMR		...	...	2769	58¼	57⅜	57⅜	−1
	47¼	34½	ARCO Chm	RCM	2.50	5.6	24	274	45	44½	45	+ ¼
	2⅜	1	ARX	ARX		...	17	2	1½	1½	1½	...
	53½	33⅞	ASA	ASA	2.00	5.7	...	307	35⅜	34⅞	35	...
	6½	¼	ATT Cap yen wt			...	...	60	1½	1¼	1¼	− ½
s	34¾	26⅛	AbbotLab	ABT	.60a	2.1	20	13224	28⅞	27⅞	28⅜	+ ⅛
n	9⅞	5⅛	Abex	ABE		...	...	376	5½	5⅛	5½	+ ⅜
▼	14	11⅞	Abitibi g	ABY	.50	...	...	2	11¾	11¾	11¾	− ⅛
	6¼	3⅞	AcmeElec	ACE		...	34	48	4⅜	4⅜	4⅜	...
	11¾	4¾	AcmeCleve	AMT	.40	5.9	13	34	6¾	6¾	6¾	...
	37⅜	14⅜	Acuson	ACN		...	11	778	16⅛	15⅝	15¾	...
	20¼	17½	AdamsExp	ADX	1.63e	8.3	...	112	19¾	19⅝	19¾	+ ⅛
	21½	7⅜	AdvMicro	AMD		...	4	4223	11⅝	11⅜	11½	...
	49⅛	29½	AdvMicro pf		3.00	8.0	...	54	37½	37	37⅜	+ ⅜
	9⅛	3¼	Advest	ADV		...	...	33	5¾	5⅝	5¾	+ ⅛
s	41⅝	28⅝	Aegon	AEG	.68i	1.7	7	24	40¾	40½	40¾	+ ⅛
	47	33¼	AetnaLife	AET	2.76	6.7	10	1496	41⅛	40¾	41	− ⅛
	12⅞	7½	AffilPub	AFP	.24	2.2	18	936	10¾	10⅝	10¾	+ ⅛
n	25¾	21½	AgriMinl	AMC	2.42	10.3	8	208	23¾	23¼	23½	− ¼
	19⅜	12⅝	Ahmanson	AHM	.88	6.4	8	1751	14	13¾	13¾	− ⅛
	27⅝	24	Ahmanson pf		2.40	9.1	...	29	26½	26¼	26½	...
	22½	4½	Aileen	AEE		...	9	179	5	4⅞	5	+ ⅛
s	49½	31¾	AirProduct	APD	.85	1.9	19	483	44½	44⅛	44⅛	− ⅜
	29¾	12½	AirbornFrght	ABF	.30	1.8	33	198	16⅞	16⅝	16¾	...
	34¼	18	Airgas	ARG		...	25	168	29⅞	29½	29¾	− ⅛
	13⅝	8⅛	Airlease	FLY	1.68	14.9	9	70	11½	11¼	11¼	− ⅛
	25⅝	24⅝	AlaPwr pfH		1.90	7.6	...	17	25	24⅞	24⅞	− ⅛
	25¾	23⅝	AlaPwr pfA		1.90	7.7	...	192	24⅞	24¾	24¾	− ⅛
	11¼	10⅛	AlaPwr pfS		.87	8.0	...	5	10⅞	10⅞	10⅞	+ ⅛
	104	94¾	AlaPwr pfC		8.16	8.0	...	z100	102⅜	102⅜	102⅜	− ⅛
	105	95½	AlaPwr pfB		8.28	7.9	...	z220	104½	104½	104½	+1
	23⅞	17⅛	AlaskaAir	ALK	.20	1.1	...	102	17¾	17½	17½	− ¼
▼	21¼	13⅞	AlbanyInt	AIN	.35	2.5	55	812	14¼	13¾	14¼	...
	32	21¼	AlbertoCl	ACV	.24	1.0	18	35	23¾	23⅜	23⅝	− ¼
	25¾	18⅝	AlbertoCl A	ACVA	.24.	1.1	17	42	22¾	22⅛	22¾	+ ⅜
	47½	32¾	Albertsons	ABS	.64	1.5	24	2504	44⅛	43	44⅛	+1
▼	22¾	17¼	Alcan	AL	.30	1.7	...	1680	17½	17⅛	17¼	− ¼
	42⅝	30¼	AlcoStd	ASN	.92	2.6	16	151	36⅜	35⅞	36	− ⅜
n	27⅛	23¼	AlcatelAsthom	ALA	.56e	2.2	...	64	26	25¾	25⅞	...
	27¾	15	AlexBrown	AB	.40	2.6	5	249	15½	15	15⅜	+ ⅜
	27⅜	18	Alex&Alex	AAL	1.00	3.9	16	860	25⅞	25½	25⅞	− ⅛
	32	8⅜	viAlexanders	ALX		...	...	681	29¼	27¼	28½	+1⅜
	129	92½	AlleghanyCp	Y	1.86t	1.5	20	2	121½	121½	121½	...
	36⅝	20¼	AllegLud	ALS	.88	2.6	25	192	33⅜	33	33⅜	+ ⅜
	48¾	41½	AllegPwr	AYP	3.20	6.8	13	1966	47	46¾	46⅞	...
	30	15	AllenGp	ALN	.20b	.8	16	60	24	23¾	23⅞	− ⅛
	27¼	18½	Allergan	AGN	.40	1.8	...	900	22⅞	22⅛	22⅝	+ ⅜
	39⅛	25¾	AllncCapMgt	AC	2.40e	7.9	12	1364	30½	29⅛	30½	+1¼
	12½	9¼	AllncGlblEnv	AEF	.18e	1.8	...	96	9⅞	9¾	9¾	− ⅛
▲	26⅛	19⅛	AlliantTech	ATK		...	7	845	26⅜	26⅛	26¼	+ ⅛
	28⅜	23¼	AlldIrishBk pf		2.97	11.2	...	88	26¾	26⅝	26⅝	− ⅛
	4	1¾	AlliedPdts	ADP		...	...	26	2	1⅞	1⅞	− ⅛
	61¼	34	AlliedSgnl	ALD	1.00	1.9	...	2884	53¼	52¼	52⅞	− ⅝
	10⅜	9½	AllmonTr	GSO	.66e	6.8	...	106	9⅞	9¾	9¾	...
	9⅞	8½	AllstMunOpp	AMO	.72	8.3	...	397	8⅞	8⅝	8⅝	− ¼
	10	8⅜	AllstMunOppII	AOT	.72	8.1	...	135	8⅞	8¾	8⅞	...
	10½	9	AllstMunOppIII	AIO	.72a	7.7	...	39	9⅜	9⅜	9⅜	+ ⅛
	11⅜	10⅛	AllstMunIn	ALM	.72a	6.7	...	202	10¾	10⅝	10¾	...
	11⅛	9¾	AllstMunInII	ALT	.69a	6.6	...	130	10⅝	10½	10½	...
	10⅛	9⅜	AllstMunInIII	ALL	.66a	6.9	...	77	9¾	9⅝	9⅝	...
	11⅜	9¾	AllstMunPrem	ALI	.75	7.1	...	267	10⅝	10½	10½	− ⅛
	43¾	34¾	ALLTEL	AT	1.48	3.4	19	609	43¾	43½	43¾	+ ⅛
	8⅝	4⅞	Allwaste	ALW		...	18	368	5¾	5½	5⅝	...
	80⅝	54⅜	Alcoa	AA	1.60	2.4	23	1256	66⅞	65⅝	65⅝	−1⅛
s	55¾	34⅝	Alza	AZA		...	58	5415	42	40½	42	+1½
	15/16	9/32	AmBase	ABC		...	...	410	7/16	⅜	7/16	+ 1/16
	12⅝	8½	AmaxGold	AU	.08	.8	31	827	9¾	9½	9⅝	− ⅛
	23⅜	15⅞	Amax	AMX	.80a	4.6	...	1358	17⅜	17⅛	17⅜	+ ⅛
	47	37½	Amax pf		3.00	6.9	...	7	44¼	43¾	43¾	− ¼
	40½	26¼	Ambac	ABK	.40	1.1	11	225	36¾	35⅝	36¾	+1⅛
	25	11⅝	AmcastInd	AIZ	.48	3.7	10	1454	13⅛	12	13	+1
			-N-N-N-									
	21⅝	11⅝	NBB Bcp	NBB	.84	4.1	10	32	20⅝	20⅜	20½	− ¼
s	31⅝	26	NBD Bcp	NBD	1.08	3.7	11	482	29¼	28⅞	29	− ¼
	74½	57½	NCH	NCH	1.00	1.4	15	3	72⅛	71½	72⅛	+ ⅝
	27	22½	NIPSCO	NI	1.24	4.8	13	2589	26	25¾	25⅞	+ ¼
▼	14⅛	6⅜	NL Ind	NL	.20	3.1	...	1160	6¾	6	6⅜	− ½
	8⅜	3¼	NS Gp	NSS	.03j	.6	...	41	5	4⅞	4⅞	− ⅛

	52 Weeks Hi	52 Weeks Lo	Stock	Sym	Div	Yld %	PE	Vol 100s	Hi	Lo	Close	Net Chg.
	25	16⅛	NUI	NUI	1.58	7.0	13	90	22⅝	22¼	22½	− ¼
	43¾	26	NWNL	NWN	1.48	3.8	11	15	38⅞	38¾	38¾	...
	28⅞	24⅞	NWNL pf		2.50	9.2	...	8	27⅜	27¼	27¼	...
	39¾	22⅜	NYMAGIC	NYM	.40	1.5	14	170	26	25⅞	26	+ ⅛
	60	35¾	NACCO	NC	.64	1.7	21	9	38¾	38½	38½	...
	42¼	30¾	Nalco	NLC	.84	2.4	19	883	35¾	35¼	35½	...
	31¼	18	Nashua	NSH	.72	3.3	544	80	22¼	21¾	21¾	− ⅛
	31⅝	25⅝	NtlAustrlBk	NAB	1.67e	6.4	...	20	26	26	26	− ¼
	46	31⅝	NtlCity	NCC	1.88	4.3	11	1190	43¾	43⅛	43⅝	+ ½
	62¾	48¾	NtlCity pf		4.00	6.5	...	4	61¼	61¼	61¼	+ ¼
	3	1/16	vjNtlConvStr	NCS		...	...	281	½	7/16	15/32	...
	44¼	4	vjNtlConvStr pf			...	...	1	7¼	7¼	7¼	...
	12¼	6½	NtlEducat	NEC		...	20	772	7	6⅝	6⅝	− ¼
	¾	1/16	NtlEnt	NEI		...	...	21	9/16	9/16	9/16	...
	29	23¼	NtlFuelG	NFG	1.50	5.8	13	928	26⅜	25⅞	26	− ⅛
	25	20	NtlHlthInv	NHI	2.08	8.7	...	57	24	23¾	24	...
	30⅞	18	NtlHlthLab	NH	.32	1.6	18	5348	20	19½	19¾	− ⅛
	1¼	1/16	NtlHeritg	NHR		...	...	39	¾	¾	¾	...
	16⅝	11⅛	NtlIntgp	NII		...	...	174	12	11½	12	...
	51½	45¾	NtlIntg pf		5.00	10.0	...	67	50⅜	49⅞	50	− ⅛
	7⅝	1⅛	NtlMedia	NM		...	...	312	6¼	6⅛	6⅛	...
s	21¾	11⅛	NtlMedEnt	NME	.48	4.2	7	4892	11½	11¼	11⅜	+ ⅛
	83	46½	NtlPresto	NPK	1.70a	3.2	11	20	53¾	53⅝	53¾	+ ⅛
	24	17	NatlRe	NRE	.12	.5	12	471	23½	23	23½	+ ¼
	12⅜	3⅞	NtlSemi	NSM		...	20	5098	11¾	11¼	11¾	+ ½
	50¾	34¼	NtlSemi pf		4.00	8.2	...	292	49	48⅜	49	+ ½
	26⅜	19	NtlSvcInd	NSI	1.00	4.0	17	588	25⅛	24¾	24⅞	...
	40¼	27½	NtlWestmin	NW	2.45e	6.5	83	31	37½	37¼	37½	+ ½
	28⅜	23¾	NtlWestmin A		2.66	9.9	...	56	26⅞	26⅝	26¾	...
	50	33	NationsBank	NB	1.48	3.4	30	3922	44¼	43½	43¾	+ ⅛
	30½	23	NatwdHlth	NHP	2.25	7.4	17	159	30⅜	29¾	30⅜	+ ½
	4⅛	1⅞	Navistar	NAV		...	...	1706	2⅛	2	2⅛	...
	1¼	¼	Navistar wtA			...	...	2	11/32	11/32	11/32	...
x	48⅛	27	Navistar pfG		6.00	21.5	...	x137	28½	27½	27⅞	−1⅝
	15⅝	10⅜	NeimanMarc	NMG	.20	1.6	...	14	12¼	12⅛	12⅛	...
	20⅝	11¼	NERCO	NER	.64	4.2	25	160	15¼	14¾	15⅛	+ ⅜
	18¼	9½	NetwkEqpt	NWK		...	...	208	11⅜	11⅛	11⅜	+ ¼
	22⅝	17⅛	NevPwr	NVP	1.60	7.2	19	415	22⅜	22¼	22⅜	+ ⅛
	4¾	3½	NewAmFd	HYB	.48	11.0	...	125	4⅜	4¼	4⅜	...
	37⅜	29¼	NewEngElec	NES	2.16	6.0	13	668	35⅞	35½	35⅞	+ ⅛
	13	9½	NewGermnyFd	GF	.33e	3.0	...	674	11⅜	11	11⅛	− ¼
	24⅛	18¼	NewJerRes	NJR	1.52	6.9	14	153	22	21⅝	21⅞	+ ¼
	25	19⅝	NewPlnRlty	NPR	1.26	5.6	23	295	22⅜	22⅛	22⅜	+ ⅛
	⅜	⅛	NewValley	NVL		...	...	194	9/64	⅛	⅛	...
▲	31¾	26⅛	NYSE&G	NGE	2.16	6.7	13	491	32	31⅝	32	+ ¼
	26⅝	23⅝	NYSE&G pfA		1.95e	7.6	...	12	25⅞	25⅝	25⅝	− ⅜
	27½	24¼	NYSE&G pf		2.12	7.9	...	1	26¾	26¾	26¾	− ¼
	53	33	Newell	NWL	.60	1.6	20	2053	37	35¾	36⅞	+ ¾
	20⅜	12	NewhallLd	NHL	.40	3.2	15	101	12½	12¼	12½	...
	51⅝	35	NewmtGold	NGC	.05a	.1	41	204	43¼	42¾	42⅞	− ¼
	53⅞	36⅛	NewmtMin	NEM	.60	1.2	32	327	48¾	48⅜	48¾	...
	36⅝	16⅝	NewsCorp	NWS	1.7e	.5	15	2986	34¾	34⅜	34¾	+ ⅛
	20½	16¾	NiaMoPwr	NMK	.80	4.1	13	2279	19⅝	19¼	19⅝	...
	47	38¼	NiaMoPwr pf		3.40	7.4	...	z60	46	46	46	+1
			-O-O-O-									
s	37	16⅛	OEA	OEA		...	30	252	20⅝	20¼	20⅜	− ⅛
	9⅞	5⅞	OHM Cp	OHM		...	46	37	7⅛	6⅞	6⅞	...
	9⅝	3⅝	OMI Cp	OMM	.14	3.7	6	107	3¾	3⅝	3¾	...
	2⅝	¾	OakInd	OAK		...	12	468	1¾	1⅝	1⅝	...
s	16½	7⅝	OakwdHome	OH	,08	.6	16	1052	14½	13⅞	14½	+ ¾
	24⅛	16⅝	OcciPete	OXY	1.00	5.6	25	4045	18⅛	17¾	17⅞	...
	17½	8⅞	OceanrgInt	OII		...	22	204	16⅝	16¼	16⅝	+ ⅛
s	31	15¼	OffcDepot	ODP		...	56	3221	28½	28	28⅛	− ⅛
	15¾	7	OffshrPipe	OFP		...	24	578	14⅞	14⅝	14⅝	− ⅛
	39⅛	24⅞	OffshrPipe pf		2.25	5.9	...	150	38⅜	37⅜	38	+ ¾
	24⅜	17⅝	Ogden	OG	1.25	6.7	14	864	18⅞	18½	18¾	− ⅛
	25½	14½	OgdenProj	OPI		...	10	153	15⅝	14⅞	15½	+ ¾
	22¾	18¾	OhioEd	OEC	1.50	6.7	14	945	22⅜	22	22⅜	+ ⅛
	59	50	OhioEd pf		4.40	7.6	...	2	58	58	58	+1
	95	83⅛	OhioEd pf		7.36	7.7	...	z200	95	95	95	+1
	107	100	OhioEd pf		9.12	8.7	...	z10	104½	104½	104½	+1½
	105	95	OhioEd pf		8.64	8.5	...	z50	102	101½	101½	− ¾
	100	91	OhioPwr pf		8.04	8.1	...	z100	99	99	99	...
	98	88	OhioPwr pfB		7.60	7.8	...	z600	98	97	97	− ½
	27½	25¾	OhioPwr pfG		2.27	8.5	...	4	26⅝	26⅝	26⅝	...
	44	30⅛	OklaGE	OGE	2.66	7.6	14	589	34⅞	34¼	34⅞	+ ½
s ▲	22⅝	15⅛	OldRepublic	ORI	.40	1.7	8	1359	23¼	22⅝	23¼	+ ⅝
	27⅜	24⅞	OldRepublic pf		2.20	8.5	...	31	26⅜	26	26	− ¼
	54¾	36⅝	Olin	OLN	2.20	5.5	12	93	40	39⅝	39⅞	+ ¼
	47½	42⅛	Olin pfA		3.64	8.4	...	77	43½	43½	43½	...
n	21	18⅝	OmegaHlthcr	OHI		...	...	138	19½	19¼	19¼	− ⅛
	28⅜	12	Omnicare	OCR	.14	.6	36	333	23¾	23⅛	23¼	− ½
	36¾	28¾	Omnicom	OMC	1.24	3.5	16	169	35⅜	35⅛	35⅜	+ ¼
	16¾	11⅜	Oneida	OCQ	.48	3.8	12	12	12½	12⅜	12½	+ ⅛
	17½	13⅜	ONEOK	OKE	1.00	5.8	15	123	17⅛	17	17⅛	− ⅛
	23	17⅞	OppenCap	OCC	1.70a	7.9	14	173	21⅝	21⅜	21½	− ⅛
	10	9	OppenGvt	OGT	.79	8.4	...	53	9½	9⅜	9⅜	...
	11¾	10⅜	OppenMlti	OMS	1.16	10.2	...	461	11½	11¼	11⅜	+ ⅛
	40	32⅜	OrangeRkl	ORU	2.46	6.2	13	70	39½	39⅜	39½	+ ⅛
n	30⅜	14½	OrbitEng	OE		...	...	2	14⅞	14⅞	14⅞	+ ⅛
	28¾	18½	OregSteel	OS	.56	2.9	11	504	19⅝	19⅛	19⅜	− ¼
	3⅝	1⅝	OrientExpr	OEH		...	...	2	1⅝	1⅝	1⅝	...
	40¼	29	OrionCap	OC	.92	2.3	7	24	39¾	39⅝	39¾	+ ⅛
	50¾	41	OrionCap pf		4.24e	8.7	...	1	48½	48½	48½	− ¼

From *The Wall Street Journal*, September 29, 1992. "Reprinted by permission of *The Wall Street Journal*, © 1992 Dow Jones & Company, Inc. All Rights Reserved Worldwide."

FIGURE 18.1

The first step in reading this table is to find the line corresponding to the company whose stock is of interest. Company names are usually abbreviated in newspapers. For example, Abbott Laboratories is abbreviated AbbotLab. Look in the stock table to find

| 52 Weeks | | | | | Yld | | Vol | | | | Net |
Hi	Lo	Stock	Sym	Div	%	PE	100s	Hi	Lo	Close	Chg
$34\frac{3}{4}$	$26\frac{1}{8}$	AbbotLab	ABT	.60a	2.1	20	13224	$28\frac{7}{8}$	$27\frac{7}{8}$	$28\frac{3}{8}$	$+\frac{1}{8}$

The numbers $34\frac{3}{4}$ and $26\frac{1}{8}$ in front of the company's name show that $34\frac{3}{4}$ ($34.75) is the highest price that the stock has reached in the last 52 weeks, while $26\frac{1}{8}$ ($26.125) is the lowest. After the name of the company and its symbol, find .60a, which means that the company pays $.60 per year per share of stock as a dividend to the owners of the stock. Dividends go up when the company is doing well and down when business is bad. The symbol a after the .60 indicates an extra dividend in addition to the regular dividend. The 2.1 in the next column is the current yield on the company's stock, in percent. The dividend of .60 per share is 2.1% of the current purchase price of the stock. After the 2.1 is 20, the price-earnings ratio, discussed later. Then comes 13224, the sales for the day in hundreds. On the day reported, a total of

$$13,224 \times 100 = 1,322,400$$

shares of Abbott Laboratories stock were sold. After 13224 comes a list of prices reached by the stock during the day. The first number, $28\frac{7}{8}$, tells the highest price reached by the stock for the day, while $27\frac{7}{8}$ was the lowest. The next number, $28\frac{3}{8}$, says the stock closed for the day at $28\frac{3}{8}$ per share. The last number is $+\frac{1}{8}$, or $\frac{1}{8}$ of a dollar more than the last price of the previous day.

NOTE In reading the stock table, the following should be noted.
(1) Price rises or declines of 5% or more are highlighted with boldface type (see Abex).
(2) Up or down arrows next to a stock indicate a new 52-week high or low (see Alcan).
(3) Stocks with unusual volume activity are underlined (see NL Ind).

EXAMPLE 1
Reading a Stock Table

Use the stock table to find (a) the highest price for the last 52 weeks for Alcoa and (b) the dividend for Nalco.

SOLUTION

(a) The abbreviation for Alcoa is AA. Find the correct line in the stock table.

| 52 Weeks | | | | | Yld | | Vol | | | | Net |
Hi	Lo	Stock	Sym	Div	%	PE	100s	Hi	Lo	Close	Chg
$80\frac{5}{8}$	$54\frac{3}{8}$	Alcoa	AA	1.60	2.4	23	1256	$66\frac{7}{8}$	$65\frac{5}{8}$	$65\frac{5}{8}$	$-1\frac{1}{8}$

The highest price in the last 52 weeks is $80\frac{5}{8}$ or 80.625, the first number on the left.

(b) In the table, the dividend is given just after the company symbol, NLC. The dividend for Nalco is $.84. ∎

The letters "pf" appear after some of the company names in the stock table. These letters represent "preferred stock," which was discussed in Section 18.1.

EXAMPLE 2

Reading a Stock Table

Find the cost for 100 shares of Ogden at the low price for the day.

SOLUTION Find the total cost of a stock purchase by multiplying the price per share by the number of shares. From the stock table, the low price of Ogden was $18\frac{1}{2}$ per share. First change $18\frac{1}{2}$ to the decimal 18.5, and multiply.

$$100 \times 18.5 = \$1850$$

The cost of 100 shares of this stock is $1850 (plus any broker's fee). ∎

3 It is necessary to use a broker to buy or sell a stock. The broker has representatives at the exchange who will execute a buyer's order. (It is sometimes possible to buy stock directly from a bank, which might sell it with no sales charge.) The broker will charge a fee, or **commission**, for executing an order. Commission rates formerly were set by stock exchange rules and did not vary from broker to broker. Now, however, commissions are competitive and vary considerably among brokers.

In the last few years, several **discount brokers** have become popular. These brokers merely buy and sell stock and offer no additional services, such as research or suggestions on stocks to buy or sell.

The rates charged depend on whether the order is for a **round lot** of shares (multiples of 100) or an **odd lot** (fewer than 100 shares). Odd lot orders often involve an **odd-lot differential**: an extra charge of $\$\frac{1}{8}$, or 12.5 cents, a share. Typical expenses in buying and selling stock are as follows. (There is often a minimum commission charge.)

Buying Stock	**Selling Stock**
Broker's commission of 2.5% of purchase price plus Any odd-lot differential	Broker's commission of 2.5% of selling price plus Any odd-lot differential plus SEC fee (see below) plus Any transfer taxes (see below)

The SEC fee is set by the Securities and Exchange Commission, a federal government agency that regulates stock markets. The fee is currently 1 cent per $500 in value (or any fraction of $500). For example, to find the fee for a sale of $1100, first divide $1100 by $500.

$$\frac{\$1100}{\$500} = 2.2$$

Since the fee is 1¢ per $500, or *fraction of $500*, round 2.2 *up* to 3. The fee is then $3 \times 1¢ = 3¢$.

NOTE Some state and local governments charge a **transfer tax** when stock is sold. The amount of this tax would be subtracted by the broker before turning over the balance of the money to the seller.

4   The next two examples show the total cost of a stock purchase and the cost of selling a stock.

EXAMPLE 3

Finding Total Cost of a Purchase

Marie Wilson bought 75 shares of stock, paying $26\frac{3}{4}$ per share. Find her total cost for the purchase.

SOLUTION   The basic cost of the stock is found by multiplying the price per share and the number of shares.

$$\text{Price per share} \times \text{Number of shares} = \$26\frac{3}{4} \times 75$$
$$= \$26.75 \times 75$$
$$= \$2006.25.$$

The broker's commission is 2.5% of this amount, or

$$\text{Broker's commission} = 2.5\% \times \$2006.25$$
$$= 0.025 \times \$2006.25$$
$$= \$50.16.$$

Since Wilson bought 75 shares (and not a multiple of 100 shares), she must pay an odd-lot differential of $\$\frac{1}{8}$, or 12.5 cents, per share. For 75 shares, this odd-lot differential amounts to

$$75 \text{ shares} \times \$\frac{1}{8} \text{ per share} = \$9.38.$$

The total cost of the shares of stock is

$2006.25	basic cost
50.16	broker's commission
+ 9.38	odd-lot differential
$2065.79	

EXAMPLE 4

Finding Total Cost of a Stock Sale

Find the amount received by a person selling 700 shares of a stock at $63\frac{5}{8}$.

SOLUTION   The basic price of the stock is

$$700 \times \$63\frac{5}{8} = 700 \times \$63.625 = \$44{,}537.50.$$

Find the SEC fee as described. First,

$$\frac{\$44{,}537.50}{\$500} = 89.075.$$

Round 89.075 up to 90. The SEC fee is then

$$90 \times 1\text{¢} = 90\text{¢}.$$

The broker's commission is 2.5% of the basic price, or

$$0.025 \times \$44,537.50 = \$1113.44.$$

Finally, the seller receives

$44,537.50	basic price
− 1,113.44	broker's fee
$43,424.06	
− .90	SEC fee
$43,423.16.	

There is no odd-lot differential since the number of shares traded is a multiple of 100. ■

Most people buy stock because they hope that the price will go up. If the price does go up, the investor can then sell the stock at a profit. Some people, however, buy a stock because of the dividend that it pays. (A dividend is usually paid quarterly.)

While there is no certain way of choosing stocks that will go up, there are a couple of **stock ratios** that can be looked at when considering a stock purchase. Two useful ratios are the **current yield** and the **price-earnings ratio**.

5   The **current yield** on a stock is used to compare the dividends paid by stocks selling at different prices. Find current yield with the following formula.

$$\text{Current yield} = \frac{\text{Annual dividend per share}}{\text{Current price per share}}$$

This result usually is converted to a percent (rounded to the nearest tenth). The annual dividend rate and the current yield can be found in the stock tables in daily newspapers.

EXAMPLE 5

Finding Current Yield

Find the current yield for each of the following stocks: (a) Olin dividend $2.20 per year, purchase price $39\frac{7}{8}$ per share, and (b) Acme Electric no dividend, purchase price $4\frac{3}{8}$.

SOLUTION

(a)   Use the formula for current yield to get

$$\text{Current yield} = \frac{\$2.20}{\$39.875} = 0.055 = 5.5\% \qquad \text{(rounded)}$$

(b)   Current yield $= \dfrac{\$0}{\$4.375} = 0 = 0\%.$ ∎

NOTE A stock pays no dividend when the company has been going through bad times or is investing in research or new plants which promise a long-term payoff. Sometimes a small new company will pay no dividends during its early years, preferring to reinvest the money for long-term growth.

6 One number that some people use to help decide which stock to buy is the **price-earnings ratio** (abbreviated **PE ratio**). This ratio is found with the following formula.

$$\text{PE ratio} = \frac{\text{Price per share}}{\text{Annual net income per share}}$$

EXAMPLE 6   Find the PE ratio for each of the following stocks: (a) Reebok: price per share $24.50,
Finding   annual earnings per share $2.46, and (b) Upjohn: price per share $32.50, annual earn-
the PE Ratio   ings per share $3.02.

SOLUTION

(a) Use the formula to get

$$\text{PE ratio} = \frac{24.50}{2.46} = 9.96, \text{ or 10 after rounding.}$$

It is usual to round the PE ratio to the nearest whole number.

(b) $\text{PE ratio} = \dfrac{32.50}{3.02} = 10.76, \text{ or 11 after rounding.}$ ∎

Sometimes a low PE ratio may indicate that the stock is a "sleeper" which has not been found by other investors. On the other hand, a high PE ratio may indicate that the stock's price is too high; as other people notice this, the stock's price could fall.

Unfortunately, the PE ratio is not a perfect guide to future stock market behavior. The PE ratio may be low, not because the stock is an undervalued sleeper, but because investors correctly see a poor future for the company. A PE ratio may be high, not because the stock is overpriced, but because investors correctly feel that company earnings will increase over the next few years.

Many daily newspapers now give the PE ratio. If no PE ratio is given for a particular stock, most probably that company has lost money during the previous year.

18.2 Exercises

Find each of the following from the stock table. Give money answers in dollars.

1. High for the day for Acme Electric
2. Low for the day for Aetna Life
3. Closing price for Navistar (NAV)
4. Change from the previous day for Airgas
5. 52-week high for Nashua
6. 52-week low for Airborne Freight
7. Dividend for Ohio Edison (not the preferred)
8. Dividend for Nevada Power
9. Low for the day for Allergan
10. High for the day for Alaska Airlines
11. Sales for the day for Air Product
12. Sales for the day for Alcoa
13. Yield for Alcan
14. Yield for Oneida

Find the price for each of the following stock purchases. Ignore any broker's fees.

	Stock	Number of Shares	Transaction
15.	Olin Corporation	200	high
16.	Nevada Power	500	close
17.	Oneida	300	low
18.	Airgas	400	low
19.	Omnicare	600	close
20.	Newscorp	300	high

Find the price for each of the following stock purchases. Use the broker's charges given in the text. (Hint: In Exercise 27, the odd-lot differential is charged on only 40 shares.)

21. 200 shares at $27\frac{5}{8}$
22. 700 shares at $19\frac{1}{8}$
23. 1200 shares at $37\frac{3}{4}$
24. 1400 shares at $16\frac{7}{8}$
25. 60 shares at $35\frac{5}{8}$
26. 90 shares at $53\frac{3}{4}$
27. 540 shares at $69\frac{1}{4}$
28. 740 shares at $32\frac{3}{8}$

Find the amount received by the sellers of the following stocks.

29. 700 shares at $29\frac{5}{8}$
30. 600 shares at $54\frac{1}{4}$
31. 1500 shares at $6\frac{7}{8}$
32. 1400 shares at $36\frac{7}{8}$
33. 830 shares at $52\frac{3}{4}$
34. 360 shares at $72\frac{1}{8}$

Find the current yield for each of the following stocks. Round to the nearest tenth of a percent.

	Stock	Current Price per Share	Annual Dividend
35.	Emerson Electronic	$21	$1.12
36.	Gillette	$34	$1.86
37.	K Mart	$48.75	$1.32
38.	General Motors	$29.25	$1.60
39.	Xerox	$32.50	$3
40.	Hewlett-Packard	$38.75	$ .34

Find the PE ratio for each of the following. Round all answers to the nearest whole number.

	Stock	Price per Share	Net Income per Share
41.	Motorola	$36.75	$3.20
42.	General Electric	$45.75	$3.10
43.	Westinghouse	$37.875	$4.25
44.	McDonald's	$46.75	$3.35

Work each of the following word problems.

45. Mindy Egbert bought 50 shares of Sears, Roebuck, selling at $39\frac{1}{2}$ per share, and 80 shares of Mobil Oil at $61\frac{1}{8}$ per share. Find the total amount that she paid, ignoring broker's commissions.

46. Wanda Wyzninski bought 80 shares of TRW at $54\frac{3}{4}$ per share, and 50 shares of Disney at $36\frac{1}{8}$ per share. Find the total amount that she paid, ignoring broker's commissions.

47. Explain the purpose of calculating a PE ratio. (See Objective 6.)

48. What does the current yield of a stock indicate? (See Objective 5.)

18.3 Bonds

OBJECTIVES

1. Know the basics of bonds.
2. Read bond tables.
3. Find the cost of bonds, including commission.

A corporation can raise money by selling additional shares of stock. The purchasers of this stock become part owners of the business. However, company management may feel that the sale of additional stock would excessively dilute the ownership rights of current stockholders. If so, management might decide to raise money by borrowing.

1 For short-term money needs, a corporation might borrow from a bank or an insurance company. For longer term borrowing (such as 5 years or more), the corporation might borrow money from the public. The corporation borrows this money by selling **bonds**. A bond is a promise to repay the borrowed money at some specified time. The bond also promises to pay interest at a certain annual rate.

For example, suppose a person buys a bond for $1000 from Duke Power. This bond promises to repay the $1000 in the year 2002 and until then to pay interest of $7\frac{3}{8}\%$ per year. For this bond, the investor would receive annual interest payments of

$$\$1000 \times 7\frac{3}{8}\% = \$1000 \times .07375 = \$73.75.$$

In this example, $1000 is the amount that the company promises to repay to the investor. This amount is called the **face value** or **par value** of the bond. Almost all corporations issue bonds with a par value of $1000.

2 The Duke Power bond will be redeemed by the company in 2002 for $1000. Suppose, however, that the bond's owner needs money now. The bond can be sold quickly through a bond dealer. However, the price for the bond is set, not by Duke Power but by market conditions. To find the selling price of a bond, look in the "Corporate Bond" section of the daily newspaper. A portion of *The Wall Street Journal* corporate bond page is reproduced in Figure 18.2.

For these Duke Power bonds, the table gives the following.

Bonds	Cur Yld	Vol	Close	Net Chg
Duke P $7\frac{3}{8}02$	7.3	10	$101\frac{1}{4}$	– – –

After the name of the company, which may be abbreviated, comes $7\frac{3}{8}02$. The $7\frac{3}{8}$ says that the bonds pay $7\frac{3}{8}\%$ interest on their face value of $1000, while 02 is an abbreviation for the year 2002. (An "s" indicates that interest is paid by the company every 6 months instead of annually.) The number 7.3 is the current yield. The 10 shows that 10 bonds with a face value of $1000 each were sold that day. The next number gives the closing price of the bonds. The bond prices in the table represent not dollar amounts but percents. Here $101\frac{1}{4}$ says that the bond is selling at $101\frac{1}{4}\%$ of its par value of $1000. An investor who sold these bonds at this price would receive

$$\$1000 \times 101\frac{1}{4}\% = 1000 \times 1.0125 = \$1012.50.$$

NOTE This selling price of $1012.50 is higher than the face value of $1000 since general interest rates are lower than the $7\frac{3}{8}\%$ of this bond.

Bonds	Cur Yld	Vol	Close	Net Chg.
DatGen 8⅜02	9.5	14	88	...
DataGn 01	cv	5	93	+ 1
Datpnt 8⅞06	cv	8	63¼	+ ¾
DaytP 8⅛01	7.8	40	103⅝	+ ¾
DetEd 6s96	6.0	45	100¼	+ ½
DetEd 6.4s98	6.4	30	100	− ¾
DetEd 8.15s00	8.0	22	102¼	+ ½
DetEd 7⅜01	7.4	10	99¾	− ⅜
Disney zr05	...	448	47⅛	+ ⅛
Dow 8½s06	8.2	3	103¼	− ⅜
duPnt 8.45s04	8.2	44	103	+ ⅛
duPnt 8½06	8.2	50	103⅞	...
duPnt dc6s01	6.3	334	94⅞	...
DukeP 7⅜01	7.1	15	103¼	+ ¾
DukeP 7⅜02	7.3	10	101¼	...
EKod zr11	...	57	29¼	− ⅛
EmbSuit 10½94	10.1	23	103¾	+ ¼
EmbSuit 10⅞02	10.3	10	105⅜	− ⅝
EBP 6¾06	cv	168	66	+ ¼
EnqStr 02	...	48	105½	+ ½
Exxon 6s97	6.0	35	100½	...
Exxon 6½98	6.4	60	101	+ ¼
FMC 9½2000	9.3	46	101⅝	...
FairCp 12¼96	12.4	10	98½	− 2
FairCp 12s01	13.0	72	92¼	− 1⅝
FairCp 13⅛06	14.2	105	92⅜	− 2⅛
FdMog 8⅜93	8.3	50	101	− ⅛
FedN zr19s	...	290	10¾	+ ⅛
FedDS 10s00	10.0	506	100⅜	...
Fldcst 6s12	cv	65	70¾	+ ½
FUnRE 8⅜94	8.4	10	100	...
Flemg 6½cld	cv	5	103¼	...
FrdC 8⅜01	8.3	75	101½	...
FrdC 8½02	8.4	18	100⅝	− ⅜
FrpMCG zr11	...	1	32½	− ½
Frpt dc6.55s01	cv	11	92	...
FreptM zr06	...	106	29⅞	...
Fuqua 9½98	9.9	51	95½	− ⅛
Fuqua 9⅞97	9.9	10	100	− ⅛
GMA 7.85s98	7.8	10	100⅞	...
GMA 8s02	7.8	25	102	...
GMA 8.65s08	8.5	6	102	...
GMA dc6s11	7.5	29	79⅞	+ ⅛
GMA zr12	...	169	169	− 1⅛
GMA zr15	...	45	135	− 1⅝
GMA 8⅞96	8.7	135	101⅝	+ ⅛
GMA 8¼16	8.4	255	98¾	...
GMA 8s93J	7.8	25	102¼	+ 1/16
GMA 8s94	7.6	100	105⅞	+ ⅞
GMA 8⅜97	7.9	1	106½	− 2¼
GTE 9⅜99	9.0	3	104⅛	...
GnCorp 02	...	33	99	− 1
GEICap 7⅞06	7.4	34	106¼	+ ½
GHost 7s94	7.0	25	100	...
GHost 11½02	10.9	15	105½	+ ¼
GHost 8s02	cv	7	113	+ 3
Genrad 7¼11	cv	51	45	+ 1
Ga Glf 15s00	13.0	6	115	...
GaPw 8⅛01	7.9	47	102¼	...
GaPw 7½02J	7.4	32	102	− 1
GaPw 7⅞03	7.7	1	102	...
GaPw 8⅝cld	...	20	103 11/32	...
GaPw 10s16J	9.4	18	105⅞	− 1⅛

Bonds	Cur Yld	Vol	Close	Net Chg.
MACOM 9¼06	cv	5	95¾	+ 1¾
MGMGrd 11¾99	11.3	73	104	− ¾
MGMGrd 12s02	11.5	363	104	− ⅝
MGMUA 13s96f	...	219	69⅝	− ⅞
Magntx 8s01	cv	15	112	− 2
MfrH 8⅛04	8.0	20	101⅞	− 1⅜
MfrH 8⅛07	8.0	15	101⅛	...
MarO 9½94	9.0	28	105⅞	...
MarO 9¾99	9.0	30	108¾	...
MarkIV 13⅜99	12.2	5	110	− 3⅛
MarkIV 07	cv	35	104½	− ½
Masco 5¼12	cv	10	88¾	+ 1¼
Maxus 8½08	9.2	5	92½	− ¾
vjMcCro 7½s94f	...	2	16½	+ ⅝
vjMcCro 7¾95f	...	4	16½	+ ¼
McDe 10s03	9.9	25	101	− ½
McDinv 8s11	cv	11	98	− 2
McDnl zr94	...	23	95⅛	...
McDnlDg 7⅞97	7.9	175	99½	+ ⅛
McDnlDg 8⅝97	8.5	30	101¾	− ⅛
McDnlDg 9¾12	9.7	100	100¼	...
MeYk 9.1s02	8.8	25	103½	+ 1½
Mead 6¾12	cv	17	98¼	...
Medpix 02	...	5	100½	− ½
Melln 8⅞98	8.7	10	102	+ ¾
MesaCap na96	...	191	94⅛	− ⅜
MesaCap 13½99	13.8	513	98	...
MichB 7¾11	7.8	6	100	− ½
MichB 7s12	7.2	20	97⅜	+ ⅝
MichB 8⅛15	7.9	45	103¼	...
MidlBk 11.35s93	11.2	100	101 11/16	− 1/16
MKT 5½33fr	...	10	60	...
MPac 5s45f	...	1	60⅜	...
Mobil 8⅝94	8.0	25	107¾	+ ¼
Mons 9⅛00	8.9	1	102¾	...
Motrla zr09	...	10	40¾	+ ¾
MtSTl 7¾13	7.8	25	100	...
MtSTl 8s17	8.0	51	100	− ¼
MtStTl 9¼14	8.8	19	105	+ ¼
NBD 7¼06	cv	20	113	− ½
NJBTl 7¼11	7.3	15	99½	+ ⅜
NJBTl 7⅜12	7.4	30	99⅜	...
NJBTl 7¾13	7.8	35	100	− ⅛
NJBTl 8¼16	8.0	20	103	− 1
NJBTl 8s16	7.8	4	102	− ⅜
NJBTl 8¾18	8.4	40	104⅝	− ¾
NRUt 9¼92	9.2	3	100⅛	...
vjNtGyp zr04	...	154	1⅞	...
NStl 8⅜06	9.3	5	90½	+ ⅜
NConv 9s08f	cv	15	40	− ½
NtEdu 6½11	cv	1	70	...
vjNEnt 4¾96f	cv	20	16	...
NavFin 7⅝93	7.9	225	96⅞	− 11/32
NavFin 7½94	8.1	90	92¼	− ¼
NavFin 11.95s95	13.4	642	89	− 1
Owlll 10½02	10.1	104	103¾	...
Ownlll 10s02	9.9	33	101	− ⅛
Ownlll 9¾04	9.8	423	99	− 1¼
OxyOG 9¾00	9.7	1	101	− 1⅛
PPG 10⅛95	9.8	5	103⅝	− ¼
PcLumb 12s96	11.8	1	101½	− ½
PcLumb 12½98	11.9	1	105	+ 1½

From *The Wall Street Journal*, September 29, 1992. "Reprinted by permission of *The Wall Street Journal*, ©1992 Dow Jones & Company, Inc. All Rights Reserved Worldwide."

FIGURE 18.2

EXAMPLE 1 *Finding the Selling Price of Bonds*

Find the current selling price of the following bonds: (a) Fuqua, $9\frac{1}{2}\%$ bonds of 1998, (b) Ford Motor Credit Company, $8\frac{1}{2}\%$ bonds of 2002, and (c) Exxon, $6\frac{1}{2}\%$ bonds of 1998.

SOLUTION

(a) The listing for Fuqua gives the following

$$\text{Fuqua}\quad 9\frac{1}{2}98 \quad 9.9 \quad 51 \quad 95\frac{1}{2} \quad -\frac{1}{8}$$

The price information for these bonds comes from the number $95\frac{1}{2}$. Only 51 of these Fuqua bonds were sold that day (look between 9.9 and $95\frac{1}{2}$). This number represents just 51 bonds, not 51 hundreds as with stocks.

Since the price for the day of Fuqua bonds is $95\frac{1}{2}$, or $95\frac{1}{2}\%$ of par value, the selling price for one bond is

$$\$1000 \times 95\frac{1}{2}\% = \$1000 \times .955 = \$955.$$

(b) Find the listing for Ford Motor Credit Company. The price for the day is given as $100\frac{5}{8}$, with one bond selling for

$$\$1000 \times 100\frac{5}{8}\% = \$1000 \times 1.00625 = \$1006.25.$$

(c) The selling price of an Exxon $6\frac{1}{2}\%$ bond of 1998 is given in the bond table as 101. The selling price of one bond is

$$\$1000 \times 101\% = \$1000 \times 1.01 = \$1010 \quad \blacksquare$$

3 Commissions charged on bond sales vary among brokers. A common charge is $5 per bond, either to buy or to sell.

EXAMPLE 2
Finding the Cost of Purchasing Bonds

Find the charge to purchase 15 bonds of Masco, $5\frac{1}{4}\%$ of 2012. Use the low price for the day and assume a sales charge of $5 per bond.

SOLUTION   From the bond table in Figure 18.2, the price is found to be $88\frac{3}{4}$, or $88\frac{3}{4}\%$. The cost to buy one bond of $1000 par value is

$$\$1000 \times 88\frac{3}{4}\% = \$1000 \times .8875 = \$887.50.$$

Fifteen of these bonds cost

$$15 \times \$887.50 = \$13,312.50.$$

Commission is $5 per bond, with a total commission of

$$15 \times \$5 = \$75.$$

The purchase price of the 15 bonds is

$$\$13,312.50 + \$75 = \$13,387.50. \quad \blacksquare$$

Bonds are a debt; a corporation owes money to its bondholders. As such, bondholders have first claim, after bankruptcy lawyers, on the assets of the corporation if it goes into bankruptcy. (Stockholders have last claim.) Even so, bonds may pay off only a few cents on the dollar in event of bankruptcy. Bondholders have lost substantial sums in recent bankruptcies. (Some investors like to buy the bonds of bankrupt and troubled companies—such **junk bonds** have been known to pay off handsomely for their holders, while other holders have lost money on them. We might mention that bond salespeople do not like the term "junk bonds," they prefer "high-yield securities.")

18.3 Exercises

Find the following prices from the bond table in Figure 18.2. Use the listing for GMA, the $8\frac{1}{4}\%$ bonds of 2016.

1. Closing price for GMA bonds
2. Number of bonds sold
3. Interest paid on the par value of the bonds, both as a percent and in dollars
4. Year when the bonds will be paid off by the company
5. Change since the previous day in the price of one bond
6. Price to buy 25 such bonds, at the closing price, with sales charges of $5 per bond

Find the cost, including sales charges of $5 per bond, for each of the following transactions.

	Bond	Number Purchased
7.	Mountain States Telephone, $7\frac{3}{4}\%$ bonds of 2013	15
8.	DOW, $8\frac{1}{2}\%$ bonds of 2006	10
9.	NBD, $7\frac{1}{4}\%$ bonds of 2006	15
10.	FairCp, $13\frac{1}{8}\%$ bonds of 2006	20
11.	Michigan Bank, 7% bonds of 2012	45
12.	Dupont, $8\frac{1}{2}\%$ bonds of 2006	30
13.	GMA, $8\frac{3}{8}\%$ bonds of 1997	10
14.	MACOM, $9\frac{1}{4}\%$ bonds of 2006	20
15.	NtEdu, $6\frac{1}{2}\%$ bonds of 2011	15
16.	Mead, $6\frac{3}{4}\%$ bonds of 2012	50

17. Explain the purpose of bonds. (See Objective 1.)
18. Explain how the annual interest payments are determined for bondholders. (See Objective 2.)

Work each word problem. Assume sales commissions of $5 per bond. Use the table of bond prices in Figure 18.2.

19. Martie Ondricka bought 15 bonds of MKT. Find the total purchase price (don't forget the sales commission).

20. Trish O'Donnell bought 60 bonds of FMC. Find the total purchase price (don't forget the sales commission).

21. Clark Dimmitt sold 55 FairCp bonds, the $13\frac{1}{8}\%$ bonds of 2006. Find the final amount received from the sale.

22. Kristie Ficker sold 75 GnCorp bonds. Find the amount received from the sale.

23. An investor has purchased 20 bonds of Maxus. (a) Find the purchase price of the bonds, including sales charges. (b) How much annual interest would the investor earn on the bonds?

24. A pension fund has purchased 35 bonds of DataGn, the $8\frac{3}{8}\%$ bonds of 2002. (a) Find the purchase price of the bonds, including sales charges. (b) How much annual interest would the fund earn on the bonds?

18.4 Distribution of Profits and Losses in a Partnership

OBJECTIVES

1. Divide profits by equal shares.
2. Divide profits by agreed ratio.
3. Divide profits by original investment.
4. Divide profits by salary and agreed ratio.
5. Divide profits by interest on investment and agreed ratio.

In a partnership, a business is owned by two or more people. These partners may have invested equal amounts of money to start the business, or one may have invested money while another invested specialized knowledge. The partners must agree on the relative amounts of money and time that will be invested in the business. They must also agree on the method by which any profits will be distributed. This section considers the various methods by which partnership profits may be distributed.

1   The partners may simply agree to share all profits equally. (In fact, if there is no formal agreement stating the terms under which profits are to be divided, most states require that profits be divided equally.)

EXAMPLE 1
Dividing Profits by Equal Shares

Three partners opened a music store, and agreed to divide the profits equally. If the store produced profits of $69,000 in one year, each partner would get

$$\frac{1}{3} \times \$69,000 = \$23,000$$

as the annual share of the profits. ■

2 Partners may agree to divide the profits using some given rule. For example, two partners might agree that profits will be divided so that 60% goes to one partner and 40% to the other. Profit divisions are sometimes given as a ratio; this division could be written 60:40, or in a reduced form, 3:2, with profits said to be divided in an **agreed ratio**.

EXAMPLE 2
Dividing Profits by Agreed Ratio

Three partners divide the profits from a business in the ratio 2:3:5. How would profits of $47,500 be divided?

SOLUTION   The ratio 2:3:5 says that the profit should be divided into $2 + 3 + 5 = 10$ equal shares. The first partner gets 2 of these 10 shares, or

$$\frac{2}{10} \times \$47,500 = \$9500$$

The second partner gets 3 of the 10 equal shares, or

$$\frac{3}{10} \times \$47,500 = \$14,250$$

Finally, the third partner gets 5 shares, or

$$\frac{5}{10} \times \$47,500 = \$23,750$$

To check, the sum of the three shares, $9500 + $14, 250 + $23,750, is the total profit, or $47,500. ∎

3 A common way of dividing the profits is on the basis of the **original investments** made by each partner. The fraction of the total original investment supplied by each partner is used to find the fraction of the profit that each partner receives.

EXAMPLE 3
Dividing Profits by Original Investment

Ed Porter, Fran Jones, and Wes Wilson formed a partnership. Porter contributed $15,000, Jones $20,000, and Wilson $25,000. The three signed an agreement that profits would be distributed based on the original investment. If the firm made a profit of $75,000, find the share received by each.

SOLUTION   The total amount contributed to start the company was

$$\$15,000 + \$20,000 + \$25,000 = \$60,000$$

Of this total, Porter gave

$$\frac{\$15,000}{\$60,000} = \frac{1}{4}.$$

Therefore, Porter is entitled to $\frac{1}{4}$ of the profits, or

$$\frac{1}{4} \times \$75,000 = \$18,750.$$

Jones gave

$$\frac{\$20,000}{\$60,000} = \frac{1}{3}$$

of the total, and gets $\frac{1}{3}$ of the profits, or $\$75,000 \times \frac{1}{3} = \$25,000$. Finally, Wilson gave

$$\frac{\$25,000}{\$60,000} = \frac{5}{12}$$

of the total, and gets $\frac{5}{12}$ of the profits or

$$\frac{5}{12} \times \$75,000 = \$31,250. \quad \blacksquare$$

NOTE Each partner's fraction or percent of the total investment must be determined before the profit distribution is calculated.

EXAMPLE 4
Dividing Losses by
Original Investment

Suppose the firm in Example 3 had a loss of $36,000 in one year. Find the share of the loss that each partner must pay.

SOLUTION   Just as partners share profits, they may be called on to share losses. Here Porter must pay $\frac{1}{4}$ of the loss (see Example 3), or

$$\frac{1}{4} \times \$36,000 = \$9000.$$

Jones must pay $\frac{1}{3}$ of the loss, or $12,000, while Wilson must pay $\frac{5}{12}$ of the loss, or $15,000. $\blacksquare$

4   Sometimes one partner contributes money to get a business started, while a second partner contributes money and also operates the business on a daily basis. In such a case, the partner operating the business may be paid a salary out of profits, with any additional profits divided in some agreed-upon ratio, called dividing profits by **salary and agreed ratio**. As mentioned in the introduction to this chapter, a partner who makes only a financial investment, but takes no part in running the business, is a **silent partner**.

EXAMPLE 5
Dividing Profits by
Salary and Original
Investment

Lin Chao and Joan Frisk start a new dry-cleaning business. Frisk contributed $50,000, while Chao contributed $25,000. The business will be run by Chao. The partners have agreed to pay Chao a salary of $14,000 per year, and then divide the remaining profits according to the original investment. Find the amount each partner would get from a profit of $26,000.

SOLUTION   The profit is first used to pay Chao's salary. Of the $26,000, Chao gets $14,000, leaving the following.

$26,000	total profit
− 14,000	Chao's salary
$12,000	profit to be divided

The balance of the profits will be divided in the ratio of the original investments, which total $50,000 + $25,000 = $75,000$. Of this total, Chao contributed

$$\frac{\$25,000}{\$75,000} = \frac{1}{3},$$

and thus receives

$$\frac{1}{3} \times \$12,000 = \$4,000$$

Frisk receives the balance of the $12,000, or $8000.

In summary, Chao receives the following.

	$14,000	salary
+	4000	share of profits after salary
	$18,000	total

Frisk receives only the $8000. ■

5   Sometimes one partner will put up a large share of the money necessary to start a firm, while other partners may actually operate the firm. In such a case, an agreement to divide profits by **interest on investment and agreed ratio** may be reached by which the partner putting up the money gets interest on the investment before any further division of profits.

EXAMPLE 6
Dividing Profits by Interest and Agreed Ratio

Laura Cameron, Jay Davis, and Donna Friedman opened a restaurant. Cameron contributed $250,000 to the opening of the restaurant, which will be operated by Davis and Friedman. The partners agree that Cameron will first receive a 10% return on her investment before any further division of profits. Additional profits will be divided in the ratio 1:2:2. Find the amount that each partner would receive from a profit of $75,000.

SOLUTION   Cameron is first paid a 10% return on her investment of $250,000. This amounts to

$$\$250,000 \times 10\% = \$250,000 \times 0.10 = \$25,000.$$

This leaves an additional

$75,000	total profit
− 25,000	amount to Cameron
$50,000	

to be divided. The additional profit of $50,000 is to be divided in the ratio 1:2:2. First divide this amount into $1 + 2 + 2 = 5$ equal shares. Cameron gets 1 of these 5 shares, or

$$\frac{1}{5} \times \$50,000 = \$10,000.$$

Davis and Friedman each get 2 of the 5 shares, or

$$\frac{2}{5} \times \$50,000 = \$20,000.$$

In summary, Cameron gets the following amount.

$25,000	return on investment
+ 10,000	share of profit
$35,000	total

Both Davis and Friedman get $20,000. ■

NOTE The return on investment is paid first and then the remaining profit is divided among the partners.

EXAMPLE 7
Dividing Losses by Agreed Rates

Suppose the restaurant in Example 6 had a profit of only $15,000. What would be the distribution of this amount?

SOLUTION The partners agreed to give Cameron a 10% return, or $25,000. The profits were only $15,000, leaving a loss of $10,000.

$25,000
− 15,000
$10,000

This loss of $10,000 will be shared in the ratio 1:2:2, just as were the profits. Cameron's share of the loss is

$$\frac{1}{5} \times \$10,000 = \$2000$$

while the share of both Davis and Friedman is

$$\frac{2}{5} \times \$10,000 = \$4000.$$

Cameron gets $25,000, minus her share of the loss.

$25,000	due to Cameron
− 2000	her share of loss
$23,000	actually received by Cameron

Both Davis and Friedman must each contribute $4000 toward the loss. The $23,000 that Cameron actually receives is made up as follows.

$15,000	profit
4000	from Davis
+ 4000	from Friedman
$23,000	total to Cameron ■

NOTE Cameron does absorb her share of the loss by accepting $23,000 instead of the $25,000 return on investment initially agreed upon.

18.4 Exercises

Divide the following profits. Round all answers to the nearest dollar.

	Partners	Investment	Method	Profits
1.	1	$12,500	Equal shares	$81,000
	2	$15,000		
	3	$18,200		
2.	1	$16,000	Ratio 3:5	$96,000
	2	$20,000		
3.	1	$25,000	Ratio of	$90,000
	2	$75,000	investment	
4.	1	$125,000	$25,000 salary to	$250,000
	2	$100,000	partner 2; balance	
	3	$80,000	divided 4:2:4	
5.	1	$40,000	10% return to	$30,000
	2	$10,000	partner 1; balance	
	3	$5000	in ratio 1:4:5	
6.	1	$30,000	12% return to	$132,000
	2	$100,000	partner 2; balance	
	3	$20,000	in ratio of	
			investment	
7.	1	$40,000	$8000 salary to	$62,000
	2	$50,000	partner 1; $12,000	
	3	$60,000	salary to partner 2;	
			balance divided	
			equally	
8.	1	$75,000	$20,000 salary to	$140,000
	2	$25,000	partner 2; 10%	
	3	$50,000	return to partner	
			3; balance divided	
			3:1:1	

Work the following word problems.

 9. Two partners make a profit of $54,000. If they have no agreement on dividing profits, find the share of the profits that each will get.

10. If five lawyers agree to divide their profits equally, find the share that each gets if the firm makes a profit of $144,000.

11. Three partners contribute $15,000, $40,000, and $65,000, respectively, to start a new company. Find the share that each gets if the profit is $80,000 and profits are divided in the ratio of the original investments.

12. Powell, Reedy, and Adams have started a new office supply firm. Powell contributed $120,000 to the firm, Reedy $80,000, and Adams $100,000. Find the division of a profit of $72,000 if profits are divided in the ratio of the original investment.

13. Four partners have agreed to divide profits in the ratio 3:5:7:9. Find the division of a profit of $180,000.

14. Suppose the partners in Exercise 13 have a loss of $96,000. How much of the loss would be paid by each partner?

15. Mary Finch and Pete Renz have started a new travel agency. Finch will run the agency. She gets a $15,000 salary, with any additional profits distributed in the ratio 1:4. Find the distribution of a profit of $57,000.

16. Beth, Maureen, and Patty have started a new bookstore to be run by Maureen. Maureen will get a salary of $17,000, with any additional profits divided in the ratio 3:1:2. Find the division of a profit of $53,000.

17. Bob Coker has invested $80,000 in a new hardware store. His partner, Will Toms, will actually run the store. The partners agree that Coker will get a 10% return on his investment, with any additional profits divided in the ratio 1:3. Find the division of profit of (a) $60,000 and (b) $6000.

18. Wilma Dickson has invested $350,000 in a small electronics plant, to be run by her partner, John Ardery. They agree that she will receive a 10% return on her investment, and that any additional profits will be divided in the ratio 2:3. Divide a profit of (a) $90,000 and (b) $30,000.

19. Three partners invest $15,000, $25,000, and $30,000 in a business. The partners agree that partner 1 will receive a 10% return on investment, with partner 2 receiving a salary of $12,000. Any additional profits will be divided in the ratio of the original investments. Divide a profit of $110,000.

20. A plumbing wholesale business has three partners. Partner 1 invested $50,000 in the business, and is given a 10% return on investment. Partner 2 invested $75,000, and earns a 6% return on investment, plus a salary of $21,000. Partner 3 invested $100,000 and earns a 12% return on investment. Any additional profits are divided in the ratio 2:1:2. Divide a profit of $180,000.

21. State the approach used to divide profits among 3 partners if partner 1 gets a fixed salary and the remaining profits are divided according to a ratio of 2:3:2. (See Objective 4.)

22. Explain the process used to allocate losses if one partner is guaranteed a fixed return on investment. (See Objective 5.)

18.5 Distribution of Overhead

OBJECTIVES

1 Allocate overhead by floor space.

2 Allocate overhead by sales value.

3 Allocate overhead by number of employees.

Businesses have many expenses in addition to the cost of the materials and labor that are actually used to make a product. Rent on the factory building must be paid, insurance premiums and executive salaries must be paid, office supplies must be ordered, and so on. These general expenses, which cannot be avoided but which do not go directly for the production of goods and services, are called **overhead**. The cost of an office typewriter would come under overhead, while the cost of sheet metal used to actually make a product would not.

A company can usually decide on the total overhead expenses fairly quickly; however, a problem often comes up in dividing the overhead among the various products or lines of business in a company. Various methods are used by different firms to divide overhead. The choice of a method often depends on industry practice.

In any case, the **allocation of overhead** is usually done by forming a ratio of each product or department to the total firm. There are several ways of forming this ratio.

1   Overhead can be allocated by department according to the **floor space** used by each department of the company.

EXAMPLE 1
*Allocating
Overhead
by Floor Space*

Lindquist Press has three departments, with floor space as shown.

Department	Floor Space
Magazine printing	50,000 square feet
Book printing	30,000 square feet
Catalog printing	20,000 square feet
Total	100,000 square feet

Allocate an overhead of $275,000.

SOLUTION   The magazine printing department has a floor space of 50,000 square feet out of a total of 100,000 square feet. Therefore, this department is allocated

$$\frac{50,000}{100,000} = \frac{1}{2}$$

of the overhead, or

$$\frac{1}{2} \times \$275,000 = \$137,500.$$

When finding the expenses of this department, the company accountants would assign an overhead expense of $137,500 for the department.

The book printing department uses

$$\frac{30,000}{100,000} = \frac{3}{10}$$

of the floor space, and so would be allocated $\frac{3}{10}$ of the overhead, or

$$\frac{3}{10} \times \$275,000 = \$82,500.$$

Finally, catalog printing would be allocated

$$\frac{20,000}{100,000} = \frac{1}{5}$$

of the overhead, or

$$\frac{1}{5} \times \$275,000 = \$55,000. \quad \blacksquare$$

NOTE Check your answer by adding the individual departmental allocations. This sum should equal the total overhead.

2 It is common to allocate overhead according to the **sales value** of each department or product, as shown in the next example.

EXAMPLE 2
Allocating Overhead by Sales Value

Acco Hardware Manufacturing produces four products, with monthly production and value as shown.

Product	Production	Value of Each
Wheelbarrows	2500	$40
Ladders	5000	$25
Shovels	6000	$10
Hammers	25,000	$3

Allocate an overhead of $50,000.

SOLUTION   First find the total value of each item.

Product	Production	Value of Each	Total Value
Wheelbarrows	2500	$40	2500 × $40 = $100,000
Ladders	5000	$25	5000 × $25 = $125,000
Shovels	6000	$10	6000 × $10 = $60,000
Hammers	25,000	$3	25,000 × $3 = $75,000
			Total $360,000

Of the value of $360,000, wheelbarrows produced $100,000. Therefore, the fraction

$$\frac{\$100,000}{\$360,000} = \frac{5}{18}$$

of the total overhead must be applied to wheelbarrows. The total overhead is $50,000, so

$$\frac{5}{18} \times \$50,000 = \$13,888.89$$

must be applied to wheelbarrows. Also,

$$\frac{\$125,000}{\$360,000} \times \$50,000 = \frac{25}{72} \times \$50,000 = \$17,361.11$$

of overhead will be applied to ladders, and

$$\frac{\$60,000}{\$360,000} \times \$50,000 = \frac{1}{6} \times \$50,000 = \$8333.33$$

to shovels. Finally,

$$\frac{\$75,000}{\$360,000} \times \$50,000 = \$10,416.67$$

is applied to hammers. Check that the sum of the various allocated overheads is the total overhead of \$50,000. ■

3 Overhead can also be allocated by the number of employees associated with a department or product.

EXAMPLE 3
Allocating Overhead by Number of Employees

Allocate an overhead of \$30,000 to each department according to the number of employees in the department.

SOLUTION   Form a ratio of the number of employees in the department to the total number of employees.

Department	Number of Employees	Ratio of Employees	Overhead of Department
1	8	$\frac{8}{20}$	$\frac{8}{20} \times \$30,000 = \$12,000$
2	3	$\frac{3}{20}$	$\frac{3}{20} \times \$30,000 = \$4500$
3	5	$\frac{5}{20}$	$\frac{5}{20} \times \$30,000 = \$7500$
4	4	$\frac{4}{20}$	$\frac{4}{20} \times \$30,000 = \$6000$
Total	20		Total \$30,000

■

18.5 Exercises
Allocate overhead as indicated. Round to the nearest dollar.

1.

Department	Floor Space
A	4000 square feet
B	5000 square feet
C	7000 square feet

Overhead: \$240,000

2.

Department	Floor Space
A	32,000 square feet
B	57,000 square feet
C	11,000 square feet

Overhead: $280,000

3.

Department	Floor Space
1	6200 square feet
2	7200 square feet
3	6800 square feet
4	9800 square feet

Overhead: $76,000

4.

Department	Floor Space
1	4200 square feet
2	13,500 square feet
3	21,800 square feet
4	3600 square feet

Overhead: $420,000

5.

Product	Number Produced	Value of Each
M	10,000	$15.00
N	20,000	$5.00
P	40,000	$2.50

Overhead $21,875

6.

Product	Number Produced	Value of Each
X	5000	$20
Y	8000	$25
Z	4000	$50

Overhead: $62,500

7.

Product	Number Produced	Value of Each
1	80	$7
2	150	$12
3	60	$20
4	160	$10

Overhead: $12,000

8.

Product	Number Produced	Value of Each
1	150	$6
2	200	$12
3	75	$3
4	125	$8

Overhead: $10,000

9.

Department	Number of Employees
A	500
B	600
C	400

Overhead: $90,000

10.

Department	Number of Employees
J	1000
K	7000
L	2000

Overhead: $900,000

11.

Department	Number of Employees
1	70
2	90
3	15
4	25

Overhead: $90,000

12.

Department	Number of Employees
1	90
2	20
3	50
4	40

Overhead: $120,000

13. Dayton Auto Parts allocates its $360,000 overhead by the floor space used by each department. Allocate the overhead for the following departments.

Department	Floor Space
Hoses	2000 square feet
Carburetors	8000 square feet
Water pumps	6000 square feet
Fuel pumps	9000 square feet
Gaskets	1000 square feet
Filters	4000 square feet

14. City Office Supply wishes to allocate its $75,000 overhead among its various departments by floor space. Allocate the overhead for the following departments.

Department	Floor Space
Typing paper	750 square feet
Copy machine paper	600 square feet
Copy machines	1000 square feet
Office furniture	1500 square feet
Filing cabinets	500 square feet
Calculators	650 square feet

15. A wholesale lumber mill wishes to allocate its overhead of $15,150 by the sales value of each product. Allocate overhead for the following products.

Product	Number Produced	Value Per Unit
Construction 2 × 4's	15	$200
Plywood	20	$400
Veneers	10	$600
Wood chips	50	$75
Furniture wood	30	$150

16. Allocate the $8732 overhead of Victor Meats by sales value of products, using the information in this chart.

Product	Number Produced	Value Per Unit
Beef	10	$800
Lamb	7	$300
Pork	5	$750
Chicken	14	$120
Sausage	12	$150
Luncheon meats	15	$300

17. Allocate an overhead of $4500 for Chalet Manufacturing according to the number of employees per department. Use the information in the following chart.

Department	Number of Employees
Office	20
Sales	35
Manufacturing	75
Finishing	12
Shipping	8

18. The Beaver Drug Company wishes to allocate an overhead of $11,400 among its departments according to the number of employees per department. Use the following chart.

Department	Number of Employees
Headache remedies	25
Pain killer	30
Cold remedies	40
Foot powder	15
Eye wash	20
Skin lotion	25

19. Define the term *overhead*. List at least three expenses that would be included in overhead.

20. What is the rationale that a company uses for selecting a specific method of allocating overhead?

CHAPTER 18 QUICK REVIEW

TOPIC	APPROACH	EXAMPLE
18.1 Determining the amounts paid to holders of preferred and common stock	To find total paid to owners of preferred stock, multiply par value by dividend rate to obtain dividend per share, then multiply by number of shares. To find the dividend paid to owners of common stock, subtract total paid to owners of preferred stock from total available to stockholders, then divide by number of shares of common stock.	A company distributes $750,000 to stockholders. It has 15,000 shares of $100 par value 4% preferred stock and 150,000 shares of common stock. Find (a) amount paid to holders of preferred stock and (b) amount per share to holders of common stock. **(a)** Dividend per share $$= \$100 \times 0.04 = \$4$$ Total to preferred $= \$4 \times 15,000$ $$= \$60,000$$ **(b)** Dividend to common $$= \frac{\$750,000 - \$60,000}{150,000}$$ $$= \$4.60$$
18.1 Finding earnings per share	Subtract dividends on preferred stock from net income, then divide by the number of shares of common stock outstanding.	A company made $500,000 last year. The company has 750,000 shares of common stock outstanding and paid $75,000 to owners of preferred stock. Find the earnings per share. $$EPS = \frac{\$500,000 - \$75,000}{750,000} = \$.57$$
18.2 Reading the stock table	Locate the stock involved and determine the various quantities required.	Use the stock table to find the following information for Allegheny Power (Alleg Pwr): dividend; high for day; low for day; total sales; yearly high; yearly low. Stock table entry is $48\frac{3}{4}$ $41\frac{1}{2}$ Alleg Pwr AYP 3.20 6.8 13 1966 47 $46\frac{3}{4}$ $46\frac{7}{8}$ — dividend is $3.20; high is 47 or $47; low is $46\frac{3}{4}$ or $46.75; total sales are 196,600; yearly high is $48\frac{3}{4}$; yearly low is $41\frac{1}{2}$

TOPIC	APPROACH	EXAMPLE
18.2 Finding the current yield on a stock	Current yield $= \dfrac{\text{Annual dividend}}{\text{Current Price}}$	Find the current yield for IBM if the purchase price is $54\frac{1}{4}$ per share and the annual dividend is $2.42. $$\text{Current Yield} = \dfrac{\$2.42}{\$54.25}$$ $$= 0.045$$ $$= 4.5\%$$
18.2 Selling shares of a stock	Find the basic price of the stock from the table. Subtract the SEC fee and the broker's commission from the basic price of the stock.	Find the amount received by a person selling 500 shares of a stock at $53\frac{3}{8}$. Basic price $= 500 \times \$53.375$ $\qquad\qquad = \$26{,}687.50$ SEC fee: $\$26{,}687.50 \div \$500 = 54$ $\qquad\qquad\qquad\qquad\qquad$ (rounded) SEC fee $= 54 \times \$.01 = \$.54$ Broker's commission $= 0.025$ $\qquad\qquad \times \$26{,}687.50 = \$667.19$ Seller's proceeds $= \$26{,}687.50$ $\qquad -\$667.19 - \$.54 = \$26{,}019.77$
18.2 Finding the price to earnings ratio (PE ratio)	To find the price to earnings ratio use the formula: $$\dfrac{\text{PE}}{\text{ratio}} = \dfrac{\text{Price per share}}{\substack{\text{Annual net income} \\ \text{per share}}}$$	Price per share, $42.50; annual net income per share, $2.75. $$\text{PE ratio} = \dfrac{\$42.50}{\$2.75} = 15.45$$
18.3 Determining the cost of purchasing bonds	Locate the bond in the table, then multiply the price of the bond by 1000 and the number of bonds purchased. Then, add $5 per bond to the total cost.	Find the cost, including sales charges, of 20 Disney bonds. $$20 \times (1000 \times .47\tfrac{1}{8}) + (20 \times \$5) = \$9525$$
18.3 Determining the amount received from the sale of bonds	Locate the bond in the table, then multiply the price of the bond by 1000 and the number of bonds sold. Subtract $5 per bond from the total selling price.	Find the amount received from the sale of 15 Eastman Kodak bonds. $$15 \times (1000 \times .29\tfrac{1}{4}) - (15 \times \$5)$$ $$= \$4312.50$$

TOPIC	APPROACH	EXAMPLE

18.4 Dividing profits in a partnership

Use one of the following methods to determine each partner's ratio of the profits:

Equal shares
Agreed ratio
Original investment
Salary and agreed ratio
Interest on investment and agreed ratio.

Multiply total profits by each partner's ratio.

Divide profits of $75,000 among 3 investors by original investment if each partner invests the following amount.

Partner	Investment
1	$12,000
2	$15,000
3	$18,000

Total initial investment

$$= \$12,000 + \$15,000 + \$18,000$$

$$= \$45,000$$

Ratios for each partner:

1. $\dfrac{12000}{45000} = \dfrac{4}{15}$

2. $\dfrac{15000}{45000} = \dfrac{1}{3}$

3. $\dfrac{18000}{45000} = \dfrac{2}{5}$

Profit for each partner:

1. $\dfrac{4}{15}(\$75,000) = \$20,000$

2. $\dfrac{1}{3}(\$75,000) = \$25,000$

3. $\dfrac{2}{5}(\$75,000) = \$30,000$

18.5 Allocating overhead by floor space

Determine the percent of floor space each department occupies. Multiply the percent by the amount of overhead to be allocated.

Department	Floor Space
Printing	40,000 sq. ft.
Cutting	25,000 sq. ft.
Binding	55,000 sq. ft.

Allocate $330,000 overhead.

Printing: $\dfrac{40,000}{120,000} \times \$330,000$

$$= \$110,000$$

Cutting: $\dfrac{25,000}{120,000} \times \$330,000$

$$= \$68,750$$

Binding: $\dfrac{55,000}{120,000} \times \$330,000$

$$= \$151,250$$

TOPIC	APPROACH	EXAMPLE

18.5 Allocating overhead by sales value

Determine the percent of sales for each department.
Multiply this percent by the amount of overhead to be allocated.

Allocate $120,000 overhead.

Product	Number Produced	Value of each
A	5000	$12
B	8000	$ 5
C	10,000	$10

Total Value = (5000)($12) + (8000)($5)
$$+ (10,000)($10) = \$200,000$$

A: $\dfrac{(5000)(\$12)}{\$200,000} \times \$120,000 = \$36,000$

B: $\dfrac{(8000)(\$5)}{\$200,000} \times \$120,000 = \$24,000$

C: $\dfrac{(10,000)(\$10)}{\$200,000} \times \$120,000 = \$60,000$

18.5 Allocating overhead by number of employees

Determine the ratio of employees in the department to total number of employees.
Multiply this ratio by the amount of overhead to be allocated.

Allocate $15,000 overhead.

Department	Number of Employees
1	5
2	6
3	9
Total	20

1. $\dfrac{5}{20} \times \$15,000 = \$3750$

2. $\dfrac{6}{20} \times \$15,000 = \$4500$

3. $\dfrac{9}{20} \times \$15,000 = \$6750$

SUMMARY EXERCISE

The Dougherty Tutoring Service, Inc., was formed with an investment of $15,000 from Trish Decker, $10,000 from Katie Shields, and $25,000 from Beth Abbot. They agreed to divide net profits in the same ratio as their investments. They also sold shares to shareholders. They have decided to give 45% of the net income to the shareholders. They have 10,000 preferred shares of $50 par value at 8% and 50,000 common shares. Last year the net income was $250,000.

(a) Find the dividend per share.

(b) If the net profit is 75% of the amount remaining after shareholders are paid, find the distribution of profits.

(c) An overhead of $34,375 has to be allocated to 3 departments based on the following number of employees.

Dept	No. of Employees
Math	7
English	5
Reading	4

Find the allocation to each department. Round to the nearest dollar.

CHAPTER 18 REVIEW EXERCISES

In each of the following find (a) the amount paid to holders of preferred stock and (b) the amount per share to holders of common stock. [18.1]

	Net Income	Reinvested Funds	Par Value	Rate	Number of Preferred Stockholders	Number of Common Stockholders
1.	$1,250,000	$500,000	$100	9%	10,000	150,000
2.	$2,375,000	$750,000	$150	8%	15,000	200,000
3.	$2,640,000	$425,000	$125	7%	22,750	750,000

In each of the following, find the earnings per share. [18.1]

	Net Income	Dividends on Preferred Stock	Number of Shares of Common Stock
4.	$725,000	0	100,000
5.	$1,425,000	$675,000	275,000
6.	$2,750,000	$900,000	500,000

Use the stock table to find each of the following. Give money answers in dollars. [18.2]

7. High for the day for Abex

8. Low for the day for NERCO

9. Closing price for Olin

10. Change from previous day for AdamsExp

11. Dividend for NewEngElec

12. Sales for the day for Airgas

13. Yield for Ogden

14. 52 week high for Newscorp

15. 52 week low for Oneida

Find the price for each of the following stock purchases. Ignore any broker's fees. [18.2]

	Stock	Number of Shares	Transaction
16.	ONEDK	200	High
17.	New AmEd	150	Low
18.	Alcan	500	Close

Find the price for each of the following stock purchases. Use the broker's fees in the text. [18.2]

19. 200 shares at $41\frac{5}{8}$

20. 340 shares at $73\frac{1}{8}$

Find the current yield for the following. Round to the nearest tenth of a percent. [18.2]

21. Aetna Life at $41 per share with a dividend of $2.76

22. NevPwr at $23 per share with a dividend of $1.60

Find the PE ratio for each of the following. Round all answers to the nearest whole number. [18.2]

23. Omnicare at $23\frac{1}{8}$ per share with a net income per share of $1.24

24. Aetna Life at $40\frac{3}{4}$ with a net income per share of $2.76

Use the bond table to find each of the following. Use the listing for Masco. [18.3]

25. Closing price for Masco Bonds
26. Number of bonds sold
27. Year when the bonds will be paid off by the company
28. Change since the previous day in the price of one bond
29. Price to buy 30 such bonds at the closing price, with sales charges of $5 per bond.
30. Interest paid on the par value of the bonds, both as a percent and in dollars

Find the cost, including sales charges of $5 per bond, for each of the following. [18.3]

	Bond		Number Purchased
31.	Fair Cp	$12\frac{1}{4}$% of 1996	35
32.	MfrH	$8\frac{1}{8}$% of 2007	70

In problems 33–35, divide the profits based on the indicated method. Round all answers to the nearest dollar. [18.4]

	Partners	Investment	Method	Profits
33.	1	$8500	Equal shares	$48,000
	2	$7000		
	3	$10,500		
34.	1	$16,000	Ratio 2:3	$120,000
	2	$25,000		
35.	1	$9000	Ratio of	$90,000
	2	$12,000	investment	

In problems 36–38, allocate the overhead to each department of the company. Round to the nearest dollar. [18.5]

36.

Department	Floor Space
A	3000 square feet
B	5000 square feet
C	4000 square feet

Overhead: $100,000

37.

Product	Number Produced	Value of Each
x	4000	$10
y	3000	$5
z	2000	$8

Overhead: $75,000

38.

Department	Number of Employees
A	70
B	55
C	45
D	60

Overhead: $85,000

Business Statistics

The word *statistics* comes from words which mean *state numbers*. State numbers refer to vital statistics or data gathered by the government. Examples include the number of births, deaths, marriages, and so on in the population. Today the word statistics is used in a much broader sense to include data from business, economics, social science, and many other fields. This chapter looks mainly at business uses of statistics.

19.1 Frequency Distributions and Graphs

OBJECTIVES

1 Construct a frequency distribution.

2 Make a bar graph.

3 Make a line graph.

4 Make a circle graph.

The sales manager of a small corporation is trying to decide on the factors that make one salesperson superior to another. She decides to first see if there is a relationship between the number of calls made on potential customers and the success of a salesperson. She begins by listing the number of sales calls made in a week by each of the firm's 50 salespeople.

22	16	14	16	17	21	15	13	22	25
19	17	16	14	11	22	14	17	23	28
20	17	20	18	25	17	13	19	24	27
14	15	18	17	18	14	12	18	22	26
17	19	19	16	16	12	15	23	27	27

1   Such a list or set of **raw data** is hard to read. There are so many numbers, arranged in a random order, that it is very difficult to see any pattern to the numbers. To help make the data easier to understand, a **frequency distribution table** is made which shows the number of times an event occurs; in this case, the sales manager makes a table which shows each possible number of sales calls and the number of salespeople who made that many calls.

TABLE 19.1   Sample Frequency Distribution

Number of Sales Calls	Tally	Frequency	Number of Sales Calls	Tally	Frequency
11	|	1	20	||	2
12	||	2	21	|	1
13	||	2	22	||||	4
14	||||	5	23	||	2
15	|||	3	24	|	1
16	||||	5	25	||	2
17	|||| ||	7	26	|	1
18	||||	4	27	|||	3
19	||||	4	28	|	1

As this frequency distribution shows, the most common number of sales calls is 17; seven salespeople made 17 sales calls during the week.

2   The next step in analyzing this information is to use it to make a graph. In statistics, a *graph* is a visual presentation of numerical data. One of the most common graphs is a *bar graph*, where the height of a bar represents the frequency of a particular value. A bar graph for the data in Table 19.1 is shown in Figure 19.1.

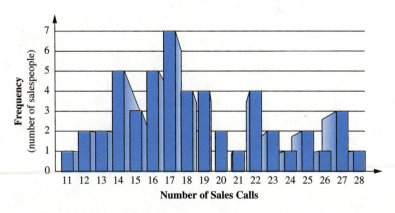

FIGURE 19.1

The frequency distribution in Table 19.1 contains a great deal of information. It may be a little hard to digest all the numbers in the graph. To simplify the information, the number of sales calls can be combined in **classes**, or intervals. Data combined in this manner are referred to as **grouped data**. The frequency of values for each class is called the **class frequency**. Table 19.2 shows grouped data for sales calls.

TABLE 19.2   Sample of Grouped Data

Number of Sales Calls (Class)	Frequency (Number of Salespeople)
11−13	5
14−16	13
17−19	15
20−22	7
23−25	5
26−28	5

NOTE The number of classes is arbitrary and usually varies between 5 and 15.

This information could also be presented in a bar graph, as shown in Figure 19.2. This bar graph shows that the most frequent number of sales calls fell in the class 17 to 19, even though 17 can no longer be identified as the most frequent number of calls.

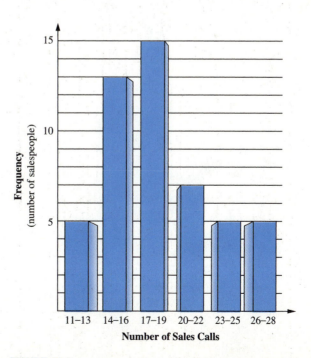

FIGURE 19.2

3   Bar graphs show which numbers occurred, and how many times, but do not necessarily show the order in which the numbers occurred. To discover any trends that may have developed, draw a *line graph*. For example, suppose Eastside Tire Sales had the following total sales.

Year	Total Sales
1991	$740,000
1992	$860,000
1993	$810,000
1994	$1,040,000

A line graph of these sales is shown in Figure 19.3.

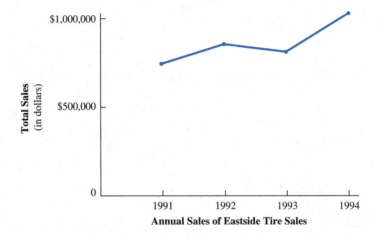

Annual Sales of Eastside Tire Sales

FIGURE 19.3

EXAMPLE 1
Interpreting a Line Graph

Based on the line graph of the sales for Eastside Tire, answer the following questions.

(a)   What year showed a decrease in sales?

(b)   What year showed the least sales?

(c)   What year showed the most sales?

SOLUTION

(a)   1993 is the only year that showed a decrease in sales.

(b)   1991 is the year with the least sales.

(c)   1994 is the year with the most sales.   ∎

One advantage of line graphs is that two or more sets of data can be shown on the same graph. For example, the managers of Eastside Tire Sales might want to compare total sales, profits, and overhead. They might first go to their past records, and produce the numbers in the following table.

Year	Total Sales	Overhead	Profit
1991	$740,000	$205,000	$83,000
1992	$860,000	$251,000	$102,000
1993	$810,000	$247,000	$21,000
1994	$1,040,000	$302,000	$146,000

Separate lines can be made on a line graph for each category, so that necessary comparisons can be made. Such a graph is called a **comparative line graph**, and is shown in Figure 19.4.

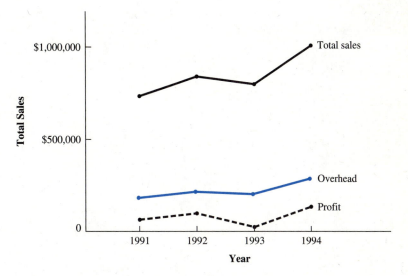

FIGURE 19.4

4 Suppose a sales manager makes a record of the expenses involved in keeping a sales force on the road. After finding the total expense, she could convert each expense into a percent of the total, with the following results.

Item	Percent of Total
Car and plane	30%
Lodging	25%
Food	15%
Entertainment	10%
Sales meetings	10%
Other	10%

The sales manager can show these percents by using a **circle graph**. A circle has 360 degrees (written 360°). The 360° represents the total expenses. Since entertainment is 10% of the total expense, she used

$$360° \times 10\% = 360° \times 0.10 = 36°$$

to represent her entertainment expense. Since lodging is 25% of the total expenses, she used

$$360° \times 25\% = 90°$$

to represent lodging. After she found the degrees that represent each of her expenses, she drew the circle graph shown in Figure 19.5.

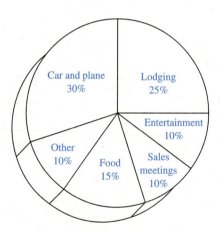

FIGURE 19.5

EXAMPLE 2   Based on the circle graph in Figure 19.5, answer the following questions.

Interpreting a   **(a)** What percent of expenses was spent on travel and entertainment?

Circle Graph   **(b)** What percent of expenses was spent on food and lodging?

SOLUTION

(a) Travel is   30% (car and plane)
     Entertainment is 10%
     ──────────────────────────
     Total spent   40%

(b) Food is   15%
     Lodging is   25%
     ──────────────────────
     Total spent   40% ▪

19.1 Exercises

Work the following problems using the information provided.

1. For Exercises 1 and 2, the following graph shows annual sales for two different stores for each of the past few years.

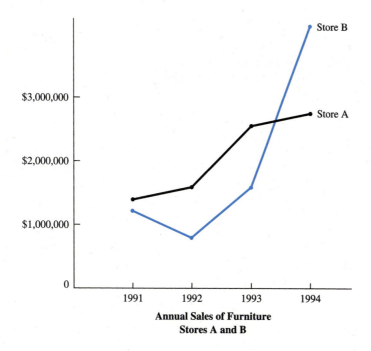

**Annual Sales of Furniture
Stores A and B**

Estimate annual sales for Store A in each of the following years: (a) 1994, (b) 1993, and (c) 1992.

2. Estimate annual sales for Store B in each of the following years: (a) 1994, (b) 1993, and (c) 1992.

3. The following set of data shows the number of college units completed by 30 of the employees of the EZ Life Insurance Company.

74	133	4	127	20	30	4	64
103	27	139	118	138	121	140	119
149	132	64	141	130	76	12	
42	50	95	56	65	104	88	

Use these numbers to complete the following table.

	Number of Units	Frequency
(a)	0–24	_____
(b)	25–49	_____
(c)	50–74	_____
(d)	75–99	_____
(e)	100–124	_____
(f)	125–149	_____

   (g) Make a line graph using the frequencies that you found.

4. The daily high temperatures in Phoenix for the month of July during one year were as follows. (The numbers are in chronological order from left to right. For example, the temperature on July 5 was 102°, and on July 12 it was 104°.)

79°	84°	88°	96°	102°	104°	110°	108°	106°	106°	92°
104°	99°	97°	92°	94°	90°	82°	74°	72°	83°	
85°	92°	100°	99°	101°	107°	111°	102°	97°	94°	

Use these numbers to complete the following table.

	Temperature	Frequency
(a)	70°–74°	_____
(b)	75°–79°	_____
(c)	80°–84°	_____
(d)	85°–89°	_____
(e)	90°–94°	_____
(f)	95°–99°	_____
(g)	100°–104°	_____
(h)	105°–109°	_____
(i)	110°–114°	_____

   (j) Make a bar graph showing the results given in the table.

   (k) Make a line graph using the original numbers.

5. List the advantages and disadvantages of using a bar graph to present data. (See Objective 2.)

6. Explain the purpose of a comparative line graph. (See Objective 3.)

7. The following numbers show the scores of 80 students on a business mathematics test.

```
79  60  74  59  55  98  61  67  83  71  69  56  84  93  63  60  68  51  73  54
71  46  63  66  69  42  75  62  71  77  50  88  76  93  48  70  39  76  95  57
78  65  87  57  78  91  82  73  94  48  63  94  82  54  89  64  77  94  72  69
87  65  62  81  63  66  65  49  45  51  51  56  67  88  81  70  81  54  66  87
```

Use these data to complete the following table.

Score	Frequency
(a) 30–39	_____
(b) 40–49	_____
(c) 50–59	_____
(d) 60–69	_____
(e) 70–79	_____
(f) 80–89	_____
(g) 90–99	_____

(h)   Make a bar graph showing the results in the table above.

(i)   How many students scored less than 60 on the exam?

(j)   How many students scored 70 or higher?

(k)   How many students scored from 60 to 89?

(l)   How many students scored from 50 to 69?

8. Southside Real Estate has 60 salespeople spread over its five offices. The number of new homes sold by each of these salespeople during the past year is shown below.

```
 9  38  14   8  17  10  25  11   4  16   3   9
15  24  19  30  16  31  21  20  30   2   6   6
 3   8   5  11  15  26   7  18  29  10   7   3
11   6  10   4   2  37  10  25   5  19  34   2
 8  13  25  15  23  26  12   4  22  12  21  12
```

Use these numbers to complete the following table.

Number Sold	Frequency
(a) 0–5	_____
(b) 6–10	_____
(c) 11–15	_____
(d) 16–20	_____
(e) 21–25	_____
(f) 26–30	_____
(g) 31–35	_____
(h) 36–40	_____

(i)   Make a bar graph showing the results in the table.

9. The following graph is used to estimate the hourly acreage covered by a farm implement when its width and speed of travel are known. For example, a $7\frac{1}{2}$ foot (90-inch) mower blade moving 4 miles per hour would cover about $3\frac{5}{8}$ acres per hour. This is found by going across the graph from the working width (90 inches) to the diagonal line for speed (4 mph), then down to the bottom to find hourly acreage.

(a) What is the hourly acreage for a 36-inch implement moving $2\frac{1}{2}$ miles per hour?

(b) What is the hourly acreage for an 8-foot-wide combine moving 4 miles per hour?

(c) How fast must a tractor pull a 48-inch plow in order to plow one acre per hour?

(d) How wide a spray pattern is needed in order to spray $4\frac{1}{2}$ acres per hour at a speed of $4\frac{1}{2}$ miles per hour?

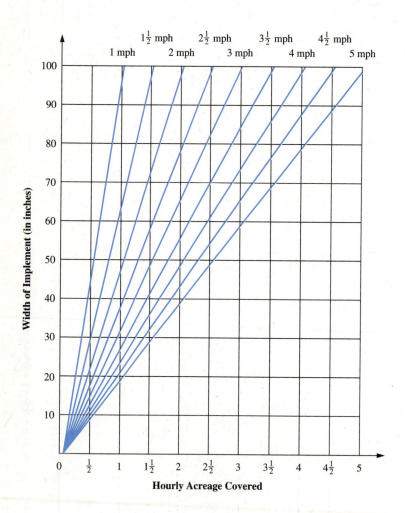

10. The comparative line graph shows the change in average weight (in pounds) for a recent 20-year period for various categories of American adults. Find the change in weight for each of the following groups of people.

    (a) Men aged 20–24 who are 5 feet 10 inches tall (Hint: first find 5′ 10″ on the horizontal line in the center of the graph.)

    (b) Women aged 40–49 whose height is 5 feet 8 inches

    (c) 5 foot tall women aged 20–24

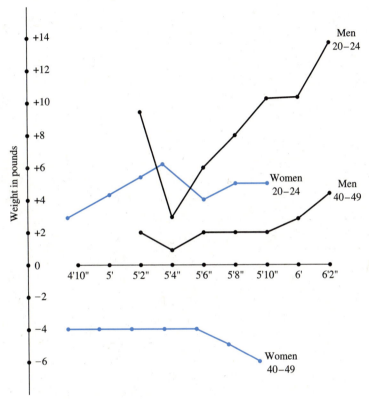

20-year change in average weight of Americans

11. During one recent period, Evie Allsot, a student, spent $1400 for expenses as shown in the following chart. Find all numbers missing from the chart.

	Item	Dollar Amount	Percent of Total	Degrees of a Circle
	Food	$350	25%	90°
(a)	Rent	$280	_____	72°
(b)	Clothing	$210	_____	_____
(c)	Books	$140	10%	_____

Item	Dollar Amount	Percent of Total	Degrees of a Circle
(d) Entertainment	$210	_____	54°
(e) Savings	$70	_____	
(f) Other	_____	_____	36°

(g) Draw a circle using this information.

12. Jensen Manufacturing Company has its annual sales divided into five categories as follows.

Item	Annual Sales
Parts	$25,000
Hand tools	$80,000
Bench tools	$120,000
Brass fittings	$100,000
Cabinet hardware	$75,000

Make a circle graph showing this distribution.

13. A book publisher had 25% of his sales in mysteries, 10% in biographies, 15% in cookbooks, 15% in romantic novels, 20% in science, and the rest in business books. Draw a circle graph with this information.

14. A family kept track of its expenses for a year, with the following results.

Item	Percent of Total
Housing	30%
Food	21%
Automobile	14%
Clothing	10%
Medical	5%
Savings	8%
Other	12%

Draw a circle graph for this distribution.

15. In Exercise 14, what percent did the family spend on food and housing?

16. In Exercise 14, what percent did the family spend on automobile and medical?

17. Make a comparative line graph for the following data from Fuller's Wholesale, Inc.

Year	Total Sales	Cost of Goods Sold	Profit
1987	$620,000	$405,000	$60,000
1988	$690,000	$470,000	$68,000
1989	$780,000	$530,000	$79,000
1990	$710,000	$460,000	$10,000
1991	$905,000	$704,000	$85,000
1992	$1,210,000	$820,000	$109,000

18. The following chart shows various expenses for Hunt Real Estate Sales. Make a comparative line graph for the data.

Year	Salaries	Rent	Taxes
1988	$125,000	$16,000	$12,000
1989	$170,000	$22,000	$18,000
1990	$225,000	$29,000	$25,000
1991	$210,000	$29,000	$22,000
1992	$160,000	$21,000	$15,000

19.2 The Mean

OBJECTIVES

1 Find the mean of a set of data.

2 Find a weighted mean.

3 Find the mean for grouped data.

Businesses are often faced with the problem of analyzing a mass of raw data. Reports come in from many different branches of a company, or salespeople may send in a large number of expense claims, for example. In analyzing all this data, one of the first things to look for is a **measure of central tendency**—a single number that is designed to represent the entire list of numbers. One such measure of central tendency is the **mean**, which is just the common **average** of everyday life.

For example, suppose the sales of carnations at Tom's Flower Shop for each of the days last week were

$86, $103, $118, $117, $126, $158, and $149.

1 To find a single number that is representative of this list, use the following formula.

$$\text{Mean} = \frac{\text{Sum of all values}}{\text{Number of values}}$$

For Tom's Flower Shop, the mean is

$$\text{Mean} = \frac{86 + 103 + 118 + 117 + 126 + 158 + 149}{7}$$

$$= \frac{857}{7}$$

$$= \$122.43 \qquad \text{rounded to the nearest cent.}$$

EXAMPLE 1
Finding the Mean

Find the mean for each of the following sets of data: (a) $25.12, $42.58, $76.19, $32, $81.11, $26.41, $19.76, $59.32, $71.18, $21.03 and (b) $374,910, $382,740, $321,872, $412,111, $242,943, $334,089, $351,147, $262,900.

SOLUTION

(a) Add the numbers and divide by 10 (since there are 10 numbers). Check that the sum of the numbers is $454.70. The mean is

$$\text{Mean} = \frac{\$454.70}{10} = \$45.47.$$

(b) The sum of the 8 numbers is $2,682,712. The mean is

$$\text{Mean} = \frac{\$2,682,712}{8} = \$335,339. \quad \blacksquare$$

2 Table 19.3 shows a frequency distribution of annual salaries received by the management employees of a medium-sized corporation.

TABLE 19.3   Sample Salaries of Management Employees

Salary	Number of Managers (Frequency)
$32,000	27
40,000	16
50,000	11
72,000	6
90,000	4
96,000	4
110,000	3
160,000	2
296,000	1

As the table shows, 27 management employees were paid $32,000 each, 16 were paid $40,000 each, and so on. The average salary paid to these employees cannot be found by just adding the salaries, since different salaries are earned by different numbers of employees. To find the mean of the salaries, it is necessary to first multiply each annual salary by the number of employees receiving that salary. This process produces a **weighted mean**, where each number (a salary here) is "weighted" by multiplying it by the number of times it occurs.

Salary	Number of Managers	Salary $\times$ Number of Managers
$32,000	27	$864,000
40,000	16	640,000
50,000	11	550,000
72,000	6	432,000
90,000	4	360,000
96,000	4	384,000
110,000	3	330,000
160,000	2	320,000
296,000	1	296,000
Totals	74	$4,176,000

By adding the numbers in the "Number of Managers" column, find that the corporation has a total of 74 management employees. Find the mean by dividing the total of all salaries, $4,176,000, by the total number of employees, 74.

$$\text{Mean salary} = \frac{\$4,176,000}{74} = \$56,432 \qquad \text{(rounded)}$$

The mean salary of a management employee is $56,432.

EXAMPLE 2

Finding a Weighted Mean

Find the weighted mean for the numbers given in the following table.

Value	Frequency
3	4
5	2
7	1
8	5
9	3
10	2
12	1
13	2

SOLUTION   According to this table, the value 5 occurred 2 times, 8 occurred 5 times, 12 occurred 1 time, and so on. To find the mean, multiply each value by the frequency for that value; then add the products. Also add the "Frequency" column to find the total number of values.

Value	Frequency	Value × Frequency
3	4	12
5	2	10
7	1	7
8	5	40
9	3	27
10	2	20
12	1	12
13	2	26
Totals	20	154

The mean is

$$\text{Mean} = \frac{154}{20} = 7.7. \quad \blacksquare$$

Weighted means are used to find a student's grade point average, as shown in the next example.

EXAMPLE 3

Finding Grade Point Average

Find the grade point average for the following student. Assume A = 4, B = 3, C = 2, D = 1, and F = 0.

SOLUTION

Course	Units	Grade	Grade × Units
Business Mathematics	3	A (=4)	4 × 3 = 12
Retailing	4	C (=2)	2 × 4 = 8
English	3	B (=3)	3 × 3 = 9
Computer Science	2	A (=4)	4 × 2 = 8
Lab for Computer Science	2	D (=1)	1 × 2 = 2
Totals	14		39

The grade point average for this student is

$$\frac{39}{14} = 2.79. \quad \blacksquare$$

NOTE It is common to round grade point averages to the nearest hundredth.

3 The mean can also be found for data that has been grouped into a frequency distribution. To do so, find the midpoint of each interval, or class. This midpoint is found by averaging the highest and lowest numbers that can go into a class. For example, the midpoint of **class mark** of the interval $100-109$ is the mean of 100 and 109.

$$\text{Class midpoint} = \frac{100 + 109}{2} = \frac{209}{2} = 104.5$$

EXAMPLE 4

Finding the Mean for Grouped Data

Find the mean for the frequency distribution shown.

Intervals	Frequency
100–109	9
110–119	12
120–129	17
130–139	28
140–149	21
150–159	16
160–169	4

SOLUTION Begin by finding the class mark for each class. As explained, the class mark or midpoint of the first class is 104.5, while the midpoint of the second class is

$$\frac{110 + 119}{2} = \frac{229}{2} = 114.5.$$

Find the other midpoints in a similar way. Then multiply the frequencies and the class marks, giving the column at the right (labeled "Frequency $\times$ Class Mark"). Next, find the totals in the "Frequency" column and the "Frequency $\times$ Class Mark" column.

Intervals	Frequency	Class Mark	Frequency $\times$ Class Mark
100–109	9	104.5	$9 \times 104.5 =$ 940.5
110–119	12	114.5	$12 \times 114.5 =$ 1374.0
120–129	17	124.5	$17 \times 124.5 =$ 2116.5
130–139	28	134.5	$28 \times 134.5 =$ 3766.0
140–149	21	144.5	$21 \times 144.5 =$ 3034.5
150–159	16	154.5	$16 \times 154.5 =$ 2472.0
160–169	4	164.5	$4 \times 164.5 =$ 658.0
	Totals 107		14,361.5

Finally, the mean is the quotient of these totals, or

$$\text{Mean} = \frac{14{,}361.5}{107} = 134.2 \text{ (to the nearest tenth).} \quad \blacksquare$$

NOTE When a set of data is divided up into classes, it is no longer possible to tell where in a class a particular item falls. For this reason, a mean found from grouped data is only approximate, although in most cases the approximation to the true mean is very good.

19.2 Exercises

Find the mean for each of the following sets of data. Round to the nearest tenth.

1. 8, 10, 16, 21, 25
2. 51, 48, 32, 43, 74, 58
3. 40, 51, 59, 62, 68, 73, 49, 80
4. 32, 26, 30, 19, 51, 46, 38, 39
5. 21,900, 22,850, 24,930, 29,710, 28,340, 40,000
6. 38,500, 39,720, 42,183, 21,982, 43,250
7. 9.4, 11.3, 10.5, 7.4, 9.1, 8.4, 9.7, 5.2, 1.1, 4.7
8. 30.1, 42.8, 91.6, 51.2, 88.3, 21.9, 43.7, 51.2

Round to the nearest dollar in Exercises 9–12.

9. The seven people at Gardner Realty earned commissions last year of $32,750, $49,811, $12,092, $17,583, $27,854, $98,253, and $37,584. Find the mean commission.

10. Life insurance sold last year by the six agents of Wilson Insurance totaled $294,000, $580,000, $722,000, $463,000, $814,000, and $1,785,000. Find the mean total of life insurance sold.

11. Last year, the value of the new cars sold by the eight salespeople at Modern Motors was $385,000, $495,000, $873,000, $1,210,000, $611,000, $802,000, $173,000, and $708,000. Find the mean value of the cars.

12. Telesales employs nine people to make telephone calls to sell magazines. Last year, these people produced total sales of $492,811, $763,455, $901,852, $179,806, $244,193, $382,574, $591,873, $1,003,058, and $473,902. Find the mean sales per employee.

Find the weighted mean for each of the following. Round to the nearest tenth.

13.

Value	Frequency
3	4
5	2
9	1
12	3

14.

Value	Frequency
9	3
12	5
15	1
18	1

15.

Value	Frequency
12	4
13	2
15	5
19	3
22	1
23	5

16.

Value	Frequency
25	1
26	2
29	5
30	4
32	3
33	5

17. Can the mean be a poor indicator of the central tendency of a list of numbers? When can this happen?

18. What is the purpose of a weighted mean? Give an example of where it is used. (See Objective 2.)

In the following problems, find the mean salary for the employees. Round to the nearest thousand dollars.

19.

Salary	Number of Employees
$16,000	7
$21,000	11
$24,000	8
$29,000	6
$38,000	4
$41,000	3
$53,000	2
$162,000	1

20.

Salary	Number of Employees
$15,000	8
$20,000	15
$22,000	13
$25,000	9
$30,000	4
$42,000	3
$57,000	2
$260,000	1

Find the grade point average for each of the following students. Assume $A = 4, B = 3,$ $C = 2, D = 1,$ and $F = 0.$ Round to the nearest hundredth.

21.

Units	Grade
4	B
2	A
5	C
1	F
3	B

22.

Units	Grade
3	A
3	B
4	B
2	C
4	D

Find the mean for the following grouped data. Round to the nearest tenth.

23.

Interval	Frequency
50–59	12
60–69	15
70–79	21
80–89	27
90–99	18
100–109	7

24.

Interval	Frequency
320–339	7
340–359	9
360–379	12
380–399	11
400–419	6
420–439	5

25.

Interval	Frequency
25–49	13
50–74	12
75–99	20
100–124	18
125–149	32
150–174	14
175–199	7

26.

Interval	Frequency
150–154	4
155–159	7
160–164	9
165–169	12
170–174	16
175–179	8
180–184	3

19.3 The Median and the Mode

OBJECTIVES

1 Find the median of a set of data.

2 Find the mode.

In everyday life, the word "average" usually refers to the mean. However, there are two other "averages" in common use, the *median* and the *mode*. Median and mode are discussed in this section.

Suppose the owner of a small company pays five employees annual salaries of

$$\$12{,}500, \$13{,}000, \$13{,}200, \$14{,}000, \text{ and } \$15{,}000.$$

The average, or mean, salary paid to the employees is

$$\text{Mean} = \frac{\$12{,}500 + \$13{,}000 + \$13{,}200 + \$14{,}000 + \$15{,}000}{5}$$

$$= \frac{\$67{,}700}{5} = \$13{,}540.$$

Now suppose that the employees go on strike and demand a raise. To get public support, they appear on television to talk about their low salaries, which average only $13,540 per year.

The television station sends a reporter to interview the owner of the company. Before the interviewer arrives, the owner decides to find the average salary of *all* employees, including the five on strike, plus his own. To do this, he adds the five salaries given above, plus his salary of $127,000. This gives an average of

$$\text{Mean} = \frac{\$12,500 + \$13,000 + \$13,200 + \$14,000 + \$15,000 + \$127,000}{6}$$

$$= \frac{\$194,700}{6} = \$32,450.$$

When the television reporter arrives, the owner is prepared to state that there is no reason for the employees to be on strike, since they have an average salary of $32,450.

There are two points to this story. First, both averages are correct, depending on what is being measured. This shows how easily statistics can be manipulated. Second, the mean is often a poor indicator of the "middle" of a list of numbers. In fact, when the mean was computed by the owner, it was greater than 5 of the 6 employees' salaries. The mean may be greatly affected by extreme values, such as the owner's salary of $127,000.

1 To avoid such a misleading result when using the mean, use a different measure of the "middle" of a list of numbers, the **median**. As a general rule, the median divides a list of numbers in half: one half of the numbers lie at or above the median and one half lie at or below the median.

Since the median divides a list of numbers in half, the fist step in finding a median is to rewrite the list of numbers as an **ordered array**, with the numbers going from smaller to larger. For example, the list of numbers 9, 6, 11, 17, 14, 12, 8 would be written in order as the ordered array

6, 8, 9, 11, 12, 14, 17.

The median is found from the ordered array as explained in the following box. Notice that the procedure for finding the median depends on whether the number of numbers in the list is *even* or *odd*.

If the ordered array has an *odd* number of numbers, divide the number of numbers by 2. The next higher whole number gives the *location* of the median.

If the ordered array has an *even* number of numbers, there is no single middle number. Find the median by first dividing the number of numbers by 2. The median is the average (mean) of the number in this position and the number in the next position.

Example 1 shows lists of numbers having an *odd* number of numbers; Example 2 shows an *even* number of numbers.

EXAMPLE 1
Finding the Median

Find the median for each set of data: (a) 7, 23, 15, 6, 18, 12, 24 and (b) 25, 23, 17, 21, 29, 40, 49, 15, 20.

SOLUTION

(a) First place the numbers in numerical order to get the ordered array:

$$6, 7, 12, 15, 18, 23, 24.$$

There are 7 numbers. Divide 7 by 2 to get

$$\frac{7}{2} = 3.5.$$

The next higher whole number is 4, so that the median is the 4th number, or 15. Here three numbers are larger than 15, and three are smaller.

(b) Write the numbers as the ordered array:

$$15, 17, 20, 21, 23, 25, 29, 40, 49.$$

There are 9 numbers, and $\frac{9}{2} = 4.5$. Since the next higher whole number is 5, the median is the fifth number, or 23. ∎

EXAMPLE 2
Finding the Median

Find the median for each set of data: (a) 7, 13, 15, 25, 28, 32, 47, 59, 68, 74 and (b) 147, 159, 132, 181, 174, 253.

SOLUTION

(a) The numbers are already written as an ordered array. Since there are 10 numbers and 10 is even, divide 10 by 2 to get 5. The median is the mean of the number in the 5th and 6th positions, or

$$\text{Median} = \frac{28 + 32}{2} = \frac{60}{2} = 30.$$

(b) Begin by writing the numbers as an ordered array:

$$132, 147, 159, 174, 181, 253.$$

There are 6 numbers, so the median is the mean of the $\frac{6}{2} = 3$rd number and the 4th number, or

$$\text{Median} = \frac{159 + 174}{2} = \frac{333}{2} = 166\frac{1}{2}. \quad ∎$$

2 The last important statistical measure is called the **mode**. The mode is the number which occurs the most often. For example, if ten students earned the following scores on a business law examination

$$74, 81, 39, 74, 82, 80, 100, 92, 74, 85,$$

then the mode is 74, since more students obtained this score than any other.

EXAMPLE 3
Finding the Mode

Find the mode for each of the following sets of data: (a) 51, 32, 49, 73, 49, 90; (b) 482, 485, 483, 485, 487, 487, 489; and (c) 10,708; 11,519; 10,972; 12,546; 13,905; 12,182.

SOLUTION

(a)   The number 49 occurs more often than any other number. Therefore, 49 is the mode. (It is not necessary to form an ordered array when looking for the mode.)

(b)   Here 485 and 487 both occur twice. This data set has *two* modes. Such sets are sometimes called **bimodal**.

(c)   No number here occurs more than once. This day set has no mode.   ∎

The mean, median, and mode are different ways of locating the middle or center of a list of numbers. Each of these three ways is a measure of central tendency.

19.3 Exercises

Find the median for each of the following sets of data.

1. 11, 17, 31, 50, 57, 91, 105
2. 596, 604, 612, 683, 719
3. 100, 114, 125, 135, 150, 172
4. 298, 346, 412, 501, 515, 521, 528, 621
5. 37, 63, 92, 26, 44, 32, 75, 50, 41
6. 7, 15, 28, 3, 14, 18, 46, 59, 1, 2, 9, 21
7. 28.4, 9.1, 3.4, 27.6, 59.8, 32.1, 47.6, 29.8
8. 0.6, 0.4, 0.9, 1.2, 0.3, 4.1, 2.2, 0.4, 0.7, 0.1

Find the mode or modes for each of the following sets of data.

9. 4, 9, 8, 6, 9, 2, 1, 3
10. 21, 32, 46, 32, 49, 32, 49
11. 80, 72, 64, 64, 72, 53, 64
12. 158, 162, 165, 162, 165, 157, 163
13. 5, 9, 17, 3, 2, 8, 19, 1, 4, 20
14. 12, 15, 17, 18, 21, 29, 32, 74, 80
15. 6.1, 6.8, 6.3, 6.3, 6.9, 6.7, 6.4, 6.1, 6.0
16. 12.75, 18.32, 19.41, 12.75, 18.30, 19.45, 18.33
17. When is the median a better average to use than the mean to describe a set of data? (See Objective 1.)
18. List some situations where the mode is the best average to use to describe a set of data. (See Objective 2.)

A chemistry student working on a lab experiment copied the following meter readings into a notebook.

$$3, 4, 5, 2, 3, 2, 2, 30, 3$$

Using these numbers, find each of the following.

19. The mean   **20.** The median

The student later decided that 30 was way out of line. He suspected the meter had been misread. The number 30 was removed from the list, giving

$$3, 4, 5, 2, 3, 2, 2, 3.$$

Using these numbers, find each of the following.

21. The mean   **22.** The median

23. If you want to avoid a single extreme value having a large effect on the average, would you use the mean or the median?

24. Suppose you own a hat shop and can only order hats in one size. You look at last year's sales to decide on the size to order. Should you find the mean, median, or mode for these sales?

19.4 Standard Deviation

OBJECTIVES

1 Find the range for a set of data.

2 Find the standard deviation.

3 Use the normal curve to estimate data.

The mean is a good indicator of the middle, or central tendency, of a set of data values, but it does not give the whole story about the data. To see why, compare distribution A with distribution B in Table 19.4.

Both distributions of numbers have the same mean (and the same median also), but beyond that they are quite different. In the first, 7 is a fairly typical value; but in the second, most of the values differ quite a bit from 7. To show this difference requires some measure of the **dispersion**, or spread, of the data.

TABLE 19.4   Comparison of Distributions A and B

	A	B
	5	1
	6	2
	7	7
	8	12
	9	13
Mean	7	7
Median	7	7

1 Two of the most common measures of dispersion, the **range** and the **standard deviation**, are discussed here.

The range for a set of data is defined as the difference between the largest value and the smallest value in the set. In distribution A in Table 19.4, the largest value is 9 and the smallest is 5. The range is

$$\text{Highest} - \text{Lowest} = \text{Range}$$

$$9 - 5 = 4.$$

In distribution B, the range is

$$13 - 1 = 12.$$

The range can be misleading if it is interpreted unwisely. For example, suppose three executives rate two employees, Mark and Myrna, on five different jobs, as shown in the following table.

Job	Mark	Myrna
1	28	27
2	22	27
3	21	28
4	26	6
5	18	27
Mean	23	23
Median	22	27
Range	10	22

By looking at the range for each person, we might be tempted to conclude that Mark is a more consistent worker than Myrna. However, by checking more closely, we might decide that Myrna is actually more consistent with the exception of one very poor score, which is probably due to some special circumstance. Myrna's median score is not affected much by the single low score and is more typical of her performance as a whole than is her mean score.

One of the most useful measures of dispersion, the standard deviation, is based on *deviation from the mean* of the data values. To find how much each value deviates from the mean, first find the mean, and then subtract the mean from each data value.

EXAMPLE 1
Finding Deviations from the Mean

Find the deviations from the mean for the data values

$$32, 41, 47, 53, 57.$$

SOLUTION   Add these numbers and divide by 5. The mean is 46. To find the deviations from the mean, subtract 46 from each data value. (Subtracting 46 from a smaller number produces a negative result.)

Data value	32	41	47	53	57
Deviation	−14	−5	1	7	11	∎

NOTE To check the work in Example 1, add the deviations. The sum of deviations for a set of data is always 0, as long as the mean was not rounded.

2 To find the measure of dispersion, it might be tempting to find the mean of the deviations. However, this number always turns out to be 0 no matter how much the dispersion in the data is, because the positive deviations simply cancel out the negative ones.

Get around this problem of positive and negative numbers adding to 0 by *squaring* each deviation. (The square of a negative number is positive.) Take Example 1 one step further.

Data value	32	41	47	53	57
Deviation from mean	−14	−5	1	7	11
Square of deviation	**196**	**25**	**1**	**49**	**121**

We can now define the **standard deviation:** it is *the square root* of the mean of the squares of the deviation.*

Continue the example, and calculate the mean of the squares of the deviations:

$$\frac{196 + 25 + 1 + 49 + 121}{5} = \frac{392}{5} = 78.4.$$

The standard deviation is the *square root* of this number, written $\sqrt{78.4}$. The letter *s* is used to represent the standard deviation.

In summary, for the numbers 32, 41, 47, 53, 57, the standard deviation is

$$s = \sqrt{78.4} = 8.9 \quad \text{(to the nearest tenth).}$$

The square root of 78.4 can be found from tables or with a calculator. In this book, we will be satisfied with either $\sqrt{78.4}$ or 8.9; both answers will be given in the answer section at the back of the book.

The next box summarizes the formula for finding the standard deviation of a list of ungrouped values. This formula uses the symbol Σ, the Greek letter *sigma*, which represents "sum of." For example, if the four values of *x* are 17, 11, 8, and 21, then Σ*x* would represent the sum of these values, or Σ*x* = 17 + 11 + 8 + 21 = 57.

*The square root of a number n is written $\sqrt{n}$. By definition, $\sqrt{n} \times \sqrt{n} = n$. For example, $\sqrt{49} = 7$, since $7 \times 7 = 49$. Also, $\sqrt{144} = 12$. Many calculators will find square roots.

> Let d represent the result of subtracting the mean of the numbers from each value in a list of numbers. Then the *standard deviation*, s, of the numbers is
>
> $$s = \sqrt{\frac{\Sigma d^2}{n}},$$
>
> where Σ represents "sum of" and n is the number of numbers.

EXAMPLE 2

Finding Standard Deviation

Find the standard deviation of the values

$$7, 9, 18, 22, 27, 29, 32, 40.$$

SOLUTION

Step 1.   Find the mean of the values.

$$\frac{7 + 9 + 18 + 22 + 27 + 29 + 32 + 40}{8} = 23$$

Step 2.   Find the deviations from the mean.

Data values	7	9	18	22	27	29	32	49
Deviations	-16	-14	-5	-1	4	6	9	17

Step 3.   Square each deviation.

Squares of deviations: 256   196   25   1   16   36   81   289

These numbers are the d^2 values in the formula.

Step 4.   Find the sum of the d^2 values.

$$\Sigma d^2 = 256 + 196 + 25 + 1 + 16 + 36 + 81 + 289 = 900$$

Now divide Σd^2 by n, which is 8 in this example.

$$\frac{\Sigma d^2}{n} = \frac{900}{8} = 112.5$$

Step 5.   Take a square root of the answer in Step 4. The standard deviation of the given list of numbers is

$$s = \sqrt{112.5} = 10.6. \quad \blacksquare$$

In some applications of statistics, it is not necessary to take the square root. Going through all the steps except the final one of taking the square root produces the *variance*. That is,

$$\text{Standard deviation} = \sqrt{\text{Variance}},$$

or

$$\text{Variance} = (\text{Standard deviation})^2.$$

3 One of the main applications of standard deviation comes in working with the **normal curve**. Many different sets of data in the real world lead to graphs which look very much like the normal curve. (See Figure 19.6.)

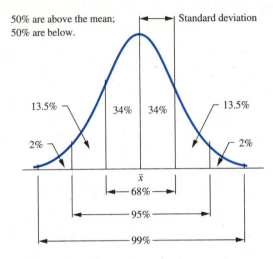

FIGURE 19.6

It turns out that if a group of data is very closely approximated by a normal curve, approximately 68% of the data will lie within 1 standard deviation of the mean. Approximately 95% will lie within 2 standard deviations of the mean; and about 99% will lie within 3 standard deviations of the mean.

EXAMPLE 3

Using the Normal Distribution

Suppose an instructor gives a test to 300 students. Suppose further that the grades are closely approximated by a normal curve with mean 75 and standard deviation 8. Find the number of scores: (a) within 1 standard deviation of the mean; and (b) within 2 standard deviations.

SOLUTION

(a) As mentioned, 68% of all scores lie within 1 standard deviation of the mean. Since there is a total of 300 scores, the number of scores within 1 standard deviation is

$$(68\%) \times (300) = (0.68) \times (300) = 204.$$

Since 1 standard deviation was given as 8, with the mean 75, there were 204 students getting scores between $75 - 8 = 67$ and $75 + 8 = 83$.

(b) A total of 95% of all scores lie within 2 standard deviations of the mean. Since there is a total of 300 scores, the number of scores within 2 standard deviations is

$$(0.95) \times 300 = 285.$$

There were 285 students getting scores between $75 - 2 \times 8 = 75 - 16 = 59$ and $75 + 2 \times 8 = 75 + 16 = 91.$ ∎

19.4 Exercises

Find the range and standard deviation for each set of data. Round answers to the nearest tenth.

1. 6, 8, 9, 10, 12

2. 12, 15, 19, 23, 26

3. 7, 6, 12, 14, 18, 15

4. 4, 3, 8, 9, 7, 10, 1

5. 42, 38, 29, 74, 82, 71, 35

6. 122, 132, 141, 158, 162, 169, 180

7. 241, 248, 251, 257, 252, 287

8. 51, 58, 62, 64, 67, 71, 74, 78, 82, 93

9. 3, 7, 4, 12, 15, 18, 19, 27, 24, 11

10. 15, 42, 53, 7, 9, 12, 28, 47, 63, 14

11. When can the range of a set of numbers be misleading?

12. Explain how to interpret the standard deviation. (See Objective 2.)

Suppose 100 different geology students measure the weight of an ore sample. Due to human error and to limitations in the accuracy of the balance, not all students get the same value. The results are found to be closely approximated by a normal curve. The mean is 37 grams, with a standard deviation of 1 gram. Use the following sketch of a normal curve and find the number of students reporting each reading in Exercises 13–20.

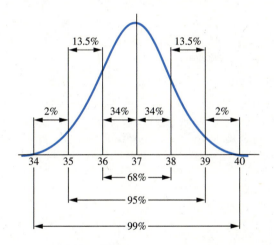

13. More than 37 grams

14. More than 36 grams

15. Between 36 and 38 grams

16. Between 35 and 39 grams

17. Between 38 and 39 grams

18. Between 36 and 39 grams

19. Within 1 gram of the mean

20. More than 2 grams away from the mean

On standard IQ tests, the mean is 100, with a standard deviation of 15. The results are very close to fitting a normal curve. Suppose an IQ test is given to a very large group of people. Find the percent of people whose IQ score is:

21. More than 100

22. Less than 100

23. Greater than 115

24. Between 85 and 115

25. Between 70 and 130

26. Between 55 and 145

27. Less than 55

28. More than 145

The bolts made by a certain factory average 2 inches in length, with a standard deviation of 0.1 inch. The lengths fit a normal curve very closely. What percent of the bolts are:

29. 1.9 inches or longer?

30. Shorter than 1.9 inches?

31. 2.2 inches or shorter?

32. Longer than 2.2 inches?

At one factory, production line workers can assemble a certain computer component with a mean time of 47.6 minutes, and a standard deviation of 2.7 minutes. The times are very closely approximated by a normal curve. What percent of the times are:

33. At least 44.9 minutes?

34. No more than 44.9 minutes?

35. No more than 53 minutes?

36. At least 53 minutes?

37. Between 44.9 minutes and 50.3 minutes?

38. Between 42.5 minutes and 53 minutes?

39. Explain the purpose of the normal distribution.

40. A student's score is 3 standard deviations above the mean. Give an interpretation of this score.

19.5 Index Numbers

OBJECTIVES

1 Find the price relative.

2 Use the Consumer Price Index to compare costs.

1 A house that cost $40,000 ten years ago now sells for $115,000. Ten years ago, a gallon of gasoline cost 85 cents; today it costs $1.35. Both items increased in price. To find out which increased more in percent, find the *price relative* for each item. A **price relative** is the quotient of the current price and the price in some past year with the quotient multiplied by 100. The past year is called the **base year**. The formula for the price relative is as follows.

$$\text{Price relative} = \frac{\text{Price this year}}{\text{Price in base year}} \times 100$$

EXAMPLE 1
Finding the Price Relative

(a) Using the prices just given, the price relative for the house is

$$\text{Price relative} = \frac{\$115,000}{\$40,000} \times 100 = 287.5.$$

The price of the house today is 287.5% of its price ten years ago. Note that a price relative is really just a percent—it gives the percent that this year's price is of the price in the base year.

(b) The price relative for gasoline, using the prices given is

$$\text{Price relative} = \frac{1.35}{.85} \times 100 = 158.8 \quad \text{(rounded)}.$$

The price of gasoline this year is 158.8% of its price ten years ago. ∎

Compare the price relatives of Example 1 to find that the price of the house has increased at a faster rate than that of gasoline.

EXAMPLE 2
Finding the
Price Relative

A small calculator cost $25 several years ago, while today a similar model sells for $9. The price relative is

$$\text{Price relative} = \frac{\$9}{\$25} \times 100 = 36.$$

The calculator sells today for 36% of its earlier selling price. This example shows that a price relative can be less than 100—a few things go down in price over the years. Such items are rare, however, with almost all price relatives being over 100 in an inflationary period. ∎

NOTE The price relative gives a way of comparing two prices and showing a percent increase.

2 The **Consumer Price Index**, published by the Bureau of Labor Statistics, gives good examples of price relatives. The Bureau keeps track of the costs of a great many items in different cities throughout the country, and publishes its findings monthly. A portion of the report for one month is included here.

TABLE 19.5 **Urban Prices Index**

	Chicago	Detroit	Los Angeles-Long Beach	New York-New Jersey	Philadelphia
All items	187.3	190.2	189.6	193.5	190.8
Food and beverages	205.0	198.6	198.5	203.0	205.8
Housing	185.8	192.0	199.3	195.6	192.7
Apparel and upkeep	145.2	147.9	145.8	157.1	143.0
Transportation	183.5	180.7	182.3	197.5	188.1
Medical	219.3	249.9	214.4	228.3	235.6
Entertainment	175.5	174.8	163.3	183.5	172.4
Other	181.1	180.4	174.6	187.6	180.7

All figures are expressed as a percentage of the 1967 base of 100.

The numbers in this table represent price relatives, with a base year of 1967. For example, in Chicago the cost of food and beverage is now 205% of the cost in 1967, or, in other words, it now costs $205 to buy the food and beverage that could have been bought with $100 in 1967. As a further example, medical care that cost $100 in Philadelphia in 1967 now costs $235.60, and so on.

The price relatives in Table 19.5 can only be used to compare prices for the given city—they *cannot* be used for comparisons between cities. For example, the cost of housing in Los Angeles is now 199.3% of what it was in 1967, while the cost of housing in Chicago is now 185.8% of what it was in 1967. However, it cannot be said that housing in Los Angeles is more expensive than in Chicago, only that it has increased at a faster rate. It is possible that housing in Los Angeles was less expensive to begin with, so that even with a greater percent increase, it is still less expensive than Chicago. The information from the table does not tell these things.

EXAMPLE 3
Using the CPI

Suppose a typical operation cost $1500 in 1967 in Detroit. Estimate its cost today.

SOLUTION From Table 19.5, medical costs in Detroit today are 249.9% of what they were in 1967. A $1500 operation should cost about

$$\$1500 \times 249.9\% = \$1500 \times 2.499$$
$$= \$3748.50,$$

or about $3800 today. ■

19.5 Exercises

Find the price relatives for the following items. Round to the nearest tenth.

	Item	Price Then	Price Now
1.	Paper	80¢ per package	$1.50 per package
2.	Eggs	49¢ per dozen	79¢ per dozen
3.	Soda Pop	$1.59 per six pack	$2.49 per six pack
4.	Rent	$200 per month	$410 per month
5.	Jeans	$10 per pair	$21 per pair
6.	Automatic Washer	$300	$380

Use the Urban Prices Index in Table 19.5 to complete the following chart.

	Urban Area	Item	$100 Worth in 1967 Will Cost Today
7.	Philadelphia	Food and beverage	_____
8.	Chicago	Transportation	_____
9.	New York-New Jersey	Medical	_____

Urban Area	Item	$100 Worth in 1967 Will Cost Today
10. Philadelphia	Entertainment	_____
11. Detroit	Apparel and upkeep	_____
12. Los Angeles-Long Beach	Housing	_____

13. Suppose a house in Chicago cost $20,000 in 1967. Estimate its cost today. Round to the nearest $500.

14. Estimate the cost today of an operation in Philadelphia that cost $1200 in 1967. Round to the nearest $500.

15. In which urban area did the cost of housing increase the fastest?

16. Where did the cost of transportation increase the least?

CHAPTER 19 QUICK REVIEW

TOPIC	APPROACH	EXAMPLE
19.1 Constructing a frequency distribution from raw data	1. Construct a table listing each value, and the number of times this value occurs. 2. For a distribution with grouped data, combine the data into classes.	For the following data, construct a frequency distribution: 12, 15, 15, 14, 13, 20, 10, 12, 11, 9, 10, 12, 17, 20, 16, 17, 14, 18, 19, 13.

Data	Tally	Frequency
9	|	1
10	||	2
11	|	1
12	|||	3
13	||	2
14	||	2
15	||	2
16	|	1
17	||	2
18	|	1
19	|	1
20	||	2

Classes	Frequency
9–11	4
12–14	7
15–17	5
18–20	4

TOPIC	APPROACH	EXAMPLE
19.1 Constructing a bar graph from a frequency distribution	Draw a bar for each class using the frequency of the class as the height of the bar.	Construct a bar graph from the frequency distribution of the previous example.

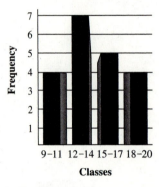

19.1 Constructing a line graph	1. Plot each year on the horizontal axis. 2. For each year, find the values for that year and plot a point for each value. 3. Connect all points with straight lines.	Construct a line graph for the following data.

Year	Value
1991	$850,000
1992	$920,000
1993	$875,000
1994	$975,000

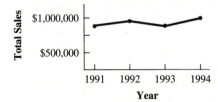

TOPIC	APPROACH	EXAMPLE

19.1 Constructing a circle graph

1. Determine the percent of the total for each item.
2. Find the number of degrees represented by each percent.
3. Draw the circle.

Construct a circle graph for the following expenses.

Item	Amount	Percent
Car	$200	20%
Lodging	$300	30%
Food	$250	25%
Entertainment	$150	15%
Other	$100	10%

Multiply each percent by 360°.

Car: $360° \times .2 = 72°$

Lodging: $360° \times .3 = 108°$

Food: $360° \times .25 = 90°$

Entertainment: $360° \times .15 = 54°$

Other: $360° \times .1 = 36°$

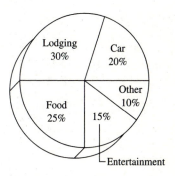

19.2 Finding the mean of a set of data

Divide the sum of the data by the number of data.

The test scores for Pat Phelan in her Business Math course were 85, 76, 93, 91, 78, 82, 87, and 85. Find Pat's test average.

Mean =
$$\frac{85 + 76 + 93 + 91 + 78 + 82 + 87 + 85}{8}$$

$$= \frac{677}{8} = 84.63$$

TOPIC	APPROACH	EXAMPLE
19.2 Finding the weighted mean	1. Multiply frequency by value. 2. Add all products obtained in Step 1. 3. Divide the sum in Step 2 by the total number of data.	

No. of School Age Children — **Frequency**

No. of School Age Children	Frequency
0	12
1	6
2	7
3	3
4	2
Total families	30

Find the mean number of school age children per family.

No.	Frequency	No. $\times$ Frequency
0	12	0
1	6	6
2	7	14
3	3	9
4	2	8
		37

$$\text{Mean} = \frac{37}{30} = 1.23$$

TOPIC	APPROACH	EXAMPLE
19.2 Finding the mean of a frequency distribution	1. Determine the class mark (the midpoint) for each class. 2. Multiply the class mark by the frequency of each class. 3. Add all the products obtained in Step 2.	

Find the mean.

Intervals	Frequency
3–5	2
6–8	10
9–11	12
12–14	9
15–17	7

Intervals	Freq.	Class Mark	Frequency $\times$ Class Mark
3–5	2	4	8
6–8	10	7	70
9–11	12	10	120
12–14	9	13	117
15–17	7	16	112
			427

$$\text{Mean} = \frac{427}{40} = 10.68$$

TOPIC	APPROACH	EXAMPLE
19.3 Finding the median of a set of data	1. Arrange the data from lowest to highest. 2. The median is the middle value or the average of the middle values.	Find the median for Pat Phelan's grades from an earlier example. The data arranged from lowest to highest is 76, 78, 82, 85, 85, 87, 91, and 93. The average of the middle two values is $$\frac{85 + 85}{2} = 85.$$
19.3 Determining the mode of a set of data	The mode is the most frequently occurring value.	Find the mode for Pat's grades in the previous example. 85 occurs most frequently (twice).
19.4 Finding the range of a set of data	Range = Highest − Lowest	Find the range of the values 7, 6, 10, 7, 9, 5, 2, 8, and 9. Range = Highest − Lowest $\quad\quad\quad$ = 10 − 2 = 8
19.4 Finding the standard deviation	1. Determine the mean of the data. 2. Subtract the mean from each value to obtain individual deviations, d. 3. Square each deviation. 4. Sum all the squared deviations. 5. Divide the sum by the number of data. 6. Take the square root of the number obtained in Step 5.	Find the standard deviation of the values, 7, 6, 10, 7, 9, 5, 2, 8, and 9. Mean = $$\frac{7 + 6 + 10 + 7 + 9 + 5 + 2 + 8 + 9}{9}$$ $$= 7$$

Data Value	Deviation d	Deviation squared, d^2
7	0	0
6	−1	1
10	3	9
7	0	0
9	2	4
5	−2	4
2	−5	25
8	1	1
9	2	4

$$\frac{\Sigma d^2}{n} = \frac{48}{9} = 5.33$$

$$s = \sqrt{5.33} = 2.31$$

TOPIC	APPROACH	EXAMPLE
19.5 Finding the price relative	Divide the price this year by the price in a base year and multiply by 100.	A car costs $4500 ten years ago. It now costs $9300. Find the price relative for the car. Price Relative $= \dfrac{\text{Price this year}}{\text{Price in base year}} \times 100$ $= \dfrac{\$9300}{\$4500} \times 100 = 206.67$
19.5 Finding cost today using the Consumer Price Index (CPI)	Multiply CPI by cost in base year to estimate current cost.	A typical house in Philadelphia cost $49,000 in 1967. Estimate its cost today. Cost today $= \$49,000 \times 192.7\%$ $= 49,000 \times 1.927 = \$94,423$

SUMMARY EXERCISE

The following 20 values give the weekly earnings of the part-time employees at a college bookstore.

$125 $121 $127 $123 $144
$132 $148 $128 $128 $136
$136 $142 $136 $130 $131
$133 $135 $139 $135 $130

(a) Use these numbers to complete the following table.

Salary	Number of Salespeople
$120–$124	_____
$125–$129	_____
$130–$134	_____
$135–$139	_____
$140–$144	_____
$145–$149	_____

(b) Use the numbers in the above table to draw a bar graph.

(c) Calculate the mean, median, and mode for the weekly salaries of the salespeople.

CHAPTER 19 REVIEW EXERCISES

Construct frequency distributions for the sets of data in problems 1 and 2. Use the table provided. [19.1]

					Number	Frequency
1. 2	5	8	6	7	1–3	_____
9	8	8	7	8	4–6	_____
3	15	8	10	12	7–9	_____
13	3	4	6	14	10–12	_____
10	11	8	15	9	13–15	_____
4	2	13	11	8		

								Number	Frequency
2. 27	23	22	38	43	24	35	24	15–19	_____
26	28	18	20	25	23	22	37	20–24	_____
52	31	30	41	45	29	27	28	25–29	_____
43	29	28	27	25	29	28	29	30–34	_____
18	26	33	25	27	25	34	32	35–39	_____
36	22	32	33	21	23	24	18	40–44	_____
48	23	16	38	26	21	23		45–49	_____
								50–54	_____

Work problems 3–6 using the information provided. [19.1]

3. Construct a bar graph for the data of Exercise 1.

4. Construct a bar graph for the data of Exercise 2.

5. Construct a circle graph for the following data.

Region	Frequency
Northeast	49,519
Midwest	58,953
South	79,539
West	45,970

6.   Construct a circle graph for the following information.

Unit	Number
A	360
B	130
C	120
D	90
E	20

Calculate the mean, median, and mode for the following sets of data. Round answers to the nearest tenth. [19.2–19.3]

7.   43, 67, 36, 52, 30, 44, 61, 39, 39

8.   18, 7, 5, 9, 12, 5, 6, 5

9.   19, 24, 26, 23, 19, 27, 46, 52, 27, 27

10.   310, 418, 512, 452, 310, 365, 570, 432

11.   2.0, 2.3, 4.1, 3.3, 1.9, 3.5, 1.8, 4.0, 2.7, 3.9, 2.6

12.   8, 9, 8, 8, 7, 7, 10, 11, 12, 10, 9, 13, 12

Calculate the mean for the frequency distribution given in problems 13–15. Round answers to the nearest tenth. [19.2]

13.

Intervals	Frequency
10–14	4
15–19	2
20–24	3
25–29	6
30–34	5
35–39	9

14.

Intervals	Frequency
0–4	7
5–9	18
10–14	23
15–19	8
20–24	4

15.

Intervals	Frequency
1–5	20
6–10	12
11–15	14
16–20	10
21–25	5

Find the range and standard deviation for problems 16–19. Round answers to the nearest hundredth. [19.4]

16. 2, 3, 4, 5, 6, 8, 10, 10

17. 17, 20, 15, 18, 21, 20, 22

18. 9, 6, 5, 6, 5, 8, 7, 6, 7, 1

19. 50, 47, 38, 62, 37, 66, 54, 42, 20, 25, 51, 60

Find the price relative for problems 20–25. Round to the nearest tenth. [19.5]

	Item	Price in Base Year	Price in Current Year
20.	Eggs	$.48 per dozen	$1.20 per dozen
21.	Rent	$100 per month	$350 per month
22.	Car	$4000	$9200
23.	Dishwasher	$495	$725
24.	Chicken	$.35 per lb.	$1.25 per lb.
25.	Chalk	$.15 per box	$.45 per box

Arithmetic Review

Even with the use of calculators, it is important to understand the fundamentals of arithmetic, since the most crucial part of solving a problem is to *set it up*—to decide on the procedure for solving the problem. This appendix reviews arithmetic, including rounding of numbers, and the addition, subtraction, multiplication, and division of whole numbers and decimals.

A.1 Whole Numbers

OBJECTIVES

1 Read whole numbers.

2 Round whole numbers.

3 Add whole numbers.

4 Subtract whole numbers.

5 Multiply whole numbers.

6 Multiply by omitting zeros.

7 Divide whole numbers.

1 The standard system of numbering is called the **decimal system**. The decimal system, based on powers of 10, uses the ten **digits**, 0, 1, 2, 3, 4, 5, 6, 7, 8, and 9. Combinations of these digits represent any number. This section discusses only **whole numbers**—the numbers used for counting. To show that a number is a whole number, a **decimal point** is sometimes placed at its right. The decimal point is the starting point in the decimal system. (Later, when discussing parts of a whole, digits will be placed to the right of the decimal point.)

Figure A.1 names the first ten places used with whole numbers. The number

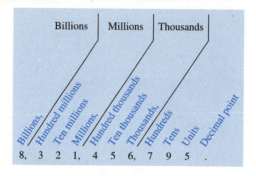

FIGURE A.1

8,321,456,795 is read as "eight billion, three hundred twenty-one million, four hundred fifty-six thousand, seven hundred ninety-five." Notice that the word *and* is not used with whole numbers. The word *and* represents the decimal point and is discussed in Section A.2.

EXAMPLE 1
Expressing Whole Numbers in Words

Express the following numbers in words.

(a) 7835   **(b)** 111,356,075   **(c)** 6,000,005

SOLUTION

(a) seven thousand, eight hundred thirty-five

(b) one hundred eleven million, three hundred fifty-six thousand, seventy-five

(c) six million, five ■

2 Business applications often require **rounding** numbers. For example, money amounts are commonly rounded to the nearest cent when prices are calculated. However, money amounts can also be rounded to the nearest dollar, hundred dollars, thousand dollars, or even hundreds of thousands of dollars and beyond.
    Use the following rules for **rounding whole numbers**.

---

1. Locate the place to which the number is to be rounded.

2A. If the digit to the right of the place being rounded is **5 or more, increase** the digit in the place being rounded by one.

2B. If the digit to the right of the place being rounded is **4 or less, do not change** the digit in the place being rounded.

3. Change all digits to the right of the place being rounded to zero.

EXAMPLE 2

Rounding Whole Numbers

Round each number.

(a)   768 to the nearest ten

(b)   67,533 to the nearest thousand

(c)   1,498,985 to the nearest million

SOLUTION

(a)   768 to tens

Step 1.   Locate the tens place.

768

↑

Step 2.   The digit after the tens place is 8, which is 5 or more, so the tens place is increased by 1.

Step 3.   Change all digits after the tens place to zero. 768 rounded to the nearest ten is 770.

(b)   67,533 rounds to the nearest thousand as 68,000

(c)   1,498,985 rounds to the nearest million as 1,000,000   ■

NOTE When rounding a number look at the digit just to the right of the digit being rounded. Do not look beyond this digit.

There are four basic *operations* that may be performed on whole numbers: addition, subtraction, multiplication, and division. The rest of this section quickly reviews these operations.

 In an addition problem, the numbers being added are called **addends**, and the answer is called the **sum** or **total** or **amount**, as follows.

8	addend
+ 9	addend
17	sum

Add numbers by arranging them in a column with units above units, tens above tens, hundreds above hundreds, thousands above thousands, and so on. Use the decimal point as a reference for arranging the numbers. If a number does not include a decimal point, the decimal point is assumed to be at its far right.

EXAMPLE 3

Adding Whole Numbers

Add the following numbers.

SOLUTION

(a)
$$
\begin{array}{r}
275 \\
713 \\
5 \\
3 \\
+\ 4173 \\
\hline
5169
\end{array}
$$

(b)
$$
\begin{array}{r}
331 \\
1 \\
74 \\
8715 \\
3 \\
+\ \ 786 \\
\hline
9910
\end{array}
$$

(c)
$$
\begin{array}{r}
2 \\
5175 \\
6890 \\
13 \\
326 \\
21 \\
+\ \ 153 \\
\hline
12{,}580
\end{array}
$$
■

4   A subtraction problem is set up much like an addition problem. The top number is the **minuend**, the number being subtracted is the **subtrahend**, and the answer is the **remainder** or **difference**.

$$
\begin{array}{r}
23 \\
-\ 7 \\
\hline
16
\end{array}
\quad
\begin{array}{l}
\text{minuend} \\
\text{subtrahend} \\
\text{difference}
\end{array}
$$

To subtract one number from another, place the subtrahend directly under the minuend. Again, use the decimal point as a reference so that units are above units, tens above tens, and so on. Then begin at the right column and subtract the subtrahend from the minuend, as shown in the following example.

EXAMPLE 4

Subtracting with Borrowing

Subtract 2894 from 3783.

SOLUTION   Write the problem as follows.

$$
\begin{array}{r}
3783 \\
-2894
\end{array}
$$

In the units column, subtract 4 from 3 by borrowing a 1 from the tens column in the minuend, to get 1 ten + 3, or 10 + 3 = 13, in the units column with 7 remaining in the tens column. Now subtract 4 from 13, for a result of 9. Complete the subtraction as follows.

$$
\begin{array}{r}
2\ \ 16\ \ 17\ \ 13 \\
\cancel{3}\ \ \cancel{7}\ \ 8\ \ \cancel{3} \\
-\ 2\ \ 8\ \ 9\ \ 4 \\
\hline
8\ \ 8\ \ 9
\end{array}
\ \blacksquare
$$

5   Multiplication is a quick method of addition. For example, 3×4 can be found by adding 3 a total of 4 times, since $3 \times 4 = 3 + 3 + 3 + 3 = 12$. However, it would not be practical to use this method to multiply large numbers. For example, 103×92 would be found by adding 103 a total of 92 times, which is not practical. Find this result with multiplication instead, as follows.

In multiplication, the number being multiplied is the **multiplicand** and the number doing the multiplying is the **multiplier**. The answer is the **product**.

$$
\begin{array}{r}
3 \\
\times\ 4 \\
\hline
12
\end{array}
\quad
\begin{array}{l}
\text{multiplicand} \\
\text{multiplier} \\
\text{product (answer)}
\end{array}
$$

When the multiplier contains more than one digit, **partial products** must be used, as shown in the following.

EXAMPLE 5
Multiplying Whole
Numbers

Multiply 57 by 23.

SOLUTION

$$
\begin{array}{r}
57 \\
\times \quad 23 \\
\hline
171 \\
114 \\
\hline
1311
\end{array}
$$

   multiplicand
   mulitplier
   partial product
   partial product (one position to the left)
   product

To find the product of 57 and 23, multiply 57 by 3 (taken from the units column of the multiplier). This gives 171, a partial product. Then multiply 57 by 2 (from the tens column of the multiplier), resulting in 114 as a partial product. Since the 2 in the multiplier is from the tens column, write the partial product 114 one position to the left with the 4 in the tens column. The final step is to add the partial products. Here the product is 1311. If the multiplier had more digits, each partial product would be found and placed one additional position to the left. ■

6   When the multiplier, multiplicand, or both end in zeros, save time by first omitting any zeros at the right of the numbers and then replace any omitted zeros at the right of the final answer. This shortcut is useful even when using calculators. For example, multiply 240 and 13 by deleting zeros, as follows.

$$
\begin{array}{r}
24\cancel{0} \\
\times \quad 13 \\
\hline
72 \\
24 \\
\hline
312
\end{array}
$$

   omit the zero in the calculation

   now replace the zero at the right of
   312 for a final answer of 3120 (product)

EXAMPLE 6
Multiplying
Omitting Zeros

Multiply the following. Omit zeros and then replace the omitted zeros to obtain the product.

SOLUTION

(a)
$$
\begin{array}{r}
150 \\
\times \ 70 \\
\hline
\end{array}
\qquad
\begin{array}{r}
15 \\
\times \ 7 \\
\hline
105 \\
10{,}500
\end{array}
$$
   +2 zeros
   product

(b)
$$
\begin{array}{r}
300 \\
\times \ 70 \\
\hline
\end{array}
\qquad
\begin{array}{r}
3 \\
\times \ 7 \\
\hline
21 \\
21{,}000
\end{array}
$$
   +3 zeros
   product ■

NOTE   A shortcut for multiplying by 10, 100, 1000, and so on is to omit the zeros before multiplying, multiply, and then replace the same number of zeros to obtain the desired answer.

7   Division is indicated by different symbols. For example, $\div$ and $\overline{)}$ both mean divide. Also a — with a number above and a number below, as in a fraction, means division. In printing and typing, and with the computer, the bar is often written /, so that 24/6 means to divide 24 by 6, for example.

The **dividend** is the number being divided, the **divisor** is the number doing the dividing, and the **quotient** is the answer.

The problem "15 divided by 5 equals 3" could be written in any of the following ways.

$$15 \;\; \div \;\; 5 \;\; = \;\; 3$$

dividend   divisor   quotient

$$\text{divisor} \quad 5\overline{)15} \quad \begin{matrix} \text{quotient} \\ \text{dividend} \end{matrix}$$

$$\frac{\text{dividend}}{\text{divisor}} \quad \frac{15}{5} = 3 \quad \text{quotient}$$

$$15/5 = 3 \quad \text{quotient}$$

dividend/divisor

EXAMPLE 7

Dividing Whole Numbers

Divide 1095 by 73.

SOLUTION Write the problem as follows.

$$73\overline{)1095}$$

Since 73 is larger than 1 or 10 but smaller than 109, begin by dividing 73 into 109. There is 1 of the 73s in 109, so place 1 over the digit 9 in the dividend, as shown. Then multiply 1 and 73.

$$\begin{array}{r} 1 \\ 73\overline{)1095} \\ \underline{73} \\ 36 \end{array}$$

When 73 is subtracted from 109, the remainder is 36. The next step is to drop down the 5 from the dividend, placing it next to the remainder 36. This gives the number 365. The divisor 73 is then divided into 365 with a result of 5, which is placed to the right of the 1 in the quotient. Since 73 divides exactly 5 times into 365, the final answer (quotient) is exactly 15.

$$\begin{array}{r} 15 \\ 73\overline{)1095} \\ \underline{73} \\ 365 \\ \underline{365} \\ 0 \end{array}$$

To check, multiply 73 and 15. The answer should be 1095. ∎

EXAMPLE 8

Dividing with a Remainder in the Answer

Divide 126 by 24.

SOLUTION The work should look like the following.

$$\begin{array}{r} 5 \\ 24\overline{)126} \\ \underline{120} \\ 6 \end{array}$$

The number 6 is called the **remainder**. Write the answer as 5 R 6. Later, we shall see the remainder written as a fraction, or a decimal. Check this result as follows.

$$
\begin{array}{r}
24 \\
\times \quad 5 \\
\hline
120 \\
+ \quad 6 \\
\hline
126
\end{array}
$$

$\leftarrow$ add the remainder

$\leftarrow$ equals the dividend ∎

A.1 Exercises

Express each of the following numbers in words.

1. 6750

2. 3675

3. 5103

4. 4408

5. 37,901

6. 11,222

Round each of the following numbers to the nearest ten, nearest hundred, and nearest thousand.

7. 7065

8. 31,321

9. 47,356

10. 59,802

11. 63,721

12. 78,784

13. 106,054

14. 359,874

15. 1,058,992

16. 3,721,518

Add each of the following.

17.
$$\begin{array}{r} 25 \\ 67 \\ 32 \\ +\ 13 \\ \hline \end{array}$$

18.
$$\begin{array}{r} 875 \\ 364 \\ 171 \\ +\ 776 \\ \hline \end{array}$$

19.
$$\begin{array}{r} 850 \\ 791 \\ 458 \\ 340 \\ +\ 507 \\ \hline \end{array}$$

20.
$$\begin{array}{r} 71 \\ 6845 \\ 8739 \\ 13 \\ +\ 847 \\ \hline \end{array}$$

21.
$$\begin{array}{r} 553 \\ 710 \\ 877 \\ 521 \\ +\ 139 \\ \hline \end{array}$$

22.
$$\begin{array}{r} 36 \\ 123 \\ 3\ 489 \\ 7\ 354 \\ +\ 61,151 \\ \hline \end{array}$$

23.
$$\begin{array}{r} 75,730 \\ 13,584 \\ +\ 79,157 \\ \hline \end{array}$$

24.
$$\begin{array}{r} 153,085 \\ 718,359 \\ +\ 373,827 \\ \hline \end{array}$$

Subtract each of the following.

25.
$$\begin{array}{r} 724 \\ -\ 138 \\ \hline \end{array}$$

26.
$$\begin{array}{r} 625 \\ -\ 315 \\ \hline \end{array}$$

27.
$$\begin{array}{r} 4718 \\ -\ 615 \\ \hline \end{array}$$

28.
$$\begin{array}{r} 7853 \\ -1679 \\ \hline \end{array}$$

29.
$$\begin{array}{r} 78,591 \\ -63,781 \\ \hline \end{array}$$

30.
$$\begin{array}{r} 337,159 \\ -184,795 \\ \hline \end{array}$$

31.
$$\begin{array}{r} 7,942,837 \\ -\ 615,995 \\ \hline \end{array}$$

32.
$$\begin{array}{r} 9,037,905 \\ -\ 259,919 \\ \hline \end{array}$$

Multiply each of the following.

33. 2725
       $\times\,73$

34.   725
       $\times 673$

35.   6375
       $\times 7259$

36.   2153
       $\times 603$

37.   567
       $\times 36$

38.   375
       $\times 28$

39.   1109
       $\times 7311$

40.   9503
       $\times 411$

41.   7300
       $\times 1600$

42.   2300
       $\times\ 760$

43. 21,000
       $\times\ \ 70$

44.   16,000
       $\times 7\,000$

45.   710
       $\times 350$

46.   130
       $\times 500$

47.   3760
       $\times 6000$

48.   7200
       $\times 1300$

Divide each of the following. Express any remainder using R.

49. $7\overline{)1491}$

50. $8\overline{)808,816}$

51. $6\overline{)132,144}$

52. $28\overline{)18,424}$

53. $32\overline{)15,584}$

54. $52\overline{)38,075}$

55. $283\overline{)89,527}$

56. $105\overline{)68,404}$

57. $462\overline{)800,821}$

58. $240\overline{)468,000}$

59. $560\overline{)1,405,600}$

60. $2154\overline{)812,853}$

Perform each operation.

61. Add 5874, 422, and 923.

62. Add 7694, 385, and 755.

63. Subtract 15,758 from 21,032.

64. Subtract 63,909 from 75,811.

65. Multiply 572 and 64.

66. Multiply 803 and 152.

67. Divide 25,488 by 531.

68. Divide 66,176 by 752.

Work the following word problems.

69. Sales at the Computer Center were $6975 today. If this is $1630 less than the sales yesterday, what were yesterday's sales?

70. Kevin Howell owes $3815 plus $268 interest on his credit union loan. If he wants to pay the loan in full, how much must he pay?

71. Cooperative Almond Growers has 785 production employees, 93 office and clerical workers, and 18 management personnel. Find the total number of employees.

72. The Natural Chocolate Works melts 385 pounds of light chocolate, 100 pounds of dark, and 22 pounds of peanut butter. They then add 18 pounds of almonds and 1 pound of confectioner's wax. What is the total weight of the candy made from these ingredients?

73. If 375 ski lift tickets are sold per day, how many tickets will be sold in a 7-day period?

74. To qualify for a real estate loan at Home Bank, a borrower must have a monthly income of at least 4 times the monthly payment on the loan. For a monthly payment of $775, find the borrower's minimum monthly income.

75. A car weighs 2425 pounds. If its 582-pound engine is removed and replaced with a 634-pound engine, find the weight of the car after the engine change.

76. Donald Cole has annual payroll deductions of $2184 for federal taxes and $372 for state taxes. If equal deductions are made each month, find his total monthly tax deductions.

77. John and Will Kellogg invented the first cold flakes cereal in 1894. Of the total 200 different types of cold cereals produced today, a large supermarket decides to sell all but 62 of the types. How many types of cereal does the supermarket sell?

78. A truck weighs 9250 pounds when empty. After being loaded with firewood, the truck weighs 21,375 pounds. What is the weight of the firewood?

79. Debbie Roper knows that her Ford Escort gives 36 miles per gallon of gasoline. How many miles can she travel on 37 gallons?

80. Management reports that 73 window frames come off the assembly line each hour. At this rate, how many window frames come off the assembly line in a 24-hour period?

81. Kelly Bell spent $286 on tuition, $176 on books, and $22 on supplies. If this money was withdrawn from her checking account, which had a balance of $785, what is her new balance?

82. How many 2-inch strips of leather can be cut from a piece of leather 3 feet in width? (Hint: 1 foot = 12 inches.)

83. If there are 43,560 square feet in an acre, and 144 square inches in a square foot, how many square inches are there in an acre?

84. Find the total cost if a college bookstore buys 17 computers at $506 each and 13 printers at $482 each.

85. A theater owner wants to provide enough seating for 1250 people. The main floor has 30 rows of 25 seats in each row. If the balcony has 25 rows, how many seats must be in each row to satisfy the owner's seating requirements?

86. Jennie makes 24 grapevine wreaths per week to sell to gift shops. She works 30 weeks a year and packages six wreaths per box. If she ships equal quantities to each of five shops, find the number of boxes each store will receive.

◣A.2 Decimals

OBJECTIVES

1 Read and write decimals.

2 Add and subtract decimals.

3 Multiply decimals.

4 Divide decimals.

1 A **decimal** is a number written with a decimal point, such as 6.8, 5.375, and 0.000982. Section 1.1 discussed how to read the digits to the left of the decimal point. Read the digits to the right of the decimal point as in Figure A.2.

FIGURE A.2

The decimal 9.7 is written in words or read as "nine and seven tenths." The word "and" represents the decimal point. Also, 11.59 is read "eleven and fifty-nine hundredths," and 72.087 is read as "seventy-two and eighty-seven thousandths."

EXAMPLE 1
Reading Decimal Numbers

Write in words the following decimals.

(a) 19.08 **(b)** 0.097 **(c)** 7648.9713

SOLUTION

(a) nineteen and eight hundredths

(b) ninety-seven thousandths

(c) seven thousand, six hundred forty-eight and nine thousand seven hundred thirteen ten-thousandths ■

2 Addition of decimals is done in much the same way as addition of whole numbers. When adding decimals, however, be careful to keep the decimal points in a line.

EXAMPLE 2
Adding Decimals

Add 9.83, 6.4, 17.592, and 3.087.

SOLUTION

$$
\begin{array}{r}
9.83 \\
6.4 \\
17.592 \\
+\ 3.087 \\
\hline
36.909
\end{array}
$$

decimal points lined up

Add in columns, as whole numbers were added. One way to keep the digits in their correct columns is to attach zeros to the right of each decimal, so that each number has the same number of digits following the decimal point. Placing zeros to the right of the decimal point does not change the value of a number. For example, 4.21 = 4.210 = 4.2100, and so on. Now rewrite the problem above and add.

$$9.830$$
$$6.400$$
$$17.592$$
$$+ \quad 3.087$$
$$\overline{36.909}\ \blacksquare$$

Subtraction is done in much the same way as addition. Line up the decimal points, and attach as many zeros after each decimal as needed.

EXAMPLE 3
Subtracting Decimals

Subtract 17.432 from 21.76.

SOLUTION

$$21.760 \quad \text{(one zero is needed)}$$
$$-17.432$$
$$\overline{4.328}$$

To check this subtraction, add the answer (difference) and the number subtracted.

$$17.432$$
$$+ \ 4.328$$
$$\overline{21.760}\ \blacksquare$$

3 Decimals are multiplied as if they were whole numbers. (It is not necessary to line up the decimal points.) The decimal point in the answer is then found as follows.

---

1. Count the number of digits to the right of the decimal point in each of the two numbers multiplied.
2. In the answer, count from right to left the number of places found in (1). It may be necessary to place zeros to the left of the answer.

EXAMPLE 4
Multiplying Decimals

Multiply.

(a) 8.34 and 4.2   **(b)** 0.032 and 0.07

SOLUTION

(a) First multiply the given numbers as if they were whole numbers.

$$8.34 \quad \leftarrow \quad \text{2 decimal places}$$
$$\times \ 4.2 \quad \leftarrow \quad \text{1 decimal place}$$
$$\overline{1668} \qquad \text{3 decimal places in answer}$$
$$3336$$

There are two decimal places in 8.34, and one in 4.2. This means there are $2 + 1 = 3$ decimal places in the final answer. Find the final answer by starting at the right and counting three places to the left.

$$35.028, \qquad \text{3 places}$$

(b) In this product it is necessary to attach zeros to the left of the answer.

$$
\begin{array}{r}
0.032 \\
\times\ 0.07 \\
\hline
0.00224.
\end{array}
$$

0.032   ←   3 decimal places

× 0.07   ←   2 decimal places

0.00224.   ←   5 decimal places in answer

Attach 2 zeros   ■

The next example uses the formula for the gross pay for a worker paid by the hour.

Gross pay = Number of hours worked × Pay per hour

EXAMPLE 5
Multiplying Two Decimal Numbers

Find the gross pay of a person working 42.6 hours at a pay of $8.55 per hour.

SOLUTION   Multiply.

$$
\begin{array}{r}
42.6 \\
\times\ 8.55 \\
\hline
2130 \\
2130\ \ \\
3408\ \ \ \\
\hline
364.230
\end{array}
$$

42.6   ←   1 place

× 8.55   ←   2 places

2130   3 places in answer

This worker's gross pay is $364.23.   ■

4 Recall that in the division problem $14 \div 7 = 2$, the number 7 is the divisor, 14 is the dividend, and 2 is the quotient. These words also are used in the division of decimals. There are two different possibilities.

Dividing a Decimal by a Whole Number.   To divide the decimal 21.93 by the whole number 3, write the division problem as if both numbers were whole numbers. (That is, ignore the decimal points at first.)

$$3\overline{)21.93}$$

Place the decimal point in the quotient above the decimal point in the dividend, and perform the division.

$$3\overline{)21.93} = 7.31$$

decimal point moves straight up

Check by multiplying the divisor and the quotient. The answer should equal the dividend.

$$\begin{array}{r} 7.31 \\ \times \quad 3 \\ \hline 21.93 \end{array} \leftarrow \text{matches dividend}$$

EXAMPLE 6

Dividing a Decimal by a Whole Number

Divide 27.52 by 32. Check the answer.

SOLUTION

Problem	*Check*

$$\begin{array}{r} .86 \\ 32\overline{)27.52} \\ 25\ 6 \\ \hline 1\ 92 \\ 1\ 92 \\ \hline 0 \end{array} \qquad \begin{array}{r} 0.86 \\ \times \quad 32 \\ \hline 172 \\ 258 \\ \hline 27.52 \end{array} \ \blacksquare$$

Dividing a Decimal by a Decimal. To divide by a decimal, first rewrite the number so that the divisor is a whole number. For example, to divide 27.69 by 0.3, convert 0.3 to a whole number by moving the decimal point one place to the right. Then do exactly the same thing to the dividend. (Moving the decimal the same number of places in both the divisor and the dividend does not change the value of the problem.)

$$0.3.\overline{)27.6.9}$$

After moving the decimal point, write the original problem as 276.9 ÷ 3. Then divide as usual.

$$\begin{array}{r} 92.3 \\ 3\overline{)276.9} \end{array}$$

Sometimes it is necessary to place zeros after the dividend. As before, attach zeros and divide until the quotient has one more digit than the desired precision, and then round.

EXAMPLE 7

Dividing a Decimal by a Decimal

Divide and check the following.

(a) 17.6 ÷ 0.25

(b) 9.43 ÷ 0.4

SOLUTION

$$
\begin{array}{r}
70.4 \\
0.25.)\overline{17.60.0} \\
\underline{17\,5} \\
10\,0 \\
\underline{10\,0}
\end{array}
$$

(a)

zeros were attached
after 17.6

Check

$$
\begin{array}{r}
70.4 \\
\times\,0.25 \\
\hline
3520 \\
1408 \\
\hline
17.600
\end{array}
$$

(b)

$$
\begin{array}{r}
23.575 \\
0.4.)\overline{9.4.300} \\
\underline{8} \\
1\,4 \\
\underline{1\,2} \\
2\,3 \\
\underline{2\,0} \\
30 \\
\underline{28} \\
20 \\
\underline{20}
\end{array}
$$

Check

$$
\begin{array}{r}
23.575 \\
\times\quad 0.4 \\
\hline
9.4300 \quad \blacksquare
\end{array}
$$

NOTE When checking an answer that has been rounded, the check will be off a little.

A.2 Exercises

Write the following decimals in words.

1. 3.15
2. 98.71
3. 21.37
4. 11.583

Write each of the following decimals using numbers.

5. one hundred eleven and five tenths
6. ninety-seven and sixty-two hundredths
7. six and four hundred eleven thousands
8. two thousand seventy-four ten-thousands

Convert each of the following decimals to fractions and reduce to lowest terms.

9. 0.36
10. 0.72
11. 0.336
12. 0.215
13. 0.805
14. 0.791
15. 0.096
16. 0.012

Add each of the following decimals.

17.	18.	19.	20.
9.71	2.98	3872.40	1489.76
4.8	6.43	9.61	21.42
3.6	7.12	3.825	19.35
5.2	14.20	+ 9.717	+ 8.1
9.17	18.97		
+ 3.42	+ 17.42		

21. 192.43 + 86.7 + 908.153 + 17.28 + 9.621

22. 743.1 + 817.65 + 2.908 + 123.76 + 21.98

23. 798.419 + 68.32 + 512.807 + 643.9 + 428

24. 749.6 + 258.12 + 9.483 + 126.40 + 8.97 + 438.215

Subtract each of the following.

25.   19.74
       − 6.53

26.   27.96
       − 8.39

27.   51.215
       −19.708

28.   37.643
       −28.547

29. 158.032 − 79.981

30. 3974.61 − 892.59

31. 8.6 − 3.571

32. 27.8 − 13.582

Multiply each of the following decimals.

33.   0.042
       ×   3.2

34.   0.571
       ×   2.9

35.   21.7
       × 0.431

36.   76.9
       × 0.903

37. 0.0408 × 0.06

38. 0.0109 × 0.03

39. 1976.2 × 0.005

40. 2481.9 × 0.003

Find the gross pay for each of the following workers. Round each answer to the nearest cent.

41. 26 hours at $10.11 per hour

42. 41.75 hours at $8.08 per hour

43. 38.75 hours at $8.12 per hour

44. 27.25 hours at $7.80 per hour

Find the total cost for each of the following items.

45. 28.5 cubic yards of concrete at $48.56 per cubic yard

46. 1526.25 running feet of lumber at $.72 per foot

47. 6.5 pounds of peaches at $.44 per pound, plus 9.5 pounds of squash at $.28 per pound, plus 3.5 six-packs at $2.62 per six-pack

48. 3760 bricks at $.146 per brick plus 9.5 cubic yards of concrete at $55.26 per yard

Divide each of the following.

49. $5)\overline{20.865}$

50. $15)\overline{19.863}$

51. 375.429 ÷ 12

52. 921.47 ÷ 25

53. $2.5)\overline{4.98}$

54. $3.2)\overline{18.72}$

55. $0.52)\overline{7.6336}$

56. $0.88)\overline{29.392}$

57. 49.5924 ÷ 0.034

58. 6.5618 ÷ 0.043

59. 0.42 ÷ 0.008

60. 0.85 ÷ 0.005

Work each of the following word problems.

61. To find the assessed value of a piece of real estate, divide the amount of taxes by the tax rate. For a certain piece of property, taxes were $4225 and the tax rate was 0.169. Find the assessed value.

62. Mae Hedding drove 352.6 miles on the 16.4 gallons of gas in the tank of her Escort. How many miles per gallon did she get?

63. An office building has 43 identical small offices that rent for $714.92 per month. Find the total monthly rental income.

64. A One-Dollar Olympic Silver Coin weighs 26.73 grams. Find the number of coins that can be produced from 2198 grams of silver. Round to the nearest whole number.

65. If a Five-Dollar Olympic Gold Coin weighs 8.359 grams, find the number of coins that can be produced from 221 grams of gold. Round to the nearest whole number.

66. Commercial grade carpet sells for $22.10 per square yard, with padding costing $2.72 per square yard. Find the cost to buy and install 106.4 square yards, if the installer charges $3.15 per square yard.

67. Cindy Yates sells office equipment. Last week, her daily sales were $11,496.12, $4892.43, $17,029.54, $18,385.14, and $2965.84. Find (a) her total sales for the week and (b) her commission on the sales. To find her commission, multiply her total sales by 0.015.

68. Yukon Department Store had daily sales for the last five days of $46,911.12, $38,253.42, $59,847.11, $32,546.19, and $51,896.15. Find (a) the total sales for the period and (b) the profit, which is found by multiplying total sales by 0.017.

69. A television shop bought 79 color televisions for $274 each. It sold 41 of the sets for the regular price of $498 each, with the balance sold on sale at $375. Find (a) the total amount received from the sale of the sets and (b) the gross profit. Subtract cost from the amount received in order to find the gross profit.

70. A manufacturer sold 148 low level computer chips for $315.24 and 275 advanced chips for $2263.25. The company's profit on the low level chips was $127.28 and the profit on the advanced chips was $899.25. Find the company's cost to make (a) a low level chip and (b) an advanced chip.

71. New claims for damage caused by asbestos are being reported at the rate of 1300 each month. Find the number of claims reported in two years.

72. There are 63,800 claims for damages caused by asbestos. Asbestos manufacturers have retained 1100 law firms around the country to defend them against these claims. If each law firm defends the manufacturers against the same number of claims, find the number defended by each firm.

SUMMARY EXERCISE

According to the National Climate Data Center, these average annual rainfall amounts in inches are given for the following cities:

Atlanta	57.56	Memphis	59.79
Buffalo	50.89	Newark	52.30
Chicago	43.12	Philadelphia	35.79
Dallas	45.27	San Francisco	10.35
Los Angeles	5.24	Seattle	44.75

(a) Find the difference in rainfall between the city with the most rainfall and the city with the least rainfall.

(b) How much total rainfall was there in the two cities with the greatest amount of rainfall?

(c) How much total rainfall was there in the two cities with the least rainfall?

(d) If an equal amount of rain falls in Seattle each month of the year, find the average amount of rainfall each month in Seattle. (Round to the nearest hundredth.)

B

Powers of e

x	e^x	x	e^x	x	e^x	x	e^x	x	e^x
0.00	1.00000000	0.55	1.73325302	1.10	3.00416602	1.65	5.20697983	2.20	9.02501350
0.01	1.01005017	0.56	1.75067250	1.11	3.03435839	1.66	5.25931084	2.21	9.11571639
0.02	1.02020134	0.57	1.76826705	1.12	3.06485420	1.67	5.31216780	2.22	9.20733087
0.03	1.03045453	0.58	1.78603843	1.13	3.09565650	1.68	5.36555597	2.23	9.29986608
0.04	1.04081077	0.59	1.80398842	1.14	3.12676837	1.69	5.41948071	2.24	9.39333129
0.05	1.05127110	0.60	1.82211880	1.15	3.15819291	1.70	5.47394739	2.25	9.48773584
0.06	1.06183655	0.61	1.84043140	1.16	3.18993328	1.71	5.52896148	2.26	9.58308917
0.07	1.07250818	0.62	1.85892804	1.17	3.22199264	1.72	5.58452846	2.27	9.67940081
0.08	1.08328707	0.63	1.87761058	1.18	3.25437420	1.73	5.64065391	2.28	9.77668041
0.09	1.09417428	0.64	1.89648088	1.19	3.28708121	1.74	5.69734342	2.29	9.87493768
0.10	1.10517092	0.65	1.91554083	1.20	3.32011692	1.75	5.75460268	2.30	9.97418245
0.11	1.11627807	0.66	1.93479233	1.21	3.35348465	1.76	5.81243739	2.31	10.07442466
0.12	1.12749685	0.67	1.95423732	1.22	3.38718773	1.77	5.87085336	2.32	10.17567431
0.13	1.13882838	0.68	1.97387773	1.23	3.42122954	1.78	5.92985642	2.33	10.27794153
0.14	1.15027380	0.69	1.99371553	1.24	3.45561346	1.79	5.98945247	2.34	10.38123656
0.15	1.16183424	0.70	2.01375271	1.25	3.49034296	1.80	6.04964746	2.35	10.48556972
0.16	1.17351087	0.71	2.03399126	1.26	3.52542149	1.81	6.11044743	2.36	10.59095145
0.17	1.18530485	0.72	2.05443321	1.27	3.56085256	1.82	6.17185845	2.37	10.69739228
0.18	1.19721736	0.73	2.07508061	1.28	3.59663973	1.83	6.23388666	2.38	10.80490286
0.19	1.20924960	0.74	2.09593551	1.29	3.63278656	1.84	6.29653826	2.39	10.91349394
0.20	1.22140276	0.75	2.11700002	1.30	3.66929667	1.85	6.35981952	2.40	11.02317638
0.21	1.23367806	0.76	2.13827622	1.31	3.70617371	1.86	6.42373677	2.41	11.13396115
0.22	1.24607673	0.77	2.15976625	1.32	3.74342138	1.87	6.48829640	2.42	11.24585931
0.23	1.25860001	0.78	2.18147227	1.33	3.78104339	1.88	6.55350486	2.43	11.35888208
0.24	1.27124915	0.79	2.20339643	1.34	3.81904351	1.89	6.61936868	2.44	11.47304074
0.25	1.28402542	0.80	2.22554093	1.35	3.85742553	1.90	6.68589444	2.45	11.58834672
0.26	1.29693009	0.81	2.24790799	1.36	3.89619330	1.91	6.75308880	2.46	11.70481154
0.27	1.30996445	0.82	2.27049984	1.37	3.93535070	1.92	6.82095847	2.47	11.82244685
0.28	1.32312981	0.83	2.29331874	1.38	3.97490163	1.93	6.88951024	2.48	11.94126442
0.29	1.33642749	0.84	2.31636698	1.39	4.01485005	1.94	6.95875097	2.49	12.06127612
0.30	1.34985881	0.85	2.33964685	1.40	4.05519997	1.95	7.02868758	2.50	12.18249396
0.31	1.36342511	0.86	2.36316069	1.41	4.09595540	1.96	7.09932707	2.51	12.30493006
0.32	1.37712776	0.87	2.38691085	1.42	4.13712044	1.97	7.17067649	2.52	12.42859666
0.33	1.39096813	0.88	2.41089971	1.43	4.17869919	1.98	7.24274299	2.53	12.55350614
0.34	1.40494759	0.89	2.43512965	1.44	4.22069582	1.99	7.31553376	2.54	12.67967097
0.35	1.41906755	0.90	2.45960311	1.45	4.26311452	2.00	7.38905610	2.55	12.80710378
0.36	1.43332941	0.91	2.48432253	1.46	4.30595953	2.01	7.46331735	2.56	12.93581732
0.37	1.44773461	0.92	2.50929039	1.47	4.34923514	2.02	7.53832493	2.57	13.06582444
0.38	1.46228459	0.93	2.53450918	1.48	4.39294568	2.03	7.61408636	2.58	13.19713816
0.39	1.47698079	0.94	2.55998142	1.49	4.43709552	2.04	7.69060920	2.59	13.32977160
0.40	1.49182470	0.95	2.58570966	1.50	4.48168907	2.05	7.76790111	2.60	13.46373804
0.41	1.50681779	0.96	2.61169647	1.51	4.52673079	2.06	7.84596981	2.61	13.59905085
0.42	1.52196156	0.97	2.63794446	1.52	4.57222520	2.07	7.92482312	2.62	13.73572359
0.43	1.53725752	0.98	2.66445624	1.53	4.61817682	2.08	8.00446891	2.63	13.87376990
0.44	1.55270722	0.99	2.69123447	1.54	4.66459027	2.09	8.08491516	2.64	14.01320361
0.45	1.56831219	1.00	2.71828183	1.55	4.71147018	2.10	8.16616991	2.65	14.15403865
0.46	1.58407398	1.01	2.74560102	1.56	4.75882125	2.11	8.24824128	2.66	14.29628910
0.47	1.59999419	1.02	2.77319476	1.57	4.80664819	2.12	8.33113749	2.67	14.43996919
0.48	1.61607440	1.03	2.80106583	1.58	4.85495581	2.13	8.41486681	2.68	14.58509330
0.49	1.63231622	1.04	2.82921701	1.59	4.90374893	2.14	8.49943763	2.69	14.73167592
0.50	1.64872127	1.05	2.85765112	1.60	4.95303242	2.15	8.58485840	2.70	14.87973172
0.51	1.66529119	1.06	2.88637099	1.61	5.00281123	2.16	8.67113766	2.71	15.02927551
0.52	1.68202765	1.07	2.91537950	1.62	5.05309032	2.17	8.75828404	2.72	15.18032224
0.53	1.69893231	1.08	2.94467955	1.63	5.10387472	2.18	8.84630626	2.73	15.33288702
0.54	1.71600686	1.09	2.97427407	1.64	5.15516951	2.19	8.93521311	2.74	15.48698510

Interest Tables

n	A Compound Interest $(1+i)^n$	B Present Value $\dfrac{1}{(1+i)^n}$	C Amount of Annuity $s_{\overline{n}|i}$	D Present Value of Annuity $a_{\overline{n}|i}$	E Sinking Fund $\dfrac{1}{s_{\overline{n}|i}}$	F Amortization $\dfrac{1}{a_{\overline{n}|i}}$
			Rate $\frac{1}{3}\%$			
1	1.00333333	0.99667774	1.00000000	0.99667774	1.00000000	1.00333333
2	1.00667778	0.99336652	2.00333333	1.99004426	0.49916805	0.50250139
3	1.01003337	0.99006630	3.01001111	2.98011056	0.33222469	0.33555802
4	1.01340015	0.98677704	4.02004448	3.96688760	0.24875347	0.25208680
5	1.01677815	0.98349871	5.03344463	4.95038631	0.19867110	0.20200444
6	1.02016741	0.98023127	6.05022278	5.93061759	0.16528317	0.16861650
7	1.02356797	0.97697469	7.07039019	6.90759228	0.14143491	0.14476824
8	1.02697986	0.97372893	8.09395816	7.88132121	0.12354895	0.12688228
9	1.03040313	0.97049395	9.12093802	8.85181516	0.10963785	0.11297118
10	1.03383780	0.96726972	10.15134114	9.81908487	0.09850915	0.10184248
11	1.03728393	0.96405620	11.18517895	10.78314107	0.08940402	0.09273736
12	1.04074154	0.96085335	12.22246288	11.74399442	0.08181657	0.08514990
13	1.04421068	0.95766115	13.26320442	12.70165557	0.07539656	0.07872989
14	1.04769138	0.95447955	14.30741510	13.65613512	0.06989383	0.07322716
15	1.05118369	0.95130852	15.35510648	14.60744364	0.06512491	0.06845825
16	1.05468763	0.94814803	16.40629017	15.55559167	0.06095223	0.06428557
17	1.05820326	0.94499803	17.46097781	16.50058970	0.05727056	0.06060389
18	1.06173060	0.94185851	18.51918107	17.44244821	0.05399807	0.05733140
19	1.06526971	0.93872941	19.58091167	18.38117762	0.05107015	0.05440348
20	1.06882060	0.93561071	20.64618137	19.31678832	0.04843511	0.05176844
21	1.07238334	0.93250236	21.71500198	20.24929069	0.04605111	0.04938445
22	1.07595795	0.92940435	22.78738532	21.17869504	0.04388393	0.04721726
23	1.07954448	0.92631663	23.86334327	22.10501167	0.04190528	0.04523861
24	1.08314296	0.92323916	24.94288775	23.02825083	0.04009159	0.04342492
25	1.08675344	0.92017192	26.02603071	23.94842275	0.03842307	0.04175640
26	1.09037595	0.91711487	27.11278414	24.86553763	0.03688297	0.04021630
27	1.09401053	0.91406798	28.20316009	25.77960561	0.03545702	0.03879035
28	1.09765724	0.91103121	29.29717062	26.69063682	0.03413299	0.03746632
29	1.10131609	0.90800453	30.39482786	27.59864135	0.03290033	0.03623367
30	1.10498715	0.90498790	31.49614395	28.50362925	0.03174992	0.03508325
31	1.10867044	0.90198130	32.60113110	29.40561055	0.03067378	0.03400712
32	1.11236601	0.89898468	33.70980154	30.30459523	0.02966496	0.03299830
33	1.11607389	0.89599802	34.82216754	31.20059325	0.02871734	0.03205067
34	1.11979414	0.89302128	35.93824143	32.09361454	0.02782551	0.03115885
35	1.12352679	0.89005444	37.05803557	32.98366898	0.02698470	0.03031803
36	1.12727187	0.88709745	38.18156236	33.87076642	0.02619065	0.02952399
37	1.13102945	0.88415028	39.30883423	34.75491670	0.02543957	0.02877291
38	1.13479955	0.88121290	40.43986368	35.63612960	0.02472808	0.02806141
39	1.13858221	0.87828528	41.57466322	36.51441488	0.02405311	0.02738644
40	1.14237748	0.87536739	42.71324543	37.38978228	0.02341194	0.02674527
41	1.14618541	0.87245920	43.85562292	38.26224147	0.02280209	0.02613543
42	1.15000603	0.86956066	45.00180833	39.13180213	0.02222133	0.02555466
43	1.15383938	0.86667175	46.15181436	39.99847389	0.02166762	0.02500095
44	1.15768551	0.86379245	47.30565374	40.86226633	0.02113912	0.02447246
45	1.16154446	0.86092270	48.46333925	41.72318903	0.02063415	0.02396749
46	1.16541628	0.85806249	49.62488371	42.58125153	0.02015118	0.02348451
47	1.16930100	0.85521179	50.79029999	43.43646332	0.01968880	0.02302213
48	1.17319867	0.85237055	51.95960099	44.28883387	0.01924572	0.02257905
49	1.17710933	0.84953876	53.13279966	45.13837263	0.01882077	0.02215410
50	1.18103303	0.84671637	54.30990899	45.98508900	0.01841285	0.02174618

	A	B	C	D	E	F
Rate $\frac{5}{12}\%$	Compound Interest	Present Value	Amount of Annuity	Present Value of Annuity	Sinking Fund	Amortization
n	$(1+i)^n$	$\dfrac{1}{(1+i)^n}$	$s_{\overline{n}\|i}$	$a_{\overline{n}\|i}$	$\dfrac{1}{s_{\overline{n}\|i}}$	$\dfrac{1}{a_{\overline{n}\|i}}$
1	1.00416667	0.99585062	1.00000000	0.99585062	1.00000000	1.00416667
2	1.00835069	0.99171846	2.00416667	1.98756908	0.49896050	0.50312717
3	1.01255216	0.98760345	3.01251736	2.97517253	0.33194829	0.33611496
4	1.01677112	0.98350551	4.02506952	3.95867804	0.24844291	0.25260958
5	1.02100767	0.97942457	5.01484064	4.93810261	0.19834026	0.20250693
6	1.02526187	0.97536057	6.06284831	5.91346318	0.16493898	0.16910564
7	1.02953379	0.97131343	7.08811018	6.88477661	0.14108133	0.14524800
8	1.03382352	0.96728308	8.11764397	7.85205970	0.12318845	0.12735512
9	1.03813111	0.96326946	9.15146749	8.81532916	0.10927209	0.11343876
10	1.04245666	0.95927249	10.18959860	9.77460165	0.09813929	0.10230596
11	1.04680023	0.95529211	11.23205526	10.72989376	0.08903090	0.09319757
12	1.05116190	0.95132824	12.27885549	11.68122200	0.08144082	0.08560748
13	1.05554174	0.94738082	13.33001739	12.62860283	0.07501866	0.07918532
14	1.05993983	0.94344978	14.38555913	13.57205261	0.06951416	0.07368082
15	1.06435625	0.93953505	15.44549896	14.51158766	0.06474378	0.06891045
16	1.06879106	0.93563657	16.50985520	15.44722422	0.06056988	0.06473655
17	1.07324436	0.93175426	17.57864627	16.37897848	0.05688720	0.06105387
18	1.07771621	0.92788806	18.65189063	17.30686654	0.05361387	0.05778053
19	1.08220670	0.92403790	19.72960684	18.23090443	0.05068525	0.05485191
20	1.08671589	0.92020372	20.81181353	19.15110815	0.04804963	0.05221630
21	1.09124387	0.91638544	21.89852942	20.06749359	0.04566517	0.04983183
22	1.09579072	0.91258301	22.98977330	20.98007661	0.04349760	0.04766427
23	1.10035652	0.90879636	24.08556402	21.88887297	0.04151865	0.04568531
24	1.10494134	0.90502542	25.18592053	22.79389839	0.03970472	0.04387139
25	1.10954526	0.90127013	26.29086187	23.69516853	0.03803603	0.04220270
26	1.11416836	0.89753042	27.40040713	24.59269895	0.03649581	0.04066247
27	1.11881073	0.89380623	28.51457549	25.48650517	0.03506978	0.03923645
28	1.12347244	0.89009749	29.63338622	26.37660266	0.03374572	0.03791239
29	1.12815358	0.88640414	30.75685866	27.26300680	0.03251307	0.03667974
30	1.13285422	0.88272611	31.88501224	28.14573291	0.03136270	0.03552936
31	1.13757444	0.87906335	33.01786646	29.02479626	0.03028663	0.03445330
32	1.14231434	0.87541578	34.15544090	29.90021205	0.02927791	0.03344458
33	1.14707398	0.87178335	35.29775524	30.77199540	0.02833041	0.03249708
34	1.15185346	0.86816599	36.44482922	31.64016139	0.02743873	0.03160540
35	1.15665284	0.86456365	37.59668268	32.50472504	0.02659809	0.03076476
36	1.16147223	0.86097624	38.75333552	33.36570128	0.02580423	0.02997090
37	1.16631170	0.85740373	39.91480775	34.22310501	0.02505336	0.02922003
38	1.17117133	0.85384604	41.08111945	35.07695105	0.02434208	0.02850875
39	1.17605121	0.85030311	42.25229078	35.92725416	0.02366736	0.02783402
40	1.18095142	0.84677488	43.42834199	36.77402904	0.02302644	0.02719310
41	1.18587206	0.84326129	44.60929342	37.61729033	0.02241685	0.02658352
42	1.19081319	0.83976228	45.79516547	38.45705261	0.02183637	0.02600303
43	1.19577491	0.83627779	46.98597866	39.29333040	0.02128295	0.02544961
44	1.20075731	0.83280776	48.18175357	40.12613816	0.02075474	0.02492141
45	1.20576046	0.82935212	49.38251088	40.95549028	0.02025008	0.02441675
46	1.21078446	0.82591083	50.58827134	41.78140111	0.01976743	0.02393409
47	1.21582940	0.82248381	51.79905581	42.60388492	0.01930537	0.02347204
48	1.22089536	0.81907102	53.01488521	43.42295594	0.01886263	0.02302929
49	1.22598242	0.81567238	54.23578056	44.23862832	0.01843801	0.02260468
50	1.23109068	0.81228785	55.46176298	45.05091617	0.01803044	0.02219711

Rate $\frac{1}{2}\%$	A Compound Interest	B Present Value	C Amount of Annuity	D Present Value of Annuity	E Sinking Fund	F Amortization
n	$(1+i)^n$	$\dfrac{1}{(1+i)^n}$	$s_{\overline{n}|i}$	$a_{\overline{n}|i}$	$\dfrac{1}{s_{\overline{n}|i}}$	$\dfrac{1}{a_{\overline{n}|i}}$
1	1.00500000	0.99502488	1.00000000	0.99502488	1.00000000	1.00500000
2	1.01002500	0.99007450	2.00500000	1.98509938	0.49875312	0.50375312
3	1.01507513	0.98514876	3.01502500	2.97024814	0.33167221	0.33667221
4	1.02015050	0.98024752	4.03010012	3.95049566	0.24813279	0.25313279
5	1.02525125	0.97537067	5.05025063	4.92586633	0.19800997	0.20300997
6	1.03037751	0.97051808	6.07550188	5.89638441	0.16459546	0.16959546
7	1.03552940	0.96568963	7.10587939	6.86207404	0.14072854	0.14572854
8	1.04070704	0.96088520	8.14140879	7.82295924	0.12282886	0.12782886
9	1.04591058	0.95610468	9.18211583	8.77906392	0.10890736	0.11390736
10	1.05114013	0.95134794	10.22802641	9.73041186	0.09777057	0.10277057
11	1.05639583	0.94661487	11.27916654	10.67702673	0.08865903	0.09365903
12	1.06167781	0.94190534	12.33556237	11.61893207	0.08106643	0.08606643
13	1.06698620	0.93721924	13.39724018	12.55615131	0.07464224	0.07964224
14	1.07232113	0.93255646	14.46422639	13.48870777	0.06913609	0.07413609
15	1.07768274	0.92791688	15.53654752	14.41662465	0.06436436	0.06936436
16	1.08307115	0.92330037	16.61423026	15.33992502	0.06018937	0.06518937
17	1.08848651	0.91870684	17.69730141	16.25863186	0.05650579	0.06150579
18	1.09392894	0.91413616	18.78578791	17.17276802	0.05323173	0.05823173
19	1.09939858	0.90958822	19.87971685	18.08235624	0.05030253	0.05530253
20	1.10489558	0.90506290	20.97911544	18.98741915	0.04766645	0.05266645
21	1.11042006	0.90056010	22.08401101	19.88797925	0.04528163	0.05028163
22	1.11597216	0.89607971	23.19443107	20.78405896	0.04311380	0.04811380
23	1.12155202	0.89162160	24.31040322	21.67568055	0.04113465	0.04613465
24	1.12715978	0.88718567	25.43195524	22.56286622	0.03932061	0.04432061
25	1.13279558	0.88277181	26.55911502	23.44563803	0.03765186	0.04265186
26	1.13845955	0.87837991	27.69191059	24.32401794	0.03611163	0.04111163
27	1.14415185	0.87400986	28.83037015	25.19802780	0.03468565	0.03968565
28	1.14987261	0.86966155	29.97452200	26.06768936	0.03336167	0.03836167
29	1.15562197	0.86533488	31.12439461	26.93302423	0.03212914	0.03712914
30	1.16140008	0.86102973	32.28001658	27.79405397	0.03097892	0.03597892
31	1.16720708	0.85674600	33.44141666	28.65079997	0.02990304	0.03490304
32	1.17304312	0.85248358	34.60862375	29.50328355	0.02889453	0.03389453
33	1.17890833	0.84824237	35.78166686	30.35152592	0.02794727	0.03294727
34	1.18480288	0.84402226	36.96057520	31.19554818	0.02705586	0.03205586
35	1.19072689	0.83982314	38.14537807	32.03537132	0.02621550	0.03121550
36	1.19668052	0.83564492	39.33610496	32.87101624	0.02542194	0.03042194
37	1.20266393	0.83148748	40.53278549	33.70250372	0.02467133	0.02967139
38	1.20867725	0.82735073	41.73544942	34.52985445	0.02396045	0.02896045
39	1.21472063	0.82323455	42.94412666	35.35308900	0.02328607	0.02828607
40	1.22079424	0.81913886	44.15884730	36.17222786	0.02264552	0.02764552
41	1.22689821	0.81506354	45.37964153	36.98729141	0.02203631	0.02703631
42	1.23303270	0.81100850	46.60653974	37.79829991	0.02145622	0.02645622
43	1.23919786	0.80697363	47.83957244	38.60527354	0.02090320	0.02590320
44	1.24539385	0.80295884	49.07877030	39.40823238	0.02037541	0.02537541
45	1.25162082	0.79896402	50.32416415	40.20719640	0.01987117	0.02487117
46	1.25787892	0.79498907	51.57578497	41.00218547	0.01938894	0.02438894
47	1.26416832	0.79103390	52.83366390	41.79321937	0.01892733	0.02392733
48	1.27048916	0.78709841	54.09783222	42.58031778	0.01848503	0.02348503
49	1.27684161	0.78318250	55.36832138	43.36350028	0.01806087	0.02306087
50	1.28322581	0.77928607	56.64516299	44.14278635	0.01765376	0.02265376

	A	B	C	D	E	F
Rate $\frac{3}{4}$%	Compound Interest	Present Value	Amount of Annuity	Present Value of Annuity	Sinking Fund	Amortization
n	$(1+i)^n$	$\dfrac{1}{(1+i)^n}$	$s_{\overline{n}|i}$	$a_{\overline{n}|i}$	$\dfrac{1}{s_{\overline{n}|i}}$	$\dfrac{1}{a_{\overline{n}|i}}$
1	1.00750000	0.99255583	1.00000000	0.99255583	1.00000000	1.00750000
2	1.01505625	0.98516708	2.00750000	1.97772291	0.49813200	0.50563200
3	1.02266917	0.97783333	3.02255625	2.95555624	0.33084579	0.33834579
4	1.03033919	0.97055417	4.04522542	3.92611041	0.24720501	0.25470501
5	1.03806673	0.96332920	5.07556461	4.88943961	0.19702242	0.20452242
6	1.04585224	0.95615802	6.11363135	5.84559763	0.16356891	0.17106891
7	1.05369613	0.94904022	7.15948358	6.79463785	0.13967488	0.14717488
8	1.06159885	0.94197540	8.21317971	7.73661325	0.12175552	0.12925552
9	1.06956084	0.93496318	9.27477856	8.67157642	0.10781929	0.11531929
10	1.07758255	0.92800315	10.34433940	9.59957958	0.09667123	0.10417123
11	1.08566441	0.92109494	11.42192194	10.52067452	0.08755094	0.09505094
12	1.09380690	0.91423815	12.50758636	11.43491267	0.07995148	0.08745148
13	1.10201045	0.90743241	13.60139325	12.34234508	0.07352188	0.08102188
14	1.11027553	0.90067733	14.70340370	13.24302242	0.06801146	0.07551146
15	1.11860259	0.89397254	15.81367923	14.13699495	0.06323639	0.07073639
16	1.12699211	0.88731766	16.93228183	15.02431261	0.05905879	0.06655879
17	1.13544455	0.88071231	18.05927394	15.90502492	0.05537321	0.06287321
18	1.14396039	0.87415614	19.19471849	16.77918107	0.05209766	0.05959766
19	1.15254009	0.86764878	20.33867888	17.64682984	0.04916740	0.05666740
20	1.16118414	0.86118985	21.49121897	18.50801969	0.04653063	0.05403063
21	1.16989302	0.85477901	22.65240312	19.36279870	0.04414543	0.05164543
22	1.17866722	0.84841589	23.82229614	20.21121459	·0.04197748	0.04947748
23	1.18750723	0.84210014	25.00096336	21.05331473	0.03999846	0.04749846
24	1.19641353	0.83583140	26.18847059	21.88914614	0.03818474	0.04568474
25	1.20538663	0.82960933	27.38488412	22.71875547	0.03651650	0.04401650
26	1.21442703	0.82343358	28.59027075	23.54218905	0.03497693	0.04247693
27	1.22353523	0.81730380	29.80469778	24.35949286	0.03355176	0.04105176
28	1.23271175	0.81121966	31.02823301	25.17071251	0.03222871	0.03972871
29	1.24195709	0.80518080	32.26094476	25.97589331	0.03099723	0.03849723
30	1.25127176	0.79918690	33.50290184	26.77508021	0.02984816	0.03734816
31	1.26065630	0.79323762	34.75417361	27.56831783	0.02877352	0.03627352
32	1.27011122	0.78733262	36.01482991	28.35565045	0.02776634	0.03526634
33	1.27963706	0.78147158	37.28494113	29.13712203	0.02682048	0.03432048
34	1.28923434	0.77565418	38.56457819	29.91277621	0.02593053	0.03343053
35	1.29890359	0.76988008	39.85381253	30.68265629	0.02509170	0.03259170
36	1.30864537	0.76414896	41.15271612	31.44680525	0.02429973	0.03179973
37	1.31846021	0.75846051	42.46136149	32.20526576	0.02355082	0.03105082
38	1.32834866	0.75281440	43.77982170	32.95808016	0.02284157	0.03034157
39	1.33831128	0.74721032	45.10817037	33.70529048	0.02216893	0.02966893
40	1.34834861	0.74164796	46.44648164	34.44693844	0.02153016	0.02903016
41	1.35846123	0.73612701	47.79483026	35.18306545	0.02092276	0.02842276
42	1.36864969	0.73064716	49.15329148	35.91371260	0.02034452	0.02784452
43	1.37891456	0.72520809	50.52194117	36.63892070	0.01979338	0.02729338
44	1.38925642	0.71980952	51.90085573	37.35873022	0.01926751	0.02676751
45	1.39967584	0.71445114	53.29011215	38.07318136	0.01876521	0.02626521
46	1.41017341	0.70913264	54.68978799	38.78231401	0.01828495	0.02578495
47	1.42074971	0.70385374	56.09996140	39.48616775	0.01782532	0.02532532
48	1.43140533	0.69861414	57.52071111	40.18478189	0.01738504	0.02488504
49	1.44214087	0.69341353	58.95211644	40.87819542	0.01696292	0.02446292
50	1.45295693	0.68825165	60.39425732	41.56644707	0.01655787	0.02405787

Rate $\frac{5}{6}\%$	A Compound Interest	B Present Value	C Amount of Annuity	D Present Value of Annuity	E Sinking Fund	F Amortization
n	$(1 + i)^n$	$\dfrac{1}{(1 + i)^n}$	$s_{\overline{n}\mid i}$	$a_{\overline{n}\mid i}$	$\dfrac{1}{s_{\overline{n}\mid i}}$	$\dfrac{1}{a_{\overline{n}\mid i}}$
1	1.00833333	0.99173554	1.00000000	0.99173554	1.00000000	1.00833333
2	1.01673611	0.98353938	2.00833333	1.97527491	0.49792531	0.50625864
3	1.02520891	0.97541095	3.02506944	2.95068586	0.33057092	0.33890426
4	1.03375232	0.96734970	4.05027836	3.91803557	0.24689661	0.25522994
5	1.04236692	0.95935508	5.08403068	4.87739065	0.19669433	0.20502766
6	1.05105331	0.95142652	6.12639760	5.82881717	0.16322806	0.17156139
7	1.05981209	0.94356349	7.17745091	6.77238066	0.13932523	0.14765856
8	1.06864386	0.93576545	8.23726300	7.70814611	0.12139955	0.12973288
9	1.07754922	0.92803185	9.30590686	8.63617796	0.10745863	0.11579196
10	1.08652880	0.92036217	10.38345608	9.55654013	0.09630705	0.10464038
11	1.09558321	0.91275587	11.46998489	10.46929600	0.08718407	0.09551741
12	1.10471307	0.90521243	12.56556809	11.37450843	0.07958255	0.08791589
13	1.11391901	0.89773134	13.67028116	12.27223976	0.07315138	0.08148472
14	1.12320167	0.89031207	14.78420017	13.16255183	0.06763978	0.07597311
15	1.13256168	0.88295412	15.90740184	14.04550595	0.06286382	0.07119715
16	1.14199970	0.87565698	17.03996352	14.92116292	0.05868557	0.06701890
17	1.15151636	0.86842014	18.18196322	15.78958306	0.05499956	0.06333289
18	1.16111233	0.86124312	19.33347958	16.65082618	0.05172375	0.06005708
19	1.17078827	0.85412540	20.49459191	17.50495158	0.04879336	0.05712669
20	1.18054483	0.84706652	21.66538017	18.35201810	0.04615659	0.05448992
21	1.19038271	0.84006597	22.84592501	19.19208406	0.04377148	0.05210482
22	1.20030256	0.83312327	24.03630772	20.02520734	0.04160373	0.04993706
23	1.21030509	0.82623796	25.23661028	20.85144529	0.03962497	0.04795831
24	1.22039096	0.81940954	26.44691537	21.67085483	0.03781159	0.04614493
25	1.23056089	0.81263756	27.66730633	22.48349240	0.03614374	0.04447708
26	1.24081556	0.80592155	28.89786721	23.28941395	0.03460463	0.04293796
27	1.25115569	0.79926104	30.13868277	24.08867499	0.03317995	0.04151328
28	1.26158199	0.79265558	31.38983846	24.88133057	0.03185744	0.04019078
29	1.27209517	0.78610471	32.65142045	25.66743527	0.03062654	0.03895987
30	1.28269596	0.77960797	33.92351562	26.44704325	0.02947808	0.03781141
31	1.29338510	0.77316493	35.20621158	27.22020818	0.02840408	0.03673741
32	1.30416331	0.76677514	36.49959668	27.98698332	0.02739756	0.03573090
33	1.31503133	0.76043815	37.80375999	28.74742147	0.02645240	0.03478573
34	1.35298993	0.75415354	39.11879132	29.50157501	0.02556316	0.03389650
35	1.33703984	0.74792087	40.44478125	30.24949588	0.02472507	0.03305840
36	1.34818184	0.74173970	41.78182109	30.99123559	0.02393385	0.03226719
37	1.35941669	0.73560962	43.13000293	31.72684521	0.02318572	0.03151905
38	1.37074516	0.72953020	44.48941962	32.45637541	0.02247725	0.03081059
39	1.38216804	0.72350103	45.86016479	33.17987644	0.02180542	0.03013875
40	1.39368611	0.71752168	47.24233283	33.89739813	0.02116746	0.02950079
41	1.40530016	0.71159175	48.63601893	34.60898988	0.02056089	0.02889423
42	1.41701099	0.70571083	50.04131909	35.31470070	0.01998349	0.02831682
43	1.42881942	0.69987851	51.45833008	36.01457921	0.01943320	0.02776653
44	1.44072625	0.69409439	52.88714950	36.70867360	0.01890818	0.02724152
45	1.45273230	0.68835807	54.32787575	37.39703167	0.01840676	0.02674009
46	1.46483840	0.68266916	55.78060805	38.07970083	0.01792738	0.02626071
47	1.47704539	0.67702727	57.24544645	38.75672809	0.01746864	0.02580197
48	1.48935410	0.67143200	58.72249183	39.42816009	0.01702925	0.02536258
49	1.50176538	0.66588297	60.21184593	40.09404307	0.01660803	0.02494136
50	1.51428009	0.66037981	61.71361131	40.75442288	0.01620388	0.02453721

	A	B	C	D	E	F
Rate 1%	Compound Interest	Present Value	Amount of Annuity	Present Value of Annuity	Sinking Fund	Amortization
n	$(1 + i)^n$	$\dfrac{1}{(1 + i)^n}$	$s_{\overline{n}\|i}$	$a_{\overline{n}\|i}$	$\dfrac{1}{s_{\overline{n}\|i}}$	$\dfrac{1}{a_{\overline{n}\|i}}$
1	1.01000000	0.99009901	1.00000000	0.99009901	1.00000000	1.01000000
2	1.02010000	0.98029605	2.01000000	1.97039506	0.49751244	0.50751244
3	1.03030100	0.97059015	3.03010000	2.94098521	0.33002211	0.34002211
4	1.04060401	0.96098034	4.06040100	3.90196555	0.24628109	0.25628109
5	1.05101005	0.95146569	5.10100501	4.85343124	0.19603980	0.20603980
6	1.06152015	0.94204524	6.15201506	5.79547647	0.16254837	0.17254837
7	1.07213535	0.93271805	7.21353521	6.72819453	0.13862828	0.14862828
8	1.08285671	0.92348322	8.28567056	7.65167775	0.12069029	0.13069029
9	1.09368527	0.91433982	9.36852727	8.56601758	0.10674036	0.11674036
10	1.10462213	0.90528695	10.46221254	9.47130453	0.09558208	0.10558208
11	1.11566835	0.89632372	11.56683467	10.36762825	0.08645408	0.09645408
12	1.12682503	0.88744923	12.68250301	11.25507747	0.07884879	0.08884879
13	1.13809328	0.87866260	13.80932804	12.13374007	0.07241482	0.08241482
14	1.14947421	0.86996297	14.94742132	13.00370304	0.06690117	0.07690117
15	1.16096896	0.86134947	16.09689554	13.86505252	0.06212378	0.07212378
16	1.17257864	0.85282126	17.25786449	14.71787378	0.05794460	0.06794460
17	1.18430443	0.84437749	18.43044314	15.56225127	0.05425806	0.06425806
18	1.19614748	0.83601731	19.61474757	16.39826858	0.05098205	0.06098205
19	1.20810895	0.82773992	20.81089504	17.22600850	0.04805175	0.05805175
20	1.22019004	0.81954447	22.01900399	18.04555297	0.04541531	0.05541531
21	1.23239194	0.81143017	23.23919403	18.85698313	0.04303075	0.05303075
22	1.24471586	0.80339621	24.47158598	19.66037934	0.04086372	0.05086372
23	1.25716302	0.79544179	25.71630183	20.45582113	0.03888584	0.04888584
24	1.26973465	0.78756613	26.97346485	21.24338726	0.03707347	0.04707347
25	1.28243200	0.77976844	28.24319950	22.02315570	0.03540675	0.04540675
26	1.29525631	0.77204796	29.52563150	22.79520366	0.03386888	0.04386888
27	1.30820888	0.76440392	30.82088781	23.55960759	0.03244553	0.04244553
28	1.32129097	0.75683557	32.12909669	24.31644316	0.03112444	0.04112444
29	1.33450388	0.74934215	33.45038766	25.06578530	0.02989502	0.03989502
30	1.34784892	0.74192292	34.78489153	25.80770822	0.02874811	0.03874811
31	1.36132740	0.73457715	36.13274045	26.54228537	0.02767573	0.03767573
32	1.37494068	0.72730411	37.49406785	27.26958947	0.02667089	0.03667089
33	1.38869009	0.72010307	38.86900853	27.98969255	0.02575744	0.03572744
34	1.40257699	0.71297334	40.25769862	28.70266589	0.02483997	0.03483997
35	1.41660276	0.70591420	41.66027560	29.40853009	0.02400368	0.03400368
36	1.43076878	0.69892495	43.07687836	30.10750504	0.02321431	0.03321431
37	1.44507647	0.69200490	44.05764714	30.79950994	0.02246805	0.03246805
38	1.45952724	0.68515337	45.95272361	31.48466330	0.02176150	0.03176150
39	1.47412251	0.67836967	47.41225085	32.16303298	0.02109160	0.03109160
40	1.48886373	0.67165314	48.88637336	32.83468611	0.02045560	0.03045560
41	1.50375237	0.66500311	50.37523709	33.49968922	0.01985102	0.02985102
42	1.51878989	0.65841892	51.87898946	34.15810814	0.01927563	0.02927563
43	1.53397779	0.65189992	53.39777936	34.81000806	0.01872737	0.02872737
44	1.54931757	0.64544546	54.93175715	35.45545352	0.01820441	0.02820441
45	1.56481075	0.63905492	56.48107472	36.09450844	0.01770505	0.02770505
46	1.58045885	0.63272764	58.04588547	36.72723608	0.01722775	0.02722775
47	1.59626344	0.62646301	59.62634432	37.35369909	0.01677111	0.02677111
48	1.61222608	0.62026041	61.22260777	37.97395949	0.01633384	0.02633384
49	1.62834834	0.61411921	62.83483385	38.58807871	0.01591474	0.02591474
50	1.64463182	0.60803882	64.46318218	39.19611753	0.01551273	0.02551273

Rate $1\frac{1}{4}\%$	A Compound Interest	B Present Value	C Amount of Annuity	D Present Value of Annuity	E Sinking Fund	F Amortization
n	$(1 + i)^n$	$\dfrac{1}{(1 + i)^n}$	$s_{\overline{n}|i}$	$a_{\overline{n}|i}$	$\dfrac{1}{s_{\overline{n}|i}}$	$\dfrac{1}{a_{\overline{n}|i}}$
1	1.01250000	0.98765432	1.00000000	0.98765432	1.00000000	1.01250000
2	1.02515625	0.97546106	2.01250000	1.96311538	0.49689441	0.50939441
3	1.03797070	0.96341833	3.03765625	2.92653371	0.32920117	0.34170117
4	1.05094534	0.95152428	4.07562695	3.87805798	0.24536102	0.25786102
5	1.06408215	0.93977706	5.12657229	4.81783504	0.19506211	0.20756211
6	1.07738318	0.92817488	6.19065444	5.74600992	0.16153381	0.17403381
7	1.09085047	0.91671593	7.26803762	6.66272585	0.13758872	0.15008872
8	1.10448610	0.90539845	8.35888809	7.56812429	0.11963314	0.13213314
9	1.11829218	0.89422069	9.46337420	8.46234498	0.10567055	0.11817055
10	1.13227083	0.88318093	10.58166637	9.34552591	0.09450307	0.10700307
11	1.14642422	0.87227746	11.71393720	10.21780337	0.08536839	0.09786839
12	1.16075452	0.86150860	12.86036142	11.07931197	0.07775831	0.09025831
13	1.17526395	0.85087269	14.02111594	11.93018466	0.07132100	0.08382100
14	1.18995475	0.84036809	15.19637988	12.77055275	0.06580515	0.07830515
15	1.20482918	0.82999318	16.38633463	13.60054592	0.06102646	0.07352646
16	1.21988955	0.81974635	17.59116382	14.42029227	0.05684672	0.06934672
17	1.23513817	0.80962602	18.81105336	15.22991829	0.05316023	0.06566023
18	1.250557739	0.79963064	20.04619153	16.02954893	0.04988479	0.06238479
19	1.26620961	0.78975866	21.29676893	16.81930759	0.04695548	0.05945548
20	1.28203723	0.78000855	22.56297854	17.59931613	0.04432039	0.05682039
21	1.29806270	0.77037881	23.84501577	18.36969495	0.04193749	0.05443749
22	1.31428848	0.76086796	25.14307847	19.13056291	0.03977238	0.05227238
23	1.33071709	0.75147453	26.45736695	19.88203744	0.03779666	0.05029666
24	1.34735105	0.74219707	27.78808403	20.62423451	0.03598665	0.04848665
25	1.36419294	0.73303414	29.13543508	21.35726865	0.03432247	0.04682247
26	1.38124535	0.72398434	30.49962802	22.08125299	0.03278729	0.04528729
27	1.39851092	0.71504626	31.88087337	22.79629925	0.03136677	0.04386677
28	1.41599230	0.70621853	33.27938429	23.50251778	0.03004863	0.04254863
29	1.43369221	0.69749978	34.69537659	24.20001756	0.02882228	0.04132228
30	1.45161336	0.68888867	36.12906880	24.88890623	0.02767854	0.04017854
31	1.46975853	0.68038387	37.58068216	25.56929010	0.02660942	0.03910942
32	1.48813051	0.67198407	39.05044069	26.24127418	0.02560791	0.03810791
33	1.50673214	0.66368797	40.53857120	26.90496215	0.02466786	0.03716786
34	1.52556629	0.65549429	42.04530334	27.56045644	0.02378387	0.03628387
35	1.54463587	0.64740177	43.57086963	28.20785822	0.02295111	0.03545111
36	1.56394382	0.63940916	45.11550550	28.84726737	0.02216533	0.03466533
37	1.58349312	0.63151522	46.67944932	29.47878259	0.02142270	0.03392270
38	1.60328678	0.62371873	48.26294243	30.10250133	0.02071983	0.03321983
39	1.62332787	0.61601850	49.86622921	30.71851983	0.02005365	0.03255365
40	1.64361946	0.60841334	51.48955708	31.32693316	0.01942141	0.03192141
41	1.66416471	0.60090206	53.13317654	31.92783522	0.01882063	0.03132063
42	1.68496677	0.59348352	54.79734125	32.52131874	0.01824906	0.03074906
43	1.70602885	0.58615656	56.48230801	33.10747530	0.01770466	0.03020466
44	1.72735421	0.57892006	58.18833687	33.68639536	0.01718557	0.02968557
45	1.74894614	0.57177290	59.91569108	34.25816825	0.01669012	0.02919012
46	1.77080797	0.56471397	61.66463721	34.82288222	0.01621675	0.02871675
47	1.79294306	0.55774219	63.43544518	35.38064224	0.01576406	0.02826406
48	1.81535485	0.55085649	65.22838824	35.93148091	0.01533075	0.02783075
49	1.83804679	0.54405579	67.04374310	36.47553670	0.01491563	0.02741563
50	1.86102237	0.53733905	68.88178989	37.01287575	0.01451763	0.02701763

Rate $1\frac{1}{2}\%$	A Compound Interest	B Present Value	C Amount of Annuity	D Present Value of Annuity	E Sinking Fund	F Amortization
n	$(1 + i)^n$	$\dfrac{1}{(1 + i)^n}$	$s_{\overline{n}|i}$	$a_{\overline{n}|i}$	$\dfrac{1}{s_{\overline{n}|i}}$	$\dfrac{1}{a_{\overline{n}|i}}$
1	1.01500000	0.98522167	1.00000000	0.98522167	1.00000000	1.01500000
2	1.03022500	0.97066175	2.01500000	1.95588342	0.49627792	0.51127792
3	1.04567838	0.95631699	3.04522500	2.91220042	0.32838296	0.34338296
4	1.06136355	0.94218423	4.09090337	3.85438465	0.24444479	0.25944479
5	1.07728400	0.92826033	5.15226693	4.78264497	0.19408932	0.20908932
6	1.09344326	0.91454219	6.22955093	5.69718717	0.16052521	0.17552521
7	1.10984491	0.90102679	7.32299419	6.59821396	0.13655616	0.15155616
8	1.12649259	0.88771112	8.43283911	7.48592508	0.11858402	0.13358402
9	1.14338998	0.87459224	9.55933169	8.36051732	0.10460982	0.11960982
10	1.16054083	0.86166723	10.70272167	9.22218455	0.09343418	0.10843418
11	1.17794894	0.84893323	11.86326249	10.07111779	0.08429384	0.09929384
12	1.19561817	0.83638742	13.04121143	10.90750521	0.07667999	0.09167999
13	1.21355244	0.82402702	14.23682960	11.73153222	0.07024036	0.08524036
14	1.23175573	0.81184928	15.45038205	12.54338150	0.06472332	0.07972332
15	1.25023207	0.79985150	16.68213778	13.34323301	0.05994436	0.07494436
16	1.26898555	0.78803104	17.93236984	14.13126405	0.05576508	0.07076508
17	1.28802033	0.77638526	19.20135539	14.90764931	0.05207966	0.06707966
18	1.30734064	0.76491159	20.48937572	15.67256089	0.04880578	0.06380578
19	1.32695075	0.75360747	21.79671636	16.42616837	0.04587847	0.06087847
20	1.34685501	0.74247042	23.12366710	17.16863879	0.04324574	0.05824574
21	1.36705783	0.73149795	24.47052211	17.90013673	0.04086550	0.05586550
22	1.38756370	0.72068763	25.83757994	18.62082437	0.03870332	0.05370332
23	1.40837715	0.71003708	27.22514364	19.33086145	0.03673075	0.05173075
24	1.42950281	0.69954392	28.63352080	20.03040537	0.03492410	0.04992410
25	1.45094535	0.68920583	30.06302361	20.71961120	0.03326345	0.04826345
26	1.47270953	0.67902052	31.51396896	21.39863172	0.03173196	0.04673196
27	1.49480018	0.66898574	32.98667850	22.06761746	0.03031527	0.04531527
28	1.51722218	0.65909925	34.48147867	22.72671671	0.02900108	0.04400108
29	1.53998051	0.64935887	35.99870085	23.37607558	0.02777878	0.04277878
30	1.56308022	0.63976243	37.53868137	24.01583801	0.02663919	0.04163919
31	1.58652642	0.63030781	39.10176159	24.64614582	0.02557430	0.04057430
32	1.61032432	0.62099292	40.68828801	25.26713874	0.02457710	0.03957710
33	1.63447918	0.61181568	42.29861233	25.87895442	0.02364144	0.03864144
34	1.65899637	0.60277407	43.93309152	26.48172849	0.02276189	0.03776189
35	1.68388132	0.59386608	45.59208789	27.07559458	0.02193363	0.03693363
36	1.70913954	0.58508974	47.27596921	27.66068431	0.02115240	0.03615240
37	1.73477663	0.57644309	48.98510874	28.23712740	0.02041437	0.03541437
38	1.76079828	0.56792423	50.71988538	28.80505163	0.01971613	0.03471613
39	1.78721025	0.55953126	52.48068366	29.36458288	0.01905463	0.03405463
40	1.81401841	0.55126232	54.26789391	29.91584520	0.01842710	0.03342710
41	1.84122868	0.54311559	56.08191232	30.45896079	0.01783106	0.03283106
42	1.86884712	0.53508925	57.92314100	30.99405004	0.01726426	0.03226426
43	1.89687982	0.52718153	59.79198812	31.52123157	0.01672465	0.03172465
44	1.92533302	0.51939067	61.68886794	32.04062223	0.01621038	0.03121038
45	1.95421301	0.51171494	63.61420096	32.55233718	0.01571976	0.03071976
46	1.98352621	0.50415265	65.56841398	33.05648983	0.01525125	0.03025125
47	2.01327910	0.49670212	67.55194018	33.55319195	0.01480342	0.02980342
48	2.04347829	0.48936170	69.56521929	34.04255365	0.01437500	0.02937500
49	2.07413046	0.48212975	71.60869758	34.52468339	0.01396478	0.02896478
50	2.10524242	0.47500468	73.68282804	34.99968807	0.01357168	0.02857168

Rate $1\frac{3}{4}\%$	A Compound Interest	B Present Value	C Amount of Annuity	D Present Value of Annuity	E Sinking Fund	F Amortization
n	$(1 + i)^n$	$\dfrac{1}{(1 + i)^n}$	$s_{\overline{n}|i}$	$a_{\overline{n}|i}$	$\dfrac{1}{s_{\overline{n}|i}}$	$\dfrac{1}{a_{\overline{n}|i}}$
1	1.01750000	0.98280098	1.00000000	0.98280098	1.00000000	1.01750000
2	1.03530625	0.96589777	2.01750000	1.94869875	0.49566295	0.51316295
3	1.05342411	0.94928528	3.05280625	2.89798403	0.32756746	0.34506746
4	1.07185903	0.93295851	4.10623036	3.83094254	0.24353237	0.26103237
5	1.09061656	0.91691254	5.17808939	4.74785508	0.19312142	0.21062142
6	1.10970235	0.90114254	6.26870596	5.64899762	0.15952256	0.17702256
7	1.12912215	0.88564378	7.37840831	6.53464139	0.13553059	0.15303059
8	1.14888178	0.87041157	8.50753045	7.40505297	0.11754292	0.13504292
9	1.16898721	0.85544135	9.65641224	8.26049432	0.10355813	0.12105813
10	1.18944449	0.84072860	10.82539945	9.10122291	0.09237534	0.10987534
11	1.21025977	0.82626889	12.01484394	9.92749181	0.08323038	0.10073038
12	1.23143931	0.81205788	13.22510371	10.73954969	0.07561377	0.09311377
13	1.25298950	0.79809128	14.45654303	11.53764097	0.06917283	0.08667283
14	1.27491682	0.78436490	15.70953253	12.32200587	0.06365562	0.08115562
15	1.29722786	0.77087459	16.98444935	13.09288046	0.05887739	0.07637739
16	1.31992935	0.75761631	18.28167721	13.85049677	0.05469958	0.07219958
17	1.34302811	0.74458605	19.60160656	14.59508282	0.05101623	0.06851623
18	1.36653111	0.73177990	20.94463468	15.32686272	0.04774492	0.06524492
19	1.39044540	0.71919401	22.31116578	16.04605673	0.04482061	0.06232061
20	1.41477820	0.70682458	23.70161119	16.75288130	0.04219122	0.05969122
21	1.43953681	0.69466789	25.11638938	17.44754919	0.03981464	0.05731464
22	1.46472871	0.68272028	26.55592620	18.13026948	0.03765638	0.05515638
23	1.49036146	0.67097817	28.02065490	18.80124764	0.03568796	0.05318796
24	1.51644279	0.65943800	29.51101637	19.46068565	0.03388565	0.05138565
25	1.54298054	0.64809632	31.02745915	20.10878196	0.03222952	0.04972952
26	1.56998269	0.63694970	32.57043969	20.74573166	0.03070269	0.04820269
27	1.59745739	0.62599479	34.14042238	21.37172644	0.02929079	0.04679079
28	1.62541290	0.61522829	35.73787977	21.98695474	0.02798151	0.04548151
29	1.65385762	0.60464697	37.36329267	22.59160171	0.02676424	0.04426424
30	1.68280013	0.59424764	39.01715029	23.18584934	0.02562975	0.04312975
31	1.71224913	0.58402716	40.69995042	23.76987650	0.02457005	0.04207005
32	1.74221349	0.57398247	42.41219955	24.34385897	0.02357812	0.04107812
33	1.77270223	0.56411053	44.15441305	24.90796951	0.02264779	0.04014779
34	1.80372452	0.55440839	45.92711527	25.46237789	0.02177363	0.03927363
35	1.83528970	0.54487311	47.73083979	26.00725100	0.02095082	0.03845082
36	1.86740727	0.53550183	49.56612949	26.54275283	0.02017507	0.03767507
37	1.90008689	0.52629172	51.43353675	27.06904455	0.01944257	0.03694257
38	1.93333841	0.51724002	53.33362365	27.58628457	0.01874990	0.03624990
39	1.96717184	0.50834400	55.26696206	28.09462857	0.01809399	0.03559399
40	2.00159734	0.49960098	57.23413390	28.59422955	0.01747209	0.03497209
41	2.03662530	0.49100834	59.23573124	29.08523789	0.01688170	0.03438170
42	2.07226624	0.48256348	61.27235654	29.56780136	0.01632057	0.03382057
43	2.10853090	0.47426386	63.34462278	30.04206522	0.01578666	0.03328666
44	2.14543019	0.46610699	65.45315367	30.50817221	0.01527810	0.03277810
45	2.18297522	0.45809040	67.59858386	30.96626261	0.01479321	0.03229321
46	2.22117728	0.45021170	69.78155908	31.41647431	0.01433043	0.03183043
47	2.26004789	0.44246850	72.00273637	31.85894281	0.01388836	0.03138836
48	2.29959872	0.43485848	74.26278425	32.29380129	0.01346569	0.03096569
49	2.33984170	0.42737934	76.56238298	32.72118063	0.01306124	0.03056124
50	2.38078893	0.42002883	78.90222468	33.14120946	0.01267391	0.03017391

	A	B	C	D	E	F
Rate 2%	**Compound Interest**	**Present Value**	**Amount of Annuity**	**Present Value of Annuity**	**Sinking Fund**	**Amortization**
n	$(1+i)^n$	$\dfrac{1}{(1+i)^n}$	$s_{\overline{n}\rvert i}$	$a_{\overline{n}\rvert i}$	$\dfrac{1}{s_{\overline{n}\rvert i}}$	$\dfrac{1}{a_{\overline{n}\rvert i}}$
1	1.02000000	0.98039216	1.00000000	0.98039216	1.00000000	1.02000000
2	1.04040000	0.96116878	2.02000000	1.94156094	0.49504950	0.51504950
3	1.06120800	0.94232233	3.06040000	2.88388327	0.32675467	0.34675467
4	1.08243216	0.92384543	4.12160800	3.80772870	0.24262375	0.26262375
5	1.10408080	0.90573081	5.20404016	4.71345951	0.19215839	0.21215839
6	1.12616242	0.88797138	6.30812096	5.60143089	0.15852581	0.17852581
7	1.14868567	0.87056018	7.43428338	6.47199107	0.13451196	0.15451196
8	1.17165938	0.85349037	8.58296905	7.32548144	0.11650980	0.13650980
9	1.19509257	0.83675527	9.75462843	8.16223671	0.10251544	0.12251544
10	1.21899442	0.82034830	10.94972100	8.98258501	0.09132653	0.11132653
11	1.24337431	0.80426304	12.16871542	9.78684805	0.08217794	0.10217794
12	1.26824179	0.78849318	13.41208973	10.57534122	0.07455960	0.09455960
13	1.29360663	0.77303253	14.68033152	11.34837375	0.06811835	0.08811835
14	1.31947876	0.75787502	15.97393815	12.10624877	0.06260197	0.08260197
15	1.34586834	0.74301473	17.29341692	12.84926350	0.05782547	0.07782547
16	1.37278571	0.72844581	18.63928525	13.57770931	0.05365013	0.07365013
17	1.40024142	0.71416256	20.01207096	14.29187188	0.04996984	0.06996984
18	1.42824625	0.70015937	21.41231238	14.99203125	0.04670210	0.06670210
19	1.45681117	0.68643076	22.84055863	15.67846201	0.04378177	0.06378177
20	1.48594740	0.67297133	24.29736980	16.35143334	0.04115672	0.06115672
21	1.51566634	0.65977582	25.78331719	17.01120916	0.03878477	0.05878477
22	1.54597967	0.64683904	27.29898354	17.65804820	0.03663140	0.05663140
23	1.57689926	0.63415592	28.84496321	18.29220412	0.03466810	0.05466810
24	1.60843725	0.62172149	30.42186247	18.91392560	0.03287110	0.05287110
25	1.64060599	0.60953087	32.03029972	19.52345647	0.03122044	0.05122044
26	1.67341811	0.59757928	33.67090572	20.12103576	0.02969923	0.04969923
27	1.70688648	0.58586204	35.34432383	20.70689780	0.02829309	0.04829309
28	1.74102421	0.57437455	37.05121031	21.28127236	0.02698967	0.04698967
29	1.77584469	0.56311231	38.79223451	21.84438466	0.02577836	0.04577836
30	1.81136158	0.55207089	40.56807921	22.39645555	0.02464992	0.04464992
31	1.84758882	0.54124597	42.37944079	22.93770152	0.02359635	0.04359635
32	1.88454059	0.53063330	44.22702961	23.46833482	0.02261061	0.04261061
33	1.92223140	0.52022873	46.11157020	23.98856355	0.02168653	0.04168653
34	1.96067603	0.51002817	48.03380160	24.49859172	0.02081867	0.04081867
35	1.99988955	0.50002761	49.99447763	24.99861933	0.02000221	0.04000221
36	2.03988734	0.49022315	51.99436719	25.48884248	0.01923285	0.03923285
37	2.08068509	0.48061093	54.03425453	25.96945341	0.01850678	0.03850678
38	2.12229879	0.47118719	56.11493962	26.44064060	0.01782057	0.03782057
39	2.16474477	0.46194822	58.23723841	26.90258883	0.01717114	0.03717114
40	2.20803966	0.45289042	60.40198318	27.35547924	0.01655575	0.03655575
41	2.25220046	0.44401021	62.61002284	27.79948945	0.01597188	0.03597188
42	2.29724447	0.43530413	64.86222330	28.23479358	0.01541729	0.03541729
43	2.34318936	0.42676875	67.15946777	28.66156233	0.01488993	0.03488993
44	2.39005314	0.41840074	69.50265712	29.07996307	0.01438794	0.03438794
45	2.43785421	0.41019680	71.89271027	29.49015987	0.01390962	0.03390962
46	2.48661129	0.40215373	74.33056447	29.89231360	0.01345342	0.03345342
47	2.53634352	0.39426836	76.81717576	30.28658196	0.01301792	0.03301792
48	2.58707039	0.38653761	79.35351927	30.67311957	0.01260184	0.03260184
49	2.63881179	0.37895844	81.94058966	31.05207801	0.01220396	0.03220396
50	2.69158803	0.37152788	84.57940145	31.42360589	0.01182321	0.03182321

Rate $2\frac{1}{2}\%$	A Compound Interest	B Present Value	C Amount of Annuity	D Present Value of Annuity	E Sinking Fund	F Amortization
n	$(1+i)^n$	$\dfrac{1}{(1+i)^n}$	$s_{\overline{n}|i}$	$a_{\overline{n}|i}$	$\dfrac{1}{s_{\overline{n}|i}}$	$\dfrac{1}{a_{\overline{n}|i}}$
1	1.02500000	0.97560976	1.00000000	0.97560976	1.00000000	1.02500000
2	1.05062500	0.95181440	2.02500000	1.92742415	0.49382716	0.51882716
3	1.07689063	0.92859941	3.07562500	2.85602356	0.32513717	0.35013717
4	1.10381289	0.90595064	4.15251562	3.76197421	0.24081788	0.26581788
5	1.13140821	0.88385429	5.25632852	4.64582850	0.19024686	0.21524686
6	1.15969342	0.86229687	6.38773673	5.50812536	0.15654997	0.18154997
7	1.18868575	0.84126524	7.54753015	6.34939060	0.13249543	0.15749543
8	1.21840290	0.82074657	8.73611590	7.17013717	0.11446735	0.13946735
9	1.24886297	0.80072836	9.95451880	7.97086553	0.10045689	0.12545689
10	1.28008454	0.78119840	11.20338177	8.75206393	0.08925876	0.11425876
11	1.31208666	0.76214478	12.48346631	9.51420871	0.08010596	0.10510596
12	1.34488882	0.74355589	13.79555297	10.25776460	0.07248713	0.09748713
13	1.37851104	0.72542038	15.14044179	10.98318497	0.06604827	0.09104827
14	1.41297382	0.70772720	16.51895284	11.69091217	0.06053652	0.08553652
15	1.44829817	0.69046556	17.93192666	12.38137773	0.05576646	0.08076646
16	1.48450562	0.67362493	19.38022483	13.05500266	0.05159899	0.07659899
17	1.52161826	0.65719506	20.86473045	13.71219772	0.04792777	0.07292777
18	1.55965872	0.64116591	22.38634871	14.35336363	0.04467008	0.06967008
19	1.59865019	0.62552772	23.94600743	14.97889134	0.04176062	0.06676062
20	1.63861644	0.61027094	25.54465761	15.58916229	0.03914713	0.06414713
21	1.67958185	0.59538629	27.18327405	16.18454857	0.03678733	0.06178733
22	1.72157140	0.58086467	28.86285590	16.76541324	0.03464661	0.05964661
23	1.76461068	0.56669724	30.58442730	17.33211048	0.03269638	0.05769638
24	1.80872595	0.55287535	32.34903798	17.88498583	0.03091282	0.05591282
25	1.85394410	0.53939059	34.15776393	18.42437642	0.02927592	0.05427592
26	1.90029270	0.52623472	36.01170803	18.95061114	0.02776875	0.05276875
27	1.94780002	0.51339973	37.91200073	19.46401087	0.02637687	0.05137687
28	1.99649502	0.50087778	39.85980075	19.96488866	0.02508793	0.05008793
29	2.04640739	0.48866125	41.85629577	20.45354991	0.02389127	0.04889127
30	2.09756758	0.47674269	43.90270316	20.93029259	0.02277764	0.04777764
31	2.15000677	0.46511481	46.00027074	21.39540741	0.02173900	0.04673900
32	2.20375694	0.45377055	48.15027751	21.84917796	0.02076831	0.04576831
33	2.25885086	0.44270298	50.35403445	22.29188094	0.01985938	0.04485938
34	2.31532213	0.43190534	52.61288531	22.72378628	0.01900675	0.04400675
35	2.37320519	0.42137107	54.92820744	23.14515734	0.01820558	0.04320558
36	2.43253532	0.41109372	57.30141263	23.55625107	0.01745158	0.04245158
37	2.49334870	0.40106705	59.73394794	23.95731812	0.01674090	0.04174090
38	2.55568242	0.39128492	62.22729664	24.34860304	0.01607012	0.04107012
39	2.61957448	0.38174139	64.78297906	24.73034443	0.01543615	0.04043615
40	2.68506384	0.37243062	67.40255354	25.10277505	0.01483623	0.03983623
41	2.75219043	0.36334695	70.08761737	25.46612200	0.01426786	0.03926786
42	2.82099520	0.35448483	72.83980781	25.82060683	0.01372876	0.03872876
43	2.89152008	0.34583886	75.66080300	26.16644569	0.01321688	0.03821688
44	2.96380808	0.33740376	78.55232308	26.50384945	0.01273037	0.03773037
45	3.03790328	0.32917440	81.51613116	26.83302386	0.01226751	0.03726751
46	3.11385086	0.32114576	84.55403443	27.15416962	0.01182676	0.03682676
47	3.19169713	0.31331294	87.66788530	27.46748255	0.01140669	0.03640669
48	3.27148956	0.30567116	90.85958243	27.77315371	0.01100599	0.03600599
49	3.35327680	0.29821576	94.13107199	28.07136947	0.01062348	0.03562348
50	3.43710872	0.29094221	97.48434879	28.36231168	0.01025806	0.03525806

	A	B	C	D	E	F
Rate 3%	Compound Interest	Present Value	Amount of Annuity	Present Value of Annuity	Sinking Fund	Amortization
n	$(1 + i)^n$	$\dfrac{1}{(1 + i)^n}$	$s_{\overline{n}|\,i}$	$a_{\overline{n}|\,i}$	$\dfrac{1}{s_{\overline{n}|\,i}}$	$\dfrac{1}{a_{\overline{n}|\,i}}$
1	1.03000000	0.97087379	1.00000000	0.97087379	1.00000000	1.03000000
2	1.06090000	0.94259591	2.03000000	1.91346970	0.49261084	0.52261084
3	1.09272700	0.91514166	3.09090000	2.82861135	0.32353036	0.35353036
4	1.12550881	0.88848705	4.18362700	3.71709840	0.23902705	0.26902705
5	1.15927407	0.86260878	5.30913581	4.57970719	0.18835457	0.21835457
6	1.19405230	0.83748426	6.46840988	5.41719144	0.15459750	0.18459750
7	1.22987387	0.81309151	7.66246218	6.23028296	0.13050635	0.16050635
8	1.26677008	0.78940923	8.89233605	7.01969219	0.11245639	0.14245639
9	1.30477318	0.76641673	10.15910613	7.78610892	0.09843386	0.12843386
10	1.34391638	0.74409391	11.46387931	8.53020284	0.08723051	0.11723051
11	1.38423387	0.72242128	12.80779569	9.25262411	0.07807745	0.10807745
12	1.42576089	0.70137988	14.19202956	9.95400399	0.07046209	0.10046209
13	1.46853371	0.68095134	15.61779045	10.63495533	0.06402954	0.09402954
14	1.51258972	0.66111781	17.08632416	11.29607314	0.05852634	0.08852634
15	1.55796742	0.64186195	18.59891389	11.93793509	0.05376658	0.08376658
16	1.60470644	0.62316694	20.15688130	12.56110203	0.04961085	0.07961085
17	1.65284763	0.60501645	21.76158774	13.16611847	0.04595253	0.07595253
18	1.70243306	0.58739461	23.41443537	13.75351308	0.04270870	0.07270870
19	1.75350605	0.57028603	25.11686844	14.32379911	0.03981388	0.06981388
20	1.80611123	0.55367575	26.87037449	14.87747486	0.03721571	0.06721571
21	1.86029457	0.53754928	28.67648572	15.41502414	0.03487178	0.06487178
22	1.91610341	0.52189250	30.53678030	15.93691664	0.03274739	0.06274739
23	1.97358651	0.50669175	32.45288370	16.44360839	0.03081390	0.06081390
24	2.03279411	0.49193374	34.42647022	16.93554212	0.02904742	0.05904742
25	2.09377793	0.47760557	36.45926432	17.41314769	0.02742787	0.05742787
26	2.15659127	0.46369473	38.55304225	17.87684242	0.02593829	0.05593829
27	2.22128901	0.45018906	40.70963352	18.32703147	0.02456421	0.05456421
28	2.28792768	0.43707675	42.93092252	18.76410823	0.02329323	0.05329323
29	2.35656551	0.42434636	45.21885020	19.18845459	0.02211467	0.05211467
30	2.42726247	0.41198676	47.57541571	19.60044135	0.02101926	0.05101926
31	2.50008035	0.39998715	50.00267818	20.00042849	0.01999893	0.04999893
32	2.57508276	0.38833703	52.50275852	20.38876553	0.01904662	0.04904662
33	2.65233524	0.37702625	55.07784128	20.76579178	0.01815612	0.04815612
34	2.73190530	0.36604490	57.73017652	21.13183668	0.01732196	0.04732196
35	2.81386245	0.35538340	60.46208181	21.48722007	0.01653929	0.04653929
36	2.89827833	0.34503243	63.27594427	21.83225250	0.01580379	0.04580379
37	2.98522668	0.33498294	66.17422259	22.16723544	0.01511162	0.04511162
38	3.07478348	0.32522615	69.15944927	22.49246159	0.01445934	0.04445934
39	3.16702698	0.31575355	72.23423275	22.80821513	0.01384385	0.04384385
40	3.26203779	0.30655684	75.40125973	23.11477197	0.01326238	0.04326238
41	3.35989893	0.29762800	78.66329753	23.41239997	0.01271241	0.04271241
42	3.46069589	0.28895922	82.02319645	23.70135920	0.01219167	0.04219167
43	3.56451677	0.28054294	85.48389234	23.98190213	0.01169811	0.04169811
44	3.67145227	0.27237178	89.04840911	24.25427392	0.01122985	0.04122985
45	3.78159584	0.26443862	92.71986139	24.51871254	0.01078518	0.04078518
46	3.89504372	0.25673653	96.50145723	24.77544907	0.01036254	0.04036254
47	4.01189503	0.24925876	100.39650095	25.02470783	0.00996051	0.03996051
48	4.13225188	0.24199880	104.40839598	25.26670664	0.00957777	0.03957777
49	4.25621944	0.23495029	108.54064785	25.50165693	0.00921314	0.03921314
50	4.38390602	0.22810708	112.79686729	25.72976401	0.00886549	0.03886549

Rate $3\frac{1}{2}\%$	A Compound Interest	B Present Value	C Amount of Annuity	D Present Value of Annuity	E Sinking Fund	F Amortization
n	$(1+i)^n$	$\dfrac{1}{(1+i)^n}$	$s_{\overline{n}\mid}i$	$a_{\overline{n}\mid}i$	$\dfrac{1}{s_{\overline{n}\mid}i}$	$\dfrac{1}{a_{\overline{n}\mid}i}$
1	1.03500000	0.96618357	1.00000000	0.96618357	1.00000000	1.03500000
2	1.07122500	0.93351070	2.03500000	1.89969428	0.49140049	0.52640049
3	1.10871788	0.90194271	3.10622500	2.80163698	0.32193418	0.35693418
4	1.14752300	0.87144223	4.21494287	3.67307921	0.23725114	0.27225114
5	1.18768631	0.84197317	5.36246588	4.51505238	0.18648137	0.22148137
6	1.22925533	0.81350064	6.55015218	5.32855302	0.15266821	0.18766821
7	1.27227926	0.78599096	7.77940751	6.11454398	0.12854449	0.16354449
8	1.31680904	0.75941156	9.05168677	6.87395554	0.11047665	0.14547665
9	1.36289735	0.73373097	10.36849581	7.60768651	0.09644601	0.13144601
10	1.41059876	0.70891881	11.73139316	8.31660532	0.08524137	0.12024137
11	1.45996972	0.68494571	13.14199192	9.00155104	0.07609197	0.11109197
12	1.51106866	0.66178330	14.60196164	9.66333433	0.06848395	0.10348395
13	1.56395606	0.63940415	16.11303030	10.30273849	0.06206157	0.09706157
14	1.61869452	0.61778179	17.67698636	10.92052028	0.05657073	0.09157073
15	1.67534883	0.59689062	19.29568088	11.51741090	0.05182507	0.08682507
16	1.73398604	0.57670591	20.97102971	12.09411681	0.04768483	0.08268483
17	1.79467555	0.55720378	22.70501575	12.65132059	0.04404313	0.07904313
18	1.85748920	0.53836114	24.49969130	13.18968173	0.04081684	0.07581684
19	1.92250132	0.52015569	26.35718050	13.70983742	0.03794033	0.07294033
20	1.98978886	0.50256588	28.27968181	14.21240330	0.03536108	0.07036108
21	2.05943147	0.48557090	30.26947068	14.69797420	0.03303659	0.06803659
22	2.13151158	0.46915063	32.32890215	15.16712484	0.03093207	0.06593207
23	2.20611448	0.45328563	34.46041373	15.62041047	0.02901880	0.06401880
24	2.28332849	0.43795713	36.66652821	16.05836760	0.02727283	0.06227283
25	2.36324498	0.42314699	38.94985669	16.48151459	0.02567404	0.06067404
26	2.44595856	0.40883767	41.31310168	16.89035226	0.02420540	0.05920540
27	2.53156711	0.39501224	43.75906024	17.28536451	0.02285241	0.05785241
28	2.62017196	0.38165434	46.29062734	17.66701885	0.02160265	0.05660265
29	2.71187798	0.36874815	48.91079930	18.03576700	0.02044538	0.05544538
30	2.80679370	0.35627841	51.62267728	18.39204541	0.01937133	0.05437133
31	2.90503148	0.34423035	54.42947098	18.73627576	0.01837240	0.05337240
32	3.00670759	0.33258971	57.33450247	19.06886547	0.01744150	0.05244150
33	3.11194235	0.32134271	60.34121005	19.39020818	0.01657242	0.05157242
34	3.22086033	0.31047605	63.45315240	19.70068423	0.01575966	0.05075966
35	3.33359045	0.29997686	66.67401274	20.00066110	0.01499835	0.04999835
36	3.45026611	0.28983272	70.00760318	20.29049381	0.01428416	0.04928416
37	3.57102543	0.28003161	73.45786930	20.57052542	0.01361325	0.04861325
38	3.69601132	0.27056194	77.02889472	20.84108736	0.01298214	0.04798214
39	3.82537171	0.26141250	80.72490604	21.10249987	0.01238775	0.04738775
40	3.95925972	0.25257247	84.55027775	21.35507234	0.01182728	0.04682728
41	4.09783381	0.24403137	88.50953747	21.59910371	0.01129822	0.04629822
42	4.24125799	0.23577910	92.60737128	21.83488281	0.01079828	0.04579828
43	4.38970202	0.22780590	96.84862928	22.06268870	0.01032539	0.04532539
44	4.54334160	0.22010231	101.23833130	22.28279102	0.00987768	0.04487768
45	4.70235855	0.21265924	105.78167290	22.49545026	0.00945343	0.04445343
46	4.86694110	0.20546787	110.48403145	22.70091813	0.00905108	0.04405108
47	5.03728404	0.19851968	115.35097255	22.89943780	0.00866919	0.04366919
48	5.21358898	0.19180645	120.38825659	23.09124425	0.00830646	0.04330646
49	5.39606459	0.18532024	125.60184557	23.27656450	0.00796167	0.04296167
50	5.58492686	0.17905337	130.99791016	23.45561787	0.00763371	0.04263371

Rate $3\frac{3}{4}\%$	A Compound Interest	B Present Value	C Amount of Annuity	D Present Value of Annuity	E Sinking Fund	F Amortization
n	$(1 + i)^n$	$\dfrac{1}{(1 + i)^n}$	$s_{\overline{n}|i}$	$a_{\overline{n}|i}$	$\dfrac{1}{s_{\overline{n}|i}}$	$\dfrac{1}{a_{\overline{n}|i}}$
1	1.03750000	0.96385542	1.00000000	0.96385542	1.00000000	1.03750000
2	1.07640625	0.92901727	2.03750000	1.89287270	0.49079755	0.52829755
3	1.11677148	0.89543834	3.11390625	2.78831103	0.32114005	0.35864005
4	1.15865042	0.86307310	4.23067773	3.65138413	0.23636875	0.27386875
5	1.20209981	0.83187768	5.38932815	4.48326181	0.18555189	0.22305189
6	1.24717855	0.80180981	6.59142796	5.28507162	0.15171219	0.18921219
7	1.29394774	0.77282874	7.83860650	6.05790036	0.12757370	0.16507370
8	1.34247078	0.74489517	9.13255425	6.80279553	0.10949839	0.14699839
9	1.39281344	0.71797125	10.47502503	7.52076677	0.09546517	0.13296517
10	1.44504394	0.69202048	11.86783847	8.21278725	0.08426134	0.12176134
11	1.49923309	0.66700769	13.31288241	8.87979494	0.07511521	0.11261521
12	1.55545433	0.64289898	14.81211550	9.52269392	0.06751230	0.10501230
13	1.61378387	0.61966167	16.36756983	10.14235558	0.06109642	0.09859642
14	1.67430076	0.59726426	17.98135370	10.73961984	0.05561317	0.09311317
15	1.73708704	0.57567639	19.65565447	11.31529623	0.05087595	0.08837595
16	1.80222781	0.55486881	21.39274151	11.87016504	0.04674483	0.08424483
17	1.86981135	0.53481331	23.19496932	12.40497835	0.04311280	0.08061280
18	1.93992927	0.51548271	25.06478067	12.92046106	0.03989662	0.07739662
19	2.01267662	0.49685080	27.00470994	13.41731187	0.03703058	0.07453058
20	2.08815200	0.47889234	29.01738656	13.89620421	0.03446210	0.07196210
21	2.16645770	0.46158298	31.10553856	14.35778719	0.03214862	0.06964862
22	2.24769986	0.44489926	33.27199626	14.80268645	0.03005531	0.06755531
23	2.33198860	0.42881856	35.51969612	15.23150501	0.02815339	0.06565339
24	2.41943818	0.41331910	37.85168472	15.64482411	0.02641890	0.06391890
25	2.51016711	0.39837985	40.27112290	16.04320396	0.02483169	0.06233169
26	2.60429838	0.38398058	42.78129001	16.42718454	0.02337470	0.06087470
27	2.70195956	0.37010176	45.38558838	16.79728630	0.02203343	0.05953343
28	2.80328305	0.35672459	48.08754794	17.15401089	0.02079540	0.05829540
29	2.90840616	0.34383093	50.89083099	17.49784183	0.01964991	0.05714991
30	3.01747139	0.33140331	53.79923715	17.82924513	0.01858762	0.05608762
31	3.13062657	0.31942487	56.81670855	18.14867001	0.01760046	0.05510046
32	3.24802507	0.30787940	59.94733512	18.45654941	0.01668131	0.05418131
33	3.36982601	0.29675123	63.19536019	18.75330063	0.01582395	0.05332395
34	3.49619448	0.28602528	66.56518619	19.03932591	0.01502287	0.05252287
35	3.62730178	0.27568702	70.06138067	19.31501293	0.01427320	0.05177320
36	3.76332559	0.26572242	73.68868245	19.58073535	0.01357060	0.05107060
37	3.90445030	0.25611800	77.45200804	19.83685335	0.01291122	0.05041122
38	4.05086719	0.24686072	81.35645834	20.08371407	0.01229159	0.04979159
39	4.20277471	0.23793805	85.40732553	20.32165212	0.01170860	0.04920860
40	4.36037876	0.22933788	89.61010024	20.55098999	0.01115946	0.04865946
41	4.52389296	0.22104855	93.97047900	20.77203855	0.01064164	0.04814164
42	4.69353895	0.21305885	98.49437196	20.98509739	0.01015286	0.04765286
43	4.86954666	0.20535793	103.18791091	21.19045532	0.00969106	0.04719106
44	5.05215466	0.19793535	108.05745757	21.38839067	0.00925434	0.04675434
45	5.24161046	0.19078106	113.10961223	21.57917173	0.00884098	0.04634098
46	5.43817085	0.18388536	118.35122269	21.76305709	0.00844943	0.04594943
47	5.64210226	0.17723890	123.78939354	21.94029599	0.00807824	0.04557824
48	5.85368109	0.17083290	129.43149579	22.11112866	0.00772609	0.04522609
49	6.07319413	0.16465800	135.28517689	22.27578666	0.00739179	0.04489179
50	6.30093891	0.15870651	141.35837102	22.43449317	0.00707422	0.04457422

Rate 4%	A Compound Interest	B Present Value	C Amount of Annuity	D Present Value of Annuity	E Sinking Fund	F Amortization
n	$(1 + i)^n$	$\dfrac{1}{(1 + i)^n}$	$s_{\overline{n}|i}$	$a_{\overline{n}|i}$	$\dfrac{1}{s_{\overline{n}|i}}$	$\dfrac{1}{a_{\overline{n}|i}}$
1	1.04000000	0.96153846	1.00000000	0.96153846	1.00000000	1.04000000
2	1.08160000	0.92455621	2.04000000	1.88609467	0.49019608	0.53019608
3	1.12486400	0.88899636	3.12160000	2.77509103	0.32034854	0.36034854
4	1.16985856	0.85480419	4.24646400	3.62989522	0.23549005	0.27549005
5	1.21665290	0.82192711	5.41632256	4.45182233	0.18462711	0.22462711
6	1.26531902	0.79031453	6.63297546	5.24213686	0.15076190	0.19076190
7	1.31593178	0.75991781	7.89829448	6.00205467	0.12660961	0.16660961
8	1.36856905	0.73069021	9.21422626	6.73274487	0.10852783	0.14852783
9	1.42331181	0.70258674	10.58279531	7.43533161	0.09449299	0.13449299
10	1.48024428	0.67556417	12.00610712	8.11089578	0.08329094	0.12329094
11	1.53945406	0.64958093	13.48635141	8.76047671	0.07414904	0.11414904
12	1.60103222	0.62459705	15.02580546	9.38507376	0.06655217	0.10655217
13	1.66507351	0.60057409	16.62683768	9.98564785	0.06014373	0.10014373
14	1.73167645	0.57747508	18.29191119	10.56312293	0.05466897	0.09466897
15	1.80094351	0.55526450	20.02358764	11.11838743	0.04994110	0.08994110
16	1.87298125	0.53390818	21.82453114	11.65229561	0.04582000	0.08582000
17	1.94790050	0.51337325	23.69751239	12.16566885	0.04219852	0.08219852
18	2.02581652	0.49362812	25.64541288	12.65929697	0.03899333	0.07899333
19	2.10684918	0.47464242	27.67122940	13.13393940	0.03613862	0.07613862
20	2.19112314	0.45638695	29.77807858	13.59032634	0.03358175	0.07358175
21	2.27876807	0.43883360	31.96920172	14.02915995	0.03128011	0.07128011
22	2.36991879	0.42195539	34.24796979	14.45111533	0.02919881	0.06919881
23	2.46471554	0.40572633	36.61788858	14.85684167	0.02730906	0.06730906
24	2.56330416	0.39012147	39.08260412	15.24696314	0.02558683	0.06558683
25	2.66583633	0.37511680	41.64590829	15.62207994	0.02401196	0.06401196
26	2.77246978	0.36068923	44.31174462	15.98276918	0.02256738	0.06256738
27	2.88336858	0.34681657	47.08421440	16.32958575	0.02123854	0.06123854
28	2.99870332	0.33347747	49.96758298	16.66306322	0.02001298	0.06001298
29	3.11865145	0.32065141	52.96628630	16.98371463	0.01887993	0.05887993
30	3.24339751	0.30831867	56.08493775	17.29203330	0.01783010	0.05783010
31	3.37313341	0.29646026	59.32833526	17.58849356	0.01685535	0.05685535
32	3.50805875	0.28505794	62.70146867	17.87355150	0.01594859	0.05594859
33	3.64838110	0.27409417	66.20952742	18.14764567	0.01510357	0.05510357
34	3.79431634	0.26355209	69.85790851	18.41119776	0.01431477	0.05431477
35	3.94608899	0.25341547	73.65222486	18.66461323	0.01357732	0.05357732
36	4.10393255	0.24366872	77.59831385	18.90828195	0.01288688	0.05288688
37	4.26808986	0.23429685	81.70224640	19.14257880	0.01223957	0.05223957
38	4.43881345	0.22528543	85.97033626	19.36786423	0.01163192	0.05163192
39	4.61636599	0.21662061	90.40914971	19.58448484	0.01106083	0.05106083
40	4.80102063	0.20828904	95.02551570	19.79277388	0.01052349	0.05052349
41	4.99306145	0.20027793	99.82653633	19.99305181	0.01001738	0.05001738
42	5.19278391	0.19257493	104.81959778	20.18562674	0.00954020	0.04954020
43	5.40049527	0.18516820	110.01238169	20.37079494	0.00908989	0.04908989
44	5.61651508	0.17804635	115.41287696	20.54884129	0.00866454	0.04866454
45	5.84117568	0.17119841	121.02939204	20.72003970	0.00826246	0.04826246
46	6.07482271	0.16461386	126.87056772	20.88465356	0.00788205	0.04788205
47	6.31781562	0.15828256	132.94539043	21.04293612	0.00752189	0.04752189
48	6.57052824	0.15219476	139.26320604	21.19513088	0.00718065	0.04718065
49	6.83334937	0.14634112	145.83373429	21.34147200	0.00685712	0.04685712
50	7.10668335	0.14071262	152.66708366	21.48218462	0.00655020	0.04655020

Rate $4\frac{1}{2}$%	A Compound Interest	B Present Value	C Amount of Annuity	D Present Value of Annuity	E Sinking Fund	F Amortization
n	$(1 + i)^n$	$\dfrac{1}{(1 + i)^n}$	$s_{\overline{n}\mid i}$	$a_{\overline{n}\mid i}$	$\dfrac{1}{s_{\overline{n}\mid i}}$	$\dfrac{1}{a_{\overline{n}\mid i}}$
1	1.04500000	0.95693780	1.00000000	0.95693780	1.00000000	1.04500000
2	1.09202500	0.91572995	2.04500000	1.87266775	0.48899756	0.53399756
3	1.14116613	0.87629660	3.13702500	2.74896435	0.31877336	0.36377336
4	1.19251860	0.83856134	4.27819112	3.58752570	0.23374365	0.27874365
5	1.24618194	0.80245105	5.47070973	4.38997674	0.18279164	0.22779164
6	1.30226012	0.76789574	6.71689166	5.15787248	0.14887839	0.19387839
7	1.36086183	0.73482846	8.01915179	5.89270094	0.12470147	0.16970147
8	1.42210061	0.70318513	9.38001362	6.59588607	0.10660965	0.15160965
9	1.48609514	0.67290443	10.80211423	7.26879050	0.09257447	0.13757447
10	1.55296942	0.64392768	12.28820937	7.91271818	0.08137882	0.12637882
11	1.62285305	0.61619874	13.84117879	8.52891692	0.07224818	0.11724818
12	1.69588143	0.58966386	15.46403184	9.11858078	0.06466619	0.10966619
13	1.77219610	0.56427164	17.15991327	9.68285242	0.05827535	0.10327535
14	1.85194492	0.53997286	18.93210937	10.22282528	0.05282032	0.09782032
15	1.93528244	0.51672044	20.78405429	10.73954573	0.04811381	0.09311381
16	2.02237015	0.49446932	22.71933673	11.23401505	0.04401537	0.08901537
17	2.11337681	0.47317639	24.74170689	11.70719143	0.04041758	0.08541758
18	2.20847877	0.45280037	26.85508370	12.15999180	0.03723690	0.08223690
19	2.30786031	0.43330179	29.06356246	12.59329359	0.03440734	0.07940734
20	2.41171402	0.41464286	31.37142277	13.00793645	0.03187614	0.07687614
21	2.52024116	0.39678743	33.78313680	13.40472388	0.02960057	0.07460057
22	2.63365201	0.37970089	36.30337795	13.78442476	0.02754565	0.07254565
23	2.75216635	0.36335013	38.93702996	14.14777489	0.02568249	0.07068249
24	2.87601383	0.34770347	41.68919631	14.49547837	0.02398703	0.06898703
25	3.00543446	0.33273060	44.56521015	14.82820896	0.02243903	0.06743903
26	3.14067901	0.31840248	47.57064460	15.14661145	0.02102137	0.06602137
27	3.28200956	0.30469137	50.71132361	15.45130282	0.01971946	0.06471946
28	3.42969999	0.29157069	53.99333317	15.74287351	0.01852081	0.06352081
29	3.58403649	0.27901502	57.42303316	16.02188853	0.01741461	0.06241461
30	3.74531813	0.26700002	61.00706966	16.28888854	0.01639154	0.06139154
31	3.91385745	0.25550241	64.75238779	16.54439095	0.01544345	0.06044345
32	4.08998104	0.24449991	68.66624524	16.78889086	0.01456320	0.05956320
33	4.27403018	0.23397121	72.75622628	17.02286207	0.01374453	0.05874453
34	4.46636154	0.22389589	77.03025646	17.24675796	0.01298191	0.05798191
35	4.66734781	0.21425444	81.49661800	17.46101240	0.01227045	0.05727045
36	4.87737846	0.20502817	86.16396581	17.66604058	0.01160578	0.05660578
37	5.09686049	0.19619921	91.04134427	17.86223979	0.01098402	0.05598402
38	5.32621921	0.18775044	96.13820476	18.04999023	0.01040169	0.05540169
39	5.56589908	0.17966549	101.46442398	18.22965572	0.00985567	0.05485567
40	5.81636454	0.17192870	107.03032306	18.40158442	0.00934315	0.05434315
41	6.07810094	0.16452507	112.84668760	18.56610949	0.00886158	0.05386158
42	6.35161548	0.15744026	118.92478854	18.72354975	0.00840868	0.05340868
43	6.63743818	0.15066054	125.27640402	18.87421029	0.00798235	0.05298235
44	6.93612290	0.14417276	131.91384220	19.01838305	0.00758071	0.05258071
45	7.24824843	0.13796437	138.84996510	19.15634742	0.00720202	0.05220202
46	7.57441961	0.13202332	146.09821353	19.28837074	0.00684471	0.05184471
47	7.91526849	0.12633810	153.67263314	19.41470884	0.00650734	0.05150734
48	8.27145557	0.12089771	161.58790163	19.53560654	0.00618858	0.05118858
49	8.64367107	0.11569158	169.85935720	19.65129813	0.00588722	0.05088722
50	9.03263627	0.11070965	178.50302828	19.76200778	0.00560215	0.05060215

	A	B	C	D	E	F
Rate 5%	**Compound Interest**	**Present Value**	**Amount of Annuity**	**Present Value of Annuity**	**Sinking Fund**	**Amortization**
n	$(1 + i)^n$	$\dfrac{1}{(1 + i)^n}$	$s_{\overline{n}|i}$	$a_{\overline{n}|i}$	$\dfrac{1}{s_{\overline{n}|i}}$	$\dfrac{1}{a_{\overline{n}|i}}$
1	1.05000000	0.95238095	1.00000000	0.95238095	1.00000000	1.05000000
2	1.10250000	0.90702948	2.05000000	1.85941043	0.48780488	0.53780488
3	1.15762500	0.86383760	3.15250000	2.72324803	0.31720856	0.36720856
4	1.21550625	0.82270247	4.31012500	3.54595050	0.23201183	0.28201183
5	1.27628156	0.78352617	5.52563125	4.32947667	0.18097480	0.23097480
6	1.34009564	0.74621540	6.80191281	5.07569207	0.14701747	0.19701747
7	1.40710042	0.71068133	8.14200845	5.78637340	0.12281982	0.17281982
8	1.47745544	0.67683936	9.54910888	6.46321276	0.10472181	0.15472181
9	1.55132822	0.64460892	11.02656432	7.10782168	0.09069008	0.14069008
10	1.62889463	0.61391325	12.57789254	7.72173493	0.07950457	0.12950457
11	1.71033936	0.58467929	14.20678716	8.30641422	0.07038889	0.12038889
12	1.79585633	0.55683742	15.91712652	8.86325164	0.06282541	0.11282541
13	1.88564914	0.53032135	17.71298285	9.39357299	0.05645577	0.10645577
14	1.97993160	0.50506795	19.59863199	9.89864094	0.05102397	0.10102397
15	2.07892818	0.48101710	21.57856359	10.37965804	0.04634229	0.09634229
16	2.18287459	0.45811152	23.65749177	10.83776956	0.04226991	0.09226991
17	2.29201832	0.43629669	25.84036636	11.27406625	0.03869914	0.08869914
18	2.40661923	0.41552065	28.13238467	11.68958690	0.03554622	0.08554622
19	2.52695020	0.39573396	30.53900391	12.08532086	0.03274501	0.08274501
20	2.65329771	0.37688948	33.06595410	12.46221034	0.03024259	0.08024259
21	2.78596259	0.35894236	35.71925181	12.82115271	0.02799611	0.07799611
22	2.92526072	0.34184987	38.50521440	13.16300258	0.02597051	0.07597051
23	3.07152376	0.32557131	41.43047512	13.48857388	0.02413682	0.07413682
24	3.22509994	0.31006791	44.50199887	13.79864179	0.02247090	0.07247090
25	3.38635494	0.29530277	47.72709882	14.09394457	0.02095246	0.07095246
26	3.55567269	0.28124073	51.11345376	14.37518530	0.01956432	0.06956432
27	3.73345632	0.26784832	54.66912645	14.64303362	0.01829186	0.06829186
28	3.92012914	0.25509364	58.40258277	14.89812726	0.01712253	0.06712253
29	4.11613560	0.24294632	62.32271191	15.14107358	0.01604551	0.06604551
30	4.32194238	0.23137745	66.43884750	15.37245103	0.01505144	0.06505144
31	4.53803949	0.22035947	70.76078988	15.59281050	0.01413212	0.06413212
32	4.76494147	0.20986617	75.29882937	15.80267667	0.01328042	0.06328042
33	5.00318854	0.19978254	80.06377084	16.00254921	0.01249004	0.06249004
34	5.25334797	0.19035480	85.06695938	16.19290401	0.01175545	0.06175545
35	5.51601537	0.18129029	90.32030735	16.37419429	0.01107171	0.06107171
36	5.79181614	0.17265741	95.83632272	16.54685171	0.01043446	0.06043446
37	6.08140694	0.16443563	101.62813886	16.71128734	0.00983979	0.05983979
38	6.38547729	0.15660536	107.70954580	16.86789271	0.00928423	0.05928423
39	6.70475115	0.14914797	114.09502309	17.01704067	0.00876462	0.05876462
40	7.03998871	0.14204568	120.79977424	17.15908635	0.00827816	0.05827816
41	7.39198815	0.13528160	127.83976295	17.29436796	0.00782229	0.05782229
42	7.76158756	0.12883962	135.23175110	17.42320758	0.00739471	0.05739471
43	8.14966693	0.12270440	142.99333866	17.54591198	0.00699333	0.05699333
44	8.55715028	0.11686133	151.14300559	17.66277331	0.00661625	0.05661625
45	8.98500779	0.11129651	159.70015587	17.77406982	0.00626173	0.05626173
46	9.43425818	0.10599668	168.68516366	17.88006650	0.00592820	0.05592820
47	9.90597109	0.10094921	178.11942185	17.98101571	0.00561421	0.05561421
48	10.40126965	0.09614211	188.02539294	18.07715782	0.00531843	0.05531843
49	10.92133313	0.09156391	198.42666259	18.16872173	0.00503965	0.05503965
50	11.46739979	0.08720373	209.34799572	18.25592546	0.00477674	0.05477674

Rate $5\frac{1}{2}\%$	A Compound Interest	B Present Value	C Amount of Annuity	D Present Value of Annuity	E Sinking Fund	F Amortization
n	$(1 + i)^n$	$\dfrac{1}{(1 + i)^n}$	$s_{\overline{n}|i}$	$a_{\overline{n}|i}$	$\dfrac{1}{s_{\overline{n}|i}}$	$\dfrac{1}{a_{\overline{n}|i}}$
1	1.05500000	0.94786730	1.00000000	0.94786730	1.00000000	1.05500000
2	1.11302500	0.89845242	2.05500000	1.84631971	0.48661800	0.54161800
3	1.17424138	0.85161366	3.16802500	2.69793338	0.31565407	0.37065407
4	1.23882465	0.80721674	4.34226637	3.50515012	0.23029449	0.28529449
5	1.30696001	0.76513435	5.58109103	4.27028448	0.17917644	0.23417644
6	1.37884281	0.72524583	6.88805103	4.99553031	0.14517895	0.20017895
7	1.45467916	0.68743681	8.26689384	5.68296712	0.12096442	0.17596442
8	1.53468651	0.65159887	9.72157300	6.33456599	0.10286401	0.15786401
9	1.61909427	0.61762926	11.25625951	6.95219525	0.08883946	0.14383946
10	1.70814446	0.58543058	12.87535379	7.53762583	0.07766777	0.13266777
11	1.80209240	0.55491050	14.58349825	8.09253633	0.06857065	0.12357065
12	1.90120749	0.52598152	16.38559065	8.61851785	0.06102923	0.11602923
13	2.00577390	0.49856068	18.28679814	9.11707853	0.05468426	0.10968426
14	2.11609146	0.47256937	20.29257203	9.58964790	0.04927912	0.10427912
15	2.23247649	0.44793305	22.40866350	10.03758094	0.04462560	0.09962560
16	2.35526270	0.42458109	24.64113999	10.46216203	0.04058254	0.09558254
17	2.48480215	0.40244653	26.99640269	10.86460856	0.03704197	0.09204197
18	2.62146627	0.38146590	29.48120483	11.24607447	0.03391992	0.08891992
19	2.76564691	0.36157906	32.10267110	11.60765352	0.03115006	0.08615006
20	2.91775749	0.34272896	34.86831801	11.95038248	0.02867933	0.08367933
21	3.07823415	0.32486158	37.78607550	12.27524406	0.02646478	0.08146478
22	3.24753703	0.30792567	40.86430965	12.58316973	0.02447123	0.07947123
23	3.42615157	0.29187267	44.11184669	12.87504239	0.02266965	0.07766965
24	3.61458990	0.27665656	47.53799825	13.15169895	0.02103580	0.07603580
25	3.81339235	0.26223370	51.15258816	13.41393266	0.01954935	0.07454935
26	4.02312893	0.24856275	54.96598051	13.66249541	0.01819307	0.07319307
27	4.24440102	0.23560450	58.98910943	13.89809991	0.01695228	0.07195228
28	4.47784307	0.22332181	63.23351045	14.12142172	0.01581440	0.07081440
29	4.72412444	0.21167944	67.71135353	14.33310116	0.01476857	0.06976857
30	4.98395129	0.20064402	72.43547797	14.53374517	0.01380539	0.06880539
31	5.25806861	0.19018390	77.41942926	14.72392907	0.01291665	0.06791665
32	5.54726238	0.18026910	82.67749787	14.90419817	0.01209519	0.06709519
33	5.85236181	0.17087119	88.22476025	15.07506936	0.01133469	0.06633469
34	6.17424171	0.16196321	94.07712207	15.23703257	0.01062958	0.06562958
35	6.51382501	0.15351963	100.25136378	15.39055220	0.00997493	0.06497493
36	6.87208538	0.14551624	106.76518879	15.53606843	0.00936635	0.06436635
37	7.25005008	0.13793008	113.63727417	15.67399851	0.00879993	0.06379993
38	7.64880283	0.13073941	120.88732425	15.80473793	0.00827217	0.06327217
39	8.06948699	0.12392362	128.53612708	15.92866154	0.00777991	0.06277991
40	8.51330877	0.11746314	136.60561407	16.04612469	0.00732034	0.06232034
41	8.98154076	0.11133947	145.11892285	16.15746416	0.00689090	0.06189090
42	9.47552550	0.10553504	154.10046360	16.26299920	0.00648927	0.06148927
43	9.99667940	0.10003322	163.57598910	16.36303242	0.00611337	0.06111337
44	10.54649677	0.09481822	173.57266850	16.45785063	0.00576128	0.06076128
45	11.12655409	0.08987509	184.11916527	16.54772572	0.00543127	0.06043127
46	11.73851456	0.08518965	195.24571936	16.63291537	0.00512175	0.06012175
47	12.38413287	0.08074849	206.98423392	16.71366386	0.00483129	0.05983129
48	13.06526017	0.07653885	219.36836679	16.79020271	0.00455854	0.05955854
49	13.78384948	0.07254867	232.43362696	16.86275139	0.00430230	0.05930230
50	14.54196120	0.06876652	246.21747645	16.93151790	0.00406145	0.05906145

	A	B	C	D	E	F
Rate 6%	Compound Interest	Present Value	Amount of Annuity	Present Value of Annuity	Sinking Fund	Amortization
n	$(1 + i)^n$	$\dfrac{1}{(1 + i)^n}$	$s_{\overline{n}\rvert i}$	$a_{\overline{n}\rvert i}$	$\dfrac{1}{s_{\overline{n}\rvert i}}$	$\dfrac{1}{a_{\overline{n}\rvert i}}$
1	1.06000000	0.94339623	1.00000000	0.94339623	1.00000000	1.06000000
2	1.12360000	0.88999644	2.06000000	1.83339267	0.48543689	0.54543689
3	1.19101600	0.83961928	3.18360000	2.67301195	0.31410981	0.37410981
4	1.26247696	0.79209366	4.37461600	3.46510561	0.22859149	0.28859149
5	1.33822558	0.74725817	5.63709296	4.21236379	0.17739640	0.23739640
6	1.41851911	0.70496054	6.97531854	4.91732433	0.14336263	0.20336263
7	1.50363026	0.66505711	8.39383765	5.58238144	0.11913502	0.17913502
8	1.59384807	0.62741237	9.89746791	6.20979381	0.10103594	0.16103594
9	1.68947896	0.59189846	11.49131598	6.80169227	0.08702224	0.14702224
10	1.79084770	0.55839478	13.18079494	7.36008705	0.07586796	0.13586796
11	1.89829856	0.52678753	14.97164264	7.88687458	0.06679294	0.12679294
12	2.01219647	0.49696936	16.86994120	8.38384394	0.05927703	0.11927703
13	2.13292826	0.46883902	18.88213767	8.85268296	0.05296011	0.11296011
14	2.26090396	0.44230096	21.01506593	9.29498393	0.04758491	0.10758491
15	2.39655819	0.41726506	23.27596988	9.71224899	0.04296276	0.10296276
16	2.54035168	0.39364628	25.67252808	10.10589527	0.03895214	0.09895214
17	2.69277279	0.37136442	28.21287976	10.47725969	0.03544480	0.09544480
18	2.85433915	0.35034379	30.90565255	10.82760348	0.03235654	0.09235654
19	3.02559950	0.33051301	33.75999170	11.15811649	0.02962086	0.08962086
20	3.20713547	0.31180473	36.78559120	11.46992122	0.02718456	0.08718456
21	3.39956360	0.29415540	39.99272668	11.76407662	0.02500455	0.08500455
22	3.60353742	0.27750510	43.39229028	12.04158172	0.02304557	0.08304557
23	3.81974966	0.26179726	46.99582769	12.30337898	0.02127848	0.08127848
24	4.04893464	0.24697855	50.81557735	12.55035753	0.01967900	0.07967900
25	4.29187072	0.23299863	54.86451200	12.78335616	0.01822672	0.07822672
26	4.54938296	0.21981003	59.15638272	13.00316619	0.01690435	0.07690435
27	4.82234594	0.20736795	63.70576568	13.21053414	0.01569717	0.07569717
28	5.11168670	0.19563014	68.52811162	13.40616428	0.01459255	0.07459255
29	5.41838790	0.18455674	73.63979832	13.59072102	0.01357961	0.07357961
30	5.74349117	0.17411013	79.05818622	13.76483115	0.01264891	0.07264891
31	6.08810064	0.16425484	84.80167739	13.92908599	0.01179222	0.07179222
32	6.45338668	0.15495740	90.88977803	14.08404339	0.01100234	0.07100234
33	6.84058988	0.14618622	97.34316471	14.23022961	0.01027293	0.07027293
34	7.25102528	0.13791153	104.18375460	14.36814114	0.00959843	0.06959843
35	7.68608679	0.13010522	111.43477987	14.49824636	0.00897386	0.06897386
36	8.14725200	0.12274077	119.12086666	14.62098713	0.00839483	0.06839483
37	8.63608712	0.11579318	127.26811866	14.73678031	0.00785743	0.06785743
38	9.15425235	0.10923885	135.90420578	14.84601916	0.00735812	0.06735812
39	9.70350749	0.10305552	145.05845813	14.94907468	0.00689377	0.06689377
40	10.28571794	0.09722219	154.76196562	15.04629687	0.00646154	0.06646154
41	10.90286101	0.09171905	165.04768356	15.13801592	0.00605886	0.06605886
42	11.55703267	0.08652740	175.95054457	15.22454332	0.00568342	0.06568342
43	12.25045463	0.08162962	187.50757724	15.30617294	0.00533312	0.06533312
44	12.98548191	0.07700908	199.75803188	15.38318202	0.00500606	0.06500606
45	13.76461083	0.07265007	212.74351379	15.45583209	0.00470050	0.06470050
46	14.59048748	0.06853781	226.50812462	15.52436990	0.00441485	0.06441485
47	15.46591673	0.06465831	241.09861210	15.58902821	0.00414768	0.06414768
48	16.39387173	0.06099840	256.56452882	15.65002661	0.00389765	0.06389765
49	17.37750403	0.05754566	272.95840055	15.70757227	0.00366356	0.06366356
50	18.42015427	0.05428836	290.33590458	15.76186064	0.00344429	0.06344429

Rate $6\frac{1}{2}\%$	A Compound Interest	B Present Value	C Amount of Annuity	D Present Value of Annuity	E Sinking Fund	F Amortization
n	$(1+i)^n$	$\dfrac{1}{(1+i)^n}$	$s_{\overline{n}|i}$	$a_{\overline{n}|i}$	$\dfrac{1}{s_{\overline{n}|i}}$	$\dfrac{1}{a_{\overline{n}|i}}$
1	1.06500000	0.93896714	1.00000000	0.93896714	1.00000000	1.06500000
2	1.13422500	0.88165928	2.06500000	1.82062642	0.48426150	0.54926150
3	1.20794963	0.82784909	3.19922500	2.64847551	0.31257570	0.37757570
4	1.28646635	0.77732309	4.40717462	3.42579860	0.22690274	0.29190274
5	1.37008666	0.72988084	5.69364098	4.15567944	0.17563454	0.24063454
6	1.45914230	0.68533412	7.06372764	4.84101356	0.14156831	0.20656831
7	1.55398655	0.64350621	8.52286994	5.48451977	0.11733137	0.18233137
8	1.65499567	0.60423119	10.07685648	6.08875096	0.09923730	0.16423730
9	1.76257039	0.56735323	11.73185215	6.65610419	0.08523803	0.15023803
10	1.87713747	0.53272604	13.49442254	7.18883022	0.07410469	0.13910469
11	1.99915140	0.50021224	15.37156001	7.68904246	0.06505521	0.13005521
12	2.12909624	0.46968285	17.37071141	8.15872532	0.05756817	0.12256817
13	2.26748750	0.44101676	19.49980765	8.59974208	0.05128256	0.11628256
14	2.41487418	0.41410025	21.76729515	9.01384233	0.04594048	0.11094048
15	2.57184101	0.38882652	24.18216933	9.40266885	0.04135278	0.10635278
16	2.73901067	0.36509533	26.75401034	9.76776418	0.03737757	0.10237757
17	2.91704637	0.34281251	29.49302101	10.11057670	0.03390633	0.09890633
18	3.10655438	0.32188969	32.41006738	10.43246638	0.03085461	0.09585461
19	3.30858691	0.30224384	35.51672176	10.73471022	0.02815575	0.09315575
20	3.52364506	0.28379703	38.82530867	11.01850725	0.02575640	0.09075640
21	3.75268199	0.26647608	42.34895373	11.28498333	0.02361333	0.08861333
22	3.99660632	0.25021228	46.10163573	11.53519562	0.02169120	0.08669120
23	4.25638573	0.23494111	50.09824205	11.77013673	0.01996078	0.08496078
24	4.53305081	0.22060198	54.35462778	11.99073871	0.01839770	0.08339770
25	4.82769911	0.20713801	58.88767859	12.19787673	0.01698148	0.08198148
26	5.14149955	0.19449579	63.71537769	12.39237251	0.01569480	0.08069480
27	5.47569702	0.18262515	68.85687725	12.57499766	0.01452288	0.07952288
28	5.83161733	0.17147902	74.33257427	12.74647668	0.01345305	0.07845305
29	6.21067245	0.16101316	80.16419159	12.90748984	0.01247440	0.07747440
30	6.61436616	0.15118607	86.37486405	13.05867591	0.01157744	0.07657744
31	7.04429996	0.14195875	92.98923021	13.20063465	0.01075393	0.07575393
32	7.50217946	0.13329460	100.03353017	13.33392925	0.00999665	0.07499665
33	7.98982113	0.12515925	107.53570963	13.45908850	0.00929924	0.07429924
34	8.50915950	0.11752042	115.52553076	13.57660892	0.00865610	0.07365610
35	9.06225487	0.11034781	124.03469026	13.68695673	0.00806226	0.07306226
36	9.65130143	0.10361297	133.09694513	13.79056970	0.00751332	0.07251332
37	10.27863603	0.09728917	142.74824656	13.88785887	0.00700534	0.07200534
38	10.94674737	0.09135134	153.02688259	13.97921021	0.00653480	0.07153480
39	11.65828595	0.08577590	163.97362996	14.06498611	0.00609854	0.07109854
40	12.41607453	0.08054075	175.63191590	14.14552687	0.00569373	0.07069373
41	13.22311938	0.07562512	188.04799044	14.22115199	0.00531779	0.07031779
42	14.08262214	0.07100950	201.27110981	14.29216149	0.00496842	0.06996842
43	14.99799258	0.06667559	215.35373195	14.35883708	0.00464352	0.06964352
44	15.97286209	0.06260619	230.35172453	14.42144327	0.00434119	0.06934119
45	17.01109813	0.05878515	246.32458662	14.48022842	0.00405968	0.06905968
46	18.11681951	0.05519733	263.33568475	14.53542575	0.00379743	0.06879743
47	19.29441278	0.05182848	281.45250426	14.58725422	0.00355300	0.06855300
48	20.54854961	0.04866524	300.74691704	14.63591946	0.00332505	0.06832505
49	21.88420533	0.04569506	321.29546665	14.68161451	0.00311240	0.06811240
50	23.30667868	0.04290616	343.17967198	14.72452067	0.00291393	0.06791393

Rate 7%	A Compound Interest	B Present Value	C Amount of Annuity	D Present Value of Annuity	E Sinking Fund	F Amortization
n	$(1 + i)^n$	$\dfrac{1}{(1 + i)^n}$	$s_{\overline{n}|i}$	$a_{\overline{n}|i}$	$\dfrac{1}{s_{\overline{n}|i}}$	$\dfrac{1}{a_{\overline{n}|i}}$
1	1.07000000	0.93457944	1.00000000	0.93457944	1.00000000	1.00000000
2	1.14490000	0.87343873	2.07000000	1.80801817	0.48309179	0.55309179
3	1.22504300	0.81629788	3.21490000	2.62431604	0.31105167	0.38105167
4	1.31079601	0.76289521	4.43994300	3.38721126	0.22522812	0.29522812
5	1.40255173	0.71298618	5.75073901	4.10019744	0.17389069	0.24389069
6	1.50073035	0.66634222	7.15329074	4.76653966	0.13979580	0.20979580
7	1.60578148	0.62274974	8.65402109	5.38928940	0.11555322	0.18555322
8	1.71818618	0.58200910	10.25980257	5.97129851	0.09746776	0.16746776
9	1.83845921	0.54393374	11.97798875	6.51523225	0.08348647	0.15348647
10	1.96715136	0.50834929	13.81644796	7.02358154	0.07237750	0.14237750
11	2.10485195	0.47509280	15.78359932	7.49867434	0.06335690	0.13335690
12	2.25219159	0.44401196	17.88845127	7.94268630	0.05590199	0.12590199
13	2.40984500	0.41496445	20.14064286	8.35765074	0.04965085	0.11965085
14	2.57853415	0.38781724	22.55048786	8.74546799	0.04434494	0.11434494
15	2.75903154	0.36244602	25.12902201	9.10791401	0.03979462	0.10979462
16	2.95216375	0.33873460	27.88805355	9.44664860	0.03585765	0.10585765
17	3.15881521	0.31657439	30.84021730	9.76322299	0.03242519	0.10242519
18	3.37993228	0.29586392	33.99903251	10.05908691	0.02941260	0.09941260
19	3.61652754	0.27650833	37.37896479	10.33559524	0.02675301	0.09675301
20	3.86968446	0.25841900	40.99549232	10.59401425	0.02439293	0.09439293
21	4.14056237	0.24151309	44.86517678	10.83552733	0.02228900	0.09228900
22	4.43040174	0.22571317	49.00573916	11.06124050	0.02040577	0.09040577
23	4.74052986	0.21094688	53.43614090	11.27218738	0.01871393	0.08871393
24	5.07236695	0.19714662	58.17667076	11.46933400	0.01718902	0.08718902
25	5.42743264	0.18424918	63.24903772	11.65358318	0.01581052	0.08581052
26	5.80735292	0.17219549	68.67647036	11.82577867	0.01456103	0.08456103
27	6.21386763	0.16093037	74.48382328	11.98670904	0.01342573	0.08342573
28	6.64883836	0.15040221	80.69769091	12.13711125	0.01239193	0.08239193
29	7.11425705	0.14056282	87.34652927	12.27767407	0.01144865	0.08144865
30	7.61225504	0.13136712	94.46078632	12.40904118	0.01058640	0.08058640
31	8.14511290	0.12277301	102.07304137	12.53181419	0.00979691	0.07979691
32	8.71527080	0.11474113	110.21815426	12.64655532	0.00907292	0.07907292
33	9.32533975	0.10723470	118.93342506	12.75379002	0.00840807	0.07840807
34	9.97811354	0.10021934	128.25876481	12.85400936	0.00779674	0.07779674
35	10.67658148	0.09366294	138.23687835	12.94767230	0.00723396	0.07723396
36	11.42394219	0.08753546	148.91345984	13.03520776	0.00671531	0.07671531
37	12.22361814	0.08180884	160.33740202	13.11701660	0.00623685	0.07623685
38	13.07927141	0.07645686	172.56102017	13.19347345	0.00579505	0.07579505
39	13.99482041	0.07145501	185.64029158	13.26492846	0.00538676	0.07538676
40	14.97445784	0.06678038	199.63511199	13.33170884	0.00500914	0.07500914
41	16.02266989	0.06241157	214.60956983	13.39412041	0.00465962	0.07465962
42	17.14425678	0.05832857	230.63223972	13.45244898	0.00433591	0.07433591
43	18.34435475	0.05451268	247.77649650	13.50696167	0.00403590	0.07403590
44	19.62845959	0.05094643	266.12085125	13.55790810	0.00375769	0.07375769
45	21.00245176	0.04761349	285.74931084	13.60552159	0.00349957	0.07349957
46	22.47262338	0.04449859	306.75176260	13.65002018	0.00325996	0.07325996
47	24.04570702	0.04158747	329.22438598	13.69160764	0.00303744	0.07303744
48	25.72890651	0.03886679	353.27009300	13.73047443	0.00283070	0.07283070
49	27.52992997	0.03632410	378.99899951	13.76679853	0.00263853	0.07263853
50	29.45702506	0.03394776	406.52892947	13.80074629	0.00245985	0.07245985

Rate $7\frac{1}{2}\%$	A Compound Interest	B Present Value	C Amount of Annuity	D Present Value of Annuity	E Sinking Fund	F Amortization
n	$(1 + i)^n$	$\dfrac{1}{(1 + i)^n}$	$s_{\overline{n}|i}$	$a_{\overline{n}|i}$	$\dfrac{1}{s_{\overline{n}|i}}$	$\dfrac{1}{a_{\overline{n}|i}}$
1	1.07500000	0.93023256	1.00000000	0.93023256	1.00000000	1.07500000
2	1.15562500	0.86533261	2.07500000	1.79556517	0.48192771	0.55692771
3	1.24229688	0.80496057	3.23062500	2.60052574	0.30953763	0.38453763
4	1.33546914	0.74880053	4.47292187	3.34932627	0.22356751	0.29856751
5	1.43562933	0.69655863	5.80839102	4.04588490	0.17216472	0.24716472
6	1.54330153	0.64796152	7.24402034	4.69384642	0.13804489	0.21304489
7	1.65904914	0.60275490	8.78732187	5.29660132	0.11380032	0.18880032
8	1.78347783	0.56070223	10.44637101	5.85730355	0.09572702	0.17072702
9	1.91723866	0.52158347	12.22984883	6.37888703	0.08176716	0.15676716
10	2.06103156	0.48519393	14.14708750	6.86408096	0.07068593	0.14568593
11	2.21560893	0.45134319	16.20811906	7.31542415	0.06169747	0.13669747
12	2.38177960	0.41985413	18.42372799	7.73527827	0.05427783	0.12927783
13	2.56041307	0.39056198	20.80550759	8.12584026	0.04806420	0.12306420
14	2.75244405	0.36331347	23.36592066	8.48915373	0.04279737	0.11779737
15	2.95887735	0.33796602	26.11836470	8.82711975	0.03828724	0.11328724
16	3.18079315	0.31438699	29.07724206	9.14150674	0.03439116	0.10939116
17	3.41935264	0.29245302	32.25803521	9.43395976	0.03100003	0.10600003
18	3.67580409	0.27204932	35.67738785	9.70600908	0.02802896	0.10302896
19	3.95148940	0.25306913	39.35319194	9.95907821	0.02541090	0.10041090
20	4.24785110	0.23541315	43.30468134	10.19449136	0.02309219	0.09809219
21	4.56643993	0.21898897	47.55253244	10.41348033	0.02102937	0.09602937
22	4.90892293	0.20371067	52.11897237	10.61719101	0.01918687	0.09418687
23	5.27709215	0.18949830	57.02789530	10.80668931	0.01753528	0.09253528
24	5.67287406	0.17627749	62.30498744	10.98296680	0.01605008	0.09105008
25	6.09833961	0.16397906	67.97786150	11.14694586	0.01471067	0.08971067
26	6.55571508	0.15253866	74.07620112	11.29948452	0.01349961	0.08849961
27	7.04739371	0.14189643	80.63191620	11.44138095	0.01240204	0.08740204
28	7.57594824	0.13199668	87.67930991	11.57337763	0.01140520	0.08640520
29	8.14414436	0.12278761	95.25525816	11.69616524	0.01049811	0.08549811
30	8.75495519	0.11422103	103.39940252	11.81038627	0.00967124	0.08467124
31	9.41157683	0.10625212	112.15435771	11.91663839	0.00891628	0.08391628
32	10.11744509	0.09883918	121.56593454	12.01547757	0.00822599	0.08322599
33	10.87625347	0.09194343	131.68337963	12.10742099	0.00759397	0.08259397
34	11.69197248	0.08552877	142.55963310	12.19294976	0.00701461	0.08201461
35	12.56887042	0.07956164	154.25160558	12.27251141	0.00648291	0.08148291
36	13.51153570	0.07401083	166.82047600	12.34652224	0.00599447	0.08099447
37	14.52490088	0.06884729	180.33201170	12.41536952	0.00554533	0.08054533
38	15.61426844	0.06404399	194.85691258	12.47941351	0.00513197	0.08013197
39	16.78533858	0.05957580	210.47118102	12.53898931	0.00475124	0.07975124
40	18.04423897	0.05541935	227.25651960	12.59440866	0.00440031	0.07940031
41	19.39755689	0.05155288	245.30075857	12.64596155	0.00407663	0.07907663
42	20.85237366	0.04795617	264.69831546	12.69391772	0.00377789	0.07877789
43	22.41630168	0.04461039	285.55068912	12.73852811	0.00350201	0.07850201
44	24.09752431	0.04149804	307.96699080	12.78002615	0.00324710	0.07824710
45	25.90483863	0.03860283	332.06451511	12.81862898	0.00301146	0.07801146
46	27.84770153	0.03590961	357.96935375	12.85453858	0.00279354	0.07779354
47	29.93627915	0.03340428	385.81705528	12.88794287	0.00259190	0.07759190
48	32.18150008	0.03107375	415.75333442	12.91901662	0.00240527	0.07740527
49	34.59511259	0.02890582	447.93483451	12.94792244	0.00223247	0.07723247
50	37.18974603	0.02688913	482.52994709	12.97481157	0.00207241	0.07707241

Rate 8% n	A Compound Interest $(1 + i)^n$	B Present Value $\dfrac{1}{(1 + i)^n}$	C Amount of Annuity $s_{\overline{n}|i}$	D Present Value of Annuity $a_{\overline{n}|i}$	E Sinking Fund $\dfrac{1}{s_{\overline{n}|i}}$	F Amortization $\dfrac{1}{a_{\overline{n}|i}}$
1	1.08000000	0.92592593	1.00000000	0.92592593	1.00000000	1.08000000
2	1.16640000	0.85733882	2.08000000	1.78326475	0.48076923	0.56076923
3	1.25971200	0.79383224	3.24640000	2.57709699	0.30803351	0.38803351
4	1.36048896	0.73502985	4.50611200	3.31212684	0.22192080	0.30192080
5	1.46932808	0.68058320	5.86660096	3.99271004	0.17045645	0.25045645
6	1.58687432	0.63016963	7.33592904	4.62287966	0.13631539	0.21631539
7	1.71382427	0.58349040	8.92280336	5.20637006	0.11207240	0.19207240
8	0.85093021	0.54026888	10.63662763	5.74663894	0.09401476	0.17401476
9	1.99900463	0.50024897	12.48755784	6.24688791	0.08007971	0.16007971
10	2.15892500	0.46319349	14.48656247	6.71008140	0.06902949	0.14902949
11	2.33163900	0.42888286	16.64548746	7.13896426	0.06007634	0.14007634
12	2.51817012	0.39711376	18.97712646	7.53607802	0.05269502	0.13269502
13	2.71962373	0.36769792	21.49529658	7.90377594	0.04652181	0.12652181
14	2.93719362	0.34046104	24.21492030	8.24423698	0.04129685	0.12129685
15	3.17216911	0.31524170	27.15211393	8.55947869	0.03682954	0.11682954
16	3.42594264	0.29189047	30.32428304	8.85136916	0.03297687	0.11297687
17	3.70001805	0.27026895	33.75022569	9.12163811	0.02962943	0.10962943
18	3.99601950	0.25024903	37.45024374	9.37188714	0.02670210	0.10670210
19	4.31570106	0.23171206	41.44626324	9.60359920	0.02412763	0.10412763
20	4.66095714	0.21454821	45.76196430	9.81814741	0.02185221	0.10185221
21	5.03383372	0.19865575	50.42292144	10.01680316	0.01983225	0.09983225
22	5.43654041	0.18394051	55.45675516	10.20074366	0.01803207	0.09803207
23	5.87146365	0.17031528	60.89329557	10.37105895	0.01642217	0.09642217
24	6.34118074	0.15769934	66.76475922	10.52875828	0.01497796	0.09497796
25	6.84847520	0.14601790	73.10593995	10.67477619	0.01367878	0.09367878
26	7.39635321	0.13520176	79.95441515	10.80997795	0.01250713	0.09250713
27	7.98806147	0.12518682	87.35076836	10.93516477	0.01144810	0.09144810
28	8.62710639	0.11591372	95.33882983	11.05107849	0.01048891	0.09048891
29	9.31727490	0.10732752	103.96593622	11.15840601	0.00961854	0.08961854
30	10.06265689	0.09937733	113.28321111	11.25778334	0.00882743	0.08882743
31	10.86766944	0.09201605	123.34586800	11.34979939	0.00810728	0.08810728
32	11.73708300	0.08520005	134.21353744	11.43499944	0.00745081	0.08745081
33	12.67604964	0.07888893	145.95062044	11.51388837	0.00685163	0.08685163
34	13.69013361	0.07304531	158.62667007	11.58693367	0.00630411	0.08630411
35	14.78534429	0.06763454	172.31680368	11.65456822	0.00580326	0.08580326
36	15.96817184	0.06262458	187.10214797	11.71719279	0.00534467	0.08534467
37	17.24562558	0.05798572	203.07031981	11.77517851	0.00492440	0.08492440
38	18.62527563	0.05369048	220.31594540	11.82886899	0.00453894	0.08453894
39	20.11529768	0.04971341	238.94122103	11.87858240	0.00418513	0.08418513
40	21.72452150	0.04603093	259.05651871	11.92461333	0.00386016	0.08386016
41	23.46248322	0.04262123	280.78104021	11.96723457	0.00356149	0.08356149
42	25.33948187	0.03946411	304.24352342	12.00669867	0.00328684	0.08328684
43	27.36664042	0.03654084	329.58300530	12.04323951	0.00303414	0.08303414
44	29.55597166	0.03383411	356.94964572	12.07707362	0.00280152	0.08280152
45	31.92044939	0.03132788	386.50561738	12.10840150	0.00258728	0.08258728
46	34.47408534	0.02900730	418.42606677	12.13740880	0.00238991	0.08238991
47	37.23201217	0.02685861	452.90015211	12.16426741	0.00220799	0.08220799
48	40.21057314	0.02486908	490.13216428	12.18913649	0.00204027	0.08204027
49	43.42741899	0.02302693	530.34273742	12.21216341	0.00188557	0.08188557
50	46.90161251	0.02132123	573.77015642	12.23348464	0.00174286	0.08174286

Rate 9%	A Compound Interest	B Present Value	C Amount of Annuity	D Present Value of Annuity	E Sinking Fund	F Amortization
n	$(1+i)^n$	$\dfrac{1}{(1+i)^n}$	$s_{\overline{n}|i}$	$a_{\overline{n}|i}$	$\dfrac{1}{s_{\overline{n}|i}}$	$\dfrac{1}{a_{\overline{n}|i}}$
1	1.09000000	0.91743119	1.00000000	0.91743119	1.00000000	1.09000000
2	1.18810000	0.84167999	2.09000000	1.75911119	0.47846890	0.56846890
3	1.29502900	0.77218348	3.27810000	2.53129467	0.30505476	0.39505476
4	1.41158161	0.70842521	4.57312900	3.23971988	0.21866866	0.30866866
5	1.53862395	0.64993139	5.98471061	3.88965126	0.16709246	0.25709246
6	1.67710011	0.59626733	7.52333456	4.48591859	0.13291978	0.22291978
7	1.82803912	0.54703424	9.20043468	5.03295284	0.10869052	0.19869052
8	1.99256264	0.50186628	11.02847380	5.53481911	0.09067438	0.18067438
9	2.17189328	0.46042778	13.02103644	5.99524689	0.07679880	0.16679880
10	2.36736367	0.42241081	15.19292972	6.41765770	0.06582009	0.15582009
11	2.58042641	0.38753285	17.56029339	6.80519055	0.05694666	0.14694666
12	2.81266478	0.35553473	20.14071980	7.16072528	0.04965066	0.13965066
13	3.06580461	0.32617865	22.95338458	7.48690392	0.04356656	0.13356656
14	3.34172703	0.29924647	26.01918919	7.78615039	0.03843317	0.12843317
15	3.64248246	0.27453804	29.36091622	8.06068843	0.03405888	0.12405888
16	3.97030588	0.25186976	33.00339868	8.31255819	0.03029991	0.12029991
17	4.32763341	0.23107318	36.97370456	8.54363137	0.02704625	0.11704625
18	4.71712042	0.21199374	41.30133797	8.75562511	0.02421229	0.11421229
19	5.14166125	0.19448967	46.01845839	8.95011478	0.02173041	0.11173041
20	5.60441077	0.17843089	51.16011964	9.12854567	0.01954648	0.10954648
21	6.10880774	0.16369806	56.76453041	9.29224373	0.01761663	0.10761663
22	6.65860043	0.15018171	62.87333815	9.44242544	0.01590499	0.10590499
23	7.25787447	0.13778139	69.53193858	9.58020683	0.01438188	0.10438188
24	7.91108317	0.12640494	76.78981305	9.70661177	0.01302256	0.10302256
25	8.62308066	0.11596784	84.70089623	9.82257960	0.01180625	0.10180625
26	9.39915792	0.10639251	93.32397689	9.92897211	0.01071536	0.10071536
27	10.24508213	0.09760781	102.72313481	10.02657992	0.00973491	0.09973491
28	11.16713952	0.08954845	112.96821694	10.11612837	0.00885205	0.09885205
29	12.17218208	0.08215454	124.13535646	10.19828291	0.00805572	0.09805572
30	13.26767847	0.07537114	136.30753855	10.27365404	0.00733635	0.09733635
31	14.46176953	0.06914783	149.57521702	10.34280187	0.00668560	0.09668560
32	15.76332879	0.06343838	164.03698655	10.40624025	0.00609619	0.09609619
33	17.18202838	0.05820035	179.80031534	10.46444060	0.00556173	0.09556173
34	18.72841093	0.05339481	196.98234372	10.51783541	0.00507660	0.09507660
35	20.41396792	0.04898607	215.71075465	10.56682148	0.00463584	0.09463584
36	22.25122503	0.04494135	236.12472257	10.61176282	0.00423505	0.09423505
37	24.25383528	0.04123059	258.37594760	10.65299342	0.00387033	0.09387033
38	26.43668046	0.03782623	282.62978288	10.69081965	0.00353820	0.09353820
39	28.81598170	0.03470296	309.06646334	10.72552261	0.00323555	0.09323555
40	31.40942005	0.03183758	337.88244504	10.75736020	0.00295961	0.09295961
41	34.23626789	0.02920879	369.29186510	10.78656899	0.00270789	0.09270789
42	37.31753197	0.02679706	403.52813296	10.81336604	0.00247814	0.09247814
43	40.67610984	0.02458446	440.84566492	10.83795050	0.00226837	0.09226837
44	44.33695973	0.02255455	481.52177477	10.86050504	0.00207675	0.09207675
45	48.32728610	0.02069224	525.85873450	10.88119729	0.00190165	0.09190165
46	52.67674185	0.01898371	574.18602060	10.90018100	0.00174160	0.09174160
47	57.41764862	0.01741625	626.86276245	10.91759725	0.00159525	0.09159525
48	62.58523700	0.01597821	684.28041107	10.93357546	0.00146139	0.09146139
49	68.21790833	0.01465891	746.86564807	10.94823436	0.00133893	0.09133893
50	74.35752008	0.01344854	815.08355640	10.96168290	0.00122687	0.09122687

Rate 10%	A Compound Interest	B Present Value	C Amount of Annuity	D Present Value of Annuity	E Sinking Fund	F Amortization
n	$(1 + i)^n$	$\dfrac{1}{(1 + i)^n}$	$s_{\overline{n}\rvert i}$	$a_{\overline{n}\rvert i}$	$\dfrac{1}{s_{\overline{n}\rvert i}}$	$\dfrac{1}{a_{\overline{n}\rvert i}}$
1	1.10000000	0.90909091	1.00000000	0.90909091	1.00000000	1.10000000
2	1.21000000	0.82644628	2.10000000	1.73553719	0.47619048	0.57619048
3	1.33100000	0.75131480	3.31000000	2.48685199	0.30211480	0.40211480
4	1.46410000	0.68301346	4.64100000	3.16986545	0.21547080	0.31547080
5	1.61051000	0.62092132	6.10510000	3.79078677	0.16379748	0.26379748
6	1.77156100	0.56447393	7.71561000	4.35526070	0.12960738	0.22960738
7	1.94871710	0.51315812	9.48717100	4.86841882	0.10540550	0.20540550
8	2.14358881	0.46650738	11.43588810	5.33492620	0.08744402	0.18744402
9	2.35794769	0.42409762	13.57947691	5.75902382	0.07364054	0.17364054
10	2.59374246	0.38554329	15.93742460	6.14456711	0.06274539	0.16274539
11	2.85311671	0.35049390	18.53116706	6.49506101	0.05396314	0.15396314
12	3.13842838	0.31863082	21.38428377	6.81369182	0.04676332	0.14676332
13	3.45227121	0.28966438	24.52271214	7.10335620	0.04077852	0.14077852
14	3.79749834	0.26333125	27.97498336	7.36668746	0.03574622	0.13574622
15	4.17724817	0.23939205	31.77248169	7.60607951	0.03147378	0.13147378
16	4.59497299	0.21762914	35.94972986	7.82370864	0.02781662	0.12781662
17	5.05447028	0.19784467	40.54470285	8.02155331	0.02466413	0.12466413
18	5.55991731	0.17985879	45.59917313	8.20141210	0.02193022	0.12193022
19	6.11590904	0.16350799	51.15909045	8.36492009	0.01954687	0.11954687
20	6.72749995	0.14864363	57.27499949	8.51356372	0.01745962	0.11745962
21	7.40024994	0.13513057	64.00249944	8.64869429	0.01562439	0.11562439
22	8.14027494	0.12284597	71.40274939	8.77154026	0.04100506	0.11400506
23	8.95430243	0.11167816	79.54302433	8.88321842	0.01257181	0.11257181
24	9.84973268	0.10152560	88.49732676	8.98474402	0.01129978	0.11129978
25	10.83470594	0.09229600	98.34705943	9.07704002	0.01016807	0.11016807
26	11.91817654	0.08390545	109.18176538	9.16094547	0.00915904	0.10915904
27	13.10999419	0.07627768	121.09994191	9.23722316	0.00825764	0.10825764
28	14.42099361	0.06934335	134.20993611	9.30656651	0.00745101	0.10745101
29	15.86309297	0.06303941	148.63092972	9.36960591	0.00672807	0.10672807
30	17.44940227	0.05730855	164.49402269	9.42691447	0.00607925	0.10607925
31	19.19434250	0.05209868	181.94342496	9.47901315	0.00549621	0.10549621
32	21.11377675	0.04736244	201.13776745	9.52637559	0.00497172	0.10497172
33	23.22515442	0.04305676	222.25154420	9.56943236	0.00449941	0.10449941
34	25.54766986	0.03914251	245.47669862	9.60857487	0.00407371	0.10407371
35	28.10243685	0.03558410	271.02436848	9.64415897	0.00368971	0.10368971
36	30.91268053	0.03234918	299.12680533	9.67650816	0.00334306	0.10334306
37	34.00394859	0.02940835	330.03948586	9.70591651	0.00302994	0.10302994
38	37.40434344	0.02673486	364.04343445	9.73265137	0.00274692	0.10274692
39	41.14477779	0.02430442	401.44777789	9.75695579	0.00249098	0.10249098
40	45.25925557	0.02209493	442.59255568	9.77905072	0.00225941	0.10225941
41	49.78518112	0.02008630	487.85181125	9.79913702	0.00204980	0.10204980
42	54.76369924	0.01826027	537.63699237	9.81739729	0.00185999	0.10185999
43	60.24006916	0.01660025	592.40069161	9.83399753	0.00168805	0.10168805
44	66.26407608	0.01509113	652.64076077	9.84908867	0.00153224	0.10153224
45	72.89048369	0.01371921	718.90483685	9.86280788	0.00139100	0.10139100
46	80.17953205	0.01247201	791.79532054	9.87527989	0.00126295	0.10126295
47	88.19748526	0.01133819	871.97485259	9.88661808	0.00114682	0.10114682
48	97.01723378	0.01030745	960.17233785	9.89692553	0.00104148	0.10104148
49	106.71895716	0.00937041	1057.18957163	9.90629594	0.00094590	0.10094590
50	117.39085288	0.00851855	1163.90852880	9.91481449	0.00085917	0.10085917

	A Compound Interest	B Present Value	C Amount of Annuity	D Present Value of Annuity	E Sinking Fund	F Amortization
Rate 11%						
n	$(1+i)^n$	$\dfrac{1}{(1+i)^n}$	$s_{\overline{n}|i}$	$a_{\overline{n}|i}$	$\dfrac{1}{s_{\overline{n}|i}}$	$\dfrac{1}{a_{\overline{n}|i}}$
1	1.11000000	0.90090090	1.00000000	0.90090090	1.00000000	1.11000000
2	1.23210000	0.81162243	2.11000000	1.71252333	0.47393365	0.58393365
3	1.36763100	0.73119138	3.34210000	2.44371472	0.29921307	0.40921307
4	1.51807041	0.65873097	4.70973100	3.10244569	0.21232635	0.32232635
5	1.68505816	0.59345133	6.22780141	3.69589702	0.16057031	0.27057031
6	1.87041455	0.53464084	7.91285957	4.23053785	0.12637656	0.23637656
7	2.07616015	0.48165841	9.78327412	4.71219626	0.10221527	0.21221527
8	2.30453777	0.43392650	11.85943427	5.14612276	0.08432105	0.19432105
9	2.55803692	0.39092477	14.16397204	5.53704753	0.07060166	0.18060166
10	2.83942099	0.35218448	16.72200896	5.88923201	0.05980143	0.16980143
11	3.15175729	0.31728331	19.56142995	6.20651533	0.05112101	0.16112101
12	3.49845060	0.28584082	22.71318724	6.49235615	0.04402729	0.15402729
13	3.88328016	0.25751426	26.21163784	6.74987040	0.03815099	0.14815099
14	4.31044098	0.23199482	30.09491800	6.98186523	0.03322820	0.14322820
15	4.78458949	0.20900435	34.40535898	7.19086958	0.02906524	0.13906524
16	5.31089433	0.18829220	39.18994847	7.37916178	0.02551675	0.13551675
17	5.89509271	0.16963262	44.50084281	7.54879440	0.02247148	0.13247148
18	6.54355291	0.15282218	50.39593551	7.70161657	0.01984287	0.12984287
19	7.26334373	0.13767764	56.93948842	7.83929421	0.01756250	0.12756250
20	8.06231154	0.12403391	64.20283215	7.96332812	0.01557564	0.12557564
21	8.94916581	0.11174226	72.26514368	8.07507038	0.01383793	0.12383793
22	9.93357404	0.10066870	81.21430949	8.17573908	0.01231310	0.12231310
23	11.02626719	0.09069252	91.14788353	8.26643160	0.01097118	0.12097118
24	12.23915658	0.08170498	102.17415072	8.34813658	0.00978721	0.11978721
25	13.58546380	0.07360809	114.41330730	8.42174466	0.00874024	0.11874024
26	15.07986482	0.06631359	127.99877110	8.48805826	0.00781258	0.11781258
27	16.73864995	0.05974197	143.07863592	8.54780023	0.00698916	0.11698916
28	18.57990145	0.05382160	159.81728587	8.60162183	0.00625715	0.11625715
29	20.62369061	0.04848793	178.39718732	8.65010976	0.00560547	0.11560547
30	22.89229657	0.04368282	199.02087793	8.69379257	0.00502460	0.11502460
31	25.41044919	0.03935389	221.91317450	8.73314646	0.00450627	0.11450627
32	28.20559861	0.03545395	247.32362369	8.76860042	0.00404329	0.11404329
33	31.30821445	0.03194050	275.52922230	8.80054092	0.00362938	0.11362938
34	34.75211804	0.02877522	306.83743675	8.82931614	0.00325905	0.11325905
35	38.57485103	0.02592363	341.58955480	8.85523977	0.00292749	0.11292749
36	42.81808464	0.02335462	380.16440582	8.87859438	0.00263044	0.11263044
37	47.52807395	0.02104020	422.98249046	8.89963458	0.00236416	0.11236416
38	52.75616209	0.01895513	470.51056441	8.91858971	0.00212535	0.11212535
39	58.55933991	0.01707670	523.26672650	8.93566641	0.00191107	0.11191107
40	65.00086731	0.01538441	581.82606641	8.95105082	0.00171873	0.11171873
41	72.15096271	0.01385983	646.82693372	8.96491065	0.00154601	0.11154601
42	80.08756861	0.01248633	718.97789643	8.97739698	0.00139086	0.11139086
43	88.89720115	0.01124895	799.06546504	8.98864593	0.00125146	0.11125146
44	98.67589328	0.01013419	887.96266619	8.99878011	0.00112617	0.11112617
45	109.53024154	0.00912990	986.63855947	9.00791001	0.00101354	0.11101354
46	121.57856811	0.00822513	1096.16880101	9.01613515	0.00091227	0.11091227
47	134.95221060	0.00741003	1217.74736912	9.02354518	0.00082119	0.11082119
48	149.79695377	0.00667570	1352.69957973	9.03022088	0.00073926	0.11073926
49	166.27461868	0.00601415	1502.49653350	9.03623503	0.00066556	0.11066556
50	184.56482674	0.00541815	1668.77115218	9.04165318	0.00059924	0.11059924

Rate 12%	A Compound Interest	B Present Value	C Amount of Annuity	D Present Value of Annuity	E Sinking Fund	F Amortization
n	$(1 + i)^n$	$\dfrac{1}{(1 + i)^n}$	$s_{\overline{n}|i}$	$a_{\overline{n}|i}$	$\dfrac{1}{s_{\overline{n}|i}}$	$\dfrac{1}{a_{\overline{n}|i}}$
1	1.12000000	0.89285714	1.00000000	0.89285714	1.00000000	1.12000000
2	1.25440000	0.79719388	2.12000000	1.69005102	0.47169811	0.59169811
3	1.40492800	0.71178025	3.37440000	2.40183127	0.29634898	0.41634898
4	1.57351936	0.63551808	4.77932800	3.03734935	0.20923444	0.32923444
5	1.76234168	0.56742686	6.35284736	3.60477620	0.15740973	0.27740973
6	1.97382269	0.50663112	8.11518904	4.11140732	0.12322572	0.24322572
7	2.21068141	0.45234922	10.08901173	4.56375654	0.09911774	0.21911774
8	2.47596318	0.40388323	12.29969314	4.96763977	0.08130284	0.20130284
9	2.77307876	0.36061002	14.77565631	5.32824979	0.06767889	0.18767889
10	3.10584821	0.32197324	17.54873507	5.65022303	0.05698416	0.17698416
11	3.47854999	0.28747610	20.65458328	5.93769913	0.04841540	0.16841540
12	3.89597599	0.25667509	24.13313327	6.19437423	0.04143681	0.16143681
13	4.36349311	0.22917419	28.02910926	6.42354842	0.03567720	0.15567720
14	4.88711229	0.20461981	32.39260238	6.62816823	0.03087125	0.15087125
15	5.47356576	0.18269626	37.27971466	6.81086449	0.02682424	0.14682424
16	6.13039365	0.16312166	42.75328042	6.97398615	0.02339002	0.14339002
17	6.86604098	0.14564434	48.88367407	7.11963049	0.02045673	0.14045673
18	7.68996580	0.13003959	55.74971496	7.24967008	0.01793731	0.13793731
19	8.61276169	0.11610678	63.43968075	7.36577686	0.01576300	0.13576300
20	9.64629309	0.10366677	72.05244244	7.46944362	0.01387878	0.13387878
21	10.80384826	0.09255961	81.69873554	7.56200324	0.01224009	0.13224009
22	12.10031006	0.08264251	92.50258380	7.64464575	0.01081051	0.13081051
23	13.55234726	0.07378796	104.60289386	7.71843370	0.00955996	0.12955996
24	15.17862893	0.06588210	118.15524112	7.78431581	0.00846344	0.12846344
25	17.00006441	0.05882331	133.33387006	7.84313911	0.00749997	0.12749997
26	19.04007214	0.05252081	150.33393446	7.89565992	0.00665186	0.12665186
27	21.32488079	0.04689358	169.37400660	7.94255350	0.00590409	0.12590409
28	23.88386649	0.04186927	190.69888739	7.98442277	0.00524387	0.12524387
29	26.74993047	0.03738327	214.58275388	8.02180604	0.00466021	0.12466021
30	29.95992212	0.03337792	241.33268434	8.05518397	0.00414366	0.12414366
31	33.55511278	0.02980172	271.29260646	8.08498569	0.00368606	0.12368606
32	37.58172631	0.02660868	304.84771924	8.11159436	0.00328033	0.12328033
33	42.09153347	0.02375775	342.42944555	8.13535211	0.00292031	0.12292031
34	47.14251748	0.02121227	384.52097901	8.15656438	0.00260064	0.12260064
35	52.79961958	0.01893953	431.66349649	8.17550391	0.00231662	0.12231662
36	59.13557393	0.01691029	484.46311607	8.19241421	0.00206414	0.12206414
37	66.23184280	0.01509848	543.59869000	8.20751269	0.00183959	0.12183959
38	74.17966394	0.01348078	609.83053280	8.22099347	0.00163980	0.12163980
39	83.08122361	0.01203641	684.01019674	8.23302988	0.00146197	0.12146197
40	93.05097044	0.01074680	767.09142034	8.24377668	0.00130363	0.12130363
41	104.21708689	0.00959536	860.14239079	8.25337204	0.00116260	0.12116260
42	116.72313732	0.00856728	964.35947768	8.26193932	0.00103696	0.12103696
43	130.72991380	0.00764936	1081.08261500	8.26958868	0.00092500	0.12092500
44	146.41750346	0.00682978	1211.81252880	8.27641846	0.00082521	0.12082521
45	163.98760387	0.00609802	1358.23003226	8.28251648	0.00073625	0.12073625
46	183.66611634	0.00544466	1522.21763613	8.28796115	0.00065694	0.12065694
47	205.70605030	0.00486131	1705.88375247	8.29282245	0.00058621	0.12058621
48	230.39077633	0.00434045	1911.58980276	8.29716290	0.00052312	0.12052312
49	258.03766949	0.00387540	2142.98057909	8.30103831	0.00046686	0.12046686
50	289.00218983	0.00346018	2400.01824858	8.30449849	0.00041666	0.12041666

Rate 13%	A Compound Interest	B Present Value	C Amount of Annuity	D Present Value of Annuity	E Sinking Fund	F Amortization
n	$(1+i)^n$	$\dfrac{1}{(1+i)^n}$	$s_{\overline{n}\rvert i}$	$a_{\overline{n}\rvert i}$	$\dfrac{1}{s_{\overline{n}\rvert i}}$	$\dfrac{1}{a_{\overline{n}\rvert i}}$
1	1.13000000	0.88495575	1.00000000	0.88495575	1.00000000	1.13000000
2	1.27690000	0.78314668	2.13000000	1.66810244	0.46948357	0.59948357
3	1.44289700	0.69305016	3.40690000	2.36115260	0.29352197	0.42352197
4	1.63047361	0.61331873	4.84979700	2.97447133	0.20619420	0.33619420
5	1.84243518	0.54275994	6.48027061	3.51723126	0.15431454	0.28431454
6	2.08195175	0.48031853	8.32270579	3.99754979	0.12015323	0.25015323
7	2.35260548	0.42506064	10.40465754	4.42261043	0.09611080	0.22611080
8	2.65844419	0.37615986	12.75726302	4.79877029	0.07838672	0.20838672
9	3.00404194	0.33288483	15.41570722	5.13165513	0.06486890	0.19486890
10	3.39456739	0.29458835	18.41974915	5.42624348	0.05428956	0.18428956
11	3.83586115	0.26069765	21.81431654	5.68694113	0.04584145	0.17584145
12	4.33452310	0.23070589	25.65017769	5.91764702	0.03898608	0.16898608
13	4.89801110	0.20416450	29.98470079	6.12181152	0.03335034	0.16335034
14	5.53475255	0.18067655	34.88271190	6.30248807	0.02866750	0.15866750
15	6.25427038	0.15989075	40.41746444	6.46237882	0.02474178	0.15474178
16	7.06732553	0.14149624	46.67173482	6.60387506	0.02142624	0.15142624
17	7.98607785	0.12521791	53.73906035	6.72909298	0.01860844	0.14860844
18	9.02426797	0.11081231	61.72513819	6.83990529	0.01620085	0.14620085
19	10.19742280	0.09806399	70.74940616	6.93796928	0.01413439	0.14413439
20	11.52308776	0.08678229	80.94682896	7.02475158	0.01235379	0.14235379
21	13.02108917	0.07679849	92.46991672	7.10155007	0.01081433	0.14081433
22	14.71383077	0.06796327	105.49100590	7.16951334	0.00947948	0.13947948
23	16.62662877	0.06014448	120.20483667	7.22965782	0.00831913	0.13831913
24	18.78809051	0.05322521	136.83146543	7.28288303	0.00730826	0.13730826
25	21.23054227	0.04710195	155.61955594	7.32998498	0.00642593	0.13642593
26	23.99051277	0.04168314	176.85009821	7.37166812	0.00565451	0.13565451
27	27.10927943	0.03688774	200.84061098	7.40855586	0.00497907	0.13497907
28	30.63348575	0.03264402	227.94989040	7.44119988	0.00438693	0.13438693
29	34.61583890	0.02888851	258.58337616	7.47008839	0.00386722	0.13386722
30	39.11589796	0.02556505	293.19921506	7.49565344	0.00341065	0.13341065
31	44.20096469	0.02262394	332.31511301	7.51827738	0.00300919	0.13300919
32	49.94709010	0.02002119	376.51607771	7.53829857	0.00265593	0.13265593
33	56.44021181	0.01771786	426.46316781	7.55601643	0.00234487	0.13234487
34	63.77743935	0.01567953	482.90337962	7.57169596	0.00207081	0.13207081
35	72.06850647	0.01387569	546.68081897	7.58557164	0.00182922	0.13182922
36	81.43741231	0.01227937	618.74932544	7.59785101	0.00161616	0.13161616
37	92.02427591	0.01086670	700.18673775	7.60871771	0.00142819	0.13142819
38	103.98743178	0.00961655	792.21101365	7.61833426	0.00126229	0.13126229
39	117.50579791	0.00851022	896.19844543	7.62684447	0.00111582	0.13111582
40	132.78155163	0.00753117	1013.70424333	7.63437564	0.00098648	0.13098648
41	150.04315335	0.00666475	1146.48579497	7.64104039	0.00087223	0.13087223
42	169.54876328	0.00589801	1296.52894831	7.64693840	0.00077129	0.13077129
43	191.59010251	0.00521948	1466.07771159	7.65215787	0.00068209	0.13068209
44	216.49681583	0.00461901	1657.66781410	7.65677688	0.00060326	0.13060326
45	244.64140189	0.00408762	1874.16462994	7.66086450	0.00053357	0.13053357
46	276.44478414	0.00361736	2118.80603183	7.66448185	0.00047196	0.13047196
47	312.38260608	0.00320120	2395.25081596	7.66768306	0.00041749	0.13041749
48	352.99234487	0.00283292	2707.63342204	7.67051598	0.00036933	0.13036933
49	398.88134970	0.00250701	3060.62576691	7.67302299	0.00032673	0.13032673
50	450.73592516	0.00221859	3459.50711660	7.67524158	0.00028906	0.13028906

Answers to Selected Exercises

Chapter 1
Section 1.1 (page 10)

1. $\frac{14}{9}$ **3.** $\frac{29}{10}$ **5.** $\frac{155}{13}$ **7.** $\frac{101}{8}$ **9.** $\frac{2}{3}$ **11.** $\frac{8}{15}$ **13.** $\frac{9}{10}$ **15.** $\frac{4}{5}$ **17.** $\frac{11}{12}$ **19.** $\frac{8}{15}$ **21.** $2\frac{4}{7}$

23. $3\frac{4}{5}$ **25.** $1\frac{3}{11}$ **27.** $3\frac{7}{11}$ **29.** $1\frac{62}{63}$ **31.** $2\frac{8}{37}$ **35.** $1\frac{1}{5}$ **37.** $\frac{17}{20}$ **39.** $1\frac{7}{60}$ **41.** $\frac{19}{22}$ **43.** $1\frac{23}{36}$

45. $2\frac{5}{24}$ **47.** $70\frac{4}{7}$ **49.** $80\frac{3}{4}$ **51.** $97\frac{7}{40}$ **53.** 187 **55.** $\frac{2}{3}$ **57.** $\frac{1}{2}$ **59.** $\frac{1}{6}$ **61.** $\frac{1}{3}$ **63.** $12\frac{1}{8}$

65. $3\frac{11}{24}$ **67.** $9\frac{1}{24}$ **69.** $3\frac{11}{12}$ **75.** $\frac{7}{8}$ interest **77.** $104\frac{5}{12}$ ft. **79.** $\frac{19}{24}$ **81.** $14\frac{23}{24}$ **83.** $14\frac{7}{16}$ tons

85. $619\frac{5}{12}$ ft. **87.** $9\frac{1}{6}$ hrs. **89.** $1\frac{23}{24}$ cu. yds.

Section 1.2 (page 19)

1. $\frac{5}{8}$ **3.** $\frac{1}{2}$ **5.** 4 **7.** 69 **9.** $\frac{1}{3}$ **11.** 90 **13.** $2\frac{1}{10}$ **15.** $\frac{35}{108}$ **17.** $1\frac{1}{2}$ **19.** $\frac{2}{3}$ **21.** $3\frac{1}{3}$

23. $\frac{8}{11}$ **27.** $2260 **29.** $1341 **31.** $1828 **33.** $\frac{9}{25}$ **35.** $\frac{42}{125}$ **37.** $\frac{12}{125}$ **39.** $\frac{7}{8}$ **41.** $\frac{51}{200}$

43. $\frac{3}{16}$ **45.** 78.4; 78.41 **47.** 0.1; 0.08 **49.** 7.4; 7.45 **51.** 59.0; 58.96 **53.** 0.625 **55.** 0.938

57. 0.167 **59.** 0.813 **61.** 0.111 **63.** 0.856 **69.** 56 bottles **71.** 35 salt shakers **73.** $\frac{1}{32}$ of the estate

75. 157 rolls **77.** $120,000

Section 1.3 (page 27)

1. 104.58 **3.** 44,904.75 **5.** 733.45 **7.** 56.51 **9.** 20.45 **11.** 58.9 **13.** .49 **15.** 133.14 **17.** 8.1

19. 566.14 **21.** 0.63 **23.** 5794.44 **25.** 0.09 **29.** $29,167.32 **31.** $829.25 **33.** (a) $1164.05

(b) $95.13

Summary Exercise (page 32)

(a) $1031.25 **(b)** $1121.25 **(c)** $1625 **(d)** $1535 **(e)** $413.75

Chapter 1 Review Exercises (page 32)

1. $\frac{4}{5}$ **2.** $\frac{1}{2}$ **3.** $\frac{1}{3}$ **4.** $\frac{1}{2}$ **5.** $\frac{9}{10}$ **6.** $\frac{11}{12}$ **7.** $\frac{1}{50}$ **8.** $\frac{8}{11}$ **9.** $3\frac{1}{6}$ **10.** $1\frac{9}{16}$ **11.** $1\frac{7}{12}$

12. $7\frac{6}{7}$ **13.** $2\frac{1}{13}$ **14.** $8\frac{1}{6}$ **15.** $2\frac{8}{37}$ **16.** $2\frac{19}{256}$ **17.** $\frac{19}{22}$ **18.** $\frac{19}{24}$ **19.** $\frac{1}{2}$ **20.** $\frac{7}{24}$ **21.** $71\frac{5}{6}$

22. $91\frac{5}{6}$ **23.** $4\frac{1}{4}$ **24.** $6\frac{29}{48}$ **25.** $4\frac{1}{8}$ cans **26.** $15\frac{1}{6}$ gal. **27.** $319\frac{1}{2}$ ft. **28.** $34\frac{11}{24}$ lbs. **29.** $\frac{9}{40}$

30. $\frac{7}{40}$ **31.** $1\frac{2}{3}$ **32.** 16 **33.** $3\frac{21}{32}$ **34.** $\frac{35}{64}$ **35.** $20\frac{5}{6}$ **36.** $6\frac{1}{6}$ **37.** $146.40 **38.** 18 bags

39. $\frac{5}{32}$ **40.** $152\frac{4}{9}$ ounces **41.** $\frac{7}{25}$ **42.** $\frac{7}{8}$ **43.** $\frac{3}{16}$ **44.** $\frac{1}{200}$ **45.** 56.2; 56.21

46. 7215.6; 7215.64   **47.** 0.7; 0.72   **48.** 8.0; 8.03   **49.** 0.625   **50.** 0.111   **51.** 0.833   **52.** 0.760

53. 476.61   **54.** 714.11   **55.** 60.04   **56.** 200.01   **57.** 192.21   **58.** 10,198.62   **59.** 3.31   **60.** 66.31

Chapter 2

Section 2.1 (page 40)

1. 5   **3.** 10   **5.** 6   **7.** 8   **9.** 35   **11.** 2   **13.** 3   **15.** 6   **17.** .8   **19.** 3.6   **21.** 20   **23.** 7   **25.** $6\frac{2}{3}$

27. 12   **29.** $\frac{5}{6}$ **31.** $\frac{2}{11}$ **33.** 5   **35.** 8   **37.** $1\frac{2}{3}$ **39.** $1\frac{3}{16}$ **41.** $\frac{2}{3}$ **43.** 9   **45.** $3\frac{1}{5}$ **47.** 13   **49.** 20

51. 3   **53.** 7   **55.** 2   **57.** 3   **59.** $\frac{2}{3}$ **61.** 1.6   **63.** 2.1   **65.** 2.1694

Section 2.2 (page 46)

1. $5 + x$ **3.** $x + 1$ **5.** $x + 16$ **7.** $x - 3$ **9.** $x - 15$ **11.** $9x$ **13.** $2x$ **15.** $\frac{x}{11}$ **17.** $\frac{x}{4}$ **19.** $8(x + 3)$

21. $7(x - 3)$ **23.** $53x$ **25.** $73 - x$ **27.** $\frac{172}{x}$ **29.** $21 - x$ **31.** $2b + 5d$ **33.** 6   **35.** 2   **37.** 1   **39.** $1\frac{3}{7}$

41. 89   **43.** 146   **45.** $300   **47.** 42—deluxe; 63—economy   **49.** $17,600—pr; $26,400—fou   **51.** 47 inches; 59 inches   **53.** 28—new; 35—exp

Section 2.3 (page 51)

1. 185   **3.** 3   **5.** 0.0625   **7.** 14   **9.** 10   **11.** 21   **13.** 2   **15.** 3   **17.** 7   **19.** 24,000   **21.** $\frac{A}{L}$ **23.** $\frac{V}{LW}$

25. $\frac{I}{PR}$ **27.** $\frac{P - 2W}{2}$ **29.** $\frac{2A}{(b + B)}$ **31.** $\frac{M - P}{PT}$ **33.** $\frac{A - P}{P}$ **35.** $117.75   **37.** $105   **39.** (a) $194.56

(b) $213.88   (c) $229.42   **41.** $60,000   **43.** $48   **45.** $90,000   **47.** 25   **49.** $15,500   **51.** 8%   **53.** 5 yrs.

55. $1400

Section 2.4 (page 58)

1. $\frac{5}{3}$ **3.** $\frac{43}{51}$ **5.** $\frac{2}{5}$ **7.** $\frac{2}{3}$ **9.** $\frac{2}{15}$ **11.** $\frac{8}{5}$ **13.** $\frac{1}{6}$ **15.** $\frac{4}{15}$ **17.** $\frac{9}{2}$ **19.** T   **21.** T   **23.** F   **25.** F

27. F   **29.** T   **31.** T   **33.** F   **35.** T   **37.** T   **39.** 16   **41.** 25   **43.** 16   **45.** $3\frac{1}{2}$ **47.** 24   **49.** 8

53. 475   **55.** 576 miles   **57.** 3850   **59.** $456,000   **61.** 15   **63.** $144   **65.** $14,000   **67.** 84   **69.** $.15

Summary Exercise (page 61)

(a) $20.85   (b) $6.95   (c) $423.95

Chapter 2 Review Exercises (page 61)

1. 27   **2.** 10   **3.** 7   **4.** $\frac{2}{3}$ **5.** 30   **6.** 30   **7.** 56   **8.** -18 **9.** $\frac{-3}{4}$ **10.** $\frac{-7}{3}$ **11.** 19.32   **12.** 4.18

13. $5x$ **14.** $\frac{1}{2}x$ **15.** $x + 6x$ **16.** $5x - 11$ **17.** $3x + 7$ **18.** $2250   **19.** 180 movies   **20.** $108—water;

$432—phone   **21.** 76   **22.** 70—child; 30—ad   **23.** $4000   **24.** $3250   **25.** 160   **26.** $\frac{P - kx^2}{v}$ **27.** $\frac{A - 2L}{2}$

28. $\frac{9}{5}C + 32$ **29.** $\frac{4}{3}$ **30.** $\frac{18}{1}$ **31.** $\frac{20}{1}$ **32.** $\frac{12}{5}$ **33.** $\frac{8}{3}$ **34.** $\frac{4}{3}$ **35.** $\frac{10}{3}$ **36.** $\frac{20}{9}$ **37.** $\frac{48}{5}$ **38.** $\frac{15}{4}$

39. 72   **40.** 14   **41.** $12.75   **42.** 105   **43.** $57,000   **44.** $139.50   **45.** 25

Chapter 3

Section 3.1 (page 67)

1. 80%   **3.** 0.7%   **5.** 140%   **7.** 37.5%   **9.** 412.5%   **11.** 0.25%   **13.** 75%   **15.** 10%   **17.** 40%
19. 62.5%   **21.** 12.5%   **23.** 0.5%   **25.** 0.18   **27.** 0.65   **29.** 0.006   **31.** 0.0025   **33.** 1.25   **35.** 2.006
41. 0.25; 25%   **43.** $\frac{1}{20}$; 0.05   **45.** $\frac{3}{4}$; 75%   **47.** 6.125; 612.5%   **49.** $7\frac{1}{4}$; 725%   **51.** $\frac{1}{400}$; 0.25%
53. 0.333 (rounded); $33\frac{1}{3}$%   **55.** $\frac{3}{400}$; 0.0075   **57.** $\frac{1}{40}$; 2.5%   **59.** $\frac{7}{20}$; 0.35   **61.** $23\frac{41}{50}$; 2382%
63. $\frac{3}{8}$; 0.375

Section 3.2 (page 74)

1. 10.92   **3.** 244.35   **5.** 4   **7.** 10,185   **9.** 121   **11.** 148.44   **13.** 5366.65   **15.** 7   **19.** $20,825
21. $645   **23.** (a) $290   (b) $3480   **25.** 46 seniors   **27.** 80 cans   **29.** $632.50   **31.** 2156 products
33. $16,574.25   **35.** $51,844.20   **37.** $510,390   **39.** $45,500

Section 3.3 (page 78)

1. 2500   **3.** 187.5   **5.** 20,000   **7.** 96   **9.** 20,000   **11.** 875   **13.** 6698.67   **15.** 130,800   **17.** 27
21. 9278 stores   **23.** 7761 students   **25.** 2,019,000 tons   **27.** $47,517.65   **29.** 48.7 gallons   **31.** $185,500

Supplementary Exercises on Base and Part (page 80)

1. 478,175 Mustangs   **3.** $288,150   **5.** $3815   **7.** $1261.50   **9.** $29,370   **11.** 193,400 teachers   **13.** $23

Section 3.4 (page 84)

1. 50   **3.** 175   **5.** 5.0   **7.** 250   **9.** 0.8   **11.** 1.4   **13.** 13.9   **15.** 6.9   **17.** 25.7   **21.** 65.9%   **23.** 15.5%
25. 8.7%   **27.** 15.1%   **29.** 32.5%

Supplementary Exercises on Rate, Base, and Part (page 85)

1. 4.9%   **3.** 16.9%   **5.** $396.05   **7.** 248.6 million   **9.** 27.2%   **11.** 24%   **13.** $97,896   **15.** .5%
17. $7970   **19.** 128%   **21.** $674.4 million   **23.** (a) 46.6%   (b) 22.0%   (c) 31.4%   **25.** 1300%   **27.** $137,023

Section 3.5 (page 92)

1. $700   **3.** $18.69   **5.** $20   **7.** $818.18   **9.**   **11.** $3660   **13.** $256   **15.** 179,000   **17.** 160 feet
19. $63.40   **21.** $9840   **23.** $58.9 billion   **25.** $3864   **27.** 78,000   **29.** 51.2 million   **31.** 20,000 students
33. $30.25 or $$30\frac{1}{4}$

Summary Exercise (page 97)

 $4; $30; $1.50; $1200; $9; $18; $25; $15

Chapter 3 Review Exercises (page 98)

1. 0.12   **2.** 37.6   **3.** 0.035   **4.** 1100   **5.** 12.6%   **6.** 5%   **7.** 0.0075   **8.** 800   **9.** 480   **10.** $6.50
11. $850   **12.** 4%   **13.** (a) higher   (b) 3.1%   **14.** $1096.70   **15.** 21.0   **16.** $762.20   **17.** 7.2%
18. 16%   **19.** 61.4%   **20.** 5000 lbs.   **21.** (a) $46,760   (b) 2.5%   **22.** 32 in.   **23.** $10,660   **24.** $8200
25. $16,800   **26.** 1,974,320 tons   **27.** $10.625   **28.** $85,375   **29.** 8.5%   **30.** $630   **31.** 27%   **32.** $128

Chapter 4

Section 4.1 (page 106)

1. $12.80   **3.** $15.50   **5.** $0   **7.** $28.40   **9.** $4517.34   **11.** $1739.54   **17.** $9519.29   **19.** $1791.39
21. $3097.49

Section 4.2 (page 112)

1. (a) $1700.42   (b) $153.58   (c) $1546.84   (d) $46.41   **3.** (a) $1591.44   (b) $189.39   (c) $1402.05
(d) $56.08   **5.** (a) $710.22   (b) $90.12   (c) $620.10   (d) $18.60

Section 4.3 (page 120)

1. $5632.97   **3.** $7690.62   **5.** $29,981.68   **7.** $7019.52   **9.** $3749.10   **11.** $4496.01   **17.** $5657.67

Summary Exercise (page 124)

$3222.54

Chapter 4 Review Exercises (page 125)

1. $34,750.23   **2.** $34,549.91   **3.** $35,392.77   **4.** $21,072.62   **5.** $16,746.95   **6.** $928.15   **7.** $114.27
8. $813.88   **9.** $20.35   **10.** $3021.58   **11.** $8992.02   **12.** $6728.20

Chapter 5

Section 5.1 (page 136)

1. 39; 0; $9.18   **3.** $38\frac{3}{4}$; 0; $9.30   **5.** 40; $3\frac{1}{4}$; $15.42   **7.** $238.68; $0; $238.68   **9.** $240.25; $0; $240.25

11. $411.20; $50.12; $461.32   **13.** $7.65; $191.25; $0; $191.25   **15.** $9.30; $248; $51.15; $299.15   **17.** $12.27;
$327.20; $42.95; $370.15   **19.** 51; 11; $2.90; $295.80; $31.90; $327.70   **21.** $52\frac{1}{4}$; $12\frac{1}{4}$; $5.30; $553.85; $64.93;
$618.78   **23.** $48\frac{1}{2}$; $8\frac{1}{2}$; $4.10; $397.70; $34.85; $432.55   **25.** 35; 5; $8.97; $209.30; $44.85; 254.15   **27.** $39\frac{1}{2}$;
$3\frac{3}{4}$; $10.05; $264.65; $37.69; $302.34   **29.** $39\frac{3}{4}$; $3\frac{1}{2}$; $15.30; $405.45; $53.55; $459   **33.** $670; $725.83;
$1451.67; $17,420   **35.** $426; $923; $1846; $22,152   **37.** $286.15; $572.31; $1240; $14,880   **39.** $618.46;
$1236.92; $1340; $32,160   **41.** $343.85; $687.69; $745; $1490   **43.** $465.50   **45.** $487.70   **47.** $703.08
49. $394.40   **51.** $335.40   **53.** $521.38   **55.** $851.20   **57.** (a) $840   (b) $910   (c) $1820   (d) $21,840

Section 5.2 (page 144)

1. $351.52   **3.** $543.30   **5.** $1941.75   **7.** $433.37   **9.** $129.60   **11.** $90.68   **13.** $62.92   **15.** $113.60
19. $3920; $235.30; $535.20   **21.** $4085; $245.10; $245.10   **23.** $3530; $105.90; $105.90   **25.** $2897;
$144.85; $354.85   **27.** $546.80   **29.** $2555   **31.** (a) $1247.50   (b) $747.50   **33.** $412.14

Section 5.3 (page 150)

1. 326; $208.64   **3.** 435; $226.20   **5.** 665; $452.20   **7.** 588; $270.48   **9.** 670; $522.60   **11.** $85.05
13. $89.04   **15.** $62.25   **17.** $92.48   **19.** $154.72   **21.** $191.44   **23.** $260.19   **25.** $254.90
27. $198   **29.** $274.80   **31.** $352.25   **33.** $354.34   **35.** $322.57   **37.** $340.73   **41.** $449.36
43. $379.71   **45.** $180.26

Section 5.4 (page 158)

1. $16.50; $3.81   **3.** $54.65; $12.61   **5.** $15.66; $3.61   **7.** $34.20; $7.89   **9.** $5.47   **11.** $278.10
13. $11.72   **15.** $370.50; 0; $370.50; $24.08; $5.56; $4.63   **17.** $323.20; $57.57; $380.77; $24.75; $5.71;
$4.76   **19.** $204; $38.25; $242.25; $15.75; $3.63; $3.03   **21.** $249.60; $63.18; $312.78; $20.33; $4.69;
$3.91   **23.** (a) $40.83   (b) $9.42   **25.** (a) $100.30   (b) $23.15   (c) $19.29   **27.** $2661.57; $614.21
29. $4265.94; $1067.53   **31.** $3039.99; $701.54

Section 5.5 (page 166)

1. $173   **3.** $61   **5.** $86   **7.** $110   **9.** $184   **11.** $8.99   **13.** $19.57   **15.** $7.28   **17.** $1.80; $22.63;
$5.22; $318.47   **19.** $170.48; $99.59; $22.98; $1239.13   **21.** $276.62; $214.66; $49.54; $2761.64   **23.** $343.82;
$256.24; $59.13; $3282.93   **25.** $91.82; $44.80; $10.34; $542.20   **27.** $44.74; $25.32; $5.84; $313.57
29. $823.56; $345.32; $79.69; $4064.02   **31.** $44.37; $28.03; $6.47; $352.38   **35.** $433.10   **37.** $440.21
39. $3270.95

Section 5.6 (page 174)

1. $593.02   **3.** $2794.04   **5.** $4522.12   **7.** $9996.26   **9.** $2579.92   **11.** $13,354.58   **13.** $13,092.06
15. $18,155.85   **19.** $7016.98   **21.** $3851.58   **23.** (a) $1120   (b) $69.44   **25.** (a) $1600   (b) $99.20

Summary Exercise (page 178)

(a) $680   **(b)** $306   **(c)** $986   **(d)** $64.09   **(e)** $14.79   **(f)** $200.57   **(g)** $12.33   **(h)** $80.08
(i) $492.14

Chapter 5 Review Exercises (page 179)

1. 40; $15\frac{3}{4}$; $426.29   **2.** 40; 8; $442   **3.** 40; $3\frac{1}{2}$; $321.28   **4.** 40; $17\frac{1}{4}$; $447.95   **5.** $750; $812.50; $1625;
$19,500   **6.** $265; $574.17; $1148.33; $13,780   **7.** $346.15; $692.31; $750; $1500   **8.** $403.85; $807.69;
$1750; $21,000   **9.** $498.75   **10.** $427.50   **11.** $1560.32   **12.** $915.48   **13.** $242.75   **14.** $382.50
15. $1968.75   **16.** $420   **17.** $382.80   **18.** $265.02   **19.** (a) $334.75   (b) $77.25   **20.** (a) $217.75
(b) $77.25   **21.** $57   **22.** $141   **23.** $208   **24.** $65   **25.** $18   **26.** $52   **27.** $1065.54   **28.** $268.05
29. $398.80   **30.** $2035.22   **31.** $19,182.41   **32.** (a) $33.44   (b) $7.72   (c) $6.43   **33.** (a) $142.60
(b) $49.19   **34.** $5451.25   **35.** (a) $913   (b) $56.61   **36.** (a) $2140   (b) $132.68

Chapter 6

Section 6.1 (page 188)

1. $.25; $.15; $5.40   **3.** $2.27; $4.16; $44.23   **5.** $8.68; $14.85; $197.03   **7.** $44.17; $58.89; $839.21
9. $1470; $504; $31,374   **11.** $31.50; $32.76   **13.** $167.20; $175.56   **15.** $330; $339.90   **17.** $540.33;
$572.75   **19.** $20.50; $.82   **21.** $119.33; $3.58   **23.** $19.81; $.79   **25.** $639.54; $31.98   **27.** $2753.05;
$192.71   **31.** (a) $.90   (b) $3.00   (c) $33.85   **33.** $368   **35.** $1980   **37.** $49.44   **39.** $6.48   **41.** $201.35
43. $24,224.75

Section 6.2 (page 194)

1. $31,050   **3.** $13,000   **5.** $1,840,000   **7.** 3%   **9.** 3.6%   **11.** 3%   **13.** (a) 2.8%   (b) $2.80   (c) $28
15. (a) $2.41   (b) $24.10   (c) 24.1   **17.** (a) 3.48%   (b) $34.80   (c) 34.8   **21.** $31,044.50   **23.** $47,498.22
25. $915   **27.** 7.6%   **29.** $8076.60   **31.** $5.25   **33.** $236,800   **35.** $5007.24   **37.** $1877.72
39. $377,175   **41.** $164,800   **43.** 8.4%   **45.** $2500

Section 6.3 (page 208)

1. $19,079   **3.** $21,710   **5.** $43,108   **7.** $13,850; $2077.50   **9.** $12,722; $1915.80   **11.** $43,050; $7634
13. $22,750; $3724.50   **15.** $26,668; $4821.54   **17.** $39,254; $6571.12   **19.** $988.22 refund
21. $796.02 due   **23.** $533.85 due   **27.** $1167.90   **29.** $4006.18   **31.** $6738   **33.** $2630.55

Summary Exercise (page 212)

(a) Anderson: $3,143,664; Bentonville: $3,488,706   **(b)** Anderson: $785,916; Bentonville: $697,741.20
(c) Anderson: $25,149.31; Bentonville: $20,583.37   **(d)** Anderson: $3,395,157.10; Bentonville: $3,694,539.70

Chapter 6 Review Exercises (page 213)

1. $11.22; $30.86; $322.58   **2.** $3; $5; $57.95   **3.** $825; $660; $17,985   **4.** $24.22; $40.19; $410.37
5. $70   **6.** $142   **7.** $189   **8.** $131.33   **9.** $138   **10.** $170   **11.** $279   **12.** $163   **13.** 1.75%; $17.50;
17.5   **14.** 2.7%; $2.70; $27   **15.** $1.27; $12.70; 12.7   **16.** 2.03%; $2.03; 20.3   **17.** $5985
18. $22.50   **19.** $46,500   **20.** 2.8%   **21.** $96,200   **22.** $2278.40   **23.** $27,733; $5119.74   **24.** $12,271;
$1840.65   **25.** $40,512; $6923.36   **26.** $41,668; $9021.54   **27.** 2.9%   **28.** $194.88   **29.** $11,825.24
30. $6605.84   **31.** $3867.02   **32.** $7819.92   **33.** $1682.96 due   **34.** $427.10 due   **35.** $1694.61 refund
36. $710.10 due

Chapter 7

Section 7.1 (page 224)

1. $670   **3.** $1097.25   **5.** $9298.72   **7.** $8973.18   **9.** $495   **11.** $228.90   **13.** $221.70   **15.** $243
17. (a) $780   (b) $780   **19.** (a) $780   (b) $1092   **21.** (a) $1904   (b) $1360   **23.** $9400   **25.** $4000
27. $33,518.75   **29.** $12,554.95   **31.** $28,800; $19,200   **33.** $60,667; $39,000; $30,333   **35.** (a) $22,500
(b) A: $15,000; B: $7500   (c) $7500   **37.** (a) $12,500   (b) 1: $7500; 2: $5000   (c) $7500   **39.** $2589.60
41. $393.05   **43.** $510   **45.** $412.50   **47.** (a) $416   (b) $832   **49.** (a) $1134   (b) $810   **53.** (a) $7366.07
(b) $133.93   **55.** (a) $24,545.45   (b) $11,454.55   **59.** A: $8636 B: $17,273 C: $12,091   **61.** (a) $37,500
(b) A: $28,125 B: $9375   **63.** (a) $75,000   (b) 1: $41,666.67   2: $20,833.33   3: $12,500

Section 7.2 (page 233)

1. $447   **3.** $405   **5.** $244.95   **7.** $507   **9.** $591   **11.** $215   **15.** $440.45   **17.** $673.75
19. (a) $15,000   (b) $7000   **21.** (a) $1778   (b) $6936   (c) $100,000   (d) $15,100   **23.** (a) $60,000
(b) $31,208

Section 7.3 (page 246)

1. $365.20; $186.25; $94.95; $33.16   **3.** $924.75; $471.62; $240.44; $83.97   **5.** $2928.25; $1493.41; $761.35;
$265.89   **7.** $354.50; $180.80; $92.17; $32.19   **9.** $255.50; $130.31; $66.43; $23.20   **11.** $1573.25; $802.36;
$409.05; $142.85   **13.** $821.70; $419.07; $213.64; $74.61   **17.** $9440   **19.** $15,690   **21.** $400
23. 23 yrs. 315 days   **25.** $115.60   **27.** 18   **29.** $143.40   **31.** (a) $1240.20   (b) $36,000   **33.** $7284
35. (a) $444.72   (b) $226.72   (c) $79.18   **37.** (a) $5660   (b) $11,580   (c) 23 yrs. 315 days   **39.** −$4904
41. (a) $211.50   (b) approx. 20 yrs.   (c) $115.75   (d) $109.50   **43.** (a) $345.50   (b) 18 yrs.   (c) $297
(d) $286.50

Summary Exercise (page 252)

(a) $18,822.90   **(b)** $705.79   **(c)** $19,528.69   **(d)** $971.31

Chapter 7 Review Exercises (page 253)

1. $1995.50   **2.** $3417.90   **3.** $434   **4.** $1028   **5.** $156   **6.** $319.80   **7.** $222.90   **8.** $1007.30
9. (a) $255   (b) $765   **10.** (a) $1424   (b) $712   **11.** (a) $792   (b) $72   **12.** (a) $464   (b) $2320
13. $19,736.84   **14.** $24,229.73   **15.** $2731.66   **16.** $35,707.69   **17.** $263   **18.** $815.30   **19.** $502.60
20. $524   **21.** $1569   **22.** $527.20   **23.** $369.90   **24.** $677.80   **25.** A: $10,500 B: $7000 C: $3500
26. (a) $125,762   (b) 1: $80,030   2: $45,732   **27.** (a) $25,000   (b) $9000   **28.** (a) $15,000   (b) $0
29. (a) $40,000   (b) $36,800   **30.** (a) $552.84   (b) $281.84   (c) $98.43   (d) $1105.68; $1127.36; $1181.16
31. $21,852   **32.** (a) $11,320   (b) $23,160   (c) 23 yrs. 315 days   **33.** −$7972   **34.** (a) $231.20
(b) about 18 yrs.   (c) $185.20   (d) $179.60

Chapter 8

Section 8.1 (page 264)

1. at   **3.** sack   **5.** great gross   **7.** case   **9.** drum   **11.** cost per thousand   **13.** each   **15.** carton
17. $12.50; $30.00; $21.60; $21.60; $125.00; $210.70; $220.60   **21.** 0.56   **23.** 0.8075   **25.** 0.75

27. 0.4025   **29.** 0.336   **31.** 0.684   **33.** $459   **35.** $4.32   **37.** $532   **39.** $384.75   **41.** $11.81   **43.** $1000
49. (a) 15/20   (b) $.55   **51.** $352.51   **53.** $164.25   **55.** $459.65   **57.** (a) 15/10/5   (b) $1090.13
59. $26.38

Section 8.2 (page 271)

1. 0.5525, 44.75%   **3.** 0.6, 40%   **5.** 0.64, 36%   **7.** 0.576, 42.4%   **9.** 0.675, 32.5%   **11.** 0.75, 25%
13. 0.648, 35.2%   **15.** 0.243, 75.7%   **17.** 0.45, 55%   **19.** 0.7, 30%   **21.** 0.5184, 48.16%   **23.** 0.5054,
49.46%   **27.** $450   **29.** $5250   **31.** $1920   **33.** (a) 20/15/10   (b) 0.012 or 1.2%   **35.** $700
37. (a) $60.17   (b) $66.85 (c) $6.68   **39.** 18.0%   **41.** $3857.14   **43.** 5.0%

Section 8.3 (page 278)

1. Dec. 8; Dec. 23   **3.** July 25; Sept. 8   **5.** Oct. 1; Oct. 11   **7.** Jan. 24; March 15   **9.** Jan. 20; Mar. 6
11. $.78; $37.97   **13.** $0; $81.25   **15.** $12.70; $675.48   **17.** $32.78; $3245.22   **19.** $19.26; $622.74
23. $1258.88   **25.** $278.48   **27.** $12.70   **29.** $2511.13   **31.** $23.29   **33.** (a) Jan. 28, Feb. 7, Feb. 17
(b) Mar. 9   **35.** (a) April 25 (b) May 5   **37.** $2170.01

Section 8.4 (page 283)

1. April 7; April 27   **3.** Dec. 22; Jan. 11   **5.** May 8; May 28   **7.** Aug. 10; Aug. 30   **9.** June 20; July 10
11. $13.80; $1366.20   **13.** $0; $194.04   **15.** $59.20; $2900.80   **17.** $10.69; $345.51   **19.** $.25; $12.13
21. $97.52; $3153.08   **23.** $68.33; $1639.85   **27.** $280; $245   **29.** $318; $557   **31.** $100; $60
35. (a) May 10   (b) May 30   **37.** (a) May 13   (b) June 2   **39.** $1695.40   **41.** (a) Nov. 10   (b) Nov. 30
43. $122.51   **45.** (a) $1000   (b) $920   **47.** $1495.58   **49.** $93.02   **51.** (a) $153.06   (b) $110.34
53. (a) $597.94   (b) $194.64

Summary Exercise (page 289)

(a) $2856.96   **(b)** Nov. 10   **(c)** Nov. 30   **(d)** $2890.05

Chapter 8 Review Exercises (page 290)

1. $142.80; $367.20   **2.** $10.78; $26.22   **3.** $164.85; $253.15   **4.** $793.80; $826.20   **5.** 0.6375; 36.25%
6. 0.729; 27.1%   **7.** 0.4; 60%   **8.** 0.4032; 59.68%   **9.** $855.36   **10.** $167.36   **11.** $537.09   **12.** $2262.11
13. Mar. 14; April 3   **14.** Nov. 21; Dec. 11   **15.** Feb. 15; Mar. 7   **16.** Aug. 7; Aug. 27   **17.** $1.48; $72.70
18. $3.55; $130.37   **19.** $35.02; $907.66   **20.** $44.21; $2166.39   **21.** $101.01; $118.99   **22.** $857.14;
$912.86   **23.** $505.05; $354.95   **24.** $2113.40; $1736.60   **25.** (a) $362.10   (b) $373.82   **26.** $348.80
27. $370   **28.** 10%   **29.** $1779.95   **30.** (a) $1875   (b) $3405   (c) $75

Chapter 9

Section 9.1 (page 298)

1. $1.20; $4.20   **3.** 60%; $19.20   **5.** $39.80; 25.1%   **7.** $67.50; 20%   **9.** $118; 56.2%   **11.** $44.55; $209.55
15. $6.53   **17.** $128   **19.** $9.07   **21.** $5.20   **23.** 17.8%   **25.** (a) 126%   (b) $5.67   (c) $1.17   **27.** 400%
29. (a) $775   (b) 12%   (c) $93   **31.** $6.63

Section 9.2 (page 305)

1. $12.48; $35.66   **3.** $131.48; $243.48   **5.** $.22; $1   **7.** $8.21; $2.74   **9.** $77.82; 35.2%   **11.** $460; $575
13. $4.23; $11.13; 61.3%   **15.** $375; $525; 28.6%   **17.** $178.76; 22%   **19.** 20%   **21.** 35.1%

23. 33.3% or $33\frac{1}{3}$%   **25.** 66.7% or $66\frac{2}{3}$%   **29.** $550   **31.** 35%   **33.** $109.62   **35.** (a) $13.50   (b) $8.64

(c) 64%   **37.** 33.3% or $33\frac{1}{3}$%   **39.** (a) $18.70   (b) $8.80   (c) 32%   **41.** (a) $13,680   (b) $6080

(c) 44.4%   **43.** (a) 45%   (b) 81.8%   **45.** (a) 87.5%   (b) 700%   **47.** (a) 43.8%   (b) 30.4%   **49.** (a) $32.40

(b) 25.9%   **51.** (a) $24.90   (b) 12.5%   (c) 14.2%

Section 9.3 (page 310)

1. $5   **3.** $2   **5.** $9   **7.** $1.65   **9.** 19; $5   **11.** 18; $22   **13.** 76 pr.; $3.75   **15.** 1900 gal.; $16.58
17. 45; 5; $3.11   **19.** 19;1; $97.89   **21.** 108;36; $4.17   **23.** 350; 150; $4.71   **27.** $4.22   **29.** $10.50
31. $3.07   **33.** $308.75   **35.** $25.40   **37.** $24.13

Summary Exercise (page 315)

(a) $8058.20   **(b)** $10,063.50   **(c)** $2005.30   **(d)** 20%   **(e)** 25%

Chapter 9 Review Exercises (page 315)

1. $3.60; $15.60   **2.** $16; $20   **3.** $97.10; 52.0%   **4.** $59; 56.2%   **5.** $39.25; $112.15   **6.** $50; 40.1%
7. $34.70; $52.05   **8.** 32.5%; $572.30   **9.** $35.20; $70.40   **10.** $22.80; 100%; 50%   **11.** $1; 46%; 31.5%
12. $512.64; $640.80; 20%   **13.** 25%   **14.** 50%   **15.** 50%   **16.** 45.9%   **17.** $1.11   **18.** $7.50   **19.** $8.24
20. $12   **21.** 45; 5; $6.44   **22.** 72 pr.; 18 pr.; $2.38   **23.** 216; 72; $4.17   **24.** 700; 300; $4.71   **25.** $14
26. 30%   **27.** $3.85   **28.** 32.5%; 24.5%   **29.** (a) $19,050.25   (b) 47%   **30.** $4   **31.** (a) 25%   (b) 33.3%
or $33\frac{1}{3}$%   **32.** $4.12

Chapter 10

Section 10.1 (page 324)

1. 50%; $370   **3.** 35%; $.27   **5.** $120; $36   **7.** $2.70; $1.62   **9.** $18.30; $18.30   **11.** $857; 20%   **13.** $6.25;
$.75; none   **15.** $16; $22; $6   **17.** $200; $140; $16   **19.** $29; $10; $39   **23.** $29.50   **25.** 46%   **27.** $.60
profit   **29.** (a) $63.62 operating loss (b) $40.75 absolute loss (c) 27%   **31.** (a) $256.50 (b) 11%

Section 10.2 (page 328)

1. $8211   **3.** $19,672.67   **5.** $24,500   **7.** 2.81; 2.83   **9.** 7.94; 7.98   **11.** 10.25; 10.25   **13.** 4.66; 4.69
17. $54,080   **19.** 5.54   **21.** 6.32   **23.** 9.29   **25.** 3.64

Section 10.3 (page 336)

1. $534   **3.** $719   **5.** (a) $161 (b) $160 (c) $159   **7.** (a) $2352 (b) $2385 (c) $2313   **9.** $1607
11. (a) $48 (b) $50 (c) $51   **13.** (a) $1252 (b) $1430 (c) $1040   **15.** (a) $6142 (b) $6784 (c) $5500   **17.** $65,300
19. $30,660

Summary Exercise (page 341)

(a) $50 **(b)** $825 **(c)** $150 **(d)** None

Chapter 10 Review Exercises (page 341)

1. $9.15; $9.15 **2.** $30; $9 **3.** $10.80; $6.48 **4.** 35%; $409.50 **5.** $3.20; $4.40; $1.20 **6.** $18.75; $2.25; none **7.** $100; $70; $8 **8.** $6.25; $.75; none **9.** $17,840 **10.** $127,864 **11.** $76,411.80 **12.** $32,859.80 **13.** 2.81; 2.83 **14.** 7.94; 7.98 **15.** 4.66; 4.69 **16.** 4.56; 4.63 **17.** $713 **18.** $351 **19.** $3640 **20.** $4969 **21.** 33% **22.** (a) $78.40 (b) 7% **23.** $11,082 **24.** 14.58 **25.** 3.45 **26.** (a) $1476 (b) $2070 (c) $910.50 **27.** $115,000 **28.** $75,600

Chapter 11

Section 11.1 (page 348)

1. $144 **3.** $189 **5.** $9.73 **7.** $24.72 **9.** $206.25 **11.** $254.58 **13.** $644.90 **15.** $3821.17 **17.** $300 **19.** $4062.50 **21.** 7% **23.** 7 **25.** $5000 **27.** $4200 **29.** 11 **31.** 8% **33.** 20 yrs. **35.** $228 **37.** 0.667 yrs. or 8 mo. **39.** 4%

Section 11.2 (page 355)

1. 214 **3.** 71 **5.** 196 **7.** Aug. 11 **9.** July 28 **11.** Feb. 12 **13.** $82.64 **15.** $70.95 **17.** $736.86 **19.** $41.25 **21.** $67.13 **23.** $16 **25.** $187.20 **27.** $568.99 **29.** $114.68 **31.** $98.40 **35.** $20.82 **37.** $237.66 **39.** $12,069.51 **41.** (a) $2169.86 (b) $2200 (c) $30.14 **43.** (a) $6464.36 (b) $6554.14 (c) $89.78 **45.** $55.67

Section 11.3 (page 361)

1. $8000 **3.** $360 **5.** $400 **7.** $45,357.19 **9.** 8% **11.** 11.5% **13.** 7.2% **15.** 72 **17.** 130 **19.** 164 **21.** 270 days **23.** 6.8% **25.** $21,000 **27.** 45 days **29.** $400 **31.** 55 days **33.** 9.0% **35.** 21.0% **37.** $13.48

Section 11.4 (page 367)

1. $480; $4480 **3.** $610.50; $8010.50 **5.** $169.31; $2749.31 **7.** $263.25; $4163.25 **9.** 120; $8624 **11.** 9%; $12,138.75 **13.** $21,000; $315 **15.** $217.89; $4435.08 **17.** $126; 180 **19.** $42,459.44; 15% **21.** $32,500; 106 **23.** $7449.17 **25.** $112,042.50 **27.** 120; $1800 **29.** $16,000; $17,200

Section 11.5 (page 373)

1. $952.38 **3.** $4097.56 **5.** $9111.28 **7.** $8013.18 **9.** $3083.92 **11.** $606.56 **13.** $1566.31 **17.** $8415.58 **19.** $1211.76 **21.** $7104.85 **23.** $14,516.42 **25.** $5800 in 150 days

Summary Exercise (page 380)

(a) $380 **(b)** $9380 **(c)** $8821.32 **(d)** $9151.22

Chapter 11 Review Exercises (page 381)

1. $216 **2.** $371.25 **3.** $3333.33 **4.** $1538.46 **5.** 9% **6.** 7.5% **7.** 9 months **8.** 30 months
9. 114 days **10.** 66 days **11.** $18.00 **12.** $187.20 **13.** $222.51 **14.** $43.17 **15.** $70.95
16. $360 **17.** $6181.82 **18.** 7% **19.** 6% **20.** 120 **21.** 480 **22.** $1452 **23.** $1980
24. $12,180 **25.** $1421.80 **26.** $20,833.33 **27.** 9% **28.** 12% **29.** $1927.71
30. $11,612.90 **31.** $5070.75 **32.** $19,550.56 **33.** $809.69 **34.** $20,522.94 **35.** $237.50 **36.** 9%
37. 175 days **38.** 15% **39.** 9.5% **40.** 17.3% **41.** 90 days **42.** $9127.31 **43.** $19,528.16
44. $11,948.33

Chapter 12

Section 12.1 (page 390)

1. Helen Spence **3.** Donna Sharp **5.** 90 days **7.** Jan. 25 **9.** Sept. 24 **11.** Sept. 30 **13.** March 17
15. April 23 **17.** Nov. 9; $6225 **19.** Oct. 21; $7038 **21.** Dec. 23; $401.47 **23.** $16,000 **25.** 120 days
27. 12% **29.** $8879.07 **33.** (a) March 28 (b) $8403.75 **35.** (a) Dec. 9 (b) $17,893.75 **37.** (a) April 7
(b) $16,915.83 **39.** $15,000 **41.** 90 **43.** 8%

Section 12.2 (page 398)

1. $360; $11,640 **3.** $61; $1464 **5.** $292.75; $11,417.25 **7.** Nov. 17; $953.55 **9.** Feb. 21; $5568
11. 8/9; $360; $15,640 **13.** 11%; 8/7; $13,740 **15.** $7200; 6%; 2/10 **17.** $133.33; $4866.67 **19.** 120
21. 15% **23.** $5689.05 **25.** $3815; 12.1% **27.** $77,980.20; 14.7% **29.** $3920; $3921.57
31. (a) $4950 (b) $5000 (c) $50 (d) 4.04%

Section 12.3 (page 403)

1. 7.53% **3.** 11.31% **5.** 9.21% **7.** 5.66% **9.** 13.08% **11.** 14.29% **15.** 13% simple interest
17. 15.86%

Section 12.4 (page 408)

1. 120 days **3.** 53 days **5.** 22 days **7.** $5840 **9.** $3560 **11.** $5626.76 **13.** 61 days; $91.63;
$3513.37 **15.** 49 days; $41.81; $2006.19 **17.** 37 days; $159.31; $10,174.02 **19.** 39 days; $209.27;
$12,668.81 **21.** (a) 60 days (b) $102.09 (c) $6023.24 **23.** (a) $23.29 (b) $1011.71 **25.** (a) $1920
(b) $1980 (c) $60 **27.** (a) $2264 (b) $2361 (c) $97

Summary Exercise (page 413)

(a) $14,550 **(b)** $14,705 **(c)** $15,000 **(d)** 9.28%

Chapter 12 Review Exercises (page 413)

1. $80; $3080   **2.** 11%; $8440   **3.** 9%; $225   **4.** Sept. 8; $1235   **5.** Oct. 12; $3247.50   **6.** $270; $11,730
7. $304.95; $11,405.05   **8.** (a) 19 days (b) $7.86 (c) $985.04   **9.** (a) 17 days (b) $120.45 (c) $16,883.72
10. 12.37%   **11.** 9.40%   **12.** $9600   **13.** (a) $45.33 (b) $7112.17   **14.** $12,454.40   **15.** 9.8%   **16.** $9555
17. $6000   **18.** 270   **19.** $7654.29   **20.** $14,500   **21.** $12,307.69   **22.** 150 days   **23.** 80 days   **24.** 15.9%
25. 11.42%   **26.** $8318.53   **27.** 270   **28.** 17.37%   **29.** 15%   **30.** $21,475.78   **31.** $16,223.19   **32.** 17.14%
33. $7951.05   **34.** $6377.09   **35.** 13.48%   **36.** 11.35%

Chapter 13

Section 13.1 (page 423)

1. $1310.80; $310.80   **3.** $16,401.65; $1401.65   **5.** $1593.85   **7.** $30,273.75   **9.** $1341.54   **11.** $82,378.99
13. $15,154.55   **15.** $7737.21   **17.** $60,484.63   **19.** $2860.57   **21.** $300; $338.23; $38.23   **23.** $3163.37;
$3775.92; $612.55   **25.** 10.25%   **27.** 12.68%   **29.** (a) $2624.77 (b) $2667.70 (c) $2689.86 (d) $2704.89
(e) $2400.00   **31.** $12,043.41   **33.** (a) $11,248.64 ; $11,268.25 (b) $19.61   **35.** $10,538.50   **37.** $17,308.67
39. $58,863.88

Section 13.2 (page 433)

1. $7.51   **3.** $18.72   **5.** $112.84   **7.** $34.53   **9.** $7283.85   **11.** $3003.93   **13.** $5488.79   **15.** $11,540.26
17. $10,307.46   **19.** $27,079.11   **23.** $83.34; $7083.34   **25.** $176.27; $11,696.27   **27.** 0   **29.** (a) 14 months
(b) $5\frac{1}{8}$%   **31.** $265.70   **33.** $1648.72; $648.72   **35.** $9281.96; $5431.96   **37.** $8621.62; $502.08   **39.** 10%
compounded semiannually; $76.03

Section 13.3 (page 439)

1. 6   **3.** 2   **5.** 8   **7.** $1800   **9.** 7%   **11.** 6%   **13.** 12%   **17.** 4   **19.** 10%   **21.** approx. 24 yrs.
23. approx. 14 yrs.   **25.** approx. 12   **27.** $40,224.30   **29.** $8101.63   **31.** $22,244.99

Section 13.4 (page 443)

1. $666.34; $333.66   **3.** $1701.46; $998.54   **5.** $5268.28; $6231.72   **7.** $12,431.12; $32,364.88
11. $3564.93; $1435.07   **13.** $23,368.76   **15.** $1520 in 5 years   **17.** $38,288.45; $31,409.86   **19.** $43,400;
$32,607.06   **21.** $434,066.51

Summary Exercise (page 449)

(a) $7346.64   **(b)** $7401.22   **(c)** $7429.74   **(d)** $7459.12   **(e)** $5880.24   **(f)** $5845.52   **(g)** $5827.57

Chapter 13 Review Exercises (page 449)

1. $9021.78; $3021.78   **2.** $18,816; $3816   **3.** $13,022.60; $3022.60   **4.** $16,162.26; $4162.26   **5.** $17,169.22;
$5169.22   **6.** $11,451.24; $3451.24   **7.** 8.30%   **8.** 8.24%   **9.** 7.12%   **10.** 10.47%   **11.** $10.85   **12.** $80.25
13. $62.75   **14.** $3534.40   **15.** $7271.12   **16.** $7206.68   **17.** $4121.52   **18.** $8739.49   **19.** $5370.95
20. $1377.13; $377.13   **21.** $2822.96; $1022.96   **22.** 8%   **23.** 10%   **24.** 8%   **25.** 3   **26.** $3\frac{1}{2}$ **27.** $583.49
28. $2751.52   **29.** $6171.51   **30.** $6733.25   **31.** $27.89; $3542.89   **32.** $40,056.23; $22,056.23   **33.** $192.77
34. $29,462.37

Chapter 14

Section 14.1 (page 456)

1. $4071.34; $71.34   **3.** $17,161.92; $1361.92   **5.** $9862.15; $507.15   **9.** $47,038.63; $1313.63
11. $41,176.11; $1876.11   **13.** $11,516.12; $316.12

Section 14.2 (page 462)

1. $3.18   **3.** $2.73   **5.** $12.01   **7.** $5.05, $338.30, $338.30, $5.75, $378.13, $378.13, $6.43, $352.30, $352.30,
$5.99, $346.49   **9.** $13.99, $853.80, $853.80, $14.51, $1002.06, $1002.06, $17.04, $985.40, $985.40, $16.75,
$958.58   **11.** $2.81   **13.** $1.35   **15.** $2.07   **17.** $605.78; $9.09   **19.** $221.44; $3.32   **21.** $682.02;
$10.23

Section 14.3 (page 473)

1. $1200; $220   **3.** $315; $40   **5.** $3274.92; $374.13   **7.** 14.0%   **9.** 12.2%   **11.** 15.75%   **13.** 14%
17. 14.5%   **19.** (a) $7640 (b) 14.75%   **21.** 15.75%   **23.** (a) $28.72 (b) 15% (c) $6.81, $106.31, $438.70,
$438.70, $5.48, $107.64, $331.06, $331.06, $4.14, $108.98, $222.08, $222.08, $2.78, $110.34, $111.74, $111.74,
$113.14, $1.40, $111.74, $0

Section 14.4 (page 478)

1. $385.52   **3.** $15.26   **5.** $139.81   **9.** $19.37   **11.** $1.94   **13.** (a) $51.82 (b) $490.58

Summary Exercise (page 482)

(a) $1820.67   **(b)** $70.67   **(c)** $529.14   **(d)** $586.35   **(e)** Yes; $813.84

Chapter 14 Review Exercises (page 483)

1. $6638.63; $138.63   **2.** $7309.87; $309.87   **3.** $915.66; $115.66   **4.** $4641.89; $141.89   **5.** $6.43
6. $10.30   **7.** $13.83   **8.** $4.75, $344.53, $344.53, $5.17, $383.51, $383.51, $5.75, $339.97, $339.97, $5.10,
$237.68   **9.** $1.69   **10.** $3.25   **11.** $5.34   **12.** $552.56; $8.29   **13.** $216.25; $3.24   **14.** $1200; $275
15. $3180; $280   **16.** $11,260; $260   **17.** 8.6%   **18.** 13.6%   **19.** 11.4%   **20.** 16%   **21.** 14.5%   **22.** 15%
23. 14.5%   **24.** $33.75   **25.** $46.05   **26.** $16   **27.** $8.72   **28.** (a) $2788.22 (b) $173.22   **29.** $57.28; $.86
30. $12,092; 15%

Chapter 15

Section 15.1 (page 492)

1. 18.59891389   **3.** 21.82453114   **5.** 22.01900399   **7.** 299.12680533   **9.** 45.11550550   **11.** $2977.81;
$977.81   **13.** $110,284.74; $30,284.74   **15.** $388,629.98; $64,533.90   **17.** $17,459.62; $4659.62
19. $281,073.15; $43,413.15   **21.** $13,305.24; $4305.24   **23.** $138,997.66; $33,733.66   **27.** $12,522.84;
$3722.84   **29.** $5303.43; $1703.43   **31.** $526.95   **33.** $952.33   **35.** 29; $9698.06   **37.** 45; $40,745.91
39. $11,863.26; $863.26   **41.** $137,895.79; $29,895.79   **43.** $34,186.78; $14,706.78   **45.** $190.47
47. 31 months; $4075.14

Section 15.2 (page 499)

1. 11.46992122   **3.** 12.65929697   **5.** 14.71787378   **7.** $3790.79   **9.** $4595.25   **11.** $11,213.01
13. $69,996.18   **15.** $259,194.02   **19.** $221,523.53   **21.** $34,008.46   **23.** $12,675.75; $4124.25
25. $5499.16; $6400; $900.84   **27.** $34,773.48; $17,617.33   **29.** $79,636.35   **31.** second offer
33. $2,500,000 today

Section 15.3 (page 504)

1. 0.03721571   **3.** 0.02401196   **5.** $434.11   **7.** $1087.31   **9.** $1868.08   **13.** $4961.09; $20,622.56
15. $9572.45   **17.** $78,541.36   **19.** $404,143.76; $766,849.92   **21.** 169.78, 4414.28, 4414.28, 353.14,
6889.67, 6889.67, 2122.25, 551.17, 9563.09   **23.** (a) $1200   (b) $6511.67

(c)

Period	Beginning of Period Accumulated Amount	Periodic Deposit	End of Period Interest Earned	Accumulated Amount
1	$0	$6511.67	$0	$6511.67
2	$6511.67	$6511.67	$260.47	$13,283.81
3	$13,283.81	$6511.67	$531.35	$20,326.83
4	$20,326.83	$6511.67	$813.07	$27,651.57
5	$27,651.57	$6511.67	$1106.06	$35,269.30
6	$35,269.30	$6511.67	$1410.77	$43,191.74
7	$43,191.74	$6511.67	$1727.67	$51,431.08
8	$51,431.08	$6511.68	$2057.24	$60,000

Section 15.4 (page 516)

1. 0.05904742   **3.** 0.09167999   **5.** $179.14   **7.** $5054.93   **9.** $5970.35   **11.** $229.54   **15.** $15,707.08;
$195,454.88

17.

Payment Number	Amount of Payment	Interest for Period	Portion to Principal	Principal at End of Period
0	—	—	—	$4000
1	$1207.68	$320	$887.68	$3112.32
2	$1207.68	$248.99	$958.69	$2153.63
3	$1207.68	$172.29	$1035.39	$1118.24
4	$1207.70	$89.46	$1118.24	$0

19.

Payment Number	Amount of Payment	Interest for Payment	Portion to Principal	Principal at End of Period
0	—	—	—	$7184
1	$211.03	$107.76	$103.27	$7080.73
2	$211.03	$106.21	$104.82	$6975.91
3	$211.03	$104.64	$106.39	$6869.52
4	$211.03	$103.04	$107.99	$6761.53
5	$211.03	$101.42	$109.61	$6651.92
6	$211.03	$99.78	$111.25	$6540.67

21. $158.30; $299.20   **23.** $238.47; $1300.92   **25.** $378.00   **27.** $682.50   **29.** (a) $488.05 (b) $461.09 (c)$26.96 (d) $56,723.04   **31.** (a) $471.51 (b) $414.38 (c) $57.13 (d) $58,442.87 (e) $471.51 (f) $413.97 (g) $57.54 (h) $58,385.33

Summary Exercise (page 525)

(a) $10,819.57   (b) $1219.57   (c) $8516.06   (d) $277.28

Chapter 15 Review Exercises (page 525)

1. $27,152.11   **2.** $37,429.11   **3.** $11,304.71   **4.** $22,370.96   **5.** $597.53   **6.** $84,668.57   **7.** $14,943.67; $2891.62   **8.** $134,489.45; $21,989.45   **9.** $9370.33   **10.** $2893.19   **11.** $17,654.09   **12.** $18,613.72 **13.** $1054.06   **14.** $1332.74   **15.** $8702.22   **16.** $623.89   **17.** $5525.24   **18.** $4191.95   **19.** $113.07; $213.68   **20.** $159.43; $939.48   **21.** $304.36; $2609.28   **22.** $290.61; $3436.60   **23.** $8644.30   **24.** $1566.27 **25.** $5596.62   **26.** $2572.38

27.

Payment Number	Amount of Payment	Interest for Period	Portion to Principal	Principal at End of Period
0	—	—	—	$8500
1	$1522.65	$510	$1012.65	$7487.35
2	$1522.65	$449.24	$1073.41	$6413.94
3	$1522.65	$384.84	$1137.81	$5276.13
4	$1522.65	$316.57	$1206.08	$4070.05
5	$1522.65	$244.20	$1278.45	$2791.60
6	$1522.65	$167.50	$1355.15	$1436.45
7	$1522.64	$86.19	$1436.45	0

28.

Payment Number	Amount of Payment	Interest for Period	Portion to Principal	Principal at End of Period
0	—	—	—	$40,000.00
1	$6664.38	$1600.00	$5064.38	$34,935.62
2	$6664.38	$1397.42	$5266.96	$29,668.66
3	$6664.38	$1186.75	$5477.63	$24,191.03
4	$6664.38	$967.64	$5696.74	$18,494.29
5	$6664.38	$739.77	$5924.61	$12,569.68
6	$6664.38	$502.79	$6161.59	$6408.09
7	$6664.41	$256.32	$6408.09	$0

Chapter 16

Section 16.1 (page 533)

1. 20%   **3.** 12.5%   **5.** 6.25%   **7.** 4%   **9.** 3%   **11.** 2%   **13.** $1400   **15.** $30   **17.** $150
19. $5000   **21.** $1480   **23.** $675   **25.** $73,000   **29.** Year 1: $(33\frac{1}{3}\% \times \$6000)$, $2000, $2000, $6000;
Year 2: $(33\frac{1}{3}\% \times \$6000)$, $2000, $4000, $4000; Year 3: $(33\frac{1}{3}\% \times \$6000)$, $2000, $6000, $2000
31. Book values: $8200; $7000; $5800; $4600; $3400; $2200   **33.** $2250; $16,000   **35.** $2527; $20,211
37. (a) $12\frac{1}{2}\%$ (b) $90   (c) $790

Section 16.2 (page 540)

1. 40%   **3.** 25%   **5.** $13\frac{1}{3}\%$ **7.** 8%   **9.** 6%   **11.** 4%   **13.** $37   **15.** $4200   **17.** $2400
19. $1680   **21.** $85   **23.** $3417   **25.** $750   **29.** Year 1: $(66\frac{2}{3}\% \times \$1680)$, $1120, $1120, $560;
Year 2: $(66\frac{2}{3}\% \times \$560)$, $360, $1480, $200; Year 3: $(66\frac{2}{3}\% \times \$0)$, $0, $1480, $200   **31.** Book values: $6375;
$4781; $3586; $2689; $2017; $1513; $1500; $1500   **33.** $1153   **35.** $235   **37.** (a) 25%   (b) $145
(c) $443   (d) $137

Section 16.3 (page 548)

1. $\frac{3}{6}$ **3.** $\frac{5}{15}$ **5.** $\frac{7}{28}$ **7.** $\frac{10}{55}$ **9.** $450   **11.** $10,000   **13.** $125   **15.** $2700   **17.** $3857   **19.** $2400
21. $650   **25.** Year 1: $(\frac{3}{6} \times \$3420)$, $1710, $1710, $2190; Year 2: $(\frac{2}{6} \times \$3420)$, $1140, $2850, $1050;
Year 3: $(\frac{1}{6} \times \$3420)$, $570, $3420, $480   **27.** Book values: $2100; $1600; $1200; $900; $700; $600   **29.** $800
31. $11,763   **33.** (a) $663 (b) $568   **35.** (a) $\frac{8}{36}$ (b) $2840 (c) $12,780 (d) $5550

Section 16.4 (page 555)

1. $.029   **3.** $.23   **5.** $.24   **7.** $30   **9.** $17,280   **11.** $5950   **13.** $2775   **15.** $640   **19.** $270   **21.** $525
23. $1667   **25.** $257   **27.** Year 1: (1350 × $1.26), $1701, $1701, $5099; Year 2: (1820 × $1.26), $2293,
$3994, $2806; Year 3: (730 × $1.26), $920, $4914, $1886; Year 4: (1100 × $1.26), $1386, $6300, $500   **29.** $3060
31. $1825   **33.** $1775; $3106

Section 16.5 (page 563)

1. 33.33%   **3.** 10%   **5.** 17.49%   **7.** 3.636%   **9.** 7.41%   **11.** 4.888%   **13.** $4478   **15.** $3226
17. $7826   **19.** $29,475   **21.** $134,509   **23.** $656   **25.** $79,364   **29.** Year 1: (33.33% × $10,980), $3660,
$3660, $7320; Year 2: (44.45% × $10,980), $4881, $8541, $2439; Year 3: (14.81% × $10,980), $1626,
$10,167, $813; Year 4: (7.41% × $10,980), $813, $10,980, $0   **31.** Book values: $110,430; $88,344;
$70,675; $56,540; $45,227; $36,184; $28,147; $20,110; $12,061; $4024; $0   **33.** $186,550   **35.** $3571;
$7144; $7144; $7144; $7144

Summary Exercise (page 567)

(a) $66,000 book value   **(b)** $132,000 dep. in 3 years   **(c)** $35,640   **(d)** $33,000 straight–line; $14,256
double–declining–balance; $22,000 sum–of–the–years'–digits

Chapter 16 Review Exercises (page 568)

1. 20%; 40%; $\frac{5}{15}$ **2.** 25%; 50%; $\frac{4}{10}$ **3.** $33\frac{1}{3}$ %; $66\frac{2}{3}$%; $\frac{3}{6}$ **4.** 10%; 20%; $\frac{10}{55}$ **5.** $16\frac{2}{3}$%; $33\frac{1}{3}$%; $\frac{6}{21}$
6. $12\frac{1}{2}$%; 25%; $\frac{8}{36}$ **7.** 44.45%   **8.** 11.52%   **9.** 5.91%   **10.** 17.49%   **11.** 3.637%
12. 3.174%   **13.** $1021   **14.** $73,680   **15.** $11,264   **16.** $2167   **17.** $1092   **18.** $4000
19. $1530   **20.** (a)$2736; $3192; $5928 (b) $24,864; $21,672; $15,744   **21.** $13,000   **22.** $33,433;
$26,747; $20,060; $13,373; $6687   **23.** $2900   **24.** $1260; $2003   **25.** $2840; $5112   **26.** $3357
27. $4746   **28.** $2520   **29.** $6222   **30.** $6533; $8712; $2903; $1452   **31.** $1157; $1984; $1417; $1012;
$723   **32.** $201,426

Chapter 17

Section 17.1 (page 574)

1. $80,000; $16,000   **3.** $228,400

5.

```
CARMICHAEL AUTO PARTS
INCOME STATEMENT
YEAR ENDING DECEMBER 31
```

Gross Sales		**$284,000**
Returns		**$6000**
Net Sales		**$278,000**
Inventory, January 1	**$58,000**	
Cost of Goods Purchased	**$232,000**	
Freight	**$3000**	
Total Cost of Goods Purchased	**$235,000**	
Total of Goods Available for Sale	**$293,000**	
Inventory, December 31	**$69,000**	
Cost of Goods Sold		**$224,000**
Gross Profit		**$54,000**
Expenses		
Salaries and Wages	**$15,000**	
Rent	**$6000**	
Advertising	**$2000**	
Utilities	**$1000**	
Taxes on Inventory, Payroll	**$3000**	
Miscellaneous Expenses	**$4000**	
Total Expenses		**$31,000**
NET INCOME		**$23,000**

7.

NORMAN'S AUTO MART
INCOME STATEMENT
FOR THE YEAR ENDING DECEMBER 31

Gross Sales		$326,000
Returns		$7,000
Net Sales		$319,000
Inventory, January 1	$22,000	
Cost of Goods Purchased	$125,000	
Freight	$5,000	
Total Cost of Goods Purchased	$130,000	
Total of Goods Available for Sale	$152,000	
Inventory, December 31	$26,000	
Cost of Goods Sold		$126,000
Gross Profit		$193,000
Expenses		
Salaries and Wages	$32,000	
Rent	$16,000	
Advertising	$29,000	
Utilities	$4,000	
Taxes on Inventory, Payroll	$7,000	
Miscellaneous Expenses	$8,000	
Total Expenses		$96,000
NET INCOME		$97,000

Section 17.2 (page 583)

1. 57.3%; 28.7%

3.

HANDY ANDY APPLIANCES

	Amount	Percent	Percent from Table 17.1
Net Sales	$750,000	100.0%	100.0%
Cost of Goods Sold	488,000	65.1%	66.9%
Gross Profit	262,000	34.9%	33.1%
Wages	85,000	11.3%	11.9%
Rent	20,000	2.7%	2.4%
Advertising	18,000	2.4%	2.5%
Total Expenses	210,000	28.0%	26.0%
Net Income	52,000	6.9%	7.2%

5.

HERNANDEZ NURSERY
COMPARATIVE INCOME STATEMENT

	This Year		Last Year	
	Amount	Percent	Amount	Percent
Gross Sales	$1,856,000	100.3%	$1,692,000	100.7%
Returns	6000	0.3%	12,000	0.7%
Net Sales	1,850,000	100.0%	1,680,000	100.0%
Cost of Goods Sold	1,202,000	65.0%	1,050,000	62.5%
Gross Profit	648,000	35.0%	630,000	37.5%
Wages	152,000	8.2%	148,000	8.8%
Rent	82,000	4.4%	78,000	4.6%
Advertising	111,000	6.0%	122,000	7.3%
Utilities	32,000	1.7%	17,000	1.0%
Taxes on Inv., Payroll	17,000	0.9%	18,000	1.1%
Miscellaneous Expenses	62,000	3.4%	58,000	3.5%
Total Expenses	456,000	24.6%	441,000	26.3%
Net Income	192,000	10.4%	189,000	11.3%

7. Net income too low; wages too high; 67.9%; 32.1%; 23.5%; 8.6%; 12.3%; 2.4%; 1.4%   **9.** Wages are high; 68.9%; 31.2%; 21.7%; 9.6%; 9.5%; 1.8%; 2.5%

Section 17.3 (page 589)

1.

OUTDOOR SHED COMPANY
BALANCE SHEET FOR DECEMBER 31

Assets		
Current Assets		
Cash	$21,000	
Notes Receivable	$28,000	
Accounts Receivable	$36,000	
Inventory	$54,000	
Total Current Assets		$139,000
Plant Assets		
Land	$42,000	
Buildings	$35,000	
Fixtures	$9,000	
Total Plant Assets		$86,000
TOTAL ASSETS		$225,000

Liabilities		
Current Liabilities		
Notes Payable	$52,000	
Accounts Payable	$42,000	
Total Current Liabilities		$94,000
Long-term Liabilities		
Mortgages Payable	$65,000	
Long-term Notes Payable	$9,000	
Total Long-term Liabilities		$74,000
Total Liabilities		$168,000

Owner's Equity		
Owner's Equity	$57,000	
TOTAL LIABILITIES AND OWNER'S EQUITY		$225,000

Section 17.4 (page 597)

1.

INTERSTATE RUBBER SUPPLY COMPARATIVE BALANCE SHEET				
	Amount This Year	Percent This Year	Amount Last Year	Percent Last Year
Assets				
Current Assets				
Cash				
Notes Receivable	$52,000	**13.0%**	$42,000	**13.1%**
Accounts Receivable	$8,000	**2.0%**	$6,000	**1.9%**
Inventory	$148,000	**37.0%**	$120,000	**37.5%**
Total Current Assets	$153,000	**38.3%**	$120,000	**37.5%**
	$361,000	**90.3%**	**$288,000**	**90.0%**
Plant Assets				
Land				
Buildings	$10,000	**2.5%**	$8,000	**2.5%**
Fixtures	$14,000	**3.5%**	$11,000	**3.4%**
Total Plant Assets	$15,000	**3.8%**	$13,000	**4.1%**
	$39,000	**9.8%**	**$32,000**	**10.0%**
TOTAL ASSETS				
	$400,000	100.0%	**$320,000**	100.0%
Liabilities				
Current Liabilities				
Accounts Payable	$3,000	**0.8%**	$4,000	**1.3%**
Notes Payable	$201,000	**50.3%**	$152,000	**47.5%**
Total Current Liabilities	**$204,000**	**51.0%**	**$156,000**	**48.8%**
Long-term Liabilities				
Mortgages Payable	$20,000	**5.0%**	$16,000	**5.0%**
Long-term Notes Payable	$58,000	**14.5%**	$42,000	**13.1%**
Total Long-term Liabilities	**$78,000**	**19.5%**	**$58,000**	**18.1%**
Total Liabilities	**$282,000**	**70.5%**	**$214,000**	**66.9%**
Owner's Equity	$118,000	**29.5%**	$106,000	**33.1%**
TOTAL LIABILITIES AND OWNER'S EQUITY	**$400,000**	**100.0%**	**$320,000**	**100.0%**

3. 1.77; 1.02   **5.** 1.74; 1.23   **7.** 2.13; 1.27   **9.** 239.0%   **11.** 39.7%   **13.** 1.8%   **15.** 16.9 times; 21.6 days

Summary Exercise (page 602)

(a) Gross Sales: $212,000; Returns: $12,500; Net Sales: $199,500; Inventory 1/1: $44,000; Cost of Goods Purchased: $75,000; Freight: $8000; Total Cost of Goods Purchased: $83,000; Total of Goods Available for Sale: $127,000; Inventory 12/31: $26,000; Cost of Goods Sold: $101,000; Gross Profit: $98,500; Salaries and Wages: $37,000; Rent: $12,000; Advertising: $2000; Utilities: $3000; Taxes on Inventory, Payroll: $7000; Miscellaneous Expenses: $4500; Total Expenses: $65,500; Net income: $33,000 **(b)** 106%; 6.3%; 50.6%; 18.5%; 6%; 1.5%

(c)

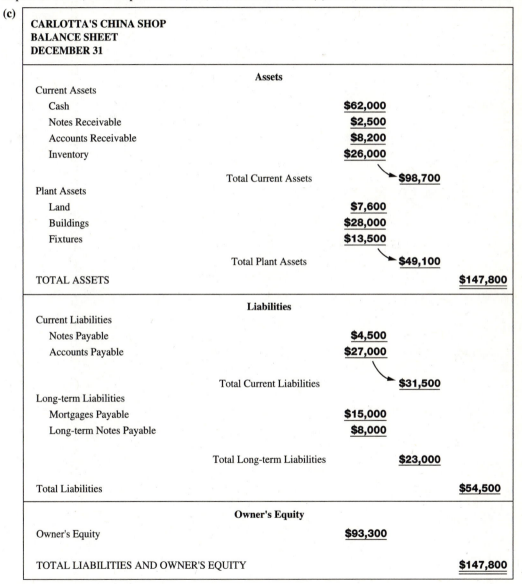

CARLOTTA'S CHINA SHOP
BALANCE SHEET
DECEMBER 31

Assets		
Current Assets		
Cash	**$62,000**	
Notes Receivable	**$2,500**	
Accounts Receivable	**$8,200**	
Inventory	**$26,000**	
Total Current Assets		**$98,700**
Plant Assets		
Land	**$7,600**	
Buildings	**$28,000**	
Fixtures	**$13,500**	
Total Plant Assets		**$49,100**
TOTAL ASSETS		**$147,800**

Liabilities		
Current Liabilities		
Notes Payable	**$4,500**	
Accounts Payable	**$27,000**	
Total Current Liabilities		**$31,500**
Long-term Liabilities		
Mortgages Payable	**$15,000**	
Long-term Notes Payable	**$8,000**	
Total Long-term Liabilities	**$23,000**	
Total Liabilities		**$54,500**

Owner's Equity		
Owner's Equity	**$93,300**	
TOTAL LIABILITIES AND OWNER'S EQUITY		**$147,800**

(d) 3.13; 2.31

Chapter 17 Review Exercises (page 605)

1. $50,000; $16,000   **2.** $56,000; $10,000   **3.** $200,000; $125,000   **4.** $110,000; $30,000   **5.** $160,000; $60,000   **6.** $150,000   **7.** $55,000   **8.** $15,000   **9.** $27,000   **10.** $30,000

11.

ROSE'S PARTY BALLOONS
INCOME STATEMENT
FOR THE YEAR ENDING DECEMBER 31

Gross Sales		**$175,000**
Returns		**$8,000**
Net Sales		**$167,000**
Inventory, January 1	**$44,000**	
Cost of Goods Purchased	**$126,000**	
Freight	**$2,000**	
Total Cost of Goods Purchased	**$128,000**	
Total of Goods Available for Sale	**$172,000**	
Inventory, December 31	**$52,000**	
Cost of Goods Sold		**$120,000**
Gross Profit		**$47,000**
Expenses		
Salaries and Wages	**$9,000**	
Rent	**$4,000**	
Advertising	**$1,500**	
Utilities	**$1,000**	
Taxes on Inventory, Payroll	**$2,000**	
Miscellaneous Expenses	**$3,000**	
Total Expenses		**$20,500**
NET INCOME		**$26,500**

12.

MIKE'S COMPUTER STORE
INCOME STATEMENT
FOR THE YEAR ENDING DECEMBER 31

Gross Sales		**$2,215,000**
Returns		**$26,000**
Net Sales		**$2,189,000**
Inventory, January 1	**$215,000**	
Cost of Goods Purchased	**$1,123,000**	
Freight	**$4,000**	
Total Cost of Goods Purchased	**$1,127,000**	
Total of Goods Available for Sale	**$1,342,000**	
Inventory, December 31	**$265,000**	
Cost of Goods Sold		**$1,077,000**
Gross Profit		**$1,112,000**
Expenses		
Salaries and Wages	**$154,000**	
Rent	**$59,000**	
Advertising	**$11,000**	
Utilities	**$12,000**	
Taxes on Inventory, Payroll	**$10,000**	
Miscellaneous Expenses	**$9,000**	
Total Expenses		**$255,000**
NET INCOME		**$857,000**

13. 84%; 41.6%   **14.** 50%; 18%   **15.** Percent: 41.7%; 58.3%; 24.0%; 4.0%; 1.9%; 41.0%; 17.3% Percent from Table 17: 48.4%; 51.6%; 26.4%; 2.8%; 1.4%; 43.7%; 7.9%

16.

WOODEN BOAT COMPANY BALANCE SHEET FOR DECEMBER 31		
Assets		
Current Assets		
Cash	$9,000	
Notes Receivable	$4,000	
Accounts Receivable	$3,000	
Inventory	$12,000	
Total Current Assets		$28,000
Plant Assets		
Land	$28,000	
Buildings	$15,000	
Fixtures	$8,000	
Total Plant Assets		$51,000
TOTAL ASSETS		$79,000
Liabilities		
Current Liabilities		
Notes Payable	$11,000	
Accounts Payable	$15,000	
Total Current Liabilities		$26,000
Long-term Liabilities		
Mortgages Payable	$22,000	
Long- term Notes Payable	$10,000	
Total Long-term Liabilities		$32,000
Total Liabilities		$58,000
Owner's Equity		
Owner's Equity	$21,000	
TOTAL LIABILITIES AND OWNER'S EQUITY		$79,000

17. 2.33; 1.2; 80%   **18.** 2.67; 1.5; 64%   **19.** 3.2; 3.0; 70%   **20.** 11.8; 30.9 days   **21.** 12.3; 29.7 days

Chapter 18

Section 18.1 (page 615)

1. $2.62 **3.** $1.03; $7 **5.** $2.92; $60 **7.** $.44 **9.** $8; $.75 **11.** $1.60; $.86 **13.** $20; $5.06
15. $5.83 **17.** $4.38

Section 18.2 (page 623)

1. 4\frac{3}{8}$ or $4.375 **3.** 2\frac{1}{8}$ or $2.125 **5.** 31\frac{1}{4}$ or $31.25 **7.** $1.50 **9.** 22\frac{1}{8}$ or $22.125 **11.** 48,300
13. 1.7% **15.** $8000 **17.** $3712.50 **19.** $13,950 **21.** $5663.13 **23.** $46,432.50 **25.** $2198.44
27. $38,334.88 **29.** $20,218.65 **31.** $10,054.48 **33.** $42,683.31 **35.** 5.3% **37.** 2.7% **39.** 9.2%
41. 11 **43.** 9 **45.** $6865

Section 18.3 (page 628)

1. $987.50 **3.** 8$\frac{1}{4}$% or $82.50 **5.** none **7.** $15,075 **9.** $17,025 **11.** $44,043.75 **13.** $10,700
15. $10,575 **19.** $9075 **21.** $50,531.25 **23.** (a) $18,600 (b) $1700

Section 18.4 (page 634)

1. $27,000 each **3.** $22,500 for 1; $67,500 for 2 **5.** $6600 for 1; $10,400 for 2; $13,000 for 3 **7.** $22,000
for 1; $26,000 for 2; $14,000 for 3 **9.** $27,000 each **11.** $10,000 for 1; $26,667 for 2; $43,333 for 3
13. $22,500; $37,500; $52,500; $67,500 **15.** $23,400 for Finch; $33,600 for Renz **17.** (a) $21,000 for Coker;
$39,000 for Toms (b) $7500 for Coker; $1500 by Toms to Coker **19.** $22,179 to 1; $46,464 to 2; $41,357 to 3

Section 18.5 (page 638)

1. $60,000; $75,000; $105,000 **3.** $15,707; $18,240; $17,227; $24,827 **5.** $9375; $6250; $6250 **7.** $1302;
$4186; $2791; $3721 **9.** $30,000; $36,000; $24,000 **11.** $31,500; $40,500; $6750; $11,250 **13.** $24,000;
$96,000; $72,000; $108,000; $12,000; $48,000 **15.** $1800; $4800; $3600; $2250; $2700 **17.** $600; $1050;
$2250; $360; $240

Summary Exercise (page 646)

(a) $4 preferred; $1.45 common
(b) Decker: $30,937.50; Shields: $20,625; Abbot: $51,562.50
(c) Math: $15,039; English: $10,742; Reading: $8594

Chapter 18 Review Exercises (page 647)

1. (a) $9; (b) $4.40 **2.** (a) $12; (b) $7.23 **3.** (a) $8.75; (b) $2.69 **4.** $7.25 **5.** $2.73 **6.** $3.70
7. 5$\frac{1}{2}$ **8.** 14$\frac{3}{4}$ **9.** 39$\frac{7}{8}$ **10.** +$\frac{3}{8}$ **11.** $2.16 **12.** $16,800 **13.** 6.7% **14.** 36$\frac{5}{8}$ **15.** 11$\frac{3}{8}$ **16.** $3425
17. $637.50 **18.** $8625 **19.** $8533.13 **20.** $25,484.06 **21.** 6.7% **22.** 7.0% **23.** 19 **24.** 15
25. $887.50 **26.** 10 **27.** 2012 **28.** +$1.25 **29.** $26,775 **30.** 5$\frac{1}{4}$% or $52.50 **31.** $34,650
32. $71,137.50 **33.** $16,000 **34.** $48,000 to 1; $72,000 to 2 **35.** $38,571 to 1; $51,429 to 2 **36.** $25,000;
$41,667; $33,333 **37.** $42,254; $15,845; $16,901 **38.** $25,870; $20,326; $16,630; $22,174

Chapter 19

Section 19.1 (page 657)

1. (a) approx. $2,800,000 (b) approx. $2,500,000 (c) approx. $1,600,000

3. (a) 4 (b) 3 (c) 6 (d) 3 (e) 5 (f) 9 (g)

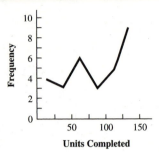

7. (a) 1 (b) 6 (c) 13 (d) 22 (e) 17 (f) 13 (g) 8 (h)

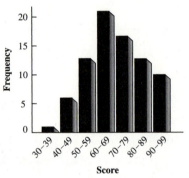

(i) 20 (j) 38 (k) 52 (l) 35 **9.** (a) almost 1 acre (b) almost $3\frac{7}{8}$ acres (c) 2 mph (d) 99 inches   **11.** (a) 20%
(b) 15%; 54° (c) 36° (d) 15% (e) 5%; 18° (f) $140; 10% (g)

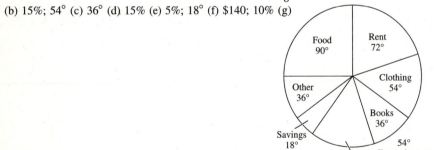

13.

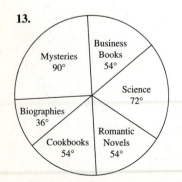

15. 51%   **17.**

Section 19.2 (page 668)

1. 16   **3.** 60.3   **5.** 27,955   **7.** 7.7   **9.** $39,418   **11.** $657,125   **13.** 6.7   **15.** 17.2   **19.** $30,000
21. 2.60   **23.** 79.0   **25.** 111.6

Section 19.3 (page 673)

1. 50   **3.** 130   **5.** 44   **7.** 29.1   **9.** 9   **11.** 64   **13.** none   **15.** 6.1 and 6.3   **19.** 6   **21.** 3
23. median

Section 19.4 (page 679)

1. 6, 2   **3.** 12, 4.3   **5.** 53, 20.2   **7.** 46, 14.7   **9.** 24, 7.7   **13.** 50   **15.** 68   **17.** 14   **19.** 68
21. 50%   **23.** 16%   **25.** 95%   **27.** $\frac{1}{2}$%   **29.** 84%   **31.** 97.5%   **33.** 84%   **35.** 97.5%   **37.** 68%

Section 19.5 (page 682)

1. 187.5   **3.** 156.6   **5.** 210   **7.** $205.80   **9.** $228.30   **11.** $147.90   **13.** $37,000   **15.** Los Angeles,
Long Beach

Summary Exercise (page 688)

(a) 2; 4; 5; 6; 2; 1

(b)
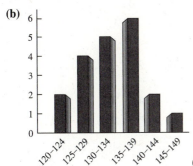

(c) Mean $132.95; Median $132.50; Mode $136

Chapter 19 Review Exercises (page 689)

1. 4; 5; 11; 5; 5   **2.** 4; 14; 19; 7; 5; 3; 2; 1

3.
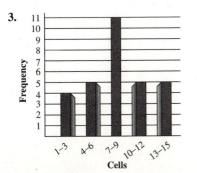

4.
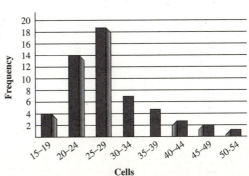

5.

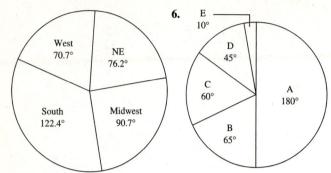

6.

7. 45.7; 43; 39   **8.** 8.4; 6.5; 5   **9.** 29; 26.5; 27   **10.** 421.1; 425; 310   **11.** 2.9; 2.7; no mode   **12.** 9.5; 9;
8   **13.** 27.7   **14.** 10.7   **15.** 10.4   **16.** 8; 2.87   **17.** 7; 2.27   **18.** 8; 2.05   **19.** 46; 13.65   **20.** 250
21. 350   **22.** 230   **23.** 146.5   **24.** 357.1   **25.** 300

Appendix A

Section A.1 (page A-7)

7. 7070; 7100; 7000   **9.** 47,360; 47,400; 47,000   **11.** 63,720; 63,700; 64,000   **13.** 106,050; 106,100; 106,000
15. 1,058,990; 1,059,000; 1,059,000   **17.** 137   **19.** 2946   **21.** 2800   **23.** 168,471   **25.** 586   **27.** 4103
29. 14,810   **31.** 7,326,842   **33.** 198,925   **35.** 46,276,125   **37.** 20,412   **39.** 8,107,899   **41.** 11,680,000
43. 1,470,000   **45.** 248,500   **47.** 22,560,000   **49.** 213   **51.** 22,024   **53.** 487   **55.** 316 R99   **57.** 1733 R175
59. 2510   **61.** 7219   **63.** 5274   **65.** 36,608   **67.** 48   **69.** $8605   **71.** 896 employees   **73.** 2625 tickets
75. 2477 pounds   **77.** 138 sold   **79.** 1332 miles   **81.** $301   **83.** 6,272,640 sq. in.   **85.** 20 seats

Section A.2 (page A-14)

1. three and fifteen hundredths   **3.** twenty-one and thirty-seven hundredths   **5.** 111.5   **7.** 6.411   **9.** $\dfrac{9}{25}$
11. $\dfrac{42}{125}$ **13.** $\dfrac{161}{200}$ **15.** $\dfrac{12}{125}$ **17.** 35.9   **19.** 3895.552   **21.** 1214.184   **23.** 2451.446   **25.** 13.21
27. 31.507   **29.** 78.051   **31.** 4.849   **33.** 0.1344   **35.** 9.3527   **37.** 0.002448   **39.** 9.881   **41.** $262.86
43. $314.65   **45.** $1383.96   **47.** $14.69   **49.** 4.173   **51.** 31.286   **53.** 1.992   **55.** 14.68
57. 1458.6   **59.** 52.5   **61.** $25,000   **63.** $30,741.56   **65.** 26 coins   **67.** (a) $54,769.07 (b) $821.54
69. (a) $34,668 (b) $13,022   **71.** 31,200 claims

Summary Exercise (page A-17)

(a) 54.55 inches   **(b)** 117.35 inches   **(c)** 15.59 inches   **(d)** 3.73 inches

Glossary

For further information on any of these terms, refer to the section indicated within the square brackets. (Also, see the index.)

absolute or **gross loss** The loss resulting when the selling price is less than the cost. [10.1]

accelerated cost recovery system (ACRS) The method of depreciation required on all federal income tax returns for property acquired after January 1, 1981 and before 1986. [16.5]

accelerated depreciation Depreciation which has a rate greater than a straight-line rate of depreciation. For example, declining balance, sum-of-the-years'-digits, or ACRS. [16.2]

accidental death benefit Coverage which pays an additional death benefit if the insured dies as the result of an accident. [7.3]

accounts receivable turnover Net sales divided by average accounts receivable. [17.4]

accumulated depreciation A running balance or total of the depreciation to date on an asset. [16 Introduction]

acid-test ratio The ratio of current assets and current liabilities. Also called quick ratio. [17.4]

actual selling price *See* Reduced price. [10.1]

actuary A person who determines insurance premiums. [7.2]

addends The number being added in an addition problem. [A.1]

adjusted bank balance This number represents the current checking account balance. [4.3]

adjusted gross income (AGI) The sum total of all income received from wages, salaries, interest, and dividends less any adjustments to income such as sick pay and moving expenses. [6.3]

adult operator A driver of a motor vehicle over a certain age, usually 25 years of age or older. [7.2]

agreed ratio Partners of a business divide the profits using some given rule. These profit divisions are sometimes given as a ratio. [18.4]

algebraic logic The logic used by most electronic calculators. [1.3]

allocation of overhead Dividing the overhead among the various products or lines of business of a company. [18.5]

amortization schedule A table showing the equal payment necessary to pay off a loan for a specific amount of money including interest, for a specific amount of time. Also called a repayment schedule. [15.4]

amortized When principal and interest are paid by a sequence of equal payments (on a loan). [15.4]

amount *See* Sum. [A.1]

amount financed The difference of the cash price of an item and the down payment. [14.3]

amount of an annuity The sum of the compound amounts of all the periodic payments into an annuity, compounded to the end of the term. [15.1]

annual meeting A meeting open to all owners of stock where the management of the firm is open to questions from stockholders, and where the board of directors is elected. [18.1]

annual percentage rate A rate of interest that must be stated for each loan, by federal regulation. This annual percentage rate is designed to help consumers compare interest rates. [12.2] This is the true or effective rate of interest. [14.2, 14.3]

annuity Periodic payments of a given, fixed amount of money. [7.3, 15.1]

annuity certain An annuity with a fixed beginning date and a fixed ending date. [15.1]

annuity due An annuity with payments made at the beginning of a time period. [15.1]

anticipation The seller's offer of interest for early payment of an invoice, in addition to a cash discount. [8.4]

AS OF An invoice which is postdated "AS OF" a future date. [8.3]

assessed The procedure whereby a local official, called the assessor, makes an estimate of the fair market value of property. [6.2]

assessed valuation The value for property tax purposes set by the tax assessor on a piece of property. [6.2]

assessment rate A certain percent used in an area to determine assessed valuation. [6.2]

assets Items of value owned by a firm. [17.3]

attached A seizure of property by court order. [18 Introduction]

automated teller machine (ATM) A machine allowing 24-hour banking. [4.1]

average *See* Mean. [19.2]

average age of accounts receivable One year (365 days) divided by accounts receivable turnover rate. [17.4]

average daily balance A method of calculating the balance owed on a revolving charge account. With this method, the balance on the account is found at the end of each day in the month and the total is divided by the number of days in the month. [14.2]

average daily balance method A method of calculating the finance charge on a revolving charge account by using the average balance at the end of each day during a month. [14.2]

average inventory Determined by dividing the sum of all inventories taken by the number of times inventory was taken. [10.2]

bad check A check that is not honored because there are insufficient funds in the checking account. [4.3]

balanced Agreement reached between the bank statement amount and the depositor's checkbook balance. [4.3]

balance brought forward The amount left in a checking account after previous checks written have been subtracted; the current balance. [4.1]

balance sheet A summary of the financial condition of a firm at one point in time. [17.3]

bank discount *See* Discount. [12.2, 12.4]

bank statement A list of all charges and deposits made against and to a checking account, usually sent out monthly by the bank. [4.3]

bank statement balance This is the checking account balance appearing on the front of the bank statement. [4.3]

banker's interest *See* Ordinary interest. [11.2]

banker's ratio *See* Current ratio. [17.4]

base In the number 3^2, the number 3 is the base. *See* Exponent. [1.3] The starting point or reference point or that to which something is being compared. [3.2]

base year Some past year, with which something today is being compared. [19.5]

basic percent equation Rate $\times$ Base $=$ Part or $R \times B = P$. [3.2]

beneficiary The person receiving insurance benefits upon the occurrence of a certain event. [7.3]

bimodal A set of data in which two numbers occur equally often. [19.3]

blank endorsement The endorsement of a check with a signature alone. [4.1]

board of directors A group of people who represent the stockholders. [18.1]

bodily injury insurance Another name for liability insurance. [7.2]

bond A promise by a corporation or government to pay a certain fixed amount of money at a certain time in the future. [15.3, 18.3]

book value The cost of an asset minus any depreciation to date. [16.1]

borrow Taking a number from one column of numbers in a problem in order to make a larger number in the column to which the borrowed number is added. [A.1]

breakeven point The cost of an item plus the operating expenses associated with the item. Above this amount a profit is made, below it, a loss is incurred. [10.1]

business checking account The type of checking account used by businesses. [4.1]

business owner's package policy A business insurance policy insuring many additional perils beyond fire. [7.1]

cancellation A process used to simplify multiplication and division of fractions using a modification of the method of writing fractions in lowest terms. [1.2]

cancellation rate Another name for short-term rate. [7.1]

capital The amount of money originally invested in a firm. [18.1]

carrier The insurance company. Also known as the insurer. [7.1]

cash discount A discount offered by the seller allowing the buyer to take a discount if payment is made within a specified period of time. [8.3]

cash settlement option Life insurance benefits which are paid in cash. [7.3]

cash value The value in cash remaining after a policy holder has canceled or borrowed against a life insurance policy. [7.3]

cashier's check A check written by the financial institution itself and having the full faith and backing of the institution. [4.2]

certificate of deposit Money placed in a time deposit account. [13.2]

chain calculation A long sequence of calculations. [1.3]

chain discount Involves two or more individual discounts. [8.1]

chargeback A fee charged to a production employee for a rejected item of production. [5.3]

check register A single page record of checks written and deposits made to a checking account. [4.1]

checks outstanding Checks written that have not reached and cleared the bank as of the statement date. [4.3]

check stub A stub attached to the check and retained for keeping a record of checks written. [4.1]

circle graph A circle broken up into various parts, based on percentages of 360°. [19.1]

classes The intervals of a frequency distribution. [19.1]

class frequency The frequency of values for each class. [19.1]

class mark The midpoint of an interval. [19.2]

C.O.D. A shipping term meaning *cash on delivery*. [8.1]

coefficient A number used to multiply a variable. [2.1]

coinsurance clause A fire insurance clause which places part of the risk of fire loss upon the insured. [7.1]

collateral Goods pledged as security for a loan—in the event that a loan is not paid off, the collateral can be seized by the lender and sold to pay the debt. [12.1]

collision insurance A form of automobile insurance that pays for repairs to the insured's car in case of an accident. [7.2]

commission A fee paid to an employee for transacting a piece of business or performing a service. [5.2] A charge for buying or selling stock. [18.2]

common denominator A number that all the denominators of a fraction problem divide into evenly. [1.1]

common stock Ordinary capital stock not sharing the privileges of preferred stock. [18.1]

companion or spouse insurance This lets the insured add a companion or spouse to a policy, resulting in both being insured. [7.3]

comparative income statement Preparation of a vertical analysis for two or more years in order to compare incomes or balance sheet items for each year analyzed. [17.2]

comparative line graph One graph which shows how several different things relate. [19.1]

compensatory time (comp time) Time off given an employee to compensate for overtime previously worked. [5.1]

complement The number which must be added to a given discount to get 1 or 100%. [8.1]

compound amount The final amount, both principal and interest, after money is deposited at compound interest. [13.1]

compound interest Interest computed on both principal and interest. [11.1, 13.1]

compounded daily Interest is paid for every day that money is on deposit in a savings account. [13.2]

comprehensive insurance A form of automobile insurance that pays for damage to the insured's car caused by fire, theft, vandalism, and so on. [7.2]

consumer The ultimate user of a product or service, the public. [8.1]

Consumer Price Index A monthly publication by the federal government showing the change in the cost of living. [19.5]

contingent annuity An annuity with a variable beginning or ending date. [15.1]

continuous compounding An account offering continuous compounding features interest compounded every instant. [13.2]

convertible preferred stock One share is convertible into a stated number of shares of common stock at some date. [18.1]

corporation A form of business organization offering limited liability—no more money may be lost than has been invested. [18 Introduction]

cost The price paid to a supplier after trade and cash discounts have been taken. This price includes transportation and insurance charges. [9.1] The amount paid for a depreciable asset. This is the amount used to determine depreciation. [16 Introduction]

cost of goods sold The amount paid by a firm for the goods it sold during the time period covered by an income statement. [17.1]

country club billing A type of billing received on revolving charge plans in which actual carbon copies of charges are returned. [14.2]

credit union share draft accounts A credit union account that may be used as a checking account. [4.2]

cross-products In the proportion $\frac{a}{b} = \frac{c}{d}$, the cross-products are ad and bc. [2.4]

cumulative preferred stock Stock requiring that any dividends not paid in the past must be paid before common stockholders receive any money. [18.1]

current assets Cash or items that can be converted into cash within a given period of time, such as a year. [17.3]

current balance See adjusted bank balance. [4.3]

current (short-term) liabilities Those items which must be paid by a firm within a given period of time, such as a year. [17.3]

current ratio The quotient of current assets and current liabilities. Also called banker's ratio. [17.4]

current yield The annual dividend per share of stock divided by the current price per share. [18.2]

debt-to-equity ratio All liabilities divided by owner's equity. [17.4]

decimal A number written with a decimal point, such as 4.3 or 7.22. [A.2]

decimal equivalent of a fraction The decimal fraction that is equal to a proper fraction. For example, $\frac{1}{2} = 0.5$, $\frac{3}{8} = 0.375$. [1.2]

decimal number A fraction with a denominator that is a power of ten, which is written with a decimal point, such as 4.3 or 7.22. [1.2]

decimal point The starting point in the decimal system (.). [A.1]

decimal system Our system of numbers; based on the digits 0, 1, 2, 3, 4, 5, 6, 7, 8, and 9. [A.1]

declining-balance depreciation An accelerated depreciation method. [16.1]

declining-balance method A method of depreciation using a declining balance rate. [16.2]

(200%) declining-balance method An accelerated method of depreciation using twice or 200% of the straight-line rate. Also called double-declining-balance method. [16.2]

(150%) declining-balance method An accelerated method of depreciation using one and one half or 150% of the straight-line rate. [16.2]

(125%) declining-balance method An accelerated method of depreciation using one and one fourth or 125% of the straight-line rate. [16.2]

decrease problem Often called a difference problem; the part equals the base minus some portion of the base. Usually the base must be found. [3.5]

decreasing term insurance A form of life insurance in which the insured pays a fixed premium until age 60 or 65 with the amount of life insurance decreasing periodically. [7.3]

deductible The amount of the deductible is paid by the insured with the balance of the loss being paid by the insurance company. [7.2]

deductions Amounts that are subtracted from the gross earnings of an employee to arrive at the amount of money the employee actually receives, net pay. [5.4]

deferred payment price The cash price of an item, plus any finance charge. [14.3]

deficit number *See* Negative number. [1.3]

denominator The number below the line in a fraction. For example, in the fraction $\frac{7}{9}$, 9 is the denominator. [1.1]

deposit slip (deposit ticket) The form used for making a bank savings or checking account deposit. [4.1]

depreciable amount The amount to be depreciated over the life of the asset. [16.1]

depreciation A method used to spread the value of an asset over the several years of its life. [16 Introduction]

depreciation fraction The fraction used with sum-of-the-years'-digits depreciation. The numerator is the year and the denominator is the sum of the years of life of the asset. [16.3]

depreciation schedule A schedule or table showing the depreciation rate, amount of depreciation, book value, and accumulated depreciation for each year of an asset's life. [16.1]

destination The city or town where goods or merchandise are being shipped. [8.1]

difference The answer in a subtraction problem. Also called remainder. [A.1]

differential-piece rate A piece rate designed to pay a greater amount for each unit of production as the number of units produced is increased. [5.3]

digits One-place numbers in the decimal system. They are 0, 1, 2, 3, 4, 5, 6, 7, 8, and 9. [A.1]

discount An amount subtracted from the price of a product or service which helps the buyer purchase at a lower cost and increase profits. [8.1] The amount of interest charged on a note. Also called a bank discount. [12.2, 12.4]

discount broker A stockbroker who charges less than full price for buying and selling stocks. [18.2]

discount note A note where interest is deducted in advance. [12.2]

discount period The period of time in the discounting process. [12.4]

discounting a note The holder of a note sometimes sells the note to a bank before its maturity date. This gives cash to the holder earlier than otherwise. [12.4]

dispersion Spread of data. [19.4]

distributive property A property of algebra that says a number on the outside of parentheses should be multiplied times each term inside the parentheses. [2.1]

dividend The number being divided by another number in a division problem. [A.1]

dividends Money paid by a company to the holders of a stock. [18.1]

divisor The number doing the dividing in a division problem. [A.1]

docking Same meaning as chargeback. [5.3]

double-declining-balance method *See* (200%) declining-balance method. [16.2]

double-time Twice the regular hourly rate. A premium often paid for working holidays and Sunday. [5.1]

down payment An amount paid when an item is bought. [14.3]

draw An amount paid by an employer to salespeople at regular intervals. This is often paid against future income. [5.2]

drawing account An account from which a salesperson can receive payment against future commissions. [5.2]

duplicate statement A duplicate of a checking account statement issued by the bank. [4.2]

early withdrawal penalty A fine or amount of money charged by the lending institution for withdrawal of money earlier than the time agreed upon by the depositor and the institution. These penalties apply only to interest, not to principal. [13.2]

earnings per share The difference of the net income of a corporation and any dividends on preferred shares, divided by the number of common shares outstanding. [18.1]

effective rate of interest The simple interest rate corresponding to a given discount rate. Also called true rate of interest. [12.3] The actual percent of interest earned during a year. [13.1]

Employer's Quarterly Federal Tax Return The form (Form 941) is sent to the IRS along with quarterly payments of FICA and withholding tax. [5.6]

end-of-month dating (EOM) In cash discounts, the time period beginning at the end of the month the invoice is dated. Proximo and prox. have the same meaning. [8.4]

endowment policy A form of life insurance guaranteeing the payment of a fixed amount of money to a given individual whether or not the insured person lives. [7.3]

equal shares Partners in a business share all profits equally. [18.4]

equation A statement that says two expressions are equal. [2.1]

equivalent cash price A single amount today equal to the present value of an annuity. [15.2]

escrow account An account maintained by real estate lenders and used to pay taxes and insurance. Also called an impound account. [15.4]

exact interest Simple interest calculated using 365 days in a year. [11.2]

excise tax A tax charged on specific items which are purchased. Tobacco, alcoholic beverages, and gasoline have an excise tax. [6.1]

executive officers President, vice president, and so on, of a corporation. [18.1]

exponent In the number 3^2 the small number 2 is the exponent. It says to multiply 3 by itself. [1.3] A number that tells how many times a number is used in a product. For example, $3^2 = 3 \times 3 = 9$. [13.1]

extended term insurance The nonforfeiture option which gives the insured term insurance for a fixed number of years and days. [7.3]

extension total On an invoice, the product of the number of items times the unit price. [8.1]

extra dating (extra, ex., or x) Extra time allowed in determining the net payment date of a cash discount. [8.4]

face value The amount shown on the face of a note. [12.1] *See* Par value. [18.3]

face value of the policy The amount of an insurance policy. [7.1]

factor A person who buys accounts receivable of a firm (accounts receivable represent money owed to the firm). [12.3]

factoring The term for when a business sells part of its accounts receivable to a financial institution. [12.4]

Fair Labor Standards Act A federal law setting work conditions and standards of employee treatment. [5.1]

fair market value The price for which a piece of property could reasonably be expected to be sold in the market. [6.2]

FAS (free alongside ship) Free alongside the ship on the loading dock with all freight charges to that point paid by the shipper. [8.1]

Federal Insurance Contributions Act (FICA) A Federal act requiring that a specified amount of money be collected from the paycheck of almost all nongovernmental employees, which is used by the federal government to pay pensions, survivors benefits, disability, and Medicare. [5.4]

Federal Truth in Lending Act An act passed in 1969 which requires that all interest rates be given as comparable percents. [12.2]

Federal Truth-in-Lending Law in 1969 (Regulation Z) A federal law passed in 1969 that establishes uniform methods of disclosing information on finance charges and interest rates. [14.3]

Federal Unemployment Tax Act (FUTA) A Federal act covering unemployment insurance. [5.6]

finance charges Charges paid to obtain credit. [14.2, 14.3]

first-in, first-out method (FIFO) Inventory valuation method following the flow of goods, first-in, first-out. [10.3]

fixed amount annuity A settlement option which pays a fixed amount per month to life insurance beneficiaries. [7.3]

fixed assets *See* Plant and equipment assets. [17.3]

fixed period annuity A settlement option for life insurance beneficiaries paying a sum of money for a fixed period of time. [7.3]

fixed rate loan A home loan made at a fixed rate of interest for a fixed period of time. [15.4]

floating decimal point A feature on electronic calculators that locates the decimal point in the answer. [1.3]

floor space Overhead is sometimes allocated among lines of business based on the amount of floor space used by each line. [18.5]

FOB (free on board) Free on board shipping point means that the buyer pays for shipping. Free on board destination means that the seller pays for shipping. [8.1]

formula A rule showing how quantities are related. [2.3]

fraction Used to indicate a part of a whole. For example, $\frac{3}{4}$ means that the whole is divided into 4 parts and we are considering three of them. [1.1]

frequency distribution table A table showing the number of times one or more events occur. [19.1]

gross cost The cost including freight, insurance, and commission in a commission purchase. [5.2]

gross earnings The total amount of money earned by an employee before any deductions are taken. [5.1]

gross loss *See* Absolute loss. [10.1]

gross proceeds The amount received before freight, insurance and commission in a commission sale. [5.2]

gross profit The difference between the amount received from customers for goods and what the firm paid for the goods. [17.1]

gross profit method A method used to estimate inventory value at cost which utilizes cost amounts. [10.3]

gross sales The total amount of money received from customers for the goods or services sold by the firm. [17.1]

group insurance plans An insurance plan which includes a group of people employed by the same company or belonging to the same organization. [7.1]

grouped data Items combined into groups (taken from a table) to simplify information for more immediate comprehension. [19.1]

guaranteed conversion privilege This provision allows the insured to convert term insurance to ordinary or variable life insurance without physical examination. [7.3]

half-year convention Under MACRS property placed in service or disposed of is allowed one-half year of depreciation. [16.5]

home banking A system that allows the customer to do banking from the home or business using the telephone and computer. [4.2]

homeowner's policy A policy for homeowners providing fire, theft, and vandalism protection. [7.1]

horizontal analysis Prepared by finding the amount of any change from last year to current year, both in dollars and as a percent. [17.2 and 17.4]

hourly wage A rate of pay expressed as so much per hour. *See* Time rate. [5.1]

impound account See escrow account. [15.4]

improper fraction A fraction with a numerator larger than or equal to the denominator. (For example, $\frac{7}{5}$ is an improper fraction; $\frac{1}{9}$ is not.) [1.1]

incentive rate A payment system based on the amount of work completed. [5.3]

income statement A summary of all the income and expenses involved in running a business for a given period of time. [17.1]

income tax method *See* Accelerated cost recovery system (ACRS). [16.5]

income tax withholding Federal income tax withheld from gross earnings by the employer. [5.5]

increase problem Often called an amount problem; the part equals the base plus some portion of the base, resulting in a new value. Usually the base must be found. [3.5]

Individual Retirement Account (IRA) An account that permits an individual to establish a retirement plan and to deduct his contributions to the account. [6.3]

installment loan A loan paid off in a series of equal payments made at equal periods of time. Car loans are examples of installment loans. [14.1]

insufficient funds Not enough funds in a checking account for the bank to honor the check. [4.3]

insured A person or business that has purchased insurance. Also known as the policyholder. [7.1]

insured money market accounts (IMMAs) Accounts which are insured up to a certain maximum by the federal government, and which offer a higher rate than passbook accounts. [13.2]

insurer The insurance company. [7.1]

interest A charge paid for borrowing money or a fee received for lending money. [11.1]

interest-in-advance note *See* Simple discount note. [12.2]

interest on investment and agreed ratio Sometimes one partner will put up a large share of money to start a firm, while other partners operate it. The partner putting up the larger share of money gets interest on the investment before any further division of profits. [18.4]

interest rate spread The difference between the interest rate charged on loans and that paid on deposits. [15.3]

inventory The value of all goods on hand for sale. [17.1]

inventory turnover The number of times each year that the average inventory is sold, also called stock turnover. [10.2]

inventory valuation Determining the value of merchandise in stock. Four common methods are: specific identification, average cost, FIFO, and LIFO. [10.3]

invoice A document which helps business keep track of sales and purchases. [8.1]

invoice total The total amount owed on an invoice. [8.1]

irregulars Items that are blemished or have flaws and must be sold at a reduced price. [9.3]

itemized billing A method of credit card billing in which purchases are listed, along with payments, with no actual receipts returned to the user. [14.2]

junk bonds Bonds of bankrupt or troubled companies. [18.3]

last-in, first-out method (LIFO) Inventory valuation method following the flow of goods, last-in, first-out. [10.3]

least common denominator The smallest whole number that all the denominators of two or more fractions evenly divide into. [1.1]

left side In the equation $4x = 28$, the left side is $4x$. [2.1]

liabilities Expenses which must be paid by a firm. [17.3]

liability or **bodily injury insurance** Coverage which provides protection from suit by an injured party. [7.2]

like fractions Two fractions that have the same denominator. [1.1]

limited liability No more money can be lost than has been invested. [18 Introduction]

limited payment life insurance A form of life insurance in which premiums are paid for only a certain fixed number of years. [7.3]

liquid assets Cash or items which can be converted to cash quickly. [17.3]

liquidity A firm is liquid if it has the ability to pay its bills as they come due. [17.4]

list price The suggested retail price or final consumer price given by the manufacturer or supplier. [8.1]

loan payoff table A table used to decide on the payment that will amortize a loan. [15.4]

long-term liabilities Those items which will be paid after one year. [17.3]

lowest terms A fraction is written in lowest terms when no number except the number 1 divides evenly into both the numerator and denominator of the fraction. [1.1]

luxury tax A name sometimes given to excise tax. [6.1]

maintenance charge per month A flat charge for maintaining a checking account. [4.1]

maker The person borrowing the money on a note. [12.1]

manufacturer The assembler of component parts or finished products. [8.1]

markdown A reduction from the original selling price. It may be expressed as a dollar amount or as a percent of the original selling price. [10.1]

marketing channels The path or steps that goods take from manufacturer to consumer. [5.2]

markup (margin or **gross profit)** The difference between the cost and the selling price. [9.1]

markup conversion formula A formula used to convert markup from one base to the other base. [9.2]

markup formula The formula used when working with markup. Cost + Markup = Selling price. [9.1]

markup on cost Markup that is calculated as a percent of cost. [9.1]

markup on selling price Markup that is calculated as a percent of selling price. [9.2]

markup with spoilage The calculation of markup including deduction for spoiled or unsaleable merchandise. [9.3]

Master Card A credit card plan. [4.2]

mathematics of buying The mathematics involving trade and cash discounts. [8.1]

maturity date The date a loan is due. [11.4]

maturity value The total amount, principal and interest, that must be repaid when a loan is paid off. [11.4] It equals face value plus interest. [12.1]

mean The sum of all the numbers divided by the number of numbers. [19.2]

measure of central tendency A number that tries to estimate the middle of a set of data. Measures of central tendency include the mean, median, and mode. [19.2]

median The middle number in an ordered array. [19.3]

medical insurance Insurance providing medical protection in the event of accident or injury. [7.2]

medicare tax Part of the social security tax (FICA) until 1991. Since 1991 medicare tax has been collected separately. [5.4]

memory keys A feature on electronic calculators which allows answers to be stored for future use and recalled. [1.3]

merchant batch header ticket A form used to deposit credit card sales in a business checking account. [4.2]

merchant deposit summary The bank form used to deposit credit card transactions. [4.2]

middlemen Those along the marketing channels, such as wholesalers, brokers, and retailers. [5.2]

mid-quarter convention When the assets purchased in the last three months of a year exceed 40% a reduced amount of depreciation is taken in the first year. [16.5]

mill A mill is one-tenth of a cent or one-thousandth of a dollar. [6.2]

minuend The number from which another number (the subtrahend) is subtracted in a subtraction problem. [A.1]

mixed number The sum of a fraction and a whole number. (For example, $1\frac{1}{5}$ or $2\frac{5}{9}$ are mixed numbers.) [1.1]

mode The most common number in a list of numbers. [19.5]

modified accelerated cost recovery system (MACRS) The Tax Reform Act of 1986 replaces the ACRS with the MACRS. [16.5]

money order An instrument which is purchased and used in place of cash. It is usually preferred over a personal or business check. [4.2]

mortality table A table showing statistics on life expectancy, survival, and death rates. [7.3]

multiple carriers More than one insurance company sharing in an insurable risk. [7.1]

multiplicand A number being multiplied. [A.1]

multiplier A number doing the multiplying. [A.1]

mutual company An insurance company owned by the policyholders who receive a dividend. [7.3]

negative number (deficit number) A number which is less than zero; a negative balance or deficit. For example, −$800 or ($800). [1.3]

net cost The cost or price after allowable discounts have been taken. [8.1]

net cost equivalent or **percent paid** The decimal number derived from the product of the complements of the trade discounts. This number may be multiplied times the list price to find the net cost (price). [8.1]

net cost of insurance policy The cost of insurance after subtracting cash values and dividends from total premiums paid over the policy life. [7.3]

net income The difference between gross profit and operating expenses. [17.1]

net pay The amount of money actually received by an employee after deductions are taken from gross pay. [5.5]

net proceeds The amount received by a seller in an account sale after all expenses are deducted. [5.2]

net profit (or **net earnings**) The difference between gross margin and expenses. After the cost of goods and operating expenses are subtracted from total sales, the remainder is net profit. [9.1]

net sales The value of goods bought by customers after subtracting goods returned. [17.1]

net worth Same as owner's equity. [17.3]

no-fault insurance Motor vehicle insurance which pays directly to the insured no matter who causes the accident. [7.2]

nominal rate *See* Stated rate. [13.1]

noncustomer check cashing A service that allows an individual who is not a bank customer to cash a check upon payment of a fee. [4.2]

nonforfeiture options Options available to the insured when canceling the insurance policy. [7.3]

nonparticipating A form of stock which will never pay dividends above the stated rate. [18.1]

nonparticipating policy The type of life insurance policy issued by a stock insurance company. [7.3]

nonsmoker's discount A discount given to nonsmokers because they are better insurance risks. [7.3]

normal curve The bell-shaped curve of statistics. [19.4]

notary service A service that provides notarization, which is required on certain business documents and transfers. [4.2]

NOW account This account uses a "Negotiable Order of Withdrawal," which works and looks like a check. [4.2]

numerator The number above the line in a fraction. (For example, in the fraction $\frac{5}{8}$, 5 is the numerator.) [1.1]

odd lot Fewer than 100 shares of stock. [18.2]

odd-lot differential An additional charge for buying or selling stocks when the number of shares is not a multiple of 100. [18.2]

open-end credit An account that is not paid off in a fixed period of time; MasterCard and Visa accounts are examples of open-end credit. [14.2]

operating expenses (or **overhead**) Expenses of operating a business. Wages, salaries, rent, utilities, and advertising are examples of operating expenses. [9.1, 17.1]

operating loss The loss resulting when the selling price is less than the breakeven point. [10.1]

order of operations The rules determining which calculations must be done first in chain calculations. [1.3]

ordered array An arrangement of a list of numbers from smallest to largest. [19.3]

ordinary annuity An annuity with payments made at the end of a given period of time. [15.1]

ordinary dating method A method for calculating the discount date and the net payment date. Days are counted from the date of the invoice. [8.3]

ordinary interest Simple interest calculated assuming 360 days in a year. Also called banker's interest. [11.2]

ordinary life insurance (Whole life insurance, straight life insurance) A form of life insurance in which the insured pays a constant premium until death or retirement, whichever occurs sooner. Upon retirement, monthly payments are made by the company to the insured until the death of the insured. [7.3]

original investment Partners divide profits of a business on the basis of original investments by each partner. [18.4]

overdraft This occurs when a customer writes a check for which there are insufficient funds in the account. [4.2]

overdraft protection The bank service of honoring checks written on an account which has insufficient funds. [4.2]

overhead *See* Operating expenses. [17.1]

override A commission received by a sales supervisor or department head based on total sales of the sales group or department. [5.2]

overtime The number of hours worked by an employee in excess of 40 hours per week, or 8 hours per day. [5.1]

overtime premium method Payment of overtime as a premium. All hours worked are paid at regular rate. Overtime hours are paid at $\frac{1}{2}$ rate. Gross earnings are the sum of these. [5.1]

owner's equity The difference between assets and liabilities. Also called proprietorship or net worth. [17.3]

paid-up insurance A nonforfeiture option which provides paid-up insurance of a certain amount. [7.3]

par value The amount printed on a stock certificate; usually the price at which a share of stock is first offered to the public. [18.1, 18.3]

part The result of multiplying the base times the rate. [3.2]

partial payment A payment which is less than the total owed on an invoice; a cash discount may be earned. [8.4]

partial product Part of the process of getting the answer in a multiplication problem. [A.1]

partial-year depreciation The amount of depreciation that is determined for the asset during a period less than one year. [16.4]

participating A type of stock that could be affected by increase in the dividend. [18.1]

participating policy The type of life insurance policy issued by a mutual insurance company. [7.3]

partnership A business formed by two or more people. [18 Introduction]

passbook account A bank account used for day-in and day-out deposit of money. These accounts usually have the lowest interest rates of any accounts, but have no penalties when money is withdrawn. [13.2]

pay period The time period for which an employee is paid. [5.1]

payee The person who loans the money and will receive payment on a note. [12.1]

payer *See* Maker. [12.1]

payment period The time between the payments into an annuity [15.1]

payments for life A life insurance settlement option which pays an annuity for life. [7.3]

payments for life with a guaranteed number of years A life insurance settlement option which pays a certain amount per month for the life of the insured but guarantees a certain length of time in the event that the insured dies before this guaranteed time period. [7.3]

payroll ledger A chart showing all payroll information. [5.1]

per debit charge A charge per check. Usually continues regardless of the number of checks written. [4.1]

percent A percent is one hundredth. For example, 2 percent means 2 parts of a hundred. [3.1]

percent or **rate of markdown** The markdown expressed as a percent of original price. [10.1]

percent formula The basic percent formula is $P = B \times R$, or Part = Base $\times$ Rate. [3.2]

percent key The electronic calculator key $\boxed{\%}$ which moves the decimal point two places to the left when used following multiplication or division. [1.3]

peril insurance Insurance which pays upon a loss by the insured. [7.1]

period of compounding Amount of time between the addition of interest to a deposit or loan. [13.1]

periodic inventory A physical inventory taken at regular intervals. [10.3]

perpetual inventory A continuous inventory system normally utilizing a computer. [10.3]

personal checking account The type of checking account used by individuals. [4.1]

personal exemption Each taxpayer currently gets a $2000 deduction for each dependent, including the taxpayer. [6.3]

personal income tax A tax charged by states and the federal government to individuals. The tax is based on income earned. [5.5]

personal property That property which is not real property such as furnishings, appliances, cars, trucks, clothing, boats, and money. [6.2]

physical inventory An actual physical count of each item in stock at a given time. [10.3]

piecework rate A method of pay by which an employee receives so much money per item completed. [5.3]

plant assets *See* Plant and equipment assets. [17.3]

plant and equipment assets Items owned by a firm which will not be converted to cash within a year. Also called fixed assets or plant assets. [17.3]

policy A contract between an insured and an insurance company. [7.1]

policy fee An annual policy fee charged by motor vehicle insurance companies to cover the cost of processing the policy. [7.2]

policyholder A person or business that has purchased insurance. Also known as the insured. [7.1]

postdating Dating in the future; on an invoice **"AS OF"** dating. [8.3]

preferred stock Stock which pays dividends before common stockholders receive any dividends. [18.1]

premium The amount of money charged for an insurance policy. [7.1, 7.2]

premium factor A factor used to convert annual premiums to either semiannual, quarterly, or monthly premiums. [7.3]

premium payment An additional payment for extra service. [5.1]

premium rate A higher amount of pay given for additional hours worked or additional units produced. [5.3]

present value An amount that can be invested today to produce a given amount in the future. [11.5, 13.4]

present value of an annuity (1) The lump sum that can be deposited today that will amount to the same final total as would the periodic payment of an annuity. (2) A lump sum that could be deposited today so that equal periodic withdrawals could be made. [15.2]

price-earnings ratio (PE ratio) The price per share of stock divided by the annual earnings per share of the stock. [18.2]

price relative The quotient of the current price and the price in some past year with the quotient multiplied by 100. [19.5]

prime cost The cost before expenses are added in an account purchase. [5.2]

prime number A number divisible without remainder only by itself or 1 (such as 7 or 13). [1.1]

principal An amount of money either borrowed, loaned, or deposited. [11.1] The initial amount of money deposited. [13.2]

proceeds The amount of money the borrower receives after subtracting the discount from the face value of a note. [12.2, 12.4]

product The answer in a multiplication problem. [A.1]

promissory note A document in which one person agrees to pay money to another person, a certain amount of time in the future, and at a certain rate of interest. [12.1]

proper fraction A fraction in which the numerator is smaller than the denominator. For example, $\frac{2}{3}$ is a proper fraction; $\frac{9}{5}$ is not. [1.1]

property damage insurance A type of automobile insurance that pays for damages caused to the property of others. [7.2]

property tax rate For property, the tax rate is found by dividing total amount needed by total assessed value. [6.2]

proportion A proportion says that two ratios are equal. [2.4]

proprietorship *See* Owner's equity. [17.3]

proximo dating In cash discounts, the time period beginning at the end of the month the invoice is dated. End-of-month dating (EOM) and "prox." have the same meaning. [8.4]

Publication 534 The Internal Revenue Service publication which gives a complete coverage of depreciation. [16.5]

purchase invoice The invoice or document received by the purchaser of goods or services from the seller. [8.1]

quick ratio *See* Acid-test ratio. [17.4]

quota bonus A plan which pays a bonus to an employee after reaching a quota. [5.2]

quotient The answer to a division problem. [A.1]

range The difference between the largest value and the smallest value in a set. [19.4]

rate A number followed by "%" or "percent." [3.2]

rate of interest The percent of interest charged for one year. [11.1]

ratio A quotient of two quantities. [2.4]

ratio of net income after taxes to average owner's equity Net income divided by average owner's equity. [17.4]

raw data A set of data before analysis. [19.1]

real property All land, buildings, and other improvements attached to the land. [6.2]

receipt of goods dating (ROG) In cash discounts, time is counted from the date that goods are received. [8.4]

reciprocal The result of interchanging the numerator and denominator of a fraction. [2.1]

reconciliation The process of checking a bank statement against the depositor's own personal records. [4.3]

recourse Merchants sometimes sell debts that are owed them. If the person owing the money is unavailable and the bank buying the debt has recourse to the merchant—the merchant is liable for the debt. [12.4]

recovery class The class into which property is placed under MACRS (3-, 5-, 10-, 15-, 20-, 27.5-, or 31.5-year class). [16.5]

recovery period The number of years over which the cost of an asset is recovered using the MACRS. [16.5]

rediscounting The process in which one financial institution discounts a note at a second institution. [12.4]

reduced net profit This occurs when a markdown decreases the selling price to a point which is still above the breakeven point. [10.1]

reduced price The selling price after subtracting the markdown, also called sale price and actual selling price. [10.1]

remainder The answer to a subtraction problem. In a division problem, the part left over when one number will not divide exactly into another. [A.1]

repayment schedule *See* Amortization schedule. [15.4]

repeating decimal A decimal which repeats one or more digits without ending. A bar is often placed over the repeating digit(s). For example, $.33\overline{33}$ and $.16\overline{16}$ are both repeating decimals. [1.2]

restricted endorsement Endorsement of a check so that only the person or company given the check may cash it. [4.1]

retail method A method used to estimate inventory value at cost which utilizes both cost and retail amounts. [10.3]

retailer The business of selling directly to the consumer. [8.1]

returned deposit item The return to the bank of an item which has been deposited, due to any number of irregularities. [4.2]

returned goods Merchandise returned due to incorrect shipment or damage. [8.3]

returns The total value of all goods returned by customers. [17.1]

revolving charge account *See* Open-end credit. [14.2]

right side In the equation $4x = 28$, the right side is 28. [2.1]

round lot Multiple of 100 shares of stock. [18.2]

rounded decimals Decimals reduced to a number with fewer decimals. [1.2]

Rule of 78 A method of calculating interest charges that need not be paid because the loan was paid off earlier than planned. [14.4]

rules for divisibility Rules which help determine whether a number is evenly divisible by another number. [1.1]

salary A fixed amount of money per pay period. [5.1]

salary and agreed ratio Same as agreed ratio, except that a salary may be allowed to one partner or the other in addition to the profit division. [18.4]

salary plus commission A commission is paid as a premium in addition to salary. [5.2]

sale price *See* Reduced price. [10.1]

sales invoice The invoice or document retained by the seller of goods or services, a copy of which is sent to the purchaser. [8.1]

sales quota An expected level of production. A premium may be paid for surpassing quota. [5.2]

sales tax A tax placed on sales to the final consumer. The tax is collected by the state, county, or local government. [6.1]

sales value Value of sales for each department of a company. [18.5]

salvage value or **scrap value** The value of an asset at the end of its useful life. For depreciation purposes, this is often an estimate. [16 Introduction]

SDI (State Disability Insurance) deduction The deduction for a state disability insurance program. [5.4]

self-employed individuals Individuals who work for themselves instead of for the government or a private company. [5.4]

selling price The price at which merchandise is offered for sale to the public. The cost of an item plus its markup. [9.1]

series discount *See* Chain discount. [8.1]

settlement options Methods of receiving life insurance benefits in addition to cash payment. [7.3]

shift-differential A premium paid for working a less desirable shift, such as swing shift or graveyard shift. [5.1]

shipping point The location from which merchandise is shipped by the seller to the buyer. [8.1]

short-term or **cancellation rate** A rate used when charging for short-term policies and the refunds given when policies are canceled by the policyholder. [7.1]

silent partner A partner who invests in a partnership, but takes no part in running it. [18 Introduction, 18.4]

simple annuity An annuity with payment dates matching the compounding period. [15.1]

simple discount note A note whose interest is deducted in advance from the face value, with only the difference given to the borrower. [12.2]

simple interest Interest computed only on the principal. [11.1]

simple interest notes Notes on which interest is found by formulas for simple interest. [12.1]

single discount A discount expressed as a single percent and not as a series or chain discount. [8.1]

single discount equivalent to a series discount A series or chain discount which is expressed as a single discount. [8.2]

sinking fund A fund set up to receive equal periodic payments in order to pay off an obligation at some fixed time in the future. [15.3]

sliding-scale commission A graduated commission plan giving a higher rate to top producing salespeople. [5.2]

SMP The abbreviation for a special multi-perils policy. This policy gives additional insurance coverage to businesses. *See* Business owner's package policy. [7.1]

snack tax A sales tax charged on certain food items which are determined by the taxing authority to be "snack foods". [6.1]

Social Security *See* Federal Insurance Contributions Act (FICA). [5.4]

sole proprietorship A business owned by one person. [18 Introduction]

solution A number that can replace a variable in an equation and result in a true statement. [2.1]

special endorsement An endorsement to a specific payee. [4.1]

specific identification method Inventory valuation method which identifies the cost of each individual item. [10.3]

split-shift premium A premium paid for working a split shift. For example, an employee who is on 4 hours, off 4 hours, and then on 4 hours. [5.1]

spoilage Merchandise which becomes unsaleable. Usually considered when calculating markup. [9.3]

square root The square root ($\sqrt{}$) of a number is a number when multiplied by itself equals that number. The square root of 9, $\sqrt{9}$, is 3, since $3 \times 3 = 9$. [1.3]

square root key The electric calculator key $\boxed{\sqrt{}}$ which calculates the square root of the number on the calculator. [1.3]

standard deduction A deduction used to reduce taxable income for taxpayers who do not itemize their deductions. [6.3]

standard deviation Found by first finding the mean, and then subtracting the mean from each data value. The square root of the mean of the squares of the deviation. [19.4]

state withholding State income tax withheld from gross earnings by the employer. [5.5]

stated rate The rate of interest quoted by a bank. Also called the nominal. [13.1]

stock A share of stock represents partial ownership of a corporation. [18.1]

stock certificates Documentation of stock ownership. [18.1]

stock company An insurance company owned by stockholders. No dividend is paid for policyholders. [7.3]

stock ratio Numbers used to compare stocks—typically the current yield and the PE ratio. [18.2]

stock turnover *See* Inventory turnover. [10.2]

stockholder A person who buys and sells stock for the public. [18.2]

stockholders The owners of a corporation. [18.1]

stockholders' equity The difference between a corporation's assets and liabilities. [17.3]

stop payment order A request that the bank not pay on a check previously written. [4.2]

straight commission A fixed amount or percent for each unit of work. Earnings are based on performance alone. [5.2]

straight life insurance Another name for ordinary or whole life insurance. [7.3]

straight-line depreciation A depreciation method where depreciation is spread evenly over the life of the asset. [16.1]

substitution Replacing the variable in an equation by the solution; substitution is used to check a solution. [2.1]

subtrahend The number being subtracted or taken away in a subtraction problem. [A.1]

suicide clause A clause which excludes suicide as an insurable cause of death (usually for the first two years of the policy). [7.3]

sum The answer in an addition problem. Also called the total, or amount. [A.1]

sum-of-the-years' digits method An accelerated depreciation method using a depreciation fraction. [16.3]

tax rate schedule A schedule which shows the individual tax rates for cash filing status. [6.3]

taxable income Adjusted gross income, minus exemptions, minus deductions. [6.3]

telephone transfer The transfer of funds with a verbal request over the telephone. [4.2]

term A single letter, a single number, or the product of a number and a letter. [2.1]

term insurance A form of insurance providing protection for a fixed length of time. [7.3]

term of an annuity The time from the beginning of the first payment into an annuity until the end of the last payment. [15.1]

term of the note The length of time until a note is due. [12.1]

time The number of years or fraction of a year for which the loan is made. [11.1]

time-and-a-half rate Many employees are paid $1\frac{1}{2}$ times the normal rate of pay for any hours worked in excess of 40 hours per week, or 8 hours per day. [5.1]

time card A card that is helpful in preparing the payroll. The time card includes such information as the dates of the pay period, the employee's name, and the number of hours worked. [5.1]

time deposit account A savings account in which the depositor agrees to leave money for a certain period of time. [13.2]

time rate Earnings based on hours worked, not work accomplished. [5.3]

time value of money, or **value of money** The average interest rate for which money is loaned at a given time. [11.5]

total *See* Sum. [A.1]

total installment cost Find the total installment cost by multiplying the amount of each payment on a loan and the number of payments; then add any down payment. [14.3]

total invoice amount The sum of all the extension totals on an invoice. [8.1]

trade discount The discount offered to businesses. This discount is expressed either as a single discount (such as 25%) or a series discount (such as 20/10) and is subtracted from the list price. [8.1]

transfer tax A tax charged by some cities and states on the purchase or sale of stock. [18.2]

true rate of interest *See* Effective rate of interest. [12.2, 12.3]

turnover at cost Found by the following formula. [10.2]

$$\frac{\text{Cost of goods sold}}{\text{Amount of inventory at cost}}$$

turnover at retail Found by the following formula. [10.2]

$$\frac{\text{Sales}}{\text{Average inventory at retail}}$$

1099 form This form is sent out by banks, savings and loans, and other financial institutions and shows interest, stock dividends, and other miscellaneous income. [6.3]

underinsured motorist insurance Insurance coverage which covers the insured when involved in an accident with a driver who is underinsured. Coverage for bodily injury above the amounts of insurance carried by the underinsured driver. [7.2]

underwriter An insurance company employee who determines the risk factors involved in the occurrence of various insurable losses. This helps determine the insurance premium. [7.1]

unearned interest The amount of interest not owed when a loan is paid off early. [14.4]

unemployment insurance tax A tax paid by employers. The money is used to pay unemployment benefits to qualified unemployed workers. [5.6]

uniform product codes (UPC) Coding which is issued per product and product size, used for efficient inventory control by stores. It also provides greater accuracy and perhaps faster service to the customer. [10.3]

uninsured motorist insurance Insurance coverage which covers the insured when involved in an accident with a driver who is not insured. [7.2]

units-of-production method A depreciation method using the units produced to determine depreciation allowance. [16.4]

United States Rule A method of handling partial loan payoffs; any payment is first applied to the interest owed on the loan, with any balance then used to reduce the principal amount of the loan. [14.1]

universal life insurance Allows the insured to vary the amount of premium and type of protection depending on changing insurance needs. [7.3]

unlike fractions Fractions having different denominators. [1.1]

unpaid balance The balance outstanding on a revolving charge account at the end of a billing period. [14.2]

unpaid balance method A method of calculating the finance charge on a revolving charge account by using the balance at the end of the previous month. [14.2]

unsaleable items Merchandise which cannot be sold. Usually considered when calculating markup. [9.3]

useful life The estimated life of an asset. The IRS gives guidelines of useful life for depreciation purposes. [16 Introduction]

U.S. Treasury bills A loan of money to the United States government. Treasury bills (or T-bills) are a very safe way to invest money. [12.2]

variable A letter that represents a number. [2.1]

variable commission A rate of commission that depends on the total amount of the sales, with the rate increasing as sales increase. [5.2]

variable life insurance Provides life insurance protection and allows the insured to select investment funds to invest the balance of the premium. [7.3]

variable rate loan A home loan made at an interest rate that varies with market conditions. [15.4]

vertical analysis The process of listing each of the important items on an income statement as a percent of total net sales or each item on a balance sheet as a percent of total assets. [17.2 and 17.4]

VISA A credit card plan. [4.2]

waiver of premium clause Allows insurance to continue without payment of premium when insured becomes disabled. [7.3]

weighted average method Inventory valuation method where the cost of all purchases during a time period is divided by the number of units purchased. [10.3]

weighted mean A mean calculated by using weights, so that each number is multiplied by its frequency. [19.2]

whole life insurance Another name for ordinary or straight life insurance. [7.3]

whole numbers Numbers made up of digits to the left of the decimal point. [A.1]

wholesaler The middleman; purchases from manufacturers or other wholesalers and sells to retailers. [8.1]

wire transfer The instant electronic transfer of funds from one account to another. [4.2]

withholding allowance These allowances, for employees, their spouses and dependents, determine the amount of withholding tax taken from gross earnings. [5.5]

worker's compensation insurance Insurance which provides payments to an employee who is unable to work due to a job related injury or illness. [7.1]

W-2 forms The wage and tax statement given to the employee each year by the employer. [6.3]

youthful operator A driver of a motor vehicle under a certain age, usually 25 years of age or younger. [7.2]

Index